The Law of Digital Content

CYBER AND TECHNOLOGY LAW COMMITTEE

Digital Media, Gaming and Entertainment Subcommittee

JON M. GARON, EDITOR

ABA
AMERICAN BAR ASSOCIATION
Business Law Section

Cover design by Catherine Zaccarine.

Printed in the United States of America.

29 28 27 26 25   5 4 3 2 1

ISBN: 978-1-63905-635-4

Discounts are available for books ordered in bulk. Special consideration is given to state bars, CLE programs, and other bar-related organizations. Inquire at Book Publishing, ABA Publishing, American Bar Association, 321 N. Clark Street, Chicago, Illinois 60654-7598.

www.shopABA.org

Contents

Introduction to the Law of Digital Content

By Jon M. Garon

The universe is made of stories not of atoms.

—Muriel Rukeyser (1913–1980)[1]

Welcome to the world of digital content and the legal framework surrounding its creation, distribution, consumption, and regulation. The title requires a brief introduction to both the meaning of digital content and an explanation as to why digital content is not just content. As used in this book and throughout various content industries, digital content is that which can be understood broadly to mean all data which are produced and supplied in digital form, ranging from computer software, and video games to databases, virtual worlds, texts, music, and videos. In fact, since celluloid film and magnetic tape are rarely used in the modern production of content, essentially all audiovisual works are digital at some stage in their development, and most remain digital throughout their life cycle.

At a more practical level, digital content has taken on an industry meaning that focuses on "media that an organization uses to engage with visitors, customers, or users of their website or applications, distributed by online delivery systems . . . The term encompasses every type of publishable media from streaming video, downloadable guides, images, live broadcasts, or a piece of gated information."[2] The coverage of the term also includes nonfungible tokens (NFTs) and therefore incorporates fungible tokens such as cryptocurrency. This concept highlights the distinction between a digital asset or digital object, such as a particular copy of an ebook owned by a consumer, and the copyright in the book retained by the author.

The law of digital content, therefore, intersects with various intellectual property laws, including copyright, trademark, publicity rights, trade secrets, and occasionally patent law. Because laws pertaining to digital content only intersect with intellectual property regulations on select provisions of law, the book can provide useful information on transactions involving digital content for both intellectual property attorneys and nonintellectual property attorneys alike.

As the introductory chapter highlights, digital content has gone from an incidental part of the economy to its heart. Videogames represent a significantly larger part of the entertainment industry than film, music, and publishing combined. Videogames are evolving

1 Muriel Rukeyser, *Speed of Darkness* (1968), in Janet Kaufman & Anne Herzog, eds., Collected Poems of Muriel Rukeyser 465 (2005).

2 *Digital Content*, Optimizely, https://www.optimizely.com/optimization-glossary/digital-content/ (last visited June 4, 2024).

into multiverse platforms that host e-commerce, concerts, and more. Nearly every business operates through its website and most use social media to promote and manage their brands. Artificial intelligence (AI) provides new opportunities and new risks in generating content directly from textual inputs rather than creative efforts. Deepfakes allow synthetic content to easily generate unauthorized content that has the potential to harm individuals, brands, and the broader public.

The book provides a framework for business attorneys, law students, and other readers to navigate the changes to contractual and legal duties that are developing from the norms surrounding the expansion of generative AI, synthetic media, Web3, digital assets including cryptocurrency and NFTs, and metaverse platforms in conducting advertising, business transactions, employment-related activities, and education. These changes significantly impact intellectual property, financial services, healthcare services, and even fields such as housing and education.

The core of the book is legal analysis, providing a robust discussion of the changes to the legal field caused by the adoption of the applicable technology. The book provides an overview and framework for how these new technologies impact each of the relevant legal fields. In each of the core industries, the book will identify the manner in which the law and practice are changed by the use of these technologies and what the practitioner (or regulator) must consider when operating in this sphere.

1
The Transformation of the Internet from Protocol to Venue

By Jon M. Garon[1]

1.1. Media Distribution and the Development of Web 1.0

The history of Western media begins with the invention of the printing press by Johannes Gutenberg from 1448 to 1450.[2] Gutenberg printed copies of the authorized Latin Bible in 1455, establishing the press as an important new tool in publication. The example grew, and the printing industry emerged over the next half century.[3] The printing press promoted the ability of publishers to expand the book business and activists to use pamphlets to spread their messages.[4] Through the use of Gutenberg's invention of movable type using metal letters, Gutenberg's press improved the print quality and increased the production rate "1,000 times more than could be done by a scribe by hand."[5] Weekly newspapers emerged over 150 years after the introduction of Gutenberg's press. Although the early weeklies did not include the name of the city in which they were published for fear of government persecution, "[b]y 1641, a newspaper was printed in almost every country in Europe as publication spread to France, Italy, and Spain."[6]

---

1 Section 1.3 of this chapter is adapted from Jon M. Garon, *Normative Copyright: A Conceptual Framework for Copyright Philosophy & Ethics*, 88 CORNELL L. REV. 101 (2003) (adapted with permission of the author).

2 Joshua J. Mark, *Johannes Gutenberg*, WORLD HISTORY ENC. (Jul. 25, 2022), https://www.worldhistory.org/Johannes_Gutenberg/.

3 *See* Elizabeth L. Eisenstein, The Printing Press as an Agent of Change 33 (1979).

4 *See, e.g.*, Joan Acocella, *How Martin Luther Changed the World*, NEW YORKER (Oct. 23, 2017), https://www.newyorker.com/magazine/2017/10/30/how-martin-luther-changed-the-world.

5 *History of Newspapers*, Understanding Media and Culture 4.2 (2010).

6 *Id.*

Newspapers expanded and transformed with the invention of the telegraph by Samuel Morse. The patent for the telegraph was filed in 1844. Within two years, a consortium of five New York newspapers formed the Associated Press to share news stories as they happened across the continent.[7] The first transatlantic cable was laid in 1858, extending the reach to Europe.[8]

Alexander Graham Bell rose to the competition, introducing the telephone in 1876.[9] In 1877, Thomas Edison's work on the telegraph and the telephone led to his creation and patent for the phonograph.[10] Edison's phonograph "became the most popular home-entertainment device of the century."[11] But that was the nineteenth century. To add visual images to the phonograph, in 1888, Edison eventually turned to one of his assistants, William Kennedy Laurie Dickson. Within a year, Dickson completed the task of producing a working motion picture camera.[12]

At the same time, national and transcontinental communication lines were augmented by wireless communication, led by the inventions by Guglielmo Marconi. Marconi's experiments began in 1894, and by 1900, he had filed patent applications for wireless radio stations.[13] Telephone systems and phonograph devices were also becoming popular. As mass communication, however, it was radio that quickly emerged as competition to newspapers. Radio operations expanded quickly, resulting in overlapping usage and signal interference. To control the amateur radio use, Congress passed the Radio Act of 1912,[14] but the law was too narrow to address the rapid growth of radio. As radio license application requests exploded across the country, the law was replaced with the Radio Act of 1927, and then again with the Communications Act of 1934, which added chapters for both radio and telephone regulation.[15]

In the first decades of the twentieth century, the leader in wireless was American Marconi (the Marconi Wireless Telegraph Company of America) but, with the advent of World War I, concerns over national security resulted in the sale of American Marconi to General Electric (GE) in 1919.[16] The newly acquired company became the Radio Corporation of America (RCA), a GE subsidiary formed at the behest of the Navy.

---

7 *See id.*

8 *See id.* at 14.

9 *Two Hundred Years of Global Communications*, World 101 from the Council on Foreign Relations, https://world101.cfr.org/global-era-issues/globalization/two-hundred-years-global-communications (last visited Jun. 18, 2024).

10 *History of the Cylinder Phonograph*, Library of Cong., https://www.loc.gov/collections/-edison-company-motion-pictures-and-sound-recordings/articles-and-essays/history-of-edison-sound-recordings/history-of-the-cylinder-phonograph/ (last visited Jun. 18, 2023).

11 Robert Sklar & David Cook, *History of Film*, Britannica (May 21, 2023), https://www.britannica.com/art/history-of-the-motion-picture.

12 *Id.*

13 Reginald Leslie Smith-Rose, *Guglielmo Marconi*, Encyc. Britannica (Apr. 29, 2024), https://www.britannica.com/biography/Guglielmo-Marconi.

14 37 Stat. 302 (1912) (superseded).

15 *See* Pub. L. 73-416, 48 Stat. 1064 (codified 47 U.S. Code § 151 *et seq.* (1934)) (superseded).

16 *100 YEARS—A Visual Memoir of RCA*, Radio Corp. of Am., https://www.rca.com/us_en/our-legacy-266-us-en (last visited Jun. 4, 2024).

As early as 1915, at American Marconi, David Sarnoff wrote an important memo describing radio as a "household utility" utilizing "Radio Music Box."[17] Sarnoff's model called for separate stations to be broadcasting at "different wavelengths, which would be changeable with the throwing of a single switch or pressing of a single button."[18] At RCA, Sarnoff fulfilled his vision. The company acquired AT&T's two radio stations in 1926 and used those licenses to form the National Broadcasting Company (NBC), which was owned co-equally by GE and RCA.[19]

The other major radio network competitor was the Columbia Broadcasting System (CBS), which launched in 1927.[20] CBS was formed by a talent agent unable to obtain client bookings on NBC, but a series of small mergers and financial difficulties led to its acquisition by "William S. Paley, whose father owned the company that made La Palina cigars, one of the network's principal advertisers."[21] The reconstituted and rebranded company went on the air in 1929. The two national networks quickly dominated the market. "In 1926, the public owned 6.4 percent of U.S. broadcasting stations; by 1931, that number had risen to 30 percent."[22] The Radio Act of 1927 reorganized and rationalized the market. For NBC and CBS, the new regulations enabled these two networks to increase their foothold to 70 percent of the marketplace.[23]

Both Paley and Sarnoff were aggressive supporters of television, understanding that adding images to voice inside the public's living room would be transformative. The motion picture industry leaders, in contrast, tended to see the emergence of television as a competitor. Combined with significant antitrust issues plaguing Hollywood and a distrust of Communists and former Communists among Hollywood's leading screenwriters and actors, the Federal Communications Commission eased the transition for radio networks to expand into television networks.[24] "Television . . . existed before World War II, but gained mainstream popularity in the 1950s. In 1947, there were 178,000 television sets made in the United States; 5 years later, 15 million were made."[25]

Television and radio dominated the media marketplace throughout much of the twentieth century. At the eve of the new century, however, new technologies were threatening the status quo of the twentieth century.

---

17 JEROME B. WIESNER, *Forward*, *in* DAVID SARNOFF, Looking Ahead, at vii (1968) (quoting letters of David Sarnoff); *see also* CAMPBELL, *supra* note 6 at 22 (Sarnoff proposed "'a radio music box' and outlin[ed] a plan of development that he believed 'would make radio a household utility.' He suggested that such a device could carry lectures, music, major national events, baseball scores, and other matters of interest . . .").

18 *Id.*

19 *See 100 Years*, *supra* note 18.

20 Harold L. Erickson, *CBS Corporation*, ENCYC. BRITANNICA (Jun. 3, 2024), https://www.britannica.com/money/CBS-Corporation.

21 *Id.*

22 Understanding Media and Culture, *supra* note 5 at 15.

23 *Id.* at 327.

24 *See* Jon M. Garon, *Hidden Hands that Shaped the Marketplace of Ideas: Television's Early Transformation from Medium to Genre*, 19 U. DENV. SPORTS & ENT. L. J. 29, 47–49 (2016).

25 Understanding Media and Culture, *supra* note 5 at 16.

The change began with the commercialization of the internet in 1994 and the promulgation of the World Wide Web in the early nineties. The project began with the "four-year old Advanced Research Projects Agency (ARPA) of the U.S. Department of Defense, a future-oriented funder of 'high-risk, high-gain' research, lays the groundwork for what becomes the ARPANET and, much later, the Internet."[26] (The word "Defense" was later added to the agency name.) The first data on the ARPANET was transmitted in 1969. Throughout the 1970s, ARPANET and other computer networks began to expand, primarily at universities. Vint Cerf and others led the process of standardizing the communication protocols so that the competing systems could communicate with each into a single network. The project moves out of Defense Advanced Research Projects Agency (DARPA), but support from the National Science Foundation continues to enable researchers to expand the network, even personal computing and the Apple II emerge in the consumer market.

As early as 1989, Tim Berners-Lee was proposing the World Wide Web as part of his work at the European Council for Nuclear Research (CERN).[27] The proposal included "a 'hypertext project' called 'WorldWideWeb' in which a 'web' of 'hypertext documents' could be viewed by 'browsers.'"[28] In 1993, Berners-Lee released the first hypertext markup language (HTML) that became the standard for internet browsers. At the same time, Marc Andreessen and Eric Brina at the National Center for Supercomputing Applications (NCSA) at the University of Illinois were transforming the early browser into a commercially viable interface. Their project became the Mosaic browser, featuring the ability to view pictures directly on the page, the ability to click on a URL rather than typing in its address, page scrolling, and buttons to move forward, backward, or refresh the browser page.[29]

Commercial use began in earnest with the Mosaic graphical user interface. Between 1993 and 1994, the web grew from five hundred web servers to over ten thousand servers, of which two thousand were for commercial use.[30] Mosaic became the most popular browser, earning InfoWorld Magazine's Product of the Year for 1993.[31] The "browser wars" erupted pitting Netscape Navigator, another product of Marc Andreessen (and Jim Clark), against the entrant of Microsoft's Explorer web browser.

The internet caught Bill Gates and Microsoft off-guard. But as with the earlier experience of radio's disruption to the newspaper, and television's disruption of the movie industry, entrenched industries have strong incentives to disavow the forces that threaten their foundations. Perhaps the more impressive aspect of the story is the recognition that Gates made. On May 26, 1995, Microsoft CEO Bill Gates responded with a memo, *The Internet Tidal Wave*, that recharted the course of media history.

---

26 *Internet History 1962 to 1992*, Computer History Museum, https://www.computerhistory.org/internethistory/ (last visited Jun. 4, 2024).

27 Conseil Européen pour la Recherche Nucléaire.

28 *Where the Web Was Born*, CERN, http://home.cern/science/computing/birth-web/short-history-web (last visited Sept. 21, 2023).

29 *NCSA Mosaic Internet Web Browser: The Complete History*, History Computer (Nov. 24, 2022), http://history-computer.com/history-of-the-ncsa-mosaic-internet-web-browser/.

30 *Where the Web Was Born*, *supra* note 28.

31 *NCSA Mosaic Internet Web Browser*, *supra* note 29.

> [D]evelopments on the Internet over the next several years will set the course of our industry for a long time to come. Perhaps you have already seen memos from me or others here about the importance of the Internet. I have gone through several stages of increasing my views of its importance. Now I assign the Internet the highest level of importance. In this memo I want to make clear that our focus on the Internet is crucial to every part of our business. The Internet is the most important single development to come along since the IBM PC was introduced in 1981. . . .
>
> Most important is that the Internet has bootstrapped itself as a place to publish content. It has enough users that it is benefiting from the positive feedback loop of the more users it gets, the more content it gets, and the more content it gets, the more users it gets. . . . Of particular interest are the sites such as "YAHOO" which provide subject catalogs and searching.[32]

For Netscape, the ability of Microsoft to bundle and distribute its browser as part of the Windows operating system proved too much. Between 1997 and 1998, Netscape witnessed a decline in market share from 72 percent down to only 20 percent.[33] The U.S. Department of Justice brought antitrust litigation over Microsoft's bundling practices, but the slow pace of antitrust litigation meant that the final resolution of the lawsuit did little to reverse the transformation of the internet browser market.[34]

Similar conflicts emerged among Internet Service Providers (ISPs) as they sought to connect customers to the internet, initially through a dial-up modem and eventually through broadband access. Through a disastrous merger between America Online and Time Warner, at least one Hollywood company tried to learn from the mistake about integrating television and the internet, but a host of miscalculations resulted in a largely failed strategy.[35]

The emergence of the web as a dominant use case for the internet is now referred to as Web 1.0. The primary use of HTML webpages was to extend publishing from print to online, dramatically reducing the costs associated with production and distribution of content. Initially, an acceptable use policy restricted the internet to academic uses, such as research and education.[36] The growth increased tremendously as private institutions and for-profit enterprises entered the market, and by 1995, academic use was taken over by individual and commercial activity.[37]

---

[32] Bill Gates, *The Internet Tidal Wave*, Microsoft (May 25, 1995), available at *Letters of Note*, http://lettersofnote.com/2011/07/22/the-internet-tidal-wave/.

[33] Jay Hoffman, *The History of the Browser Wars: When Netscape Met Microsoft*, History of the Web (Jun. 19, 2017), https://thehistoryoftheweb.com/browser-wars/.

[34] *See* United States v. Microsoft Corp., 253 F.3d 34, 47 (D.C. Cir. 2001) (reversing divestiture order against Microsoft); U.S. v. Microsoft Corp., 147 F.3d 935 (D.C. Cir. 1998) (finding Microsoft's bundling of Internet Explorer 3.0 and 4.0 with Windows '95 did not violate the consent decree of the previous United States v. Microsoft); U.S. v. Microsoft Corp., 56 F.3d 1448 (D.C. Cir. 1995) (settled under a consent decree).

[35] *See* Tim Arango, *How the AOL-Time Warner Merger Went So Wrong*, N.Y. Times (Jan. 10, 2010), https://www.nytimes.com/2010/01/11/business/media/11merger.html.

[36] Henry Perritt, Jr., Law and the Information Superhighway 7 (2d ed., 2001).

[37] *Id.* at 7.

Since the web began as a publishing platform, it was logical for Time Warner to move into the field, given its status as a leading publisher. In the mid-to-late 1990s, the web provided not only an opportunity for all print purveyors to extend their reach but also a threat because the access to online content began the inevitable restructuring of much of the print-base industry.

The best measure of the internet's effect on the newspaper industry, for example, is not the number of newspapers but the number of journalists. This reflects the overall health of the newspaper, rather than merely its ability to remain in business.

> In just a few years' time, many newspapers cut their reporting staffs by half and significantly reduced their news coverage. *The Baltimore Sun*'s newsroom shrank to about 150 journalists from more than 400; the *Los Angeles Times*'s to fewer than 600 journalists from more than 1,100. Overall, according to various studies, the number of newspaper editorial employees, which had grown from about 40,000 in 1971 to more than 60,000 in 1992, had fallen back to around 40,000 in 2009.[38]

Newspapers suffered an aggregate loss of one-third of their editorial staff in the digital transformation. Newspapers also began losing their classified ad revenue to online companies, including Craigslist, Angie's List, Yelp, and other services. Newspapers suffered. "Newspaper classified advertising peaked in 2000 at $19.6 billion. In 2012, classified advertising brings in $4.6 billion. That is a 77 percent drop in revenues just from classified advertising, primarily due to shifts in classifieds to such Internet entities as Craigslist."[39]

Web 1.0 transformed the way mass media operated in the field of print content. Publishers struggled to retain revenue or fully monetize the content being placed on websites. Online advertising began in 1994 with a banner ad for AT&T on HotWired website (now wired.com).[40] Banner ads and display ads provided new revenue, but they could not replace the loss of print subscription revenue for magazines and newspapers.

The content of Web 1.0 remained predominantly static and noninteractive. It replicated print onto the home computer but remained primarily a publication platform. To find content, most users relied on the content offered by the user's ISP or web portals. America Online dominated the internet during the period before widespread adoption of broadband, and portals including Yahoo!, GeoCities, and Netscape provided the primary navigation for users on the web.[41] By comparison, Google became a top-10 destination for the first time in 2001, became the top destination in 2006 when it competed with Yahoo!

---

38 Leonard Downie, Jr., & Michael Schudson, *The Reconstruction of American Journalism*, Colum. Journ. Rev. (Oct. 19, 2009), https://www.cjr.org/reconstruction/the_reconstruction_of_american.php.

39 Media Ownership in the 21st Century: Hearing before the Subcomm. on Commc'ns & Tech. of the H. Comm. on Energy & Com., 113th Cong. (Jun. 11, 2014) (Serial No. 113–152), http://www.govinfo.gov/content/pkg/CHRG-113hhrg91517/html/CHRG-113hhrg91517.htm.

40 *The History of Digital Advertising Technology*, Clear Code, https://adtechbook.clearcode.cc/history-advertising-technology/ (last visited Jun. 5, 2024).

41 *See* Corey Hammond, *The Most Visited Websites Every Year since 1995*, A2 Hosting (Jan 24, 2024), https://www.a2hosting.com/blog/the-most-visited-websites-every-year-since-1995/.

for the top spot, and has remained the top destination since 2011.[42] (Yahoo! remains in the top 10 even today.)

Static webpages were not the only technology under development. In 1998, the first dedicated ebook readers were sold for reading digital books, and in 1999, Napster launched a peer-to-peer file sharing service for digital music files.

Digital books were not new. "[In]1971, Michael S. Hart launched Project Gutenberg and digitized the U.S. Declaration of Independence, becoming the first eBook in the world. (To put the date into context, 1971 was the year that the first email message was ever sent—between two mainframe computers!)"[43] eBooks emerged commercially in 1999 with Simon & Schuster's digital imprint, iBooks. That same year, "Oxford University Press offered a selection of its books over the internet through netLibrary."[44] Amazon's Kindle and Apple's iPad translated the potential into reality. Although ebooks were predicted to essentially replace books in print, that has not been the case. According to a Pew Research survey, "75% of U.S. adults say they have read a book in the past 12 months in any format, whether completely or part way through, a figure that has remained largely unchanged since 2011."[45] Sixty-five percent said they read the book or books in print compared to 30 percent who read an ebook and 23 percent who listened to the book as an audiobook.[46] The dominance of print is even more striking when looking at revenue.

"Publishers of books in all formats made almost $26 billion in revenue . . . in the U.S., with print making up $22.6 billion and e-books taking $2.04 billion, according to the Association of American Publishers' annual report 2019. Those figures include trade and educational books, as well as fiction."[47] The failure of ebooks to meet the glowing early expectations is important to understanding the shape of the digital content economy. Print books are collectibles for the purchaser and form an important part of the objects that people display to others. "The book lover loves to have a record of what they've read, and it's about signaling to the rest of the world. It's about decorating your home, it's about collecting, I guess, because people are completists aren't they, they want to have that to indicate about themselves."[48]

Where newspapers and magazines felt the transformative impact of digitization, books have not. Likely this is due to the aspects of book buying that are unrelated to reading. The tactile aspects of book collecting are not satisfied with ebooks. One cannot wrap an ebook as a present or hand someone a copy. eBook sales continue to decline. Print does

---

42 *Id.*

43 *The History of eBooks from 1930's "Readies" to Today's GPO eBook Services*, U.S. Gov't Printing Off. (Mar. 10, 2014), https://govbooktalk.gpo.gov/2014/03/10/the-history-of-ebooks-from-1930s-readies-to-todays-gpo-ebook-services/.

44 James Hardy, *A History of eBooks*, History Cooperative (Feb. 5, 2024), https://historycooperative.org/the-history-of-e-books/.

45 Michelle Faverio & Andrew Perrin, *Three-in-Ten Americans Now Read e-Books*, Pew Rsch. Ctr. (Jan. 6, 2022), https://www.pewresearch.org/short-reads/2022/01/06/three-in-ten-americans-now-read-e-books/.

46 *Id.*

47 Lucy Handley, *Physical Books Still Outsell e-Books—and Here's Why*, CNBC (Sept. 19, 2019), https://www.cnbc.com/2019/09/19/physical-books-still-outsell-e-books-and-heres-why.html.

48 *Id.* (quoting Meryl Halls, Managing Director of the Booksellers' Association in the United Kingdom).

well, particularly in fields where book collections matter, including "nature, cookery and children's books."[49]

Unlike ebooks, the advent of digital music was much more disruptive. The sound recording industry—the side of the music business that packaged and sold recording music—had enjoyed a resurgence in the transition from vinyl records to digital sound recordings on compact discs (CDs).

Napster truly launched a revolution. The free service offered peer-to-peer file sharing for anyone with an internet connection and free account. Although the service touted its use and value for the discovery of new artists, more than 90 percent of the traffic was for illegally shared music files that have been commercially released by artists and record labels.[50] Legitimate computer companies including Apple encouraged consumers to "Rip, Mix, Burn" their CDs,[51] lending further rationalization to the often espoused complaints that CD prices were too high, that album sales forced consumers to buy tracks they didn't really want, and that the money never went to the artists.[52] Although the legal case against Napster seems obvious in hindsight, the size of the cultural phenomenon turned this into an open question at the time.

Although Napster and the music sharing companies that tried to serve as replacements all lost their legal battles, the consequences for the music business were devastating for more than a decade. Revenues declined every year from 1999 to 2015 before slowly recovering. Twenty years later, "worldwide recording revenue [was] a fraction of what it was at its peak in 1999. In that banner year the industry claimed some $39 billion in global revenue . . . . In [2019's] dollars, the 1999 sum approaches $60 billion, two thirds higher than 2018's revenue harvest of $19.1 billion."[53]

The music industry recovery was not a recovery for record sales. Instead, an entirely new disruptive force eventually rendered the business model of CD sales and digital downloads largely moot. According to the Recording Industry Association of America, "[r]ecorded music revenues in the U.S. in 2023 continued strong growth for the eighth consecutive year. Total revenues grew 8% to a record high $17.1 billion at estimated retail value."[54] Although the revenue has not returned to pre-Napster levels, the continued increase is a positive development. But the primary growth is not in sales. "Streaming continued to be the biggest driver of growth with record levels of engagement in paid subscriptions, continued growth in ad-supported revenues, and growing contributions

---

49 *Id.*

50 A&M Records, Inc. v. Napster, Inc., 114 F. Supp. 2d 896, 917 (N.D. Cal. 2000), *aff'd in part*, 239 F.3d 1004 (9th Cir. 2001).

51 *See* John Borland, *Gateway ads urge "Rip, Burn, Respect"* CNET (Mar. 28, 2003), https://www.cnet.com/tech/home-entertainment/gateway-ads-urge-rip-burn-respect/.

52 Eamonn Forde, *Oversharing: How Napster Nearly Killed the Music Industry*, GUARDIAN (May 31, 2019), https://www.theguardian.com/music/2019/may/31/napster-twenty-years-music-revolution.

53 Bill Hochberg, *The Record Business Is Partying Again, But Not Like It's 1999*, FORBES (Apr. 11, 2019), https://www.forbes.com/sites/williamhochberg/2019/04/11/the-record-business-is-coming-back-but-its-not-1999-yet/?sh=1549bd5b3257.

54 Matthew Bass, "Year-End 2023 RIAA Revenue Statistics," RIAA (2024), https://www.riaa.com/reports/2023-year-end-music-industry-revenue-report-riaa/.

from new platforms and services."[55] Physical sales, in the legacy CD sales and the growing collectible vinyl market, represent just slightly more than 10 percent of the revenue.[56] Digital downloads are fading away, representing less than 2 percent of the market.[57]

To the extent there is a vinyl record resurgence, it reflects the same consumer behaviors that shape book purchases. Collectors want tactile experiences. They want to display works that have personal meaning, and they want to be able to share their collections with friends through common experiences and opportunities to give gifts. While music is the perfect medium to share through listening (or dancing) together, vinyl records had a much more engaging presence compared to five-inch plastic discs.

1.2. Web 2.0 and Whatever Comes Next

A variety of forces converged to transition the web from its static origins to the modern, social-media-driven sharing platform. These included the bursting of the dotcom bubble, the growth of Wikipedia and community-written content, the improvement of search functionality led by Google, and the further transition from blogging to micro-blogging to posting through Facebook, Twitter, and social media. The disruption created by the market crash provided an opening for new content ventures to compete—and quickly dominate—the web and the internet.

Economic disruption drove the transformation. The dotcom bubble burst, destroying a great deal of financial value and resetting the corporate pecking order regarding power and resources. For example, after peaking in March 2000, over the next two years, "the Nasdaq index fell 76.81 percent in the next two years."[58] The AOL merger with Time Warner and other corporate strategies simply could not survive in the face of such broad-based economic losses.

The economic decline dissuaded large traditional media companies from going deeper into the new technologies. Companies that had already done so were suddenly chasing losing investments. That gap, in turn, created opportunities for alternative content, particularly as the size of the online community continued to grow.

As the economic conditions hobbled the media giants' investments, the businesses on the internet were beginning to expand the potential of the technology. Mass media approached the internet as a delivery platform. New companies, however, saw the webpage as a new medium.

Darcy DiNucci coined the terms Web 1.0 and Web 2.0 in a 1999 article to explain the transformation occurring on the web.[59] "What we need to remember, though, is that the Web, as we know it now, is a fleeting thing. The relationship of Web 1.0 to the Web of

---

55 *Id.*

56 *See id.*

57 *Id.*

58 Adam Hayes, *Dotcom Bubble Definition*, INVESTOPEDIA (Jun. 13, 2023), http://www.investopedia.com/terms/d/dotcom-bubble.asp.

59 Darcy Dinucci, *Fragmented Future*, 53 Print 32 (1999), http://darcyd.com/fragmented_future.pdf.

tomorrow is roughly the equivalent of Pong to *The Matrix*."[60] DiNucci correctly anticipated that "[t]he Web we know now, which loads into a browser window in essentially static screenfuls, is only an embryo of the Web to come."[61]

DiNucci explained that the web was more than what appeared on the screen. Instead, "[t]he Web will be identified only by its underlying DNA structure—TCP/IP (the protocol that controls how files are transported across the Internet), HTTP (the protocol that rules the communication between computers on the Web), and URLs (a method for identifying files)."[62] Added to the DNA, DiNucci explained the need to connect large seventeen-inch screens and two-inch personal digital assistants (PDAs) using touch screens, joysticks, pens, or keyboards.[63]

The technology enabled users to communicate with other users just as effectively as it provided traditional media the ability to communicate with audiences. This shift from mass media to social media was nearly impossible to imagine prior to the advent of the web browser, but it quickly became inevitable.

In 2000, for example, Jimmy Wales and Lawrence Sanger launched a free online encyclopedia site, Nupedia. The free online service provided "peer-reviewed and edited content written by experts. However, Nupedia's process proved very slow: In the first six months, only two articles were published."[64] The team switched gears to take advantage of the public participation on the internet. They replaced Nupedia with a wiki. "[A]long came Wales' and Sanger's Wikipedia, which allowed anyone to write an article without review, generating massive growth: The website had more than 20,000 articles in 18 languages by the end of its first year, and a million by 2006."[65]

Wiki publication captured the benefit of social capital. "The idea behind Berners-Lee's Internet embraced the creation and expansion of social capital through technologically mediated communication. While there are many variations on the definition of social capital, one powerful definition focuses on 'features of social organization such as networks, norms, and social trust that facilitate coordination and cooperation for mutual benefit.'"[66]

The process of participating in wiki writing and shared anonymous writing quickly gave way to self-published writing—and posting of images and video—through personal web logs or blogs. The blogosphere quickly and massively outpaced wiki publishing. In 2010, for example, wikis had approximately 91,000 contributing authors, a small fraction of the 20 million bloggers.[67] That same year Twitter had 180 million users.[68]

---

60 *Id.* at 32.

61 *Id.*

62 *Id.*

63 *See id.*

64 *Wikipedia Launches*, History (Jan. 9, 2024), https://www.history.com/this-day-in-history/wikipedia-launches.

65 *Id.*

66 Jon M. Garon, *Wiki Authorship, Social Media, and the Curatorial Audience*, 1 Harv. J. & Ent. L. 96, 96–97 (2010) quoting Anita Blanchard & Tom Horan, *Virtual Communities and Social Capital* 7, in Social Dimensions of Information Technology: Issues for the New Millennium 6–22 (G. David Garson ed., 2000).

67 *Id.* at 104.

68 José van Dijck, *Tracing Twitter: The Rise of a Microblogging Platform*, 7 Int'l J. Media & Cultural Pol. 333 (2012).

The importance of social capital was reflected in the community shared by the users. Social media, including the friends and posts on Friendster, MySpace, and Facebook, offered direct connections, while Twitter's open architecture expanded the world further. Google's acquisition and transformation of YouTube fueled video as another medium for social media exchange.

Much of the content seems inane, but the small posts create a compelling mosaic for the regular participants. "Each little update—each individual bit of social information—is insignificant on its own, even supremely mundane. But taken together, over time, the little snippets coalesce into a surprisingly sophisticated portrait of your friend's and family member's lives, like thousands of dots making a pointillist painting."[69] The dominance of Facebook over MySpace has often been linked to inefficiencies, excessive advertising, and slow load times,[70] but Facebook also benefited from understanding that the Facebook News Feed became the "killer app" for social engagement.[71] Together, the social media landscape integrated the personal reflections on the user's community with news and most importantly personalized public opinion.[72]

Futurist J. G. Ballard shared a glimpse of this future, describing a dystopian world to come in a 1987 interview for *i-D Magazine*.[73] Ballard suggested that television was warping the European public's sense of reality, and inevitably "[e]very home will be transformed into its own TV studio. We'll all be simultaneously actor, director and screenwriter in our own soap opera. People will start screening themselves. They will become their own TV programmes."[74] Ballard's description has largely become the reality.

Adding to economic disruption and self-interested social capitalism as drivers of Web 2.0, the third was a massive shift in the online economy fueled by Google and exemplified by Amazon and eBay. Google's success as a search engine was based on the simple technological innovation that better search results would flow from prioritizing the pages with the most traffic. Yahoo! and other web portals were hierarchical in nature, publishing pages of links. By using its "backrub" algorithm, Google prioritized the pages that appeared most frequently through hypertext links. The search experience improved.[75] Google's ranking was fueled by the public's interest in each page ranked.

Unlike Yahoo! and other popular portal sites, Google was not a publisher, so it was not trying to promote its own pages and content. The many-to-many model of communication

---

69 *Id.* quoting Clive Thompson, *Brave New World of Digital Intimacy*, N.Y. Times (Sept. 5, 2008), https://www.nytimes.com/2008/09/07/magazine/07awareness-t.html?pagewanted=all.

70 *See* Evan Tarver, *3 Social Media Networks before Facebook*, Investopedia (Sept. 13, 2022), https://www.investopedia.com/articles/markets/081315/3-social-media-networks-facebook.asp.

71 *See* Thompson, *supra* note 69.

72 *See* Jan H. Kietzmann et al., *Social Media? Get Serious! Understanding the Functional Building Blocks of Social Media*, 54 Bus. Horizons 241 (2011).

73 *See* J.G. Ballard, *Predicted Social Media in i-D 27 Years Ago*, i-D (Jun. 12, 2014), https://i-d.vice.com/en_gb/article/jg-ballard-predicted-social-media-in-i-d-27-years-ago.

74 *Id.* quoting J. G. Ballard.

75 *See* Mark Hall & William L. Hosch, *Google*, Encyc. Britannica (Jun. 7, 2024), https://www.britannica.com/money/Google-Inc.

was more valuable than the mass media model of Web 1.0 and broadcast. In addition, Google grew in popularity in part because from 2000 to 2004, Yahoo! adopted Google as its search engine. The ads provided by Google did not dominate the search results, making it a much friendlier tool for consumers. As the volume of content on the web grew, portals became increasingly outmoded. With Google's search engine usurping portals for navigation, it quickly came to dominate the internet.

eBay and Amazon also embraced aspects of social communications in their platforms. Amazon did this through customer reviews while eBay initiated customer-to-customer transactions.[76] Web 2.0 had become a new medium based on the transcendence of many-to-many, social communications in place of the prior model of mass communication which had dominated since the advent of Gutenberg's press.

The dark side of Web 2.0 has been the growth of the advertiser economy and consolidation to three dominant ad platforms. While consumers benefit from free services, this comes at the cost of pervasive data tracking. By 2021, Google, Meta (Facebook), and Amazon accounted for 74 percent of all global digital advertising expenditures.[77] That concentration, however, seems to be in decline as digital payments to influencers and new competitors begin to erode the market dominance.[78] The use of persistent cookies and "dark patterns" further tracks and manipulates online users.[79]

"The pervasive nature of data collection techniques, which allow companies to gather massive amounts of information about consumers' identities and online behavior, enables businesses to adapt and leverage advertisements to target a particular demographic or even a particular consumer's interests."[80] These manipulative techniques pose heightened consumer risk because they are hard to detect and embarrassing to admit.[81]

The modern internet, or Web 2.0, has therefore become a new medium and marketplace in which news, data, information, digital objects, personal information, and behavioral patterns are all up for auction. The laws regulating digital content must therefore address the ownership, privacy, public disclosure, and reliability of that information as it is used by individuals and enterprises in every aspect of the public's daily lives.

---

76 *See How companies Are Benefiting from Web 2.0*, McKinsey Quarterly (Sept. 1, 2009), http://www.mckinsey.com/capabilities/mckinsey-digital/our-insights/how-companies-are-benefiting-from-web-20-mckinsey-global-survey-results#/.

77 Seb Joseph, *The Rundown: Google, Meta and Amazon Are on Track to Absorb More than 50% of All Ad Money in 2022*, Digiday (Feb. 4, 2022), http://digiday.com/marketing/the-rundown-google-meta-and-amazon-are-on-track-to-absorb-more-than-50-of-all-ad-money-in-2022/.

78 *See* Ethan Cramer-Flood, *US Ad Spending 2023*, Inside Intelligence (May 2023).

79 *See* FTC, Bringing Dark Patterns to Light (Sept. 2022), https://www.ftc.gov/reports/bringing-dark-patterns-light.

80 *Id.* at 2 (footnotes omitted).

81 *Id.* at 2–3.

1.3. The Economic Nature of Digital Objects

There are a number of fallacies about digital content, many of them stemming from pseudo-economic treatment of intangibles. Ideas, and perhaps factual information, are pure public goods in that they are nonrivalrous and nonexclusive.[82] Nonrivalrous means that the enjoyment of the idea by one recipient does not diminish the enjoyment of any earlier or later recipient.[83] Nonexclusive means that the enjoyment cannot be selectively delivered, but rather everyone within the zone of delivery will receive the benefit, whether the supplier desires such a broad distribution or not.[84] This was the core of the famous quote by Thomas Jefferson that "[h]e who receives an idea from me, receives instruction himself without lessening mine; as he who lights his taper at mine, receives light without darkening me. The light of the public ideas brightens the entire world."[85] The concept of public goods is consistent with the Roman property models. Air, sea, and free-flowing water are nonrivalrous in that no user generally reduces the enjoyment of each other.[86] None of these types of property can be held exclusively.[87]

Those properties which are both nonrivalrous and nonexclusive can be diminished by any individual, and therefore society does not respect any claims of ownership. Regardless of legal construct, social justice dictates that public goods are not subject to ownership and control. In the 1980s, before the advent of commercially viable digital content, William M. Landes & Richard Posner suggested that intellectual property is a public good.[88] They explained that intellectual property takes on this attribute because of its delivery aspects.

> While the cost of creating a work subject to copyright protection—for example, a book, movie, song, ballet, lithograph, map, business directory, or computer software program—is often high, the cost of reproducing the work, whether by the creator or by those to whom he has made it available, is often low. And once copies are available to others, it is often inexpensive for these users to make additional copies.[89]

For their work, the perfect illustration of copyrighted works as public goods was the over-the-air broadcasting of radio and television signals. Reception of amplitude

---

82 Adam R. Fox, *The Economics of Expression and the Future of Copyright Law*, 25 Ohio N.U.L. Rev. 5, 10 (1999); Richard Watt, *supra* n. at 3 ("[a] public good is characterized by admitting more than one user, with no user's consumption requiring any less consumption by any other user.").

83 *Id.*

84 *Id.* at 10–11.

85 Graham v. John Deere Co., 383 U.S. 1, 8 (1966) (quoting VI Writings of Thomas Jefferson at 180–81 (Washington ed. 1854)).

86 See Alfred C. Yen, *Restoring the Natural Law: Copyright as Labor and Possession*, 51 Ohio St. L. J. 517, 522–23 (1990) (discussing the potential limiting value on natural public goods and how overuse diminishes their value without affecting individual interests, but noting that access to such goods, like coastlines, can be privately controlled).

87 *Id.*

88 William M. Landes & Richard A. Posner, *An Economic Analysis of Copyright Law*, 18 J. Legal Stud. 325, 326 (1989).

89 *Id.* (noting that peer-to-peer networks and other technological advancements have reduced reproduction costs to nearly zero, with only an overhead cost for the computer, which is relevant only if the computer was purchased exclusively for copying copyrighted works).

modulation (AM), frequency modulation (FM), and broadcast television are each nonrivalrous. The addition of more television sets and radio receivers does not diminish the broadcast signal in any manner. The broadcasters also recognized that the signal is nonexclusive, so that the broadcaster had only general control over the ability to select recipients of the signal.[90] As a result, over-the-air broadcasting is a public good.

The problem with this description of over-the-air broadcasting is that it suggests that radio and television programming—the content being distributed—is a public good as well. The public good nature of the distribution model does not transform the underlying work's property attributes. Traditionally, the delivery of some copyrighted works such as books and phonorecords was treated as public goods because the manufacturing costs were low while the development costs were high.[91] These were not true public goods, since each copy of the work is exclusive. However, the ability of either the copyright owner or the infringer to cheaply expand the number of copies closely approximates the nature of true public goods. Each additional copy does have some costs, however, and legal regimes such as copyright retain the exclusivity to stop pirates and keep the copyrighted works from becoming public goods. Unlike over-the-air broadcasting, newspapers, CDs, and other distribution methods are not truly public goods.

Similarly, live indoor public performances in movie theaters and stage theaters are exclusive because each seat for the performance is sold individually. As a result, indoor public performances of copyrighted works have never been public goods. Nonetheless, the preeminence of over-the-air broadcasting as an entertainment and communications medium has influenced the public's perception that copyright protects public goods.

Here is where the advances in technology require that economic and normative models begin to differentiate between the delivery mechanism and the underlying interest. In the earlier cases of *Fortnightly Corp. v. United Artists*[92] and *Sony v. Universal*,[93] the Court was swayed, at least in part, by the public good nature of the delivery mechanism.

In *Fortnightly Corp.*, a local community antenna television (CATV)[94] system retransmitted broadcast signals from the local, over-the-air broadcasters to subscribers' homes using coaxial cable. United Artists sued, claiming that the rebroadcasts of its copyrighted motion pictures to the CATV company's paying subscribers were a public performance engaged in for profit by the CATV system.[95] The Court refused to find liability. As the Court explained, "a CATV system no more than enhances the viewer's capacity to receive the broadcaster's signals; . . . It is true that a CATV system plays an 'active' role in making

---

90 *Id.* (noting that broadcasters may have limited ability to control the outlaying audience by choice of signal strength and through placement of the transmitting tower).

91 Landes & Posner, *supra*, note 90 at 326.

92 Fortnightly Corp. v. United Artists, 392 U.S. 390 (1968); *See also* Teleprompter Corp. v. CBS, 415 U.S. 394 (1974).

93 Sony Corp. v. Universal City Studios, Inc., 464 U.S. 417, 429 (1984).

94 This is the precursor of modern cable broadcasting.

95 *See* 17 U.S.C. §1(c) (superseded) (providing for the copyright owner's exclusive right to "perform . . . in public for profit"). Fortnightly, 392 U.S. at 394.

reception possible in a given area, but so do ordinary television sets and antennas."[96] By providing the broadcaster's audience with the same content delivered through a similar vehicle, the Court found that no performance had taken place. This was heavily disputed by the dissent, which pointed out that over forty years of case law had supported the notion that retransmission was a public performance.[97] The dissent cited *Buck v. Jewell-LaSalle Realty Corp.*,[98] which the majority held was limited to its facts.[99] The significant distinction, according to the majority opinion, was that the original broadcast had been unauthorized—suggesting that had the original broadcast been a lawful one, rebroadcasting the signals to the public in the nonexclusive audience could not be a copyright violation.[100] The outcome is inconsistent with most, if not all, case law addressing public performance, because the unauthorized person has no legal right to expand, enhance, modify, or alter the public performance offered by the copyright owner, even if the target audience would not otherwise have changed.[101]

Although the Court never discussed the public good nature of the broadcast, it strongly suggested that if a member of the public has the access to a signal, then the intermediate actions to provide that same signal cannot violate the copyright owner's interest, even when conducted by an unauthorized third party. The result can best be explained as reflecting the understanding that the broadcast is essentially a public good, for which no copyright injury can be compensated by the court. Congress responded to *Fortnightly* and *Teleprompter* with a revision to the Copyright Act to make it clear that the public good approach to broadcasting was never the intent of the law.[102] As the Supreme Court later explained, under the copyright law revisions, "*both* the broadcaster *and* the viewer of a television program 'perform,' because they both show the program's images and make audible the program's sounds. . . . Congress also enacted the Transmit Clause, which specifies that an entity performs publicly when it 'transmit[s] . . . a performance . . . to the public.'"[103]

---

96 *Id.* at 399.

97 *Id.* at 406 (Fortas, J., dissenting).

98 283 U.S. 191 (1931).

99 *Id.* ("But in *Jewell-LaSalle*, a hotel received on a master radio set an unauthorized broadcast of a copyrighted work and transmitted that broadcast to all the public and private rooms of the hotel by means of speakers installed by the hotel in each room. The Court held the hotel liable for infringement but noted that the result might have differed if, as in this case, the original broadcast had been authorized by the copyright holder. 283 U.S., at 199, n. 5. The Jewell-LaSalle decision must be understood as limited to its own facts.")

100 Fortnightly, 392 U.S. at 396 n.18.

101 NFL v. Primetime 24 Joint Venture, 211 F.3d 10 (2d Cir. 2000) cert. denied, 2001 U.S. LEXIS 2486 (2001) (interception of broadcast signal); Columbia Pictures Industries, Inc. v. Aveco, Inc., 800 F.2d 59 (3d Cir. 1986) (rental of viewing room and video cassettes); Columbia Pictures Industries v. Redd Horne, 749 F.2d 154 (3d Cir. 1984) (rental of viewing rooms); WGN Continental Broad. Co. v. United Video, Inc., 693 F.2d 622, 624–25 (7th Cir. 1982) (retransmission of cable system); Hubbard Broad., Inc. v. Southern Satellite Sys., Inc., 593 F. Supp. 808, 813 (D. Minn. 1984), *aff'd* 777 F.2d 393 (8th Cir. 1985) (retransmission of cable system).

102 *See* Am. Broad. Companies, Inc. v. Aereo, Inc., 573 U.S. 431, 439 (2014) ("Congress also enacted the Transmit Clause, which specifies that an entity performs when it 'transmit[s] . . . a performance . . . to the public.'").

103 *Id.* at 441 (quoting 17 U.S.C. §101 (2024)).

Unfortunately, the *Fortnightly* approach was still adopted, at least in part, even after the revision of the copyright law. In *Sony Corp. v. Universal City Studios*,[104] the Court, in discussing whether the unauthorized, temporary copying of broadcast programming, known as time-shifting, could be deemed a fair use, invoked a variation of the public goods analysis:

> Theft of a particular item of personal property of course may have commercial significance, for the thief deprives the owner of his right to sell that particular item to any individual. Time-shifting does not even remotely entail comparable consequences to the copyright owner. Moreover, the time-shifter no more steals the program by watching it once than does the live viewer, and the live viewer is no more likely to buy prerecorded videotapes than is the time-shifter. Indeed, no live viewer would buy a prerecorded videotape if he did not have access to a VTR.[105]

The public goods approach to time-shifting was a central part of the thin majority's analysis. According to the evidence relied upon by the Court, time-shifting accounted for as much as 96 percent of the Betamax use, according to defendants, and at least 75.4 percent according to plaintiff's evidence.[106] No significant evidence was given to provide a percentage balance between authorized and unauthorized time-shifting, though some anecdotal evidence suggested that 20 to 56 percent would have been authorized, at least in part.[107] As a result, the fair use determination was critical to the outcome that Sony was not contributorily liable for the unauthorized time-shifting of its consumers. Had unauthorized time-shifting been found infringing, the Court would have had a much more difficult time determining if the Betamax machine was nonetheless noninfringing. The explanation that the time-shifting was not comparable to the theft of property undermined the important fair use factors, enabling the Court to find fair use for Sony.[108]

As digital distribution has become more widely understood, the Court has moved away from these critical decisions. In *ABC v. Aereo*,[109] the Court recognized that the 1976 Copyright Act specifically reversed the prior case law in *Teleprompter* and *Fortnightly*. In Aero, the cable broadcast redistributor tried to avoid creating a public performance by installing individual mini-antennas for each customer. The theory was that each individual retransmission would therefore constitute a private performance for just that single subscriber. While perhaps technically true, the same can be said of the copy shop that makes reproductions for one customer at a time. Nonetheless, the business of the copy shop would violate copyright if it were engaged in large-scale reproduction

---

[104] *See* JOHN LARDNER, FAST FORWARD: HOLLYWOOD, THE JAPANESE, AND THE ONSLAUGHT OF THE VCR (2d Ed. 2002); PAUL GOLDSTEIN, COPYRIGHT'S HIGHWAY: FROM GUTENBERG TO THE CELESTIAL JUKEBOX 149–58 (1994) (detailing reversal of majority of court from a finding of infringement to a finding of fair use).

[105] Sony Corp., 464 U.S. at 450 n.33.

[106] *Id.* at 424 n.4.

[107] *Id.*

[108] *Id.* at 450 (comparing infringement to jewelry theft).

[109] ABC v. Aereo, Inc., 573 U.S. 431 (2014).

of copyrighted works.[110] In the forty years that separated the decisions, the arguments that the public had free access to content simply because it had been broadcast disappeared. On the contrary, Aereo's technology demonstrated that companies could actually control even broadcast content at the individual customer level. The collection of individual performances constituted a public performance, making the rebroadcast a violation of copyright law.

The public good characterization ascribed to copyrighted works may also help to explain the congressional balancing regarding Section 110(5) with respect to rights granted to stores and restaurants to publicly perform broadcasts, so long as space and equipment limitations are met. Congress implicitly chose to acknowledge that broadcasting is a public good.[111] No market inefficiencies required Congress to provide this balance in favor of the stores and restaurants. The performing rights societies, such as American Society of Composers, Authors and Publishers (ASCAP) and Broadcast Music, Inc. (BMI), are quite efficient at licensing such uses.[112] Congress also treated broadcasting separately from live public performances, limiting the scope of Section 110(5) to broadcast rights only.[113]

Section 110(5) illustrates that where Congress and the courts provide statutory exemptions or fair use defenses for activities delivered under a regime of nonrivalrous, nonexclusive use, the regulations will result in the lowest impact on the copyright owner. Where the exemptions and defenses impinge on exclusively controlled activities, the copyright owner's economic and natural interests are more highly taxed. When the copyright owner cannot control the use of the work, congressional authorization of that conduct has only marginal impact; when Congress bars the copyright owner from exploiting an exclusive right which the copyright owner can control, however, the cost to the copyright owner is much greater. This practical reality may allow Congress and the copyright owners to agree on new rules that cost copyright owners relatively little but may serve to redraw that line which was crossed in *Sony*.

The transformation in the music industry underscores the concerns Universal first raised in its lawsuit against Sony Betamax. Industry leaders were concerned that the philosophy underlying home taping would change the public's relationship with copyright owners. The public goods attributes of ideas and broadcasting have been extended in the public's mind to copyrighted works more generally. The public goods imprimatur of copyright law was elevated into a philosophical agenda in 1987 with Steward Brand's

---

[110] *See* Princeton Univ. Press v. Mich. Doc. Servs., Inc., 99 F.3d 1381, 1385 (6th Cir.1996) (en banc); Blackwell Publg., Inc. v. Excel Research Group, LLC, 661 F. Supp. 2d 786, 792 (E.D. Mich. 2009); Basic Books, Inc. v. Kinko's Graphics Corp., 758 F. Supp. 1522, 18 U.S.P.Q.2d 1437 (S.D.N.Y. 1991).

[111] Congress did not go so far as to declare over-the-air broadcasting as a public good but instead provided a safe harbor for certain types of uses. 17 U.S.C. §110(5) (1999). *See supra* n. 82 and accompanying text.

[112] Economic Analysis of Copyright, *supra* note, 88 at 358.

[113] *Id.*

emphatic declaration that "information wants to be free."[114] This burgeoning approach exploded with the allegedly unregulable internet that developed thereafter.[115] The very phrase "information wants to be free" suggests that information is presently imprisoned, both in its physical trappings of books, celluloid, and polymer, and legally imprisoned in copyright's ever-expanding straightjacket.[116]

---

[114] Marci A. Hamilton, *Symposium: Copyright Law as Communications Policy: Convergence of Paradigms and Cultures: The Distant Drumbeat: Why the Law Still Matters in the Information Era*, 20 CARDOZO ARTS & ENT. L.J. 259, 260 (2002) (quoting Stewart Brand, *Finding a Balance in the Slippery Economics of an Information Age: Depending on Your Perspective, Data's Free—Or Priceless*, L.A. TIMES, Nov. 8, 1987, at C3 ("The Information Era was officially initiated when Stewart Brand of the Electronic Frontier Foundation declared that 'information wants to be free.'")).

[115] *Id.* at 260 ("This mesmerizing, utopian call [Brand's statement] has had a powerful impact, leading otherwise law-abiding citizens to declare that copyright law—the hackers' most hated legal regime—was dead, that national boundaries are ephemeral, and that privacy was impossible. They have treated the collection of new technologies we have dubbed an 'era' as the path to democracy, the path to free creative products, and the path to radical egalitarianism.").

[116] *Id.* Hamilton frames the anarchistic approach as follows: "The hackers who initiated the Information Era have touted an anti-government, anti-law, and anti-big business mentality that challenges the fundamentals of the modern legal, creative culture. The fertile ground of their radical posture has generated arguments against any regulation of the Web (even including child pornography regulations), arguments against sales taxes on the Web as though sales that happen to occur via the Web are categorically different from other types of sales, and, most vociferously of all, arguments that copyright laws are simply obsolete." *Id.*

2 Copyright's Power and Limitation over Digital Assets

By Vicenç Feliú

2.1. Introduction

The "Digital Age," beginning in the late twentieth century with the rise of personal computers and continuing into the early twenty-first century, has fundamentally altered the landscape of copyright law. This period, marked by the widespread use of digital electronics, digital devices, and the internet, has introduced a new era where it becomes much more difficult to judge whether someone's work is too similar to another's and if it has been directly copied. The issue of protection is no longer just about the tangible object but also the intangible manifestation of expression. While the aim of copyright law has always been to protect these intangible expressions, the scope has extended to include intangible digital creations alongside traditional, tangible objects. The concept of digital media is nothing new. It has been around for quite some time with the internet really propelling it to the forefront. Older forms, such as compact discs (CDs), digital photographs, and digital video discs (DVDs), were considered "perfect copies," because of their faithful reproduction of original works. The consensus remains that copying the protectable elements of a work constitutes copyright infringement, though the concern often revolves more around the existence of identical copies than economic impact. With the advent of the internet and peer-to-peer (P2P) file sharing, this concept mushroomed into something of astronomical proportions. Since files can be transferred easily at little to no cost, there is a higher chance of widespread distribution of copyrighted works without permission from the owners. While P2P has been one of the most controversial ways to share files due to its ease and widespread use, any form of digital media that is publicly displayed over the internet is susceptible to unlawful use. This could range from someone downloading a picture and using it to make a profit to bargain bin Flash artists who rip off each other's game coding. Enormous inflations in digital media have paved the way for the Recording Industry Association of America (RIAA), Motion Picture Association of America (MPAA), and other copyright protection entities to lobby for more stringent copyright laws and the ways in which they are enforced. A good number of these laws are still in debate, yet some have caused quite an impact on how copyright laws are used today.

The growth of the digital world has prompted many changes in the methods of creating, distributing, and using digital information. The changes have affected many categories of players in the information industry, including authors, publishers, musicians, recording companies, and software developers. The changes have also affected many users of digital information, including teachers, professors, students, and consumers of all kinds. The digital age is taking over, offering the world many wondrous opportunities to look up information and express intellectual endeavors. Digital media is in abundance and other social digital media sharing has become a haven for those seeking to take part in new and exciting ways to communicate. At the same time, innovation has flourished and the age-old fight for the creators' rights still rages on. To better understand the impact copyright laws have on digital media, one should look at how copyright started, how it has affected the current digital landscape, and how it will continue to be enforced in the future.

Changes in the information industry have prompted changes in copyright law. Generally, copyright law protects the rights of creators—such as authors, composers, and artists—against unauthorized uses of their works.[1] Copyright law provides a number of legal rules and remedies that can be used to enforce the rights of copyright owners. As the information industry evolves, so do the types of unauthorized uses that occur, which can also affect the costs and challenges of enforcing the rights of copyright owners. Therefore, it should not be surprising that changes in the information industry often prompt changes in the laws of copyright to address new forms of infringement and the growing complexities of enforcement.

2.1.1. Overview of the Digital Landscape

The rise of new communications technologies, particularly the growth of the internet, has created a new set of issues for copyright law. The ease with which digital works can be copied and transmitted has led to an increasing tension between the interests of copyright owners and the public's desire for free access to copyrighted works.

The nature of digital technologies and their potential for replication and dissemination of information have always posed a significant challenge to copyright law. In the 1960s, photocopying brought about a need to reassess the balance between the rights of copyright owners and the needs of information users. Conventional law focused on protecting the economic interests of the copyright owner, with protection being contingent upon

---

1 17 U.S.C. § 106; U.S. Copyright Office, *What Is Copyright*, COPYRIGHT.GOV, http://www.copyright.gov/what-is-copyright/#:~:text=U.S.%20copyright%20law%20provides%20copyright,rental%2C%20lease%2C%20or%20lending (last visited Apr. 28, 2024).

fixation, meaning the work must be written or recorded in some manner. Most digital works are fixed, though transiently (e.g., displayed on a screen). However, copyright law varies in different jurisdictions as to whether transient works are protected. The consensus is that to be protected, a work must be fixed for a period longer than that of a transitory duration.[2] The law was ill-equipped to deal with the shift toward global, instantaneous, and cost-free replication and dissemination of information made possible by digital technologies. This led to a shift in legislation toward protecting the interests of consumers and information users so as to not inhibit beneficial uses of information, though some have argued that legislative changes have swung too far in the opposite direction. This debate is particularly relevant in recent times due to the advent of Web 2.0, wherein user-generated content (UGC) and social networking frequently involve the use of existing copyrighted material.

Two key economic features of digital technology have greatly complicated the task of copyright owners in controlling the uses of their works. First, the cost of producing additional copies of a digital work is very low, possibly close to zero. This is because digital works are generally reduced to a string of binary digits that can be readily and faithfully copied by computers. Consequently, it is highly inefficient, if not impossible, for copyright owners to try to prevent unauthorized copying by reducing the supply of their works, a common method in the pre-digital era. For example, books are in short supply if a publisher prints only a small number of copies, but the advent of photocopying techniques forced publishers to rethink this strategy. Now, the publishers of digital works are faced with a choice between two different strategies for reducing the availability of their works and, therefore, limiting unauthorized copying. Publishers can use effective technological protection measures (TPMs) to prevent unauthorized access to their works, or they can rely on the fact that many consumers will not pay for something that they can get for free. This second strategy involves making the work available at a low cost while relying upon the threat of legal action to prevent consumers from copying instead of purchasing.

2.1.2. Importance of Understanding Copyright Law

How we access, download, store, and subsequently reuse files has vastly changed due to the shift from an analog to a digital society. The legal definition of a "copy" does not require an identical or literal reproduction but merely the copying of protectable elements from a protected work.[3] As technology advances, it is crucial to understand how copyright law relates to digital assets and how copying is facilitated by the digital environment. Users often disregard copyright issues regarding digital material, yet just because a work is available does not mean that it is free to copy. Copyright law is often seen as outdated and ill-suited for its intended purpose given the ease with which digital material is so easily reproduced and transmitted at no cost. However, this is a mistaken view, and it is often the case that those who feel free to copy would quickly change their stance and understand the importance of copyright if their own digital creations or livelihood were in jeopardy. People often forget that years of time, money, and effort

---

[2] 17 U.S.C. § 101.
[3] 17 U.S.C. § 101.

go into creating digital material, and for some, producing such work is their livelihood. While digital files can be easily and faithfully copied, retain their perfect condition after copying, and be accessible to further reproduction, this does not change the fact that the material may be protected by copyright law.

Understanding the fundamental concepts of copyright is essential to preserving the commercial incentives that drive the creation of new creative work. Although many may disagree with the ethics of copyright law, it remains an integral part of modern business, particularly affecting those who create digital material, such as artists and software developers. The fact that copyright is automatic means that any original work created and set in a fixed form is copyrighted, regardless of whether the creator is aware of this legal function.[4] This can lead to complications for those who decide to use the free culture known as "open source," where creators may find that their work has been built upon or reproduced without their consent. While open source is not illegal, it may contradict the intentions of the creator and may conflict with the potential for future earnings regarding the material.

Copyright law protects the rights of those who produce original work, covering various types of creations such as literature, music, drama, art, films, sound recordings and broadcasts, and architectural works.[5] This protection ensures that the original creator of the work is automatically safeguarded from their work being used or exploited without permission. The creator of the work can grant this permission through a license, either for a fee or by waiving the fee, which can also serve as a promotional tool for the creator. Permission for use may also be given in the form of a statement that the work is free to use, as is common in the open-source culture. For example, a particular piece of music might be made available for any purpose, a practice known as an indirect method of permission. However, even in such cases, permission would still need to be sought if the work were to be commercially exploited.

2.1.3. Purpose and Structure of Chapter

The subsequent sections will establish the basic framework of copyright law and its evolution in response to technological advancements. This will allow for a better understanding of its current authority. Subsequently, we will analyze economic theories of intellectual property and their parallels to the public good of data. This analysis is particularly relevant to digital media, as it will help assess the effectiveness of protected rights on consumer surplus, the cost of pirated and copied material, and the dynamic efficiency in the creation of cultural works. At this point, we will present the argument that current copyright laws are not aligned with the public good of culture and arts. This will set the foundation for examining the present challenges with digital media and their effects on both producers and consumers of copyrighted material.

---

[4] 17 U.S.C. § 102; Valancourt Books, LLC v. Garland, 82 F.4th 1222 (D.C. Cir. 2023).

[5] 17 U.S.C. § 102(a).

The primary purpose of the chapter is twofold: first, to present and examine the current impact of copyright laws on the production, dissemination, and consumption of digital media material. The chapter will focus on significant issues that question the effectiveness of copyright laws in an age where advanced technology has made accessing digital media almost effortless. It is argued that today's copyright laws are not adequately protecting the rights of authors and that piracy remains too effortlessly achievable. This has negatively affected not only the cost of digital media material but also the incentive to create, making it increasingly difficult for consumers to access legal copies of material, a critical characteristic of the second digital landscape.

The second purpose of the chapter is to analyze and propose changes to copyright laws that could restore balance and facilitate fair access to copyrighted material. This is important because much of the existing body of law that exists today is not because of deliberate policy choices but rather a by-product of incremental changes and pragmatic adaptations to past technological shifts. Given the rapid speed at which technology continues to change, it has become increasingly challenging for law and policymakers to ensure that copyright laws continue to fulfill their original purpose: to encourage the development of culture and arts while providing incentives to creators through rights protection.

2.2. Foundations of Copyright Law

The origins of copyright law can be traced back to early eighteenth-century England when the rise of the printing press brought about the need to protect the rights of its owners. The Statute of Anne, enacted in in 1710[6] and often regarded as the "birth of copyright law," marked the first formal attempt to restrict the unauthorized copying of printed books. The statute granted authors exclusive rights to their works for a limited time, making it the first law in history to define a specific duration of time for copyright protection. This legislation was largely a result of heavy lobbying by the "Stationer's Company," a group of individuals who were once sellers of manuscript books but found themselves by the printing press and sought a way to regain control over the book trade.

In the United States, the principles of the Statute of Anne were adopted by individual states before the federal government implemented its own copyright law, following the ratification of the Constitution in 1787.[7] The Constitution empowered Congress "[t]o promote the Progress of Science and useful Arts, by securing for limited Times to Authors and Inventors the exclusive Right to their respective Writings and Discoveries."[8] Over time, the notion of providing an "exclusive right" has been strengthened and extended, with modern copyright law placing greater emphasis on protecting not only an author's commercial interests but also personal reputation. By the end of the nineteenth century, there was a growing movement for the unification of copyright laws to address the

---

6 *Statute of Anne, 8 Ann., c. 19 (1710).*

7 U.S. Copyright Office, *The 18th Century Timeline*, COPYRIGHT.GOV, http://www.copyright.gov/timeline/timeline_18th_century.html (last visited Apr. 29, 2024).

8 U.S. CONST. art. I, § 8, cl. 8.

protection of foreign works. This culminated in the Berlin Text of the Berne Convention in 1908, which remains a foundational element of international copyright law today.[9]

2.3. Brief History of Copyright Law

In the fifteenth century, the British crown responded to the advent of the printing press by granting monopoly rights to publishers, thereby providing them exclusive rights to texts in order to protect their business interests. This monopoly, granted to the Stationer's Company, was the first form of copyright regulation in England that laid the foundation for the modern copyright system. The massive power of censorship by the Tudor and Stuart monarchs prompted a reaction from the English parliament, which led to the establishment of a statutory right of first publication and a right of copy for authors. This development culminated in the Statute of Anne, which, while ostensibly designed to regulate the printing industry and benefit the public, also served as a tool for the crown to selectively grant privileges to printers. In essence, the statute effectively replaced earlier rights and regulations, positioning the crown's control over information as being in the public's interest.

Modern copyright law traces its roots to the British printers' guilds of the late fifteenth century. These craft organizations formed around the printing of a specific type of written information, creating a monopoly by granting exclusive rights to their members and suppressing the printing of information outside their guild. The crown sought to assert control over these guilds through a series of restrictive acts, and the printers responded with petitions for independent privileges to control the printing of the works they specialized in. This early copyright was an expression of regulation and control by the dominant political and economic regime, not an effort by authors to protect their own intellectual creations. It was a tool used by the state and crown to suppress information outside the official system and to regulate the quality and content of published opinions. In this early stage, copyright was not considered an exclusive right or form of property, but rather a mechanism of censorship and state control.

There are records of authors attempting to restrain freedom of information and free competition through monopolies, dating back as far as ancient Greece. Philosophers have noticed that censorship and copyright are mirror images of each other: censorship regulates the public's access to information, and copyright regulates the public's access to the creator's information. Much like censorship, the impetus for copyright law has often come from an individual's desire to control or suppress dissenting information.

The Statute of Anne was set to expire around the time of the end of the Seven Years' War and the French and Indian War, raising questions about whether the regulation of colonial printers would revert to the Crown's copyright and the Acts of Trade and Navigation. In response, the Printers' Guild of New York sought to create a perpetual copyright through the key provisions of the 1767 and 1790 New York state copyright acts. Ultimately, a

---

9 *See* J. H. Reichman, *Design Protection in Domestic and Foreign Copyright Law: From The Berne Revision of 1948 to The Copyright Act of 1976*, 1983 Duke L. Rev. 1143 (1983).

compromise was reached, granting authors the right to secure a longer term of regulation and control over their works. This would make U.S. copyright different from all prior copyright and would make copyright something distinct from censorship, regulation, and control. This highly ideological transformation was strongly opposed by the crown and its print monopolies, but it became a cornerstone of the U.S. law, enshrined in the U.S. Constitution with the first Copyright Act. Today, the most current form of copyright law is embodied in the Berne Convention and its adherent international copyright treaties and conventions.

2.4. Core Principles of Copyright Law

The concept of authorship builds on the idea of subject matter in that, for a piece of work to be protected, it must have an identifiable author or authors, though the author can be anonymous or pseudonymous.[10] Authorship can serve as proof of ownership in the event of a dispute, though copyright is transferable, meaning the authorship does not always imply current ownership. In the case of a computer program, the term "author" can be substituted for "programmer." Since copyright is a property right, it is possible to transfer the rights of ownership from one person to another through a written agreement, which is particularly significant in the commercial industry where work is often carried out on a contractual basis. The duration of copyright will generally hinge on the lifetime of the author, with the exception of works made for hire, pseudonymous, or anonymous works.[11]

Subject matter concerns the types of works that qualify for copyright protection. Literary works, musical scores, films, and computer programs are all protected by copyright. It is essential to note that it is the expression of an idea that is protected, not the idea itself. Patent law, by contrast, protects ideas that can be expressed in a process, machine, manufacture, or composition of matter.[12] Although copyright protection is automatic, it is sensible to assert that a record should be kept of when a piece of work was created. In the event of a dispute pertaining to work that has been published, it is the date of the publication that is held as evidence. This poses problems for digital works which are subject to change in the absence of a clear publication, though the situation is analogous to an unpublished draft manuscript.

The core principles of copyright law can be classified under five areas: subject matter, authorship, infringement, ownership, and duration. Subject matter in copyright law refers to the types of works that are eligible for federal copyright protection, focusing on originality and fixation.[13] Authorship is the principle that copyright vests initially in the author or authors of the work.[14] Infringement involves the violation of the exclusive rights of copyright owners, such as the rights to reproduce, distribute, and develop derivative

---

10 17 U.S.C. § 102; 17 U.S.C. § 201(a).

11 17 U.S.C. § 302.

12 Mazer v. Stein, 347 U.S. 201 (1954).

13 17 U.S.C. § 102(a).

14 *Id.*; 17 U.S.C. § 201(a).

works.[15] Ownership is the principle that the owner of a valid copyright has a protectable property interest in their creative works. Duration corresponds to the "limited times" provision in the Constitution, ensuring that the property interest eventually transfers to the public domain.

2.5. Transition to the Digital Era

When copyright law was first codified, the world was vastly different from what it is today. The founders of the U.S. Constitution had a clear vision for what copyright was intended to achieve, and it is a far cry from what copyright has become today. To get a clear perspective on what copyright was intended to protect, we must go back to the U.S. Constitution. Article 1, Section 8 of the Constitution states that Congress shall have the power "[t]o promote the Progress of Science and useful Arts, by securing for limited Times to Authors and Inventors the exclusive Right to their respective Writings and Discoveries."

Copyright was originally designed to be an agreement between the public and an author. The author would be given copyright protection on their work for a limited amount of time, after which the work would enter the public domain. The author would be given an economic incentive to produce more works, ensuring financial reward for a limited amount of time. In turn, the public benefited by gaining access to new and innovative works. Once the copyright expired, the work would go into the public domain, and the public would have free access to build upon it and develop new works.

The system of protecting copyright in the United States was quite simple and stayed almost unchanged for nearly two hundred years. An author would go down to the Library of Congress, fill out a form, and pay a fee to copyright their work. Before the Copyright Act of 1976, this protection lasted for an initial twenty-eight-year term, with the option to renew for another twenty-eight years. At that time, an average of only about 15 percent of published works were actually copyrighted because it was an opt-in system that required the author to take action to secure their rights.[16]

With the advent of new technology, copyright law has changed drastically, shifting from an opt-in system to what is now an opt-out system. When international copyright standards from the Berne Convention were put into place in U.S. law with the Copyright Act of 1976 ("the Act"), copyright protection became automatic, granted to an author as soon as a work is fixed in a tangible medium. This means that an author no longer has to fill out forms or pay fees; copyright is automatically assumed, though it can be challenged based on the originality of the work. While registration is not required to enjoy the benefits of copyright, in the United States, registration is necessary to assert those rights in court.

---

15 17 U.S.C. § 106; 17 U.S.C. § 501.

16 *See* Duke Law School's Center for the Study of the Public Domain, *The Incredible Shrinking Public Domain*, Public Domain Day 2021 Shrinking (2021) http://web.law.duke.edu/cspd/publicdomainday/2021/shrinking; Brad A. Greenberg, *More Than Just a Formality: Instant Authorship and Copyright's Opt-Out Future in the Digital Age*, 59 UCLA L. Rev. 1028 (2012).

The duration of copyright has also significantly increased. For works created after January 1, 1978, when the Act came into effect, copyright protection lasted for the life of the author plus an additional fifty years. However, with the implementation of the Copyright Term Extension Act (CTEA) of 1998, an additional twenty years was added, making the duration of protection now in effect the life of the author plus seventy years. This represents a substantial shift from the original Copyright Act of 1790, which provided a fourteen-year term with an option to renew for an additional fourteen years. The extended duration was largely a result of efforts to harmonize U.S. copyright laws with the laws of other Berne Convention signatories.

2.6. Power of Copyright Law over Digital Assets

One way of understanding the power of copyright law over digital assets is to examine the extent to which digital assets are protected by the law. Copyright law has become the dominant form of regulation in relation to most internet content. The role of copyright law in internet content represents a significant shift in the power structures that surround the creation and distribution of content from the traditional paradigm. A key feature of copyright law is that it protects content at the point of creation, regardless of whether the creator wishes to protect it. This contrasts with the default perception of most digital content, which appears to be freely available for anyone to change or reproduce. Copyright law effectively creates property rights for "original works of authorship," and these rights are conferred on any content that meets the criterion of originality and is "fixed in a tangible medium of expression."[17] This very broad definition allows digital assets, from personal webpages to virtual chess games, to be protected by copyright, depending on the relevant jurisdiction and the level of originality in the content.

The scope of a "digital asset" is indeed wide, encompassing everything from computer source code to online video footage of a sports game. The defining characteristic of a digital asset, for copyright law purposes, is that it results from digitalization, the process of encoding information into discrete units. Because digital assets are typically complex and composed of various files and formats, determining the precise boundaries of the asset in question can be challenging. This complexity impacts the degree of protection offered by copyright law, and courts often interpret legislation through case law to distinguish between "original" and infringing works.

2.7. Defining Digital Assets

Digital assets are electronic records in which an individual has a right or interest. This term does not include an underlying asset unless it is itself an electronic record. They can be any information about a person, belonging to a person, or created by a person that exists in digital form, either online or on an electronic storage device, including the information necessary to access the digital asset. Digital assets can also be any form of valuable right that exists in a dematerialized electronic form, such as virtual currencies

---

[17] 17 U.S.C. § 106.

and other forms of electronic tokens. They include things like social media accounts, photographs stored in the cloud and on a computer, cryptocurrency, digital music libraries, loyalty points, gaming, bank accounts, medical records, and Nonfungible Tokens (NFTs). In the context of blockchain technology, digital assets often refer to cryptocurrencies and "altcoins." Digital assets are intangible goods that have been designed or generated utilizing computerized technology. They exist in binary form and are reliant on the computer environment for their existence. These assets are susceptible to many of the same contingencies that are found in the tangible world and are in some cases even more vulnerable because of their nature. Digital assets are not constant and what is here today may be gone tomorrow because technological changes will cause compatibility issues between hardware and software storage. These characteristics of digital assets make them vulnerable to the processes of degradation, planned destruction, and obsolescence. As digital technology continues to progress and the use of digital assets becomes more prevalent, the volume of digital assets that are at risk of contingencies will increase. However, there are measures that can be taken to safeguard digital assets in a similar way to tangible possessions. One example is through the use of copyright law.

2.8. Copyright Protection of Digital Assets

Copyright protection exists for a wide array of digital information, from digitally copied content to the content on websites. Copyright law can protect all types of digital information that meet the requirements for protection of other works. It gives the authors the right to control the ways in which their digital material is used. In the context of the digital environment, the reproduction right is particularly affected. It is the essence of the exclusive right that Congress is concerned about when it creates the right of copyright, for the protection of the copyright owner is the object of the constitutional provision.[18] The technology used to create and disseminate information in digital format has facilitated access to copyrighted work in its digital form. Copying for many types of works is as simple as a click of the mouse on a web page. This ready access to copying has introduced new considerations for copyright owners to consider regarding their copyrights. The ease with which a work can be reproducible may only be matched by the difficulty in preventing the copying of the work, and the potential economic impact may be proportional to the size of the audience since each recipient of a copied work usually constitutes an act of infringement.[19]

Moreover, streaming audio and video files has become a popular way to bypass the right to make a copy and the right to distribute and create a market for the downloading of such files. The streaming of these files is considered analogous to a public performance of the work and constitutes a transmission of the work to the public. This implies a right to retransmission, and a retransmission of a work to a new audience constitutes a new transmission. The transmission of works to the public via any media or method is

---

[18] Feist Publications, Inc., v. Rural Telephone Service Co., 499 U.S. 340, 361 (1991).

[19] U.S. Copyright Office, DMCA Section 104 Report (2001), http://www.copyright.gov/reports/studies/dmca/sec-104-report-vol-1.pdf.

crucial when considering the evolving technologies that involve digital assets, reinforcing the scope of copyright law.

Additionally, even a "linked" file can be considered a copy, as users are only a few automated steps away from downloading the original file to their devices. The right of public display and the right of public performance are also relevant when discussing the use of digital assets on the internet. Many hypertext markup language (HTML) files contain links to other files; the use of digital assets is such that the user is navigating through a series of pages, and an image or portion of text is displayed on the user's monitor. Such actions could implicate the right of public display of the work, further extending the relevance of copyright in the digital age.

The U.S. Copyright Act provides a copyright owner the exclusive right to authorize the use of his or her work on a computer to create a second copy of the work, such as a backup copy, or to load the work into temporary memory. This is known as the right to reproduce the work in copies. The right to distribute copies to the public is implicated when digital assets are placed on a website, and the files containing the pictures or articles are transmitted electronically to the viewer's computer. The downloading of these files would constitute the copying of the files, and the files are considered to be in "copy form." This occurs when the owner of a foreign website places a link on his site to a file contained on the owner's native website.

Copyright protection for digital assets is important in discussing the power of copyright law. Other exclusive rights, provided in § 106 of the Copyright Act, are the rights to reproduce the copyrighted work and to distribute copies of the copyrighted work to the public by sale or other transfer of ownership, or by rental, lease, or lending. This means that if one has a picture on his or her computer that is copyrighted, that person cannot print out a copy of that picture without the permission of the copyright holder.

2.9. Works Eligible for Protection

Under U.S. Federal law, copyright protection applies to original works of authorship that are fixed in a tangible medium of expression. This includes digital works that fall under the subject matter of copyright covered in Section 102 of the Copyright Act. However, to be eligible for copyright protection, a work must be original in the sense that it was not copied from another's work, and it shows creativity. The creativity requirement does not present a high bar, but it is not satisfied if the creative spark is utterly lacking or so trivial as to be virtually nonexistent.[20] For instance, a digitally remastered sound recording made as a copy of the original analog sound recording will rarely exhibit the necessary originality to qualify for independent copyright protection.[21] Similarly, a work is eligible for copyright protection if it is "original to the author," meaning that the work was independently created by the author and that it possesses at least some minimal degree of creativity. Furthermore, a work must have an "author" to be eligible for copyright, and

---

[20] Bleistein v. Donaldson Lithographing Co., 188 U.S. 239 (1903).

[21] Abs Entm't v. CBS Corp., 908 F.3d 405 (9th Cir. 2018).

this author must be a human being. Finally, collective works and compilations, including digital ones, are also eligible for copyright protection if the selection and arrangement are original. In essence, protection for digital works is no different than any other work falling within the scope of copyright.

2.10. Exclusive Rights of Copyright Holders

The granting of copyright to creators of their digital works gives them a bundle of exclusive rights to control the use of their works and the ability to distribute those rights to others. The copyright owner has the exclusive right to authorize or prevent the use of their work in specific ways. Because these rights can overlap, the violation of one of the rights in the bundle may lead to the violation of some or all the other rights. If another person wants to use the copyrighted work in a way covered by these exclusive rights, he or she must get permission from the copyright owner. One must keep in mind that most of the rights given in the bundle are technology-neutral, which means that they apply equally to physical and digital works. Given the global nature of digital works, the fact that the copyright owner's exclusive rights apply to works in their digital form means that the right holder has the same level of protection for the work, despite its nature.

2.10.1. Reproduction

The copyright owner is granted the exclusive right to reproduce the work in any medium, whether it is a photograph copied onto paper or scanned into a digital file. This right applies to new copies of the work, and in the context of digital assets, it carries considerable importance since digital copies can be reproduced without any loss of quality. It is conventional wisdom that the ability to prevent copying is the cornerstone of the copyright holder's exclusive rights but that is not all.

2.10.2. Derivative Works

The copyright owner also has the exclusive right to prepare derivative works based upon the copyrighted work. A derivative work is any new creation that is based on or derived from one or more existing works. Common derivative works include translations, musical arrangements, and dramatizations of a literary work. An often-cited example in today's digital world would be the various modifications of computer software programs. Given the global reach of digital works, the copyright owner's exclusive rights extend to digital forms, ensuring that any derivative digital work, such as software modifications, receives strong protection for the original right holder.

2.10.3. Distribution

The owners of copyrighted works have the exclusive right to distribute copies of such works and to perform those works via digital audio transmission. This right allows the copyright owner to sell, rent, lease, or lend a copyrighted work and to prevent the distribution of unauthorized copies. The distribution right is limited by the first-sale doctrine, which permits a third party to resell a copy of a work that was acquired lawfully. It would appear that the right of distribution applies equally to the physical or digital distribution of a work; however, the application of the first-sale doctrine to digital content is not straightforward. While physical copies of works in a digital format, such as CDs or DVDs, are subject to the first-sale doctrine, the conduct of transmitting the work digitally, so that another person receives a copy of the work, may not fall within the scope of the defense. This is because the digital transmission results in reproductions of the works involved, creating a new copy in the possession of a new person, which implicates the copyright owner's reproduction right as well as the distribution right. Furthermore, the World Intellectual Property Organization (WIPO) Copyright Treaty, which the United States has ratified, provides that authors have the exclusive right to authorize any communication to the public of their works, including making available to the public their works in such a way that members of the public may access these works from a place and at a time individually chosen by them.

2.10.4. Public Digital Performance

The digital performance right grants sound recording owners the ability to publicly perform their works through digital audio transmissions. However, this right is more restricted than other exclusive rights and is subject to exemptions such as compulsory licensing. A digital audio transmission includes the transmission of a sound recording in a digital or nonanalog format, like streaming music, but excludes the transmission of any audiovisual work. However, this right is limited to public performances, meaning that downloading music over the internet is not considered a public performance, but streaming music is.

The Digital Performance Right in Sound Recordings Act of 1995 (DPRA) creates two rights: a public performance right in sound recordings limited to certain "digital audio transmissions" and a compulsory license for "digital phonorecord delivery." The public performance right is limited to performances that occur "publicly" and is limited to sound recordings, which are excluded from the public performance right created under Section 106(4) of the Copyright Act.[22]

2.10.5. Public Display

The Act grants authors the exclusive right to display their copyrighted work publicly. This right is technology-neutral, covering displays made directly or utilizing any device or process "now known or later developed."[23] The right of public display is available for literary, musical, dramatic, and choreographic works; pantomimes; and pictorial, graphic, or sculptural works, including the individual images of a motion picture or other audiovisual

---

[22] The Copyright Act, 17 U.S.C. § 106(4), grants creators of music and audiovisual works the exclusive right to perform their copyrighted musical works publicly. 17 U.S.C. § 106(6) grants the right to perform copyrighted sound recordings publicly by means of digital audio transmissions.

[23] Nicklen v. Sinclair Broad. Grp., Inc., 551 F. Supp. 3d 188 (S.D.N.Y. 2021).

work. To infringe this exclusive right to public display, the infringer must show a copy of the work, either directly or by means of a film, slide, television image, or any other device or process.[24] A work is displayed publicly when it is shown at a place open to the public or at any place where a substantial number of persons outside of a normal circle of a family and its social acquaintances is gathered, transmitted, or otherwise communicated to the public regardless of whether members of the public receive it in the same place, separate place, and at the same time or different times. Therefore, unauthorized display on television or over the internet, or unauthorized display at a restaurant or other public place, can violate the public display right.

2.11. Protection Mechanisms for Digital Assets

Digital Rights Management (DRM) systems encompass a range of technologies designed to package content with encryption and various access control mechanisms, regulating how, when, and by whom a work can be used. DRM systems are increasingly being deployed in applications beyond commercial music and are now integrated with the operating systems of consumer electronics and PCs. At the highest level of integration, operating systems can enforce access controls developed by content providers. For instance, recent versions of Microsoft Windows Media Player can enforce access control restrictions specified by content owners through the DRM feature built into Windows Media Audio and Video. Adobe has similarly incorporated DRM technology into the PDF format, embedding document security controls that govern access, and prevent copying and pasting. Beyond encryption and access controls, DRM systems may also include monitoring technologies, such as installable software that tracks the use of unprotected works, or web server plug-ins that log all access to protected web pages. These monitoring tools aim to provide information about possible infringers and uses of a work that fall outside the scope of the access control measures.

The change in the nature of digital assets has led many to question the viability of the current copyright law for protecting these assets. In the twentieth century, the rapid expansion of computer and internet technology resulted in the severe devaluation of intellectual property through ease of reproduction and distribution. These concerns prompted the search for mechanisms to supplement copyright laws by offering self-help technologies that copyright owners could use to prevent unauthorized use and distribution of their works. These new mechanisms operate by controlling access to the protected works and by monitoring, and in some cases preventing unauthorized uses.

2.11.1. DRM Systems

While most legislators and industries agree that the extension of copyright to digital works is both necessary and beneficial, disagreement arises over the best method for achieving this. Technological protection measures (TPMs) seek to prevent unauthorized uses of works and run the gamut from the control of consumer behavior to more secure

[24] Hunley v. Instagram, LLC, 73 F.4th 1060 (9th Cir. 2023).

methods designed to prevent infringement. Perhaps the most widely known and understood DRM system is region coding on DVDs. By preventing DVDs purchased in one country from being played on machines bought in another, the movie industry can control the release dates of films in different markets. While this system generated hostility among consumers, it is a relatively mild form of DRM and served to maximize profits during the all-important initial release of a film. More sophisticated TPMs involve encrypting a work so that it can only be accessed and/or altered using a specific application. For example, ebooks purchased from NetLibrary could only be read using the free Adobe Reader and cannot be printed or saved. This is a high-security method designed to prevent dissemination of the work and has become more prevalent as the distribution of pirated ebooks increases. At the extreme end of the scale lie TPMs that seek to control consumer behavior itself to prevent infringement from occurring. For example, in the infamous Sony BMG scandal in 2005, Sony BMG placed rootkit software on music CDs, allegedly to prevent unauthorized copying. This software was installed without consumer knowledge and created serious security vulnerabilities in affected machines.[25] The sheer overtness of DRM in these cases provoked hostile consumer and industry reactions, including a class-action lawsuit against Sony BMG and a boycott of its products. However, given the high stakes involved in digital content industries, it is likely that such methods will continue to be used as industries view the loss prevention benefits as outweighing the costs of damage to consumer relations and security.

2.11.2. Watermarking and Fingerprinting Techniques

Watermarking is a well-known method for protecting multimedia assets. A watermark is a visible or invisible marker that is embedded in the original media to signify the ownership of the content. Visible watermarks are often logos or text placed over a picture or video and are the least secure form of watermarking because they can be removed by cropping the image or covering the mark. Invisible watermarks have been implemented for images, audio, and video, and tend to be robust against tampering. The method involves making slight modifications to media content in such a way that the changes are noticeable when extracting the watermark but imperceptible to a viewer. If the content is stolen or used without permission, the watermark can be extracted and used as evidence of ownership. This method is supported by several companies such as Digimarc and Mediabolic, who provide services for embedding and extracting watermarks in content. Similarly, fingerprinting involves creating a unique identifier for a piece of content that is derived from the content itself. If the content is found elsewhere on the internet, the fingerprint can be used to detect a match and identify the owner of the content. Digimarc also provides a service for audio and video fingerprinting, and there are a few other companies that offer various fingerprinting methods for different types of content. Both watermarking and fingerprinting only provide a means of proving ownership of media and do not prevent unauthorized use.

---

[25] Free Software Foundation Europe, *Revisiting the Sony Rootkit*, http://fsfe.org/activities/drm/sony-rootkit-fiasco.en.html.

2.11.3. Encryption and Access Control Measures

One of the most debated aspects of copyright law in the digital environment is the use of access control technologies to restrict unauthorized use of copyrighted works. As previously outlined by the WIPO Copyright Treaty, protection and enforcement of digital copyright are of great importance. It can be argued that the more effective the access control technology is, the more likely the copyright owner will be able to enforce their copyright. This means that strong access control technology may act as a deterrent to copyright infringement. On the other hand, technologies that prevent consumers from copying and using digital content in ways not authorized by the right holder may be a mixed blessing for copyright owners. This is because if access control is too effective, it may prevent the making of legitimate private copies and the use of copyrighted works, which copyright law allows. Access control is linked to encryption where one access control method is to provide the consumer with a decryption key that allows access to an encrypted file. This can assure high security as the consumer is prevented from sharing the encryption key with others. An example of access control technology is regional encoding on DVDs as discussed above. This could have a negative effect as it may even cause consumers to infringe copyright by modifying their DVD player to bypass the regional encoding.

Encryption involves the transformation of the contents of a file into another form using an algorithm. It provides a high level of security and is regarded as one of the most effective methods for protecting digital content. When a file is encrypted, a key is needed to read the contents. This is useful for content owners because encryption prevents unauthorized access and reproduction of protected works. It is also effective in preventing the alteration of files. However, encryption has the disadvantage that the strength of protection is proportional to the cost. Stronger encryption methods not only provide higher security but also prevent legitimate access to content since current encryption methods cannot distinguish between legal and illegal viewers. This has significance in relation to private copying exceptions. If encryption methods are too strong, they may prevent consumers from making copies for their own private use.

2.11.4. Notice and Takedown Procedures

In addition to the above technical measures, the Digital Millennium Copyright Act of 1998 (DMCA), as discussed below, provides a "safe harbor" for online service providers who meet certain conditions. Realizing the potential impact of legal measures on the technical advances, the WIPO Copyright Treaty and the WIPO Performances and Phonograms Treaty were adopted in 1996 and came into force in 2002. These treaties allow contracting parties to provide adequate legal protection and effective legal remedies against the circumvention of effective technological measures and against devices, products, or components primarily designed to circumvent these protections.

If copyright infringement continues despite these protections, the DMCA also provides remedies for copyright holders. This involves taking legal action against an infringing party. However, the copyright owner is only able to take this action if they can locate the infringing site or individual. This creates a need for a system to effectively track and locate the location of copyright infringements. An extension of this would require the infringing party to cease their activities and remove the infringing data or content. This is the exact intention of a notice and takedown procedure which provides a quick and efficient way for copyright owners to require an online service provider to remove copyrighted content.

2.12. Enforcement Mechanisms

When copyright owners find someone using their work without permission, what can they actually do to prevent further damage? The simplest way is to directly contact the infringing party and request that they stop using the asset. If this fails, the copyright owner can take legal action. At this point, copyright laws come into play. The legal framework for copyright enforcement in the United States is basically provided by the Copyright Act. The Act covers various key provisions to ensure copyright enforcement. First, it defines what are the subject matter that can be copyrighted in Section 102. Then, it defines the rights of the copyright owner providing a clear set of exclusive rights in Section 106. In the sections between 107 and 122, the Act also defines the limitation to the bundle of rights and the works that are not protected by copyright, thereby making it a differentiating factor from other laws. The Act also covers provisions for the duration of copyright for different works.

When infringement happens, copyright owners can seek injunctions to prevent the use of their works while seeking a resolution through the courts. In some cases, the infringement may concern a criminal offense or may involve parties outside the jurisdiction of the Copyright Act. The Agreement on Trade-Related Aspects of Intellectual Property Rights (TRIPS) requires that enforcement procedures be implemented so that infringing acts involving the importation of infringing materials are treated as a criminal offense. Civil remedies are available to the copyright owner which can include damages, injunctions, and recovery of legal costs. It is worth noting that in any legal action, global enforcement can always be possible as long as both countries in question are members of the agreement concerned.

To enforce their rights, copyright owners must stay vigilant about unauthorized uses of their works. Digital assets can be monitored through the use of specialized search engines designed for this purpose. Multimedia asset search systems enable copyright owners to search the web for multimedia files by using queries based on text, images, and sounds. These systems help right holders protect their copyright and make sure that the use of their media is being properly compensated for.

Monitoring the unauthorized use of digital assets involves actual observation and keeping track of the usage of the asset, and there are various ways to do this. Copyright owners can use digital watermarks to embed information in the asset that identifies the owner and user of the asset. This information can then be retrieved and used to prove that the user is infringing copyright. For example, there are many services that provide digital watermarks with imperceptible digital information added to a file that is unique to the file and its owner.

The DMCA has been a significant addition to U.S. law marking the beginning of a new era in U.S. copyright enforcement. The DMCA was enacted to strengthen copyright protection in the digital age. It prohibits circumventing a technological measure that effectively controls access to a copyrighted work and trafficking in services or devices that aid an individual to circumvent a technological measure.[26] In general, it has been noted that the DMCA tips the balance of U.S. copyright law more heavily toward the interests of copyright owners by providing them with new enforcement tools while placing greater responsibility on service providers for policing online copyright infringement. Title II of the DMCA, the Online Copyright Infringement Liability Limitation Act (OCILLA), creates a safe harbor for online service providers by limiting their liability for copyright infringement by their users. To qualify for the safe harbor, service providers must adhere to and qualify for the limitations on liability set forth in the section. A service provider is defined as a provider of online services or network access, or the operator of facilities therefore, and includes an entity offering the transmission, routing, or providing of connections for digital online communications between or among points specified by a user, of material of the user's choosing, without modification to the content of the material as sent or received.

2.12.1. Legal Remedies for Copyright Infringement in the Digital Realm

Under the Act, copyright infringement claims can include direct infringement of the exclusive rights of copyright owners, infringement of attribution or integrity rights under the Visual Artists Rights Act (VARA), secondary infringement, and violations of the DMCA. In the digital realm, statutory secondary liability for copyright infringement may arise when a person provides a service primarily for the purpose of facilitating copyright infringement over the internet or another digital network.

Civil remedies for copyright infringement claims under the Act include injunctions, various types of monetary relief, impoundment, and reasonable attorneys' fees. Both the Act and DMCA give courts discretion to award reasonable attorneys' fees to the prevailing party in cases brought under either statute. The Act also contains provisions designed to prevent the circumvention of digital copyright protection systems under 17 U.S.C. §§ 1201 and 1202. Violations of these sections are subject to civil remedies under § 1203, which include the recovery of actual damages and the defendant's profits, or statutory damages.

Additionally, a copyright owner may seek an injunction to stop the infringement, sue for damages and profits, or pursue both remedies in a single action. If actual damages and profits are sought, the parties are entitled to a jury trial on the matter. The most commonly used measure of actual damages is the extent of the injury to the market value of the copyrighted work.

---

[26] Yout, LLC v. Recording Indus. Ass'n of Am., Inc., 633 F. Supp. 3d 650 (D. Conn 2022).

Civil remedies for copyright infringement are outlined in the Act itself. Section 501 defines copyright infringement as the violation of any of the exclusive rights granted to the copyright owner. Under Section 502, a copyright owner may seek an injunction to prevent further infringement, as well as recover damages, including profits, actual damages, and, in some cases, statutory damages. An infringer who is found liable for statutory damages may be required to pay a minimum of $750 per work infringed and a maximum of $30,000 per work infringed, or if the infringement was committed willfully, a maximum of $150,000 per work infringed. An award of reasonable attorney's fees and costs is also available to the prevailing party. This fee-shifting provision gives copyright owners a significant advantage over those in other civil cases, increasing the likelihood of being able to find and afford competent legal representation. Copyright cases are also attractive to attorneys because of the potential for a high dollar award, encouraging many attorneys to take cases on a contingency fee basis.

The Act provides four primary remedies for infringement: (1) preliminary and final injunctive relief, (2) court orders to impound the allegedly infringing work pending completion of the trial and to destroy same upon a successful verdict, (3) the recovery of either actual damages suffered as a result of the infringement and any infringer profits or statutory damages if the infringement is found to be willful, and (4) full costs by or against any party (other than the United States or an officer thereof) and a reasonable attorney's fees.[27] However, copyright owners who fail to register their work with the Copyright Office, or who have registered their copyright more than three months of its first publication, may not be entitled to statutory damages.

While civil remedies are most common, criminal enforcement of copyright is perhaps the most dramatic and controversial method of protecting the rights of copyright owners. However, the public interest in this area is growing—a fact evidenced by recent changes and emphasis on the part of the U.S. government and copyright owners. The criminal enforcement of copyright is addressed in Section 506 of the Act which is titled "Criminal Offenses." Under this provision, the government, on behalf of the copyright owner, may criminally prosecute a defendant who willfully infringes a copyright for purposes of commercial advantage or private financial gain. The burden of proof in a criminal copyright case is higher than in a civil case. The government must show that the defendant acted with an intent to defraud the right holder. If convicted, the defendant will be subject to the forfeiture of any property used or intended to be used in committing the crime and will face up to five years in prison. Intent can often be inferred from conduct, such as using camcorders to copy movies in a theater for piracy purposes. The use of cameras in such a setting is typically sufficient evidence of the infringer's intent to copy and distribute the work for financial gain.

---

27 17 U.S.C. § 502.

2.13. Case Studies Illustrating Copyright Law's Power over Digital Assets

Case studies of recent high-profile events involving music-related digital assets illustrate the power of copyright law vis-à-vis digital technology. Technological advances have had a profound effect on the music industry. This industry was the first to be fundamentally altered by the development of technologies for the recording, manipulation, and transmission of sound. In many respects, technological change has eroded copyright law's ability to provide effective protection for the rights of certain copyright holders. The events detailed in the case studies below, however, show that the basic structure of copyright law remains intact. Despite radical changes in the recorded music industry, copyright law still operates to confer a set of exclusive rights to copyright holders, and still provides mechanisms for enforcing those rights against unauthorized uses of protected material, even when that material is transformed into digital form.

In *MGM Studios, Inc. v. Grokster, Ltd.*,[28] a group of copyright holders in the film and music industries brought legal action against the distributors of popular P2P file-sharing applications Grokster and StreamCast. The copyright holders claimed that the companies profited from widespread copyright infringement and, therefore, were secondarily liable for infringement committed by individuals who used their software. The case eventually made its way to the U.S. Supreme Court, where the court found that the distribution and promotion of a device or service used to infringe would render the promoter contributorily liable for the infringement.[29]

The RIAA later filed several lawsuits against individuals who were suspected of copyright infringement via P2P networks such as Kazaa and LimeWire. In *RIAA v. Verizon Internet Services, Inc.*,[30] the RIAA sought to subpoena the personal information of Verizon customers who were suspected of copyright infringement. This case resulted in a landmark decision on the issue of when it is proper for a subpoena to be issued to an Internet Service Provider (ISP) and what the plaintiff must demonstrate.[31]

Section 4(2)(3)(B) of the DMCA created a cause of action for copyright infringement against individuals who circumvent technology designed to control access to or protect copyrighted works. An example of such activity would be the distribution of a program or code that disabled encryption on certain types of audio or video files.

In *RIAA v. Diamond Multimedia, Inc.*,[32] the RIAA took legal action against Diamond Multimedia for producing the Rio, a device that allowed individuals to play MP3 files. The RIAA claimed that because MP3 files of copyrighted songs could be stored on a computer and later transferred to the Rio, the device facilitated copyright infringement. However,

---

[28] Metro-Goldwyn-Mayer Studios, Inc. v. Grokster, Ltd., 545 U.S. 913 (2005).

[29] *Id.*

[30] Recording Indus. Ass'n of Am., Inc. v. Verizon Internet Servs., Inc., 351 F.3d 1229 (D.C. Cir. 2003).

[31] *Id.*

[32] Recording Indus. Ass'n of Am. v. Diamond Multimedia Sys., Inc., 180 F.3d 1072 (9th Cir. 1999).

the court found that although the potential for copyright infringement was great, the Rio was capable of substantial noninfringing uses and thus did not, in itself, constitute copyright infringement.[33]

Online copyright infringement has become a significant issue in recent years. With the increased popularity of the internet, social media networks, and digital media players, copyrighted materials have become increasingly accessible to large numbers of individuals. As a result, the record and film industries have claimed that the volume of copyright infringement has caused substantial harm to their markets and distribution channels.

2.14. Limitations and Exceptions

Sections 107 through 122 of the Act delineate the limitations and exceptions to the exclusive rights held by the copyright owner. Historically, copyright law has prevented individuals from exercising their rights as consumers by appropriating commercial works for their personal use. To address the perceived imbalance, the "doctrine" of fair use was codified into U.S. copyright law (and similar laws in other nations) through a series of judicial decisions and statutes.

The contemporary fair use doctrine creates a limited privilege for certain uses that would otherwise constitute infringement. Determining whether a particular use qualifies as fair use is determined by a case-by-case inquiry into four factors: (1) the purpose and character of the use, (2) the nature of the copyrighted work, (3) the amount and substantiality of the portion used, and (4) the effect of the use upon the potential market for the copyrighted work.

The fair use doctrine has played a significant role in the development of a number of digital technologies in recent years. Courts have found fair use to permit reproductions of copyrighted works as thumbnails in internet search engines[34] and the incidental inclusion of cultural artifacts in the backgrounds of photographs and videos.[35] In perfect harmony with the creative spirit of fair use, digital artists have found new and innovative ways to comment upon and criticize popular culture through the manipulation of copyrighted works. However, judicial decisions involving fair use in the context of emerging technology are often criticized for being ad hoc and unpredictable. The absence of bright-line rules is said to chill investment in the very technologies that a robust fair use doctrine would seek to protect. This has led to calls from certain consumer groups and technology industries for a more flexible exception that would allow any use that does not directly compete with the original work.

---

[33] *Id.*

[34] Perfect 10 v. Amazon, 487 F.3d 701 (2007).

[35] Peter Jaszi, *Copyright, Fair Use and Motion Picture*, 3 Utah L. Rev. 715 (2007); Trevor G. Reed, *Fair Use as Cultural Appropriation*, 109 Cal. L. Rev. 1373 (2021).

2.14.1. Fair Use Doctrine

The fair use doctrine, as established by the Act, permits the use of copyrighted materials in a manner that does not infringe or violate the original creator's copyright. This doctrine is not unique to U.S. law and has been the subject of debate and legislation in many other jurisdictions. In Common Law countries, fair use has been the subject of case law to determine and test whether the use of certain copyrighted material is fair or unfair. Essentially, fair use provides "a privilege in others than the owner to use the copyrighted material in a manner which does not infringe the copyright."[36]

In U.S. law, the fair use doctrine originated from a string of judicial holdings going back to the earlier part of the nineteenth century that have been codified in Section 107 of the Act. The statute explicitly distinguishes between fair use and copyright infringement. To ascertain whether a use is "fair," courts are required to consider four factors, as previously mentioned above: (1) the purpose and character of the use, including whether such use is of a commercial nature or is for nonprofit educational purposes; (2) the nature of the copyrighted work; (3) the amount and substantiality of the portion used in relation to the copyrighted work as a whole; and (4) the effect of the use upon the potential market for or value of the copyrighted work.

Notably, some courts have specifically stated that the final factor, which concerns market impact, is the "most important."[37] The fair use doctrine is complex, fact-specific, and ambiguous, making it difficult to advise clients with a great deal of certainty. This uncertainty poses a cost to right holders by increasing the risk of litigation and may also diminish the value of their copyrights. However, in *Campbell v. Acuff-Rose Music, Inc.*, the U.S. Supreme Court found that the fourth statutory factor should be evaluated within terms of market substitution, rather than the mere diminution of economic value.[38] Thus, a use will likely only be considered infringing if its fair use has substituted the copied work for the original work, offering some degree of certainty for right holders.

2.14.2. Transformative Use

Transformative use goes beyond the original work, for example, when the audience for a work is changed in some way and the work is used for a completely different purpose from the original, or a new work is created that does not harm the market for the original. Demonstrating transformative use can be more difficult than traditional fair use because the new work often qualifies as a derivative work. In copyright law, a derivative work is one based upon one or more preexisting works, such as a translation, musical arrangement, dramatization, fictionalization, motion picture version, sound recording, art reproduction, abridgment, condensation, or any other form in which a work may be recast, transformed, or adapted.

---

36 Sharon K. Black, Telecommunications Law in the Internet Age 243 (2002).

37 Campbell v. Acuff-Rose, 510 U.S. 569 (1994).

38 *Id.*

Courts have also favored fair use findings under the fourth factor when a work is being used for educational purposes. If the nature of the original work is more informational than expressive, this will be weighed with the second factor in favor of fair use. If the material is presented as part of an exercise to teach students how to look at culture through the lens of another era, permitting students to review actual examples of that culture might be deemed essential to the educational objective. In such cases, the use is likely to be viewed as superseding the original work.

2.14.3. Public Domain

When a creative work's copyright term expires or when a copyright holder decides not to enforce their rights, the work enters the public domain and can be freely used by anyone in any way. Unlike copyrighted material, which is privately owned and cannot be used without permission, public domain works are considered public property and can be utilized in any way. This gives a tremendous amount of freedom to public domain works. Any part of a public domain work can be used and edited to create a new work. For example, Benjamin Franklin's article "An Economical Project" is a public domain work, available for anyone to copy and use without restriction since no one holds the rights to it.

With copyrighted works, only specific portions of the work can be used loosely under fair use. Literal copying of an entire copyrighted work cannot be considered fair use. The use of portions of a protected work must be examined, on a case-by-case basis, to determine whether the use qualifies as fair. These boundaries and rules do not apply to public domain works, which can be adapted with complete creative freedom. With so many restrictions and rules set on copyrighted works, digital asset managers may find that it is easier to work with public domain works and create new works from them. With public domain works having fewer restrictions, the margin for creativity is much wider as compared to working with copyrighted works under the fair use doctrine.

2.15. Emerging Issues and Challenges

The traditional copyright system has become increasingly complex with the introduction of digital assets, and as a result, it has led to various emerging issues and challenges in the copyright world. This part of the chapter will explore these emerging issues and challenges that have arisen, or may arise, from the application of long-standing copyright law to new and innovative media.

One of the most significant challenges involves user-generated content (UGC) in the digital world. Often, UGC may imitate or recreate copyrighted material without proper permission to do so. Although copyright law was originally designed to protect content creators, the public policy behind encouraging public use of said material may lead to a law reform in which it may be too harsh to persecute UGC creators for copyright breaches. This shift may further diminish the rights of copyright owners should the courts determine that UGC is not a breach of copyright or that the penalties for doing so are lesser than "professional" copyright infringements.

Likewise, Artificial Intelligence (AI)-generated works present significant challenging issues in copyright in the digital world. At the very heart of copyright protection for AI-generated content lies issues pertaining to ownership, authorship, and infringement. U.S. copyright law does not have a specific copyright regime addressing AI-generated works; rather, the act of creation, determination of authorship, and originality are paramount in deciding the subsistence of copyright. Since copyright requires a "creative spark" tied to human authorship, only works created by human authors are currently protectable by U.S. copyright law.

However, the U.K. model offers a potential framework for addressing ownership of AI-created works. While there is no explicit regime for AI under U.K. copyright law, the Copyright, Designs, and Patents Act (CDPA) of 1988 states that in the case of a computer-generated work, the author shall be deemed to be the person who made the arrangements necessary for the creation of the work.[39] This blurs the line between machine and human authorship and will require substantial navigation and case law to determine who the owner of the work is and what this means for copyright protection.

The biggest issue concerning generative AI is not authorship, however, but rather the large datasets required for machine learning. Generative AI systems "learn" by processing vast quantities of data to produce outputs. In a closed dataset, the AI utilizes a finite dataset that the programs feed to the system. This type of learning tends to be an issue because the dataset can be regulated to contain only materials from open sources or the public domain thereby avoiding infringement usage. In an open dataset, however, the AI has access to a universe of learning data that is very likely to contain incredible quantities of protected materials. This unsupervised learning can result in the creation of new content that may mimic human authorship but could potentially infringe upon existing copyrighted works by deriving from protected materials.

Finally, the challenges posed by DRM issues, online piracy, and their implications for the future of copyright in digital content continue to evolve. These issues, along with the complexities of AI-generated work and UGC, represent key areas of concern. In this section, we will look at these four issues in more detail, examining their current impact and potential future developments in copyright law.

2.15.1. User-Generated Content

User-generated content is a broad term often used to describe media content that has been created by the end user of an online system or service and is publicly available to other consumers. It is a by-product of Web 2.0, facilitated through various forms of social networking media software, such as blogs, wikis, forums, instant messaging, video- and photo-sharing platforms, content creation services, and voice and picture communication. UGC content may also take the form of audio, video, and animation created and

---

[39] Copyright, Designs and Patent Act 1998, Authorship and Ownership of Copyright, Ch. 48 § 9, 3 (UK) (stating "[i] n the case of a literary, dramatic, musical or artistic work which is computer-generated, the author shall be taken to be the person by whom the arrangements necessary for the creation of the work are undertaken.").

published using applications geared toward consumers. Examples include video games like *LittleBigPlanet*, where users are able to create and share their own levels, characters, and game modifications, or applications such as TikTok, X (formerly Twitter), and Instagram, where users create content, sometimes incorporating copyright-protected materials, with followers. These platforms encourage interactive creation and sharing of content, often involving the integration of third-party materials, such as copyrighted music, into user-created videos.

UGC allows individuals to express themselves in various ways. Younger generations are particularly motivated to produce UGC for various reasons, including developing technical skills, creative expression, forming alternative identities, and achieving social status. They are also the most voracious consumers of this type of content. A notable example is the rise of YouTube and TikTok celebrities honing their video-making skills for self-promotion and entertainment. These activities are not much different than consumers of the past recording personal videos using copyrighted songs, but there is a significant increase in availability and ease of mixing copyrighted content with new UGC due to the vast expansion of easily accessible user-friendly digital editing capabilities. With the increase in popularity and activities involving UGC, there is a higher propensity for potential copyright infringement.

2.15.2. Artificial Intelligence

Ownership is generally associated with the creators of works, but in the realm of AI-generated content, determining the creator or owner may not be so clear. As noted, creations produced by unsupervised AI systems could bypass human involvement altogether. In some cases, the designer of the AI system may not be directly responsible for the creation, having merely set the AI in motion to generate output. Additionally, the work may be created through a collaboration between a human and AI, or even the product of multiple AI systems from different sources. Complicating the issue further, AI itself is often the result of human creation, and AI systems may evolve or improve independently through machine learning. This creates a complex web of causality and authorship, much of which does not fit into the standard model of copyright ownership. The idea that AI could potentially be the autonomous owner of its creations may be unsettling to some. Given that a primary motivation behind the development of AI might be to create a cheap and efficient replacement for human productivity, it is conceivable that corporations could push for laws that would assign ownership to AI systems, rather than allowing those creations to fall into the public domain, in order to protect corporate interests. Ultimately, ownership of AI-generated works will likely depend on agreements between the entities involved, unless future laws are enacted to address these challenges.

On the other hand, if we assume that AI is capable of replicating human work and its use becomes normalized, we may see a future where human creators leverage AI to accelerate content production. For instance, a professional writer might use AI to automate written articles. Even if the human directs the AI, the resulting work will technically be created by the AI, raising questions about authorship. It is reasonable to assume that the human directing the AI would want ownership attributed to themselves. This differs from current practices, where subcontracting work to third parties still allows the individual to retain authorship if it was understood that the work was created under the direction of the individual. In the case of AI-generated content, unless there is a contractual arrangement to the contrary, ownership might default to the person responsible for the AI, with the rights treated as if the AI's work were produced by an employee under a work-for-hire arrangement.[40]

To reflect on the numerous ways that AI and copyright law are likely to intersect in the coming years, Congress might consider a wholesale review of the fundamentals of copyright law and the implications of those laws when applied to works created by machines. AI-generated works might not fit into the preexisting idea/expression dichotomy, but that dichotomy has been criticized as being overly ambiguous and complex analysis. A more appropriate standard tailored to AI's unique capabilities may be necessary, potentially through the promulgation of separate rules for copyrighted computer-generated works or a redefinition of copyright infringement that accounts for the inevitable similarity between AI-generated works and the works it draws upon.

AI software represents a potentially transformative technology that could be severely hindered if developers are unable to build upon existing works to create new and better technologies. To address this, Congress might consider expanding the scope of fair use to permit broader copying, particularly in cases where AI's ability to understand and learn from existing works is essential for the creation of new content. On the other hand, the law of fair use might need tighter restrictions to prevent AI software from creating works that are highly similar to existing works but socially or economically wasteful. Balancing these competing interests will be critical in shaping the future of AI and copyright law.

2.15.3. Digital Rights Management

As previously discussed, DRM is a systematic approach to protecting digital media from unauthorized distribution and limiting how consumers can interact with purchased content. DRM serves to safeguard the intellectual property of content creators by embedding controls into the digital products they distribute. These controls can include information about the author, copyright details, expiration dates, and specific details on the consumer usage rights of the content. A DRM system typically consists of three components: content protection technologies, a server that distributes the content and rights information, and a consumer device used to view or manipulate the content.

DRM is everywhere today, embedded into various digital products to regulate consumer use. One prevalent example is the video game industry where they offer a trial version of a game to download directly from the web. The web-based game has DRM integrated into it that disables functions of the game and terminates the game after a period of time. Once a consumer is persuaded to purchase the product, they are given a key to unlock the game on their PC. This then enables them to use the same game file but with

---

[40] Vicenç Feliú, *Our Brains Beguil'd: Copyright Protection for AI Created Works*, 25 Intell. Prop. & Tech. L.J. 105 (2021).

the restrictions removed. This method of distribution is less costly for the publisher as they have saved on hard-copy distribution and have prevented an illegal sale of a copied game via the internet.

The main issue with DRM lies in its compliance with consumer law, particularly the balance between preventing unauthorized copying and ensuring a consumer's right to use a product they have purchased. Even if a product is restricted from copying, consumers still retain certain usage rights. Additionally, there is concern about whether DRM impedes the fair use of copyrighted material. Currently, with no case law on this specific issue, DRM is an effective way for copyright owners to protect their material from illegal use. However, if courts find that DRM breaches consumer law or fair use provisions, it may lead to a new era of copyright infringement cases.

2.15.4. Online Piracy

The widespread unauthorized copying and distribution of copyrighted material through digital means across the internet, including the uploading of pirated software to servers, remains an enormous problem in many countries. These activities have caused massive financial losses for copyright holders and have drastically shortened the lifespan of many copyright-protected works to the extent that the affected industries have referred to piracy as a threat to their economic survival. With the exponential increase in the use of social media platforms, copyrighted material is becoming more accessible, transferable, and duplicable. At the same time, global laws and regulations have been enacted to protect and preserve the rights of those who hold copyright in their products, making it increasingly important to address the issue of online piracy and its impact on creators and industries.

Advances in streaming technology have made it easier for individuals to stream copyright-protected content to potentially millions of views. The process of streaming involves the transfer of data over a computer network in real time, in which the user can view the content without having to download it to their device. This eliminates the need for potential viewers to download large video files and makes it very quick and convenient to view the content. Streaming also allows a degree of privacy for the user, as the data is not stored on the device and can be viewed through encrypted methods, making it harder to detect. Live streaming has also become popular in the streaming community, allowing users to broadcast events and other content in real time, potentially reaching vast audiences with minimal barriers to access.

With the rise of high-speed internet and ever-improving technology, streaming platforms have become a mainstay in today's digital age. In recent times, popular platforms such as YouTube, Vimeo, TikTok, and Netflix have seen an increase in use, resulting in a decline in the purchase and rental of physical media. Streaming has overtaken other methods as the dominant form of content consumption, with YouTube boasting over 1 billion users who watch millions of hours of streaming videos every day. However, the surge in streaming has also led to an increase in both authorized and unauthorized streaming of copyrighted works.

A widely held view among copyright owners is that current legal enforcement mechanisms are neither deterring infringement nor providing adequate remedies to right holders. The development of digital technology for the distribution of copyrighted works has resulted in an apparent weakening of copyright protection and increasing instances of infringement. Right holders argue that in comparison to "traditional" forms of piracy (i.e., hard-copy reproduction), prosecution of digital pirates is minimal because it is difficult to detect perpetrators and current criminal penalties for copyright infringement are not being carried out. The United States has been a leader in pursuing stronger copyright enforcement mechanisms and has faced criticism from other countries on this issue because of concerns regarding the potentially detrimental effects on consumer rights and fair use of copyrighted works.

With the enactment of new laws designed to protect copyrights, there also needs to be increased efforts to enforce these laws. This involves tracking down and taking legal action against those who infringe copyrights. Increased policing of intellectual property rights is a costly venture. It is reported that intellectual property theft costs the United States alone between $200 and $250 billion annually. However, the cost of not enforcing copyright laws and potentially allowing the collapse of industries that rely on copyright is far greater. High-profile lawsuits against individual copyright infringers often serve as a method to deter others from committing similar acts. This was evidenced by the RIAA's legal campaign against users of file-sharing software, which saw a sharp decline in the use of such software. Such litigation can also be targeted at copyright violators of a larger scale, which can potentially disrupt vast networks of piracy and have a significant impact.

2.16. Future Directions and Conclusion

Copyright infringement in the digital age has become increasingly prevalent due to the emergence of new digital technologies. Many individuals who commit copyright infringement by sharing or adapting protected works on social media, for example, do not believe that it is a crime and do not see themselves as criminals. This could be attributed to the fact that they do not consider the impact their actions have on the individual copyright owners.

The legal landscape surrounding copyright protection is also subject to change as a result of digital technologies. National laws and international conventions provide the basic framework for copyright protection, but the specifics of that protection are defined by the actions of copyright owners and users, and by the nature of the copyrighted works themselves. To the extent that changes in technology affect the relative costs and benefits of various types of copyright protection, the specifics of copyright law will change in response. Enhanced levels of protection could influence the behavior of users and owners, prompting changes in the ways copyrighted works are created, distributed, and consumed.

As the digital environment advances, so will the use and exploitation of digital assets. This change has significant implications for copyright owners' ability to control the use of their works. Technological change affects the basic costs of creating, using, and distributing digital content, as well as the legal environment surrounding such activities. Digital technologies reduce the costs of production and distribution in two ways: first, by eliminating the need for many physical embodiments of a work (such as a CD) and second, by automating many processes. As the expense of creating new versions of a work and of moving existing works to new markets decreases, a rational economic analysis suggests that owners will be more willing to invest in development and will seek greater returns from their works. This increased level of investment will likely be coupled with increased pressure to strengthen copyright protection, in order to maximize the return on the investment.

The next ten to twenty years are likely to witness a great deal of experimentation in the development of business models that enable the enjoyment of creative works in digital form. The success of these ventures, and their consistency with copyright's underlying principles, will be ascertained based on how well they help to enrich the store of human knowledge and culture. Many business interests will continue to view the control of information as a primary source of profit, and they may feel threatened by legal doctrines and consumer trends that support the free flow of information that fosters creativity and competition. But society's interest in the creation of positive legal doctrines for the digital age suggests that there may be a very different balance of public and private ordering in the next ten to twenty years. A vast amount of human creativity may continue to be expressed and disseminated in complete disregard for copyright, simply as an end in itself or for communication with friends and family.

If copyright's goal is to encourage an ever-richer tapestry of creativity by providing economic incentives, this should be of little concern. However, those forms of creative expression that depend on commercial exploitation or sponsorship will require rules that assure a viable economic foundation. A continued examination of how best to maintain the delicate balance of private and public ordering in copyright will be crucial to the development of cultural and information policies for the digital age.

While the challenges posed by the digital environment might suggest that copyright law is outdated and insufficient for protecting the rights of authors, the system has proven to be flexible and adaptable to new uses and technologies, legislative changes, judicial interpretations, and industry cooperation. There is no simple panacea for the problem of protecting intellectual property in the digital era. But attempts to apply new layers of protection for copyright owners, especially if they limit the rights of the public, should be viewed with skepticism, for they will likely produce unintended consequences and further tensions in the system. A better approach is to build on the foundation of long-standing copyright principles, allowing them to evolve in ways that best serve the fundamental goal of advancing knowledge and culture.

3 Trademarks and Digital Assets

By Zachary L. Catanzaro

3.1. Introduction

The recent consumer adoption of nascent technologies like blockchain ledgers and nonfungible tokens (NFTs) has promoted the development of new marketplaces for new forms of digital assets. These advances in computing technologies have ushered in a new era of digital innovation commonly referred to as Web 3.0. Whether sold in the metaverse or in the real world, the ephemeral nature of these new digital assets poses many unsettled questions under existing trademark law.

As early internet technologies required modernization of traditional trademark principles, the proliferation of these new forms of digital assets requires reexamination of existing law. Growing consumer demand for digital assets provides new opportunities and challenges to businesses selling their products and services online. Web 3.0 promises unparalleled consumer provenance, reduced search costs, and streamlined marketplaces for digital goods. Just as the advent of ecommerce revolutionized the purchasing of goods in an online space, these new forms of digital assets empower a novel marketplace for unique digital goods and services.

This chapter explores the impact of Web 3.0 technologies on trademark law, examining the opportunities and challenges, and offering potential solutions to these novel legal issues. By drawing on trademark law's venerable history, recent case studies, emerging best practices, and a modern recontextualization of long-standing trademark principles, this chapter provides a comprehensive understanding of the impact that digital assets and Web 3.0 have, and will continue to have, on trademark protection and brand management.

3.2. Legal Foundations of Trademarks

3.2.1. Trademarks in the Digital Age

In 1946, the Lanham Act was signed into law, modernizing and reforming the fractured patchwork approach of predominantly state common law protection and limited federal protection provided to marks used in foreign commerce. Drawing on the Commerce Clause, Congress fashioned a system of federal registration and administration of trademarks that passed constitutional review. Since enactment, the Lanham Act has seen several important amendments, including (1) the Trademark Counterfeiting Act of 1984 (criminalizing commercial counterfeiting of marks and creating additional ex parte seizure remedies);[1] (2) the Trademark Law Revision Act of 1988 (permitting registration for intent to use applications);[2] (3) the Federal Trademark Dilution Act of 1995 (creating a cause of action for dilution of famous marks);[3] and (4) the Anticybersquatting Consumer Protection Act of 1999 (prohibiting certain forms of domain squatting).[4]

The advent of the internet in the later part of the twentieth century had a lasting impact on trademark law. Where a business was once limited to its immediate geographic and distribution channels, the internet made it possible for small retailers to have international reach. As companies began to expand their online offerings, trademark law had to quickly adapt to this new channel of distribution. Yet despite the large impact the internet would have on commerce, consumer adoption of this technology was slow: it took online commerce more than fifty years to overtake traditional brick and mortar store revenues.

The internet and online commerce owe their birth to a federal Cold War military research program started as a response to growing national concerns about information blackouts in the event of a nuclear war. In 1969, the Advanced Research Projects Agency (now known as Defense Advanced Research Projects Agency (DARPA)) spearheaded the development of the modern civilian internet's grandfather, ARPANET, the first network of remote computer systems. The first message was transmitted on October 29, 1969, and by the end of the year, computers at UCLA, SRI, UC Santa Barbara, and University of Utah were connected to the network.

Commercial adoption of the technology was slow, with the first online shopping program offered in the United Kingdom using a device attached to a home television set coming a decade later in 1979. In 1982, Boston Computer Exchange launched the world's first online marketplace. The World Wide Web became available to the general public with the 1993 launch of Mosaic, and consumer access to computers and the internet expanded rapidly in the early part of the 1990s. Amazon and eBay launched in 1995

---

1 18 U.S.C. § 2320.

2 H.R.5372—Trademark Law Revision Act of 1988.
H.R. Res. 5372, 100th Cong. (1988) (enacted).

3 H.R.1295—Federal Trademark Dilution Act of 1995.
H.R. Res. 1295, 104th Cong. (1995) (enacted).

4 15 U.S.C. § 1125 (d) (2002).

(Amazon handles between 9 and 10 million transactions per day as of 2024). Both platforms completed a million consumer transactions within a few years of launch. In 1998, PayPal launched, providing consumers with a new trusted intermediary for online commercial transactions. Google AdWords launched in October 2000, revolutionizing online marketing. Ecommerce had entered its first Gilded Age, and business was booming. Until it wasn't.

A combination of artificially low interest rates and over-investment in online retailers led to the Dot-com era bubble bursting in 2000. Between 1995 and the mid-2000s, the NASDAQ rose 800 percent, only to crash to 82 percent of its peak in 2002. Many online retailers went bankrupt, and consumer confidence waned. Several notable fraud prosecutions followed allegations of fraudulent misuse of investor funds, with notable executives Bernard Ebbers, Jeffrey Skilling, and Kenneth Lay all sentenced to serious prison time for their conduct in this period. Approximately 58 percent of existing online retailers at this time went out of business.

The following decade was defined by market consolidation, mergers, and rapid expansion of existing online brands. Amazon, for example, announced its first year earning profit in 2001. In 2011, the brand employed just thirty thousand U.S. workers; today, it employs over a million worldwide. In 2019, online sales surpassed brick and mortar sales for the first time. In 2023, the total value of online sales in the United States crossed the one trillion U.S. dollars mark, representing 15.4 percent of the United States' 7 trillion annual retail trade. Furthermore, it is estimated that total online advertising amounted to $601 billion (about $1,800 per person in the United States) in 2023.

Parallel to the birth, growth, and import of the internet was the adoption, and eventual market domination, of the smartphone. The FCC (Federal Communications Commission) approved the first cellular phone, the Motorola DynaTAC 8000X, in 1983. The first commercially available smartphone, the IBM Simon Personal Communicator, was sold in 1994. In 2001, the 3G network standard launched, connecting phones to the internet for the first time. 2007 saw the launch of the seminal Apple iPhone, with Android entering the market the following year. Just three years later, smartphones overtook sales of personal computers and laptops, and by 2016, mobile browsing surpassed desktop browsing. In 2023, there were 310 million smartphone users in the United States.

Parallel to the cell phones evolution, the internet saw periods of growth and exponential technological advancement. The early internet, Web 1.0, was defined by static, informational websites. Online websites were primarily a branding exercise, lacking much of the modern interactivity and user-rich content found in today's more modern internet. Slow connection speeds limited the amount of information that could be transmitted, with many businesses operating limited, if any, online commercial presence. Consumers had not come to trust online shopping, and the lack of a trustworthy online payment processor meant that the few then-existing shopping options were mostly run as online mail order style catalogs.

Around 1999, Web 2.0 came to define the emerging shift toward dynamic and interactive websites. Social media began its slow rise to prominence, giving consumers a means to share information and attitudes toward products and advertisements. Data analytics and data mining practices served as a means of collecting and targeting consumers for granular advertising campaigns. The launch of the first true ecommerce websites occurred in this period, with consumers being able to not only purchase goods and services online but also interact with businesses and other consumers about their purchasing decisions. The speed of information sharing reduced consumer search costs for products, and the market saw rapid growth and investments leading up to the Dotcom era bubble bursting.

As with most speculative investment bubbles, the recovery that followed was relatively muted. Consumers slowly embraced online shopping technology over the next fifteen years. Widespread adoption rates of the smartphone coupled with advancements in mobile internet gave consumers a newfound convenience in their shopping behaviors. Brands became more online savvy in the later part of the Web 2.0 era as data analytics became more sophisticated. Now, after over two decades of refinement, most companies have come to rely on this specialized form of data mining as a means of connecting consumers with their product offerings. Today, these technologies are sophisticated enough that they have become predictive in application, with many algorithms capable of knowing what a consumer may be interested in before the consumer is. (The privacy ramifications are immeasurable and outside the scope of this chapter.)

3.2.2. Trademarks in the Web 3.0 Era

Web 3.0 owes its origins to technology developed to solve a problem inherent to online commerce. One of the key challenges to the growth of online commerce has been, and continues to be, the problem of double spending of digital accounts.[5] In an ordinary banking transaction, when a consumer wires funds from one account to another, the antiquated Automated Clearing House (ACH) has a built-in delay designed to prevent consumers from double spending funds from an account until a verification is made that the funds have been debited from the origin account. This system worked well before the internet, when businesses and consumers were accustomed to delays in sales and the shipping of products. But as the internet reduced the transaction costs of doing business with others, it rapidly increased communication speeds. As more and more consumers embraced online shopping, the slow speeds of the ACH system were becoming unwieldy in operation given the rapid growth and volume of online shopping transactions. Many consumers turned to third-party intermediaries in this period, with services like PayPal and various Credit Card companies stepping in to fill this need in the marketplace.

In 2008, an anonymous person using the pseudonym Satoshi Nakamoto published *Bitcoin: A Peer-to-Peer Electronic Cash System* with a proposal to solve the double spend problem.[6] By chaining records into a series of blocks of data using encryption technologies, Satoshi envisioned a ledger system of auditing that would both safeguard against

---

5 CFI Team, *Double-Spending*, Corp. Fin. Inst., https://corporatefinanceinstitute.com/resources/cryptocurrency/double-spending/ (last visited Jul. 12, 2024).

6 Satoshi Nakamoto, *Bitcoin: A Peer-to-Peer Electronic Cash System*, BITCOIN (2008), https://bitcoin.org/bitcoin.pdf.

double spending and incentivize neutral third parties to audit the transaction history of a particular ledger of transactions through financial incentives. Though the white paper does not use the term, Satoshi's proposal was instrumental in the development of blockchain ledger technologies. Satoshi's white paper is notable for suggesting that such a decentralized network of self-auditing nodes could solve the double-spend problem, which would drastically increase both the speed of online commercial transactions and reduce the transaction costs inherent to dealing with anonymous or pseudo-anonymous parties online.

If Web 2.0 was defined by the centralization of commerce into large economic actors, the allure of Web 3.0 lies in the ability to decentralize commerce and reduce (or eliminate) the need for third-party intermediaries in online transactions.[7] Absent the need for a particular clearing house, online marketplace, or other intermediary, a freely decentralized online marketplace for consumers promises further reductions in transaction costs. By eliminating these intermediaries, Web 3.0 promises a shopping experience in which companies can market directly to their customers.

Web 3.0 changes the relationship of consumers to their digital files. A consumer who "purchases" a digital file is not acquiring ownership rights. Instead, a consumer who purchases a digital file is acquiring a market inalienable and usually revocable contractual license to use that particular digital file.[8] Generally, these files contain contractual provisions that prohibit the resale of these files. While a consumer who purchases a physical compact disc (CD) is free to resell that CD on the marketplace, that same right has not been extended to the purchase of a digital file. Both the Courts and the Copyright Office have thoroughly rejected the notion of a digital right of resale under the venerable doctrine of first sale.[9] Therefore, a consumer who purchases a digital file, absent an agreement to the contrary with the creator of that file, has no right to resell that particular file in the marketplace.[10]

Yet, when a company sells a digital asset as a market alienable good, trademark law offers broader first sale protections after the seller has exhausted their rights. Blockchain and other distributed ledger technologies allow content creators of digital files to sell a particular and *uniquely* identifiable digital file rather than just another digital copy of a particular work. By specifically identifying the unique hard drive on which a particular copy has been stored, these new Web 3.0 technologies have created an entirely new class of digital assets, raising questions about the application of trademark law to these new forms of digital goods.[11] Further complicating this inquiry is the rather novel practice

---

7 Scott Clark, How Is Web3 Decentralized? CMSWIRE (Feb. 2, 2022), https://www.cmswire.com/information-management/how-is-web3-decentralized/.

8 *Macy's Web3 Offerings Terms of Use*, MACY'S (Aug. 29, 2023), https://www.macys.com/social/mstylelab/termsofservice/ (might be interesting to include an actual Terms of Use by a big-box retailer that directly addresses the purchase of NFTs as giving the purchaser a revocable license).

9 Capitol Recs., LLC v. ReDigi Inc., 910 F.3d at 649, 658 (2d Cir. 2018); *see also* U.S. Copyright Office's Digital Millennium Copyright Act, § 104 Report at xix (Aug. 29, 2001) ("Works in digital format can be reproduced flawlessly, and disseminated to nearly any point on the globe instantly and at negligible cost.").

10 Josh Hendrickson, What Is the Deal with NFTs? ECONOMIC FORCES (Dec. 30, 2021), https://www.economicforces.xyz/p/what-is-the-deal-with-nfts.

11 Angela Kalsi, *Trademark Law and NFTs: The IP Implications of Emerging Technology*, UB GREENSFELDER (Mar. 16, 2023), https://www.ubglaw.com/news-and-media/trademark-law-and-nfts-the-ip-implications-of-emerging-technology.

of linking these particular offerings to some form of utility service offered by the original seller of that particular file structure.

A digital asset is a uniquely identifiable, digitally recorded, and stored intangible property interest. Because these files are uniquely identifiable, they are non-fungible and can offer monetary or other abstract value to their owner. Digital assets have existed since the early days of computer technologies, but recent advancements, such as tokenization on blockchain ledgers, can create artificial scarcity in a way that helps facilitate a marketplace for these intangible digital files. Whether these digital assets should be protectable at law is a matter of public policy.[12]

3.3. Public Policy Goals of Trademarks

The historical goals of trademark law provide context to the question of protection of trademark rights in digital assets. Historically, different public policy arguments have been advanced to justify the need for trademarks. The oldest of these arguments is found in efforts to protect standards of fair dealing and commercial morality.[13] Others have argued that trademarks are a form of property under a natural rights or personality approach.[14] Some believe that trademarks reward businesses for their labors in cultivating the associated goodwill with a particular mark.[15] But the dominant theory justifying the U.S. system of trademarks today is as a means of protecting the public from a specific type of fraud called "consumer source identification confusion."[16] Consumer confusion results in deadweight losses in the marketplace in that they (1) increase search costs for consumers; (2) disincentivize companies from bringing products and services to market; (3) cause lost sales from counterfeiting, passing, or palming a product off; and (4) cause reputational harm to the legitimate seller.[17] So, unlike the Copyright and Patent Acts, which exist to promote the advancement of the sciences and arts, trademark law exists to protect consumers from fraud in the marketplace.

In a trademark infringement case, it is not the trademark that is infringed.[18] "What is infringed is the right of the public to be free of confusion and the synonymous right of a trademark owner to control his product's reputation." In serving that function,

---

12 Mark P. McKenna & Lucas S. Osborn, *Trademarks and Digital Goods*, 92 Notre Dame L. Rev. 1425, 1462 (2017).

13 R. Anthony Reese, *Copyright and Trademark Law and Public Interest Lawyering*, 2 UC Irvine L. Rev. 911, 912 (2012), https://heinonline.org/HOL/Page?collection=usjournals&handle=hein.journals/ucirvlre2&id=925&men_tab=srchresults.

14 Sheldon W. Halpern, *Trafficking in Trademarks: Setting Boundaries for the Uneasy Relationship between Property Rights and Trademark and Publicity Rights*, 58 DePaul L. Rev. 1013, 1018 (2009).

15 Mark McKenna, *The Normative Foundations of Trademark Law*, 82 Notre Dame L. Rev. 1839 (2007), https://scholarship.law.nd.edu/law_faculty_scholarship/226/.

16 Daphne Leeds, *Confusion and Consumer Psychology*, 37 J. Pat. Off. Soc'y 894, 898 (1955). https://heinonline.org/HOL/Page?public=true&handle=hein.journals/jpatos37&div=149&start_page=894&collection=usjournals&set_as_cursor=4&men_tab=srchresults.
Arthur M. Handler & Eileen P. McCarthy, *Conopco—Consumer Confusion Remains the Touchstone of Trade Dress Infringement*, 86 Trademark Rep. 595, 599 (1996), https://heinonline.org/HOL/Page?public=true&handle=hein.journals/thetmr86&div=54&start_page=595&collection=usjournals&set_as_cursor=9&men_tab=srchresults.

17 Staff Editor, *Post-Sale Confusion*, N.Y.U. J. Intell. Prop. & Ent. L. JIPEL Blog (Mar. 6, 2019), https://jipel.law.nyu.edu/post-sale-confusion/.

18 James Burrough Ltd. v. Sign of the Beefeater, Inc., 540 F.2d 266, 274 (7th Cir. 1976).

trademarks benefit consumers and producers alike.[19] A source-identifying mark enables customers to select "the goods and services that they wish to purchase, as well as those they want to avoid."[20] The mark "quickly and easily assures a potential customer that this item—the item with this mark—is made by the same producer as other similarly marked items that he or she liked (or disliked) in the past."[21] And because that is so, the producer of a quality product may derive significant value from its marks.[22] Trademarks ensure that the producer itself—and not some "imitating competitor"—will reap the financial rewards associated with the product's good reputation.[23]

Trademarks thus serve an important market function as a means of source and quality identification for consumers. They are utilitarian in function and application. Trademarks primarily provide a benefit to the consuming public, a means of protecting against a species of fraud called source identification confusion.[24] This type of commercial fraud causes deadweight losses in the economy, as in their absence of protectable trademarks it becomes more expensive for consumers to search out and find products that carry the quality attached to a particular brand and its resultant goodwill.[25] Any economic benefits to the trademark holder are seen as secondary to the rights of the public. Thus, a trademark holder has an affirmative obligation to police their trademark against potential infringing uses.[26]

3.4. Trademark Protection

The Lanham Act defines a trademark as:

> any word, name, symbol, or device, or any combination thereof—
>
> (1) used by a person, or
>
> (2) which a person has a bona fide intention to use in commerce and applies to register on the principal register established by this chapter,
>
> to identify and distinguish his or her goods, including a unique product, from those manufactured or sold by others and to indicate the source of the goods, even if that source is unknown.[27]

---

19 Jack Daniel's Props. v. VIP Prods. LLC, 599 U.S. 140, 146 (2023).

20 Jack Daniel's Props. v. VIP Prods. LLC, 599 U.S. 140, 146 (2023) (quoting Matal v. Tam, 582 U.S. 218, 224, 137 S. Ct. 1744, 198 L. Ed. 2d 366 (2017)).

21 Jack Daniel's Props. v. VIP Prods. LLC, 599 U.S. 140, 146 (2023) (quoting Qualitex Co. v. Jacobson Products Co., 514 U.S. 159, 164, 115 S. Ct. 1300, 131 L. Ed. 2d 248 (1995)).

22 Jack Daniel's Props. v. VIP Prods. LLC, 599 U.S. 140, 146 (2023).

23 *KP Permanent Make-Up, Inc. v. Lasting Impression I, Inc.*, 543 U.S. 111, 125 S. Ct. 542 (2004).

24 United States PTO v. Booking.com B.V., 591 U.S. 549, 140 S. Ct. 2298 (2020).

25 R. Bone, Hunting Goodwill: A History of the Concept of Goodwill in Trademark Law, 86 B. U. L. REV. 547, 575 (2006).

26 Josh Gerben, *How to Police and Enforce Trademark Rights*, GERBEN IP (Jul. 24, 2020), https://www.gerbenlaw.com/blog/how-to-police-and-enforce-trademark-rights/.

27 15 U.S.C. § 1127.

Anything capable of associating a good or service with a mark can serve as a trademark.[28] These include marks such as the National Broadcasting Corporation (NBC) jingle, the color green-gold for dry-cleaning press pads, the taste of strawberry for bank envelopes, the sound of Darth Vader's robotic breathing, and Usain Bolt's "lightning bolt" gesture.

While often used synonymously and interchangeably, the terms trademark and service mark are not, by definition, technically so. A trademark is any mark used to identify goods, while a service mark is a mark used to identify services.[29] Trademark protection also extends to (1) collective marks (which refer to members of a coop or association), (2) certification marks (which refer to regional or other quality aspects of a product), (3) device marks (which covers logos and other nonword marks), and (4) trade dress (which protect the commercial look and feel of a product and its packaging).[30]

At common law, a trademark vests to whomever uses a distinctive mark in commerce as a source identifier in a particular marketplace first.[31] This common law protection extends to the geographic boundaries of where the marked products are sold or advertised, for those areas in which the trademark owner has established a reputation or otherwise created goodwill and a consumer association connecting their specific goods or service offerings to their mark.[32] To use a mark in commerce, a business must do more than merely announce an intention to claim a particular name. To permit otherwise would allow a free-for-all attempt at monopolization of language, which would cause catastrophic harm to the public in their right to search out products and services by their names. Additionally, a trademark owner must win the race to market. The venerable property law doctrine of "first in time, first in right" controls in trademark law absent operation of the registration systems.[33] Being economically larger or more established is not enough, the law of trademarks does not allow for larger firms to bully smaller but older companies out of business.

Distinctiveness is the heart of trademark law; a mark must be distinctive to be protectable. In the seminal case *Abercrombie & Fitch Co. v. Hunting World*, the Second Circuit Court of Appeals considered the inherent strength of the usage of a particular mark as being indicative of its distinctiveness in commerce.[34] In its holding, the Court developed the aptly named *Abercrombie* spectrum, a system of measuring the inherent distinctiveness of a mark and its protectability as such. Note that these categories, "like tones in a

---

[28] *Trademark Examples*, U.S. Patent & Trademark Off. OFFICE (Nov. 30, 2023, 04:35 PM), https://www.uspto.gov/trademarks/basics/trademark-examples.

[29] *What Is a Trademark?* U.S. Patent & Trademark Off. (Nov. 30, 2023, 04:36 PM), https://www.uspto.gov/trademarks/basics/what-trademark.

[30] *What Are the Types of Trademarks*, Dunlap Bennet & Ludwig (last visited Jul. 12, 2024), https://www.dbllawyers.com/types-of-trademarks/.

[31] Uli Widmaier, *Use, Liability, and the Structure of Trademark Law*, 33 Hofstra L. Rev. 603, 605–6 (2004).

[32] Joseph M. Levy, *The Confusion of Trademark Territoriality*, 18 Chi. Kent J. Intell. Prop. 324, 327–29 (2019).

[33] Vic Lin, *What Is Trademark Priority?* Patent Trademark Blog (last visited Jul. 12, 2024), https://www.patenttrademarkblog.com/trademark-priority/#:~:text=Trademark%20rights%20in%20the%20US,is%20known%20as%20trademark%20priority.

[34] Abercrombie & Fitch Co. v. Hunting World, Inc., 537 F.2d 4, 9 (2d Cir. 1976).

spectrum, tend to blur at the edges."[35] From weakest to strongest, those types of marks are classified as (1) generic, (2) descriptive, (3) suggestive, (4) arbitrary, and (5) fanciful.

A generic mark is one that simply refers to the product or service. At common law, a generic mark is unprotectable. No company can claim ownership of words like "smartphone" to describe a smart phone, or "oranges" to describe oranges. A mark that becomes generic loses protection under the doctrine of "genericide." It is therefore incumbent on a trademark holder to police against both infringing and generic uses of the mark. A trademark owner has no legal right to stop the consuming public from rendering a mark generic at law. The recourse is usually limited to educational efforts.[36]

A descriptive mark is one that describes aspects of an article, its qualities, ingredients, or characteristics. A merely descriptive mark is unprotectable but can become protectable if it has acquired distinctiveness in the minds of consumers. Coca-Cola, for example, is a descriptive mark that describes an ingredient (coca leaf extract used in cola) with unquestionably acquired distinctiveness, but a soft drink that attempted to claim "carbonated" as a mark would fall short as the consuming public does not attach any meaning to this mark beyond what it describes. To make this determination, a Court will look at the context in which the mark is being used and the significance the consumer places on that use.

The difference between a generic and descriptive mark is one of degree. Courts have fashioned a number of interchangeable tests for the boundaries between the generic and merely descriptive marks and those that have. One approach is the dictionary test, in which the dictionary definition of the word is measured against the relevant indication of the ordinary significance and meaning of the words to the consumer.[37] Other courts, like the Ninth Circuit, apply the imagination test, which measures the relationship between the actual words of the mark and the product to which they are applied.[38] Another approach is found in the needs test, which changes the focus to the risk of monopolization of the word on competition in that particular industry.[39] Finally, the last approach is to simply look at to what extent other competitors have used the word in marketing a similar service or product.[40]

The last means of contextualizing the usage of the mark is found in the secondary meaning test. This concept recognizes that words with an ordinary and primary meaning may, after long-term use, become associated with a particular mark. Secondary meaning can be established through consumer survey evidence or circumstantial evidence, like

---

35 Zatarains, Inc. v. Oak Grove Smokehouse, Inc., 698 F.2d 786 (5th Cir. 1983).

36 Ryan Williams, *Genericide: How an Excess of Popularity Can End Your Trademark*, MARQVISION (Aug. 8, 2023), https://www.marqvision.com/blog/genericide-how-an-excess-of-popularity-can-end-your-trademark; see also Bayer Co. v. United Drug Co., 272 F. 505 (S.D.N.Y. 1921) (holding that the name "Aspirin" had passed into the public domain, allowing defendant drug company to market "acetyl salicylic acid" as "Aspirin" to the public without qualification).

37 Enrique Bernat F., S.A. v. Guadalajara, Inc., 210 F.3d 439 (5th Cir. 2000).

38 Boost Beauty, LLC v. Woo Signatures, LLC, No. 2:18-cv-02960-CAS-Ex, 2022 U.S. Dist. LEXIS 24515 (C.D. Cal. Feb. 7, 2022).

39 Engineered Tax Servs. v. Scarpello Consulting, Inc., 958 F.3d 1323 (11th Cir. 2020).

40 Promatek Indus., Ltd. v. Equitrac Corp., 300 F.3d 808 (7th Cir. 2002).

showing the amount and manner of advertising, volume of sales, and length and manner of use. The Circuits are split on the nonexhaustive factors to consider, but the majority test for secondary meaning asks whether the average consumer associates the mark with identifying the product or service offering, and has the Court consider the following nonexhaustive factors: (1) the extent of sales and advertising leading to buyer association, (2) length of use, (3) exclusivity of use, (4) the fact of copying, (5) customer surveys, (6) customer testimony, (7) the use of the mark in trade journals, (8) the size of the company, (9) the number of sales, (10) the number of customers, and (11) actual marketplace confusion.[41] A minority of courts, however, have eliminated this test if the plaintiff can show bad faith by the defendants.[42]

Suggestive marks, as the name suggests, are marks that suggest something about the product. This suggestion is relative to the use of the product but does not directly describe the intended use or features of the product.[43] Put differently, these marks allow the consumer to draw a connection between the suggestion and the product using the consumer's imagination, thought, or perception. Netflix (a place to watch "flicks" on the "net"), Coppertone (a sunscreen that can cause a copper tan), and Microsoft (software for microcomputers) are all suggestive marks. Suggestive marks are inherently distinctive and do not require proof of acquired distinctiveness or secondary meaning to be protectable.

Arbitrary marks are those with an agreed upon meaning in the English language but are used in a manner that bears no logical or suggestive relationship to the actual characteristics or use of the goods. Apple, as used in common vernacular, refers to a fruit and the tree that bears it but has been used as a trademark to refer to both Apple Computers and Apple Records. Delta has definitions in geology (the delta of a river), mathematics (as a variable), science (the delta brain wave function), and is also a Greek letter. However, in commerce, it is associated with airlines and faucets.[44] The only major limitation of the arbitrary mark is in priority of use, an issue that led Apple Records to sue Apple Computers several times for trademark infringement, as Apple Computers expanded its product lines in a manner that crossed into Apple Records' channels of distribution.

Fanciful marks are the strongest of all. These marks have no prior definition and are invented solely to refer to the good or service. These include brands such as Exxon (for oil and gas), Pepsi (for soda), and Lexus (for automobiles).[45] As with suggestive marks, the secondary meaning in arbitrary and fanciful marks is presumed in favor of the mark holder. There is no risk of priority because the invented word has no prior usage in language. The downside of the fanciful mark is that it may take time for the public to learn to associate the invented word with the offering.

---

41 Commerce Nat'l Ins. Servs. v. Commerce Ins. Agency, Inc., 214 F.3d 432, 438 (3d Cir. 2000).

42 Jeanne C. Fromer, Against Secondary Meaning, 98 NOTRE DAME L. REV. 211, 248 (2022), https://ndlawreview.org/against-secondary-meaning/.

43 Strong Trademarks, U.S. PATENT & TRADEMARK OFF. (Nov. 30, 2023, 04:34 PM), https://www.uspto.gov/trademarks/basics/strong-trademarks.

44 *Id.*

45 *Id.*

Outside the *Abercrombie* spectrum are special categories of marks that are unprotectable for public policy reasons. Deceptive marks are those that mislead or confuse the consumer about the origin, composition, manufacture, or location of a product or service work; in other words, they work a fraud upon the public that runs contrary to the very purposes of trademark protection. A mark for "Animal Free" for a leather product when the product in fact contains animal products would be deceptive. A mark for "Luxe Parisian Furs" sold from Canada farms would be geographically deceptively misdescriptive and, therefore, unprotectable.

Likewise, a mark that serves a functional or utilitarian purpose fails to function as a trademark.[46] If the mark is an important ingredient in the commercial success of a product, and is otherwise in the domain of patent law, trademark law will not serve to extend that limited monopoly into perpetuity. A design is considered legally functional if it is one of a limited number of equally efficient options in the marketplace, and monopolization of that mark would hinder free competition.[47]

Portions of the Lanham Act's prohibition on registration of scandalous or immoral marks were struck down in the Supreme Court's 2017 *Matel v. Tam* decision.[48] There, the Supreme Court found that the disparagement clause of Section 1052(a) of the Lanham Act unconstitutionally infringed on the First Amendment rights of an Asian punk-rock band called *The Slants*. However, in 2024, the Court unanimously upheld portions of Section 1052(a) pertaining to the use of a living person's name in the use of a federal registration without that person's authorization over a dispute involving the mark "Trump too Small."[49] Other statutory bars contained in Section 1052 are beyond the scope of this chapter.[50]

The First Amendment provides a final check on the outer boundaries of trademark protection. Trademarks are private, not public, government speech. Therefore, the United States Patent and Trademark Office (USPTO) registration system must reinforce the goals of the Free Speech Clause in application. Over extension of the Lanham Act for artistic works intrudes heavily on the goals of the First Amendment.[51] Where the name of an artistic work is so intertwined with that good that a business is limited in the terms it can use, the Courts are hesitant to permit the monopolization of language.

3.5. Registration

Under federal and state law, trademark rights do not vest in a trademark owner upon registration. As explained previously, use in commerce vests rights in a mark. Registration serves as a notice system of recording, similar to the recording acts enacted to reform real property title recordation. Application to the USPTO, by itself, does not create effective

---

46 Alexandra J. Roberts, *Trademark Failure to Function*, 104 Iowa L. Rev. 1977, 1982 (2019), https://ilr.law.uiowa.edu/print/volume-104-issue-4/trademark-failure-to-function.

47 Two Pesos, Inc. v. Taco Cabana, Inc., 505 U.S. 763, 112 S. Ct. 2753 (1992).

48 Matal v. Tam, 582 U.S. 218, 137 S. Ct. 1744 (2017).

49 Vidal v. Elster, 602 U.S. 286, 144 S. Ct. 1507 (2024).

50 *See* 15 U.S.C. § 1052 (a).

51 Rogers v. Grimaldi, 875 F.2d 994, 998 (2d Cir. 1989).

notice of a claim to a mark, rather, the USPTO has, through the Lanham Act, developed a system of federal registration. Issuance of a valid registration from the office serves as prima facie evidence of the validity of that registered mark and of use in commerce as of the date of the application.

While trademark rights vest applying the property rule of "first in time, first in right," registration provides many tangible benefits to the applicant. Under the Lanham Act, issuance of registration creates a presumption of validity in the trademark.[52] Issuance of registration will backdate priority to the date of the application and extend the applicants' rights to the boundaries of the United States. Federal registration also comes with other benefits, including a right to *ex parte* seizure of counterfeit articles by customs, a bar to state dilution claims, and a right to later claim incontestability in the mark claimed in the valid registration. Notably, most international jurisdictions follow a "first to file" system of registration, a common trap for the unwary business looking to expand into international marketplaces.

Under the Lanham Act, trademarks can be registered on either the "principal register" or the "supplemental register." The principal register is available for those marks that are being actively "used in commerce" as a source identifier for a particular good or service. The supplemental register can be used for "marks capable of distinguishing [an] applicant's goods or services and not registrable on the principal register . . . which are in lawful use in commerce by the owner thereof," that is, those marks that have not acquired distinctiveness at law.[53] Additionally, the Lanham Act allows for applicants to file a "intent to use" registration application with the U.S. Patent and Trademark Office.

Application for a federal trademark is a multistep process. While most domestically domiciled trademark applicants choose to work with an attorney, they are not required to do so. Foreign-domiciled applicants must, by USPTO rule, work with a U.S. based counsel.[54] This recent change to office practice was enacted to fight back against voluminous fraudulent filings from foreign troll entities.

Every trademark applicant should start by considering the costs and benefits of seeking federal registration. As a trademark owner must police their mark to retain rights in the mark, some smaller companies may suffer a Pyrrhic victory in defending their mark from competing claims. For this reason, experienced counsel (or the services of a third-party clearing house) should be utilized to start a lawyer's due diligence period and ensure that there are no prior senior claims to a particular mark before money is invested in cultivating the mark and registering it with the USPTO. Potential challenges, based on priority or similarity in use, should be identified at this early stage in the registration process.

A company's common channels of distribution, along with state and federal registrations, should be examined for conflicts with a planned or existing use. Should a potential

---

[52] About Trademark Infringement, U.S. Patent & Trademark Off. (Nov. 30, 2023), https://www.uspto.gov/page/about-trademark-infringement.

[53] 15 U.S.C. § 1091(a).

[54] 37 C.F.R. § 2.11(a) (2021).

conflict arise, counsel must advise their client of the inherent risks of moving forward with a new or continuing an existing use of a mark. But the discovery of a potential challenger does not mean that the trademark holder is out of options. Some companies prefer entering into concurrent use agreements rather than the expense of litigation, particularly if the two uses do not operate in the same channels of commerce or offer a different enough product that the average consumer will not be confused by the two uses.[55]

A common area of confusion for start-ups and *pro se* applicants is that each State separately maintains a registry of trademarks and a registry of business entities. The creation of a business entity by a State governing authority, such as a Department of Corporations, does not vest any rights in a particular mark. These agencies simply note the records of claim to a name; they do not vet or otherwise police competing claims to a name. In other cases, a company may not actually still be in business or may operate in a different channel of commerce than the putative registrant may have originally realized.

Applicants to the office may show that they are currently using the mark in commerce or that they have a bona fide intent to do so within the statutorily defined time period[56] (six months as of the publication of this chapter). A good is considered "used in commerce" when it has been placed or affixed onto the goods, their containers, displays, or associated documents (if branding is impractical), and the goods are then sold or transported in commerce.[57] A service is deemed used in commerce when used or displayed in the sale of advertisements of a particular service rendered in commerce.[58]

An intent to use, by itself, is not enough to establish a bona fide intent to use a mark. An applicant must show some tangible efforts to launch the good or service offering in commerce, and typically does this through proof of marketing expenditures, actual marketing efforts, or other proof of premarket efforts to develop a product or service offering. Once an intent to use registration is approved, the applicant has a six-month period to show actual use to consummate the registration (subject to limited discretionary extensions of time for cause). Once the declaration of use is filed with the office, the priority of use will backdate to the date of application for registration with the USPTO.[59]

3.6. Trademark Litigation

3.6.1. Trademark Infringement

In the United States, both Congress and the States have concurrent power to regulate trademarks. Active trademark litigation might involve a claim seeking to enforce a common law right to a trademark, a state trademark claim to sales of a product in *intra*state

55 David S. Barrett, *The Future of the Concurrent Use of Trademarks Doctrine in the Information Age*, 23 UC L. SF Comm. & Ent. L. J. 687, 688 (2001), https://repository.uclawsf.edu/hastings_comm_ent_law_journal/vol23/iss4/2/.

56 15 U.S.C. § 1127.

57 *Id.*

58 *Id.*

59 Trademark Applications—Intent-to-Use (ITU) Basis, U.S. Patent & Trademark Off. (Mar. 20, 2024), https://www.uspto.gov/trademarks/apply/intent-use-itu-applications.

commerce, and a federal Lanham Act claim related to sales of a product in *inter*state trade, foreign trade, or trade involving the Indian nations. This also means that the Federal District Courts and state courts have concurrent subject matter jurisdiction over trademark claims. The Lanham Act provides several contextual causes of action to protect trademarks.

A trademark infringement action is one in which a plaintiff claims that the defendant is using their mark without authorization.[60] In a typical case, the owner of a mark sues someone using a mark that closely resembles its own. As the *Jack Daniels* Court explained:

The court must decide whether the defendant's use is "likely to cause confusion, or to cause mistake, or to deceive."[61] The "keystone" in that statutory standard is "likelihood of confusion." And the single type of confusion most commonly in trademark law's sights is confusion "about the source of a product or service." Confusion as to source is the *bête noire* of trademark law—the thing that stands directly opposed to the law's twin goals of facilitating consumers' choice and protecting producers' good will.[62] Where a good allegedly competes with the original, infringement will be found if the marks are sufficiently similar that confusion can be expected as between the two. The putative defendant's intent in such a case is highly probative of the likelihood of confusion and as a matter of equity. Where the goods are related but not competitive, the question becomes whether the products would be reasonably thought of by the consumer as coming from the same source, that is, whether it results in consumer source identification confusion. This question asks for more than a showing of mere literality, and the Circuits are split as to the appropriate factors for consideration on this question, but they often include questions of (1) the class of purchasers, (2) the strength of the mark and its acquired distinctiveness, (3) the proximity of the goods in commerce, (4) the similarity of the marks, (5) similarity of the marks, (6) evidence of actual confusion through surveys or testimonials, (7) the marketing channels used, (8) the types of goods and the degree of care exercised by a buyer of ordinary caution, (9) the putative defendant's intent in selecting the mark, and (10) the likelihood of expansion of product lines into competitive channels.[63]

---

60 Under the Lanham Act:

Any person who shall, without the consent of the registrant—

(a) use in commerce any reproduction, counterfeit, copy, or colorable imitation of a registered mark in connection with the sale, offering for sale, distribution, or advertising of any goods or services on or in connection with which such use is likely to cause confusion, or to cause mistake, or to deceive; or

(b) reproduce, counterfeit, copy, or colorably imitate a registered mark and apply such reproduction, counterfeit, copy, or colorable imitation to labels, signs, prints, packages, wrappers, receptacles or advertisements intended to be used in commerce upon or in connection with the sale, offering for sale, distribution, or advertising of goods or services on or in connection with which such use is likely to cause confusion, or to cause mistake, or to deceive . . . is liable in a civil action for trademark infringement.

15 U.S.C. § 1114.

61 Jack Daniel's Properties, Inc. v. VIP Prod. LLC, 599 U.S. 140, 147, 143 S. Ct. 1578, 1584, 216 L. Ed. 2d 161 (2023) (citing 15 U.S.C. §§ 1114(1)(A), 1125(a)(1)(A)).

62 *Id.*

63 Polaroid Corp. v. Polarad Elecs. Corp., 287 F.2d 492 (2d Cir. 1961).

3.6.2. Trademark Dilation

The Federal Trademark Dilution Act of 1995 prohibits the unauthorized use of a famous mark in a manner that weakens the famous mark.[64] A famous mark is one that "is widely recognized by the general consuming public of the United States as a designation of source of the goods or services of the mark's owner."[65] Dilution can occur through blurring or tarnishment of the famous mark. Blurring occurs when a junior mark is used in a manner that impairs or otherwise diminishes the goodwill of the senior mark. "Coda-Cola" baseball bats that are hypothetically sold by a company other than the Coca-Cola Company but using the distinctive Coca-Cola trade dress blurs the goodwill associated with the soft drink. Tarnishment occurs when someone associates a lower quality or scandalous use of a mark with the original product. In 2001, Rapper Lil Nas X's recent "Satan sneakers," which featured demonic iconography, an inverted cross, and a drop of blood on Nike Air-Max Sneakers, was enjoined for tarnishing the Nike trademark.[66]

3.6.3. Cybersquatting

Domain names are one of the oldest forms of protectable digital assets in trademark law. The Anticybersquatting Protection Act of 1999 (ACPA) was enacted to combat the practice of buying a domain name without any intention to use the name in commerce in an effort to sell the name for an inflated price to a trademark owner. Prior to its enactment, trademark owners would rely on the Federal Trademark Dilution Act of 1995. When discussing the adoption of the bill, Senator Leahy remarked that "it is my hope that this anti-dilution statute can help stem the use of deceptive Internet addresses taken by those who are choosing marks that are associated with the products and reputations of others."[67] The ACPA allows for *in rem* proceedings against the domain name in cases where the court lacks personal jurisdiction over the registrant. The ACPA, along with Internet Corporation for Assigned Names and Numbers' (ICANN) Uniform Domain Name Dispute Resolution Policy, provides trademark holders with a powerful tool for defending their rights against unlawful cybersquatting conduct.

---

64 Cite to 1125 and amendment (Revision Act).
15 U.S.C. § 1125; see also H.R. Res. 683, 109th Cong. (2006) (enacted) (amending the Trademark Act of 1946 by defining various forms of trademark dilution).

65 15 U.S.C. § 1125. The relevant factors for determining the fame of a mark include the following:

(i) The duration, extent, and geographic reach of advertising and publicity of the mark, whether advertised or publicized by the owner or third parties.
(ii) The amount, volume, and geographic extent of sales of goods or services offered under the mark.
(iii) The extent of actual recognition of the mark.
(iv) Whether the mark was registered under the Act of March 3, 1881, or the Act of February 20, 1905, or on the principal register.

Id.

66 Jonathan Stempel, *Nike Ends Lawsuit Over Lil Nas X "Satan Shoes," Which Will Be Recalled*, Reuters (Apr. 8, 2021), https://www.reuters.com/article/business/nike-ends-lawsuit-over-lil-nas-x-satan-shoes-which-will-be-recalled-idUSKBN2BV303/.

67 Panavision Int'l L.P. v. Toeppen, 141 F.3d 1316, 1326 (9th Cir. 1998); TeleTech Customer Care Mgmt., Inc. v. Tele-Tech Co., 977 F. Supp. 1407, 1413 (C.D. Cal. 1997).

3.7. The Intersection of Trademark and Copyright Law in Digital Assets

3.7.1. Nonfungible Tokens

Unlike physical goods and services, a digital asset has no tangible presence. Digital assets are considered economically nonrivalrous and nonexcludable intangibles. These intangibles are, in the absence of an intervening intellectual property, contract right, or digital rights management tool, freely copyable by others. Property is said to be rivalrous if its consumption by one consumer prevents simultaneous consumption by other consumers, or if consumption by one party reduces the ability of another party to consume it. Property is subject to exclusion when one's possession of a good necessarily limits another's ability to solely possess that thing. Absent the tools of intellectual property or a contract provision, these assets belong to the public domain.

A digital file is a product of applied physics. Modern computers use advanced electrical circuitry to arrange charges in binary patterns of 0s and 1s. These 0s and 1s then translate directly into math, language, computer programs, audiovisual representations, pictures, movies, games, and more. In the 1960s, it was unclear exactly how intellectual property rights would extend to these electrical impulses. Many argued that patent laws would best protect computer inventions. Patent law protects novel and nonobvious inventions. And a computer program is, in a literal sense, a utilitarian application of an invention to solve a problem with a digital application.

However, the Supreme Court's holding in *Alice v. CLS Bank* narrowed the subject matter of patents, making it harder to protect these programs under patent law. Additionally, in the 1960s, Congress decided that computer files would be best protected by copyright and contract law. Prior to recent advances in generative artificial intelligence (AI) techniques, digital files could only be the product of human authorship. A human computer programmer had to write the lines of code necessary for the execution of a particular program. These early programs were protected as writings under the Copyright Act. The outputs of these programs, such as the audiovisual display of the work, are also protected under copyright law.

In recognizing the artistry of computer programs, Congress sought to cultivate a marketplace for such works. Once commodified, the protections of trademark law were extended onto these new inventions. However, some curiosities that emerged in copyright law cause ongoing tensions with trademark law. Because computer code is easily copyable, and because the storage and copying of code tends to not degrade the integrity of the original file, Congress and the Copyright Office have historically taken the position that the first sale doctrine (or exhaustion) does not apply to the resale of digital files.[68] The vast majority of computer files sold prior to the advent of Web 3.0 are

---

[68] Zachary Catanzaro, *Beyond Incentives: Copyright in the Age of Algorithmic Production*, 13 N.Y.U. J. Intell. Prop. & Ent. L. 1, 53 (2023). https://jipel.law.nyu.edu/beyond-incentives-copyright-in-the-age-of-algorithmic-production/#:~:text=ByZachary%20L.,Catanzaro&text=The%20theory%20predicates%20that%2C%20without,with%20intrinsic%20intentionality%20and%20experiences.

subject to licensing agreements. Consumers do not own the digital files they purchase. Be it a program, a picture, a movie, or song, nearly all sales of computer code grant the consumer a nonexclusive and revocable license to that particular work.[69] And because a consumer's rights are governed by contract rather than property law, the rules governing restraints on alienation of chattels do not apply.

Web 3.0 changes this dichotomy. Emergent technologies like blockchain ledgers provide a means in which a seller of a digital asset can tokenize a particular asset on a ledger,[70] linking the digital asset to a specific token that can be alienated on a secondary marketplace. In the case of a traditional digital file, the token acts as a digital rights management tool, providing access and rights control to a specific hard drive on which the digital asset has been stored. These NFTs can also be tethered to physical assets, like gold, art, or other commodities, allowing for their resale online without the need to physically move the chattel. Now, rather than selling copies of specific files, consumers are able to identify specific portions of a magnetic drive on which a particular file has been appended. Additionally, many sellers of these types of digital assets sell utility NFTs, thereby linking the token to a service offering in the real or digital world.

There is no consensus as to what a blockchain ledger is.[71] In lay terms, a blockchain ledger is a digital record-keeping system. In technical terms, a blockchain ledger is a type of a distributed ledger system in which files are stored redundantly on a decentralized, peer-to-peer network. A blockchain ledger works by hashing the transaction history of the ledger onto blocks of data in redundant copies across the network. At a predetermined time, each node on the network asks for consensus as to the integrity of the ledger records, verifying the legitimacy of each transaction through proof of work or proof of stake cryptography. A lack of consensus among the nodes as to a transaction means that the transaction is kept off the chain of blocks of data that comprise the ledger.

While peer-to-peer networks are not novel, what is novel about blockchain ledgers are the additional technological controls and safeguards the construction of the system creates. Because the records are stored in a decentralized, redundant manner, the system creates trust through automation of auditing protocols. Because the records are appended to the system independently through a consensus mechanism, the records are immutable or substantially immutable. And because no one node on the system can independently alter the data on the ledger, the cryptography that runs on the back end of the system prevents fraud.

These technologies transform digital assets by changing a fundamental economic rule of intangible property rights.[72] A nonfungible tokenized representation of ownership, whether in a digital asset or tethered to a physical good or service, is both rivalrous

---

69 Kyle Orland, *After You Die, Your Steam Games Will Be Stuck in Legal Limbo*, Ars Technica (May 24, 2024), https://arstechnica.com/gaming/2024/05/after-you-die-your-steam-games-will-be-stuck-in-legal-limbo/.

70 The concept of tokenization of assets is an old one in property law, with common examples being a deed tokenizing ownership of real property or a security in a physical chattel.

71 Zachary Catanzaro & Robert Kain, *Patients as Peers: Blockchain Based EHR and Medical Information Commons Models for HITECH Act Compliance*, 44 Nova L. Rev. 289, 292 (2020), https://nsuworks.nova.edu/nlr/vol44/iss3/2/.

72 Bragg v. Linden Lab, 487 F. Supp. 2d 593 (E.D. Pa. 2007) (considering property rights in virtual real estate in the video game *Second Life*).

and excludable. This revolutionizes the marketplace for digital assets. What was once exclusive to Copyright and Contract law is now alienable as a species of property. This means that NFTs and blockchain ledgers require a recontextualization of trademark rights in digital files as a result.

Consider a purely expressive photograph of a physical Hermès Birkin handbag, without the photographer claiming an association with the brand, as a work of art. The photographer has a fair use right to take this photograph under copyright law. The photograph is also capturing something factual about the physical world, which copyright law does not protect under the idea-expression dichotomy. Additionally, the photographer can sell this picture without infringing Hermès' trademark because they are not using the Hermès mark in commerce in a manner that trademark law prohibits.[73] This is no risk of consumer confusion in this context. And to the extent there is a risk of dilution or tarnishment, the photographer has a fair use right under Trademark law as well.

In *Rogers v. Grimaldi*, the Second Circuit developed a two-prong test of artistic or expressive works using trademarked products.[74] The *Rogers* court found that the "balance [between trademark interests and First Amendment speech interests] will normally not support application of the [Lanham] Act unless [the use of the trademark] has no artistic relevance to the underlying work whatsoever, or, if it has some artistic relevance, unless [the use of the trademark] explicitly misleads as to the source or the content of the work." While *Rogers* addressed the use of a work's title, the Second Circuit extended the *Rogers* test to all works in *Cliffs Notes v. Bantam Doubleday*.[75]

However, the 2023 Supreme Court decision in *Jack Daniels Properties, Inc. v. VIP Products, Inc.* curtails use of the *Rodgers* defense where the defendant is parodizing a product line using a source identifier for their own product.[76] At issue in this case was the line of "Bad Spaniel" dog toys, made to resemble the trade dress of bottles of Jack Daniels whiskey. There, the Supreme Court held that traditional consumer confusion analysis was applicable, and that the conduct was not immediately excused under fair use. Likewise, the Court held that a parodizing product that results in dilution by blurring or tarnishment, when used as a source identifier for the defendant's product, also remained subject to traditional consumer confusion analysis.[77]

Suppose now that instead of just selling an expressive photograph, the photographer is selling a digital picture tethered to an NFT that draws a direct association with the brand. The digital file at issue is tokenized (and in other cases tethered to some utility service offering). Now the photographer is selling more than just a representation of the physical world. This was the heart of the dispute in *Hermès International, et al. v. Mason Rothschild*.[78] There, Rothschild purposely sought (with some success) to con-

[73] AM General LLC v Activision Blizzard, Inc. et al. (applying Rogers v. Grimaldi, 875 F.2d 994 (2d Cir. 1989)).
[74] *Rogers v. Grimaldi*, 875 F.2d 994 (2d Cir. 1989).
[75] *Cliffs Notes v. Bantam Doubleday Dell Publ'g Grp.*, 886 F.2d 490, 495 (2d Cir. 1989).
[76] Jack Daniel's Properties, Inc. v. VIP Prod. LLC, 599 U.S. 140, 143 S. Ct. 1578, 216 L. Ed. 2d 161 (2023).
[77] *Id.* at 161.
[78] Hermès International, et al. v. Mason Rothschild, 22-cv-384, D.E. 191 (S.D.N.Y. 2022) (order on parties' post-trial motions and entering permanent injunction against Rothschild). https://fingfx.thomsonreuters.com/gfx/legaldocs/

fuse consumers into believing that his NFTs, labeled "MetaBirkins," and his associated website, "metabirkins.com," were affiliated with Hermès' iconic "Birkin" trademarks.

Rothschild argued at trial and again in his motion for a new trial that the First Amendment protected his NFT offerings, but the Court and jury disagreed. Predicting the Supreme Court's coming decision in *Jack Daniels,* one juror remarked "that legitimate digital artists would have "no need to hide under the cloak of the 1st amendment" so long as they kept in mind "the goodwill of the brand and the consumer in mind.'"[79] As did the *Jack Daniels* court, the Southern District of New York agreed that Rothschild had "used a trademark to designate the source of its own goods—in other words, has used a trademark as a trademark." Yet, as the jury verdict was reached prior to the *Jack Daniels* decision, the court, in applying *Rodgers*, applied a stronger standard at trial defining "explicitly misleading" to include an intent to mislead.[80]

The Court then noted that the First Amendment does not shield fraud. Trademark law, as noted above, protects against a specific type of fraud: source identification confusion. So in labeling his NFT offering "MetaBirkins," Rothschild sought to defraud the consuming public into the origins of the source of his product offering. In applying the *Polaroid* factors, the Court held that Rothschild only contested Hermes evidence on the issue of actual of confusion, ignoring the presentation of evidence on "the similarities between the design of the Birkin handbag and the MetaBirkins NFTs; testimony that confirms the Birkin bag's distinctive place in American cultural life; and statements suggesting that Hermes intended to 'bridge the gap' by entering the NFT space."[81]

However, a different conclusion was reached a few years before *Jack Daniels* abrogated the *Rodgers* test in *AM Gen. LLC v. Activision Blizzard, Inc.*[82] Since 1983, AM Gen (AMG), has served as the U.S. Military Contractor for the manufacturer of the High Mobility Multipurpose Wheeled Vehicle (the Humvee™). Since the early 1990s, AMG has also granted licenses to other companies to use the Humvee trademark "on or in connection with a wide variety of products," including toys and at least four video games.[83] When AMG learned that Activision planned on including depictions of the Humvee in the upcoming *Call of Duty 4: Modern Warfare*, it sent a letter objecting to the appearances of Humvees in *Call of Duty* games and toys. When Activision refused to remove the depictions, AMG sued.

On summary judgment, the Court applied *Rodgers* and *Polaroid*, holding that "merely insinuating that a commercial motivation might exist is not enough—an artist can sell

---

akpeqbebbpr/HERMES%20NFTS%20LAWSUIT%20pi.pdf; *See* Hermès v. Rothschild, 2023 WL 1458126 at *1-3 (S.D.N.Y. Feb. 2, 2023).

79 Hermès Int'l v. Rothschild, 678 F. Supp. 3d 475, 483 (S.D.N.Y. 2023).

80 Hermès (citing Twin Peaks Productions, Inc. v. Publications Int'l, Ltd., 996 F.2d 1366, 1379 (2d Cir. 1993)).

81 Hermès Int'l v. Rothschild, 678 F. Supp. 3d 475, 486 (S.D.N.Y. 2023).

82 AM Gen. LLC v. Activision Blizzard, Inc., 450 F. Supp. 3d 467, 475 (S.D.N.Y. 2020).

83 Fred Meyer, Review of the Jungle Strike Humvee, JOEBATTLELINES.COM (2003), https://www.joebattlelines.com/reviews/toys/valorvsvenom/junglestrikehumvee.htm.

her art without the First Amendment abandoning her."[84] In applying *Rodgers*, the Court held that the first prong had been satisfied as the defendant sought to "evoke[] a sense of realism and lifelikeness to the player who 'assumes control of a military soldier and fights against a computer-controlled or human-controlled opponent across a variety of computer-generated battlefields.'" The Court then, as *Jack Daniels* would instruct several years after the fact, applied the traditional *Polaroid* consumer confusion analysis.

In applying *Polaroid*, the Court first noted that "[n]o one of the Polaroid factors is dispositive, and the list is not exhaustive; 'the analysis of the factors is not a mechanical process.'"[85] In application, the Court held that the strength of the mark factor and slight evidence of confusion favored AMG, and little else. When counterbalanced against First Amendment concerns and application of the remaining factors, the Court found that the parties used Humvees for different purposes; the parties did not serve the same purpose or share proximity in the marketplace; that AMG lacked a *bona fide* intention to enter into the video game marketplace, even in light of sporadic licensing to other video game and toy manufacturers; a lack of bad faith on the part of Activision; that Activision's product was not of a low or inferior quality that could cause dilution; and that consumers in both marketplaces, militaries (for Humvees) and video gamers (for *Call of Duty*), were sufficiently sophisticated enough in their respective channels of commerce.

3.7.2. Metaverse

These same principles apply in the metaverse and in augmented reality offerings. The metaverse is a hypothesized version of the internet, in which an interconnected virtual reality allows consumers to mesh the physical and digital worlds into one space using a combination of technologies. A key attribute of the metaverse (and augmented reality) is the ability for users to create content beyond what Web 2.0 currently permits. A consumer who makes a digital representation of a trademark good—as Rothschild did with his "metabirkens"—may be liable under the Lanham Act. Likewise, the unauthorized incorporation of brands or brand identities into the creation of avatars in the metaverse may falsely suggest sponsorship or affiliation with a brand. Trade dress of physical locations is protected under trademark law, such that a virtual recreation of such a location in the metaverse could give rise to liability.[86]

While the metaverse provides a powerful tool for collaboration online, the use of online meeting spaces could run afoul of a brand's existing trademark rights. Just as the National Football League (NFL) polices the use of the "Super Bowl" trademark in connection with unauthorized live events, an online performance would run afoul of the NFL's trademarks and copyrights in the big game. Virtual counterfeiting operations could expand across product segments in a way that dilutes a brand's virtual offerings. National Basketball Association's (NBA) Top Shot NFTs, for example, allow people to collect, trade, and sell their favorite NBA highlights as digital tokens. A hypothetical infringer selling their own

---

84 AM Gen. LLC v. Activision Blizzard, Inc., 450 Supp. 3d 467, 485 (S.D.N.Y. 2020) (citing City of Lakewood v. Plain Dealer Publ'g Co., 486 U.S. 750, 755-56 n.5 (1988)).

85 AM Gen. LLC v. Activision Blizzard, Inc., 450 F. Supp. 3d 467, 480 (S.D.N.Y. 2020) (citing Estee Lauder, Inc. v. The Gap, 108 F.3d 1503, 1510 (2d Cir. 1997)).

86 Two Pesos, Inc. v. Taco Cabana, Inc., 505 U.S. 763 (1992).

counterfeit NBA video clip NFTs now raises trademark concerns, even if the underlying footage is fair use or in the public domain. Likewise, a competing NFT of an inferior quality, for example, one that injects spyware onto a consumer's computer, could give rise to a dilution claim against that seller.

An unsettled issue here is the protection of non-traditional marks. Trademark law protects anything that serves as a source identifier, and this may extend to new forms of three-dimensional marks, motion marks, video marks, and holographic marks. Territorial-based rights may become murkier in spaces where the metaverse seeks to virtualize real-world locations, and it is unsettled whether, for example, virtual rights in a mark for *Champagne*, protected under French law as a mark for sparkling wines coming from that region in France, would likewise extend into virtual spaces. The borderless nature of the metaverse also raises jurisdictional challenges that bear some similarities to existing questions of sovereignty and comity but may differ in the wholly virtual nature of the product and service offering.

Finally, brand holders themselves could run into problems in trying to expand their offerings into this space without properly identifying what the actual product they are bringing to the marketplace. The NBA is already in the business of producing live and recorded film footage of NBA games. But as other companies look toward this new marketplace, many early efforts failed to translate existing product lines to these virtual worlds. A clothing company looking to sell virtual versions of their clothing for use by metaverse avatars is not looking to sell virtual clothing—rather, they are selling artistic representations of clothing, an entirely different type of product under the Nice Classification system. A branded product extended in such a manner would fail to function in this fashion. So, if a pharmaceutical company wanted to sell a digital form of aspirin, the resulting product is *not* a pharmacologic product anymore, rather, it is digital art.

3.7.3. Artificial Intelligence

Artificial intelligence is an umbrella term that refers to a branch of computer science that seeks to replicate aspects of human reason, learning, and volition. The term artificial intelligence was coined to secure funding for the seminal Dartmouth Conference on Artificial Intelligence in 1956, widely considered the foundations of the modern artificial intelligence field. Since then, the field experienced unprecedented growth, particularly since around the mid-2010s, with the advent of generative adversarial models and large language models (a subset type of GANs).

Generative artificial intelligence is the latest and perhaps largest leap forward in predictive algorithms. Unlike previous AI systems, which traditionally worked by brute-forcing solutions to given problems, generative AI can be used to create new and novel content, including text, sound, video, code, simulations, and more. While the technology caught the public's attention for its revolutionary leaps in the content creation industries, the technology has also enabled breakthroughs in other fields, including medical imaging, genomic sequencing, weather forecasting, legal analysis and drafting, education, data analytics, and marketing.

In marketing and advertising industries, these tools can automate much of the creative process in generating marketing content, including the creation of synthetic social media posts, image generation, advertising copy, product descriptions, and more. A recent McKinsey report estimated that generative AI could create up to $4.4 trillion in annual global productivity, with marketing and sales representing one of four groups that together could reap an estimated 75 percent of that value.[87] The report goes on to find that generative AI could increase the productivity of marketing by 5 to 15 percent of total marketing spend, worth about $463 billion annually.[88]

In addition to content generation, generative AI and other advancements in artificial intelligence offer additional cost-saving benefits in the enforcement of trademarks in a brand portfolio. The use of these technologies can significantly hasten the speed and accuracy of trademark searches, which in turn reduces the costs of effective trademark clearance searches and marketplace policing efforts. These cost-saving benefits could offer a way for smaller entities to police their brands in a manner that would otherwise be infeasible and cost prohibitive.

By using automated trademark monitoring software, AI can be leveraged to crawl the internet looking for potential infringing uses domestically and internationally. Automation can also provide a much-needed link between marketing departments and legal departments, allowing the two to better cooperate through more accurate and dynamic valuation of trademark portfolios. As these tools cut search times and costs, businesses can realize efficiency gains in the race to be first to bring new product lines to market, allowing companies to better capture new market segments.

In addition to these new opportunities for developing competitive and comparative advantages in the marketplace, these tools will also automate aspects of the procedural aspects of trademark enforcement. Mechanizing the routine aspects of registration application, opposition, and enforcement proceedings promises to reduce the legal costs of effective trademark prosecution. AI tools promise both automation of and enhancement in consumer survey evidence presentations. These systems may find patterns in consumer behavior data more efficiently or in areas in which previous human authored surveys would have missed. Finally, predictive analytics tools, when linked to robust marketing data, offer a new way to engage in sophisticated trademark search analysis. This, in turn, can provide a new means of detecting potential infringers and overt threats to brands.

But generative AI tools create many legal challenges as well. These technologies have already tested existing trademark law and the USPTO's practices. In September 2019, the USPTO promulgated the U.S. Counsel Rule, requiring all foreign domiciled trademark applications to engage the services of U.S. counsel to combat against an unprecedented

---

[87] Lisa Harkness et al., *How Generative AI Can Boost Consumer Marketing*, McKinsey & Co. (Dec. 5, 2023), https://www.mckinsey.com/capabilities/growth-marketing-and-sales/our-insights/how-generative-ai-can-boost-consumer-marketing.

[88] *Id.*

rise of computer-generated troll applications.[89] It had become a common practice for foreign agents, particularly in China, to register thousands of fake trademarks with the office, in the hopes that some of those applications would stick. The Rule was designed to combat this by requiring a U.S. licensed attorney to file and represent them in filing and registering trademarks with the office. But some foreign troll entities have turned to hiring U.S. counsel to aid in their fraudulent practices with the office, which can result in serious sanctions from the office, including monetary fines, suspension from practice before the USPTO, and referral to state and federal bar associations for further investigation.

These problems have contributed to increased operational costs at the USPTO, resulting in the office raising filing fees for certain classes of administrative actions. Worse, inundation of the principal and supplemental registers threatens to reduce the accuracy and efficiency of the trademark clearance process, raising the risk of inadvertent infringement by good faith actors. A proverbial cat and mouse game between the USPTO and these bad faith troll entities ultimately harms the efficacy of the office's efforts, diminishing the strength of and ultimately harming trademark's goals in protecting the consuming public from source identification confusion.

Generative AI systems' ability to produce vast amounts of unfiltered text, images, video, and sound can inadvertently resemble existing trademarks. While the production of an image or audiovisual file is not infringing in and of itself, use of these outputs without proper trademark clearance could easily result in inadvertent infringement by those seeking to capitalize on the labor and cost-saving advantages of these systems. Additionally, the large volume of material can result in a near endless stream of immaterial variations on existing marks, making comparison searching difficult as established brands are drowned in a sea of content. The ability of generative AI systems to rapidly generate content thus threatens to erode trademark distinctiveness.

Another consequence will be felt in enforcement actions, similar to the issues the USPTO faces in vetting good faith applications for registrations from AI-generated troll applications. The sheer volume of AI-generated content presents a strain on existing trademark enforcement mechanisms, which may require a reexamination of the procedural tools used to combat counterfeiters and foreign-based entities that attempt to escape the jurisdiction of the U.S. Federal District Courts. With the burden of policing one's trademarks placed on the holder of the trademark, the new tools, strategies, and detection systems needed to detect and police these new AI-generated infringers will come at a cost to manufacturers and service providers—a cost that will ultimately be passed onto the consumer of such offerings.

The boundaries of the use in commerce requirement are less clear as a result of these technologies. As companies use generative AI tools to produce marketing and branding strategies and content, the failure to function doctrine becomes harder to apply.

---

89 Tommy SF Wang, *USPTO Disciplines Two Los Angeles Attorneys for Allowing Trademark Trolls to Use Their Bar Registrations*, Wang IP Law Group (Jul. 8, 2022), https://www.thewangiplaw.com/blog/2022/07/uspto-disciplines-two-los-angeles-attorneys-for-allowing-trademark-trolls-to-use-their-bar-registrations/.

A company that inadvertently crosses into unintentional marketplace channels as a result of AI-based content generation could unwittingly expose themselves to liability as an accidental infringer of established marks. Additionally, the misuse of generative AI could result in accidental dilution through tarnishment or blurring of existing brands.

3.8. Conclusion

As the sale and use of physical brands blur into the virtual world, these types of disputes will become more common. Regardless of the technology used to facilitate new virtual marketplaces and the sale of virtual products, technology does not vest rights to parties—application of existing or proposed laws does. As novel as NFTs are, they do not create trademarks or other forms of intellectual property rights—the Lanham Act and Copyright Act do. While lingering questions concerning use in commerce, fair use and the First Amendment post-*Jack Daniels*, and the failure to function doctrine remain, proper risk assessment and thoughtfulness toward these new technologies will allow businesses to continue blending the boundaries between the physical and digital worlds.

Thus, while digital assets and the metaverse create challenges to trademark law, they also create novel and immersive marketplaces for consumers to express themselves. As this technology continues to improve, it is important for trademark law to remain adaptable to emergent technologies and trends, striking the necessary balance between protecting consumers from confusion in the marketplace and protecting the goodwill of companies that invest in the development of these new offerings. The coming years will undoubtedly bring further developments in this field, and practitioners, scholars, and policymakers must remain vigilant in addressing the evolving intersection of trademarks and digital assets.

4

Publicity Rights in Digital Content

By Jon M. Garon

Digital personas are one of the fastest growing fields for synthetic content generated by artificial intelligence (AI) systems. They populate metaverses, virtual worlds, and videogames. They also perform as extras in films and are increasingly becoming the featured players in new content. This chapter provides an overview of digital personas as well as traditional publicity rights. It also explores how changes to the technology are triggering significant legislative changes at state and federal levels.

4.1. The Evolution of Publicity Rights

In 1905, the Georgia Supreme Court became the first jurisdiction to recognize an individual's right to protect oneself from the unauthorized commercial exploitation of one's name, image, or likeness.[1] Although recognition of this privacy right was considered novel and newly invented by some courts, the Georgia Supreme Court recognized the legal right as part of the common law tradition. "Publicity in one instance, and privacy in the other, are each guaranteed. If personal liberty embraces the right of publicity, it no less embraces the correlative right of privacy, and this is no new idea in Georgia law."[2]

Georgia's pioneering approach to publicity rights owed its origins, at least in part, to the seminal law review article by Samuel Warren and Louis Brandeis, simply titled *The Right to Privacy*.[3] Warren and Brandeis, in the best of common law tradition, did not purport to create new law but instead strove to identify a common law tradition that had been enforced using other names. They built upon "the right to be let alone" identified in

---

1 Pavesich v. New England Life Ins. Co., 50 S.E. 68 (Ga. 1905).

2 *Id.* at 70.

3 Samuel D. Warren & Louis D. Brandeis, *The Right to Privacy*, 4 Harv. L. Rev. 193, 195 (1890).

Judge Thomas Cooley's *Treatise on Torts*.[4] Cooley wrote, "[t]he right to one's person may be said to be a right of complete immunity: to be let alone." Judge Cooley also provided an expanded understanding of libel law by framing it as "right to security in [a person's] reputation."[5]

Emphasizing the rapid expansion of media and communications technologies developing at the end of the nineteenth century, Warren and Brandeis described the "inevitable" development of privacy law as an effort to protect "intangible property, in the products and processes of the mind, as works of literature and art, goodwill, trade secrets, and trade-marks."[6]

Warren and Brandeis referenced the injunction granted to Marion Manola in a New York trial court.[7] The New York trial court found the stage performer had a right to limit the unauthorized use of her photograph for promotional purposes.[8] Other lower courts had done the same, but despite these rulings, the New York Court of Appeals rejected the Warren and Brandeis argument.

Instead, in *Roberson v. Rochester Folding Box Co.*,[9] the New York Court of Appeals reversed a decision to protect publicity rights, holding instead that a non-libelous, unauthorized likeness of a young woman used to sell flour did not constitute a cause of action.

The outcome was short-lived. One year later, in 1903, New York enacted legislation to reverse the *Roberson* decision. The newly enacted New York Civil Rights law provided that "[a] person, firm or corporation that uses for advertising purposes, or for purposes of trade, the name, portrait or picture of any living person without having first obtained the written consent of such person, or, if a minor, of his or her parent or guardian, is guilty of a misdemeanor."[10]

The early case law discussed by Warren and Brandeis based the right to be let alone on a combination of property theories and tort theories, particularly the rights for individuals to control private letters and other unpublished works protected by common law copyright. In the twentieth century, however, the primary focus of publicity rights became an extension of tort law. First, the protection of publicity rights was featured in the article *The Right to Privacy*. Second, influential scholar and Reporter to the Restatement on Torts, William Prosser, identified the right of publicity as one of the four distinct subcategories of privacy law.[11] Since protection against unauthorized commercial exploitation of one's name and likeness was an essential part of protecting and managing one's reputation, the tort analogy was not inappropriate.

---

4 Thomas Cooley, *A Treatise on the Law of Torts or the Wrongs Which Arise Independent of Contract*, 29 (1879).

5 *Id.* at 30.

6 Warren & Brandeis, *supra* note 3 at 194–95.

7 *Id.*

8 *Id. See* Dorothy Glancy, *Privacy and the Other Miss M*, 10 N. Ill. U. L. Rev. 401, 405 (1990).

9 *Roberson v. Rochester Folding Box Co.*, 64 N.E. 442 (N.Y. 1902).

10 Rhodes v. Sperry & Hutchinson Co., 85 N.E. 1097 (N.Y. 1908), affirmed, 220 U.S. 502 (1911).

11 William L. Prosser, *Privacy*, 48 Calif. L. Rev. 383, 389 (1960).

More recently, however, the comparison of publicity rights to intellectual property rights has again emphasized the property aspects of the doctrine. In some cases, these rights are created and defined by state statute.[12] In addition, some courts treat "the common law right of publicity forms a species of property right."[13] Although the analogies are helpful, publicity rights have attributes that are similar to both property interests and tort protections, so it is best to treat the law as *sui generis*.

The term "right of publicity" is derived from a Second Circuit opinion in 1953. In *Haelan Laboratories, Inc. v. Topps Chewing Gum, Inc.*,[14] the court explained that "in addition to and independent of that right of privacy . . . , a man has a right in the publicity value of his photograph, i.e., the right to grant the exclusive privilege of publishing his picture . . ."[15] By framing the interest as the "right in the publicity value," the Second Circuit acknowledged long-standing practices in the media and sports industries to exploit names and identities for their goodwill value.

The U.S. Supreme Court concurred and endorsed this approach in a few decisions. In 1977, a family circus act known as the Human Cannon Ball was performing in Ohio. Hugo Zacchini and members of the Zacchini family objected to the broadcast of their entire performance on the nightly news. The broadcaster claimed it had the right to do so because the fifteen-second feature was of public interest.[16] The Supreme Court sided with the Zacchini family. The Court noted that the Ohio Supreme Court had already recognized the right of publicity in Ohio, so the only question was the extent to which the First Amendment provided journalists a right to impede this right when covering a matter of public interest. The Court recognized that the press has such a right but that it is limited in scope.

The Court explained, "The broadcast of a film of petitioner's entire act poses a substantial threat to the economic value of that performance. As the Ohio court recognized, this act is the product of petitioner's own talents and energy, the end result of much time, effort, and expense."[17] As a result, the Supreme Court made clear that "a news broadcaster's First Amendment rights" do not authorize the elimination of a performer's right of publicity, particularly when the appropriation goes to "the very activity by which the entertainer acquired his reputation in the first place."[18]

Although the Supreme Court has not addressed the question again, the Court has recently offered at least oblique support. The Supreme Court addressed the prohibitions placed by the National Collegiate Athletic Association (NCAA) on student athletes' ability to earn pay related to their sports activities through licensing and endorsements as well as other earning opportunities.

---

12 *See, e.g.*, Rev. Code Wash. 63.60.010 (2024) (Use of name, voice, signature, photograph, or likeness is a property right.).

13 Parks v. LaFace Records, 329 F.3d 437, 459 (6th Cir. 2003).

14 Haelan Laboratories, Inc. v. Topps Chewing Gum, Inc., 202 F.2d 866 (2d Cir. 1953).

15 *Id.* at 868.

16 Zacchini v. Scripps-Howard Broad. Co., 433 U.S. 562 (1977).

17 *Id.* at 575.

18 *Id.* at 576.

The case came to the Supreme Court after the Ninth Circuit upheld the rights of publicity—increasingly referred to as name, image, and likeness rights—in the videogame representations of student athletes in a pair of cases brought by student athletes Ed O'Bannon and Sam Keller.[19] The Ninth Circuit held that the "use of the likenesses of college athletes like Samuel Keller in its video games is not, as a matter of law, protected by the First Amendment."[20] These cases were not explicitly addressed in the subsequent litigation regarding antitrust concerns raised by the NCAA's limit on student athlete competition,[21] but it was precisely those NCAA restrictions that led videogame companies to refuse to pay the athletes. In ruling that the NCAA violated antitrust laws by prohibiting student athletes from receiving compensation for outside activities, the Supreme Court knowingly opened the door to funding student athletes through publicity rights in videogames and in social media activities.[22]

4.2. The Scope of Publicity Rights—First Amendment and Preemption Limitations

"A majority of states now recognize the right of publicity by statute, common law, or both."[23] The wording and rationale vary somewhat from state to state, with some emphasizing the intrusion into reputation and identity, while others focus on commercial misappropriation. While some state laws are less clear than others, in the modern era, no state has rejected all causes of action for misappropriation of one's name or likeness for unauthorized commercial exploitation.[24]

In his 1960 article, *Privacy*, William Prosser defined the tort of misappropriation as being violated when one "appropriate[s] for the defendant's benefit or advantage, of the plaintiff's name or likeness."[25] The Restatement (Third) of Unfair Competition provides a simple cause of action: "One who appropriates the commercial value of a person's identity by using without consent the person's name, likeness, or other indicia of identity for purposes of trade is subject to liability . . ."[26] Neither consumer confusion nor an intent to deceive are required elements of the cause of action.[27]

Some commentators see the right of publicity as encompassing two different but closely related rights. "[T]he [misappropriation of name tort] protects against intrusion upon an

---

19 *See* In re NCAA Student–Athlete Name & Likeness Licensing Litig. ("Keller"), 724 F.3d 1268, 1284 (9th Cir. 2013); O'Bannon v. Natl. Collegiate Athletic Ass'n, 802 F.3d 1049, 1055 (9th Cir. 2015).

20 In re NCAA Student–Athlete Name & Likeness Licensing Litig. ("Keller"), 724 F.3d 1268, 1284 (9th Cir. 2013).

21 *See* Natl. Collegiate Athletic Assn. v. Alston, 594 U.S. 69, 77 (2021) (In 1948, the NCAA . . . adopted the "Sanity Code." The code reiterated the NCAA's opposition to "promised pay in any form.").

22 *See id.*

23 Shira Perlmutter, *Copyright and Artificial Intelligence, Part 1: Digital Replicas*, 11 U.S. Copyright Off. (Jul. 2024), https://www.copyright.gov/ai/Copyright-and-Artificial-Intelligence-Part-1-Digital-Replicas-Report.pdf (citing J. Thomas McCarthy & Roger E. Schechter, The Rights of Publicity and Privacy § 6:2 (2d ed. 2024)).

24 *See, e.g.*, Minnifield v. Ashcraft, 903 So. 2d 818, 826 (Ala. Civ. App. 2004).

25 Prosser, *supra* note 11 at 401.

26 Restatement (Third) of Unfair Competition § 46 (1995).

27 *Id.*

individual's private self-esteem and dignity, while the right of publicity protects against commercial loss caused by appropriation of an individual's [identity] for commercial exploitation."[28] Both versions of the cause of action protect the individual's exclusive right to exploit the person's identity. They differ regarding the limits of the protection and the purpose for the protection. The protection for commercial identity is much more like the trademark or goodwill interest in a person's name while the misappropriation claim identifies harm even if there is no direct commercial exploitation.[29]

Because the two aspects of the claim protect different interests, courts suggest that they allow for different measures of damages. "In a misappropriation of name action, a plaintiff may recover damages not only for pecuniary loss, but also for mental or emotional distress and suffering. . . . By contrast, in a right of publicity action, 'the measure of damages properly focuses on the pecuniary loss to the plaintiff or the unjust pecuniary gain to the defendant.'"[30]

However, despite the potential difference in the measure of damages, courts that try to split the cause of action into two separate actions also recognize that the elements of the claim are largely identical. "In a right of publicity action, the plaintiff must prove the same elements as in a misappropriation suit, with the minor exception that the plaintiff must prove that the defendant used the name to obtain a *commercial* advantage."[31]

Prior to the advent of social media and deepfakes, the primary focus of publicity rights had been protection against unauthorized commercial exploitation. Most of the controversy surrounding publicity rights focuses on the scope of those rights and the conflicting interests between publicity rights and free speech, as well as the preemption issues between federal copyright law and state publicity rights laws.[32]

In both Prosser's explanation of misappropriation and the Restatement's definition of the right of publicity, commercial advantage provides an important element of the cause of action. Prosser describes these uses as including advertising of the defendant's product, accompanying a product upon sale, presumably on packaging or hang tags, "to add luster to the name of a corporation, or for other business purposes."[33]

Out of concern for the chilling effect of an unbridled right of publicity, courts tend to seek out ways of constraining the right of publicity in order to allow for a robust First Amendment out of the concern that "[courts] cannot indulge in the facile assumption that one can forbid particular words without also running a substantial risk of suppressing

---

28 Doe v. TCI Cablevision, 110 S.W.3d 363, 368 (Mo. 2003) (quoting 4 J. Thomas McCarthy, McCarthy on Trademarks and Unfair Competition, Sec. 28.6 (4th ed.2003)); *See Use of a Natural Person's Identity; the Right of Publicity*, 4 Callmann on Unfair Comp. § 22:34. (4th ed.).

29 *See* 4 Callmann on Unfair Comp. § 22:34, *supra* note 28.

30 Doe v. TCI Cablevision, 110 S.W.3d at 368 (quoting Restatement (Third) of Unfair Competition § 49 cmt. b. (1995)).

31 *Id.* at 369.

32 *See* Bonito Boats, Inc. v. Thunder Craft Boats, Inc., 489 U.S. 141 (1989) (addressing statutory preemption of patent and copyright laws).

33 Prosser, *supra* note 11 at 401–02.

ideas in the process."[34] For example, since there is no requirement that a plaintiff prove consumer confusion, there is no legal requirement that the unauthorized use results in any public harm. Considering the lack of a consumer confusion element, courts have noted that "[b]ecause a plaintiff bears a reduced burden of persuasion to succeed in a right of publicity action, courts and commentators have recognized that publicity rights carry a greater danger of impinging on First Amendment rights than do rights associated with false advertising claims."[35]

In the case of a plaintiff's name being used in the title of a book or film, a state would not "permit the right of publicity to bar the use of a celebrity's name in a movie title, unless the title was 'wholly unrelated' to the movie or was 'simply a disguised commercial advertisement for the sale of goods or services.'"[36] This approach should apply to all communicative works, including books, magazines, and other works. "[I]n addressing right of publicity claims, courts have been mindful that the First Amendment provides greater protection to works of artistic expression such as movies, plays, books, and songs, than it provides to pure 'commercial' speech."[37] "[C]ourts, citing their concern for free expression, have refused to extend the right of publicity to bar the use of a celebrity's name in the title and text of a fictional or semi-fictional book or movie."[38] Increasingly, as discussed in the next section, courts are using copyright preemption as an alternative basis to find that defendants are free to use names and likenesses within copyright-protected works.

The same courts, however, have not applied this approach to videogames, another form of protected speech.[39] Instead, California and the Ninth Circuit have taken a balancing approach between First Amendment concerns and questions of commercial appropriation of a person's name or likeness.[40]

The initial adoption of the transformative use test was an expansion of First Amendment considerations. It was used for pictures of The Three Stooges sold on t-shirts. Under traditional rights of publicity doctrine, such a depiction fell well within the plaintiff's publicity rights claim. The California Supreme Court, however, explained that "when a work contains significant transformative elements, it is not only especially worthy of First Amendment protection, but it is also less likely to interfere with the economic interest protected by the right of publicity."[41]

---

[34] *See* Cardtoons, L.C. v. Major League Baseball Players Ass'n, 95 F.3d 959, 971 (10th Cir. 1996) quoting Cohen v. California, 403 U.S. 15, 26 (1971).

[35] Parks v. LaFace Records, 329 F.3d 437, 460 (6th Cir. 2003).

[36] Rogers v. Grimaldi, 875 F.2d 994, 1004 (2d Cir. 1989).

[37] Seale v. Gramercy Pictures, 949 F. Supp. 331, 337 (E.D. Pa. 1996).

[38] *Id. See* Hicks v. Casablanca Records, 464 F. Supp. 426 (S.D.N.Y. 1978); Frosch v. Grosset & Dunlop, Inc., 75 A.D.2d 768, 427 N.Y.S.2d 828 (1st Dep't 1980); Guglielmi v. Spelling–Goldberg Productions, 25 Cal. 3d 860, 160 Cal. Rptr. 352, 603 P.2d 454, 455 (1979) (Bird, C. J., concurring).

[39] Brown v. Entertainment Merchants Association, 564 U.S. 786 (2011).

[40] *See* Comedy III Productions, Inc. v. Gary Saderup, Inc., 25 Cal. 4th 387, 106 Cal. Rptr. 2d 126, 21 P.3d 797 (2001); In re NCAA Student-Athlete Name & Likeness Licensing Litig., 724 F.3d 1268 (9th Cir. 2013).

[41] Comedy III Productions, Inc. v. Gary Saderup, Inc., 25 Cal. 4th 387 at 405.

Had the tee-shirt images been sufficiently transformative, making the pictures of the Three Stooges more like source material for the original artwork of the designer, the California Supreme Court may have found the use was protected even though it was a depiction on a noncommunicative commercial product. Instead of using the transformative use test as a supplement when the item sold was a commercial product rather than a communicative work, the courts instead substituted the test for all balancing between First Amendment and publicity rights claims.

Consequently, videogames in particular receive lower free speech protections in those jurisdictions that follow the transformative use test. For videogames that use avatars to depict real individuals, the transformative use factors weigh strongly against fair use. Avatars that realistically depict actual individuals set in real-world environments in videogames or metaverse experiences will be somewhat literal.[42] The Third Circuit also applied the transformative use test for a collegiate football videogame and came to the same result.[43]

The protection for communicative works is sometimes established by statute or judicial opinion.[44] California's statutory right of publicity does not apply to use of an individual's voice or likeness "in connection with any news, public affairs, or sports broadcast or account, or any political campaign."[45] California, however, does not extend the statutory protection to fictional works. In contrast, Ohio provides a much broader carveout, extending to "literary work, dramatic work, fictional work, historical work, audiovisual work, or musical work regardless of the media in which the work appears or is transmitted."[46]

For claims that do not rely on the commercial exploitation of the work and instead focus on the harm to the plaintiff's reputation, there are fewer tools to balance the First Amendment considerations. Many jurisdictions do not recognize this tort, while others require an actual malice standard.[47] Perhaps a better limitation would require an "extreme and outrageous" requirement that the conduct was at least reckless.[48] Expanding on defamation decisions, the Supreme Court recently explained that a standard of "recklessness" was sufficient to protect First Amendment considerations when enforcing a statute criminalizing threatening speech. Where there is no commercial use requirement, any liability must meet constitutional standards, so the use of a reckless *mens rea* requirement should achieve that goal. The need for this cause of action is discussed below in the context of deepfakes.

---

42 *See* In re NCAA Student–Athlete Name & Likeness Licensing Litig., 724 F.3d 1268 at 1278.

43 Hart v. Electronic Arts, Inc., 717 F.3d 141 (3d Cir. 2013).

44 *See* Perlmutter, *supra* note 23 at 14.

45 Cal. Civ. Code § 3344 (West 2024).

46 Ohio Rev. Code Ann. § 2741.09(A)(1)(a) (West 2024).

47 *See* Doe v. TCI Cablevision, 110 S.W.3d 363 at 369–70.

48 *See* Counterman v. Colorado, 600 U.S. 66, 80 (2023) ("Using a recklessness standard also fits with the analysis in our defamation decisions.").

The other important restriction on the scope of publicity rights is the preemption that occurs when a name or likeness is used within a copyright-protected work.[49] The statute provides for express preemption:

The Act states in relevant part:

> (a) [A]ll legal or equitable rights that are equivalent to any of the exclusive rights within the general scope of copyright as specified by section 106 in works of authorship that are fixed in a tangible medium of expression and come within the subject matter of copyright as specified by sections 102 and 103 . . . are governed exclusively by this title. . . . [N]o person is entitled to any such right or equivalent right in any such work under the common law or statutes of any State.
>
> (b) Nothing in this title annuls or limits any rights or remedies under the common law or statutes of any State with respect to—
>
> (1) subject matter that does not come within the subject matter of copyright as specified by sections 102 and 103, including works of authorship not fixed in any tangible medium of expression; or . . .
>
> (3) activities violating legal or equitable rights that are not equivalent to any of the exclusive rights within the general scope of copyright as specified by section 106 . . .[50]

Congress did not intend full field preemption when it enacted the statute. "Congress did not, however, preempt the field when it enacted the Copyright Act. . . . Consequently, claims are not preempted if they fall outside the scope of § 301(a)'s express preemption and are not otherwise in conflict with the Act."[51]

The prevailing test for conflict involves the existence of an extra element in the state-law claim. Copyright provides exclusive rights under § 106 to (i) reproduce the copyrighted work, (ii) prepare derivative works, (iii) distribute copies of the work, (iv) perform certain works publicly, (v) display certain works publicly, and (vi) perform sound recordings publicly by means of a digital audio transmission.[52] "Federal law will preempt a state-created right if that right may be abridged by an act which, in and of itself, would infringe one of the exclusive rights established by federal law."[53] Instead, under the extra element test, "if a state cause of action requires an extra element, beyond mere copying, preparation of derivative works, performance, distribution or display, then the state cause of action is qualitatively different from, and not subsumed within, a copyright infringement claim and federal law will not preempt the state action."[54]

---

49 *See, e.g.*, In re Jackson, 972 F.3d 25, 38 (2d Cir. 2020); Dryer v. Nat'l Football League, 814 F.3d 938, 943 (8th Cir. 2016).

50 17 U.S.C. § 301(a) (2024).

51 Ryan v. Editions Ltd. W., Inc., 786 F.3d 754, 760 (9th Cir. 2015).

52 17 U.S.C. § 106.

53 Gates Rubber Co. v. Bando Chem. Industries, Ltd., 9 F.3d 823, 847 (10th Cir. 1993) (internal quotation omitted).

54 *Id.*

As a practical matter, courts typically look to the nature of the activities to determine whether a plaintiff is trying to assert copyright authority over the defendant or truly protecting the limitations on the commercial exploitation as an extra element of the claim.

> Many works of authorship that fall within the subject matter of the Copyright Act include either depictions of real persons or appearances by real persons—such as actors or musicians in the performance of the work. To the extent that publication, reproduction, or performance of a work that either refers explicitly to a real person or exhibits real persons in its performance could support a suit for invasion of that real person's right of publicity, the potential for impairment of the ability of copyright holders and licensees to exploit the rights conferred by the Copyright Act is obvious and substantial.[55]

A documentary, for example, does not run afoul of the right of publicity for its depiction of relevant photographs of the people discussed within the documentary. Provided the photographs are lawfully used under a copyright license or under the doctrine of fair use (or even if the photographs have fallen into the public domain), the publicity rights in those photographs are preempted by copyright.

In contrast, if the same photographs were reproduced in a calendar or on a mug, then that commercial exploitation of the photograph would also include the commercial misappropriation of the likeness of the person depicted in the photograph. "[T]o avoid preemption, a plaintiff must state a claim of invasion of personal, state-law rights that are distinct from copyright protections."[56] The misappropriation for commercial advantage provides that right. If the only use is incorporated into a copyrighted work, then only the § 106 rights are being exploited, and generally, this type of claim will be preempted.

One exception to this line drawing is where the use of the unauthorized content is for a radio or television advertisement. Here, the work being made is itself a copyright-protected work, but the use of that work is to sell items such as automobiles and snack chips. In two "sound-alike" cases, Bette Midler and Tom Waits were successful in bringing claims against the unauthorized exploitation of the sound of their voice when recreated in advertising campaigns.[57] The exploitation of the ad agency involved in these cases was to take advantage of the popularity of each singer to create the false impression of an endorsement or other participation in the campaign.[58]

---

55 In re Jackson, 972 F.3d 25, 39–40 (2d Cir. 2020).

56 Romantics v. Activision Pub., Inc., 574 F. Supp. 2d 758, 767 (E.D. Mich. 2008) (internal quotations omitted).

57 Midler v. Ford Motor Co., 849 F.2d 460 (9th Cir. 1988); Waits v. Frito–Lay, 978 F.2d 1093 (9th Cir. 1992).

58 *But see* Sinatra v. Goodyear Tire & Rubber Co., 435 F.2d 711 (9th Cir. 1970).

4.3. Digital Replicas and the Application of Privacy Law to Digital Spaces

Throughout the previous decade, many researchers and companies have been using various forms of machine learning and other AI technologies to create highly realistic audio and video reproductions. In 2017, a subreddit thread used the term deepfake to represent deep learning systems used to create fake or synthetic content.[59] As deepfakes rapidly improved in quality, they became associated with their use in nonconsensual pornographic content. The Copyright Office has adopted the term "Digital Replica" instead of deepfake to help separate out the broad range of uses for synthetic content and to distinguish the technology from its early relationship to pornographic content often used to harass women who did not consent to be depicted in sexualized situations.[60]

Like the Copyright Office, this chapter "uses the term 'digital replica' to refer to a video, image, or audio recording that has been digitally created or manipulated to realistically but falsely depict an individual. A 'digital replica' may be authorized or unauthorized and can be produced by any type of digital technology, not just AI."[61] For authorized digital replicas, the word "staged" may serve better than "false." Since the inception of still and motion photography, some visual artists have staged their subjects to create works that do more than merely duplicate reality.

Television and motion picture industries use various mechanical techniques and computer-generated imagery (CGI) to achieve breathtaking special effects and transport audiences to fantastical worlds. For example, CGI and digital replicas can be used to change the age or appearance of actors.[62] The AI company Metaphysic reports that it can create "high-resolution photorealistic faceswaps and de-ageing effects on top of actors' performances live and in real time without the need for further compositing or VFX work."[63]

In contrast to the increasingly important role AI technology plays in entertainment, the term deepfake continues to have strong associations with its darker past. "Deepfakes are, more often than not, associated with nefarious motives, including creating misinformation and generating confusion about politically important matters. They have been used to demean, intimidate, and harass and have targeted not only celebrities, politicians, and CEOs, but ordinary citizens as well."[64]

Since CGI is an industry term and deepfake is associated with harmful content, digital replicas provide a neutral description for the field. "Digital replicas may have both beneficial and harmful uses. On the positive side, they can serve as accessibility tools for people with disabilities, enable 'performances' by deceased or non-touring artists,

---

59 Laura Payne, *Deepfake*, ENCYC. BRITANNICA (Aug. 27, 2024), https://www.britannica.com/technology/deepfake.
60 *See* Perlmutter, *supra* note 23 at 1–2.
61 *Id.*
62 David Smith, *"We're Going through a Big Revolution": How AI Is De-Ageing Stars on Screen*, GUARDIAN (Feb. 6, 2023), https://www.theguardian.com/film/2023/feb/06/de-ageing-on-screen-ai-artificial-intelligence-film.
63 *Id.* (quoting Metaphysic's website).
64 Payne, *supra* note 59.

support creative work, or allow individuals to . . . be compensated for the use of their voice, image, and likeness."[65]

There are many issues with the unauthorized use of digital replicas, many of which are not implicated by publicity rights. Some of these concerns focus on threats to political discourse and journalism,[66] while others highlight the risk of terroristic threats and libelous or defamatory content.[67]

To the extent that a deepfake is used as part of a scheme to defraud individuals, the various laws against fraud are sufficient to address that criminal and civil misconduct. There have been multiple instances of celebrities being falsely depicted as endorsing products or using the voice of teens to defraud their parents and grandparents.[68] In what appears to be the largest dollar amount stolen so far, a deepfake was deployed in an online meeting setting in order to convince a company employee to send an unauthorized wire transfer of $25.6 million.[69] In another major incident, a deepfake-based financial swindle operating under the name Quantum AI falsely utilized deepfake content featuring Tucker Carlson, Elon Musk, the president and prime minister of Singapore, and many others to

---

65 *See* Perlmutter, supra note 23 at 2 (internal citations omitted).

66 *E.g.*, Regina Rini & Leah Cohen, Deepfakes, *Deep Harms*, 22 J. Ethics & Soc. Phil. 143, 148 (2022) ("Deepfakes do not have to trick anyone in order to be harmful. Even if a deepfake is ultimately debunked, or never believed at all, it can still hurt the person it falsely depicts by changing the discursive context around them."); Nina I. Brown, *Deepfakes and the Weaponization of Disinformation*, 23 Va. J.L. & Tech. 1, 12 (2020) ("Even the most ardent supporters of journalism will be forced to question the authenticity of video and audio footage relied on by journalists, without additional evidence that the depicted events occurred. When people cannot tell the difference between what is true and false, it reduces trust in traditional media . . ."); Jared Schroeder, *Free Expression Rationales and the Problem of Deepfakes within the E.U. and U.S. Legal Systems*, 70 Syracuse L. Rev. 1171, 1179 (2020) (addressing two harms: "(1) The creation of widely believable false statements or facts that mislead and distort the search for consensus or shared truth in society and (2) the unique power of video clips to provide credibility to false messages and to enrage and enflame citizens into action."); Holly Kathleen Hall, *Deepfake Videos: When Seeing Isn't Believing*, 27 Cath. U. J. L. & Tech. 51, 52 (2018) ("The extraordinary success of fake news being accepted in the marketplace creates grave concerns for individuals and democracy. This is exacerbated when a video is added to the equation.").

67 *E.g.*, Cass R. Sunstein, *Falsehoods and the First Amendment*, 33 Harv. J. L. & Tech. 387, 405 (2020) ("To be sure, many falsehoods can be harmful even if they do not fall in the traditional categories. . . . If social welfare is the goal, we would want to measure the benefits against the costs of allowing the false statement in question, or perhaps the category of statements of which it is a part."); Jon M. Garon, *When AI Goes to War: Corporate Accountability for Virtual Mass Disinformation, Algorithmic Atrocities, and Synthetic Propaganda*, 49 N. Ky. L. Rev. 181, 192 (2022) ("The expansion and reliance on artificial intelligence technologies are among the greatest advances in the twenty-first century and greatest threats for misuse."); Rachel E. VanLandingham, *Jailing the Twitter Bird: Social Media, Material Support to Terrorism, and Muzzling the Modern Press*, 39 Cardozo L. Rev. 1, 13 (2017) ("The link between social media platforms and terrorism competes with privacy concerns as one of the most discussed and most concerning, dynamics emanating from modern society's explosive utilization of these communication technologies.").

68 *See id.* at 5; Charles Bethea, *The Terrifying A.I. Scam that Uses Your Loved One's Voice*, New Yorker (Mar. 7, 2024), https://www.newyorker.com/science/annals-of-artificial-intelligence/the-terrifying-ai-scam-that-uses-your-loved-ones-voice; Megan Cerullo, *AI-Generated Ads Using Taylor Swift's Likeness Dupe Fans with Fake Le Creuset Giveaway*, CBS (Jan. 16, 2024), https://www.cbsnews.com/news/taylor-swift-le-creuset-ai-generated-ads/.

69 Heather Chen & Kathleen Magramo, *Finance Worker Pays Out $25 Million after Video call with Deepfake "Chief Financial Officer,"* CNN (Feb. 4, 2024), https://www.cnn.com/2024/02/04/asia/deepfake-cfo-scam-hong-kong-intl-hnk/index.html.

promote a nonexistent cryptocurrency trading platform reaching hundreds of thousands of people across the globe.[70]

Another significant problem is the use of synthetic content for the purpose of defamation.[71] "Even though courts and visually literate observers know that photography is not self-validating, it is often very hard to discern truth from deception."[72] Inauthentic video is unique in its psychological impact on the viewer.[73] "Since people tend to believe what they see, 'images and other forms of digital media are often accepted at face value.'"[74] As a result, falsified video is uniquely harmful. Nonetheless, traditional libel law can take this additional level of harm into account.

Unlike criminal acts or well-recognized torts, such as fraud or libel, traditional laws do not fully address issues of misappropriation of a person's identity when done for the purpose of harm to one's reputation, invasion of privacy by placing a person in a false light, using the misappropriation to harass, or to fully address the range of commercial misappropriations.

As noted earlier, identity misappropriation is better understood to be two discrete torts, one applicable to harm to a person's reputational interests and another that creates a harm to a person's commercial or financial interests. The harm to a person's reputational interests should be understood as one of three closely related torts, which goes along with false light invasion of privacy and libel.

The Supreme Court's leading case of non-libelous but harmful content is *Time, Inc. v. Hill*.[75] *Time Magazine* mischaracterized the novel "Desperate Hours," and the subsequent play, as being based on the life of the Hill family, who had suffered a similar but factually quite different experience when the family was held hostage by criminals. The family had shunned publicity and had even moved to another state to avoid the unwanted attention. But *Time* highlighted and distorted the story to sensationalize the coverage.[76] The litigation that went to the Supreme Court took eleven years, only for the Court to order a new trial. Although the case was settled thereafter, the result of the legal

---

70 Lucas Hu et al., *The Emerging Dynamics of Deepfake Scam Campaigns on the Web*, Palo Alto Networks (Aug. 29, 2024), https://unit42.paloaltonetworks.com/dynamics-of-deepfake-scams/.

71 *See* Jon M. Garon, Article, *An AI's Picture Paints a Thousand Lies: Designating Responsibility for Visual Libel*, 3 UCLA J. Free Speech L. 425 (2023), https://ssrn.com/abstract=4543822.

72 *Id.* at 432. *See* Lisa Fazio, *Out-of-Context Photos Are a Powerful Low-Tech Form of Misinformation*, The Conversation (Feb. 14, 2020), https://theconversation.com/out-of-context-photos-are-a-powerful-low-tech-form-of-misinformation-129959 ("[I]mages are a powerful tool for swaying popular opinion and promoting false beliefs. Psychological research has shown that people are more likely to believe true and false trivia statements, such as "turtles are deaf," when they're presented alongside an image.").

73 *See* Taurus Myhand, *Once the Jury Sees It, the Jury Can't Unsee It: The Challenge Trial Judges Face When Authenticating Video Evidence in the Age of Deepfakes*, 29 Weidner L. Rev. 171, 174 (2023).

74 *Id.* at 175 quoting Marie-Helen Maras & Alex Alexandrou, *Determining Authenticity of Video Evidence in the Age of Artificial Intelligence and in the Wake of Deepfake Videos*, 23 Int'l Evid. & Proc. 255, 257 (Jul. 2019).

75 Time, Inc. v. Hill, 385 U.S. 374 (1967).

76 *See id. See also* Samantha Barbas, *When Privacy Almost Won: Time, Inc. v. Hill*, 18 J. Con. L. 505 (2015), https://scholarship.law.upenn.edu/cgi/viewcontent.cgi?article=1587&context=jcl.

trauma on top of the sensationalism was too much and Elizabeth Hill committed suicide a few years after the Supreme Court decision.[77]

Particularly during the 1960s, the Supreme Court was extremely protective of First Amendment interests and deeply concerned about the use of tort law to constrain public discourse on matters of public opinion. In *New York Times Co. v. Sullivan*,[78] the Supreme Court created the "actual malice" standard "for libel in actions brought by public officials against critics of their official conduct."[79] The Court then extended this First Amendment protection to speakers criticizing public figures.[80] In these cases, "[f]actual error, content defamatory of official reputation, or both, are insufficient for an award of damages for false statements unless actual malice—knowledge that the statements are false or in reckless disregard of the truth—is alleged and proved."[81]

As highlighted by the conflict in the plurality of *Rosenbloom v. Metromedia, Inc.*,[82] however, the focus of Justice Brennen—author of *Times v. Sullivan*—was not on the status of the target of the false statement but instead the public interest involved. For Justice Brennen, "protection should extend to defamatory falsehoods relating to private persons if the statements concerned matters of general or public interest."[83] Others in the *Rosenbloom* plurality focused on the privilege journalists have in covering news stories, specifically for the established news media.[84]

Much has changed since the plurality decision of *Rosenbloom* or the introduction of a negligence standard for private individuals in *Gertz v. Robert Welch, Inc.*[85] Looking at these cases in the context of modern social media marketplaces and the potential for invasions of privacy and use of digital replicas to foster harassment and predatory conduct, the Supreme Court jurisprudence and state-law interpretation should likely have parameters along these lines.

Although the Supreme Court has never fully addressed the question, the First Amendment is generally understood to preclude strict liability or liability without fault for defamation and invasion of privacy even in those situations where there is no matter of public interest at stake.[86] While there is some inconsistency with regard to this outcome,[87] most public policies lean toward the protection of the First Amendment and express concerns about chilling speech if strict liability could result in monetary damages.

---

77 Barbas, *supra* note 76 at 580.

78 New York Times Co. v. Sullivan, 376 U.S. 254 (1964).

79 *Id.* at 279-280; Time, Inc. v. Hill, 385 U.S. at 387.

80 Curtis Publishing Co. v. Butts, 388 U.S. 130 (1967).

81 Time, Inc. v. Hill, 385 U.S. at 387.

82 Rosenbloom v. Metromedia, Inc., 403 U.S. 29 (1971).

83 Gertz v. Robert Welch, Inc., 418 U.S. 323, 337 (1974).

84 *Id.*

85 *Id.*

86 *See* Levinsky's, Inc. v. Wal-Mart Stores, 127 F.3d 122 (1st Cir. 1997) ("It is unclear whether the First Amendment prohibits a state from imposing strict liability in a defamation case brought by a private plaintiff concerning statements that implicate a matter of private concern. Because Maine has articulated a minimum negligence standard for all defamation actions, we need not ponder the constitutional issue here.").

87 *See* Snead v. Redland Aggregates, Ltd., 998 F.2d 1325, 1334 (5th Cir. 1993) (First Amendment "imposes no minimum standard of fault in private/private libel cases").

The Supreme Court adopted an actual malice standard for *Time, Inc. v. Hill* because the history of the case made it a matter of public concern, and courts tend to follow this doctrine rather broadly. Nonetheless, defamation law continued to develop beyond *New York Times v. Sullivan*. That additional constitutional interpretation applies with equal weight to the field of privacy, or at least it should. This may not occur simply through the common law evolution of privacy standards, so to address the significant harms created by digital replicas, state and federal lawmakers are considering a wide range of proposals and new laws to create liability for the use of a digital replica in a manner that violates the privacy of an individual, portrays that individual in a false light, or results in the misappropriation of that person's identity in a manner that causes substantial harm.

Proposals to provide this level of protection will meet their constitutional obligations provided that the appropriate level of First Amendment protection is provided. In matters that do not involve any public interest and only involve private parties, the use of a negligence standard should suffice to meet the long-standing First Amendment jurisprudence. If the matter involves a topic of public concern, then the minimum *mens rea* requirement must be that of actual malice or recklessness. The Supreme Court has made clear that this standard is sufficient even for criminal liability, provided the speech results in harm that is itself within the realm of criminal liability.[88]

Third, the proposals to protect individuals from unauthorized misappropriation of their identity through digital replicas for noncommercial purposes should be clear to limit such liability to situations where the use is "outrageous" or otherwise consistent with the development of common law doctrines of invasion of privacy and false light, in order to balance the need to protect individuals from harassment and harm with an understanding of the general dynamics expected on a social media platform. Legislation and courts should take into account the community standards of each platform to help inform what conduct is part of the expectations within the platform, whether the plaintiff had agreed to those standards by joining the platform (as opposed to being harassed even though the person was not part of that online community), whether the plaintiff is a minor, and similar factors that address the outrageousness of the conduct. Without this common law balancing, courts may find that the attempts to protect individuals from the harm caused by unauthorized digital replicas exceed the protection limits placed by the First Amendment and undermine any efforts to protect the individual.

Meeting an outrageousness requirement or similar statutory requirements that define specific harms such as harassment or nonconsensual sexualized content should readily meet this test. First Amendment values must keep ample opportunities for parody and satire, such as that produced by Saturday Night Live and the Onion. This is equally true when the satire involves nonpublic individuals, such as student organizations at college or civic organizations. But at the same time, the need to promote free speech values should not create an unlimited right to harass, bully, or cause emotional trauma. Proposals to balance protections for unauthorized misappropriation of

---

88 *See* Counterman v. Colorado, 600 U.S. at 80.

one's identity must carefully consider this balance without ignoring limits on the First Amendment when dealing with private individuals and matters that are outside the sphere of public interest.

In addition to new and proposed legislation, in many online settings, the Internet Service Providers (ISPs) themselves make efforts to enforce their community standards and terms of service by limiting unauthorized digital replicas. These efforts are welcome and appreciated. The adoption of the Communications Decency Act was designed to both permit and promote the control of user-generated content by providing the IPSs tort immunity for the choices they made to manage their users' content.[89]

> "Section 230 contains findings and policy statements . . . that Congress sought to promote the free development of the internet, while also 'remov[ing] disincentives' to implement 'blocking and filtering technologies . . .'"[90] Congress hoped the ISPs would voluntarily restrict "children's access to . . . inappropriate online material" and "ensure vigorous enforcement of Federal criminal laws to deter and punish trafficking in obscenity, stalking, and harassment online."[91] Section 230 continues to apply to digital replicas posted for violations of privacy rights.

4.4. Digital Replicas and the Expansion of Publicity Rights in Digital Spaces

Unauthorized commercial use of digital replicas is quite similar to other violations of publicity rights. The digital replica uses an individual's name, likeness, voice, or other well-known attributes in a commercial setting that constitutes an endorsement of a product or service or part of a good or service, then the individual's rights have been breached. Generally, this means that the patchwork of rights will likely be sufficient to protect individuals from the commercial misappropriation of their identity through digital replicas.

Even though the patchwork of publicity rights is sufficient to provide legal protection, the inconsistencies create gaps in some states and confusion in the marketplace. Inconsistent statutes and common law interpretations have resulted in publicity rights having different scope from state to state. Although all states protect a person's name and likeness, jurisdictions may vary on nicknames, catch phrases, voice, and other discerning features.[92]

---

89 *See* Communications Decency Act, Pub. L. No. 104-104, Tit. V, 110 Stat. 133 (1996) (in Telecommunications Act of 1996).

90 Valerie C. Brannon & Eric N. Holmes, *Section 230: An Overview*, R46751, Cong. Res. Serv. 3 (Jan. 4, 2024), https://crsreports.congress.gov (citing various statutory sections).

91 *Id.*

92 *See* Mark Roesler & Garrett Hutchinson, *What's in a Name, Likeness, and Image? The Case for a Federal Right of Publicity Law*, ABA Landslide (Sept. 16, 2020), https://www.americanbar.org/groups/intellectual_property_law/publications/landslide/2020-21/september-october/what-s-in-a-name-likeness-image-case-for-federal-right-of-publicity-law/?login#ref23.

A second challenge is understanding what it means to constitute a commercial use. Under the decisions involving videogames,[93] digital replicas have received publicity rights protection when the same reproduction in books, magazines, film, or television uses would not be considered a commercial use.[94] When Olivia de Havilland sued to object to her portrayal in the TV series *Feud: Bette and Joan*, the court was quite adamant.

> Authors write books. Filmmakers make films. Playwrights craft plays. And television writers, directors, and producers create television shows and put them on the air—or, in these modern times, online. The First Amendment protects these expressive works and the free speech rights of their creators. Some of these works are fiction. Some are factual. And some are a combination of fact and fiction. That these creative works generate income for their creators does not diminish their constitutional protection. . . . Books, films, plays, and television shows often portray real people. Some are famous and some are just ordinary folks. Whether a person portrayed in one of these expressive works is a world-renowned film star—"a living legend"—or a person no one knows, she or he does not own history. Nor does she or he have the legal right to control, dictate, approve, disapprove, or veto the creator's portrayal of actual people.[95]

This strong statement does not yet apply to videogames and presumably to virtual worlds and metaverse environments. Since they are all afforded the same First Amendment protection, courts and legislators must struggle either to reconcile the disparate treatment or justify the different outcomes.

One could try to rationalize the different outcomes by drawing a line between those works that are about the subject from those that use the publicity rights. In other words, a story about a football player would be content protected by the First Amendment while an unrelated story that included football players in the story would be deemed a commercial use that was subject to publicity rights. This line drawing, however, makes little sense. States could try to distinguish on the basis of the packaging by providing that a DVD of a videogame was a commercial product while a broadcast or streamed movie or television show was protected speech. But films are sold on DVDs, and videogames are available online. The nature of the consumer payment also provides little difference since there are ad-based videogames and pay-based television and streaming services.

The distinction between videogames as commercial products and films as communicative products is simply an anachronism that highlights the ambivalence of the courts toward the new medium of videogames and virtual worlds. Inevitably, this will change over time. The change comes more quickly as the line between interactive content blurs for episodic, story-based game play.

---

93 *See* Keller, 724 F.3d at 1284; Hart v. Electronic Arts, Inc., 717 F.3d at 141; No Doubt v. Activision Publ'g, Inc., 122 Cal. Rptr. 3d 397 (Cal. Ct. App. 2011).

94 Matthews v. Random House, 15 F.3d 432 (5th Cir. 1994) (book); De Havilland v. FX Networks, LLC, 230 Cal. Rptr. 3d 625 (Cal. App. 2d Dist. 2018) (film and television); Hoffman v. Capital Cities/ABC, Inc., 255 F.3d 1180, 1186 (9th Cir. 2001) ("altered 'Tootsie' photograph [for magazine] was not commercial speech").

95 De Havilland v. FX Networks, LLC, 230 Cal. Rptr. 3d 625, 630 (Cal. App. 2d Dist. 2018).

The better distinction is to look past the format and instead create statutory categories for commercial uses and for communicative uses. States already carve out some communicative activities.[96] California, the leading market for publicity rights, excludes protection for those rights "in connection with any news, public affairs, or sports broadcast or account, or any political campaign."[97] New York has gone even further to limit its post-mortem rights for digital replicas, by excluding

> parody, satire, commentary, or criticism; works of political or newsworthy value, or similar works, such as documentaries, docudramas, or historical or biographical works, regardless of the degree of fictionalization; a representation of a deceased performer as himself or herself, regardless of the degree of fictionalization, except in a live performance of a musical work; de minimis or incidental; or an advertisement or commercial announcement for any of the foregoing works.[98]

The categorical exclusions are very helpful to limit and focus the rights. Even the New York law seems to treat the outcome of the videogame cases as the correct outcome, which they are only if videogames have less First Amendment protections than other forms of media or are somehow more commercial than newspapers and movies purchased by the public.

There are two additional alternatives to consider. The first is to explain why the videogame is different. Although all content is treated equally by the First Amendment, one could treat those characters that can be controlled and played within a game as being incapable of expressing the game publisher's First Amendment interests. In a motion picture, every character plays a part to tell the story crafted by the author, director, editor, and producer. All the characters collectively serve as representatives of the authorial voice that is subject to First Amendment protection. In contrast, when the user of videogame manipulates an avatar, it is the user's speech rather than the speech in the game. The avatars are digital building blocks. A Lego movie is protected by the First Amendment, but a Lego building set is not. The avatar could be understood in this fashion.

Louisiana suggests yet a different distinction. In its law exempting audiovisual works, films, and television from its digital replica law, it excludes from the exemption "unauthorized digital replicas that substitute for a professional performer who did not actually appear in the work."[99] One could argue that the athletes are the performers in the work and the wholesale substitution for their participation exceeds what free speech requires much like the Supreme Court recognized that the First Amendment does not permit journalists to reproduce an artist's entire act.[100]

---

96 *See, e.g.*, CAL. CIV. CODE § 3344 (West 2024); ARK. CODE ANN. § 4-75-1110 (2024); N.Y. CIV. RIGHTS LAW § 50-f(2)(d) (McKinney 2024); LA. STAT. ANN. § 51:470.5 (2024); NEV. REV. STAT. § 597.790 (2023). *See* Perlmutter, *supra* note 23 at 14.

97 CAL. CIV. CODE § 3344(d).

98 N.Y. CIV. RIGHTS LAW § 50-f(2)(d)(ii) (McKinney 2024).

99 La. Stat. Ann. § 51:470.2(11) (2024).

100 Zacchini v. Scripps-Howard Broad. Co., 433 U.S. 562 (1977).

If either of these is going to be the legislative distinction, then it will be important for states or federal legislators to articulate the basis for the distinction between videogames and movies. Both the performance example and the building block example—alone or in conjunction—help do so. California's transformative use test is not helpful and would not be appropriate when discussing a newspaper story or motion picture, so it should be limited to the commercial products like tee-shirts and mugs for which it was useful.

If this model is too esoteric, then a simpler solution is to return to a much narrower understanding of commercial. In this model, a digital replica or right of publicity is implicated if the avatar is used to sell a good or service or advertise a good or service. This means that the athletes in videogames are not entitled to payment under rights of publicity laws, but avatars that are shown wearing goods and services sold by the publisher (or for which the publisher receives a commission) would be. The Federal Trade Commission (FTC) has extensive guidance for online endorsements.[101] Any activity that would trigger the FTC's disclosure requirements would be a commercial activity for these purposes as well. But merely showing the realistic information and statistics of athletes in games would not be an exploitation of their publicity rights. This is the case for fantasy sports leagues,[102] and the usage by fantasy sports leagues is very similar to the usage in a videogame.

Still, as has been evident by the support for paying student athletes, there are strong arguments that student and professional athletes who are featured in videogames should be compensated. These arguments, however, are not significantly different from the arguments that the subjects of films and magazine stories should be compensated. But unlike unauthorized biographies, there are also strong market forces that suggest the athletes will receive compensation. Among them, the publishers for the games may find it hard to market the products to fans if the athletes themselves do not support the effort. Paying the athletes for their endorsement is distinct from paying them for their permission.

In addition, the athletes may play an important role in both the production and promotion of the videogames. Paying some but not all the athletes would create other challenges for these publishers, and the marketplace may evolve to pay all athletes because their participation, endorsements, and support for the games would benefit both the athletes and the publishers, but not always, depending on the editorial goals of the publishers. This is why additional clarity around commercial use should be associated with clear statutory protection from misappropriation of a person's identity when used in a harmful and harassing manner, as detailed earlier.

Endorsements are treated separately from mere participation. In the case of false endorsements, the use of the digital replica will violate the § 43(a) of the Lanham Act

---

[101] *See* FTC Endorsement Guidelines, 88 Fed. Reg. 48102 (Jul. 26, 2023), https://www.ecfr.gov/current/title-16/chapter-I/subchapter-B/part-255; FTC's Endorsement Guides: What People Are Asking, Fed. Trade. Comm'n, https://www.ftc.gov/business-guidance/resources/ftcs-endorsement-guides-what-people-are-asking.

[102] *See, e.g.*, Daniels v. FanDuel, Inc., 109 N.E.3d 390, 392 (Ind. 2018) ("online fantasy sports operators . . . do not violate the Indiana right of publicity statute when those organizations use the names, pictures, and statistics of players without their consent because the use falls within the meaning of 'material that has newsworthy value,' an exception under the statute").

as an unauthorized false endorsement or false designation of origin.[103] The Lanham Act false endorsement claim requires the plaintiff prove both the commercial use and "a likelihood of consumer confusion, mistake, or deceit."[104] As a result, false endorsement claims have a significantly higher evidentiary requirement, increasing the cost of enforcement. In addition, for a person who is not famous, the unauthorized commercial use will associate the person's identity with the product, but the lack of fame will make it hard for the plaintiff to establish consumer confusion.

Given the many limitations on false endorsement claims, the Copyright Office does not believe it provides an adequate substitute for a federal right to protect against unauthorized digital replicas. "It may be difficult for many individuals, including artists and performers, to prove that the challenged conduct is likely to confuse consumers regarding the plaintiff's association with, or approval of, the defendant's commercial activities."[105]

Yet another challenge with state right of publicity claims is the question of third-party liability for web hosts, ISPs, and online services. As already noted, Communications Decency Act section 230 provides broad immunity for ISPs from liability for the torts triggered by the content of users who post the content. At the same time, however, Congress included a series of limitations on the broad tort immunity which includes intellectual property law[106] as well as federal criminal law[107] and communications privacy laws.[108]

Federal circuits have struggled to reach a consistent understanding as to whether rights of publicity are intellectual property rights for the purpose of section 230. Most recently, in *Hepp v. Facebook*,[109] the Third Circuit found that the use of a newscaster's likeness making the rounds for ads featuring convenience stores and erectile dysfunction drugs was a use "pertaining to intellectual property" and therefore not preempted by section 230.[110] In contrast, in *Perfect 10, Inc. v. CCBill LLC*,[111] the Ninth Circuit took the position that the exclusion from immunity under section 230 applied only to federal intellectual property laws.[112] Separate from the debate whether section 230 should be limited to federal intellectual property laws rather than state and federal laws, there is also the possibility that some state laws treat publicity rights as intellectual property interests while other treat them as privacy protections. The inconsistencies simply cannot be rationalized, highlighting the need for clarity at both the state and federal levels.

---

[103] *See* 15 U.S. Code §1125(a) (2024) (false designation of origin).

[104] Perlmutter, *supra* note 23 at 20.

[105] *Id.*

[106] 47 U.S. Code § 230(e)(2) (2024).

[107] *Id.* at § 230(e)(1). The express provision excludes federal criminal statutes but since the limitation of liability only extended to tort liability, Congress did not appear to preempt state criminal law. *See* Voicenet Commc'ns, Inc. v. Corbett, No. 04-1318, 2006 WL 2506318, at *3 (E.D. Pa. Aug. 30, 2006) (Section 230(e)(1) does not preempt state criminal laws). Other courts have struggled with this question. *See* Brannon & Holmes, *supra* note 90 at 27.

[108] *Id.* at § 230(e)(4).

[109] Hepp v. Facebook, 14 F.4th 204 (3d Cir. 2021).

[110] *Id.* at 210.

[111] Perfect 10, Inc. v. CCBill LLC, 488 F.3d 1102 (9th Cir. 2007).

[112] *Id.* at 1119.

To address these and related concerns, the Copyright Office has called for federal legislation in the area of protection of digital replicas. The Copyright Office is concerned that "the laws are written too narrowly to cover all types of digital replica uses. Some states restrict the right to limited groups of individuals, from professional performers, to soldiers or the deceased."[113] The Copyright Office suggests that any new federal law will also clarify the inconsistencies of secondary liability for ISPs.

4.5. What the Future Might Hold

As highlighted in this chapter, digital replica protection is really an attempt to protect both a privacy intrusion and a commercial opportunity. Since these are distinct interests, it may be better to break the protection into two parts, whether as two separate laws or as two subsections.

States are already taking action. In less than a decade since revenge porn and nonconsensual pyrography emerged as a social threat, all but two states have adopted laws to combat it, and the two states without specific statutes have other laws that likely lead to the same criminalization.[114] In the field of commercial exploitation of a digital replica, new laws and proposals are being developed. The first of the digital replica laws is the Tennessee ELVIS (Ensuring Likeness Voice and Image Security) Act. In March 2024, Tennessee adopted the ELVIS Act to replace the state's Personal Rights Protection Act of 1984.[115] "Described as 'first-of-its-kind legislation,' the ELVIS Act prohibits people from using AI to mimic a person's voice without their permission, and violations can be criminally enforced as Class A misdemeanors. The law also authorizes civil action against any person who violates this law."[116]

The law covers both direct reproductions and simulations. "'Voice' means a sound in a medium that is readily identifiable and attributable to a particular individual, regardless of whether the sound contains the actual voice or a simulation of the voice of the individual."[117] The law extends a property right to a person's voice in addition to the person's name, photograph, and likeness.[118] Tennessee offers a postmortem right for ten years following the life of the individual.[119]

The law provides civil liability for look-alikes and sound-alikes. "A person is liable to a civil action if the person publishes, performs, distributes, transmits, or otherwise makes

---

113 Perlmutter, *supra* note 23 at 12. *See, e.g.*, Ky. Rev. Stat. Ann. § 391.170 (limiting right of publicity to public figures); Ariz. Rev. Stat. Ann. § 12-761 (providing publicity protection to the armed service members).

114 *See State Revenge Porn Laws*, FindLaw (Oct. 23, 2023), https://www.findlaw.com/criminal/criminal-charges/revenge-porn-laws-by-state.html ("In Massachusetts, for example, someone may be prosecuted for revenge porn under invasion of privacy laws. In South Carolina, by contrast, one may be prosecuted for the same offense under obscenity laws.").

115 Tenn. Code Ann. § 47-25-1101 (2024).

116 *Artificial Intelligence and Copyrights: Tennessee's ELVIS Act Becomes Law*, Armstrong Teasdale (Mar. 27, 2024), https://www.armstrongteasdale.com/thought-leadership/artificial-intelligence-and-copyrights-tennessees-elvis-act-becomes-law/.

117 Tenn Code Ann. § 47-25-1102.

118 *Id.* at § 47-25-1103.

119 *Id.* at § 47-25-1104.

available to the public an individual's voice or likeness, with knowledge that use of the voice or likeness was not authorized by the individual."[120] This is broader than traditional publicity rights because the provision is not restricted to commercial purposes. To limit the scope of the law, the statute includes First Amendment and Fair Use exemptions.[121]

New York and Louisiana have followed suit,[122] primarily responding to concerns about disruption to the musical industry caused by sound-alike content being produced without the performers' authorization.[123] "[M]usic AI shops now appear to be using generative AI models . . . with a license for commercial use to create over versions of copyrighted songs. . . . The bad actor engaging in creating AI generated covers can rack up millions of plays and substantial royalties through the unauthorized cover versions."[124] State protections help artists respond to this significant economic upheaval and fraud on their customers. It is not surprising that states with strong music economies are at the forefront of the new legislation.

In addition to the states, there is also a great deal of interest at the federal level. Many of the comments provided to the Copyright Office were in support of a federal law, but of course others opposed such protections.[125] Some were also concerned that a federal law would preempt those states that had more expansive protections.

These are a few key features that state or federal legislators should consider. First, the protection against misappropriation is a personal right that should be available to all persons. There is no reason to restrict the commercial exploitation aspect of the law to celebrities either, so the protections should apply to any person. The rights should be freely transferable and separable, so that a person may transfer the commercial exploitation right while retaining the right to protect against harassment. The goals for the misappropriation protection and the commercialization rights are equally important and must be protected distinctly.

Second, although the Copyright Office did not support or reject postmortem rights, most states have recently expanded rights into the postmortem realm. Assuming there are also strong First Amendment limitations, then some postmortem right should be included to protect against the effect of harassment of the decedent's family and to help manage the digital marketplace. At the same time, many states have extended the postmortem right beyond twenty years to fifty or even hundred years.[126] Another

---

120 *Id.* at § 47-25-1105(2).

121 *Id.* at § 47-25-1107.

122 *See* La. Stat. Ann. § 51:470.4(C) (2024); N.Y. Civ. Rights Law § 50-f(1)(a)–(b), (2)(b) (McKinney 2024).

123 *See* Ethan Shanfeld, *Ghostwriter's "Heart on My Sleeve," the AI-Generated Song Mimicking Drake and the Weeknd, Submitted for Grammys*, Variety (Sept. 6, 2023), https://variety.com/2023/music/news/ai-generated-drake-the-weeknd-song-submitted-for-grammys-1235714805/.

124 Ashley King, *Is Spotify Getting Flooded with AI Covers & Fake Bands?* Digital Music News (Aug. 27, 2024), https://www.digitalmusicnews.com/2024/08/27/is-spotify-getting-flooded-with-ai-covers-fake-bands/.

125 *See* Perlmutter, *supra* note 23 at Preface ("an August 2023 Notice of Inquiry, formally seeking public input on the full range of copyright issues that had been raised. In response, we received more than 10,000 comments representing a broad range of perspectives . . .").

126 *See, e.g.*, Va. Code Ann. § 8.01-40 (2024) (20 years); Ky. Rev. Stat. Ann. § 391.170 (West 2024) (50 years for public figures); Ind. Code § 32-36-1-6 (2024) (100 years).

possibility is to continue extending the rights, conditioned upon a registration and renewal system much like a trademark. Under such a proposal, the initial term would be twenty years, but thereafter additional renewals could occur for each subsequent ten-year term either indefinitely or until a statutory cap has been reached. The benefits for lengthy postmortem rights are for the estates of those artists, of course, and to increase the cost of famous deceased digital replicas to help the marketplace for the living. The latter purpose is really a form of tariff on the deceased to help promote the economic opportunity of the living.

Third, there is an open question whether any federal law should preempt state law or supplement them as a floor for the level of protection needed. Assuming the federal law gets the balance correct between the recognized protection and First Amendment considerations, then it would be generally beneficial to have a single national standard. If the law is too restrictive, however, then the new legislation will undermine the states by being preemptive. In consequence, the federal government would benefit the public by initially creating a floor for protection and then, as the case law develops, explore whether future amendments and changes to state law would make preemption beneficial. As an alternative, advocates for new legislation could consider adopting both federal, non-preemptive legislation and a uniform or model law to achieve better alignment and consistency in a manner that does not divest current expectations.

Fourth, a federal law has an opportunity to address both the copyright preemption issue as well as the First Amendment balancing. If there is a federal law, copyright will not preempt it, so the balance between the two regimes should be clarified by Congress.[127] To the extent that the law uses express categories, the Copyright Office proposes that a "use of a balancing framework, rather than categorical exemptions, would avoid overbreadth and allow greater flexibility."[128] The challenge with flexibility is that it really means uncertainty, which adds expense and tends to result in self-censorship.

The Copyright describes Louisiana's categorical approach, which seems to work rather nicely.

> Louisiana's law similarly exempts several categories of uses: those made in connection with "a news, public affairs, sports transmission or account, or political campaign," in works of "political, public interest, educational, or newsworthy value," and in "a play, book, magazine, newspaper, literary work, musical composition, single and original work of art or photograph, or visual work." The law also exempts "a sound recording, audiovisual work, motion picture, or radio or television program," but not if they include unauthorized digital replicas that substitute for a professional performer who did not actually appear in the work.[129]

---

[127] *See, e.g.*, Dastar Corp. v. Twentieth Cent. Fox Film Corp., 539 U.S. 23 (2003).

[128] Perlmutter, *supra* note 23 at iv.

[129] *Id.* at 16 quoting La. Stat. Ann. §§ 51:470.2-5 (2024).

As indicated above, it would be better to exempt "communicative works, including without limitation, a sound recording, audiovisual work (including videogames virtual worlds and metaverse platform), motion picture, radio, television program, book, magazine, or newspaper . . ."

Fifth, any new federal law should also amend section 230 to provide consistency and clarity on the relationship between the ISP immunity and liability for unauthorized digital replicas. The Copyright Office notes that "[s]ince digital replicas are generally distributed and displayed online through the services of various intermediaries, the treatment of secondary liability will be an important element of a new federal law."[130] More than just address the Section 230 carve-out, the Copyright Office pointed out that "[i]n many circumstances, OSPs [(Online Service Providers)] are best positioned to prevent the continuing harm from the availability of such replicas."[131] Based on their critical role in distributing unauthorized replicas, the "Copyright Office believes that exclusion from section 230 is advisable to encourage prompt removal of unauthorized digital replicas from online platforms."[132]

To create incentives to remove unauthorized digital replicas quickly and reduce unnecessary litigation, the Copyright Office and many of the parties offering comments proposed some method of notice-and-take-down that would provide the ISPs (or OSPs) immunity from financial damages if they responded in a timely manner to a takedown request. The version of this system used for copyright has many critics, so the details of a notice-and-takedown system for digital replicas should be informed by lessons learned in the copyright context.[133]

Most importantly, in building the notice-and-takedown system for digital replicas (and fixing the system for copyright), Congress should replace the "red flag" rules that suggest there are times when the ISP should act even before it is notified with an affirmative obligation that the ISP rather than the victim is required to provide every instance of the infringing or unauthorized content on the ISP system. If an ISP uses a content management system that enables it to find multiple instances of the same picture, song, or video (which most do as part of their monetization strategy), then the same technology should require the ISP to remove all the unauthorized copies, not merely the ones flagged by the right holder. This would create a much more equitable notice-and-takedown regime than the one that originally expected red flag knowledge to create an incentive for self-policing.

There are other considerations suggested by the Copyright Office and the ten thousand comments the Copyright Office received, but these highlight the central issues that will drive the development of new state and federal law.

---

[130] Perlmutter, *supra* note 23 at 36.

[131] *Id.* at 38.

[132] *Id.*

[133] *See* U.S. Copyright Office, Section 512 of Title 17 164 (2020), https://www.copyright.gov/policy/section512/section-512-full-report.pdf.

4.6. Conclusion

As the digital marketplace and the ease with which digital replicas can exploit publicity rights both expand, the need to provide meaningful controls becomes essential. Publicity rights have grown substantially in the century since Georgia first recognized them by name. They have evolved in response to the changes of the judiciary's understanding of the First Amendment, the expansion of other intellectual property laws, and the economic value of celebrities and social media influencers.

The increasing ubiquity of digital replicas requires legislators to act. This goes beyond the quick response to a threat to the music industry or an outrage at the harms of nonconsensual pornography. The very medium of human interaction is changing with AI-generated avatars, chatbots, and metaverse platforms. Respecting human dignity through protections of digital replicas plays a critical role for commercial activity and personal reputations. These efforts, therefore, are fundamental to a healthy public sphere.

Publicity rights have come of age. Fortunately, as the Copyright Office report and new state laws show, regulators and legislators are doing their part to bring transparency and consistency to the field. More changes, however, will be coming.

5

Data: Building Blocks of Digital Assets

By Candace Jones

5.1. Introduction

Data are building blocks of digital assets. Understanding the various approaches to asserting legal rights in data is vital for effectively developing and commercializing digital assets. When the rush to develop the next "killer app" sidesteps the legal underpinning for its data components, the consequences can be significant.[1]

This chapter steps back from the complexity of "digital assets" to the fundamentals of data and legal rights in data. Here, "data" refers to basic factual elements such as identifiers, weights and measures, dates, scores and ratings, and transaction details like prices, quantities, and item numbers. Data can be presented in various formats, including text, tables, and graphs. The chapter uses the terms "information" and "content" to refer to material built with or around data, such as compilations, articles, and audio or video recordings.

As this chapter will explain, U.S. copyright law does not protect facts, and it offers only limited protection for data compilations. It is essential to differentiate the minimal intellectual property protection for data and the protection offered for content (a broader term), which can qualify for copyright protection if it embodies sufficient originality and creativity or for trademark protection if it garners enough consumer brand awareness.

The limitations of U.S. intellectual property law are not, however, a pass to use all data freely as if it were in the public domain. Various laws may restrict data use depending on the nature of the data. These include a patchwork of state and federal privacy laws, national security laws restricting access and disclosure, and export controls defining

---

1 *See* Bloomberg Fin. L.P. v. UBS AG, Case No. 18-CV-06334, Complaint ¶ 1 (S.D.N.Y. Jul. 12, 2018), *infra* note 82 and accompanying text.

certain data as a restricted technology.[2] Data may also be protected under trade secret laws or restricted by contracts (licenses), enforced by some combination of technical mechanisms (e.g., license keys) and legal action. In addition, confidentiality obligations established by contract or rules of professional conduct may also restrict data sharing.

Digital asset creators should account for all potential legal restrictions as they select data. They should also be cognizant of the sources they mine for data and account for various legal rights and obligations.

The goal of this chapter is to help readers recognize and understand the range of legal protections for data. For a more comprehensive discussion of intellectual property laws as they relate to protection of digital assets, refer to chapters 2 and 3.

5.2. Categorizing "Data"

"Data" and related terms are used in business and advertising without rigor, and the meanings attributed to those words tend to evolve to capture the logic and imagination of marketers, explainers, technical writers, and contract drafters in the moment. In legal practice, expect to encounter data-related terms like those in the following illustrative list. Be aware of terms purporting to denote data "ownership."[3]

- Collected and Observed Data: These terms refer to data obtained by collection activities, which could be manual or automated, from various sources, including, for example, individuals responding to surveys or completing applications, sensors and counters placed strategically to detect conditions in the environments they occupy, and financial or other transaction records.
- Derived and Resultant Data: Both terms typically refer to data obtained by manipulating[4] other data through aggregation, calculation, computation, and other forms of analysis, abstraction, or arrangement. Think of "derived data" as a second-generation data set.[5] Data licenses commonly define derived data with the additional

---

2 Privacy, national security, and export control restrictions are each book-length subjects. Comprehensive treatment of those topics is beyond the scope of this chapter. Anyone collecting, licensing, or using data must be mindful of the nature and source of the data and consider whether and how subject matter legal restrictions apply.

3 In the author's experience, navigating assertions of "ownership" is frustrating and unproductive. Consider, for example, a transaction history, which includes data like party identifiers, transaction date/time, item number, volume, and price. Who owns those data—the buyer, the seller, the platform used to process the transactions and compile the transaction history, or the service used to store the transaction history for accounting or other purposes? Each of those entities may assert some rights to the transaction data, which might be expressed using words suggesting ownership. Ultimately, competing claims of data ownership are addressed more productively by establishing among the transaction participants how each of them may or may not use the data.

4 "Manipulated" is used here in a neutral sense not to imply deception.

5 Compare the definition of "derivative work" in U.S. copyright law.

A "derivative work" is a work based upon one or more preexisting works, such as a translation, musical arrangement, dramatization, fictionalization, motion picture version, sound recording, art reproduction, abridgment, condensation, or any other form in which a work may be recast, transformed, or adapted. A work consisting of editorial revisions, annotations, elaborations, or other modifications, which, as a whole, represent an original work of authorship, is a "derivative work."

17 U.S.C. § 101 (2010).

qualifications that they cannot be reverse engineered to reveal the licensed raw data and are sufficiently different from the raw data that they are not a substitute for the raw data.

- Raw Data: This term refers to data as they are initially collected or observed, *i.e.*, without being adjusted, calculated, or otherwise manipulated.[6]
- Synthetic Data: These are data generated through estimation or prediction, such as the output of a model. While synthetic data may prove to be an accurate representation of actual conditions, they are not observed in the sense of collected data. Synthetic data may be predicted based on related conditions, context, and surrounding observed data.[7] While some might describe synthetic data as "made up," that characterization diminishes the value of synthetic data. Like any other data, the value (usefulness) of synthetic data depends on the rigor with which they are created and how well suited they are for the purpose the synthetic data are to be used.[8]

5.3. Why Are Data Not Copyrightable in the United States?

The U.S. Copyright Act provides, "In no case does copyright protection for an original work of authorship extend to any idea, procedure, process, system, method of operation, concept, principle, or discovery, regardless of the form in which it is described, explained, illustrated, or embodied in such work."[9]

The seminal decision on copyright and data is *Feist Publications, Inc. v. Rural Telephone Service Co., Inc.*[10] In *Feist*, the U.S. Supreme Court explained why neither the Constitution nor the Copyright Act of 1976 supports copyright protection for data.

Rural Telephone ("Rural") was a public utility that provided telephone service and was required by state regulation to publish a telephone directory, including basic customer information such as names, addresses, and phone numbers.[11] Rural culled directory details from its customer records.[12] Feist Publications ("Feist"), a company

---

6 *See, e.g.*, Feist Pubs., Inc. v. Rural Tele. Serv. Co., Inc., 499 U.S. 340, 361 (1991) (referring to facts that were copied as "raw data").

7 *See, e.g.*, Nat'l Inst. of Standards & Tech., NIST Spec. Pub., NIST SP 800-188, De-Identifying Government Datasets: Techniques and Governance 108 (2023) (defining "synthetic data generation" as "[a] process in which seed data are used to create artificial data that have some of the statistical characteristics of the seed data" and describing techniques to use partially or fully synthetic data for deidentifying datasets).

8 *See* U.S. Census Bur. Fact Sheet, What are Synthetic Data? (May 27, 2021), https://www.census.gov/library/-fact-sheets/2021/what-are-synthetic-data.html (last visited May 26, 2024).

Synthetic data can mean many different things depending upon the way they are used. Sometimes, as in computer programming, the term means data that are completely simulated for testing purposes. Other times, as in statistics, the term means combining data, often from multiple sources, to produce estimates for more granular populations than any one source can support.

9 17 U.S.C. § 102(b).

10 *Feist*, 499 U.S. 340.

11 *Id.* at 342.

12 *Id.* at 343.

that published regional telephone directories, requested a license from Rural to use its "white page" listings.[13] Other telephone companies in the region agreed to license their white page listings to Feist, but Rural refused. Feist nevertheless extracted listings from Rural's directory, verified them, enhanced certain listings with independently collected information, and then published the data in its regional directory.[14]

Rural sued Feist for copyright infringement, arguing that its telephone directory was copyrightable. The District Court sided with Rural and granted it summary judgment.[15] The Circuit Court affirmed in an unpublished opinion.[16] The case eventually reached the Supreme Court where the key question was whether copyright law protects factual information, such as the names and phone numbers Feist copies from Rural.[17] The Supreme Court reversed.

The Supreme Court positioned the case as an opportunity to reconcile the tension between "the interaction of two well-established propositions. The first is that facts are not copyrightable; the other, that compilations of facts generally are."[18]

Regarding facts, the Court noted:

> That there can be no valid copyright in facts is universally understood. The most fundamental axiom of copyright law is that "[n]o author may copyright his ideas or the facts he narrates."[19]

Compilations of facts, however, are within the scope of copyright protection—at least potentially. According to the Court in *Feist*:

> The key to resolving the tension [between facts, which are not copyrightable, and compilations, which are] lies in understanding why facts are not copyrightable. The *sin qua non* of copyright is originality. To qualify for copyright protection, a work must be original to the author . . .[20]
>
> "No one may claim originality as to facts." [1 M. Nimmer & D. Nimmer, Copyright] § 2.11[A], p. 2–157. This is because facts do not owe their origin to an act of authorship. The distinction is one between creation and discovery: The first person to find and report a particular fact has not created the fact; he or she has merely discovered its existence.[21]

---

13 *Id.* at 342-43. Acknowledging the generation(s) of readers who grew up without telephone books, the directories followed a standard format with an alphabetical listing of telephone subscribers printed on flimsy white paper (the "white pages") and a separate business advertising section arranged by subject matter and printed on flimsy yellow paper (the "yellow pages"). *See id.* at 342.

14 *Id.* at 343.

15 *Id.* at 344.

16 *Id.*

17 *Id.*

18 *Id.*

19 *Id.* at 344-45 (quoting Harper & Row, Pub., Inc. v. Nation Enter., 471 U.S. 539, 556 (1985)).

20 *Id.* at 345 (citation omitted). The Court explained that "[o]riginality is a constitutional requirement." *Id.* at 346.

21 *Id.* at 347. Consider in this context the notion of synthetic data and model output, generally. Synthetic data are created, not discovered, but their creation is typically the work of a machine not a human author.

A compilation of facts may be copyrightable because it could "possess the requisite originality."[22] "[C]hoices as to selection and arrangement [of facts], so long as they are made independently by the compiler and entail a minimal degree of creativity, are sufficiently original that Congress may protect such compilations through the copyright laws."[23] Copyright protection in the compilation is limited, however, to those elements of the work that are original to the author. The original elements may be commentary or arrangement and formatting, but "the facts themselves do not become original through association."[24]

The Court explained that the Constitution's protection for copyright supports this distinction between facts and expression:

> The primary objective of copyright is not to reward the labor of authors, but "[t]o promote the Progress of Science and useful Arts." Art. I, § 8, cl. 8 . . . To this end, copyright assures authors the right to their original expression, but encourages others to build freely upon the ideas and information conveyed by a work . . . [Allowing raw facts to be copied at will from a compilation] is neither unfair nor unfortunate. It is the means by which copyright advances the progress of science and art.[25]

The Court in *Feist* went on to recount and reject cases allowing copyright protection of factual compilations under the "sweat of the brow," or "industrious collection," theory.[26] It analyzed in detail revisions in the Copyright Act of 1976 clarifying "that copyright requires originality, § 102(a); that facts are never original, § 102(b); that the copyright in a compilation does not extend to the facts it contains, § 103(b); and that a compilation

---

At this time (April 2025), the U.S. Copyright Office considers it to be "well-established that copyright can protect only material that is the product of human creativity. Most fundamentally, the term 'author,' which is used in both the Constitution and the Copyright Act, excludes non-humans. The Office's registration policies and regulations reflect statutory and judicial guidance on this issue." U.S. Copyright Off., Copyright Registration Guidance: Works Containing Material Generated by Artificial Intelligence, 88 Fed. Reg. 16190 (Mar. 16, 2023).

22 *Feist*, 499 U.S. at 348.

23 *Id.* (citing Nimmer).

24 *Id.* at 349.

25 *Id.* at 349–50 (citations omitted).

26 *Id.* at 351–54.

For comparison, nationals of, and residents in, the European Union (EU) are entitled to protection of database content under a *sui generis* right authorized by Directive 96/9/EC of the European Parliament and of the Council of March 11, 1996, on the Legal Protection of Databases, art. 7, 1996 O.J. (L 77) 1, 4, http://data.europa.eu/eli/dir/1996/9/2019-06-06 (last visited May 12, 2024) (the "Database Protection Directive").

In the "Doing Business" section of the EU website, the EU explains in plain language its protections for database content:

To obtain sui generis protection, you need to prove that you have made a substantial investment (financial, material, and/or human) in either obtaining the verification or the presentation of the database content.

The sui generis database right protects the content of your database. You or the maker of the database can prevent the extraction and/or reuse of the whole or a substantial part of the database's content. When you create the database and it meets the requirements for the sui generis protection, you are automatically granted this protection for 15 years, starting either from the creation date or from when the database was first made publicly available.

Database Protection, EU, https://europa.eu/youreurope/business/running-business/intellectual-property/database-protection/index_en.htm (last visited May 12, 2024).

Analogous to U.S. copyright protection of data compilations, the Database Protection Directive extends copyright protection to database structure. Database Protection Directive, Directive 96/9/EC, art. 3, 1996 O.J. (L 77) 2.

is copyrightable only to the extent that it features an original selection, coordination, or arrangement, § 101."[27] The Court also observed that "[t]he 1976 revisions have proven largely successful in steering courts in the right direction," away from the "sweat of the brow" theory.[28]

As for Rural's claim against Feist, the Court found no real dispute that the "raw data" Feist used did not satisfy the originality requirement for copyright protection.[29] Beyond that, the Court determined that Rural's selection, coordination, and arrangement of names in an alphabetical list with corresponding telephone numbers also did not meet the low threshold of creativity sufficient for copyright protection.[30] "Because Rural's white pages lack the requisite originality, Feist's use of the listings cannot constitute infringement."[31]

5.4. How Are Data Protected in U.S. Law?

5.4.1. The Early-Internet Grab Bag of Legal Theories

The early history of internet commerce offers useful illustrations of data-driven businesses adapting to the challenge of making data readily accessible to enable online transactions while seeking to protect valuable data assets from competitors. Paywalls, license keys, and other technological measures can be effective mechanisms for restricting content to legitimate subscribers, but barriers to access can also be inconsistent with customer service objectives. Also, the concept that publicly accessible information (facts and other content) is not necessarily freely available to use for any purpose is confusing to many people.[32]

Two early legal skirmishes were *Ticketmaster Corp. v. Tickets.com, Inc.*[33] and *Register.com, Inc. v. Verio, Inc.*[34] In subsequent years, those cases have been cited often for their analyses of contract formation through online interactions.[35] The underlying subject matter of the contracts in those cases was access to and use of published data, and the contract claims proved more productive for plaintiffs seeking to protect their data assets than numerous other theories they advanced, including copyright infringement.

---

27 *Feist*, 499 U.S. at 360.

28 *Id.*

29 *Id.* at 361.

30 *Id.* at 363.

31 *Id.* at 364.

32 Copyright Off. Frequently Asked Question: "Where is the public domain? The public domain is not a place. A work of authorship is in the 'public domain' if it is no longer under copyright protection or if it failed to meet the requirements for copyright protection. Works in the public domain may be used freely without the permission of the former copyright owner." https://www.copyright.gov/help/faq/faq-definitions.html (last visited May 23, 2024).

33 54 U.S.P.Q. 2d 1344 (C.D. Cal. 2000).

34 356 F.3d 393 (2d Cir. 2004).

35 Christina L. Kunz et al., *Click-through Agreements: Strategies for Avoiding Disputes on Validity of Assent*, 57 Bus. Law. 401 (2001); Christina L. Kunz et al., *Browse-Wrap Agreements: Validity of Implied Assent in Electronic Form Agreements*, 59 Bus. Law. 279 (2003). For commentary about the significance of these early articles, see Nancy S. Kim et al., *Notice and Assent through Technological Change: The Enduring Relevance of the Work of the ABA Joint Working Group on Electronic Contracting Practices*, 75 Bus. Law. 1725 (2020).

In 1999, Ticketmaster sued Tickets.com ("Tickets") alleging that Tickets scraped event data from Ticketmaster's website and engaged in deep linking to individual event pages, practices which bypassed the terms of use on Ticketmaster's website and enabled Tickets to avoid displaying Ticketmaster's advertising and homepage content.[36] The court's ruling on Tickets's motion to dismiss Ticketmaster's complaint describes myriad theories of the case:

- Copyright Infringement: Motion to dismiss denied because Ticketmaster alleged copying, but the court "reject[ed] Ticketmaster's basic contention that it is copyright infringement to take basic facts from its publicly available web pages and use those facts (if the expression and method of presentation is not copied)."[37] The court also determined that hyperlinking does not violate the Copyright Act because "no copying is involved" in hyperlinking.[38]
- Breach of Contract: Motion to dismiss granted with leave to amend because Ticketmaster failed to allege facts showing that website users agreed to the terms and conditions linked at the bottom of the home page without requiring a click to "agree" or other indicator of assent.[39] The court contemplated that an amended complaint might allege facts showing Tickets had knowledge of the terms and agreed to them in some fashion.[40]
- Lanham Act Claims (passing off, reverse passing off, and false advertising): Motion to dismiss denied because elements of the claims were sufficiently alleged to state a claim.[41]
- State Law Claims for Misappropriation and Trespass: Motion to dismiss granted. The court found these claims, rooted in Tickets's taking factual information, preempted by the Copyright Act.[42] Furthermore, the court observed, "it is hard to see how entering a publicly available web site could be called a trespass, since all are invited to enter."[43]
- State Law Unfair Business Practices: Motion to dismiss denied. Ticketmaster's allegation of false advertising "suppl[ied] the 'extra element'" that precluded preemption by federal copyright law.[44]
- Unjust Enrichment: Motion to dismiss granted because the claim was based on taking factual information from the Ticketmaster website and "copyright preemption covers the subject of taking factual data without taking the mode of expression of same."[45]

---

36 Ticketmaster, 54 U.S.P.Q. 2d at 1345.

37 *Id.* at 1346.

38 *Id.*

39 *Id.* Compare the Second Circuit's analysis of Register's contract claim against Verio. Register.com, 356 F.3d at 401–03. Verio conceded it was aware of Register's terms restricting use of its WHOIS domain registration data and nevertheless proceeded to use data it had taken from Register in a manner prohibited by the terms. *Id.* at 402.

40 Ticketmaster, 54 U.S.P.Q. 2d at 1346.

41 *Id.*

42 *Id.* at 1347.

43 *Id.* For a more detailed discussion of the "trespass to chattels" theory, *see* Register.com, 356 F.3d at 404 & 436-39.

44 Ticketmaster, 54 U.S.P.Q. 2d at 1347.

45 *Id.*

- Tortious Interference with Prospective Business Advantage: Motion to dismiss denied at this early stage because there were "virtually no cases on deep linking" at the time, and the interference with advertising Ticketmaster alleged to be a consequence of deep linking might prove sufficient to support the theory.[46]

The court subsequently denied Ticketmaster's motion for preliminary injunction.[47] The court found that the material Tickets copied from Ticketmaster, such as event details and URLs, were facts and functional elements not protected by copyright. The limited copying done by Tickets to obtain nonprotectable information was also potentially considered fair use.[48] The court noted Ticketmaster's trespass theory as "demand[ing] serious consideration."[49] On balance, though, the court determined Ticketmaster's chance of prevailing at trial was sufficiently low that an injunction was not warranted.[50]

Register's claims against Verio asserted several of the theories advanced by Ticketmaster against Tickets, including allegations that Verio's actions caused customer confusion, constituted trespass to chattels, and breached Register's contract terms.[51] In addition, Register alleged that Verio violated the federal Computer Fraud and Abuse Act, 18 U.S.C. § 1030, by accessing Register's computers without authorization.[52]

In sum, copyright did not provide the protection Ticketmaster and Verio sought for the data exposed on their websites.

5.4.2. Trade Secrets

The court in *Ticketmaster* noted the logical challenge of arguing trespass in a space to which the public is invited. It can be similarly challenging to reconcile access to electronic data with confidentiality and trade secret protections. If data are distributed for purposes that are inherently public or distributed so widely that it is a practical impossibility to keep the data from seeping into public awareness, a key element for trade secret protection is missing. Trade secret owners must make reasonable efforts to keep trade secrets secret. On the contrary, closely held information shared with a vendor or service provider for a particular project, for example, can retain its character as a trade secret.

Forty-nine states have enacted the Uniform Trade Secrets Act (UTSA).[53] "Trade secret," under the UTSA, "means information, including a formula, pattern, compilation, program, device, method, technique, or process, that: (i) derives independent economic value, actual or potential, from not being generally known to, and not being readily

---

46 Ticketmaster Corp. v. Tickets.com, Inc., No. CV99-7654, minute order at 7 (C.D. Cal. Mar. 27, 2000). The order published at 54 U.S.P.Q. 1344 omitted the final paragraph of the minute order ruling on tortious interference.

47 Ticketmaster Corp. v. Tickets.com, Inc., No. CV99-7654, 2000 WL 1887522, at *1 (C.D. Cal. Aug. 10, 2000).

48 *Id.* at *3.

49 *Id.*

50 *Id.* at *5.

51 Register.com, 356 F.3d at 404-05 & 436-43 (Appendix including draft opinion of Judge Fred I. Parker who indicated his disagreement with the Court's decision but died before opinions in the case were issued).

52 *Id.* at 397 & 439–40.

53 Uniform Law Commission Trade Secrets Act Enactment Map, https://www.uniformlaws.org/committees/community-home?communitykey=3a2538fb-e030-4e2d-a9e2-90373dc05792 (last visited May 22, 2025).

ascertainable by proper means by, other persons who can obtain economic value from its disclosure or use, and (ii) is the subject of efforts that are reasonable under the circumstances to maintain its secrecy."[54]

An accompanying Comment explains that reasonable efforts to keep information secret do not preclude all sharing:

> [R]easonable efforts to maintain secrecy have been held to include advising employees of the existence of a trade secret, limiting access to a trade secret on "need to know basis," and controlling plant access. On the other hand, public disclosure of information through display, trade journal publications, advertising, or other carelessness can preclude protection.[55]

The Federal Defend Trade Secrets Act of 2016 created a federal private right of action for misappropriation of trade secrets related to a product or service used or intended for use in interstate or foreign commerce.[56] Federal law defines "trade secret" as:

> all forms and types of financial, business, scientific, technical, economic, or engineering information, including patterns, plans, compilations, program devices, formulas, designs, prototypes, methods, techniques, processes, procedures, programs, or codes, whether tangible or intangible, and whether or how stored, compiled, or memorialized physically, electronically, graphically, photographically, or in writing if—
>
> (A) the owner thereof has taken reasonable measures to keep such information secret; and
>
> (B) the information derives independent economic value, actual or potential, from not being generally known to, and not being readily ascertainable through proper means by, another person who can obtain economic value from the disclosure or use of the information.[57]

If trade secrets are incorporated into digital assets, failure to implement adequate measures to maintain secrecy poses a significant risk of forfeiting trade secret protection. When an object of a digital asset is to publish content, developers should consider and account for the value of giving up trade secret protection for any information they choose to disclose. Developers must also take appropriate measures to avoid disclosure of third-party data developers promise to keep confidential. A more difficult lesson in the trade secret realm may be for end users of third-party digital assets who, knowingly or unknowingly, allow the third party to take the end user's data for development or enhancement of the digital asset without fully understanding the potential for the end user's data to be disclosed to other users of the digital asset in a manner that could destroy the character of the end user's data as a trade secret.[58]

---

54 Unif. Trade Secrets Act, § 1(1) (Unif. Law Comm'n 1979 & 1985 Amd.).

55 *Id.* § 1 cmt.

56 Pub. L. 114–153 § 2(b)(1), 130 Stat. 376 (2016) (codified at 18 U.S.C. § 1836(b)).

57 18 U.S.C. § 1839(3).

58 For further discussion of trade secrets, see Chapters 4 and 13.

For example, if trade secrets are included in data used to train artificial intelligence tools, those data are at risk of being exposed. Is enabling use of trade secrets in training data consistent with taking reasonable measures to keep the data secret? Is there an effective remedy for disclosing trade secrets short of destroying the body of training data and outputs that may contain the trade secrets? Those cases will be challenging and expensive to litigate. When an organization relies on trade secret protections, a more prudent course will be to avoid technology that ingests trade secrets into datasets that could be used for training, development, or testing.

5.4.3. Licenses, Subscriptions, and Confidentiality Obligations

Widely and readily accessible data are often published subject to restrictive licenses or subscription terms typically documented in "Terms of Use" or "Terms & Conditions." The *Ticketmaster* and *Register.com* cases discussed above were early illustrations. This section includes a few more recent examples of such legal terms. Some data accessible online may be used for any purpose or for some purposes (but not others) without charge, while other data must be accessed through "paywalls" that restrict data use and impose fees. Whether or not a court would find restrictions in any of the examples below to be enforceable contractual obligations requires factual inquiries and legal analyses specific to the circumstances.[59]

Websites can also use "Robots Exclusion Protocol" (REP), or "robots.txt file," to restrict automated web crawlers deployed to harvest website content. REP is a technical corollary to terms of use.

> The REP, first introduced in 1995 and codified in 2022, has become the default mechanism for website owners to indicate to web crawlers what parts of their website, if any, they consent to have crawled. While it is not legally enforceable, it is respected by all major search engines, as it prevents website servers from getting overloaded by crawlers, it allows websites to signal pages that are undesirable to crawl (for example, calendar sites that could lead to infinite loops), and by respecting it, crawlers disincentivize adversarial tactics designed to impede crawlers.[60]

The 2024 article *Consent in Crisis* reports on an extensive survey of thousands of websites that are crawled by providers of foundational training data—"content" in the vernacular of this chapter—for AI development.[61] Much like developments in the early years of the commercial internet prompted technological mechanisms to deter objectionable competitor tactics,[62] the website survey found that website publishers in 2023 tweaked

---

59 Readers should refer to the articles cited in Note 35 for excellent analysis of online contracting practices.

60 Shayne Longpre et al., *Consent in Crisis: The Rapid Decline of the AI Data Commons* § 2 at 4 (2024) (accessed at https://arxiv.org/abs/2407.14933v2, Aug. 24, 2024) ["*Consent in Crisis*"].

61 *Id.* § 2 at 3–4.

62 *See* Ticketmaster, 2000 WL 1887522, at *1 (ruling on Ticketmaster's motion for preliminary injunction). In ruling on the motion, the court took notice of "some significant turns" during the five months elapsed since the court ruled on a motion to dismiss, including technical measures devised by Ticketmaster to block deep linking by Tickets. *Id.*

their legal terms and REP settings to deter data scraping for AI training.[63] Those tweaks were not entirely effective, however.

Consent in Crisis provides quantitative support for the proposition that legal terms and REP are inadequate tools for permissioning use of website content. REP is not designed to capture nuances that may be reflected in legal terms, and enforcing legal terms is burdensome (if not impractical on a large scale) without supporting technology.[64] "The inconsistencies and omissions between robots.txt and terms of service pages suggest a data ecosystem ill-equipped to signal or enforce preferences."[65]

Consent in Crisis is a useful reminder that technology is not a complete solution to rights management. Organizations building systems using data taken from third parties must read legal terms to know how and where they may encounter legal challenges. The following are examples from various sectors.

- **Retail Catalogs:**

  Amazon.com Conditions of Use, License and Access Section

  Subject to your compliance with these Conditions of Use and any Service Terms, and your payment of any applicable fees, Amazon or its content providers grant you a limited, non-exclusive, non-transferable, non-sublicensable license to access and make personal and non-commercial use of the Amazon Services. **This license does not include** any resale or commercial use of any Amazon Service, or its contents; **any collection and use of any product listings, descriptions, or prices; any derivative use of any Amazon Service or its contents**; any downloading, copying, or other use of account information for the benefit of any third party; **or any use of data mining, robots, or similar data gathering and extraction tools** . . .[66]

  The Home Depot Terms of Use, Use License Section

  The Home Depot, Inc. ("The Home Depot" or "Home Depot") and HDPA [Home Depot Product Authority, LLC] jointly grant you permission to view and use this

---

63 *Id.* § 3.1 at 5–6.

64 *Id.* § 3.2 at 7–8. The *Consent in Crisis* authors are particularly concerned that increasing restrictions on scraping website content harm academic and other noncommercial users.

A new wave of robots.txt and Terms of Service pages have not, or cannot, distinguish the various uses of their data. For instance, having to individually prohibit a plethora of AI crawlers has motivated many domains to simply blanket prohibit any crawling with the wildcard "*" marker. Or domains have also limited crawlers from non-profit archives such as the Common Crawl Foundation or Internet Archive, in order to prevent other organizations from downloaded [*sic*] their data for training. However, these archives are also used for non-commercial uses of AI, as well as academic research, knowledge, and accountability, well beyond the scope of AI. For instance, the Common Crawl is reported to be cited in 10,000+ research articles from varying fields.[5] This tension between data creators and, predominantly, commercial AI developers has left academic and non-commercial interests as secondary victims. As web consent continues to evolve, we believe it is essential that these often essential facilities not be marginalized or severely hampered.

Id. § 4 at 11.

65 *Id.* § 6.

66 Amazon.com Conditions of Use, Sept. 14, 2022, https://www.amazon.com/gp/help/customer/display.html?nodeId=508088&ref_=footer_cou (emphasis added) (last visited Jun. 1, 2024).

Site and to print individual pages from this Site for your own personal, non-commercial use, provided that you agree to and accept without modification the notices, terms and conditions set forth herein. **You may not modify, copy (except as set forth in the preceding sentence), distribute, transmit, display, perform, reproduce, publish, license, create derivative works from, transfer or sell any information, material, software, products, or services from this Site.**[67]

- **Geographic and Weather Information:** Compare rights granted by a commercial provider to those granted by the U.S. government.

  Environmental Systems Research Institute, Inc. (ESRI) Master Agreement

  Unless otherwise authorized in writing, Customer may only use Data with the Products for which Esri has provided the Data.[68] . . . Customer may not act directly or authorize its customers to cobrand Data, use Data in any unauthorized service or product, or offer Data through or on behalf of any third party.[69] Customer may not use or allow third parties to use Data, for the purpose of compiling, enhancing, verifying, supplementing, adding to, or deleting from compilation of information that is sold, rented, published, furnished, or in any manner provided to a third party.[70] . . . Certain Data licensors require Esri to flow down additional attribution requirements and terms of use to Customer. These terms supplement and amend the terms of this Agreement and are available at www.esri.com/legal/third-party-data.[71]

  National Centers for Environmental Information ("NCEI"), National Oceanic & Atmospheric Administration ("NOAA")[72]

  [NCEI's Data Access provides] Free access to NCEI's archive of global coastal, oceanographic, geophysical, climate, and historical weather data. These data include quality controlled hourly, sub-hourly, daily, monthly, seasonal, and yearly measurements of NOAA's archived environmental data. Data are available through direct download or sub-setting services. Customers can also order most of these data as certified hard copies for legal use.[73]

---

67 The Home Depot Terms of Use (2016), https://www.homedepot.com/c/Terms_of_Use (emphasis added) (last visited Jun. 1, 2024).

68 Environmental Systems Research Institute, Inc. (Esri) Master Agreement: Product and Services (Feb. 9, 2024) § 3.2(a), https://www.esri.com/content/dam/esrisites/en-us/media/legal/ma-full/ma-full.pdf (last visited Jun. 1, 2024).

69 *Id.* § 3.3(a).

70 *Id.* § 3.3(b).

71 *Id.* § 3.4.

72 NCEI is NOAA's data archiving center. "NCEI maintains one of the most significant archives on Earth, with comprehensive oceanic, atmospheric, and geophysical data. We archive over 229 terabytes of data each month from over 130 observing platforms." https://www.ncei.noaa.gov/ (last visited Jun. 1, 2024).

73 *See* https://www.ncei.noaa.gov/access/search/index. NCEI provides attribution guidance for the datasets it archives. NCEI also makes data available through the Registry of Open Data on AWS. *See, e.g.*, NOAA Global Historical Climatology Network Daily (GHCN-D) accessible at both https://www.ncei.noaa.gov/metadata/geoportal/rest/metadata/item/gov.noaa.ncdc:C00861/html and https://registry.opendata.aws/noaa-ghcn/ (both last visited Jun. 1, 2024).

NOAA is a bureau within the U.S. Department of Commerce. The Commerce Department publishes a website with links to public data maintained by the Department and its various bureaus and offices. https://data.commerce.gov/

- **Sports Scores and Statistics:**

  NCAA Statistics Terms & Conditions

  All content, including photographs, statistics, and charts, are property of the NCAA and cannot be rebroadcast, repurposed, reposted, or duplicated in any form without the expressed written consent of the NCAA.[74]

  National Basketball Association NBA.com Terms of Use

  NBA STATISTICS. The Operator of the Services may make available through the Services statistics, including statistics generated and/or calculated by the Operator using proprietary calculations and analyses, relating to or arising out of the performance of players during or in connection with League and/or Women's National Basketball Association ("WNBA") games, competitions, or events (collectively, "NBA Statistics"). By using such NBA Statistics, you agree that: (i) any use, display, or publication of the NBA Statistics shall include a prominent attribution to NBA.com in connection with such use, display, or publication; (ii) **the NBA Statistics may only be used, displayed, or published for legitimate news reporting or private, non-commercial purposes**; (iii) the NBA Statistics may not be used in connection with any sponsorship or commercial identification; (iv) the NBA Statistics may not be used in connection with any gambling activity (including legal gambling activity); (v) the NBA Statistics may not be used in connection with any fantasy game or other commercial product or service; (vi) the NBA Statistics may not be used in connection with any product or service that presents a live, near-live, or other real-time or archived play-by-play account or depiction of any NBA game; and (vii) **the NBA Statistics may not be used in connection with any website, product, or service that features a database (in any medium or format) of comprehensive, regularly updated statistics from NBA, WNBA or G-League games, competitions, or events without the Operator's express prior consent**.[75]

(accessed Jun. 1, 2024). The Commerce Data Hub is designed to "support[] Commerce's strategy to enable more efficient data access and analysis, and it meets the requirements of the Evidence Act of 2018 and the Open Data Policy." *Id.*

The OPEN Government Data Act, enacted as part of the Foundations for Evidence-Based Policymaking Act of 2018, "requires public government data assets to be published as machine-readable data." Pub. L. 115-435 § 202, 132 Stat. 5529, 5534 (2019). The Open Data Policy refers to OFFICE OF MGMT. & BUDGET, EXEC. OFFICE OF THE PRESIDENT, MEMORANDUM M-13-13, OPEN DATA POLICY—MANAGING INFORMATION AS AN ASSET (May 9, 2013), which was issued pursuant to the Executive Order, *Making Open and Machine Readable the New Default for Government Information*, Exec. Order No. 13,642, 78 Fed. Reg. 28,111 (May 14, 2013). The Open Data Policy provided federal agencies "a framework to help institutionalize the principles of effective information management at each stage of the information's life cycle to promote interoperability and openness." OMB MEMO M-13-13 at 1.

74 http://fs.ncaa.org/Docs/terms_and_conditions.html (last visited Jun. 1, 2024).

75 NBA.com Terms of Use (Feb. 20, 2023) § 9, https://www.nba.com/termsofuse#nba-statistics (emphasis added) (last visited Jun. 1, 2024).

- **Financial Industry Data:**

  American Bankers Association Routing Numbers Lookup—Terms for Access and Use of the ABA Routing Number Web Query Service

  This website[76] allows for single lookups of routing numbers. It is intended for use by individuals who need to look up their financial institution's routing number. Users of this service are allowed no more than two lookups per day and are limited to ten lookups per month. Users who need additional lookups or need a more robust tool for accessing the ABA Routing Number database should contact LexisNexis Risk Solutions, the Official Routing Number registrar.

  The ABA and its licensors are the owners of all right, title and interest in and to ABA Routing Number data, including the nine digit ABA Routing Number. The Official Routing Number Registrar, LexisNexis Risk Solutions, offers additional data products and delivery options for ABA Routing Numbers and other forms of licenses for the use of ABA Routing Numbers and related data beyond the uses permitted by this agreement.[77] . . . User is not entitled to incorporate or store any ABA RTN Data in its own internal databases or storage systems. A User wishing to take such actions must contact the Official Registrar, LexisNexis Risk Solutions, for details about securing the appropriate license for such use and paying the appropriate fees.[78]

  ICE Data Services—ICE Report Center Terms and Conditions[79]

  Subject to provisions as prescribed by applicable law or relevant regulatory requirements, your receipt of the proprietary data from this website is contingent upon your acknowledgement and agreement that **you shall not disclose, transmit, distribute or disseminate, either directly or indirectly through any third parties, the market data and information contained herein to any person or entity without the express written consent of ICE Data Services. The market data and information contained herein constitutes confidential information and valuable property owned by ICE Data Services, its affiliates, licensors and/or other relevant third parties.** Furthermore, you acknowledge that you have read and agree to all terms presented in the following document: ICE Report Center Terms and Conditions.[80]

---

[76] *See ABA Routing Numbers Lookup*, Am. Bankers Assoc. https://routingnumber.aba.com/default1.aspx (last visited Jun. 1, 2024). Users encounter this text and a clickthrough agreement as the landing page for the Routing Number website.

[77] *Id.* (Terms for Access & Use, License).

[78] *Id.* (Terms for Access & Use, Restrictions on Dissemination and Use § 3).

[79] *See Ice Report Center Terms & Conditions*, https://www.ice.com/publicdocs/data/ICE_Report_Center_Click_Through_Agreement.pdf ("ICE T&Cs") (last visited Jun. 1, 2024). ICE Data Service is a subsidiary of Intercontinental Exchange, Inc., which operates futures, equity, and option exchanges, including the New York Stock Exchange, and clearing houses. *See Global Clearing Services*, ICE, https://www.ice.com/about/exchanges-clearing (accessed Jun. 1, 2024).

[80] *See Report Center*, ICE, https://www.ice.com/report-center (emphasis added) (last visited Jun. 1, 2024). Users encounter this text and a clickthrough agreement as the landing page for the ICE Report Center website.

The ICE Report Center Terms and Conditions also characterize ICE "Content," which includes market data and other material, as ICE Confidential Information.[81]

5.4.4. Bloomberg Finance L.P. v. UBS AG

Bloomberg Finance L.P. (Bloomberg) is another major supplier of financial market data. In 2018, Bloomberg sued the financial services firm UBS AG (UBS) alleging UBS violated data license agreements between them.[82] Bloomberg sought both damages and injunctive relief to prevent UBS from unauthorized use and dissemination of Bloomberg's proprietary financial data.[83]

The parties' licensing arrangement was complicated, involving multiple data licenses that had been in place for almost twenty years.[84] The standard licensing terms had been amended to permit UBS's use of Bloomberg data within certain applications developed by UBS.[85] Bloomberg asserted that UBS exceeded the scope of the licenses, as amended, violating "the fundamental requirement that the licensee [UBS] not use the licensed data in any manner that would result in the licensee effectively becoming a source of or a substitute for Bloomberg's proprietary data, or in any manner that would result in the licensee competing with Bloomberg."[86]

In its complaint, Bloomberg described its data as "curated, high quality market and reference data for over 50 million instruments across a range of asset classes, such as fixed income and equities."[87] Bloomberg said it "spends enormous resources collecting, screening, curating, and normalizing information relating to millions of financial instruments in a variety of industries and asset classes," which results in "highly valuable proprietary data compilations . . ."[88] Bloomberg explained that it, "like other market data providers, uses a unique and proprietary set of methods and processes to aggregate, organize, and curate financial data."[89]

Bloomberg alleged in the UBS complaint that Bloomberg's license agreements included a number of restrictions designed to keep its data from being passed on to third parties. The licenses prohibited distribution and use of Bloomberg data in any manner that the licensee could become a substitute source of the data,[90] use of Bloomberg data in any manner that competes with Bloomberg,[91] and storage of Bloomberg data in databases

---

[81] ICE T&Cs § 3.

[82] Bloomberg Fin. L.P. v. UBS AG, Case No. 18-CV-06334, Complaint ¶ 1 (S.D.N.Y. Jul. 12, 2018).

[83] *Id.* In addition to legal remedies, data licensors may use technological measures, such as license keys and limitations on printing and download, and business practices, such as periodic compliance audits, to enforce license restrictions. *See, e.g., id.* ¶ 61.

[84] *Id.* ¶¶ 3–6.

[85] *Id.* ¶ 6.

[86] *Id.* ¶ 4.

[87] *Id.* ¶ 17.

[88] *Id.* ¶ 2.

[89] *Id.* ¶ 17.

[90] *Id.* ¶ 28.

[91] *Id.* ¶ 29.

accessible by third parties.[92] These restrictions were tempered for UBS in an addendum to the license agreements which permitted UBS "a limited right to use a specified subset of UBS's licensed Bloomberg data with certain UBS software products that were made available to third party clients of UBS."[93]

In 2017, Bloomberg learned that UBS was selling the software product, UBS Delta, enabled by Bloomberg data.[94] The public announcement of that sale set off Bloomberg inquiries revealing, according to Bloomberg's complaint, that the UBS software product "facilitated the redistribution of Bloomberg data directly to unlicensed third parties, in violation of the [parties' license agreements]."[95] Demonstrations of the UBS software "confirmed that UBS Delta clients could access and download reference data associated not just with those users' actual portfolio holdings, but with the *entire universe* of Bloomberg reference data made available to UBS under [the license Addendum]."[96]

In addition to its objections to the UBS Delta product, Bloomberg alleged that UBS breached the license agreements by giving employees of the UBS Delta purchaser access to the Bloomberg terminals licensed by UBS.[97] Bloomberg was also concerned that UBS's strategy to transition the UBS Delta product from Bloomberg data to data sourced from another data supplier would expose Bloomberg data and proprietary elements of its compilation to a competitor.[98]

Notwithstanding Bloomberg's description of its service as "highly valuable proprietary data compilations"—words suggesting a foundation for copyright protection—Bloomberg did not allege copyright infringement. Bloomberg alleged breach of contract based on four theories: unauthorized redistribution of Bloomberg data to UBS Delta clients,[99] unauthorized use of licensed data to compete with Bloomberg,[100] unauthorized redistribution of Bloomberg data to the purchaser of the UBS Delta software,[101] and unauthorized redistribution of Bloomberg data to competing data vendors.[102]

UBS moved to dismiss the complaint on grounds of *forum non conveniens* and, in the alternative, to dismiss each count except the one based on sharing access to Bloomberg terminals.[103] The court denied the motion.[104] UBS argued that the parties' agreements permitted the uses of Bloomberg data about which Bloomberg complained, but the court determined that UBS's assertions about the text of the agreements did not preclude

---

92 *Id.* ¶ 30.
93 *Id.* ¶ 36.
94 *Id.* ¶ 40.
95 *Id.* ¶ 54.
96 *Id.* ¶ 68 (emphasis in original).
97 *Id.* ¶ 55.
98 *Id.* ¶ 81.
99 *Id.* ¶¶ 90–92.
100 *Id.* ¶¶ 97–100.
101 *Id.* ¶¶ 104–09.
102 *Id.* ¶¶ 114–20.
103 Bloomberg Fin. L.P. v. UBS AG, Case No 18-CV-6334, Opinion & Order at 1 (S.D.N.Y. Dec. 19, 2018).
104 *Id.*

Bloomberg's complaint as a matter of law.[105] In other words, UBS would have to pursue its defense to a factfinding stage of litigation. The case proceeded to discovery, and Bloomberg and UBS ultimately settled in September 2020.

The Bloomberg case against UBS demonstrates that data licenses can be effective legal protection (or impediments, depending on a party's point of view) for data. While the licenses between Bloomberg and UBS appear to have been the product of meaningful negotiation, data licenses are often presented as "take it or leave it" terms—contracts of adhesion—which are routinely overlooked or bypassed by users clicking without reading.

5.5. Subject Matter Restrictions in the Law

Data can be subject to laws that impose conditions and restrictions on their use based on the nature of the content or the circumstances of the data's use. Data obtained for one purpose may be limited or restricted for other uses or in other markets. The following list is not exhaustive. It is included here to alert readers to cast a wide due diligence net when introducing new data sources and types of data into digital assets. Privacy restrictions are widely recognized as needing attention. Other restrictions may not be as familiar.

5.5.1. Privacy

A complex mosaic of federal, state, local, and foreign laws restrict the use of personal information. Some lawyers and compliance personnel dedicate their careers to tracking and managing privacy restrictions. Even summary treatment of privacy laws is beyond the scope of this chapter.[106] Anyone creating, training, testing, or commercializing digital assets using data that could, alone or in combination with other data, identify individuals should study privacy laws of the various jurisdictions in which the subject individuals reside, the personal data are collected, and the resulting digital assets and related services are offered for sale or license.

5.5.2. U.S. Export Controls

The Export Administration Regulations (EAR)[107] define "technology" and "controlled technology" very broadly in terms that could include data.

> Technology means: Information necessary for the "development," "production," "use," operation, installation, maintenance, repair, overhaul, or refurbishing (or other terms specified in ECCNs [Export Control Classification Number] on the CCL [Commerce Control List] that control "technology") of an item . . .

---

105 *Id.* at 19, 22, & 25.

106 *See generally* Chapters 4, 6, 9, and 13 for discussions of privacy rights.

107 15 C.F.R. ch. VII(C), pts. 730–786 (2024).

NOTE 1 TO DEFINITION OF TECHNOLOGY: "Technology" may be in any tangible or intangible form, such as written or oral communications, blueprints, drawings, photographs, plans, diagrams, models, formulae, tables, engineering designs and specifications, computer-aided design files, manuals or documentation, electronic media or information revealed through visual inspection; . . .[108]

Under the International Traffic in Arms Regulations (ITAR), "technical data" related to defense articles are also defense articles subject to ITAR controls.[109] Similar to "technology" under the EAR, "technical data" under ITAR is broadly defined.[110]

(a) Technical data means for purposes of this subchapter:

(1) Information, other than software as defined in § 120.40(g), which is required for the design, development, production, manufacture, assembly, operation, repair, testing, maintenance, or modification of defense articles. This includes information in the form of blueprints, drawings, photographs, plans, instructions, or documentation; . . .

5.5.3. Professional Responsibility

Lawyers owe a duty of confidentiality to their clients[111] and former clients.[112] Model Rule 1.6(c) requires lawyers to "make reasonable efforts to prevent the inadvertent or unauthorized disclosure of, or unauthorized access to, information relating to the representation of a client."[113] Digital assets built, trained, or used with seemingly anonymous data about clients, such as billing records, could reveal enough information for someone to identify a client or matters in which a client is involved.

5.6. Severe Consequences Can Follow from Overlooking Data Restrictions

Digital assets are created using data, they consume data to operate and evolve, and many exist for the purpose of rendering derived or synthetic data or other content that is a byproduct of the rendered data. Digital assets created without attention to rights and restrictions in underlying data are a house of cards.

---

[108] 15 C.F.R. § 772.1.

[109] 22 C.F.R. § 120.31(a) (2024) ("Defense article means any item or technical data designated in §121.1 of this subchapter and includes: (1) Technical data recorded or stored in any physical form, models, mockups or other items that reveal technical data directly relating to items designated in §121.1 of this subchapter; . . .").

[110] 22 C.F.R. § 120.33(a) ("Technical data means for purposes of this subchapter: (1) Information, other than software as defined in §120.40(g), which is required for the design, development, production, manufacture, assembly, operation, repair, testing, maintenance, or modification of defense articles. This includes information in the form of blueprints, drawings, photographs, plans, instructions, or documentation; . . .").

[111] MODEL RULES OF PROF'L CONDUCT, r. 1.6 (ABA 1983).

[112] *Id.* r. 1.9(c).

[113] *Id.* r. 1.6(c).

Data rights and data licenses are not difficult conceptually; they are challenging because the work to identify, document, and track rights and restrictions through the entire data life cycle is tedious. Someone must follow data flows and the chain of "title" to establish the nature, scope, and conditions of permitted use. The work to track data rights and restrictions and manage access and use accordingly are tasks in addition to the data science work of determining if datasets are fit for purpose and in a format that can be processed effectively.

A 2024 U.S. Department of Treasury report about AI describes Treasury's own effort to manage its data to maximum advantage. Treasury describes an approach that combines organizational commitment, governance, and technology, a framework that can be adapted by any entity to lay a solid foundation for data management.

> In Treasury's own AI adoption strategy, Treasury has broadly leveraged the Chief Data Officer role to empower both technology transformation and AI development. For example, Treasury established a CDO position for the Office of Terrorism and Financial Intelligence (TFI), which includes FinCEN, the Office of Foreign Assets Control (OFAC), the Office of Intelligence and Analysis (OIA), the Office of Terrorist Financing and Financial Crimes (TFFC), and Treasury Executive Office for Asset Forfeiture (TEOAF). The TFI CDO was empowered to create an executive-level data governance board to drive decision making on cloud adoption strategies, federated data lake development, and AI use cases with a focus on scalability, accessibility, access control, and protection of data required to enable the future development of AI models.
>
> In 2023, this multi-year effort led by TFI CDO resulted in the launch of the CACHE platform, a consolidated data platform for open source, subscription, and proprietary Treasury data sources. Treating data as the foundation for AI development coupled with the availability of large quantities of curated data enabled the rapid development of AI models by Treasury data scientists. As a result, the technical, legal, and security aspects of this work were integrated into the technical and data transformation infrastructure, enabling employees to develop solutions in a secure environment.[114]

For comparison, Bloomberg's lawsuit against UBS is an instructive example of potential losses arising when business and technology drivers get out of sync with data rights. While that lawsuit was settled, the injunction Bloomberg sought would undoubtedly have caused substantial business disruption for UBS.[115]

Digital asset developers should also take heed of warnings provided by Federal Trade Commission (FTC) enforcement actions. The FTC has obtained orders in consumer cases mandating the destruction of work product derived from data that were improperly

---

[114] U.S. Dept. of the Treasury, Managing Artificial Intelligence-Specific Cybersecurity Risks in the Financial Services Sector 28–29 (2024).

[115] *See* Bloomberg Fin. L.P. v. UBS AG, *supra* note 82 and accompanying text.

obtained or used beyond the scope of consumers' consents. The loss of such work product can be a significant setback for both technology development and the business that seeks to profit from it.

In *In re Everalbum, Inc.*, the FTC alleged Everalbum enabled face recognition for all users of its mobile app by default, without user consent, and without a mechanism to turn off the face recognition feature.[116] In phases over a couple of years, Everalbum added pop-up messages requesting user consent covering face recognition.[117] Everalbum used the facial images it extracted from users' photos without consent to develop facial recognition technology.[118] Also, Everalbum failed to delete users' photos, as it had committed to do, when users deactivated their accounts.[119]

The FTC settled the case against Everalbum with an Order compelling Everalbum to delete photos and video collected from users with deactivated accounts and users who had not affirmatively consented to Everalbum's use of facial recognition.[120] In addition, the Order compelled Everalbum to delete or destroy models and algorithms Everalbum developed in whole or in part using biometric information Everalbum collected without user consent.[121] Everalbum is also subject to recordkeeping requirements and compliance monitoring.[122] The Order continues in effect for twenty years.[123]

More recently, the FTC settled a case it brought against Ring LLC, a maker of home security surveillance systems.[124] Similar to Everalbum, Ring collected, shared, and used customers' surveillance video beyond the scope of the consents Ring obtained from them.[125] Under a Stipulated Order entered in the case, Ring is required to delete audio, video, and photographic data it collected without adequate customer consents, as well as facial recognition data Ring derived from those data.[126] The Stipulated Order also mandates that Ring delete affected work product, including its models and algorithms, "developed in whole or in part from review and annotation of [the recordings made without proper consent]" except work product which Ring certifies to the FTC cannot technically be deleted.[127]

---

116 In re Everalbum, Inc., F.T.C. No. C-4743, Complaint ¶ 5 (May 7, 2021), https://www.ftc.gov/system/files/documents/cases/1923172_-_everalbum_complaint_final.pdf (last visited Jun. 1, 2024).

117 *Id.* ¶¶ 6–10.

118 *Id.* ¶ 12.

119 *Id.* ¶¶ 17–22.

120 F.T.C. Decision & Order, § III (A)-(B) (May 5, 2021), https://www.ftc.gov/system/files/documents/cases/1923172_-_everalbum_decision_final.pdf (last visited Jun. 1, 2024).

121 *Id.* § III(C).

122 *Id.* §§ VI–VII.

123 *Id.* § VIII.

124 Fed. Trade Comm'n v. Ring LLC, No. 1:23-cv-1549, Stip. Order for Injunction & Monetary Judgment (D.D.C. Jun. 16, 2023), https://www.ftc.gov/system/files/ftc_gov/pdf/Ring-OrderEntered-6.16.2023%28003%29.pdf (last visited Jun. 1, 2024).

125 Fed. Trade Comm'n v. Ring LLC, No. 1:23-cv-1549, Complaint (May 31, 2023) https://www.ftc.gov/system/files/ftc_gov/pdf/complaint_ring.pdf (last visited Jun. 1, 2024).

126 Ring Stip. Order § II(A).

127 *Id.*

In addition, the Stipulated Order requires Ring to implement a privacy and security program, subject to biennial third-party assessments for twenty years after the Order's entry.[128] Ring must certify to the FTC Ring's compliance with the Order annually during its twenty-year term and self-report Ring's discovery of any security incidents relating to customers' home security recordings it collects and stores.[129] The Stipulated Order also requires Ring to notify customers who had accounts during the relevant period,[130] pay a judgment of $5.8 million to the FTC to be used for consumer redress,[131] submit annual compliance reports and create certain records for ten years,[132] and remain subject to FTC compliance monitoring for the twenty-year term of the Stipulated Order.[133]

The FTC announced on April 23, 2024, that it would be sending 117,044 PayPal payments totaling more than $5.6 million to affected Ring users.[134]

5.7. Data Life Cycle Checklist

Readily accessible data are not necessarily freely available for use without legal restrictions or significant adverse consequences. To assist readers in navigating the complexity of data use, this chapter concludes with a *Data Life Cycle Checklist* published by the Business Law Section of the American Bar Association in its *Business Law Today* Tools section.[135]

5.7.1. Checklist Introduction

Much has been written about records management and the life cycle of records. Data have a similar life cycle. At each point in the data life cycle, an organization needs to consider its rights in the data relative to the rights and interests of third parties, as well as steps it should take to secure and control data so that they are not misappropriated or used intentionally or inadvertently in ways that are unauthorized or contrary to the organization's policy or business interests.

This checklist describes the life cycle in five segments: getting data, storing data, using and sharing data, processing data—creating new data, and purging data. Specific life cycles for individual datasets vary. An organization should take care when combining datasets to account for the life cycle of the constituent datasets.

---

128 *Id.* §§ III–IV.

129 *Id.* §§ VI–VII.

130 *Id.* § VIII.

131 *Id.* § XI.

132 *Id.* §§ XIII–XIV.

133 *Id.* § XV.

134 Press Release, Fed. Trade Com., FTC Sends Refunds to Ring Customers Stemming from 2023 Settlement over Charges the Company Failed to Block Employees and Hackers from Accessing Consumer Videos (Apr. 23, 2024), https://www.ftc.gov/news-events/news/press-releases/2024/04/ftc-sends-refunds-ring-customers-stemming-2023--settlement-over-charges-company-failed-block (last visited Jun. 1, 2024).

135 Candace M. Jones, *Data Life Cycle Checklist: Cloud Computing and Cloud Marketplace Toolkit Project*, Bus. L. Today Tools (Jul. 5, 2023), https://businesslawtoday.org/tool/data-life-cycle-checklist-cloud-computing-marketplace-toolkit-project/.

Throughout the data life cycle, the organization needs to consider third-party interests that may affect data handling and controls placed on datasets to manage appropriate use. Third parties with interests in data may include one or more persons, such as data subjects, data licensors, and regulatory authorities.

Where U.S. laws control, attempting to frame data rights with principles of "ownership" is usually a distraction. The landscape for claims of data ownership could change, however, with developments in privacy law that attach property rights to personal information and developments in intellectual property law that extend protection to the outputs of emerging data-driven technologies.

5.7.2. Getting Data

The manner in which data are acquired often sets the foundation for handling data throughout their life cycle. Interests of third parties may be intertwined in a single dataset. For example, individual-level data about prospective customers licensed from a data broker should be evaluated and handled both as personal information and licensed information.

Data may be acquired in the following ways:

- Collected from third parties through commercial transactions, business processes (like onboarding subscribers), and surveys
- Licensed from third-party data brokers
- Obtained from business partners for processing (which is also a form of licensing)
- Created through business operations, such as financial data and data generated by control systems and operating equipment
- Collected from employees, contractors, equipment, and systems as performance data

5.7.3. Storing Data

Think locally and globally and consider communication channels. Managing storage locations is increasingly important given developments in privacy law allowing data subjects to obtain information about their personal data stored by organizations. Retrieving information efficiently and effectively whenever it is needed for any reason should be an essential element of an organization's data management strategy.

Data may be stored, for example, in the following ways:

- Locally on equipment that includes desktop computers as well as copiers, printers, and other networked equipment
- On machinery and SCADA (supervisory control and data acquisition) systems that monitor and control equipment, sensors, processes, and environments
- In mobile devices (laptops, smartphones, tablets, external data storage)

- In the cloud—directly or through service providers
- With service providers however they store data
- With business partners, vendors, and professional service firms
- In paper files

5.7.4. Using and Sharing Data

Data are only worth keeping if they can be put to use to satisfy a business objective, policy goal, or legal obligation. Using data effectively includes sharing data consistent with both the business, policy, or legal need and any applicable third-party rights.

Consider the following:

- Least-privilege access—*i.e.*, sharing the minimum data needed to achieve the use objective—as a sharing-management principle
- Policies and workflows that track to the approved sharing and use
- Systems (including people, processes, and technologies) that monitor and enforce the approved sharing and use
- Written agreements with third parties entrusted to handle and use data that describe permitted and prohibited uses and allow for verification of compliance
- Systems to administer and enforce use agreements with third parties
- Systems to administer and enforce the organization's compliance as the licensee of third-party data

5.7.5. Processing Data—Creating New Data

Data processing begets new data of some kind most of the time. Even if it is not the objective to create new data through analysis, the organization will generate information about how data are used, where they are processed and stored, etc. Where it is the object to create new data through analysis, calculation, or other changes, the organization should consider the extent to which the new data (sometimes called *output* or *derived data*) carry with them restrictions on underlying data (sometimes called *input*).

Consider the following:

- Will it be possible for new data to be used directly or in combination with other readily available data to identify individuals?
- If so, is that kind of use acceptable or not?
- Do new data reveal information that could be considered trade secrets of the organization or a third party?
- Are new data for the organization's use only or will they be published or licensed to third parties? If published or licensed, on what terms?

5.7.6. Purging Data

Just like records should be subject to a retention policy that includes scheduled destruction, so too data should be managed to a planned end. The plan and timeline for purging data need to be considered in the arrangements for storage, processing, and use.

Consider the following:

- Data licensors often expect data to be purged upon termination of a data license; retention of some data for some period of time may be an important negotiation point.
- Privacy laws increasingly require organizations to be able to respond to requests of data subjects, which could include purging inaccurate information.
- Regulatory requirements and other legal obligations need to factor into the data retention schedule.
- When data are used in a project or business process, some data may be needed for later reference to validate and support outcomes and decisions.
- Data destruction procedures need to be part of the organization's data storage plans and any arrangements it has with third parties given access to process and store data.

5.7.7. Checklist Conclusion

The data-driven economy heightens attention to the value of data in all of its forms and uses. On the upside, organizations with data management agility will be better equipped to evaluate and capitalize on opportunities. On the downside, as data increase in value, disputes and regulation are likely to increase as well. Attention to data management throughout the data life cycle can mitigate that risk.

6
Defamation and Tort Law Protections from Harm

By Shannon Taub

6.1. Introduction

In the age of artificial intelligence (AI), machines are increasingly taking on creative roles, generating speech that influences and impacts real lives. Consider the rapid rise of AI-driven chatbots, capable of writing essays, recommending content, writing social media posts, and engaging in seemingly human-like conversations. These technologies have sparked both fascination and concern. OpenAI's ChatGPT, for instance, became the fastest-growing consumer application in history, reaching 100 million users in just two months.[1] Generative AI models such as ChatGPT have transformed our interaction with technology, allowing machines to generate human-like text and audiovisual responses across a wide range of topics. ChatGPT uses vast amounts of data to recognize patterns in language.[2] ChatGPT and other large language models (LLMs) analyze vast datasets and generate new responses based on patterns identified during its training.[3]

While these tools represent groundbreaking advancements in natural language processing, they also introduce unintended consequences, such as the creation of false and harmful content. AI's ability to generate speech means it can also generate defamatory statements. When this happens, who is liable?[4] This question sits at the heart of this chapter, which explores how defamation law, traditionally concerned with human expression, now faces new challenges in an era where chatbots and AI systems can produce defamatory content without direct human input. Furthermore, AI's capability to replicate a person's likeness through deepfakes or digital replicas raises additional legal

1 Nina Brown, *Bots Behaving Badly: A Products Liability Approach to Chatbot-Generated Defamation*, 3 J. Free Speech L. 389, 392–97 (2023).
2 *Id.* at 390.
3 *Id.* at 393.
4 *See id.*

concerns, particularly when a person's image or voice is manipulated to create false and damaging content.[5] The protection of individuals from false representations of their identity will become a central issue as AI continues to expand into areas once dominated solely by human expression.[6]

This chapter explores the foundation of defamation law, focusing on the challenges posed by the evolving media landscape, such as distinguishing private individuals from public figures, navigating the blurred lines between fact and opinion, and addressing the informal nature of communication on social media. From there, this chapter addresses the critical role of Section 230 of the Communications Decency Act (CDA), a landmark statute that has long shielded internet platforms from liability for user-generated content, but now faces scrutiny in the context of AI-generated speech. Next, this chapter addresses the court's interpretation of Section 230, its exceptions, and its relevance to AI systems such as ChatGPT. As AI-generated speech blurs the lines between user-generated and machine-generated content, new questions about intermediary liability are emerging. As this chapter reveals, the legal system must now grapple with the implications of AI-generated speech and develop frameworks to assign responsibility in this rapidly changing landscape. Balancing innovation in AI technology with the protection of individuals' rights will be central to addressing these emerging challenges.

6.2. Overview of Defamation Law

Defamation law is a significant area of tort law, aimed at protecting individuals from damaging false statements that could harm their reputation.[7] Most states follow the Restatement of Torts standard for defamation claims, which defines defamatory communication as something that harms a person's reputation, lowering them in the eyes of the community or discouraging others from associating with or dealing with them.[8]

Proving a defamation claim requires establishing four elements: publication, falsity, harm, and fault.[9] Publication occurs when a defamatory statement is communicated to a third party.[10] Falsity means the statement must be untrue, as true statements cannot be defamatory.[11] Harm involves showing that the false statement caused damage to the plaintiff's reputation, which may include financial loss, loss of social standing, or emotional distress.[12] Fault depends on the plaintiff's status: for public figures, it typically involves proving "actual malice," meaning the defendant knew the statement was false

5 *See* Jon M. Garon, *An AI's Picture Paints a Thousand Lies: Designating Responsibility for Visual Libel*, 3 J. Free Speech L. 425 (2023) (exploring the legal implications of AI-generated images).

6 *See id.*

7 See Gertz v. Robert Welch, Inc., 418 U.S. 323, 349 (1974).

8 Restatement (Second) of Torts § 559 (Am. Law. Inst. 1977).

9 *See id.* § 558.

10 *See id.* § 557.

11 *See* Philadelphia Newspapers, Inc. v. Hepps, 475 U.S. 767, 777 (1986).

12 *See Gertz*, 418 U.S. at 350.

or acted with reckless disregard for its truth, while private individuals need only show that the defendant acted negligently.[13]

Public figures—those with prominent influence or who engage in public controversies—must prove actual malice because they have more access to media to refute false claims.[14] Defamation law recognizes two types of public figures: all-purpose public figures, who hold positions of influence across all contexts, and limited-purpose public figures, who are involved in specific public controversies.[15] These limited-purpose figures only need to prove actual malice in relation to issues linked to the controversy.[16] Additionally, states can define their own liability standards for defamation affecting private individuals, meaning the actual malice standard may vary depending on jurisdiction.[17]

The rise of social media platforms such as X (formerly Twitter), Instagram, and YouTube has allowed ordinary people to gain wide-reaching influence quickly, complicating the courts' ability to determine when someone should be treated as a public figure.[18] Bloggers and micro-influencers present a unique challenge in defamation cases due to their growing influence in public discourse. Unlike traditional public figures, their fame is often limited to niche audiences, but their content can have a significant impact within those circles. Under the framework established by *Gertz v. Robert Welch, Inc.*, the central question in these cases is whether the individual has "voluntarily thrust themselves into a public controversy" with the intent to influence its outcome.[19] If a micro-influencer gains viral attention by commenting on a significant public issue, they may be classified as a public figure for the purposes of that controversy, subjecting them to the higher standard of proving *actual malice* in defamation claims. The ability to counteract defamatory content through social media platforms also weighs in favor of applying the actual malice standard, as these individuals often have the tools to respond publicly.[20]

The rise of internet trolls and anonymous defamation further complicates this distinction, as individuals targeted by trolls may inadvertently become public figures by engaging in public controversies or being thrust into the spotlight through no choice of their own.[21] Trolls who engage in defamatory attacks may exploit this legal distinction, knowing their targets face a tougher legal standard, particularly in cases where the victim has gained significant public attention through the controversy.[22] Thus, when individuals respond publicly to defamatory attacks, comment on controversial issues, or become unwilling

---

13 *See id.* at 347–48; *New York Times Co. v. Sullivan*, 376 U.S. 254, 279–80 (1964).

14 *See Sullivan*, 376 U.S. at 279–80.

15 *Id.* at 345.

16 *Id.* at 351.

17 *Id.* at 347–48.

18 *See* Reighard v. ESPN, Inc., 991 N.W.2d 803, 827–28 (the court noted that "private citizens can become 'public figures' on social media overnight"); Berisha v. Lawson, 141 S. Ct. 2424, 2428–30 (2021) (Gorsuch, J., dissenting) (noting that modern media, including social media platforms, has blurred the distinction between public and private figures, complicating the application of the "actual malice" standard).

19 *Gertz*, 418 U.S. at 345.

20 *Id.* at 344.

21 *See* Garon, *An AI's Picture Paints a Thousand Lies*, *supra* note 5, at 435 (". . . in the age of social media and influencers, easy-to-achieve public figure status may well have swallowed the distinctions espoused in *Gertz*").

22 *See id.*

figures in a public controversy, courts may classify them as limited-purpose public figures, complicating their defamation claims against internet trolls.

Before the advent of the internet, defamation cases primarily involved media such as newspaper articles, magazines, letters to the editor, and television or radio broadcasts.[23] However, with the rise of social media, "just over half of U.S. adults (54%) say they at least sometimes get news from social media."[24] The shift in how people receive their news—from traditional media outlets to social media—significantly impacts how courts analyze defamation claims, particularly when it comes to publication, reach, harm, and fault.

Unlike traditional media, where publishers were professionally obligated to fact-check and carefully edit content, social media thrives on the instant sharing of information.[25] Ordinary social media users now act as reporters, capturing and sharing real-time information that news outlets often amplify. Unlike professional journalists, these users are generally unaware of the risks involved in sharing unverified information. Courts now must determine whether users knowingly shared false information or acted recklessly by failing to verify its accuracy, which can be challenging given the informal and spontaneous nature of social media platforms.

This shift in the media landscape also introduces new challenges for courts, such as distinguishing between factual assertions and protected opinions. Opinions, unless they imply an underlying false fact, generally cannot be the basis for defamation.[26] This requires courts to assess whether a reasonable person would interpret the statement as a factual assertion or an opinion.[27] Perhaps the casual nature of social media, where opinions, jokes, and exaggerations are often shared freely, without professional editorial standards, makes it difficult to discern between fact and opinion.[28] As a result, courts must carefully evaluate the context and tone of the communication, the platform used, and how an average person might understand the statement.[29] This analysis is crucial in determining whether the statement falls under protected speech, such as opinion, hyperbole, or satire, and is therefore not actionable.[30]

---

23 David Goguen, *Social Media and Online Defamation*, Nolo (Feb. 20, 2024), https://www.nolo.com/legal-encyclopedia/social-media-online-defamation.html.

24 *Social Media and News Fact Sheet*, Pew Rsrch. Ctr. (Sept. 17, 2024), https://www.pewresearch.org/journalism/fact-sheet/social-media-and-news-fact-sheet/.

25 *See* Hadley M. Dreibelbis, *Note, Social Media Defamation: A New Legal Frontier amid the Internet Wild West*, 16 Duke J. Const. L. & Pub. Pol'y 245, 256–57 (2021), https://scholarship.law.duke.edu/cgi/viewcontent.cgi?article=1176&context=djclpp.

26 *See Gertz*, 418 U.S. at 339–40 (stating that opinions cannot be defamatory under the First Amendment); *but see* Milkovich v. Lorain Journal Co., 497 U.S. 1, 19 (1990) (holding that even statements framed as opinions may be actionable as defamation if they imply provable false facts).

27 *See, e.g.*, Summit Bank v. Rogers, 142 Cal. Rptr. 3d 40, 62 (Cal. Ct. App. 2012) (discussing whether a reasonable person would view a statement on social media as a factual assertion or hyperbole).

28 *See* Dreibelbis, *supra* note 25, at 256.

29 *See, e.g.*, Glob. Telemedia Int'l, Inc. v. Doe 1, 132 F. Supp. 2d 1261, 1270 (C.D. Cal. 2001); Feld v. Conway, 16 F. Supp. 3d 1, 4 (D. Mass. 2014).

30 *Hustler Magazine, Inc. v. Falwell*, 485 U.S. 46, 50–51 (1988) (holding that satirical statements, even when offensive, are protected by the First Amendment because they do not assert factual claims); *Milkovich*, 497 U.S. at 20 (finding that "imaginative expression" and "rhetorical hyperbole" are not actionable under defamation law).

Some courts stress the importance of context when evaluating online statements, recognizing that readers often interpret speech on informal platforms as opinion rather than factual claims.[31] Other courts have applied traditional defamation standards, treating online statements similar to statements made in traditional media, potentially overlooking the casual, informal tone typical of online communication.[32] The latter approach can be problematic in the context of social media.

For instance, in *Jacobus v. Trump*, the court dismissed a defamation claim based on tweets by Donald Trump, where he referred to political commentor Cheri Jacobus as a "dummy" and claimed she had "begged us for a job" but "went hostile" after being rejected.[33] The court explained that the context of social media—particularly Twitter's fast-paced and informal tone—supports an expectation of exaggeration and rhetorical hyperbole, making Trump's statements more likely to be seen as nonactionable opinion rather than factual assertions.[34] The court also examined the context of the statements by considering the wording, intent, surrounding circumstances, and tone.[35] It further noted that statements made "during the course of a heated public debate" are generally nonactionable, even if they seem factual, because the audience expects hyperbole and rhetorical language in such settings.[36]

In contrast, in *Unsworth v. Musk*, the court rejected Elon Musk's defense that his tweets, in which he referred to Vernon Unsworth as a "pedo guy," were simply social media banter and hyperbole.[37] Instead the court allowed the defamation claim to proceed, finding that a reasonable jury could interpret Musk's statements as assertions of fact, despite the informal Twitter (now known as X) context.[38]

Online anonymity creates additional obstacles for plaintiffs seeking to recover damages in defamation cases. Anonymous users can post defamatory content without fear of immediate identification, making it challenging to identify and serve them with legal action. In a case between Sandals Resorts and Google, Sandals sought a court order to compel Google to reveal the identity of a Gmail user who had sent emails criticizing the company.[39] The court analyzed the email's context, tone, and purpose, ultimately viewing it as rhetorical opinion rather than factual assertion.[40] The court concluded that while certain parts of the email might appear factual, they served only to support the writer's

---

31 *See, e.g.*, Matter of Konig v. WordPress.com, 978 N.Y.S.2d 92, 94 (N.Y. App. Div. 2013) (holding that given the context of an internet blog during a contested election, the statement "downright criminal actions" was deemed opinion, not a factual accusation); Sandals Resorts Int'l Ltd. v. Google, 925 N.Y.S.2d 407, 415–16 (N.Y. App. Div. 2011) (highlighting the informal and rhetorical nature of online discourse, recognizing that readers typically interpret such statements as opinions rather than factual claims).

32 *See, e.g.*, Bently Reserve LP v. Papaliolios, 160 Cal. Rptr. 3d 423 (Cal. Ct. App. 2013) (applying traditional defamation standards to an online review).

33 *Jacobus v. Trump*, 51 N.Y.S.3d 330, 334 (N.Y. Sup. Ct. 2017).

34 *Id.* at 339.

35 *Id.* at 336–37.

36 *Id.*

37 Unsworth v. Musk, No. 2:18-cv-08048-SVW-JC, 2019 U.S. Dist. LEXIS 167626 (C.D. Cal. 2019).

38 *Id.*

39 *Sandals*, 925 N.Y.S.2d at 409.

40 *Id.* at 414.

opinion.[41] This characterization meant that the entire email was considered "pure opinion" and therefore not subject to defamation claims.[42] Even when courts allow subpoenas to unmask these users, the process can be time-consuming and costly. Additionally, anonymous defendants may lack the financial resources to pay damages, further complicating the plaintiff's ability to recover any awarded compensation.

6.3. Direct versus Intermediary Liability

Defamatory statements are often reposted, shared, or otherwise disseminated through a web of secondary actors, raising questions about whether these third parties—such as websites, social media platforms, and even individual users—can be held liable. As such, liability is primarily determined by distinguishing between direct and intermediary actors.

Direct liability attaches to the person or entity that initially publishes a defamatory statement. Typically, the original publisher is not liable for republication by others unless it was a "natural and probable consequence" of their initial act.[43] For example, if a user posts defamatory content on a public social media platform and uses hashtags or tags prominent users, it may be foreseeable that others will share the post, potentially making the original publisher liable. This principle has become more complex in the digital age, where content can go viral instantly, significantly expanding its reach and amplifying potential harm.[44]

Liability for individuals who share or repeat defamatory content often hinges on whether they are classified as *primary publishers*, *republishers*, or *passive intermediaries*. A primary publisher is directly responsible for creating or originating the defamatory statement, while a republisher adopts the content as their own by repeating or disseminating it, and thus incurs the same level of liability as the original author.[45] Courts treat each repetition of a defamatory statement as a new publication, making the republisher directly liable if they distribute the content in a manner that contributes to the harm.[46] In contrast, a *passive intermediary*—such as an individual who simply forward a defamatory email or shares a third-party link without adding new defamatory content—is less likely to face liability.

---

41 *Id.* at 416.

42 *Id.*

43 *See* Restatement (Second) of Torts § 577(1) (1977) ("Publication of defamatory matter is its communication intentionally or by a negligent act to one other than the person defamed"); *See Weaver v. Beneficial Fin. Co.*, 199 Va. 196, 201 (1957) (holding that the original publisher is liable for repetition if such repetition is a "natural and probable consequence" of the initial publication).

44 Force v. Facebook, Inc., 934 F.3d 53, 66–67 (2d Cir. 2019) (noting the complexities in applying traditional liability standards to social media platforms that use algorithms to amplify content, potentially increasing the reach and impact of harmful material).

45 Restatement (Second) of Torts § 578 (1977).

46 Salzano v. N. Jersey Media Grp. Inc., 201 N.J. 500, 514 (2010).

Whether liability attaches often depends on the degree of involvement in reshaping or amplifying defamatory content. In *Jones v. Dirty World Ent. Recordings LLC*,[47] the court found that liability does not attach if the defendant does not materially contribute to the defamatory nature of the content. However, if an individual actively selects, edits, or recontextualizes defamatory content, they may be considered a republisher and treated as a primary speaker.[48] This distinction becomes complex in the digital context, where reposting, sharing, and adding commentary are commonplace. Courts must determine whether a defendant merely disseminated preexisting content or transformed it to create new harm.[49] Some scholars argue that simply reposting content verbatim does not typically result in liability, as the individual acts as a "neutral conduit" rather than contributing to the defamatory nature of the statement.[50] However, combining elements from multiple sources to create new defamatory content could lead to liability.[51] Scholars also extend this analysis to AI systems, suggesting that if an AI assembles defamatory content independently, it may be treated as the developer of the content rather than as a passive host.[52]

Contributory liability arises when a third party, knowing of the defamatory nature of the content, provides substantial assistance in its dissemination.[53] For example, in *Gersh v. Anglin*,[54] Tanya Gersh, a Jewish real estate agent, was targeted by Andrew Anglin, founder of *The Daily Stormer*, who published her contact information and encouraged his followers to harass her.[55] The posts led to thousands of anti-Semitic messages, threats, and calls directed at Gersh and her family.[56] The court found Anglin liable for defamation among other claims, awarding Gersh over $14 million in damages.[57] Although Anglin did not personally send the harassing messages, by publicizing Gersh's personal details and urging his followers to act, he materially contributed to the defamation and harassment that followed.[58] The court emphasized that Anglin's actions went beyond passive transmission of information; he actively facilitated defamatory and harmful content.[59] This case illustrates how courts may impose contributory liability when individuals use online platforms to incite harmful conduct. This principle could also apply to other digital

---

47 755F.3d 398, 414 (6th Cir. 2014).

48 *See id.*

49 *See* Weaver, 199 Va. at 201; Catalano v. Pechous, 83 Ill. 2d 146, 155 (1980) (finding that a subsequent statement made months later to a reporter, which was then published in a newspaper, constituted a separate publication, creating distinct liability due to its altered context and timing).

50 Eugene Volokh, *Large Libel Models? Liability for AI Output*, 3 J. Free Speech L. 489, 495–97 (2023).

51 *Id.* at 496 ("If I post to my blog some third-party-written text that was intended for use on the Internet ('For instance, because it's already been posted online'), I'm immune from liability. But of course if I instead myself write a new defamatory post about you, I lack § 230 immunity even if I copied each word from a different web page and then assembled them together: I'm responsible in part (or even in whole) for creating the defamatory information. Likewise for AI programs").

52 *See id.* at 495–98.

53 *See* Restatement (Second) of Torts § 876(b) (1979).

54 No. CV-17-50-M-DLC, 2019 U.S. Dist. LEXIS 33533 (D. Mont. Mar. 14, 2019).

55 *Id.* at 3–5.

56 *Id.* at 5–7.

57 *Id.* at 22–23.

58 Gersh, *supra* note 92, at 8–10.

59 *Id.* at 10–12.

influencers, platform operators, or users who organize campaigns against a target or create an environment that encourages third parties to engage in defamatory behavior.

Media defendants, including broadcasters, are generally not liable for defamatory statements made by third parties unless they fail to exercise due care in preventing harmful content from being published.[60] In modern defamation cases, the concept of due care must evolve to address how digital platforms use algorithms to recommend or amplify content, potentially increasing the reach of defamatory material. As the courts continue to explore the liability of digital platforms, due care will likely hinge on factors such as the intentional design of algorithms, the foreseeability of harmful content being promoted, and whether platforms actively participated in the dissemination rather than simply hosting the content.[61]

Liability for defamatory content can extend to Internet Service Providers (ISPs) and websites, but they are typically immune from liability under Section 230 of the Communications Decency Act (CDA) as long as they do not actively participate in creating or modifying the content.[62] However, with the increasing integration of generative AI models into search engines and platforms (e.g., OpenAI's ChatGPT technology embedded in Microsoft's Bing), the legal landscape is reevaluating the scope of Section 230 immunity.[63] The next section will delve into how Section 230 grants immunity under certain conditions, defining the boundaries of intermediary liability.

6.3.1. Overview of Section 230 of the Communications Decency Act (CDA) in the United States

Under common law, liability for sharing defamatory content depended on whether an entity was classified as a "publisher" or "distributor." Publishers were liable for defamatory material even if unaware of it, while distributors were only liable if they knew or should have known the content was defamatory.[64] This distinction allowed entities such as bookstores to avoid liability unless they circulated content already known to be defamatory. Early courts struggled to apply these traditional distinctions to the rapidly evolving world of internet platforms, where content distribution occurred on a much larger scale.[65] Unlike traditional media outlets that exercised direct control over curated content, internet platforms enabled widespread dissemination of user-generated material, raising novel questions of liability. Recognizing the need for platforms to moderate

---

60 Costello v. Ocean Cnty. Observer, 136 N.J. 594, 610 (1994).

61 *See* Gonzalez v. Google LLC, 2 F.4th 871, 891-92 (9th Cir. 2021) (analyzing whether Google's algorithmic recommendations of harmful content could transform the platform into a direct participant rather than a neutral intermediary); *see* Jones v. Dirty World Ent. Recordings LLC, 755 F.3d 398, 414 (6th Cir. 2014) (holding that liability does not attach unless the platform's actions materially contribute to the unlawful nature of the content).

62 *See id.;* 47 U.S.C. § 230(c)(1).

63 *See* Volokh, *supra* note 50, at 496.

64 Restatement (Second) of Torts § 581 (Am. L. Inst. 1977).

65 *See* Cubby, Inc. v. CompuServe, Inc., 776 F. Supp. 135, 140 (S.D.N.Y. 1991) (holding CompuServe not liable for defamatory content because it did not moderate its forums, acting as a distributor); *but cf.* Stratton Oakmont, Inc. v. Prodigy Servs. Co., 1995 WL 323710, at *4 (N.Y. Sup. Ct. May 24, 1995) (holding Prodigy liable as a publisher because it moderated its message boards).

harmful, obscene, or defamatory content without risking liability, Congress enacted Section 230 of the CDA in 1996, shielding platforms from liability for third-party content and encouraging responsible moderation practices to protect against harmful material.[66]

The key provision in Section 230(c)(1) states that "[n]o provider or user of an interactive computer service shall be treated as the publisher or speaker of any information provided by another information content provider."[67] This language has been widely interpreted to grant immunity to platforms from liability for third-party content, as long as they act as passive intermediaries, hosting rather than creating or actively participating in the harmful content.

The statute defines an "interactive computer service" as "any information service, system, or access software provider that provides or enables computer access by multiple users to a computer server, including specifically a service or system that provides access to the Internet."[68] In other words, it covers platforms that serve as conduits for users to access information, such as social media sites or search engines. In contrast, an "information content provider" is defined as "any person or entity that is responsible, in whole or in part, for the creation or development of information provided through the Internet."[69] Courts emphasize this distinction to clarify that Section 230 protects platforms that merely host third-party content but not those that act as co-creators or developers of that content.[70] Platforms can become an "information content provider" by contributing to or creating the harmful content and lose its immunity, as section 230 applies only when the platform functions as a neutral "interactive computer service."

To determine whether Section 230 immunity applies to a claim, courts typically evaluate three elements: (1) whether the defendant is a provider or user of an interactive computer service, (2) whether the claim treats the defendant as a publisher or speaker of the content, and (3) whether the content at issue was created by a third-party information content provider.[71] If all three conditions are met, Section 230 generally provides immunity.[72]

Klayman v. Zuckerberg[73] illustrates how Section 230 has been applied to provide social media companies with broad immunity. In this case, Larry Klayman sued Facebook for allowing the publication of an anti-Semitic page titled "Third Palestinian Intifada,"

---

66 *See* 47 U.S.C. § 230.

67 *Id.* § 230(c)(1).

68 *Id.* § 230(f)(2).

69 *Id.* § 230(f)(3).

70 *See* Fair Hous. Council of San Fernando Valley v. Roommates.com, LLC, 521 F.3d 1157, 1166-67 (9th Cir. 2008) (en banc).

71 Zeran v. Am. Online, Inc., 129 F.3d 327, 330 (4th Cir. 1997) (establishing the foundational elements of Section 230 immunity by holding that a defendant must be an interactive computer service provider and must be treated as a publisher or speaker of the offensive content); Batzel v. Smith, 333 F.3d 1018, 1031 (9th Cir. 2003) (affirming that Section 230 applies when the defendant is not the original creator or developer of the content at issue); Doe v. Internet Brands, Inc., 824 F.3d 846, 851–52 (9th Cir. 2016) (clarifying that Section 230 does not protect a platform from liability for its independent failure to warn of offline risks).

72 *See id.*

73 10 F. Supp. 2d 314 (D.D.C. 2012).

which called for violence against Jews.[74] Klayman alleged harm from the page, even though Facebook removed it three days after receiving complaints.[75] The court found that Section 230 provided Facebook with immunity from the suit. It held that Facebook qualified as an interactive computer service and that any liability would be based on Facebook's decisions to modify, alter, or remove the content—actions protected by the statute. Finally, the court noted that Facebook was not the author of the harmful content. As a result, Facebook could not be liable for hosting third-party content, even if the content was knowingly false or could potentially incite anti-Semitic attacks by readers.[76]

Although Section 230 provides broad protections, its immunity has certain limitations. Congress did not intend to provide blanket immunity to platforms actively engaging in harmful or illegal activities, as evidenced by Congress's exceptions and amendments to Section 230, including intellectual property and federal criminal law carve-outs and the Fight Online Sex Trafficking Act (FOSTA) amendment on sex trafficking. Rather, Congress intended for platforms to have the freedom to curate and remove harmful content in "good faith" while still retaining immunity as neutral intermediaries. However, the line can blur when platforms engage in extensive content moderation or algorithmic curation, which may raise questions about whether they are acting as "information content providers" by shaping or influencing the content rather than merely hosting it. Courts frequently consider this intent when addressing cases that test the boundaries of Section 230 immunity.[77] They strive to balance protecting platforms from excessive liability for third-party content with ensuring that immunity is not so broad that it shields platforms from accountability if they actively contribute to or shape harmful content.[78] Thus, Congress's intent remains a guiding principle as courts navigate new issues related to platform liability and the scope of Section 230.

In *Fair Housing Council of San Fernando Valley v. Roommates.com, LLC*, the Ninth Circuit established that Section 230 immunity does not apply to platforms that "contribute materially to the alleged illegality of the conduct."[79] Roommates.com, a roommate-matching website, required users to complete a questionnaire disclosing protected characteristics such as sex, family status, and sexual orientation and then used this information to facilitate roommate matches.[80] The court stated, "A website helps to develop unlawful content, and thus falls within the exception to Section 230, if it contributes materially to

---

74 *See id.* at 315.

75 *Id.* at 315–16.

76 *See id.* at 321.

77 *See e.g.*, Roommates.com, 521 F.3d at 1164 ("The Communications Decency Act was not meant to create a lawless no-man's-land on the Internet."); Barnes v. Yahoo!, Inc., 570 F.3d 1096, 1102 (9th Cir. 2009) ("The immunity provided by § 230 was intended only to protect service providers from being treated as the publisher or speaker of content provided by others. It was not meant to immunize them from liability for their own wrongful acts."); Force v. Facebook, Inc., 934 F.3d 53, 63 (2d Cir. 2019) ("Section 230 was enacted, in part, to maintain the robust nature of Internet communication . . . and, accordingly, to keep government interference in the medium to a minimum.").

78 *See e.g.*, Zeran v. America Online, Inc., 129 F.3d 327, 330-31 (4th Cir. 1997) ("Congress made a policy choice . . . not to deter harmful online speech through the separate route of imposing tort liability on companies that serve as intermediaries for other parties' potentially injurious messages.").

79 Roommates.com, 521 F.3d at 1168.

80 *Id.*

the alleged illegality of the conduct."[81] The court further clarified that merely providing a forum for third-party content is protected, but Roommates.com's active role in requiring users to disclose protected characteristics and matching users based on those characteristics constituted material contribution to the illegality.[82] Therefore, Roommates.com was not acting as a passive intermediary; instead, it was actively involved in developing the content, making it an "information content provider" for that content and removing Section 230 protection. The court explains this distinction:

> Roommate's own acts—posting the questionnaire and requiring answers to it—are entirely its doing and thus section 230 of the CDA does not apply to them. Roommate's classification of individuals based on sex, family status and sexual orientation are also its own doing, and Section 230 of the CDA does not immunize conduct related to that content.[83]

In essence, the court found that Roommates.com's violation of federal law (the Fair Housing Act) did not, by itself, remove Section 230 protections. Instead, it was Roommates.com's active participation in developing and structuring discriminatory content that stripped it of immunity. By soliciting and organizing users' discriminatory preferences through its mandatory questionnaires, the platform played an active role in creating the illegal content. This direct solicitation of unlawful information meant that Roommates.com was not just passively hosting content but was actively involved in creating illegal content.

For a platform to be similarly liable in a defamation context, it would need to do more than just encourage feedback. Perhaps a platform involved in designing questions or prompts that explicitly solicit defamatory statements would cross the line. For instance, if a platform asked, "What illegal or unethical actions has this person engaged in?" or provided structured categories such as "criminal behavior" or "dishonest practices," it could be seen as actively encouraging users to make defamatory claims, rather than allowing open-ended answers.

Similarly, in *FTC v. Accusearch, Inc.*, the Tenth Circuit denied Section 230 immunity to Accusearch for its active role in obtaining and selling unlawfully acquired private information.[84] In this case, the FTC sued Accusearch, a company that operated a website selling confidential telephone records and other private information.[85] The court denied Section 230 immunity, reasoning that Accusearch was not acting as a passive intermediary but had actively sought out and purchased confidential telephone records. By "marketing and selling" this unlawfully obtained data, Accusearch became more than just a host, as it was "responsible, in whole or in part, for the creation or development of information" that violated privacy rights.[86]

---

81 *Id.* at 1168.
82 *Id.*
83 *Id.* at 1164.
84 FTC v. Accusearch, Inc., 570 F.3d 1187 (10th Cir. 2009).
85 *Id.* at 1199–200.
86 *Id.* at 1200.

In analyzing defamation cases, *Accusearch* provides a useful analogy. If a platform not only hosts defamatory content but also takes actions that enhance, transform, or commercialize that content, the platform could lose its immunity. For example, if a website adds defamatory tags, manipulates context, or otherwise changes user-generated statements in a way that alters their meaning or impact, *Accusearch* suggests that courts might treat the platform as more than just a passive intermediary, thus exposing it to defamation liability.

More recently, in *G.G. v. Salesforce.com, Inc.*,[87] the court found Salesforce ineligible for Section 230 immunity for actively supporting Backpage.com's illegal operations. While this case involved sex trafficking rather than defamation, it highlights that Section 230 does not protect platforms that provide active assistance in illegal activities. Salesforce provided customized software and technical support that enabled Backpage to expand its illegal business and maintain data on sex trafficking victims.[88] The Seventh Circuit found that Salesforce's conduct constituted active participation, not passive hosting, and amounted to "knowing assistance" in the trafficking scheme, rendering it ineligible for Section 230 immunity.

In defamation cases, *G.G. v. Salesforce* suggests that courts may look beyond the nature of the content itself and focus instead on the defendant's role in supporting or amplifying harmful statements. For example, if a software provider actively designs tools or features that promote defamatory content—such as algorithms that prioritize or recommend defamatory posts—the provider could be seen as playing a role similar to Salesforce's, potentially making it liable for defamation as an "information content provider." The *Salesforce* decision underscores the importance of examining the extent to which a platform's conduct contributes to the harm alleged, whether through direct involvement in content creation, targeted software solutions, or business strategies that amplify defamatory content.

Consider the following hypothetical scenario: PoliticoPro, a software company that provides a custom tool designed to post and amplify content targeting political opponents. A client uses the software to automatically post defamatory statements about a political rival, with the algorithm specifically prioritizing controversial and harmful content to generate engagement. If PoliticoPro had knowledge that its software was being used for this purpose or specifically designed it to target and promote defamatory statements, it could be viewed as actively contributing to the defamation. Much like in *G.G. v. Salesforce.com*, where Salesforce's active involvement disqualified it from Section 230 protections, a software company or platform that actively curates or promotes defamatory content via algorithms could similarly lose immunity. Algorithms that prioritize content for profit, user engagement, or based on targeted data analytics could be seen as editorial tools, making the platform responsible for the content's broader dissemination.

More recent cases have begun to explore whether algorithmic recommendations and other automated content sorting mechanisms fall within Section 230's protections. For

---

[87] 2023 WL 4944011 (7th Cir. 2023).

[88] *Id.* at 950.

example, in *Anderson v. TikTok, Inc.*,[89] the Third Circuit Court addressed the legal responsibility of social media platforms when their algorithms promote harmful content. In this case, a ten-year-old girl, Nylah Anderson, died after attempting a dangerous "Blackout Challenge" video that TikTok's algorithm recommended to her through its "For You Page."[90] The lawsuit filed by her mother claimed that TikTok's recommendation system played an active role in promoting harmful content to minors.[91] The court acknowledged that while Section 230 protects platforms from being held liable for content created by third parties, TikTok's algorithm, which recommended the dangerous video to Nylah, could be considered TikTok's own "expressive activity."[92] Citing the Supreme Court's decision in *Moody v. NetChoice, LLC*, the court reasoned that TikTok's curation and recommendation of third-party content via its algorithm could be classified as first-party speech.[93] The Court, therefore, allowed Anderson's claims related to TikTok's algorithmic recommendations to proceed.[94]

This reasoning could pave the way for defamation plaintiffs to argue that a platform's role in amplifying defamatory statements—through its recommendation systems or other automated tools—constitutes active participation, making the platform liable as if it were a publisher or speaker of the harmful content. For instance, if a platform's algorithm is designed to prioritize highly defamatory content because it generates more engagement, that algorithmic amplification could be viewed as "developing" the harmful content. In such a case, the platform might be treated as a co-creator and thus be subject to direct defamation claims.

Courts have also addressed failure-to-warn claims and design-related claims in the context of Section 230, examining whether these claims fall outside the statute's immunity when they involve a platform's independent duty or product design choices rather than its role in publishing third-party content.[95] For example, in *Doe v. Internet Brands, Inc.*, Jane Doe, a user of ModelMayhem.com, was lured by two men using the site's services, leading to her being assaulted.[96] The plaintiff claimed that Internet Brands had prior knowledge of the scheme but failed to warn its users.[97] The Ninth Circuit ruled that Section 230 did not apply because the claim focused on Internet Brands' independent duty to warn users based on offline knowledge, rather than its

---

89 No. 22-3061 (3d Cir. Aug. 27, 2024).

90 *Id.*

91 *Id.*

92 Anderson v. TikTok, Inc., No. 22-3061, 11 n.11 (3d Cir. Aug. 27, 2024) ("We recognize that TikTok's first-party speech captures certain third-party speech. However, "'exercis[ing] editorial discretion in the selection and presentation' of content" qualifies as "'speech activity' . . . [whether] the content comes from third parties [or] it does not." NetChoice, 144 S. Ct. at 2402 (first alteration in original) (quoting Ark. Educ. Television Comm'n v. Forbes, 523 U.S. 666, 674 (1998))").

93 *Anderson*, No. 22-3061, at 8–9 (citing Moody v. NetChoice, LLC, 144 S. Ct. 2383 (2024)).

94 *Id.*

95 *But see* Doe v. MySpace, 528 F.3d at 419–20 (holding that Section 230 barred claims based on MySpace's failure to implement safety measures, as such decisions were treated as publishing functions, and distinguishing claims that challenge a platform's design choices versus claims based on its role as a publisher).

96 Doe v. Internet Brands, Inc., 824 F.3d 846, 848 (9th Cir. 2016).

97 *Id.* at 848–49.

role in publishing third-party content.[98] This decision emphasizes that Section 230 immunity is not a blanket shield against all claims but is limited to those arising from a platform's function as a publisher or speaker.

For defamation claims, *Doe v. Internet Brands* provides a potential avenue for holding platforms accountable when their liability stems from offline conduct or a separate duty that exists independently of third-party content. A failure-to-warn claim could theoretically circumvent Section 230 if framed as an independent duty unrelated to the platform's role in publishing or distributing the defamatory content. The plaintiff would argue that the platform had a duty to warn users about a particular known risk, independent of its role as a publisher of third-party content.

The Ninth Circuit has also found that certain design-related claims may also fall outside the scope of Section 230's protections, particularly when they do not directly relate to the platform's role in publishing or moderating third-party content.[99] In *Lemmon v. Snap, Inc.*, for example, the Ninth Circuit held that Section 230 did not bar a negligent design claim against Snapchat, related to its "Speed Filter" feature.[100] The case arose after three teenage boys died in a high-speed car crash while using Snapchat's Speed Filter to record themselves driving at over 100 mph.[101] The boys' parents sued Snap, arguing that the app's design encouraged dangerous behavior and contributed to their sons' deaths.[102] The court ruled that these claims did not treat Snapchat as a publisher or speaker of third-party content but instead as a product manufacturer responsible for a design defect.[103]

In defamation cases, plaintiffs often challenge a platform's role in distributing or hosting harmful statements. However, *Lemmon* suggests that if the focus shifts from the content itself to a platform's features or tools that facilitate harmful behavior, such as algorithms or filters that encourage or amplify defamatory speech, the platform could potentially be held liable outside of Section 230's protections. For example, if a defamation claim involved a social media platform that designed an algorithm specifically to promote harmful or defamatory posts, *Lemmon* suggests that the platform could be viewed as a product manufacturer responsible for a defective design, rather than a publisher protected under Section 230. This would be especially relevant if the alleged harm arose from the design defect itself rather than the content.

However, the Fifth Circuit has taken a broader approach to Section 230 immunity, generally viewing decisions involving user interactions, safety measures, or platform design as part of the protected "publishing" functions.[104] In *Doe v. MySpace*, the plaintiff sued MySpace, alleging negligence for failing to implement adequate safety measures to protect minors after a minor user was sexually assaulted by someone she met on the

---

98 *Id.* at 852–53.

99 *See* Lemmon v. Snap, Inc., 995 F.3d 1085 (9th Cir. 2021).

100 *Id.* at 1091.

101 *Id.* at 1087.

102 *Id.* at 1088.

103 *Id.* at 1092.

104 Doe v. Myspace, Inc., 528 F.3d 413 (5th Cir. 2008).

platform.[105] The court granted MySpace Section 230 immunity, reasoning that decisions about user safety and platform design were part of MySpace's role as a publisher of third-party content, which is protected under Section 230.[106] This difference can significantly impact whether platforms are held liable for harms resulting from offline risks or safety failures, creating a circuit split on the scope of Section 230 protection.

These cases highlight that Section 230 is not a blanket shield and does not protect platforms from all forms of liability. Instead, immunity hinges on whether the platform acted as a passive intermediary or played an active role in creating or promoting harmful content. However, courts vary in their interpretation of Section 230's scope, particularly regarding what is considered a publishing function. This variation influences whether certain actions—such as algorithmic amplification or design choices—are viewed as activities covered by Section 230 immunity or as actions that could expose a platform to liability.

As technology advances, particularly with the rise of AI and chatbots, questions arise about how Section 230 applies to content generated autonomously by machines rather than by human users. The next section examines recent cases involving AI-generated defamation and explores the potential liabilities companies may face when their AI systems produce defamatory content, challenging the traditional boundaries of Section 230 protections.

6.3.2. Application of CDA § 230 to Company Chatbots and AI-Generated Defamation

The immunity provided by Section 230 is unlikely to extend to AI companies for content generated by their AI systems.[107] When an AI model outputs defamatory statements, the company behind it is not acting as an uninvolved intermediary. Rather, it is the direct developer of the harmful content, subject to the same standards of liability as traditional publishers. An AI company that designs and distributes a program capable of generating false and reputation-damaging accusations that did not preexist would likely be considered as materially contributing to the unlawful nature of that content. AI companies cannot claim immunity simply because their outputs are constructed from preexisting words[108] After all, human authors also rely on preexisting words and phrases, arranging them into new sentences based on what they have read.[109] However, assembling those words into a defamatory statement still exposes a human writer to liability.[110] The same logic should apply to AI programs.[111]

---

105 *Id.* at 416.
106 *Id.* at 418–20.
107 *See* Volokh, *supra* note 50, at 497.
108 *Id.* at 493.
109 *Id.*
110 *Id.*
111 *Id.*

The first defamation lawsuit arising from ChatGPT's output was recently filed against OpenAI.[112] Mark Walters, host of *Armed America Radio*, sued OpenAI after ChatGPT allegedly generated a false statement accusing him of embezzling funds from the Second Amendment Foundation (SAF), a nonprofit organization with which he has no connection.[113] A journalist prompted ChatGPT to summarize a legal complaint involving SAF, and the chatbot generated a fabricated and detailed response, incorrectly alleging that Walters was accused of embezzling funds from SAF.[114] The hallucination included invented details, such as Walters being SAF's Treasurer and CFO, his alleged misappropriation of funds, and his attempted removal from the SAF board—none of which had any basis in fact.[115]

OpenAI develops and distributes ChatGPT, which generated the false and defamatory accusations. The fact that the defamatory content was not contained in the original complaint provided to ChatGPT indicates that its output went beyond mere summarization. If an AI system creates defamatory content based on otherwise neutral input (such as summarizing a complaint), the developer could be seen as contributing to or transforming the content into something defamatory. Just as in *Accusearch*, where the platform's involvement went beyond passive facilitation, an AI that generates defamatory statements—rather than merely hosting third-party content—could be seen as playing an active role, thus losing immunity under Section 230.[116]

OpenAI aims to avoid liability, suggesting that ChatGPT's hallucinations do not qualify as a "publication" because the user owns and controls the output, and thus should bear the responsibility for its distribution.[117] However, OpenAI's assertion that users control the output does not negate the fact that it "published" the content by transmitting it to a third party. Under defamation law, publication occurs when defamatory material is communicated to someone other than the person defamed.[118] OpenAI's act of providing the output to the user qualifies as publication, regardless of who controls or owns the content afterward. This makes OpenAI responsible for the defamatory statement reaching a third party.

In *Moody*, the Supreme Court recognized that algorithmic curation can be akin to editorial choices, which suggests that OpenAI's decisions about how ChatGPT generates and presents information may be viewed as an editorial function. If the platform's use of algorithms is deemed *expressive conduct*, the platform could be liable for defamation as a primary publisher rather than a neutral intermediary.[119] If the AI system's configuration, training data, or algorithms contribute to the defamatory nature of

---

[112] *See* Complaint, Walters v. OpenAI, L.L.C., No. 23-A-04860-2 (Ga. Super. Ct. Gwinnett Cty. filed Jun. 5, 2023), removed to Walters v. OpenAI, L.L.C., No. 1:23-cv-03122 (N.D. Ga. Jul. 14, 2023).

[113] *Id.*

[114] *Id.*

[115] *Id.*

[116] *See* Accusearch, 570 F.3d at 1187.

[117] *Walters*, No. 1:23-cv-03122 (N.D. Ga. Jul. 14, 2023).

[118] Restatement (Second) of Torts § 577(1).

[119] Moody, 144 S. Ct. at 2402.

the statements, the developer could be viewed as an active co-publisher, similar to *Accusearch* and *Salesforce*.[120]

OpenAI argues that their outputs are "probabilistic" and inherently unreliable, which complicates their classification as factual statements.[121] However, courts evaluate defamation based on the statement's effect and how it would be interpreted by a reasonable person. If an AI-generated output presents information in a way that appears factual and harms an individual's reputation, the fact that it was generated "probabilistically" does not eliminate the potential for defamation. Additionally, AI companies often promote their tools as sophisticated and reliable, encouraging users to rely on their outputs. If users perceive these statements as credible and factual, AI developers cannot later assert that the content is inherently unreliable to evade liability.

OpenAI's defense rests on the assertion that there was no intent to defame, and the content was generated without malice.[122] However, in *Accusearch*, the court emphasized that when a platform's actions go beyond passive hosting and it actively encourages or participates in illegal activity, it can be seen as acting with intent or reckless disregard for the resulting harm. This suggests that evidence of *recklessness* or *willful blindness* in developing or deploying the AI system could establish fault, even if the developer did not specifically intend to defame. For instance, an absence of rigorous negative testing could surely suggest recklessness or willful blindness on the part of AI developers.

During the AI development process, negative testing, sometimes referred to as adversarial testing or red teaming, is a crucial practice for ensuring that AI systems do not generate harmful, defamatory, or otherwise damaging content. Negative testing involves challenging the AI with unfavorable, unusual, or edge-case inputs to identify if and how it might produce unintended, potentially harmful outputs.[123] By simulating unfavorable prompts—such as biased questions, controversial topics, or incomplete information—developers can understand and mitigate situations where the AI may stray into harmful territory.[124] For instance, negative testing could expose whether the AI system tends to respond in a speculative or defamatory manner when given prompts about sensitive topics or public figures. This proactive approach allows developers to recognize failure points and set boundaries or filters within the AI model to prevent harmful responses.

Furthermore, if the AI tool's structure inherently results in defamatory associations, this defective design could be the basis for *negligent design liability*, similar to the "Speed Filter" in *Lemmon*.[125] It is arguable that ChatGPT's architecture is flawed and that the developer should have foreseen the potential for defamation.

---

120 *See* Accusearch, 570 F.3d at 1187; *see* Salesforce.com, 83 Cal. App. 5th at 231.

121 *Walters*, No. 1:23-cv-03122 (N.D. Ga. Jul. 14, 2023).

122 *Id.*

123 *See What Is Negative Testing? Test Case Examples and Best Practices*, LambdaTest (Jul. 13, 2023), https://www.lambdatest.com/learning-hub/negative-testing.; Kathy Meier-Hellstern, *Responsible AI at Google Research: Adversarial Testing for Generative AI Safety*, Google Research Blog (Nov. 16, 2023), https://blog.research.google/2023/11/responsible-ai-at-google-research_16.html.

124 *See id.*

125 *See* Lemmon, 995 F.3d 1085.

In a similar case, *Battle v. Microsoft*,[126] Jeffery Battle is suing Microsoft for AI-generated misinformation from Bing, which falsely linked him to a convicted terrorist.[127] The lawsuit alleges that Bing's summarization feature, powered by ChatGPT, made unfounded connections between the two individuals.[128] However, as a Microsoft user, Battle had agreed to a Terms of Service that included an arbitration clause, which the court upheld, compelling the case into arbitration despite the apparent disconnect between the claim and the user agreement.[129] This case, while a strong theoretical example, underscores a critical issue: plaintiffs often cannot overcome the enforcement of arbitration clauses, which prevent cases from being adjudicated in court and from setting legal precedent. As a result, despite the potential for AI tools to generate defamatory content, the legal landscape remains unclear due to the absence of judicial decisions in such cases.

AI developers are more likely to rely on terms of service agreements as their primary defense for immunity, rather than depending on Section 230, which is more commonly invoked by platform deployers—those hosting the AI services.[130] These hosting platforms typically do not modify or control the content directly.[131] Instead, they are generally shielded from liability under Section 230, unless they engage more directly with the content in a way that would cause them to lose the protection of the statute's safe harbor.[132]

Some scholars argued that, had the case not been compelled to arbitration, the actual malice standard could have been satisfied if an AI company receives actual notice of the defamatory content being produced and refuses to act.[133] Bing, which integrates GPT-4 technology, produced a response that falsely combined information about two distinct individuals: Jeffery Battle, a technology professional known as "The Aerospace Professor," and Jeffrey Battle, a convicted terrorist.[134] The output listed details about the professional accomplishments of Jeffery Battle, such as his role as CEO of Battle Enterprises and his background as an adjunct professor and Air Force veteran.[135] However, it also stated that Battle was sentenced to eighteen years in prison for seditious conspiracy against the United States—information related to the criminal record of Jeffrey Battle, a different individual with a slightly different spelling of his first name.[136] This incorrect mash-up resulted in a misleading portrayal, making it appear as though the entire description referred to one person.[137]

---

[126] Battle v. Microsoft Corp., No. 1:23-cv-01822, 2024 WL 4555687, at *1 (D. Md. Oct. 23, 2024) (compelling arbitration).

[127] *Id.* at complaint. https://storage.courtlistener.com/recap/gov.uscourts.mdd.540279/gov.uscourts.mdd.540279.1.0.pdf.

[128] *Id.*

[129] *Id.*

[130] Jon M. Garon, The Law and Regulation of Artificial Intelligence in a Nutshell (2025).

[131] *Id.* at 197.

[132] *Id.*

[133] *See* Volokh, *supra* note 50, at 493.

[134] *See* Complaint, Battle v. Microsoft Corp., No. 1:23-cv-01822-JRR (D. Md. filed Jul. 7, 2023).

[135] *Id.*

[136] *Id.*

[137] *But see* Battle v. Microsoft Corp., No. 1:23-cv-01822, 2024 WL 4555687, at *1 (D. Md. Oct. 23, 2024) (compelling arbitration). Few cases, if any, are surviving to trial as a result of compelled arbitration under user agreements incorporated into terms of service agreements.

Negative testing could have helped prevent such errors by examining how the AI handled similar names, underscoring the need for preemptive safeguards. This could involve simulating various inputs designed to probe the AI system's handling of individuals with similar names or overlapping professional titles.[138] This type of negative test would aim to expose how the system responds to prompts that might trigger confusion between distinct individuals, especially those who share similar names but have vastly different backgrounds. For example, developers could run tests with inputs that ask the AI for information on "Jeffery Battle" and "Jeffrey Battle" separately, assessing if it differentiates based on contextual details such as occupations, criminal records, or any other unique identifiers. Additionally, negative testing could include prompts with ambiguous language that the system might misinterpret, to determine if it can properly distinguish biographical information across individuals with similar identifiers.[139] Through these tests, developers could refine the AI to prioritize accuracy in name-based distinctions, especially when outputs involve sensitive or reputational information.

The companies offering access to AI models such as ChatGPT and Bard are often the same entities that created these programs or are closely affiliated partners, such as Microsoft's integration of GPT-4 in Bing.[140] This integration imposes a duty of care on Microsoft to prevent reputational harm by implementing rigorous testing and filtering measures to prevent the AI from producing false associations or generating misleading information.[141] Theoretically, courts could interpret a lack of such preventive measures as recklessness or willful blindness.[142] If Microsoft continued using and promoting the summarization feature without adequate safeguards—despite being aware that its integration of GPT-4 could lead to inaccuracies or defamatory content—this would likely demonstrate reckless disregard.[143]

However, this remains a hypothetical scenario, as most users have agreed to Microsoft's Terms of Service, which include arbitration clauses, thereby limiting public litigation avenues. Even so, if such a situation were considered in a legal context, Microsoft's liability could be argued to be heightened by the fact that it was notified of the error after Jeffery Battle discovered the defamatory output linking him to a convicted terrorist. Such notice would impose a duty on Microsoft to take reasonable corrective action, especially given the severe reputational harm caused by conflating Battle's professional history with a criminal record. In this analysis, Microsoft's failure to act could be compared to *Doe v. Internet Brands*, where the platform was held liable for not warning users despite having prior knowledge of a specific risk.[144] Similarly, a hypothetical failure by Microsoft to respond to a foreseeable danger after being alerted to the issue

---

138 *See* LambdaTest, supra note 123.

139 *See id.*

140 *See* Volokh, *supra* note 50, at 500.

141 *See generally* Ryan Abbott, *The Reasonable Computer: Disrupting the Paradigm of Tort Liability*, 86 Geo. Wash. L. Rev. 1, 14–16 (2018) (arguing that as autonomous systems become safer, companies may be held to a heightened duty of care, including rigorous safety measures, to prevent harm).

142 *See id.* ("It should not be necessary for a computer tortfeasor to physically replace a human operator for negligence to apply. It should be sufficient that a computer is performing a task which a person could reasonably do").

143 *See* Accusearch, 570 F.3d at 1187.

144 *See* Internetbrands, 824 F.3d at 853–54.

could be likened to Internet Brands' breach of duty, illustrating a comparable lapse in addressing known risk.[145]

Additionally, the integration of GPT-4 into Bing, despite its potential to produce misleading or false biographical data, could suggest that Microsoft's role extended beyond mere passive facilitation. This active involvement in deploying a system known to generate defamatory content might indicate a level of knowing participation, similar to that seen in *G.G. v. Salesforce.com, Inc.*[146] In *Salesforce*, the court determined that providing customized software solutions to support illegal activities negated Section 230 immunity.[147] Similarly, Microsoft's deliberate implementation of an AI tool with foreseeable risks, without incorporating sufficient safeguards, could establish fault under the same rationale as in *Salesforce*, showing that Microsoft knowingly participated in disseminating potentially defamatory content.[148]

With the introduction of Gemini, alongside other advanced AI tools, companies continue to include disclaimers warning users of potential inaccuracies in AI-generated content. Gemini API terms of services warn users to "[u]se discretion before relying on, publishing, or otherwise using content provided by the Services."[149] Similarly, Bard includes a notice that its outputs "may display inaccurate or offensive information that doesn't represent Google's views," while ChatGPT cautions that it "may produce inaccurate information about people, places, or facts."[150] However, such disclaimers do not function as legal shields.[151] Even if users are considered to have assumed the risk by interacting with the AI despite these warnings, the rights of third parties who are defamed are not waived by these disclaimers.[152] Courts have previously held that disclaimers must be more than just general warnings about potential inaccuracies. The Supreme Court noted that even statements labeled as opinion could be actionable if they imply a provably false assertion of fact.[153] Thus, a disclaimer would likely need to explicitly state that the output is fictional, parody, or a hypothetical scenario.

However, AI developers such as OpenAI and Google do not market their products as generating fictional content. On the contrary, they emphasize the reliability and factual accuracy of their systems, creating the impression that the statements produced are truthful.[154] To effectively mitigate liability, AI companies need to reframe their marketing and explicitly characterize the content as speculative or incapable of verification.[155]

---

145 *See id.*

146 *See G.G.*, 76 Cal. App. 5th 441.

147 *See id.*

148 *See id.*

149 Google Gemini API Additional Terms of Service, GOOGLE AI (May 2, 2024), https://ai.google.dev/gemini-api/terms-archive/terms_05_02_24.

150 Google Gemini API Cookbook, GitHub, https://github.com/google-gemini/cookbook (last visited Nov. 12, 2024); OpenAI, ChatGPT, https://chat.openai.com/ (last visited Nov. 12, 2024); *See* Volokh, *supra*, note 50, at 500 (arguing "such disclaimers can't operate as contractual waivers of liability").

151 *Id.*

152 *Id.*

153 *Milkovich*, 497 U.S. at 16.

154 *Id.*

155 *See* Volokh, *supra*, note 50, at 500.

Without such clarifications, disclaimers alone may provide insufficient protection, particularly in hypothetical litigation scenarios where users have bypassed arbitration clauses.

In *Moody v. NetChoice*, the U.S. Supreme Court highlighted the importance of protecting platforms' editorial discretion under the First Amendment. If courts view AI-generated content as an extension of editorial functions, platforms could assert that promoting or displaying AI-created content falls under protected speech.[156] However, even if AI outputs are granted First Amendment protections, AI companies would still be liable for defamatory content if certain conditions are met. If the company knows that certain statements produced by its AI are false and defamatory, or if it recklessly disregards the high probability of their falsity, it may be liable under the actual malice standard.[157] When the content involves private individuals and a matter of public concern, AI companies may be liable if they are merely negligent in allowing the defamatory content to be communicated.[158] If the defamatory content concerns a purely private matter, a stricter standard of liability may apply, although most states still require a showing of negligence.[159]

Arbitration's dominance in resolving these disputes means public scrutiny of these decisions will remain limited, leaving broader questions about AI accountability unresolved in the public legal domain. As these disputes are funneled into arbitration due to the broad arbitration clauses in user agreements, they are unlikely to reach public courts. Notably, in cases where plaintiffs did not directly use the AI system but interacted with other Microsoft products, such agreements have still been deemed sufficient to compel arbitration. This effectively prevents these cases from setting public legal precedents.

In cases forced into arbitration, broader questions about whether protections under Section 230 extend to AI-generated content are unlikely to be publicly resolved. However, the issue may ultimately depend on how AI's role in content creation is interpreted in the rare cases that reach public courts or if Congress enacts amendments to explicitly address the statute's applicability to AI technologies. Bipartisan proposals to amend Section 230[160] to exclude AI-generated content underscore the growing urgency of addressing these issues.

Building on these considerations, maintaining a database of confirmed false statements and designing filters to flag these statements when they appear in connection with specific names would be a reasonable approach.[161] Once an AI company becomes aware that its system is producing false and defamatory content—such as falsely attributing a crime to an individual—it should implement mechanisms to prevent further dissemination of that content.[162] This could involve using post-processing filters to identify

---

156 Moody, 144 S. Ct. at 2402.

157 New York Times Co. v. Sullivan, 376 U.S. 254 (1964).

158 Gertz v. Robert Welch, Inc., 418 U.S. 323 (1974).

159 Restatement (Second) of Torts § 558(c) (1977).

160 Bipartisan Bill, U.S. Senate Bill to Exclude AI from Section 230 Protections (2024), https://www.reuters.com/technology/bipartisan-us-bill-would-end-section-230-immunity-generative-ai-2023-06-14/.

161 *See* Volokh, *supra* note 50, at 515.

162 *See id.*

and block specific problematic statements without altering the underlying model. Such efforts may not eliminate every variation of the harmful content, but defamation law typically requires only reasonable efforts, not perfect solutions.[163] Arguments that such filtering would be too burdensome or technically infeasible seem less convincing given the sophistication of current AI technology,[164] especially considering that AI companies already build various safeguards into their systems to avoid generating harmful or inappropriate outputs.[165] OpenAI, for example, already employs such filters for other types of harmful outputs and could extend them to address known defamatory content.[166]

6.4. Deepfakes and Digital Replicas

Deepfake technology has introduced a significant challenge for defamation law, particularly in the context of visual libel, which involves false visual representations that harm an individual's reputation.[167] Unlike text-based defamation, deepfakes can depict individuals in fabricated scenarios with such realism that the public is more likely to perceive the visual content as factual, thereby heightening the risk of reputational harm.[168] Given that visual content is often perceived as more credible than written statements, deepfakes and other AI-generated visuals can inflict severe reputational damage before the victim has a chance to respond or seek legal recourse.[169] The sheer volume and speed with which these false images can spread means that, by the time the content is removed, the reputational damage is often irreversible.[170] For example, in 2024, AI-generated explicit images of Taylor Swift went viral, amassing over 45 million views in just seventeen hours before being taken down.[171] The rapid spread of such content emphasizes the importance of legal frameworks that protect not only celebrities but also everyday individuals, including minors.

Deepfakes first gained attention in 2017 when a Reddit user posted realistic pornographic videos featuring celebrities.[172] Soon after, another user developed "FakeApp," making deepfake technology easily accessible to the public.[173] Previously, creating doctored

---

163 *See id.* at 516.

164 *See id.* at 514–15 (suggesting that a company could implement post-processing content filtering to prevent false and defamatory output once it becomes aware of the issue, without altering the underlying LLM, as OpenAI reportedly already does for other purposes).

165 *Id.* at 517–18 ("Given that AI companies are capable of doing something to diminish the production of constitutionally protected 'racist fantasies,' they should be capable of doing something to diminish the repetition of constitutionally unprotected libelous allegations to which they have been specifically alerted").

166 *See id.*

167 *See* Garon, *An AI's Picture Paints a Thousand Lies*, *supra* note 5 at 670–74 (exploring the legal implications of AI-generated images).

168 *See id.* at 673 (discussing the psychological impact and believability of visual misinformation).

169 *See id.*

170 *See id.* at 680 (emphasizing the irreparable harm caused by the rapid spread of false visual content).

171 Brian Day, *California Cracks Down on AI-Generated "Sexually Explicit Deepfakes,"* Ventura County Star (Sept. 25, 2024), https://www.vcstar.com/story/news/local/california/2024/09/25/california-cracks-down-on-ai-generated-deepfake-porn/75383103007/.

172 Rebecca A. Delfino, *Pornographic Deepfakes: The Case for Federal Criminalization of Revenge Porn's Next Tragic Act*, 88 Fordham L. Rev. 887, 893 (2019).

173 *Id.*

videos was a complex and costly process limited to Hollywood studios.[174] FakeApp simplified the process, allowing users without technical expertise to manipulate images using AI deep learning.[175] The app extracts images from platforms such as Google and Instagram to create face-swapped videos, leading to a surge in celebrity deepfakes.[176]

The Copyright Office has introduced "the term 'digital replica' to refer to a video, image, or audio recording that has been digitally created or manipulated to depict an individual realistically but falsely. A 'digital replica' may be authorized or unauthorized and can be produced by any type of digital technology, not just AI. The terms 'digital replicas' and 'deepfakes' are used here interchangeably." The Copyright Office noted concerns for three categories of harm from digital replicas beyond the creative sector:

> "First, there have been many reports of generative AI systems being used to produce sexually explicit deepfake imagery . . ." Second, the ability to create deepfakes offers a "potent means to perpetrate fraudulent activities with alarming ease and sophistication . . . Finally, there is a danger that digital replicas will undermine our political system and news reporting by making misinformation impossible to discern."[177]

Drawing on principles from traditional defamation law, courts may struggle to apply existing standards such as "actual malice" or negligence to AI-generated content.[178] In *Masson v. New Yorker Magazine*,[179] the Supreme Court recognized that falsified attributions could cause distinct reputational harm by suggesting the victim's endorsement or involvement in the falsehood. Similarly, AI-generated visual depictions create a dual harm: they present a false reality while also implying that the victim engaged in the depicted behavior.[180] This dual harm complicates liability issues for platforms and AI developers.[181]

Moreover, the dissemination of these images raises the question of who should be held liable—the platform that hosts the content, the developer of the AI technology, or the individual user who prompts the AI to create such harmful content.[182] Section 230 immunity may not extend to cases where the platform itself has "materially contributed to the unlawfulness of the information" by using AI systems that are inherently prone to generating defamatory or harmful content.[183] If the platform's design or algorithm actively

---

174 *Id.*

175 *Id.*

176 *Id.* at 894.

177 U.S. Copyright Office, *Copyright and Artificial Intelligence: Part 1—Digital Replicas Report*, at 4–5 (Jul. 2024), https://www.copyright.gov/ai/Copyright-and-Artificial-Intelligence-Part-1-Digital-Replicas-Report.pdf.

178 *See* Garon, *An AI's Picture Paints a Thousand Lies, supra* note 5, at 684 (examining the challenges in applying traditional defamation standards to AI-created content).

179 501 U.S. 496, 517 (1991).

180 Garon, *An AI's Picture Paints a Thousand Lies, supra* note 5, at 687 (explaining the unique reputational damage caused by visual falsifications).

181 *See id.* at 689 (discussing the complexities of assigning liability for synthetic visual content).

182 *See id.* at 690.

183 *See id.* at 692.

contributes to the creation of the false visual content, it could lose its immunity and be treated as a publisher or creator of the defamatory material.[184]

Without clear liability standards and updated legislation, victims—whether celebrities or ordinary individuals—may have no effective remedy against the widespread harm caused by synthetic media.[185] This gap in legal protection calls for a reevaluation of Section 230's scope and the development of new legal doctrines that address the unique risks posed by AI-generated visual content.[186] Until such reforms are implemented, the law will continue to lag behind technology, leaving victims vulnerable to the swift and devastating impact of AI-generated visual defamation.[187]

Traditional defamation law, which distinguishes between factual statements and opinions, is also ill-equipped to handle the complexities posed by manipulated imagery.[188] With deepfakes, the realistic nature of manipulated visuals blurs this distinction, complicating the application of core defamation standards such as "actual malice" and negligence.[189]

Courts have noted that when a platform materially contributes to the development of defamatory content, it can be treated as a co-creator and lose its Section 230 immunity.[190] This principle directly applies to AI-generated defamation, as the entity that designs, programs, and deploys the AI may be deemed to have "developed" the defamatory content if the system was created in a way that predictably leads to false and harmful outputs.[191] Deepfake technology, therefore, challenges the core protections afforded by Section 230, raising questions about whether the statute's immunity should extend to AI systems that operate with minimal human oversight.[192]

The use of an individual's identity to perpetrate a fraud, such as generating false visual or textual depictions that imply endorsement of a fraudulent scheme, also satisfies the defamation standard because it misrepresents the person's involvement in illegal or unethical conduct.[193] Courts have found that false statements implying criminal behavior are defamatory per se, meaning they are presumed to cause harm without requiring the plaintiff to show specific damages.[194] By associating an individual with unlawful activity, such as fraud or deception, these false depictions can substantially damage one's

---

184 *See id.* (explaining how platforms may lose immunity by contributing to the development of unlawful content).

185 *See* Garon, *An AI's Picture Paints a Thousand Lies*, *supra* note 5, at 698.

186 *See id.* at 700 (proposing reforms to Section 230 to address AI-related harms).

187 *See id.* at 702.

188 *See Milkovich*, 497 U.S. at 20 (holding that statements must be verifiable facts to be actionable under defamation law).

189 *Id.* at 19–20.

190 *See* Accusearch, *570* F.3d at 1199 (10th Cir. 2009).

191 *Id.* at 1198–99.

192 *See* Garon, *An AI's Picture Paints a Thousand Lies*, *supra* note 5, at 687 (arguing that AI systems could stretch Section 230 immunity beyond its intended scope).

193 *See* Restatement (Second) of Torts § 570 (explaining that falsely imputing criminal conduct is actionable without proof of special harm).

194 *Id.*

reputation, making the content defamatory even if the creator's intent was not to deceive but merely to create sensational content.[195]

Moreover, misinformation in political contexts—such as false claims regarding a candidate's position, conduct, or qualifications—may satisfy the actual malice standard set forth in *New York Times Co. v. Sullivan*,[196] where a plaintiff must show that the false statements were made "with knowledge of their falsity or with reckless disregard for whether they were false."[197] In the context of political elections, misinformation not only undermines the integrity of the democratic process but also inflicts reputational harm on the targeted individual, whether a candidate or a public figure.[198] Courts have determined that political falsehoods aimed at discrediting a candidate's character or public standing are inherently damaging and, when disseminated with actual malice, constitute actionable defamation.[199]

Indeed, these categories of harmful content—sexually explicit depictions, fraudulent misrepresentations using one's identity, and political misinformation—are defamatory.[200] Each involves a form of falsehood that goes beyond mere insult or hyperbole, entering the realm of legally cognizable harm.[201]

The current legal standards, which are based on human-generated content, must evolve to address the distinct risks posed by AI systems, which can independently create highly realistic, yet false visual and textual content.[202]

The increasing prevalence of digital replicas, particularly those involving nonconsensual sexual content and political manipulation, has prompted both state and federal lawmakers to take action.[203] Beginning in 2019, several states also began passing laws targeting deepfakes.[204] These laws are not limited to AI-created deepfakes but cover deceptive manipulated audio or visual media created maliciously to falsely depict individuals without their consent.[205] Many of these laws focus on sexually explicit or pornographic images, while others prohibit the distribution of deceptive media aimed at damaging

---

[195] *See* Gertz, 418 U.S. at 349 (noting that false imputations of criminal behavior have a "disproportionate impact" on reputational interests).

[196] 376 U.S. 279–80 (1964).

[197] *Id.* at 280.

[198] *See* Monitor Patriot Co. v. Roy, 401 U.S. 265, 275 (1971) (holding that defamatory statements related to a candidate's fitness for office are subject to constitutional protections but can still cause reputational harm).

[199] *See* Garrison v. Louisiana, 379 U.S. 64, 75 (1964) (holding that knowingly false statements attacking a public official's conduct constitute defamation when made with actual malice).

[200] *See* Restatement (Second) of Torts § 559.

[201] *See* Milkovich, 497 U.S. at 16 (noting that defamatory content must convey false assertions of fact to be actionable).

[202] *See* Garon, *An AI's Picture Paints a Thousand Lies*, *supra* note 5, at 690 (calling for an updated regime to address the unique challenges of AI-generated defamation).

[203] Kyra Paul-Fowler, *2024 Trending Legislation: Federal and State Attempts to Curb Deepfakes*, VILL. L. REV. BLOG (Aug. 21, 2024), https://www.villanovalawreview.com/post/2642-2024-trending-legislation-federal-and-state-attempts-to-curb-deepfakes.

[204] National Conference of State Legislatures, Deceptive Audio or Visual Media ("Deepfakes") 2024 Legislation, NCSL (May 7, 2024), https://www.ncsl.org/technology-and-communication/deceptive-audio-or-visual-media-deepfakes-2024-legislation.

[205] *Id.*

a candidate's reputation or misleading voters.[206] In 2024, forty states have pending deepfake-related legislation, with twenty states having already enacted laws.[207]

"The Copyright Office concludes that new federal legislation is urgently needed. As numerous commenters noted, generative AI technology enables the production and dissemination of digital replicas at a speed and scale that calls for a national response."[208] On the federal front, the introduction of the COPIED Act (Content Origin Protection and Integrity from Edited and Deepfaked Media Act) in 2024 marked a significant step toward broader legislative control over deepfakes.[209] This bipartisan legislation seeks to protect content creators by requiring platforms to implement digital watermarks and "content provenance" technologies, ensuring that AI-generated media cannot be used without appropriate disclosure or for unauthorized purposes, such as training AI systems.[210] The federal government's focus on protecting creative content and preventing the misuse of AI-generated media is an acknowledgment of the far-reaching impact of deepfakes on various sectors, from entertainment to politics.[211]

6.5. Conclusion

Defamation and tort laws, originally designed for human actors, now face significant gaps when applied to AI-generated content. To effectively protect individuals from digital harm, the legal system must adapt by creating clearer standards for liability and ensuring that victims of defamation and false representation have viable paths to justice.

The ubiquity of platforms such as Microsoft and other major AI developers, coupled with the prevalence of arbitration clauses in their terms of service, significantly limits the ability of courts to publicly address the legal challenges posed by AI-generated content. With many disputes resolved in private arbitration, judicial precedent necessary for developing clear standards for AI accountability is unlikely to emerge. This underscores the importance of regulatory interventions and legislative reforms to fill the gaps in the legal framework.

A negligence-based liability approach remains an important tool for addressing harm caused by AI-generated content.[212] While such a framework might primarily influence decisions within arbitration, it would still allow for assessing whether developers implemented safeguards, such as testing and monitoring, to reduce the risk of AI-generated defamatory statements. Liability would focus on whether developers exercised due care to prevent foreseeable reputational harm, striking a balance between

---

206 *Id.*

207 *Id.*

208 U.S. Copyright Office, *Copyright and Artificial Intelligence: Part 1—Digital Replicas Report*, at 22 (2024), available at https://www.copyright.gov/ai/Copyright-and-Artificial-Intelligence-Part-1-Digital-Replicas-Report.pdf.

209 National Conference of State Legislatures, Deceptive Audio or Visual Media ("Deepfakes") 2024 Legislation, NCSL (May 7, 2024), https://www.ncsl.org/technology-and-communication/deceptive-audio-or-visual-media-deepfakes-2024-legislation.

210 *Id.*

211 *Id.*

212 *See* Volokh *supra* note 50, at 522–26.

holding developers accountable for preventable harm and allowing technological innovation to flourish responsibly.

To align with this standard, developers would need to proactively address the risks associated with deploying AI systems.[213] For instance, if an AI model is used in contexts where it is expected to generate biographical statements (e.g., chatbots answering questions about public figures), developers must anticipate and mitigate risks of defamation. Failure to do so could suggest recklessness or a lack of reasonable care, opening the door for liability, even in arbitration. Unlike strict liability, which holds developers responsible for all harmful outputs regardless of precautions taken, a negligence-based approach scrutinizes whether developers were reckless or willfully blind to foreseeable risks.[214] This ensures accountability for clear negligence while allowing for isolated, unpredictable incidents without stifling innovation.

Additionally, a legally mandated takedown notice system would provide an efficient pathway for individuals to report harmful content, request its removal, and seek redress, balancing free expression and personal reputation.[215] This requirement would align with existing legal frameworks, such as the Digital Millennium Copyright Act (DMCA), which established takedown procedures for copyrighted material online.[216] Individuals could notify AI platforms of false or defamatory information produced by a chatbot or integrated search feature. The platform would then be required to assess the flagged content, and if found harmful or misleading, developers would need to establish a process to refine the model using negative testing, filtering, and built-in controls. Instead of simply removing problematic content upon notification, developers could identify patterns in flagged content, leading to more precise and lasting adjustments to the model. This approach would help address root causes in the AI's training or responses, thereby improving overall accuracy and reliability.

The risk of liability for failing to act on takedown requests would promote responsible development practices, such as training AI models to avoid generating or amplifying defamatory or misleading information. This dual approach—combining negligence-based liability with a robust regulatory framework—would hold platforms accountable for their outputs while fostering technological innovation within a framework that safeguards individual rights and public trust.

---

[213] *See id.* at 523–24 ("the question would be whether the company was negligent, and the answer would be analogous to the analysis of a negligent design product liability claim . . . even if products liability law doesn't directly apply to AI libel claims, it offers a useful analogy").

[214] *See id.*

[215] *See* Garon, *An AI's Picture Paints a Thousand Lies, supra* note 5, at 448 ("A somewhat improved version of the takedown regime that incorporates the recent suggestions of the Copyright Office[108] could go even further to provide relief for the victims on nonconsensual pornography and other libelous content without the need for protracted litigation that fails to remedy the underlying harm").

[216] *See* 17 U.S.C. §§ 512 *et seq.* (1998).

7

Privacy Regulation of Artificial Intelligence in the United States[1]

By Reena R. Bajowala

The United States lacks a comprehensive data protection or data privacy law. Instead, a patchwork of federal agencies have issued guidance, while legislative action has primarily occurred at the state level. Regulation of privacy, of course, does not equate to regulation of artificial intelligence (AI) or other automated technologies.

That said, viewing AI through the lens of privacy may offer a new perspective for regulators aiming to minimize privacy harms that legislatures have attempted to regulate through privacy laws. This viewpoint-taking requires a fundamental baseline of key privacy and data concepts.

Accordingly, in this chapter, we will begin with a section discussing key privacy and data concepts. In the next section, we will cover fundamental features of U.S. state privacy laws, as applicable to AI. Then, we will address best governance practices that arise from those fundamental features, some of which are mandated by U.S. state privacy laws. And, finally, we will address significant guidance issued by federal regulators attempting to keep pace with the way AI interacts with the industries and laws they are tasked to enforce.

---

1 The author of this chapter wishes to thank senior contributors Brett Doran and Diane Reynolds, and contributor Mackenzie Cannon of Greenberg Traurig LLP, as well as Talia Boiangin and Abigail Walker, formerly of Greenberg Traurig LLP, for their contributions to this chapter.

7.1. Key Privacy and Data Concepts

7.1.1. Personal Information

Compliance with laws that create privacy rights also requires understanding what data is relevant. These laws protect "personal information," which does not include all information that relates to an identifiable person. As discussed elsewhere, information included in training AI datasets is often scraped from publicly available webpages. "Publicly available" data receives distinct treatment in some states and is excluded from the definition of personal information altogether in other states. This means publicly available information is not subject to data subject rights like comparable elements of personal information.[2] What constitutes publicly available information differs slightly across state data privacy laws. The California Consumer Privacy Act (CCPA), as amended by the California Privacy Rights Act (CPRA), has the broadest definition for U.S. state privacy laws.[3] The major elements for defining publicly available information include government sourced information made available from federal, state, or local government records;[4] media-sourced information;[5] information made available by a person to whom the consumer has disclosed the information without restriction;[6] or data-subject-sourced information made available to the general public by the data subject.[7] Information that meets any of these criteria is not protected by data subject rights.

7.1.2. Sensitive Data

Sensitive personal information may be subject to heightened protection under state privacy laws.[8] This can include certain biometric information (e.g., voiceprints, facial geometry, fingerprints) that can be used for identification, protected health information, sexual orientation, trade union membership, religious affiliation, precise geolocation, racial or ethnic origin, genetic data, government identifying numbers like a Social Security number, account access information, and others.[9]

Under the CCPA, for example, individuals have the right to limit the use of their sensitive personal information.[10] A business must pay close attention to whether it is processing sensitive data, and whether that processing is in the form of input data, training data, or output data. Several states, including Virginia, Colorado, and Connecticut, require

---

2 Cal. Civ. Code § 1798.140 (v)(2).

3 David Zetoony, *What is "Publicly Available Information" under the State Privacy Laws* Data Privacy Dish Blog (Sept. 13, 2023), https://www.gtlaw-dataprivacydish.com/2023/09/what-is-publicly-available-information-under-the-state-privacy-laws/.

4 Cal. Civ. Code § 1798.140(v)(2) (2021), Va. Code § 59.1-571 (2021), C.R.S. § 6-1-1303(17)(b) (2021), Utah Code Ann. § 13-61-101(29)(a) (2022), Conn. Gen. Stat. § 42-515(33)(A).

5 Cal. Civ. Code § 1798.140(v)(2), Va. Code § 59.1-571 (2021), Utah Code Ann. § 13-61-101(29)(b) (2022), Conn. Gen. Stat. § 42-515(33)(B).

6 Cal. Civ. Code § 1798.140(v)(2), Va. Code § 59.1-571 (2021), Utah Code Ann. § 13-61-101(29)(c) (2022).

7 Cal. Civ. Code § 1798.140(v)(2) (West 2021), Va. Code § 59.1-571 (2021), C.R.S. § 6-1-1303(17)(b) (2021), Utah Code Ann. § 13-61-101(29)(b) (2022), Conn. Sub. Bill No. 6, § 1(25).

8 *See, e.g.*, Va. Code § 59.1-575 (2023), Colo. Rev. Stat. 6-1-1308(7), Conn. Gen. Stat. § 42-520(a)(4).

9 *See, e.g.*, Cal. Civil Code § 1798.140(ae), Utah Code § 13-61-101(32).

10 Cal. Civil Code § 1798.121.

controllers involved in processing activities that create a "heightened risk of harm" to the individual to conduct a data protection assessment.[11] A data protection assessment weighs the risks and benefits that processing creates for the individual, relevant stakeholders, and the public.

7.1.3. Aggregate and Deidentified Data

Aggregated consumer information "relates to a group or category of consumers, from which individual consumer identities have been removed, which is not linked or reasonably linkable to any consumer or household, including via a device."[12] The CCPA states that in the aggregate, personal information can be processed by entities without being subject to the personal information processing restrictions.[13] Other states, including Utah, exclude aggregated data from the definition of personal information.[14] Further, where states define personal information as "linked or reasonably linked to an identified or identifiable natural person,"[15] data in the aggregate form can reasonably be considered not to be personal information.[16]

Importantly, "'aggregate consumer information' does not include data about one or more individuals that have been deidentified."[17] Aggregate information refers to data about a group used to communicate information about a set of individuals. However, depending on the size of group and the nature of the information collected, individuals within the group may still be identifiable despite the aggregate status.[18]

Personal information that is "deidentified" has information removed such that the remaining data is no longer capable of being attributed to an identifiable person through an identifier such as a name. The CCPA defines this as information that cannot reasonably be used to infer information about, or otherwise be linked to, a particular consumer.[19] However, reidentification may remain possible based on the information that remains. If a business deidentifies data, it should address this in a privacy policy and in contracts with third parties that relate to processing this data.[20]

In the context of AI, entities should consider whether data are identifiable information, aggregate, deidentified, or anonymous. Data leakage and the contractual nuances involved in transferring personal information as well as the possible risks of sharing

---

11 *See, e.g.*, Colo. Rev. Stat. § 6-1-1309, Conn. Gen. Stat. § 42-522(a), Va. Code § 59.1-580.

12 Cal. Civ. Code § 1798.140(a).

13 Cal. Civ. Code § 1798.145(a)(6).

14 Utah Code 13-61-101(24)(b) (2022).

15 Va. Code § 59.1-575 (2023).

16 David Zetoony, *What Is Aggregated Data?*, Data Privacy Dish (Oct. 21, 2022), available at https://www.gtlawdataprivacydish.com/2022/10/what-is-aggregated-data/#_ftn2.

17 Cal. Civ. Code § 1798.140(a).

18 For example, consider a political poll in a small town. If the results are presented in such a way that they can be narrowed, filtering the results by sex, age, education, neighborhood, marital status, and so on could leave the reader with few enough individuals represented that it becomes possible to infer information about individual poll respondents.

19 Cal. Civ. Code § 1798.140(m).

20 *See, e.g., id.*, Va. Code § 59.1-581. Conn. Gen. Stat. § 42-516(c), Cal. Civ. Code § 1798.140(m).

personal information with an AI system must be kept in mind. If this information has been deidentified, the data processing addendum (DPA) between the business supplying the information and the business that operates the AI system will need to include language stating that the receiving business will not attempt to reidentify the information.[21] Similarly, if identifiable personal data is shared as input data and will be retained by the AI system, this may need to be addressed in a privacy notice.

7.1.4. Input, Training, and Output Data

The National Institute of Standards and Technology (NIST) Artificial Intelligence Risk Management Framework defines an AI system as a "machine-based system that can, for a given set of objectives, generate outputs such as predictions, recommendations or decisions influencing real or virtual environments."[22] The objectives could be instructions, a query, a dataset, an image, etc. This is called "input data," which is fed into the machine.

An AI system is built to respond to input data, but to produce useful results, it must first be trained to identify correct responses. Through this "training data," an AI system learns patterns and associations, which it can then apply to input data to create useful "output data," the resulting content.[23]

Datasets created from publicly available personal information, such as government records, media coverage, and publicly available profiles, are often excluded from state data protection laws.[24] However, building AI training datasets from personal information directly collected from individuals or obtained from other nonpublic sources may implicate state data protection laws. Output data generated by an AI system may also qualify as personal information under data protection laws if reasonably linked to an identifiable individual or individuals.[25]

7.2. Fundamental Features of U.S. State Privacy Laws, as Applied to AI

7.2.1. The Parties

Similar to Europe's General Data Protection Regulation (GDPR), state data privacy laws apply to two types of entities: "controllers" and "processors." California's privacy laws refer to these parties as "businesses" and "service providers."[26]

---

21 *Id.*

22 NIST AI RMF 1.0 at 1.

23 David Zetoony, *Do Data Privacy Laws Govern the Use of Artificial Intelligence?*, Data Privacy Dish Blog (Jun. 20, 2023), available at https://www.gtlaw-dataprivacydish.com/2023/06/do-data-privacy-laws-govern-the-use-of-artificial-intelligence/.

24 Cal. Civ. Code § 1798.140(v)(2) (2021), Va. Code § 59.1-575 (2023), Colo. Rev. Stat. § 6-1-1303(17)(b) (2021), Utah Code § 13-61-101(29)(a) (2022), Conn. Gen. Stat. § 42-515(33)(A).

25 Cal. Civ. Code § 1798.140(v)(1).

26 Cal. Civ. Code §§ 1798.140(d)(1), (ag) (West 2023). The CCPA creates a separate definition—"third party"—that contemplates an organization that is not the business, service provider, or a contractor.

Whether an organization that uses personal data to train an artificial intelligence/machine learning (AI/ML) model is deemed a controller or processor depends on the degree to which the organization determines the purpose for which the data will be used and the essential means of processing.[27] For example, if the organization is developing the AI/ML model for its own internal or commercial use and is therefore making the decision to use personal data to train an AI/ML model, the organization is likely a "controller" under state data privacy laws. If the organization has been retained by a third party to develop the AI/ML tool according to that third party's instructions, then the organization may be a "processor" while the third party is a "controller."

7.2.2. The Reason for the Processing

Organizations that use personal data for AI/ML training should carefully examine how these tools will process data, what safeguards are required for protection of personal data, and whether notice and consent is required for the use of personal data in the AI/ML model.[28]

A controller must provide a privacy notice to consumers from whom data is directly collected. The privacy notice states the purposes for which personal data is collected or used, and whether such data may be sold or shared.[29] Certain state laws require that an organization's collection, use, retention, and/or sharing of a consumer's personal data shall be "reasonably necessary and proportionate to achieve: (1) The purpose(s) for which the personal information was collected or processed, . . . or (2) Another disclosed purpose that is compatible with the context in which the personal information was collected. . . ."[30] To use personal data collected for *additional purposes* that are incompatible with the disclosed purpose for which the personal data was collected may be inconsistent with privacy laws.[31]

Therefore, not only is it important for organizations to understand their use of data and ensure the privacy notice accurately portrays the same for AI/ML tool processing, but the organization should also consider how the consumer interacts with the business on its website. A consumer is likely to expect that the purpose for collecting or processing the personal data is to provide the sought-after good or service.[32] For example, a consumer who purchases apparel on a clothing brand's ecommerce store would not reasonably expect their billing information to be used beyond the purpose of fulfilling the order.

---

[27] David A. Zetoony & Carsten A. Kociok, *Under the GDPR, Are Companies that Utilize Personal Information to Train Artificial Intelligence (AI) Controllers or Processors?* Data Privacy Dish Blog (Jun. 21, 2023), available at https://www.gtlaw-dataprivacydish.com/2023/06/under-the-gdpr-are-companies-that-utilize-personal-information-to-train-artificial-intelligence-ai-controllers-or-processors/.

[28] William Ridgway et al., *Artificial Intelligence Tools: Privacy Pitfalls*, available at Bloomberg Law (Aug. 2023), https://www.bloomberglaw.com/external/document/XBLS8B9K000000/data-collection-management-professional-perspective-artificial-i.

[29] *See, e.g.*, Cal. Civ. Code § 1798.100(a)(1) (West 2023).

[30] Cal. Code Regs. tit. 11 § 7002(a) (2024).

[31] *See, e.g.*, Cal. Civ. Code § 1798.100(a)(1) (West 2023).

[32] Cal. Code Regs. tit. 11 § 7002(b)(1) (2024).

However, a consumer who seeks to use a generative AI tool to create, for example, a weekly meal plan and grocery shopping list based on the consumer's weight, age, and other specificities the consumer inputs into the tool would expect their personal data to be used in a way that provides a service powered by AI/ML. Organizations that employ AI/ML-powered chatbots for customer support may also disclose that the customer support agent is a chatbot so the consumer reasonably understands any personal data it provides would be processed for the purpose of providing a response. Indeed, certain state law deems it illegal to deceive consumers into thinking they are interacting with a human.[33]

Additionally, the DPA between the organization and AI/ML service provider must ensure that the service provider uses personal data collected by the organization solely for the organization's operational purpose—purposes that must be disclosed in the organization's privacy notice to the relevant consumer—or for a "business purpose."[34] If an organization discloses personal data for a business purpose, then the organization does not need to provide the consumer with a right to opt out of the use or disclosure of their personal information for business purposes. However, if the disclosure of the personal data is considered a "sale" or "sharing" to the service provider, then a consumer would have the right to opt out of the use of such processing.[35]

Rights to opt out give rise to a crucial question—can an AI/ML tool provide effective and accurate results while also allowing for data subjects to delete their personal information from the datasets? Under the GDPR, for example, when receiving a request to erase a data subject's personal information, biobanks—which require the collection, use, and reuse of large quantities of biological samples and data—would need to remove all personal data about a subject from ongoing research and would not be able to use such data in "any future research or share[] with other data controllers."[36] This may pose a challenge to data that culminate in published results. AI/ML developers would face the same obstacles with output data without a processing purpose exception.[37]

It is less clear whether an organization must distribute a privacy notice to consumers with whom it has no direct connection. For example, under the GDPR, if the personal data used to train an AI/ML technology has been collected from a third-party source (e.g., scraped from the internet or received from another controller), "the GDPR generally permits the controller (with a few exceptions) to provide a copy of its privacy notice 'within a

---

33 *See., e.g.*, CAL. BUS. & PROF. CODE § 17941 (2023).

34 *See, e.g.*, CAL. CIV. CODE § 1798.140(e) (West 2023) (Business purposes include the following: "Helping to ensure security and integrity to the extent the use of the consumer's personal information is reasonably necessary and proportionate for these purposes"; "Debugging to identify and repair errors that impair existing intended functionality"; Performing services on behalf of the business, including maintaining or servicing accounts, providing customer service, processing or fulfilling orders and transactions, verifying customer information, processing payments, providing financing, providing analytic services, providing storage, or providing similar services on behalf of the business"; and "Undertaking internal research for technological development and demonstration.").

35 CAL. CIV. CODE § 1798.120(a) (West 2023).

36 CIARA STAUNTON, *Individual Rights in Biobank Research under the GDPR*, in 43 L. GOV.& TECH. SERIES: GDRP & BIOBANKING 91, 96–7 (Santa Slokenberga et al. eds., Springer 2021).

37 GDPR, Art. 17(3)(d). The GDPR is an instructive example as many U.S. states have modeled their privacy laws after the GDPR.

reasonable period, but at latest within one month' after the data is collected."[38] However, the regulations implementing the CCPA state that an organization is *not* required to distribute its privacy notice when information is collected indirectly (e.g., scraped from the internet), so long as the organization that collected the data does not attempt to sell it or share it for cross-context behavioral advertising.[39] Other state privacy laws do not distinguish between direct data collection and indirect data collection, nor do those statutes explain what it means for information to be "reasonably accessible."[40]

7.2.3. Automated Decision Making

Increasingly under the regulatory spotlight is automated decision making or "profiling." Under Colorado and Connecticut law, for instance, "profiling" refers to any form of automated processing of personal data to evaluate, analyze, or predict personal aspects concerning an identified or identifiable individual's economic situation, health, personal preferences, interests, reliability, behavior, location, or movements.[41] Organizations using personal data for profiling must, prior to the collection of a consumer's personal data, provide the consumer with a privacy notice explaining how profiling is used in the decision-making processing, including the role of human involvement.[42] They must also provide a method for opting out of the processing of the consumer's personal data for purposes of "profiling in furtherance of decisions that produce legal or similarly significant effects concerning" the consumer.[43]

Additionally, data protection assessments must be conducted prior to the processing of personal data for purposes of profiling that presents "(A) unfair or deceptive treatment of, or unlawful disparate impact on, consumers, (B) financial, physical or reputational injury to consumers, (C) a physical or other intrusion upon the solitude or seclusion, or the private affairs or concerns, of consumers, where such intrusion would be offensive to a reasonable person, or (D) other substantial injury to consumers."[44]

An example of a high-risk use of AI/ML tools is during the hiring process. AI/ML tools have been developed to assist in reviewing resumes, tracking potential candidates during the

---

38 GDPR, Article 14(3)(a); David A. Zetoony, *Under Modern US Privacy Laws, Is an Organization Required to Distribute Its Privacy Notice to Every Individual Whose Information Is Used to Train an AI?* Data Privacy Dish Blog (Sep. 7, 2023), available at https://www.gtlaw-dataprivacydish.com/2023/09/under-modern-us-privacy-laws-is-an-organization-required-to-distribute-its-privacy-notice-to-every-individual-whose-information-is-used-to-train-an-ai/.

39 Cal. Code Regs. tit. 11 § 7012(h) (2023); GDPR, Article 14(3)(a); David A. Zetoony, *Under Modern US Privacy Laws, Is an Organization Required to Distribute Its Privacy Notice to Every Individual Whose Information Is Used to Train an AI?* Data Privacy Dish Blog (Sep. 7, 2023), available at https://www.gtlaw-dataprivacydish.com/2023/09/under-modern-us-privacy-laws-is-an-organization-required-to-distribute-its-privacy-notice-to-every-individual-whose-information-is-used-to-train-an-ai/.

40 *See, e.g.*, Va. Code Ann. § 59.1-578(C) (2023); Colo. Rev. Stat. § 6-1-1308(1)(a) (2024); Del. Code tit. 6 § 12D-106(c) (2024); GDPR, Art. 14(3)(a); David A. Zetoony, *Under Modern US Privacy Laws, Is an Organization Required to Distribute Its Privacy Notice to Every Individual Whose Information Is Used to Train an AI?* Data Privacy Dish Blog (Sep. 7, 2023), available at https://www.gtlaw-dataprivacydish.com/2023/09/under-modern-us-privacy-laws-is-an-organization-required-to-distribute-its-privacy-notice-to-every-individual-whose-information-is-used-to-train-an-ai/.

41 Colo. Rev. Stat. § 6-1-1303(20) (2024); Conn. Gen. Stat. § 42-515(30) (2023).

42 Colo. Code Regs. §§ 6.03 (A)(2), 9.03 (A)(2)(C) (2024).

43 Colo. Rev. Stat. § 6-1-1306(1)(A)(I)(C) (2024); Conn. Gen. Stat. § 42-518(a)(5)(C) (2023).

44 Conn. Gen. Stat. § 42-522(a)(3) (2023); Colo. Rev. Stat. § 6-1-1309(1)-(2)(a) (2024).

hiring process, interviewing candidates, and performing "game-based assessments (measure relevant skills through computer 'games')."[45] During interviews conducted by the AI/ML tools, the AI/ML tool extracts personal data, including biometric data and data about the interviewee's personality, characteristics, and verbal and nonverbal language abilities, in order to analyze the candidate.[46] Organizations who have deployed such tools have reported a 75 percent reduction in hiring time, a reduced time-to-hire from six weeks to seven days, and a 16 percent increase in new-hire diversity.[47] Organizations must ensure that candidates in states like Colorado and Connecticut obtain the proper notice and consent of personal data processing as early as the application submission process, given that AI/ML tools are used to review and rule out an applicant's experience found on the resume.

The United States is also seeing a rise in antidiscrimination laws aimed at addressing bias in AI-driven decision making. For example, New York City's Local Law 144, in effect as of July 5, 2023, implemented requirements for employees who use automated employment decision tools (AEDT) to assist with employment decisions.[48] Such requirements include conducting a bias audit within one year of an AEDT being used, even if the AEDT is not being used to make the final hiring decision.[49] A bias audit calculates the rate at which individuals who meet certain criteria classified by the U.S. Equal Employment Opportunity Commission (EEOC) are either selected to move forward in the hiring process or assigned a classification by AEDT based on the listed categories in the EEO-1 Component 1 report.[50]

While not as advanced as the GDPR's regulation of profiling, which produces legal effects concerning a consumer, U.S. state legislatures have begun to implement regulations to combat the type of bias that can result from AI/ML's profiling results. These regulations seek to impose additional obligations on organizations and developers of such tools to enhance minimization of such discrimination.

---

[45] Brittany Kammerer, *Hired by a Robot: The Legal Implications of Artificial Intelligence Video Interviews and Advocating for Greater Protection of Job Applicants*, 107 Iowa L. Rev. 817, 821–22 (2022) (citing Ameya Deshmukh, *AI Resume Screening vs Recruiting Chatbots vs Conversational AI*, Mya (Mar. 1, 2020), available at https://www.mya.com/blog/ai-resume-screening-avoiding-common-pitfalls (discussing advantages and disadvantages of different types of resume screening AI); Rebecca Heilweil, *Artificial Intelligence Will Help Determine if You Get Your Next Job*, Vox Recode (Dec. 12, 2019, 8:00 AM), available at https://www.vox.com/recode/2019/12/12/20993665/artificial-intelligence-ai-job-screen (discusses how different AI recruitment platforms such as ZipRecruiter keeps tracking candidates for similar positions)).

[46] Brittany Kammerer, *Hired by a Robot: The Legal Implications of Artificial Intelligence Video Interviews and Advocating for Greater Protection of Job Applicants*, 107 Iowa L. Rev. 817, 821–22 (2022).

[47] David J. Garraux, *From the Jetsons to Reality, or Almost: What Employers Need to Know about Robots and AI in the Workplace*, Nat'l L. Rev. (Sept. 16, 2019), available at https://www.natlawreview.com/article/jetsons-to-reality-or-almost-what-employersneed-to-know-about-robots-and-ai.

[48] David A. Zetoony et al., *NYC's Local Law 144 and the Final Regulations: Regulation of AI-Driven Hiring Tools in the United States*, Data Privacy Dish (Jun. 30, 2023), available at https://www.gtlaw-dataprivacydish.com/2023/06/nycs-local-law-144-and-the-final-regulations-regulation-of-ai-driven-hiring-tools-in-the-united-states/#_ftn5.

[49] David A. Zetoony et al., *NYC's Local Law 144 and the Final Regulations: Regulation of AI-Driven Hiring Tools in the United States*, Data Privacy Dish (Jun. 30, 2023), available at https://www.gtlaw-dataprivacydish.com/2023/06/nycs-local-law-144-and-the-final-regulations-regulation-of-ai-driven-hiring-tools-in-the-united-states/#_ftn5; N.Y.C. Dep't of Consumer & Worker Prot. Rules § 5-30(1)(a) (2023).

[50] N.Y.C. Dep't of Consumer & Worker Prot. Rules § 5-30(1)(a) (2023).

7.2.4. Consumer Rights

States that have passed comprehensive data privacy laws have followed the model set by the GDPR, in that they have granted data subject rights that are generally quite similar. The core rights provided by these laws are the individual's right to delete, correct, and access the personal information an entity holds about them. Entities acting as controllers—or, to use the CCPA's terminology, the businesses—are responsible for addressing consumer requests related to these rights and must also inform individuals about how to submit those requests.[51] State laws require businesses that process personal information to include elements of these rights in consumer-facing privacy notices, along with relevant contact information or other methods for submitting requests. States have also set requirements for how long a business has to respond to a request and the form a response may take. Given the possibility of abuse, responding to these requests also requires businesses to create a process for authenticating the identity of the individual making the request.

These data subject rights remain relevant in the context of AI. Businesses should consider the personal information used in their training datasets, the personal information contained in the input data that goes into an AI system, and output data that contains personal information. A business's obligation to consumers may vary based on whether it collected the personal information directly from the consumer or used a dataset created by another entity. A business's obligation may also shift depending on whether it trained an AI system using its own data and controlled the training dataset or relied on an AI system trained by a vendor.

7.2.4.1. Right to Delete

Sometimes referred to as the right to erasure, individuals covered by state comprehensive data privacy laws have the right to request that a business delete the personal information it holds about them. Businesses are also required to disclose this right within a privacy policy, along with qualifiers that outline the limitations of this right. Those limitations are discussed below.

Subject to certain limitations, an entity that receives a deletion request from an individual who is covered by a comprehensive state data privacy law must delete the individual's personal information from its records. In addition, a business receiving such a request must instruct service providers or contractors to delete the individual's personal information from their records and instruct all third parties to whom the business has sold or shared the personal information to delete it—unless doing so proves impossible or involves disproportionate effort. However, there are exceptions. For example, under California law, deletion is not required of the service provider or the business that receives the request when the information is (1) necessary to complete a transaction with the individual; (2) when it is used to ensure security and integrity, and the personal information retained is reasonably necessary and proportionate for those purposes; (3) it is

---

[51] *See, e.g.*, Cal. Civ. Code § 1798.130(a)(1), Va. Code Ann. § 59.1-578(e), Colo. Rev. Statutes § 6-1-1308 (1)(a)(III), Conn. Gen. Stat. § 42-518(b).

used to debug to identify and repair errors that impair existing intended functionality; (4) when it is used to exercise free speech rights; (5) to comply with the California Electronic Communications Privacy Act; (6) engage in public or peer-reviewed scientific, historical, or statistical research that conforms or adheres to all other applicable ethics and privacy laws when the business's deletion of the information is likely to render impossible or seriously impair the ability to complete such research, if the consumer has provided informed consent; (7) to enable solely internal uses that are reasonably aligned with the expectations of the consumer based on the consumer's relationship with the business and compatible with the context in which the consumer provided the information; or (8) to comply with a legal obligation.[52]

When applied to training AI systems, the right to deletion requires entities using AI to maintain an inventory of the data used to train their models. If an individual submits a deletion request, their data may need to be removed from the training dataset. However, compliance depends on the applicable state law and the nature of the information.

The language of California's statute creates some ambiguity when it limits the application to data *collected from* the individual.[53] Businesses are required to comply with a request when it relates to personal information they have collected directly from an individual, but not necessarily if the information comes from another source. Other states do not have the same language regarding the source of information. Under data protection laws from states other than California, entities processing information—regardless of whether it was collected directly—are not exempt from fulfilling a deletion request.

This distinction is particularly relevant for training datasets compiled by third parties. When these datasets are created by scraping publicly available information from the internet, requests from data subjects will have to be analyzed against the relevant state law first to determine if the information is included in the definition of "personal information" and second to determine if a noncollector controller must comply with such a request.

7.2.4.2. Right to Access

Under the CCPA as amended by the CPRA, a consumer's right to know what personal information is collected about them is supported by the right to access their personal information.[54] Consumers may request that a business disclose to them the categories of personal information collected; the categories of sources from which the personal information is collected; the business or commercial purpose for collecting, selling, or sharing personal information; the categories of third parties to whom the business discloses personal information; and the specific pieces of personal information the business has collected about that consumer. The directive is simpler in other state laws. For example, Virginia's law simply states that a controller must comply with an authenticated

---

52 Cal. Civ. Code § 1798.105.

53 Cal. Civ. Code § 1798.105(a) ("A consumer shall have the right to request that a business delete any personal information about the consumer which the business has collected from the consumer").

54 Cal. Civ. Code § 1798.110.

consumer request to exercise the right to confirm whether or not a controller is processing the consumer's personal data and to access such personal data.[55]

When considering how the right to access applies to AI, controllers should consider what the relevant law requires of them: where the statute gives individuals the right to know the purpose for which their information is used, the controller should be able to report what data is used in a training model or as input data. Where consumers have a right to know how their data is used, some principles of explainability and transparency will apply; an entity should be able to tell a consumer the type of output their data is used to inform.

7.2.4.3. Right to Correction

Across all state comprehensive data privacy laws, consumers have the right to rectification, which is sometimes called the right to update, modify, or correct.[56] A product of the principle that individuals have a right to accurate data, is that this right allows individuals to request that their information be amended. The entity that receives such a request does not have to honor it if the changes are not accurate—such as if an individual wished to change their records to show an inaccurate history. Businesses are to use "commercially reasonable efforts" to make corrections to inaccuracies, which is to say that businesses have some discretion to weigh the impact of inaccurate information against the cost of correction.

7.2.5. Disclosures

7.2.5.1. Disclosures and Notice at Collection

State privacy laws generally require disclosure in connection with the collection or processing of personal data. The disclosure requirement is to "provide consumers with a reasonably accessible, clear, and meaningful privacy notice" including the categories of personal information collected or processed, a description of the personal information collected or processed, the purpose of the collection or processing, and whether the personal information will be shared with any third parties.[57]

For example, the CPRA requires notice *at collection*, which directs businesses in the manner of disclosure.[58] A notice is to be "readily available" to consumers at or before collection of personal information. For instance, a commonly used method is posting a conspicuous link to the privacy notice on the home page of a website and on all pages that collect personal information. If the business sells or shares personal information, then a link to a notice about the consumer's right to opt out of any sale or sharing may also be included.

---

55 Va. Code Ann. § 59.1-577(A)(1).

56 Cal. Civ. Code § 1798.106(b); Va. Code Ann. § 59.1-578(C)(3), Va. Code Ann. § 59.1-577(A)(2); Colo. Rev. Statutes § 6-1-1306(1)(c); Colo. Rev. Statutes § 6-1-1308(a)(III); Conn. Gen. Stat. § 42-518 (a)(2).

57 *See, e.g.*, Va. Code 59.1-578(C); Colo. Rev. Stat. 6-1-1308(1)(a); Cal. Civ. Code § 1798.130.

58 Cal. Code Regs. tit. 11 § 712(c)(2023).

However, there is less uniformity in whether disclosure is required from only the entity collecting the information directly from the individual or whether entities that *use* but do not *directly collect* individuals' personal information must also provide disclosure.[59] The CPRA explicitly addresses this obligation for entities that indirectly obtain the information: unless the entity intends to sell or share the information for cross-contextual behavioral advertising, these entities are generally not obligated to provide notice.[60] Outside of California, the law is less clear, as other states do not specifically address data collected indirectly.

Training datasets for AI, particularly generative AI which needs enormous amounts of training data, often come from "scraping" pages that are publicly available on the internet.[61] Such publicly available information may not be deemed to be personal information under many state privacy laws and is therefore excluded from an express disclosure requirement.

7.2.5.2. Explainability

Explainability seeks to address biases in AI as well as consumer privacy concerns.[62] In 2021, NIST published four principles that form the fundamental tenets of explainable AI systems: explanation, meaningfulness, accuracy of explanation, and knowledge limits.[63] The first tenet, explanation, is that evidence or reasons for an AI system's output can be given. The second, meaningfulness, is that the explanation is understandable to the intended audience, which is to say, not overly technical. Explanation accuracy, intuitively, indicates that the explanation given is the correct reason behind an outcome. Finally, knowledge limits confine a system to operating under the conditions it was designed to operate under and only when it has sufficient confidence in the generated output.[64]

Transparency is especially important when AI is used to make decisions such as credit worthiness or loan approvals. In instances where there are trends toward inequitable

---

59 David Zetoony, *Under Modern US Privacy Laws, Is an Organization Required to Distribute Its Privacy Notice to Every Individual Whose Information Is Used to Train an AI?* DATA PRIVACY DISH (Sept. 7, 2023), available at https://www.gtlaw-dataprivacydish.com/2023/09/under-modern-us-privacy-laws-is-an-organization-required-to-distribute-its-privacy-notice-to-every-individual-whose-information-is-used-to-train-an-ai/.

60 David Zetoony, *Under Modern US Privacy Laws, Is an Organization Required to Distribute Its Privacy Notice to Every Individual Whose Information Is Used to Train an AI?* DATA PRIVACY DISH (Sept. 7, 2023), available at https://www.gtlaw-dataprivacydish.com/2023/09/under-modern-us-privacy-laws-is-an-organization-required-to-distribute-its-privacy-notice-to-every-individual-whose-information-is-used-to-train-an-ai/ (discussing CAL. CODE REGS. TIT. 11 § 712(h) (2023)). If these entities do intend to sell this information for advertising, they can avoid distributing a privacy notice by registering as a data broker. CAL. CODE REGS. TIT. 11 § 7012(i) (2023).

61 CONGRESSIONAL RESEARCH SERVICE, "Generative Artificial Intelligence and Data Privacy: A Primer," R47569, (May 23, 2023), https://crsreports.congress.gov/product/pdf/R/R47569.

62 Nicol Turner Lee *Making AI More Explainable to Protect the Public from Individual and Community Harms*, BROOKINGS (Nov. 29, 2023), available at https://www.brookings.edu/articles/making-ai-more-explainable-to-protect-the-public-from-individual-and-community-harms/.

63 P. Jonathon Phillips et al., *Four Principles of Explainable Artificial Intelligence*, NAT'L INST. STANDARDS & TECH. (Sept. 2021), available at https://nvlpubs.nist.gov/nistpubs/ir/2021/NIST.IR.8312.pdf.

64 P. Jonathon Phillips et al., *Four Principles of Explainable Artificial Intelligence*, NAT'L INST. STANDARDS & TECH. (Sept. 2021), available at https://nvlpubs.nist.gov/nistpubs/ir/2021/NIST.IR.8312.pdf.

outcomes, individuals subjected to those decisions and individuals tasked with governing those systems must be able to understand and correct for biased output.[65] Transparency is likely to be one of the main premises for future regulation at the state level[66] and federal level.[67] Those charged with consumer protection have stated that "if companies don't even understand how their AI is making decisions, they can't really use it."[68] The White House's *Blueprint for the AI Bill of Rights* addresses the need for transparency as a counter to algorithmic discrimination, with emphasis on plain language reporting and impact assessments.[69] The publication received state support when California's state senate voted to show commitment to the five principles outlined in the *Blueprint for the AI Bill of Rights*.[70] These principles are "Safe and Effective Systems," "Algorithmic Discrimination Protections," "Data Privacy," "Notice and Explanation," and "Human Alternatives, Consideration, and Fallback."

In the *Blueprint for the AI Bill of Rights*, creating guidelines that give consumers the tools to understand and advocate for fair systems is at the heart of Notice and Explanation. Although federal data privacy law trails state law, and the same can be expected with AI legislation, California's commitment to the principles outlined in the *Blueprint for the AI Bill of Rights* indicates that these principles may shape enforceable standards. In this framework, entities that use AI, designers, and developers are instructed to provide "generally accessible plain language documentation" to describe the AI systems and the role automation plays within the AI systems. The framework stresses that these explanations are to be "timely" and "accessible." Instances where the automated system is not the sole determiner of the outcome receive special attention, calling to mind the many examples where human-made decisions exacerbated already flawed automated decisions.[71] Further underscoring that explainability is a tool for consumers to self-advocate is the notion that an AI system should provide technically valid explanations that are meaningful and useful to the individual and to any others who need to understand the system.

Companies investing in AI to process personal information should pay careful attention to how the AI is trained and why the systems produce each result. Preparing standards for consumer-appropriate content to explain the output of AI will be an important function of a company's AI governance. Strong governance programs may also include regular assessments of the performance of AI for the business's purposes, which will be

---

65 Edmund Andrews, *Credit denial in the age of AI*, Brookings (Apr. 6, 2021), available at https://www.brookings.edu/articles/credit-denial-in-the-age-of-ai/.

66 Titus Wu, *California's Draft AI Privacy Rules Show Ambitious Approach*, Bloomberg L. (Dec. 4 2023), available at https://news.bloomberglaw.com/privacy-and-data-security/californias-draft-ai-privacy-rules-show-ambitious-approach.

67 Cora Lewis, *Regulators Take Aim at AI to Protect Consumers and Workers*, Associated Press (May 26, 2023), available at https://apnews.com/article/artificial-intelligence-ai-consumer-finance-rules-8f5a450bd05e6079c742a9ce00b5c576.

68 *Id.* (quoting Rohit Chopra).

69 The White House, Blueprint for an AI Bill of Rights: Making Automated Systems Work for the American People (Oct. 2022), available at https://bidenwhitehouse.archives.gov/ostp/ai-bill-of-rights/.

70 S. Con. Resol. 17, 2023 (Cal. 2023).

71 *See, e.g.*, Kashmir Hill, *Wrongfully Accused by an Algorithm*, N.Y. Times, Jun. 24, 2020, available at https://www.nytimes.com/2020/06/24/technology/facial-recognition-arrest.html.

necessary for efforts to explain AI's results. Companies that choose to engage with AI as a service rather than to develop their own systems should not count on outsourcing this obligation. Contracts with AI as a service providers should include comparable requirements for transparency, governance, and monitoring.

7.3. Guardrails under Privacy Law

7.3.1. Data Minimization

The principle of data minimization is a staple of data protection policy worldwide, largely due to its inclusion in the Fair Information Practice Principles (FIPPs). The Organization for Economic Corporation and Development (OECD) adopted the FIPPs in 1980, and the nonbinding principles continue to guide practice around the world today. The principle of data minimization is important on two fronts: privacy and security. On the privacy front, data minimization restricts the amount of personal information that can be collected and requires that entities specify clear and justifiable purposes for processing data. On the security front, data minimization also drives retention policies that limit how long entities may maintain certain records. By restricting what information can be kept, this principle limits vulnerable information that is susceptible to breaches by bad actors.

Under the CPRA, a business's *collection*, *use*, *retention*, and *sharing* of a consumer's personal information must be reasonably necessary and proportionate to achieve the purposes for which the personal information was collected or processed.[72] Under Virginia's law, this is phrased as the controller's duty to limit the *collection* of personal data to what is adequate, relevant, and reasonably necessary in relation to the purposes for which such data is processed, as disclosed to the consumer.[73] Under Colorado law, personal data processed by a controller must be *processed* solely to the extent that the processing is necessary, reasonable, and proportionate to the specific purpose.[74] (The Colorado definition of "process" includes collection, use, sale, storage, disclosure, analysis, deletion, or modification as well as instructions to a processor.)[75]

As previously discussed, training datasets compiled by a third party—particularly the large, publicly available datasets used for training generative AI systems—tend to come from scraping the internet for information. Although this mass collection and processing of data initially seems at odds with the data minimization principle, the exclusion of publicly available information from state law definitions of personal information narrows the present discussion of minimization to personal information. Many companies that use AI will be using it with their own data both for training and for input, which risks rewarding strategies that are misaligned with minimization principles. This creates its

---

72 Cal. Civ. Code § 1798.100(c).
73 Va. Code Ann. § 59.1-578.
74 Colo. Rev. Statutes § 6-1-1304(4)(a)-(b).
75 Colo. Rev. Statutes § 6-1-1303(18).

own challenges and opportunities. Businesses will need to be able to show why processing is necessary and proportionate to the purpose for which personal data was collected.

Data minimization generally serves consumer interests by limiting overreach by businesses and also by minimizing the amount of data available for bad actors to obtain. The other side of minimizing the collection of data to what is necessary is limiting the retention of data after it is no longer necessary. Retention schedules as part of a governance scheme will be considered further in the following section, but they bear consideration here as well. Retention policies are often written such that information is to be retained for a set period of time after it is no longer in use. With the potential value of retaining information for use with AI, businesses will need to be vigilant about creating retention schedules they will adhere to and that comply with the state laws that codify the minimization principle.

7.3.2. Governance

The term "data governance" describes the practices an entity uses to manage the quality and integrity of its data. NIST describes it as "a framework of policies, rules, and processes for ensuring direction, management and accountability."[76] In the same publication, NIST notes that governance does not only focus on the technical elements like AI systems but on the human sides such as organizational process and cultural competencies that affect the people who train, deploy, and monitor AI.[77] In a technology-focused landscape that changes quickly, the policies and people involved in governance are a reasonable target for regulation. As legislators and regulators seek to write policies that ensure responsible development and deployment of AI in a way that is flexible enough to grow with changing technological capabilities, setting requirements for responsible governance is a likely approach. Watch for regulations that require oversight by certain levels of leadership, cross-functional capabilities, written policies about data handling and personal information protection, and regular assessments that are to be reviewed by leadership.

Regulating a fast-moving, technology-centric function via requirements for governance will be familiar to those with knowledge of information security compliance. For example, companies regulated by the New York Department of Financial Services have been required to comply with governance requirements outlined in 23 NYCRR 500 since 2017. Among the many requirements from this regulation are requirements that the regulated financial services entities have individuals named to key roles like the Chief Information Security Officer, that the board of directors receive updates on certain matters at certain intervals, that staff receive trainings to develop certain competencies, and that certain types of security measures are in place.[78] Beyond personnel and concrete practices, the regulation requires policies such as a written information security policy, which is to be approved by a senior officer, the board of directors (or a committee), or an equivalent

---

[76] Reva Schwartz et al., *Towards a Standard for Identifying and Managing Bias in Artificial Intelligence*, NAT'L INST. STANDARDS & TECH., 1270 (Mar. 2022), https://nvlpubs.nist.gov/nistpubs/SpecialPublications/NIST.SP.1270.pdf.

[77] *Id.* at 47.

[78] *See* 23 NYCRR § 500.4.

governing body. This policy must cover a dozen topics, including access controls, customer data privacy, vendor management, incident response plans, and more.[79] Annual certification of compliance is required.

Governance as the target for AI legislation was solidified in 2023 when Colorado adopted first-of-its-kind regulations for the use of AI by life insurers.[80] Here, the concern addressed is the potential for biased output from AI. The regulation requires a "risk-based governance structure" and "risk management system" to monitor whether the systems deployed potentially result in unfair discrimination based on race. Further, insurers are to remediate the discrimination if it is detected. The requirements emphasize written policies, procedures, systems, and controls. The regulation specifies roles for the board of directors (or committee), senior management, and a cross-functional group tasked with governance. Where outside vendors use customer personal data, the regulation still requires the insurers assess for compliance with their governance and risk management framework, from selection to oversight. Each year, life insurers that are within the scope of the regulation will file an annual report to the state's department of insurance that demonstrates compliance with the regulations. Further, this annual report will name the individuals involved in the governance and their respective responsibilities.

Testing for bias while complying with data privacy laws will require an intentional approach. The principle of data minimization is echoed in the distinctions for sensitive personal information; however, this may also create challenges in assessing for bias. Limitations on the collection of sensitive data aim to increase consumer privacy and minimize the risk of bias. For instance, many compliant entities now limit the collection of information that reveals sexuality, race, religion, and others covered by the sensitive information label. In industries such as consumer credit, some parties are not permitted to collect certain demographic information. In these instances, good governance will require foresight and strategy. As they develop internal policies, entities will need to strike a balance—adhering to minimization, while also retaining enough information to assess, identify, and correct for trends that reveal biased output from AI systems.

Companies that wish to avoid collecting sensitive information for bias testing may be able to test the results of their AI systems through other means including the use of proxies. The Consumer Financial Protection Bureau (CFPB) has shown support for this method by publishing their recommended methodology for using proxy indicators of sensitive categories.[81] Alternatively, since consent is a legitimate reason to process sensitive data, asking for demographic information and consent to process it from a sample of customers may be an effective approach to test an AI system.

---

79 *See* 23 NYCRR § 500.3.

80 3 CCR § 702-10.

81 Consumer Financial Protection Bureau, *Using Publicly Available Information to Proxy for Unidentified Race and Ethnicity* (Summer 2014), https://www.consumerfinance.gov/data-research/research-reports/using-publicly-available-information-to-proxy-for-unidentified-race-and-ethnicity/ (consumerfinance.gov).

With governance as the likely next frontier for AI regulation, businesses should consider focusing on developing workable policies and assembling teams of qualified leaders with diverse backgrounds in oversight and testing now.

7.3.3. Vendor Management

A controller may engage an AI/ML vendor when it does not have the internal capability to build training datasets or provide AI/ML-powered results to its customers and/or employees. Organizations engaging AI/ML service providers as processors should consider how the organization can protect itself against misuse of personal data and other sensitive company data. Inclusion of protective privacy safeguard, warranty, limitation of liability, and indemnification provisions minimize an organization's liability of heavy regulatory fines. Further, statutory requirements related to the processing of personal data are plentiful and must be reviewed regularly for ongoing compliance. Organizations should establish and execute a thorough vendor diligence procedure for engaging AI/ML service providers. Simultaneously, policies related to data collection, management, and retention must be implemented and followed by internal and external stakeholders.

Vendors developing AI/ML tools face both contractual and regulatory risks in relation to the use and results of these tools. A vendor should seek to contractually disclaim express or implied warranties that the performance of the AI/ML tool will be error-free or produce accurate results. The vendor may nevertheless have exposure to consumers.[82] In the case of laws regulating consumer personal data, a vendor may not avoid private liability for harm caused by a data breach or misuse of personal data. This may be true whether the vendor is engaging directly with a consumer (e.g., the vendor requires an organization's end user to create an account on the vendor's website) or the organization is providing a white-labeled version of the vendor's AI/ML technology.

While a vendor has an interest in its customer—the organization—obtaining the proper notice and consent in its role as a controller, the organization may look to its vendor as responsible for third-party harms related to the use of the vendor's AI/ML tool, and carefully examine the warranty, limitation of liability, and indemnification provisions of the services agreement with the vendor.

Unless the vendor is providing the tool in a white-labeled version, a vendor may seek to require organizations to provide the organization's end users with terms to ensure acceptance of the vendor's public-facing Terms and Conditions, End User License Agreement, or Terms of Service. These agreements may still attempt to mitigate or absolve liability for inaccurate results, data breaches, or other harm associated with data processing. Agreements such as a Terms of Service help set expectations of the AI/ML tool's capabilities and serve as a guideline for the type of data a consumer should expect to be shared with the vendor and organization who engaged such vendor.

---

[82] Iris H.-Y. Chiu & Ernest W. K. Lim, *Managing Corporations' Risk in Adopting Artificial Intelligence: A Corporate Responsibility Paradigm*, 20 Wash. U. Global Stud. L. Rev. 347, 360–61 (2021).

Where state privacy laws apply to a controller, a written agreement must be executed that governs the processor's data processing procedures with respect to processing performed on behalf of the controller.[83] A DPA includes restrictions surrounding the use of the personal data being provided to the service provider in its role as a processor.[84] While most state privacy laws govern restrictions with respect to a vendor's processing of personal data, parties often seek to negotiate certain provisions that are not explicitly stated in the laws. For example, a vendor may seek to limit the requirement to notify the organization of any *confirmed* security breach of the organization's personal data, whereas an organization would seek to receive notification immediately upon a confirmed *or suspected* security breach. A middle ground may be reached, for example, requiring notification, in no event later than forty-eight to seventy-two hours, of an "actual or suspected (after reasonable investigation)" security breach. Negotiations usually involve how to define a security breach, time periods to provide written notice of objections of subprocessors, the right for the organization to take reasonable and appropriate steps to stop and remediate unauthorized use of personal data, or other notification requirements under the laws.[85]

Additionally, vendors may be required to cooperate with consumer requests to delete any personal data they have collected, used, processed, or retained. However, as discussed further below, when a vendor uses a consumer's personal data to train an AI/ML tool to obtain certain outputs, complexities exist as to how to properly delete personal data from a training dataset without affecting the accuracy, systematic bias, or even discriminatory results (e.g., algorithmic credit scoring).[86]

An organization may also consider obtaining an enterprise license, instead of standard vendor Terms and Conditions which the vendor may modify unilaterally. Contracts with AI/ML service providers typically mandate that customers secure all necessary rights and consents to supply the personal data to the provider for their use. An AI/ML service provider who intends to rely on data collected on behalf of a business may intend to use this data to improve and enhance its AI/ML model.[87] Hence, organizations contemplating the use of AI/ML tools should consider revising their vendor due diligence processes to uncover such uses of data and categorize the relevant risk.

Reasonable due diligence includes investigating matters such as (1) what data fields the vendor anticipates receiving, (2) in which countries the vendor will be storing or accessing an organization's personal data, (3) internal personnel who will oversee the process (e.g., Chief Privacy Office, Privacy Counsel, Data Protection Officer), and (4) technical and organizational measures to protect against unauthorized access to an organization's

---

[83] *See* CAL. CIV. CODE § 1798.140(ag)(1) (West 2021); VA. CODE ANN. § 59.1-579(B) (2023); COLO. REV. STAT. § 6-1-1305(5) (2024); CONN. GEN. STAT. § 42-521 (2023); UTAH CODE ANN. § 13-61-301(2) (West 2024).

[84] *See, e.g.*, CAL. CIV. CODE § 1798.140(ag)(1) (West 2021).

[85] *See, e.g.*, CAL. CIV. CODE § 1798.100(d) (West 2023).

[86] Iris H.-Y. Chiu & Ernest W. K. Lim, *Managing Corporations' Risk in Adopting Artificial Intelligence: A Corporate Responsibility Paradigm*, 20 WASH. U. GLOBAL STUD. L. REV. 347, 367 (2021).

[87] William Ridgway et al., *Artificial Intelligence Tools: Privacy Pitfalls*, available at BLOOMBERG L. (Aug. 2023), https://www.bloomberglaw.com/external/document/XBLS8B9K000000/data-collection-management-professional-perspective-artificial-i.

data. The development of a process at the outset of searching for a vendor ensures that the organization is prepared to comply with its own requirements regarding sharing and disclosure of an organization's customers' personal data.

7.4. Federal Regulation of AI in the United States

As noted above, there is no federal privacy law. Apart from the discussions that bubble up periodically regarding the latest federal privacy law, companies typically have to follow a patchwork of federal privacy laws that apply based on the company's industry. AI is no different and in fact farther behind at the federal level. The high-level guidance—in the form of legislation, regulations, enforcement actions, bulletins, and other alerts—issued by the regulator or regulators that apply to AI and automated decision making is still fairly new. The most recent federal pronouncement regarding AI thus far has been the Trump administration's Executive Order on Removing Barriers to American Leadership in Artificial Intelligence,[88] which reverses the Biden administration's Executive Order on the Safe, Secure, and Trustworthy Development and Use of Artificial Intelligence, and shifts from the focus of from safe and trustworthy AI to promoting human flourishing, economic competitiveness, and national security, and ensuring AI systems are free from "ideological bias or engineered social agendas.".[89] The empty regulatory field has resulted in potential federal regulators rushing the field, but without a corresponding influx of binding, concrete guidance for companies wishing to employ AI technologies, including machine learning and predictive analytics.

For example, in April 2023, four federal agencies—the CFPB, the Department of Justice (DOJ), the EEOC, and the Federal Trade Commission (FTC)—issued a *Joint Statement on Enforcement of Civil Rights, Fair Competition, Consumer Protection, and Equal Opportunity Laws in Automated Systems* expressing that they would coordinate on enforcement efforts against discrimination and bias in "automated systems."[90] In terms of substance, the statement is aspirational and sparse, reiterating that "[e]xisting legal authorities apply to the use of automated systems and innovative new technologies just as they apply to other practices." The joint statement identifies that unlawful discrimination may "come from different sources, including problems with" (a) data and datasets that are skewed because they are unrepresentative or imbalanced, incorporate historical bias, or contain other types of errors; (b) automated systems that are "black boxes" with internal workings that are unclear and lack sufficient transparency to know whether the system is fair; and (c) developers that may design automated systems on

---

88 Executive Order on Removing Barriers to American Leadership in Artificial Intelligence, Jan. 23, 2025, 2025-02172 (90 FR 8741), available at https://www.whitehouse.gov/presidential-actions/2025/01/removing-barriers-to-american-leadership-in-artificial-intelligence/.

89 Executive Order on the Safe, Secure, and Trustworthy Development and Use of Artificial Intelligence, Oct. 23, 2023, 2023-24283 (88 FR 75191), available at https://www.federalregister.gov/documents/2023/11/01/2023-24283/safe-secure-and-trustworthy-development-and-use-of-artificial-intelligence.

90 Joint Statement on Enforcement of Civil Rights, Fair Competition, Consumer Protection, and Equal Opportunity Laws in Automated Systems, U.S. Equal Employment Opportunity Commission, April 2023, available at https://www.eeoc.gov/joint-statement-enforcement-civil-rights-fair-competition-consumer-protection-and-equal-0.

basis of flawed assumptions about the system's usage.[91] The joint statement then briefly addresses the mission of each organization and noted at a high level their application to AI technologies.[92]

One year later, on April 3, 2024, an amended *Joint Statement on Enforcement of Civil Rights, Fair Competition, Consumer Protection, and Equal Opportunity Laws in Automated Systems* was issued. While the original four regulators (CFPB, DOJ, EEOC, and FTC) remained involved, the amended statement included five additional regulators: the Department of Education (DOE), the Department of Health and Human Services (DHHS), the Department of Homeland Security (DHS), the Department of Housing and Urban Development (HUD), and the Department of Labor (DOL).[93] Despite the inclusion of these new agencies, the amended joint statement did not introduce material changes to its content.[94]

In this section, we cover the key federal regulators and their guidance in this space. Ultimately, the regulators generally seem to be sending two messages. First, the types of harms they are regulating are still present when evaluating AI technology. And second, the existing laws are just as applicable to those technologies.

7.4.1. The Federal Trade Commission

The FTC has emerged as a leading privacy regulator, despite the absence of an omnibus "privacy" regulation for it to enforce. Whether the FTC will assume a central role in the regulation of AI remains to be seen, but the agency has been the most active of the federal agencies in this space. Under its umbrella, the FTC regulates numerous consumer-facing regulations applicable broadly to various industries and data practices.[95]

Perhaps the FTC's signature legal tool for regulating AI is the Federal Trade Commission Act (FTCA).[96] While the FTCA does not explicitly mention privacy, it does provide the FTC with the authority to address "unfair or deceptive acts or practices" and to draft rules

---

91 *Id.*

92 *Id.*

93 Joint Statement on Enforcement of Civil Rights, Fair Competition, Consumer Protection, and Equal Opportunity Laws in Automated Systems | U.S. Equal Employment Opportunity Commission, April 4, 2024, available at https://www.eeoc.gov/joint-statement-enforcement-civil-rights-fair-competition-consumer-protection-and-equal-opportunity.

94 *Id.*

95 The FTC also enforces the Financial Modernization Act of 1999, also known as the "Gramm–Leach–Bliley Act" (GLBA). The GLBA regulates when a "financial institution" may disclose a consumer's "nonpublic personal information" to nonaffiliated third parties. The definitions of "financial institution and "nonpublic personal information" are both broad. For instance, the law covers a broad range of financial institutions (FIs), including many companies not traditionally considered to be FIs because they engage in certain "financial activities." FIs must notify their customers about their information-sharing practices and tell consumers of their right to "opt-out" if the consumers do not want their information shared with certain nonaffiliated third parties. In addition, any entity that receives a consumer's financial information from an FI may be restricted in its reuse and re-disclosure of that information. While the FTC has not issued specific guidance on AI under the GLBA, it is worth noting that the definition of NPI is so broad that any information derived from nonpublic information is covered by the term; accordingly, even a list of customers without further detail is subject to the GLBA's restrictions.

96 Section 5(a) of the FTC Act, 15 U.S.C. § 45(a).

that define specific unfair or deceptive practices. Historically, the FTC has leveraged this authority to address claims made by companies in its privacy policy and other public disclosures. The FTC is now extending these same principles to the regulation of AI and "automated decision systems," even when such systems do not involve the actual or claimed use of AI.[97]

Emphasizing the needed transparency with respect to AI tools, the FTC's Staff in the Office of Technology and the Division of Privacy and Identity Protection issued a blog post cautioning that "[i]t may be unfair or deceptive for a company to adopt more permissive data practices—for example, to start sharing consumers' data with third parties or using that data for AI training—and to only inform consumers of this change through a surreptitious, retroactive amendment to its terms of service or privacy policy."[98]

The FTC Staff in the Office of Technology and the Division of Advertising Practices also issued a blog post that emphasized the need for "safety" when discussing risks of AI causing harm.[99] Looking at safety "through the lens of [its] consumer protection and competition mission," the FTC recommended:

1. Taking necessary steps to prevent harm before and after deploying a product, including regularly monitoring or testing the accuracy of the technology and implementing procedures for tracking false results. Companies offering AI tools should assess and mitigate potential downstream harm before and during deployment of their tools, which includes addressing the use and impact of the technologies that are used to make decisions about consumers.

2. Taking preventable measures to detect, deter, and halt AI-related impersonation, fraud, child sexual abuse material, and non-consensual intimate imagery, which can be "turbocharged with AI-generated deepfakes." Measures cited include applying effective real-time detection or monitoring measures, using solutions to evaluate existing content, preventing and deterring AI-enabled scams and fraud, and leveraging solutions to build robust guardrails that provide authentication or prevent upstream harm

3. Avoiding deceptive claims about AI tools that result in people losing money or put users at risk of harm. Pursuant to the FTC's enforcement authority under the FTCA, advertising statements and representations in privacy policies or other external statements regarding the collection, use, retention, and sharing of data, as well as the functionality of the AI tool, are likely to be scrutinized.

4. Ensuring privacy and security by default, with a particular emphasis on the safeguards associated with processing highly sensitive data as part of the algorithm training

---

[97] FTC, FTC Report to Congress: Combatting Online Harms through Innovation 2 (2022).

[98] AI (and other) Companies: Quietly Changing Your Terms of Service Could Be Unfair or Deceptive FTC (Feb. 13, 2024), available at https://www.ftc.gov/policy/advocacy-research/tech-at-ftc/2024/02/ai-other-companies-quietly-changing-your-terms-service-could-be-unfair-or-deceptive.

[99] AI and the Risk of Consumer Harm, FTC (Jan. 3, 2025), available at https://www.ftc.gov/policy/advocacy-research/tech-at-ftc/2025/01/ai-risk-consumer-harm.

process for large language models, as well as conspicuous and accurate disclosures relating to data practices.[100]

While this guidance is helpful, an important aspect is the FTC's enforcement approach and focus. The FTC provided further guidance into its analytical approach to evaluating AI claims in a February 2023 blog post titled "Keep Your AI Claims in Check."[101] In this blog post, the FTC indicates that if a company claims that their AI product or service is "better than" a non-AI product or service, the FTC will want specific evidence of qualitative superiority.[102] Similarly, if a claim is evaluated for being deceptive, the FTC will compare the claim to the AI product to "see if what's inside matches up with [the Company's] claims."[103] Notably, no intentionality is required; rather, the fact that there is a disconnect may itself be sufficient. In what it termed Operation AI Comply, the FTC brought enforcement actions against companies it claimed relied on AI to "supercharge deceptive or unfair contact that harms customers."[104] Targets of this enforcement effort included companies who the FTC claimed were "promoting an AI tool that enabled its customers to create fake reviews, []claiming to sell 'AI Lawyer' services, and [] claiming that they could use AI to help consumers make money through online storefronts."[105] Sometimes called "AI washing," such practices have also caught the attention of regulators such as the U.S. Securities and Exchange Commission.[106]

One notable area of attention for the FTC is the handling of sensitive data, including children's data and biometric data. In May 2023, the FTC released a policy statement regarding the misuse of biometric information and its potential harm to consumers.[107] While the statement does not directly address AI, recent enforcement actions have illustrated the FTC's focus on the allegedly surreptitious collection of biometric data.

---

100 *Id.*

101 *Keep Your AI Claims in Check*, FTC (Feb. 27, 2023), available at https://www.ftc.gov/business-guidance/blog/2023/02/keep-your-ai-claims-check.

102 *Id.*

103 *Id.*

104 *FTC Announces Crackdown on Deceptive AI Claims and Schemes*, FTC (Sept. 25, 2024), available at https://www.ftc.gov/news-events/news/press-releases/2024/09/ftc-announces-crackdown-deceptive-ai-claims-schemes#:~:text=%E2%80%9CThe%20FTC's%20enforcement%20actions%20make,and%20consumers%20are%20being%20protected.%E2%80%9D.

105 *Id.* The decision of the FTC to move forward in filing a complaint in these matters often is supported unanimously by FTC. The action against the company alleged to enable customers to write fake reviews, Rytr, was however only supported by three of the five FTC commissioners. In a Dissenting Statement authored by Commissioner Melissa Holyoak, and joined by the other dissenting commissioner Andrew N. Ferguson, it is noted that the FTC's complaint does not allege that users actually posted any of the draft reviews generated by Rytr, so the complaint "centers on alleging speculative harms." *In re Rytr, LLC*, Matter No. 2323052 at p. 2, available at https://www.ftc.gov/system/files/ftc_gov/pdf/holyoak-rytr-statement.pdf. Furthermore, there is no proof that Rytr itself made any misrepresentations; rather the FTC pursued a "means and instrumentalities" approach that is ill-fitting to the service Rytr provided. *See id.* at p. 3. It remains to be seen if this expansion will become the norm for FTC enforcement.

106 The SEC settled charges against two investment advisors, claiming that they made false statements about their purported use of AI, in exchange for $400,000 in civil penalties. *SEC Charges Two Investment Advisers with Making False and Misleading Statements about Their Use of Artificial Intelligence*, SEC.gov (Mar. 18, 2024), available at https://www.sec.gov/newsroom/press-releases/2024-36.

107 Press Release, FTC, FTC Warns about Misuses of Biometric Information and Harm to Consumers (May 18, 2023).

The FTC recently filed an enforcement action against a company who offered a weight-management and tracking service application directed at children. The FTC alleged that the company violated the Children's Online Privacy Protection Act (COPPA) by failing to provide direct notice to parents of information collection practices. In the complaint, the FTC seeks an order that the company delete any algorithm which was trained on personal information collected from children under thirteen years of age.[108]

The use of biometrics in connection with facial recognition technology has also become a key area of enforcement for the FTC. In a 2021 settlement with Everalbum, Inc., the FTC alleged that the company improperly used photos and videos of deactivated members to train its facial recognition technology.[109] As part of the remedy, the FTC required Everalbum to delete any "models or algorithms developed in whole or in part" using biometric information collected from deactivated member accounts.

In the FTC's March 2023 blog post on "Chatbots, deepfakes, and voice clones: AI deception for sale," the FTC provides specific advice in connection with security measures.[110] In this blog post, the FTC cautions companies to implement "durable, built-in features and not bug corrections or optional features" that can be undermined via modification or removal. To meet their obligations, the FTC advises companies to evaluate products starting at the design stage for "reasonably foreseeable . . . ways [the AI system] could be misused for fraud or cause other harm."[111]

The FTC has further emphasized that companies will be held to a standard of "real accountability" when benefiting from AI systems. That is, companies "must bear the responsibility of (1) conducting regular audits and impact assessments and (2) facilitating appropriate redress for erroneous or unfair algorithmic decisions."[112]

7.4.2. Consumer Fraud Protection Bureau

The CFPB enforces numerous federal consumer financial laws, including under the Consumer Financial Protection Act, which prohibits "unfair, deceptive, and abusive acts or practices" and the ECOA,[113] which makes it unlawful for any creditor to discriminate against any applicant, with respect to any aspect of a credit transaction, on the basis of race, color, religion, national origin, sex or marital status, age (provided the applicant has the capacity to contract), because all or part of the applicant's income derives from any public assistance program, or because the applicant has in good faith exercised any right under the Consumer Credit Protection Act.[114] ECOA provides that a creditor must provide a statement of specific reasons in writing to applicants against whom

---

108 Stipulated Order, *United States v. Kurbo, Inc.*, No. 22-CV-00945 (N.D. Cal. Mar. 3, 2022), at Section III (p. 7).

109 Decision and Order, *In the Matter of Everalbum, Inc.*, Dkt. No. C-4743 (May 6, 2021), at Section III (p. 4).

110 *Chatbots, Deepfakes, and Voice Clones: AI Deception for Sale*, FTC (Mar. 20, 2023), available at https://www.ftc.gov/business-guidance/blog/2023/03/chatbots-deepfakes-voice-clones-ai-deception-sale.

111 *Id.*

112 Combatting Online Harms, at 50-51, *supra* note 96.

113 12 U.S.C. 5511; 12 U.S.C. 5536(a)(1)(B); 12 U.S.C. 5481(12).

114 15 U.S.C. 1691(a). 15 U.S.C. 1691(d)(2)(A), (B); *see also* 15 U.S.C. 1691(d)(3).

adverse action is taken.[115] "Adverse action[s]" include denying an application for credit, terminating an existing credit account, making unfavorable changes to the terms of an existing account, and refusing to increase a credit limit.[116] Pursuant to Regulation B, a statement of reasons for adverse action taken "must be specific and indicate the principal reason(s) for the adverse action."[117]

On May 26, 2022, the CFPB issued guidance relating to complex algorithms used in connection with credit decisions.[118] The CFPB published a circular regarding the use of, and reliance upon, a complex algorithm to make decisions regarding the decision to deny credit or take other adverse actions. The specific question in the circular was whether a creditor that uses complex algorithms that they reply upon to make credit decisions need to comply with the ECOA's requirement to provide a statement of specific reasons that the adverse decision was taken. The CFPB opined that:

> Creditors who use complex algorithms, including artificial intelligence or machine learning, in any aspect of their credit decisions must still provide a notice that discloses the specific principal reasons for taking an adverse action. Whether a creditor is using a sophisticated machine learning algorithm or more conventional methods to evaluate an application, the legal requirement is the same: Creditors must be able to provide applicants against whom adverse action is taken with an accurate statement of reasons.[119]

Rather, the "mere fact that the technology it employs to evaluate applications is too complicated or opaque to understand" is not a defense for violating these laws.[120] Accordingly, the "ECOA and Regulation B do not permit creditors to use complex algorithms when doing so means they cannot provide the specific and accurate reasons for adverse actions."

7.4.3. Equal Employment Opportunity Commission

The EEOC is responsible for enforcing federal laws that prohibit discrimination against job applicants or employees based on race, color, religion, sex (including pregnancy, childbirth or related conditions, gender identity, and sexual orientation), national origin,

---

[115] *Id.*

[116] 4 12 CFR 1002.2(c).

[117] 5 12 CFR 1002.9(b)(2); *see also* 12 CFR Part 1002 (Supp. I), sec. 1002.9, para. 9(b)(2)-9 ("The Fair Credit Reporting Act (FCRA) requires a creditor to disclose when it has based its decision in whole or in part on information from a source other than the applicant or its own files. . . . The FCRA also requires a creditor to disclose, as applicable, a credit score it used in taking adverse action along with related information, including up to four key factors that adversely affected the consumer's credit score (or up to five factors if the number of inquiries made with respect to that consumer report is a key factor). Disclosing the key factors that adversely affected the consumer's credit score does not satisfy the ECOA requirement to disclose specific reasons for denying or taking other adverse action on an application or extension of credit.")

[118] CFPB Circular 2022-03, available at https://files.consumerfinance.gov/f/documents/cfpb_2022-03_circular_2022-05.pdf.

[119] *Id.* at p. 3.

[120] *Id.* at p. 4.

age (40 or older), disability, or genetic information.[121] Recognizing the evolving role of AI in employment practices, the EEOC has issued two publications regarding the interplay of the laws it enforces and AI.[122]

The EEOC issued a nonbinding technical assistance document explaining how the Americans with Disabilities Act (ADA) applies to the use of software, algorithms, and AI to make employment-related decisions about job applicants and employees.[123] In 2022, the EEOC issued a publication titled "The Americans with Disabilities Act and the Use of Software, Algorithms, and Artificial Intelligence to Assess Job Applicants and Employees" (the 2022 EEOC Publication).[124] The 2022 EEOC Publication noted that AI systems are used in a myriad of ways in the employment lifecycle of hiring, performance evaluation, promotion, and termination—including filtering resumes and applications, video interviewing software, and test software that creates "job fit" scores.[125] Further, the 2022 EEOC Publication identified some common ways in which employers could violate the ADA by using algorithmic decision-making tools, including

- Not providing a "reasonable accommodation" so that the job applicant or employee can be rated fairly and accurately by the algorithm.
- Relying on an algorithmic decision-making tool that intentionally or unintentionally "screens out" an individual with a disability despite their being able to do the job with a reasonable accommodation.
- Adopting an algorithmic decision-making tool that violates the ADA's restrictions on disability-related inquiries and medical examinations.[126]

In addition, the publication clarifies that the employer remains responsible even if the AI solution was created by an outside vendor and "may be held responsible for the actions of their agents, which may include entities such as software vendors, if the employer has given them authority to act on the employer's behalf."[127] In such a case, among other advice, the EEOC recommends asking the vendor "whether the tool was developed with individuals with disabilities in mind."[128]

Almost exactly one year later, the EEOC issued "Select Issues: Assessing Adverse Impact in Software, Algorithms, and Artificial Intelligence Used in Employment Selection

---

[121] Overview,U.S. Equal Employment Opportunity Commission (accessed Nov. 11, 2024).

[122] The EEOC's publication defines AI as set forth in the National Artificial Intelligence Initiative Act of 2020 at Section 5002(3) as a "machine-based system that can, for a given set of human-defined objectives, make predictions, recommendations or decisions influencing real or virtual environments."

[123] The ADA and AI: Applicants and Employees, EEOC-NVTA-2022-2, issued 05-12-2022, available at https://www.eeoc.gov/laws/guidance/americans-disabilities-act-and-use-software-algorithms-and-artificial-intelligence.

[124] *Id.*

[125] *Id.*

[126] *Id.* at #2; Question 13 ("An assessment includes 'disability-related inquiries' if it asks job applicants or employees questions that are likely to elicit information about a disability or directly asks whether an applicant or employee is an individual with a disability. It qualifies as a 'medical examination' if it seeks information about an individual's physical or mental impairments or health.").

[127] *Id.* at #3.

[128] *Id.* at Question 12.

Procedures under Title VII of the Civil Rights Act of 1964" (the 2023 EEOC Publication).[129] The 2023 EEOC Publication addresses questions employers may have about whether and how to monitor the newer algorithmic decision-making tools "to determine whether these procedures cause disproportionately large negative effects on the basis of race, color, religion, sex, or national origin under Title VII of the Civil Rights Act of 1964 ('Title VII')."[130] As with the 2022 EEOC Publication, this publication is nonbinding and does not have the effect of law.[131] While Title VII applies to a variety of phases of the employment lifecycle, the 2023 EEOC Publication is limited in application to whether an employer's "selection procedures," that is, the procedures it uses to make employment decisions such as hiring, promotion, and firing, have a "disparate impact" or "adverse impact" that is prohibited by Title VII.[132] A "selection procedure" is any "measure, combination of measures or procedure if it is used *as a basis for* an employment decision."[133] Thus, when algorithmic decision-making tools are "used to make or inform" decisions, the 2023 EEOC Publication applies.[134]

A selection procedure adversely impacts a particular protected group where the selection rate for individuals in that group is "substantially" less than the selection rate for individuals in another group, provided the employer cannot show that such use is "job related and consistent with business necessity pursuant to Title VII."[135] Like with the ADA, employers remain liable for a vendor's actions, particularly where the employer relies on the results of the vendor who acts as the employer's agent under Title VII.[136] Among other advice, the EEOC recommends that employers directly ask the vendor, at a minimum, "whether steps have been taken to evaluate whether use of the tool causes a substantially lower selection rate for individuals with a characteristic protected by Title VII."[137] However, the EEOC clarifies that an employer cannot blindly rely upon the vendor's assessment. Indeed "if the vendor is incorrect about its own assessment and the tool does result in either disparate impact discrimination or disparate treatment discrimination, the employer could still be liable."[138]

---

129 Select Issues: Assessing Adverse Impact in Software, Algorithms, and Artificial Intelligence Used in Employment Selection Procedures under Title VII of the Civil Rights Act of 1964 | U.S. Equal Employment Opportunity Commission (Short Title: Title VII and AI: Assessing Adverse Impact), EEOC-NVTA-2023-2, Issue Date 05-18-2023, available at https://www.eeoc.gov/laws/guidance/select-issues-assessing-adverse-impact-software-algorithms-and-artificial.

130 *Id.*

131 *Id.*

132 *Id.*

133 *Id.* at Question 1 (citing 29 C.F.R. § 1607.16(Q)).

134 *Id.*

135 *Id.* at Question 2. In addition, employers should drill down to understand the basis for the vendor's determination. For example, prior EEOC guidance sets forth a four-fifths rule, which is a rule of thumb for determining whether an impact violates Title VII. Employes should "ask the vendor specifically whether it relied on the four-fifths rule of thumb when determining whether use of the tool might have an adverse impact on the basis of a characteristic protected by Title VII, or whether it relied on a standard such as statistical significance that is often used by courts."

136 *Id.* at Question 3.

137 *Id.*

138 *Id.*

7.4.4. Department of Health and Human Services

The DHHS enforces the Health Information Portability and Accountability Act (HIPAA) through its Office for Civil Rights (OCR). HIPAA regulates "protected health information," which is information created or received by a HIPAA "covered entity," including a health plan, provider, employers (in certain functions), or health care clearinghouse that "relates to the past, present, or future physical or mental health or condition of an individual; the provision of health care to an individual; or the past, present, or future payment for the provision of health care to an individual" and identifies or is identifiable (i.e., there is a reasonable basis to believe the information can be used to identify the individual).[139]

While there is not significant guidance from DHHS, the agency set up an Office of the Chief Artificial Intelligence Officer (OCAIO), whose primary functions are to, among other things, drive implementation of the DHHS AI Strategy, stand up an AI governance structure within HHS, and coordinate HHS response to AI-federal mandates.[140]

7.4.5. The Future of Federal Regulatory Guidance

The fate of the guidance issued by regulatory agencies hangs in the balance due to the U.S. Supreme Court's opinion in *Loper Bright Enterprises v. Raimondo.*[141] In *Loper*, the Supreme Court struck down the nearly four-decade old precedence in *Chevron.*[142] Under *Chevron*, courts were to give deference to an agency's interpretation if "based on a permissible construction of the statute" after finding a statute is "silent or ambiguous with respect to the specific issue at hand."[143] *Loper* held that *Chevron* is inconsistent with the rules set forth for judicial review of agency action by the Administrative Procedure Act (APA).[144] Accordingly, it found that "courts need not and under the APA may not defer to an agency interpretation of the law simply because a statute is ambiguous."[145] Federal courts are still required to give deference to policymaking or agency fact-finding.[146] And the Supreme Court offered that "although an agency's interpretation of a statute 'cannot bind a court,' it may be especially informative 'to the extent it rests on factual premises within [the agency's] expertise.'"[147]

For regulatory agencies that have been leading efforts to issue guidance on AI—particularly the FTC—*Loper* could slow the ability to promptly address the guardrails needed to corral fast-moving technologies such as AI. Further, the implications of the Trump Administration's shift in focus to rooting out "ideological bias and engineered

---

139 45 CFR § 160.103.

140 *About the HHS Office of the Chief Artificial Intelligence Officer (OCAIO)*, HHS.gov, available at https://www.hhs.gov/programs/topic-sites/ai/ocaio/index.html (last accessed Nov. 18, 2024).

141 Loper Bright Enterprises v. Raimondo, 603 U.S. ____ (2024), 2024 WL 3208360 (Jun. 28, 2024).

142 Chevron U.S.A. Inc. v. Natural Resources Defense Council, Inc., 467 U.S. 837 (1984).

143 *Id.* at *14 (quoting *Chevron, U.S.A. v. Nat. Res. Def. Council, Inc.*, 467 U.S. 837, 843 (1984)).

144 5 U.S.C. §551 *et seq.* (1946).

145 *Id.*

146 *Id.*

147 *Id.* (quoting Bureau of Alcohol, Tobacco and Firearms v. FLRA, 464 U.S. 89, 98, n. 8 (1983)).

social agendas" are still unfolding.[148] As a result, unless Congress reaches consensus on a bipartisan bill, the future of AI regulation may continue at the state level.

However, one area in which federal agencies could forge an important leadership role with respect to AI technologies is raising the profile of innovators developing privacy and security-enhancing AI solutions. A key example is the FTC's Voice Cloning Challenge, an exploratory initiative designed to encourage the development of multidisciplinary approaches to protect consumers from AI-enabled voice cloning harms, such as fraud and the broader misuse of biometric data and creative content.[149] The FTC accepted applications from companies developing innovative technologies to prevent, monitor, and evaluate malicious voice cloning.[150] By awarding prizes to three companies and granting honorary mentions to several others, the FTC highlighted and elevated these technologies as the future of security-enhancing AI technologies.[151]

---

148 Executive Order on Removing Barriers to American Leadership in Artificial Intelligence, Jan. 23, 2025, 2025-02172 (90 FR 8741), available at https://www.whitehouse.gov/presidential-actions/2025/01/removing-barriers-to-american-leadership-in-artificial-intelligence/.

149 The FTC Voice Cloning Challenge, FTC, available at https://www.ftc.gov/news-events/contests/ftc-voice-cloning-challenge.

150 *Id.*

151 *Id.* The winning submissions uses AI algorithms to (1) differentiate between genuine and synthetic voice patterns, (2) add carefully crafted perturbations to voice samples to hinder the cyber criminal's cloning process, and (3) use off-the-shelf sensors already integrated in many devices to simultaneously measure speech acoustics and the co-occurring biosignals in the throat and mouth as a person is speaking, thus authenticating the human origin of voice recordings at the point of creation and embedding this authentication as a watermark or signature in the stream.

8 International Obligations for Privacy and Data Protection

By Reena R. Bajowala[1]

Global regulation of artificial intelligence (AI) and similar technologies has been rapidly accelerating, with almost 150 laws passed globally by the end of 2023.[2] Globally, Europe has taken the lead with enacting comprehensive AI legislation, but Asia, Latin America, and Canada are not far behind.

8.1. Europe at the Forefront

8.1.1. Same Law, New Tech: Application of the European Union's General Data Protection Regulation to the Flourishing AI Landscape

AI is not new.[3] Or perhaps more aptly, having existed in some form or another for decades, it is not as new as the General Data Protection Regulation (GDPR), Europe's landmark

---

1 The author thanks senior contributors Liz Harding and John Londot, and contributors Mark Bhuptani, Arda Goker, and Sarah Stein from Greenberg Traurig, LLP for their work in researching and drafting this chapter.

2 *Artificial Intelligence Index Report 2024*, Stanford, https://hai-production.s3.amazonaws.com/files/hai_ai-index-report-2024-smaller2.pdf.

3 Kurt Gödel, Alonzo Church, and Alan Turing established important theoretical underpinnings for AI in the 1930s. Wolfgang Ertel, Introduction to Artificial Intelligence 34 (2d ed., 2017). Then in 1955, American computer scientist and AI pioneer John McCarthy became one of the first to define the term "artificial intelligence," claiming "[t]he goal of AI is to develop machines that behave as though they were intelligent." *Id.* at 1. Elaine Rich, another early AI computer scientist, more poignantly captured the potential of AI, stating that "*artificial intelligence* . . . is the study of how to make computers do things at which, at the moment, people are better." W. Keith Robinson, *Enabling Artificial Intelligence*, 60 Hous. L. Rev. 331, 333 (2022–2023) (quoting Elaine Rich, Artificial Intelligence 1 (Eric M. Munson & Joseph M. Murphy, eds., 1983)).

data protection law that went into effect in May 2018.[4] Nevertheless, the explosive rise of exciting new AI technologies, particularly large language models and generative AI tools, has focused a regulatory spotlight on AI.[5] While the GDPR does not expressly mention AI, it does govern AI to the extent an AI technology ingests personal data[6] about individuals in the European Economic Area (EEA)[7] and the United Kingdom.[8] This section aims to highlight key aspects of how AI fits into the GDPR's regulatory framework, which is the "house foundation" for data protection in Europe.[9]

An official study for the European Parliament concluded, after analyzing the relationship between the GDPR and AI, that the use of AI is generally compatible with the GDPR.[10] European regulators, such as the UK Information Commissioner's Office (ICO) and the French Data Protection Authority (CNIL), have similarly recognized this compatibility and issued guidance addressing the interaction between AI and the GDPR's legal framework.[11] Each of these authorities at some level analyzed AI through the lens of the GDPR's overarching data processing[12] principles, which are set forth in Article 5 and provide a roadmap for the below discussion of the GDPR's application to AI.

---

4 Regulation 2016/679 of the European Parliament and of the Council of April 27, 2016, on the Protection of Natural Persons with Regard to the Processing of Personal Data and on the Free Movement of Such Data, and Repealing Directive 95/46/EC (General Data Protection Regulation), 2016 O.J. (L 119) 1 (EU) [hereinafter GDPR].

5 Müge Fazlioglu, *Consumer Perspectives of Privacy and Artificial Intelligence*, IAPP (Feb. 2024), https://iapp.org/resources/article/consumer-perspectives-of-privacy-and-ai/.

6 The GDPR defines "personal data" as "any information relating to an identified or identifiable natural person ('data subject'); an identifiable natural person is one who can be identified, directly or indirectly, in particular by reference to an identifier such as a name, an identification number, location data, an online identifier or to one or more factors specific to the physical, physiological, genetic, mental, economic, cultural or social identity of that natural person." GDPR at article 4(1).

7 The EEA includes the EU's Member States and Iceland, Liechtenstein, and Norway. *Glossary: European Economic Area*, European Comm'n, https://ec.europa.eu/eurostat/statistics-explained/index.php?title=Glossary:European_Economic_Area_(EEA) (last visited Feb. 29, 2024).

8 Following Brexit, with respect to the personal data of individuals in the United Kingdom, the provisions of the European Union's (EU) GDPR were incorporated into the law of the United Kingdom "as the UK GDPR." *Overview—Data Protection and the EU*, UK Info. Comm'n Off., https://ico.org.uk/for-organisations/data-protection-and-the-eu/overview-data-protection-and-the-eu/ (last visited Feb. 29, 2024). For purposes of this section, references to the "GDPR" apply equally to the "UK GDPR."

9 Although the GDPR is the cornerstone piece of legislation governing personal data protection in Europe, "it operates in a much larger, ever-evolving context that includes at the very least dozens of regulators' guidelines, courts[] ruling at [the] national and European level[s], as well as legislation that addresses other aspects and challenges of responsible (personal) data governance." Eduardo Ustaran et al., European Data Protection Law and Practice, at Introduction (3d ed., 2023).

10 European Parliamentary Research Service, *The Impact of the General Data Protection Regulation (GDPR) on Artificial Intelligence*, Eur. Parl. 87 (Jun. 2020), https://www.europarl.europa.eu/RegData/etudes/STUD/2020/641530/EPRS_STU(2020)641530_EN.pdf [hereinafter *Parliamentary Study*].

11 *E.g.*, *Guidance on AI and Data Protection*, ICO, https://ico.org.uk/for-organisations/uk-gdpr-guidance-and-resources/artificial-intelligence/guidance-on-ai-and-data-protection/ (Mar. 15, 2023); *AI: Ensuring GDPR Compliance*, CNIL (Sept. 21, 2022), https://www.cnil.fr/en/ai-ensuring-gdpr-compliance; *AI Practical Sheets*, CNIL, https://cnil.fr/fr/les-fiches-pratiques-ia (last visited Feb. 29, 2024).

12 The GDPR defines "processing" as "any operation or set of operations which is performed on personal data or on sets of personal data, whether or not by automated means, such as collection, recording, organisation, structuring, storage, adaptation or alteration, retrieval, consultation, use, disclosure by transmission, dissemination or otherwise making available, alignment or combination, restriction, erasure or destruction." GDPR, article 4(2).

8.1.1.1. Lawfulness, Fairness, and Transparency

With respect to AI-assisted data processing, fairness and transparency are crucial.[13] The fairness principle has two separate dimensions: informational fairness and substantive fairness.[14]

Informational fairness is directly connected to the notion of transparency and requires that data subjects must not be misled about the processing of their personal data.[15] Importantly, a specific aspect of transparency in the context of AI systems is a data subject's ability to access information about an AI's training data, which could reveal potential unfairness caused by biased data or algorithms.[16] This conception of transparency is particularly important when AI systems are used to make automated decisions about individuals.[17] Indeed, as the ICO observed, "[i]f an AI-assisted decision is made about someone without some form of explanation of (or information about) the decision, this may limit their autonomy and scope for self-determination."[18] Also in the spirit of transparency/informational fairness, Articles 13 and 14 require controllers[19] to provide individuals with information about the existence of automated decision making, including profiling, that produces legal and/or other significant effects, as well as information about the logic involved and the potential consequences of the processing on the individual.[20] Similarly, Article 15 grants data subjects the right to affirmatively request and obtain the same information from the controller.[21]

On the other hand, the notion of substantive fairness relates to the content and effect of an automated inference or decision.[22] Under the GDPR, data subjects "should have the right not to be subject to a decision, which may include a measure, evaluating personal aspects . . . based solely on automated processing and which produces legal effects . . . or similarly affects [the data subject], such as automatic refusal of an online credit application or e-recruiting practices without any human intervention."[23] This dimension of fairness includes processing of personal data for purposes of profiling, and considers whether the combination of criteria involved has produced an automated decision that has "discriminatory effects . . . on the basis of racial or ethnic origin, political opinion,

---

13 "Personal data shall be . . . processed lawfully, fairly and in a transparent manner in relation to the data subject." GDPR, article 5(1)(a); Moreover, "[t]he principle of transparency requires that any information addressed to the public or to the data subject be concise, easily accessible and easy to understand, and that clear and plain language and, additionally, where appropriate, visualisation be used." GDPR recital 58.

14 *Parliamentary Study*, *supra* note 8, at 44–45; *see also* GDPR recital 60 ("The principles of fair and transparent processing require that the data subject be informed of the existence of the processing operation and its purposes.").

15 *Parliamentary Study*, *supra* note 8, at 44.

16 *Id.*

17 *Id.*

18 *Legal Framework*, ICO, https://ico.org.uk/for-organisations/uk-gdpr-guidance-and-resources/artificial-intelligence/explaining-decisions-made-with-artificial-intelligence/part-1-the-basics-of-explaining-ai/legal-framework/ (last visited Feb. 29, 2024) [hereinafter *Legal Framework*].

19 The GDPR defines the term "controller" as "the natural or legal person, public authority, agency or other body which, alone or jointly with others, determines the purposes and means of the processing of personal data." GDPR, art. 4(7).

20 GDPR art. 13(2)(f); GDPR art. 14(2)(g); *see also* GDPR art. 22(1); *Legal Framework*, *supra* note 16.

21 GDPR art. 15(1)(h).

22 *Parliamentary Study*, *supra* note 8 at 45.

23 GDPR recital 71.

religion or beliefs, trade union membership, genetic or health status or sexual orientation."[24] One aspect of the problem leading to such discriminatory effects is AI systems being trained on past human judgments, and therefore baking into training datasets the biases of the humans who made these judgments (e.g., a loan eligibility determination program trained on decisions by a racially prejudiced loan officer outputting biased eligibility determinations instead of evaluating applicants' relevant characteristics).[25] If past decisions were influenced by prejudice, the system will reproduce the same logic.[26] These biased results may persist even if forbidden discriminatory features are not used as inputs for the AI system.[27] For example, assume a recruitment software is trained on hiring decisions by a racially biased HR manager, and the HR manager's racially motivated hiring decisions correlate to fewer selections from neighborhoods with a high representation of members of the race the manager dislikes.[28] Under those circumstances, even if race is not an input criterion for hiring decisions, the AI system may disfavor candidates from those neighborhoods, which in turn would result in racially biased results (because those neighborhoods contain a high representation of the race the manager dislikes).[29] Recital 71 requires controllers to implement technical and organizational measures that prevent such effects.[30] One such measure is incorporating human review of AI-generated decisions.[31] This is reflected in Article 22, which gives individuals the right to not be subject to solely automated decisions if they produce legal or other significant effects.[32]

8.1.1.2. Purpose Limitation

The GDPR requires personal data to be "collected for [only] specified, explicit and legitimate purposes and not further processed in a manner that is incompatible with those purposes."[33] This purpose limitation also relates to Article 6, which requires the controller to be able to justify its processing of personal data on a specifically enumerated legal basis.[34] One of the main purpose limitation concerns implicated by the operation of AI technologies is the repurposing of personal data for purposes other than those for which the data was originally collected.[35] For such repurposing to be lawful under the GDPR,

---

24 GDPR recital 71.
25 *Parliamentary Study*, *supra* note 8 at 20.
26 *Id.*
27 *Id.*
28 *Id.*
29 *Id.*
30 *Id.*
31 *Id.* at 22.
32 GDPR art. 22(1).
33 GDPR art. 5(1)(b).
34 The legal bases for processing set forth in Article 6 are consent, necessity for performance of a contract to which the data subject is a party, necessity of processing for the controller's compliance with a legal obligation, necessity for the protection of any individual's vital interests, necessity for the performance of a task carried out for the public's interest or by virtue of the exercise of official authority, and necessity for the controller's or a third party's legitimate interests (except where the data subject's interests or fundamental rights or freedoms would require his or her personal data's protection). GDPR art. 6(1).
35 *Parliamentary Study*, *supra* note 8, at 45.

the new purpose must be compatible with the original purpose.[36] For example, an online retailer may collect personal data from a data subject for the purpose of processing an order. But it may then want to use personal data involved in the transaction to train an AI system it utilizes to better serve its customers. Such repurposing could only be carried out if the new collection and processing purposes are compatible with the original ones, or with a newly obtained consent.

8.1.1.3. Data Minimization

The GDPR requires that personal data be "adequate, relevant, and limited to what is necessary in relation to the purposes for which they are processed."[37] It also requires that data minimization measures are implemented "by design" and "by default."[38] AI systems inherently involve data analytics and the processing of large quantities of data to discover and apply new correlations to achieve desired outcomes.[39] Naturally, this appears to cause tension with the data minimization principle.[40] However, such apparent tension is decreased when considered in light of the minimization principle's link to the notion of proportionality.[41] In that regard, inclusion and retention of additional data for processing will be justifiable if the benefits conferred by the additional data processing by an AI system outweigh the risks to data subjects, and adequate security measures, which may include pseudonymization,[42] are in place.[43] Additionally, where personal data is used only as training data input (or as part of a statistical database), and not used to make individualized predictions or decisions, the data minimization principle is relaxed and such processing lies outside the GDPR's protective scope.[44]

8.1.1.4. Accuracy

The accuracy principle requires that personal data be "accurate and, where necessary, kept up to date," and that all inaccurate data "are erased or rectified without delay."[45] Accuracy concerns arise when personal data is used as input into AI systems.[46]

---

[36] The criteria relevant to determining whether a new purpose is compatible with the original purpose are as follows: (1) the distance between the two purposes, (2) the new purpose's alignment with the expectations of the data subject, and (3) the controller's safeguards adopted to ensure fair processing and prevention of undue impacts; Parliamentary Study, *supra* note 8, at 46 (citing *Opinion 3/2013 of the Article 29 Data Protection Working Party on "Purpose Limitation,"* 00569/13/EN WP 203 (Apr. 2013)).

[37] GDPR art. 5(1)(c). The considerations pertaining to the data minimization principle apply equally to the closely related storage limitation principle, which is therefore not discussed separately in this section. *See* GDPR art. 5(1)(e).

[38] GDPR Recital 78.

[39] *Parliamentary Study, supra* note 10, at 47.

[40] *Id.*

[41] *Id.*

[42] The GDPR defines "pseudonymisation" as "the processing of personal data in such a manner that the personal data can no longer be attributed to a specific data subject without the use of additional information, provided that such additional information is kept separately and is subject to technical and organisational measures to ensure that the personal data are not attributed to an identified or identifiable natural person." GDPR art. 4(5).

[43] *Parliamentary Study, supra* note 8, at 47; Ensuring adequate security of personal data in AI processing is required by the integrity and confidentiality principle. GDPR art. 5(1)(f); Since this principle permeates every aspect of AI development and use, it is not separately addressed in this section.

[44] *Parliamentary Study, supra* note 8, at 47.

[45] GDPR art. 5(1)(d).

[46] *Id.*

AI-assisted decisions made using inaccurate personal data could harm data subjects by outputting results that are misaligned with the individual's profile. Such accuracy concerns decrease when personal data is used in a training dataset and not as input for generating individualized decisions/outputs.[47] In either case, adherence to the accuracy principle is necessary not only to reduce the risk of data subject harm but also to promote the efficacy of AI tools.

The drive to use newer and better AI tools in virtually every commercial industry and every facet of daily life is the new global reality. While AI usage is not inherently inconsistent with the GDPR, to avoid regulatory enforcement and protect personal data, entities subject to the GDPR must adhere to its principles when using personal data in AI systems.

8.1.2. Enter the EU's Artificial Intelligence Act

As a result of the fast development of AI technologies, European Union (EU) policymakers pledged to develop a human-centered approach to AI to ensure innovation flourishes while protecting fundamental rights. In April 2021, the European Commission (the "Commission") unveiled the first ever legal framework on AI called the Artificial Intelligence Act (the "AIA").[48] Parliament reached an agreement on the AIA in December 2023, which would be the first regulation in the world that makes a substantial contribution to the development of global rules and principles for AI. The AIA was formally adopted by the European Parliament on March 13, 2024, came into effect on August 1, 2024, and will be fully enforceable in August 2026.

The main priority of AIA is to make sure that AI systems used in the EU are "safe, transparent, traceable, non-discriminatory and environmentally friendly."[49] The AI systems should also be "overseen by people, rather than by automation to prevent harmful outcomes."[50] The general objective of the AIA is to ensure that the development and use of AI systems are trustworthy and sustainable to use in the long run.

8.1.2.1. To Whom Does the AI Act Apply?

The AIA primarily applies to (1) providers of AI systems established in the EU or established in a third country placing AI systems on the EU market to put them into service in the EU (e.g., a developer of a CV-screening tool), (2) users of AI systems located in the EU (e.g., a company using the CV-screening tool), and (3) providers and users of AI systems located in a third country where the output produced by the systems is used in the EU. In other words, the AIA will apply to both public and private actors inside and out of the EU as long as the AI system is placed on the EU market, or its use affects people within the EU. What counts is whether the AI system or service has an impact on European citizens, not where the company that provides the AI system or service is located (physically

---

47 *Id.*

48 *Regulation (EU) 2024/1689 of the European Parliament and of the Council of 13 June 2024 laying down harmonised rules on artificial intelligence, OJ L 119 [hereinafter the EU AI Act]*.

49 *EU AI Act: first regulation on artificial intelligence*, EUR. PARLIAMENT: TOPICS (Jun. 8, 2023, 11:45 AM), https://www.europarl.europa.eu/topics/en/article/20230601STO93804/eu-ai-act-first-regulation-on-artificial-intelligence.

50 *Id.*

or legally).[51] This means that the EU will likely serve as a single decider for the management of AI applications (much like it is for personal data under the GDPR).[52] All companies and vendors will have to deal with the EU rather than individual Member States when proving compliance with the regulation.[53]

8.1.2.2. How Is AI Defined?

The AIA regulates "AI systems," the definition of which has been heavily criticized.[54] AI is defined as "software that is developed with one or more of the techniques and approaches listed in Annex I and can, for a given set of human-defined objectives, generate outputs such as content, predictions, recommendations, or decisions influencing the environments they interact with."[55] Annex I further contains a list of AI techniques and approaches such as machine learning, logic and knowledge based, and statistical approaches.[56] This definition is broad by any standard.

Subsequent guidance from the European Commission (EC) details the seven main elements of an "AI system" as: (1) a machine-based system; (2) that is designed to operate with varying levels of autonomy; (3) that may exhibit adaptiveness after deployment; (4) and that, for explicit or implicit objectives; (5) infers, from the input it receives, how to generate outputs (6) such as predictions, content, recommendations, or decisions (7) that can influence physical or virtual environments."[57] While most of these elements are required, including the "capability to infer," note that adaptiveness is not a "decisive condition" to a system being an "AI system."[58] Further, the EC expanded upon Article 12 of the AIA, which noted systems outside of the scope of the definition of "AI systems," including systems for improving mathematical optimization, basic data processing, systems based on class heuristics, and simple prediction systems.[59]The AIA does not clarify how various components of AI systems should be treated. In practice, AI systems are not isolated technologies and often integrate into larger technical systems that encompass organizations, people, infrastructure, and processes.[60] In other words, AI systems involve several steps (often connected) performed by both humans and AI where decisions are

---

51 Luciano Floridi, *The European Legislation on AI: A Brief Analysis of Its Philosophical Approach*, 34 Phil. & Tech. 215, 216 (2021).

52 *Id.*

53 Note that the AIA is a *regulation* like the GDPR where Member States must strictly comply compared to the ePrivacy Directive which is a *directive* that sets a minimum standard for each Member State to comply with.

54 Tambiama Madiga, *EU Legislation in Progress: Artificial Intelligence Act*, Eur. Parl. Research Service 1, 8 (Jun. 2023); Martin Ebers et al., *The European Commission's Proposal for an Artificial Intelligence Act—A Critical Assessment by Members of the Robotics and AI Law Society (RAILS)*, 4 Multidisciplinary Sci. J. (Special Issue) 589, 590 (2021).

55 *EU AI Act, supra* note 48, at art. 3(1).

56 *Commission Annexes to the Proposal for a Regulation of the European Parliament and of the Council Laying Down Harmonised Rules on Artificial Intelligence (Artificial Intelligence Act) and Amending Certain Union Legislative Acts*, Annex I COM (2021) 206 final (Apr. 21, 2021) [hereinafter *Annexes to the EU AI Act*].

57 *Commission Guidelines on the definition of an artificial intelligence system established by Regulation (EU) 2024/1689 (AI Act)*, Annex C (2025) 924 final (Feb. 2, 2025) at art. II(9).

58 *Id.* at art. II(3)(23), II(5)(26).

59 *Id.* at art. II(5.2).

60 Amit K. Chopra & Munindar P. Singh, *Sociotechnical Systems and Ethics in the Large*, in AIES '18: Proceedings of the 2018 AAAI/ACM Conference on AI, Ethics, & Society 48, 48, 53 (Dec. 27, 2018).

made by both technical properties and human involvement.[61] The AIA does not clarify whether separate components of the AI systems would be individually required to conform to the AIA or what the implications would be if a stand-alone component was not compliant.[62]

8.1.2.3. Risk Levels

The AIA fundamentally focuses on use cases and sets forth a four-tiered risk categorization for AI applications that focuses on risks to the health, safety, and fundamental rights of natural persons concerned.[63] The four types of risks are unacceptable risk, high risk, limited risk, and minimal risk. Each category is given a set of regulations proportionate to the potential harm associated with the AI system. High-risk AI systems are the main focus of the AIA regulation.

I. Unacceptable Risk: Prohibited AI Practices

If an AI system is classified as an "unacceptable risk," it is prohibited from entering the EU market. The AIA contains four prohibited categories, three of which are banned in their entirety (two relating to manipulation and one related to social scoring). The other category includes "real time" and "remote" biometric identification systems that are prohibited except for specific law enforcement purposes.[64]

The two manipulative scenarios include AI systems that (1) deploy subliminal techniques beyond a person's consciousness in order to materially distort a person's behavior that is likely to cause that person or another person physical or psychological harm, and (2) exploit any of the vulnerabilities of a specific group of persons due to demographics in a manner that is likely to cause physical or psychological harm.[65]

The social scoring prohibition includes AI systems that are (1) used by or on behalf of public authorities, (2) to generate a "trustworthiness" score, and (3) lead to either unjustified or disproportionate treatment of individuals or groups, or detrimental treatment, which while justifiable and proportionate occurs in an unrelated "context" from the input data. The "context" exemption in (3) appears to be designed to keep reputation systems out of scope.[66] If viewed narrowly, the social scoring can only relate to input data surrounding public authorities. Taken more broadly, however, this social scoring may implicate credit card records and welfare support since both involve the flow of finances.[67] Employment in the public sector may also be affected, for example, where automated

---

61 Min Chen & Amos Golan, *What May Visualization Processes Optimize?* 22(12) IEEE Transactions on Visualization & Computer Graphics 2619, 2632.

62 Ebers et al., *supra* note 54, at 591.

63 Sebastian Felix Schwemer et al., *Legal AI Systems in the EU's proposed Artificial Intelligence Act*, in Proc. of the Second Int'l Workshop on AI and Intel. Assistance for Legal Prof. in the Digital Workplace (LegalAIIA 2021), held in conjunction with ICAIL 2021 1, 3 (Jul. 8, 2021).

64 Michael Veale & Frederik Zuidrveen Borgesius, *Demystifying the Draft EU Artificial Intelligence Act*, 4 Computer L. R. Int'l 97, 98 (2021).

65 *EU AI Act*, *supra* note 48, at art. 5(1)(a–b); *Id.* at Recital 15.

66 Veale & Zuiderveen Borgesius, *supra* note 61, at 100.

67 *Id.*

"social media background checks" used to score the online lives or job applicants could concern aspects of trustworthiness.[68]

Lastly, the AIA bans some uses of "real-time" biometric systems in publicly available spaces by law enforcement. For example, a large-scale CCTV network coupled with facial recognition technology that instantaneously, or without significant delay, captures, prepares, and identifies individuals.[69] The risk is that the use of AI systems involving biometric information may pose a serious proportionality problem since they may process data from an indiscriminate number of individuals for the identification of only a few individuals (e.g., a large-scale CCTV network in an airport or train station that scans biometric information).[70] Issues of properly providing notice to individuals about the processing of their personal data in this scenario, along with difficulties for such individuals to exercise their rights (e.g., access, correct, deletion, etc.), raise complex challenges for these systems.[71]

The EC issued guidance detailing these prohibited AI practices in February of 2025.[72]

II. High Risk: Highly Regulated

The AIA stipulates that AI systems that pose a "high risk" to the "health, safety, and fundamental rights" must fulfill rigorous requirements before entering the market. This is the main focus of the AIA.[73] This category includes AI systems that are (1) products or safety components of products already covered by certain EU health and safety legislation (for example, medical devices and toys)[74] and (2) implemented in crucial sectors such as biometric identification systems (e.g., a building uses fingerprints to enter), critical infrastructures, education, employment, law enforcement, and migration.[75] In other words, the high-risk category aims to ensure that systems that produce outputs with potentially significant societal impacts are held to the highest standards of transparency, reliability, and accountability.

Most of the requirements that come along with a "high risk" designation will fall on the provider of the AI system (i.e., the developer of the AI system). Before putting a high-risk AI system into the EU market, a provider must conduct a conformity assessment to demonstrate compliance and that the AI system is trustworthy AI.[76] Providers of high-risk AI systems are also required to register their systems in an EU database managed by the

---

68 *Id.*

69 *Id.*

70 *Joint Opinion 5/2021 of Eur. Data Protection Board [EDPB] & Eur. Data Protection Supervisor [EDPS] on the "proposal for a Regulation of the European Parliament and of the Council Laying Down Harmonized Rules on Artificial Intelligence (Artificial Intelligence Act)"* (Jun. 18, 2021), at ¶ 30.

71 *Id.*

72 *Commission Guidelines on prohibited artificial intelligence practices established by Regulation (EU) 2024/1689 (AI Act)*, Annex C (2025) 884 final (Feb. 4, 2025)

73 *EU AI Act, supra* note 48, at Recital 15; *Id.* at art. 7(2).

74 *See Annexes to the EU AI Act*, Annex II COM (2021) 206 final (Apr. 21, 2021).

75 *Annexes to the EU AI Act*, Annex III COM (2021) 206 final (Apr. 21, 2021).

76 *Artificial Intelligence—Questions and Answers*, Eur. Commission, https://ec.europa.eu/commission/presscorner/detail/en/QANDA_21_1683 (Aug. 1, 2024).

Commission.[77] Any AI system already governed by existing EU legislation will fall under those third-party conformity frameworks (e.g., medical devices).[78] If an AI system is not already governed by EU legislation, it will need to conduct its own conformity assessment where the provider self-assesses its compliance with relevant law. Only biometric systems that are high risk require a conformity assessment conducted by a "notified body."[79]

Once a high-risk AI system enters the EU marketplace, compliance obligations continue, namely, risk management systems put in place to track risks associated with the AI system. The obligations include, first, creating a *quality management system*, which is already widely practiced (e.g., ISO).[80] Second, if a provider trains models, the AI systems will need to meet *data quality criteria*, including relevance, representativeness, accuracy, completeness, and application-area-specific properties. Datasets that are trained only need to meet these obligations "sufficiently" and "in view of the intended purpose of the system."[81] Third, the AIA contains obligations regarding the *accuracy, robustness, and cybersecurity* of AI systems. Fourth, providers will need to create *technical documentation*. The requirements are extensive, but the provider does not need to publish the technical documentation—it only needs to provide it to regulators or organizations involved in the conformity assessment. Fifth, providers must *log* certain data in order to allow traceability based on the AI system's risks. For example, if HR uses a facial recognition technology to ensure individuals who apply for a job are the same as those who show up to a virtual interview, the provider must include the periods of use, any input data leading to a match of the applicant and interviewee, and implement a mechanism to record the identities of the job applicant and the individual in the virtual interview.[82] Lastly, providers must ensure there is *human oversight* incorporated into the AI system. The goal here is to minimize risks to health, safety, and fundamental rights.[83]

Concerns had been expressed by both industry and governments that foundational models underpinning generative AI systems would be designated as "high risk" under the AIA, meaning that each would have to meet the ongoing requirements that come along with a "high risk" rating as discussed above.[84] The AIA did not make that designation. Rather, foundational models have certain recordkeeping and documentation requirements and may have enhanced obligations if they carry "systemic risk" but do not automatically get a high-risk rating.[85]

---

77 Madiga, *supra* note 54, at 5.
78 *Id.*
79 *Id.* A notified body is an organization designated by an EU country to assess the conformity of certain products before being placed on the market.
80 *EU AI Act*, *supra* note 48, at art. 17.
81 *EU AI Act*, *supra* note 48, at Recital 44.
82 *EU AI Act*, *supra* note 48, at arts. 12(4), 14(5).
83 *EU AI Act*, *supra* note 48, at art. 14(2).
84 Will Henshall, *E.U.'s AI Regulation Could Be Softened after Pushback from Biggest Members*, TIME MAGAZINE (Nov. 22, 2023), https://time.com/6338602/eu-ai-regulation-foundation-models/.
85 *EU AI Act*, *supra* note 49.

III. Limited and Minimal Risk: Transparency Requirements and No Obligations

AI systems that fall into the "limited risk" category must adhere to transparency guidelines. This category includes AI systems like chatbots which must disclose that they are not run by humans and any other systems that interact with humans. This also includes AI systems that generate or manipulate images, audio, or video content—also known as "deep fakes." Minimal risk AI systems can be developed and used in the EU without conforming to any additional requirements. "Limited" and "minimal" risk AI systems would be encouraged but not required to adhere to the "high-risk" obligations.[86]

The AIA is the first of its kind and the world's first attempt to create an AI regulation that promotes innovation while protecting the fundamental rights of individuals. The risk levels create parameters and specific regulation for each type of AI system for providers and users to follow and to ensure they create an ethical AI system.

8.2. Canada: Moving from "Soft Law" to a Regulatory Framework for Artificial Intelligence

The AI sector in Canada has received considerable attention and funding from federal and provincial governments, as well as from universities investing in AI research.[87] In the past, much of the attempt to regulate AI focused on "soft law" rather than clear legal guidelines designed specifically for AI.[88] For example, the Canadian government released a set of principles relating to its use of AI.[89] Since there is no AI-specific regulation, AI is default-governed by data protection laws such as the Personal Information Protection and Electronic Documents Act (PIPEDA) and Quebec's Law 25. Neither PIPEDA nor Law 25 specifically mentions AI, but each captures the rise of newer technology and sets out rules and principles that consider the impact of AI.

---

86 *See, e.g.*, *EU AI Act*, *supra* note 48, at art. 69 (providing for the establishment of "codes of conduct intended to foster the voluntary application to AI systems other than high [ ] risk AI systems of the requirements [applicable to high risk AI systems under the Act]").

87 *See, e.g.*, Christina Aguis, *AI Funding in Canada & Major Research Cities*, Medium (Feb. 13, 2019), https://medium.com/datadriveninvestor/ai-funding-in-canada-major-research-cities-d4c41ede55a3; *Canadian Researchers Connect with Business and International Peers to Train Next Generation of Science and Engineering Leaders*, Nat. Sci. & Eng'g Rsch. Council of Can. (Jul. 16, 2018), https://www.nserc-crsng.gc.ca/Media-Media/NewsDetail-DetailNouvelles_eng.asp?ID=996; *Launch of Special Call for Research on Artificial Intelligence, Health and Society*, Soc. Sci. & Human. Rsch. Council, https://www.sshrc-crsh.gc.ca/news_room-salle_de_presse/latest_news-nouvelles_recentes/2018/ai_health_society-ia_sante_societe-eng.aspx (May 9, 2018); *Artificial Intelligence: Ensuring the Ethical, Transparent and Accountable Design of AI Technologies*, Univ. of Ottawa, https://research.uottawa.ca/special-projects/artificialintelligence (last visited Feb. 26, 2024); Geoffrey Vendeville, *Eight U of T Artificial Intelligence Researchers Named CIFAR AI Chairs*, Univ. Of Toronto (Dec. 9, 2019), https://www.utoronto.ca/news/eight-u-t-artificial-intelligence-researchers-named-cifar-ai-chairs; *Artificial Intelligence*, Univ. of Alberta, https://www.ualberta.ca/research/our-research/key-strengths/ai.html (last visited Feb. 26, 2024); *Artificial Intelligence*, Université de Montréal, https://www.umontreal.ca/en/artificialintelligence/ (last visited Feb. 26, 2024).

88 Teresa Scassa, *AI and Data Protection Law*, in Artificial Intelligence and the Law in Canada 1, 7 (Florian Martin-Bariteau & Teresa Scassa, eds., LexisNexis Canada, 2021).

89 *Guiding Principles for the Use of AI in Government,* Gov't of Canada, https://www.canada.ca/en/government/system/digital-government/digital-government-innovations/responsible-use-ai/principles.html (May 30, 2024).

8.2.1. Federal Framework: PIPEDA

PIPEDA does not expressly address AI or automated decision making, but elements of the law do apply to companies' use of technology with respect to personal information. PIPEDA is based on principles that are intended to be technologically neutral, allowing it to evolve as technology develops.[90] PIPEDA's provisions, for example, have been applied to the collection, use, and disclosure of personal information by automated means.[91]

8.2.1.1. PIPEDA Principles

Consequently, while PIPEDA does not expressly address AI, developers and companies that use AI systems must comply with PIPEDA and its fair information principles.[92] Primarily, all parties need to ensure valid consent is obtained and the collection, use, and disclosure of personal information is for an appropriate purpose.[93]

Numerous issues have arisen regarding the collection of personal information in the context of AI. One question is whether personal information is collected if it is not also recorded, or if it is obtained from publicly available information on the internet.[94] In Alberta, a controversy arose over the collection of information using facial recognition technology from cameras in a shopping center. The shopping center owner asserted the information was not about individuals, since only aggregate demographic data was recorded (e.g., age and gender). But the Office of the Privacy Commissioner (OPC) found that the technology captured and stored images (even if just for a short time), and that this constituted a collection of information.[95]

8.2.1.2. PIPEDA Reform

PIPEDA dates back to 2001, and due to resistance from the private sector at the time, the government adopted a soft approach to enforcement.[96] There has been considerable discussion to modernize and bring PIPEDA into alignment with the GDPR, which is more

---

[90] *A Regulatory Framework for AI: Recommendations for PIPEDA Reform*, Off. of the Privacy Comm'r of Can., https://www.priv.gc.ca/en/about-the-opc/what-we-do/consultations/completed-consultations/consultation-ai/reg-fw_202011/ (Nov. 12, 2020).

[91] *Social Media Companies Should Take Steps to Prevent Unlawful Data Scraping, Global Privacy Authorities Say*, Off. of the Privacy Comm'r of Can. (Aug. 24, 2023), https://www.priv.gc.ca/en/opc-news/news-and-announcements/2023/nr-c_20230824/.

[92] These principles include accountability, appropriate purposes, consent, limitation on collection, use, disclosure, retention, accuracy, security, openness, individual access, and a process for individuals to challenge compliance. *See PIPEDA fair information principles*, Off. of the Privacy Comm'r of Can., https://www.priv.gc.ca/en/privacy-topics/privacy-laws-in-canada/the-personal-information-protection-and-electronic-documents-act-pipeda/p_principle/ (May 1, 2024).

[93] *Principles for Responsible, Trustworthy and Privacy-Protective Generative AI technologies*, Off. of the Privacy Comm'r of Can., https://www.priv.gc.ca/en/privacy-topics/technology/artificial-intelligence/gd_principles_ai/ (Dec. 7, 2023).

[94] Scassa, *supra* note 84, at 11.

[95] Madeline Smith, *Did Malls Violate Privacy with Facial Recognition Tech? Alberta, Federal Privacy Commissioners Investigate*, Toronto Star (Aug. 3, 2018), https://www.thestar.com/calgary/did-malls-violate-privacy-with-facial-recognition-tech-alberta-federal-privacy-commissioners-investigate/article_2b91612f-4d75-59fb-903f-be7fba75498a.html.

[96] Scassa, *supra* note 84, at 7.

human rights oriented.[97] There is also a push to address the use of personal information in relation to AI, which falls within the purview of a PIPEDA reform. The recent Bill C-27 embodies the proposed changes to PIPEDA and would establish stronger privacy protections while allowing responsible innovation. The Bill contains three parts, one of which is the Artificial Intelligence and Data Act (AIDA).[98]

The AIDA was designed to align with the evolving international norms within AI, including the European AIA, by implementing a risk-based approach and adopting key definitions reflected in other AI laws.[99] Like the AIA, AIDA's primary concern is regulating high-impact AI systems that present a risk of harm to the health and safety of individuals or a risk of adverse impact on human rights.[100] The obligations for high-impact systems would be guided by principles such as transparency, fairness, safety, accountability, and robustness.[101] The high-impact systems must also be designed and developed in such a way to enable meaningful human oversight and continual measurement and assessment of the AI systems and their output.[102]

8.2.2. Provincial Frameworks: Quebec's Law 25

On September 21, 2021, the Quebec National Assembly officially adopted Law 25, ushering in a number of new privacy requirements for companies doing business in Quebec. As part of the new privacy obligations, a number of provisions apply to AI systems. Most significant are Section 12.1, which handles automated decision making; Section 8, which regulates profiling; and the requirement of Privacy Impact Assessments (PIAs).

8.2.2.1. Automated Decision Making

Section 12.1 of Law 25 governs automated decision making and establishes transparency as well as accountability requirements for applicable automated decision-making processes. Notably, the provision only applies to automated decision-making outputs that use personal information and are *exclusively* automated (i.e., no human involvement in decision making). This may include the use of AI such as OpenAI and other technologies that may be used by an organization to make decisions about, for example, whether to grant access to a product or service based on an assessment of an individual's financial or medical situation.[103]

---

97 *Id.*

98 Note that at the time of this drafting, AIDA is still being considered in Parliament and has not passed yet. Experts do not expect it to pass until 2025 at the earliest. *See* Alex LaCasse, *Canadian Parliament's Bill C-27 hearing delves deeper into AIDA*, IAPP (Dec. 8, 2023), https://iapp.org/news/a/canadian-parliaments-bill-c-27-hearing-delves-deeper-into-aida/.

99 *The Artificial Intelligence and Data Act (AIDA)—Companion document*, GOV'T OF CAN, https://ised-isde.canada.ca/site/innovation-better-canada/en/artificial-intelligence-and-data-act-aida-companion-document (Mar.13, 2023).

100 The types of technologies that are of high concern to the government include screening systems that impact access to services or employment, biometric systems used for identification, applications like AI online content recommendation systems, and applications that make critical decisions based on information collected from sensors (e.g., autonomous vehicles or health sector technology). *See id.*

101 *Id.*

102 *Id.*

103 Note that "automated processing" is not defined under Law 25. While the target of Law 25 is likely AI-type technologies, the drafting is broad enough that it may include targeted advertising.

Section 12.1 requires companies to inform individuals when their personal information is being used to render a decision based solely on automated processing. This notice must come no later than at the time the individual is informed of the decision itself, which creates some flexibility as to the exact timing of the notice. Section 12.1 also requires that, upon request, a company must inform individuals of the personal information used to render the decision, the reasons that led to the decision, and the right to have the personal information used to render the decision corrected. One important note is that the phrasing of Section 12.1 does not limit the rights mentioned to the personal information about the affected individual, given that AI systems that make decisions about individuals may need to process large amounts of other information. While it is unlikely the law would require personal information of other individuals to be disclosed to another individual affected by the decision of the AI system, it is possible that companies will need to disclose the nature of all the personal information used (e.g., the fact that the AI used information from job applicants).

Another requirement under Section 12.1 is that concerned individuals must be given the opportunity to "submit observations to a member of the personnel of the organization who is in a position to review the decision made by automated means." This means that companies will need to ensure the right personnel with power and sufficient knowledge are able to reassess automated decisions. Section 12.1, however, does not grant individuals the right not to be subject to decisions based solely on automated processing but merely the right to present observations. This means that while the organization must review the decision, it does not need to come to an independent decision or provide reasons why a new decision should be reached.

8.2.2.2. Profiling and Collecting Information through Technological Means

Law 25 requires enhanced transparency from those who collect personal information using technology that allows individuals to be identified, located, or profiled. Companies must inform the individual of the use of such technology and the means of activating these functions.[104] "Profiling"[105] is broadly defined and may apply to various technologies as well as in different settings (e.g., generative AI, employee monitoring tools, cookies, and similar technologies used for targeted advertising, etc.). The Commission d'accès à l'information du Quebec (CAI) notes that these technologies cannot be activated by default, and that it will be up to the person concerned to activate them if so desired.[106] In other words, the individual must take an affirmative action to show intent to activate a specific function.

If a company collects personal information through technological means, it is required to publish a privacy notice in clear and simple language on the company's website

---

[104] Act Respecting the Protection of Personal Information in the Private Sector, C.Q.L.R., c P-39.1, s. 8.1(1) (Can.).

[105] Profiling is defined as the collection and use of personal information to "assess certain characteristics of a natural person, in particular for the purpose of analyzing that person's work performance, economic situation, health, personal preferences, interests or behavior." *See id.* at s. 8.2.

[106] *Main changes to privacy laws*, COMM'N D'ACCÈS À L'INFO. DU QUÉBEC, https://www.cai.gouv.qc.ca/protection-renseignements-personnels/sujets-et-domaines-dinteret/principaux-changements-loi-25?thematiques/technologie-identification-localisation-profilage/ (last visited Mar. 1, 2024).

and disseminate it by appropriate means that will reach the individual concerned.[107] "Appropriate means" is meant to encourage companies to inform individuals of information handling practices using means that are convenient and easily accessible. For example, if the company has a website, then posting the privacy notice on the website is likely an "appropriate means."

8.2.2.3. Privacy Impact Assessment

A privacy impact assessment ("PIA") is a preventive process that seeks to better protect personal information and ensure the privacy of individuals is taken into account prior to engaging in a project involving the processing of personal information. Companies will be required to conduct a PIA prior to the acquisition, development, or redesign of an information system involving the collection, use, disclosure, retention, or destruction of personal information.[108] The Privacy Impact Assessment Accompanying Guide[109] clarifies that a PIA will be required prior to the use of AI systems, surveillance cameras, fingerprints, geolocation, facial recognition, and machines that use sensors (i.e., automated cars).

The scope and content of the PIA will depend on the context but will generally include a description of the project and data processing operations (e.g., types of information collected, used, or disclosed, and the purpose for which information is processed), an evaluation of the project's compliance with privacy principles and requirements (e.g., privacy policies, proof of consent, and data security), and the identification of privacy risks resulting from the project (e.g., whether obtaining consent from or notifying affected individuals will be difficult). The CAI highly recommends conducting the PIA early on in the project's development to manage any privacy risks before they arise.

Although there is no current law that explicitly discusses AI in Canada, it is clear that existing law reaches many of the issues raised by AI. PIPEDA, while dated, implements fairness principles that AI systems must abide by, and Quebec's Law 25 targets various issues that many AI systems include, such as automated decision making and profiling. AIDA still has a long way to go, but the fact that the Canadian government is prioritizing an overhaul of PIPEDA signifies that Canada may have an AI law in place within the coming years.

8.3. East Asia: How Data Protection Regulators Are Managing the AI Boom

Although American tech giants are currently leading the AI development charge, no discussion of AI advancement and regulation would be complete without considering China,

---

[107] Act Respecting the Protection of Personal Information in the Private Sector, *supra* note 108, at s. 8.2.

[108] *Id.* at s. 3.3(1).

[109] *Guide d'accompagnement—Réaliser une évaluation des facteurs relatifs à la vie privée* [Accompanying Guide—Conduct a privacy impact assessment], Comm'n d'acces a l'info. du Quebec (Sept. 22, 2023), https://www.cai.gouv.qc.ca/uploads/pdfs/CAI_GU_EFVP.pdf.

the United States's primary competitor in the battle for global AI dominance, as well as Japan and South Korea.[110] In fighting to keep up with the United States in the global AI market, companies in these East Asian countries must navigate some of the strictest national data privacy and protection regimes on the planet.[111] As the AI race intensifies, regulators in these countries are introducing new measures governing the development and use of AI. This section discusses the AI landscape in China, Japan, and South Korea, including the data privacy and protection laws and recent AI-focused regulatory trends in those countries.

8.3.1. China's Data Protection Framework

In 2021, China passed its comprehensive data privacy and protection legislation, the Personal Information Protection Law (PIPL).[112] The PIPL harmonizes two existing data security laws (DSLs)[113] by incorporating familiar data protection concepts, such as obtaining consent before collecting personal information and establishing a classified data protection system with enhanced protection for sensitive information.[114] The PIPL covers processing activities conducted within China, applies extraterritorially to overseas processing of personal data about individuals in China, and allows China's data protection authority, the Cyberspace Administration of China (CAC), to restrict or ban overseas entities who infringe the rights of Chinese citizens or endanger China's interests from receiving Chinese personal information.[115]

Relevant to AI-assisted processing and decisions, entities using personal information for automated decision making[116] must ensure such decision making is transparent to data subjects, its results are fair and impartial, and its results are not used to unreasonably differentiate between individuals in setting transaction prices or conditions.[117] The PIPL also confers data subjects the right to request clarification about automated decision

---

110 Xuan-Thao Nguyen, *Tech Supremacy: The New Arms Race between China and the United States*, 49 J. Corp. L. 103, 103 (2023); Bhaskar Chakravorti et al., *Chartering the Emerging Geography of AI*, Harv. Bus. Rev. (Dec. 12, 2023), https://hbr.org/2023/12/charting-the-emerging-geography-of-ai; James Manyika & Michael Spence, *The Coming AI Economic Revolution: Can Artificial Intelligence Reverse the Productivity Slowdown?* 102 Foreign Aff. 70, 85 (Nov./Dec. 2023).

111 *See generally* Eva Xiao, *China Passes One of the World's Strictest Data-Privacy Laws*, WSJ (Aug. 20, 2021), https://www.wsj.com/articles/china-passes-one-of-the-worlds-strictest-data-privacy-laws-11629429138; Alex Wall, *GDPR Matchup: South Korea's Personal Information Protection Act*, iapp (Jan. 8, 2018), https://iapp.org/news/a/gdpr-matchup-south-koreas-personal-information-protection-act/.

112 Personal Information Protection Law of the People's Republic of China (中华人民共和国个人信息保护法) (promulgated by the Standing Comm. Nat'l People's Cong., Aug. 20, 2021, effective Nov. 1, 2021) [hereinafter PIPL].

113 *See* Cybersecurity Law of the People's Republic of China (中华人民共和国网络安全法) (promulgated by the Standing Comm. Nat'l People's Cong., effective Nov. 7, 2016) [hereinafter CSL]; Data Security Law of the People's Republic of China (中华人民共和国数据安全法) (promulgated by the Standing Comm. Nat'l People's Cong. Jun. 10, 2021, effective. Sept. 1, 2021) [hereinafter DSL].

114 George Qi, *China Promulgates Personal Information Protection Law*, Greenberg Traurig (Sept. 22, 2021), https://www.gtlaw.com/en/insights/2021/9/china-promulgates-personal-information-protection-law#_ftnref2.

115 PIPL arts. 3, 42 (China).

116 The PIPL defines "automated decision making" as "the activities of automatically analyzing and evaluating personal behaviors, hobbies, or economic, health, and credit status, among others, through computer programs, and making decisions." PIPL art. 73(2) (China).

117 PIPL art. 24 (China).

making based on the use of their personal information, as well as the right to request that they not be subject to a fully automated decision if that decision would significantly impact their rights and interests.[118]

The PIPL is comparable to other comprehensive data protection laws like the GDPR[119] in many respects.[120] However, while such laws are generally focused on protecting individual data rights, in contrast, the PIPL "elevates China's control over data akin to control over national property."[121] This sentiment is reflected in the PIPL's onerous cross-border transfer provisions.[122] This restrictive national oversight over and control of personal data flows is also apparent in the PIPL's imposition of stricter requirements on critical internet platform service providers, involving large user bases and complex businesses.[123]

Through such treatment of personal data, the PIPL can be viewed not only as a general data protection measure but also as a mechanism to rein in powerful Chinese tech titans, thereby promoting common prosperity.[124] China's enormous, tech-centric population is primed to utilize emerging technologies early and often, which provides a wealth of data that can be leveraged to propel China to the forefront of AI innovation.[125]

In furtherance of these objectives, in 2023, the CAC, along with other state agencies, approved new rules ("AI Measures") governing generative AI.[126] The AI Measures apply to those using generative AI technologies to provide services generating "text, pictures, audio, video, and other content **to the public** within" China.[127] In providing generative AI services to the public, organizations must, among other things, adhere to core socialist values and not subvert state power, endanger national security interests, or promote ethnic hatred, terrorism, violence, or obscenity.[128] When engaged in processing activities related to AI pre-, optimization, and other training, providers must use basic models and data only from legal sources; not violate intellectual property rights; obtain consent from data subjects when their personal information is involved unless such personal information processing is otherwise permitted by law; take measures to enhance the training data's quality, accuracy, objectivity, and diversity; and comply with China's data

---

118 *Id.*

119 GDPR.

120 *E.g., compare* PIPL arts. 5–10 (setting forth the data protection principles), *with* GDPR art. 5 (same); *compare* PIPL art. 13 (setting forth legal bases for processing), *with* GDPR art. 6 (same); *compare* PIPL Ch. IV (setting forth data subject rights), *with* GDPR, Ch. 3 (same).

121 Nguyen, *supra* note 113, at 127.

122 *See generally* Qi, *supra* note 117 (citing PIPL art. 38).

123 *Id.* (citing PIPL art. 58).

124 Nguyen, *supra* note 113, at 124; *see also* Arjun Kharpal, *In a Quest to Rein in Its Tech Giants, China Turns to Data Protection*, CNBC (Apr. 11, 2021), https://www.cnbc.com/2021/04/12/china-data-protection-laws-aim-to-help-rein-in-countrys-tech-giants.html; Qi, *supra* note 117 (recognizing relationship between regulation of critical internet platform service providers and the rise of "technology innovation and significant growth of tech giants in China").

125 Nguyen, *supra* note 113 at 125.

126 Interim Measures for the Management of Generative Artificial Intelligence Services (promulgated by the CAC, Nat'l Dev. & Reform Comm'n, Ministry of Educ., Ministry of Sci & Tech., Ministry of Info. Tech., Ministry of Pub. Sec., State Admin. of Radio & T.V., May 23, 2023, effective Aug. 15, 2023) (rough English translation) [hereinafter AI Measures].

127 AI Measures art. 2 (emphasis added) (China).

128 AI Measures art. 4 (China).

protection laws such as the PIPL, DSL, and CSL (Cybersecurity Law).[129] When annotating data during the development of generative AI, providers must establish clear labeling rules to ensure quality and accuracy.[130]

The AI Measures assign providers responsibilities as producers and moderators of the AI-generated content as well as data processor obligations to the extent the AI-platform ingests personal information.[131] The spirit of these requirements is captured in specific duties related to user protection, such as entering into service agreements with users that clarify the parties' respective rights and obligations;[132] protecting minors from generative AI addiction or overreliance;[133] complying with the PIPL with respect to personal information, including observing the data minimization principle and fulfilling data subject rights requests;[134] complying with China's "Regulations on the Management of Deep Synthesis of Information Services," which essentially require AI-generated deep fake content to be conspicuously labeled as such;[135] ensuring service continuity;[136] and establishing and improving complaint and reporting mechanisms.[137]

Lastly, the AI Measures expressly mandate compliance with Chinese laws and regulations regarding foreign investment in generative AI services[138] and require industry regulators to "strengthen the management of generative artificial intelligence services in accordance with their respective responsibilities and laws."[139] The AI Measures do not set forth specific penalties and instead indicate that liability for violations will be as contemplated in the PIPL, DSL, CSL, and other laws.[140] These new AI Measures signal China's continued interest in keeping a close eye on tech providers and likely are the precursor to an influx of similar AI-directed measures in the near future.

8.3.2. Japan and South Korea: Upcoming AI Powerhouses

Like China, Japan and South Korea are also technology powerhouses in East Asia.[141] However, their national data pools are not growing as quickly as other East Asian countries with younger populations and rising numbers of internet users, and, as a result,

---

129 AI Measures art. 7(China).

130 AI Measures art. 8; *see also China: CAC Publishes Interim Measures on Generative AI*, OneTrust DataGuidance (Jul. 13, 202) https://www.dataguidance.com/news/china-cac-publishes-interim-measures-generative-ai [hereinafter AI Measures Data Guidance Insight].

131 AI Measures arts. 9, 14 (China).

132 AI Measures art. 9 (China).

133 AI Measures art. 10 (China).

134 AI Measures art. 11 (China).

135 AI Measures art. 12 (China); AI Measures Data Guidance Insight, *supra* note 134.

136 AI Measures art. 13 (China).

137 AI Measures art. 15 (China).

138 AI Measures art. 23 (China).

139 AI Measures art. 16 (China).

140 AI Measures art. 21 (China).

141 *See generally* Chakravorti, *supra* note 113; Silvia Appelt et al., *A Global Powerhouse in Science and Technology*, OECD (Oct. 25, 2021), https://www.oecd.org/country/korea/thematic-focus/a-global-powerhouse-in-science-and-technology-61cbd1ad/.

they currently lag behind China in AI progress.[142] While Japan and South Korea share these challenges, they each face unique difficulties. For example, Japan's deficit of software engineers and inadequate access to supercomputing capabilities are impeding its advancement in generative AI technologies and deep learning software.[143] Although South Korea has certain advantages like the strength of its semiconductor industry and wealth of AI patents, like Japan, it faces a talent shortage, and it also has to deal with significant state budget cuts for AI research and development.[144]

Despite these challenges, Japan and South Korea are still considered global AI frontrunners and therefore require the addition of AI-specific measures to their respective data privacy and protection regulatory environments. In that regard, Japan and South Korea both have comprehensive data privacy and protection laws: the Act on the Protection of Personal Information (APPI) in Japan and the Personal Information Protection Act (PIPA) in South Korea.[145] Japan's and South Korea's data protection regulators are both called the Personal Protection Commission and Personal Information Protection Commission (hereinafter "PPC" refers to Japan's regulator, and "PIPC" refers to South Korea's regulator).

South Korea's PIPC has actively been pushing out AI-related regulatory initiatives. In August 2023, the PIPC published its Policy Direction for Safe Use of Personal Information in the Artificial Intelligence Era, which explains how to interpret and apply the PIPA in the context of AI.[146] The guidance focuses on, among other things, establishing a Privacy Team to facilitate communications with businesses developing and providing AI services and models, and processing standards for the stages of AI development and service.[147] Additionally, in October 2023, the PIPC announced that it was beginning to pilot its

---

142 Chakravorti, *supra* note 113 (ranking Japan in fourth place and South Korea in ninth place in the Harvard Business Review's Top-Ranked AI Nations ("TRAIN") index, which considers four factors, including innovation (i.e., "[a] dvances in AI models, techniques, creative sourcing of data, and new applications"), capital (i.e., "[t]he human, financial, and digital foundations for building AI"), rules (i.e., "[h]ow data can be accessed"), and data (i.e., "[v]olume and complexity of the core resource used to train and improve algorithms")).

143 *Id.*; *see also* Audrey Wan, *Why Japan Is Lagging behind in Generative A.I.—and How It Can Create Its Own Large Language Models*, CNBC (Jul. 6, 2023), https://www.cnbc.com/2023/07/07/why-japan-is-lagging-behind-in-generative-ai-and-creation-of-llms.html; Yuki Okoshi, *Japan's Fugaka Supercomputer to Help Develop Homegrown Generative AI*, NikkeiAsia (May 23, 2023), https://asia.nikkei.com/Business/Technology/Japan-s-Fugaku-supercomputer-to-help-develop-homegrown-generative-AI.

144 Chakravorti, *supra* note 113.

145 Act on the Protection of Personal Information, Act No. 57 of 2003, https://www.japaneselawtranslation.go.jp/en/laws/view/4241/en (Japan) [hereinafter APPI]; Personal Information Protection Act of 2011, Act No. 19234, as amended Mar. 14, 2023, [hereinafter PIPA] (S. Kor.) *translated in* Korean Legislation Research Institute's online database, https://elaw.klri.re.kr/eng_service/lawView.do?hseq=53044&lang=ENG.

146 *See* Press Release, Seonjeong Kwon, Spokesman, PIPC, Taking the First Steps Towards Trust-Based Artificial Intelligence Data *Norms* (Aug. 8, 2023), https://www.pipc.go.kr/np/cop/bbs/selectBoardArticle.do?bbsId=BS074&mCode=C020010000&nttId=9083 (rough English translation) (last visited Mar. 2, 2024) (S. Kor.).

147 *Id.*; *see also South Korea: PIPC Publishes Guidance for the Safe Use of Personal Information in the Age of AI*, OneTrust DataGuidance, Aug, 3, 2023, https://www.dataguidance.com/news/south-korea-pipc-publishes-guidance-safe-use-personal (last visited Mar. 2, 2024); Press Release, Seonjeong Kwon, Spokesman, PIPC, Personal Information Commission Launches Artificial Intelligence Privacy Team (Oct. 5, 2023), https://www.pipc.go.kr/np/cop/bbs/selectBoardArticle.do?bbsId=BS074&mCode=C020010000&nttId=9216 (rough English translation) (S. Kor.).

Preliminary Adequacy Review System, which sets forth a voluntary procedure for the PIPC to review new AI technologies in development for PIPA compliance.[148]

Further, South Korea passed the "Basic Act on the Development of Artificial Intelligence and Establishment of Foundation for Trust," (the "Basic Act") which is loosely patterned after the EU AI Act.[149] The "Basic Act" adopts a risk-based approach that apply increased obligations on developers and deployers of "high-impact" use cases, though it lists no "prohibited" uses.[150] Further, there are rules set forth regarding the use of generative AI and for large language models.[151] Unlike the EU AI Act, all AI systems – regardless of risk rating – have certain obligations, such as registration of an agent, risk assessment, and implementation of ethics and safety measures. [152] The Basic Act is set to come into force on January 22, 2026.

Although it does not have a comprehensive law specifically governing AI, Japan's ruling party has announced that, in 2024, Japan's government will introduce a new law governing generative AI.[153] While Japanese AI-specific legislation is currently limited, in 2019, Japan's Cabinet Office released a document titled "Social Principles of Human-Centric AI," which is geared toward transforming Japan into an "'AI-Ready Society,' where AI can be used effectively and safely."[154] More recently, Japan's Ministry of Internal Affairs and Communications and its Ministry of Economy, Trade and Industry published, and are requesting public comment on, draft AI Business Guidelines.[155] The guidelines generally encourage developers to consider, among other things, using appropriate data in training AI, taking steps to manage bias, and implementing appropriate security measures while setting forth similar guidance for AI business users.[156] These developments suggest a coming increase in Japanese regulatory activity surrounding the development and use of AI.

---

148 Press Release, Seonjeong Kwon, Spokesman, PIPC, Personal Information Commission Begins Pilot Operation of "Prior Appropriateness Review System" (Oct. 11, 2023), https://www.pipc.go.kr/np/cop/bbs/selectBoardArticle.do?bbsId=BS074&mCode=C020010000&nttId=9227 (rough English translation) (S. Kor.).

149 *Act on the Development of Artificial Intelligence and Establishment of Trust ("Basic Act"),* Law No. 20676, enacted on January 21, 2025, available in Korean at https://likms.assembly.go.kr/bill/billDetail.do?billId=PRC_R2V4H1W1T2K5M1O6E4Q9T0V7Q9S0U0.

150 *Id.* at Art. 33.

151 *Id.* at Art. 31.

152 *Id.* at Art. 32–36.

153 *Japan's Ruling Party Pushes for AI Legislation within 2024, Nikkei Reports*, REUTERS (Feb. 15, 2024), https://www.reuters.com/technology/japans-ruling-party-pushes-ai-legislation-within-2024-nikkei-reports-2024-02-15/?taid=65cdd87288998b0001e323c9&utm_campaign=trueAnthem:+Trending+Content&utm_medium=trueAnthem&utm_source=twitter.

154 *Social Principles of Human-Centric AI,* Cabinet Office, https://www.cas.go.jp/jp/seisaku/jinkouchinou/pdf/humancentricai.pdf (English translation) (last visited Mar. 2, 2023) (Japan).

155 *Japan: MIC and METI Request Public Comments on Draft AI Business Guidelines,* ONETRUST DATA GUIDANCE (Jan. 22, 2024), https://www.dataguidance.com/news/japan-mic-and-meti-request-public-comments-draft-ai.

156 *Id.*

8.4. Latin America: Finding Its Bearings in Regulating Data and AI

8.4.1. Chile: Taking Steps

The Chilean Constitution, along with the Chilean Data Privacy Act (CDPA),[157] set forth the general principles for the protection of privacy and personal data. The CDPA, approved in 1999, is generally considered to be toothless, though it was of the first of its kind in Latin America. Given the lack of practical enforcement mechanisms, lack of a dedicated data privacy authority, and low fines, it quickly became obsolete. In 2018, however, data protection was incorporated into the Chilean Constitution as a fundamental right, establishing the legal foundation for protecting personal data.

8.4.1.1. Current Data Protection Framework

Chile does not currently have a dedicated authority responsible for overseeing data protection; general courts have wide powers to oversee data protection. However, a Congressional Bill[158] is currently under discussion calling for data protection reform by seeking to create a national data protection authority. Nevertheless, as a private right of action, if an entity with responsibility for personal data (e.g., a registry or bank holding personal data) fails to respond within two business days to a data-protection-related request involving accessing, modifying, eliminating, or blocking personal data, a summary proceeding may be initiated.

A number of national entities also have power in matters relating to protection of personal data: the Chilean Consumer Protection Agency (SERNAC), the Council for Transparency, and the Financial Market Commission (CMF). These entities correspond to the protection of data privacy for individuals, the public sector, and the financial sector, respectively. SERNAC controls matters related to personal data protection in the context of consumer relations, and is authorized to supervise, inspect, investigate, issue interpretations of relevant regulations and laws, and bring individual or class action suits. SERNAC has already issued interpretations on best e-commerce practices, equity and fairness in adherence contracts that refer to collecting and processing personal consumer data (e.g., terms and conditions of use, and end user license agreements, etc.), and consumer protection against the use of AI systems. SERNAC was enhanced by the "Pro-Consumer Law,"[159] which went into effect in December 2021 and focuses on protection from AI systems. The Pro-Consumer Law requires that accurate, timely, and transparent information be provided to consumers, in support of freedom of choice, safety, and prohibition against arbitrary discrimination, and protection of consumers' personal data.

---

157 Law No. 19628, Sobre Proteccion de la Vida Privada, Agosto 18, 1999, as amended by Law No. 21504, Novembre 4, 2022 (Chile).

158 *See infra* note 161.

159 Law No. 21.398, Establece Medidas para Incentivar la Protección de los Derechos de los Consumidores, Deciembre 13, 2021 (Chile).

The Council for Transparency is responsible for enforcing the CDPA in the public sector, i.e., by state entities. The CMF has supervisory powers over personal data protection as well as information security and cybersecurity in the financial sector. The CMF ensures that financial institutions put in place appropriate internal policies on security and managing debtor information, which are required to follow international principles and best practices for personal data processing. Financial institutions that provide an Open Banking System must also comply with specific CMF standards related to cybersecurity and personal data protection, as required by the Fintech Law.[160]

Data breaches can lead to administrative sanctions as well as financial and other penalties. Financial penalties and fines are determined in summary proceedings in courts of general jurisdiction. In cases where willful misconduct or negligence can be found in the processing of personal data, both monetary and nonmonetary damages may be awarded. A civil judge in charge of the summary proceeding considers the circumstances and facts of a case to determine damages. The personal data protection Bill, pending in the Chilean Congress, proposes a list of "minor," "serious," and "very serious" infractions. Companies found liable may be fined up to 4 percent of their annual income, with a maximum of US$ 1.56 million, depending on the circumstances and seriousness of the breach.

8.4.1.2. Legislative Developments Regarding AI

A Congressional bill based on the EU's AI Act was sent by Chilean President of the Republic to the Chamber of Deputies to address legal and ethical issues as they arise in the creation, distribution, commercialization, and use of AI systems.[161] The bill also seeks to ensure a balance is reached where the protection of fundamental rights of citizens is guaranteed without hindering development and access to these technologies. Structured over fifteen articles, the Bill seeks to define AI and related terms; establish risk criteria where use of AI systems is considered unacceptable or high risk; create a National Commission for AI under the Ministry of Science, Technology, Knowledge and Innovation; task the new National Commission for AI with reviewing and adapting regulatory instruments; implement early-stage mechanisms and processes related to the development, commercialization, and use of AI systems; and establish monetary and nonmonetary penalties for noncompliance.

The Chilean Ministry of Science, Technology, Knowledge and Innovation published guidelines for the use of AI tools in the public sector in December 2023, which went into effect January 2024.[162] These guidelines generally provide recommendations promoting responsible use of AI tools, especially as they relate to creating people-centered AI tools, transparency, and data privacy. Specifically,

---

[160] Law No. 21.521, Promueve la Competencia e Inclusión Financiera a Través de la Innovación y Tecnología en la Prestación de Servicios Financieros, Ley Fintec, Deciembre 22, 2022 (Chile).

[161] Bulletin Number 16821-19, recast with 15869-19, introduced May 7, 2024, https://www.camara.cl/legislacion/ProyectosDeLey/tramitacion.aspx?prmID=17429&prmBOLETIN=16821-19.

[162] Machine translated excerpt from "Of. Circ. No. 711," Guidelines for the use of artificial intelligence tools in the public sector, (Dec. 11, 2023), https://minciencia.gob.cl/uploads/filer_public/ae/9a/ae9a7ce7-807b-4781-9ac3-9b253bfbe735/of_n711_2023_dis_lin_ia_minciencia.pdf (Chile).

> These guidelines will constitute a first step to arrive at a common framework, as they provide general guidelines and recommendations to promote the responsible, ethical, safe and transparent use of tools based on artificial intelligence systems in the public sector. Its monitoring will allow us to have preliminary and detailed information about the regulatory and coordination challenges at stake and, if necessary, determine which instruments are most efficient and effective to address them.[163]

As of November 2021, UNESCO member states have been working to adopt UNESCO's "Recommendation on the Ethics of AI" as a global standard aiming to leverage the positive impact of AI while addressing its inherent risks.[164] As a result of this effort, UNESCO has identified the following shortcomings in Chile's existing and proposed legislation related to AI:

- The scope of application lacks clarity, with ambiguous definitions for areas such as domestic data and foreign service providers operating in Chile from other countries.
- The definition of personal data is both insufficient and broad, encompassing any information related to an identified or identifiable natural person, making it challenging to distinguish from statistical data.
- Various actors involved in the data treatment process are not adequately addressed in the law, resulting in deficient assignment of responsibility.
- The rules of consent are outdated and require integration with the contemporary context of new digital technologies.
- Ambiguity exists regarding publicly accessible sources of data, leading to unclear boundaries.
- An excessive number of exceptions for the use of sensitive data.
- Inadequate limitations on the use and treatment of personal data by public entities.
- A weak enforcement system due to ineffective procedures, insufficient penalties, and an inadequate responsible authority.[165]

8.4.2. Peru: Following the EU's Lead

Like Chile, Peru introduced data protection as a constitutional right, stating that "information services, whether computerized or not, whether public or private, will not provide information affecting personal and family privacy."[166] To effectively guarantee this right, a "habeas data" procedure was first created in 1994 and updated in 2004, providing all individuals with the right to "access, update, cancel, or rectify their personal information stored or registered, whether manual, mechanical, or informatics, in files,

---

163 *Id.* at ¶ 7 (Chile).

164 UNESCO, Chile: Artificial Intelligence Readiness Assessment Report, SHS/BIO/2023/AI-RAM/CR/1 (2023), https://unesdoc.unesco.org/ark:/48223/pf0000387216/PDF/387216eng.pdf.

165 *Id.* at 16.

166 Article 2(6), Peruvian National Constitution.

databases, and registries of public or private entities, which provide services or access to third parties."[167] In 2011, a formal data protection framework was implemented, allowing enforcement to be entrusted to an administrative body, which allowed for more expeditious mechanisms.[168] As a result, the Peruvian Data Protection Authority (APDP) supervised and controlled data protection, and directly reported to the Office of Justice at the Ministry of Justice and Human Rights. In July 2023, a law to promote the use of AI in economic and social development was promulgated.[169] The law established that the use of AI would be promoted under an approach that properly privileges the person and human rights—guaranteeing ethical, sustainable, transparent, and responsible use of AI. As a result, AI and other technologies were to be promoted in an effort to improve education, health, justice, and national security.

In February 2024, a more comprehensive legal framework was introduced, modeled on the EU's AI Act, for the use and regulation of AI. The framework stresses unrestricted respect for human rights and fundamental rights, including the right to privacy and data protection.

The proposed bill, over nine sections, seeks to encompass a wide scope: a law applicable to people or legal entities who develop, research, innovate, or apply AI in Peru, regardless of where they are physically located. Developers, providers, and users of AI systems are to be held responsible for decisions and actions from the use of AI—including errors. Developers of AI systems will also be required to document and disclose algorithms used in their systems.

Similar to the EU's AI Act, the bill categorizes potential risks arising from AI systems into four risk levels: "unacceptable," "high," "limited," or "insignificant/minimal." In order to ensure quality and safety, companies will be required to undergo rigorous verification and certification prior to launch. The proposed bill prohibits certain practices related to the use of AI, including any AI system that "manipulate or exert undue influence, including on electoral processes or public opinion, biometric categorization using sensitive characteristics, untargeted scraping of facial images from the internet or audiovisual recordings to create facial recognition databases, and emotion recognition in the workplace and education."[170]

---

[167] *See* Law No. 26301, later substituted by Law No. 28237, Constitutional Procedural Code, https://www.tc.gob.pe/wp-content/uploads/2021/05/Codigo-Procesal-Constitucional-TC.pdf (Peru).

[168] *See* Law No. 29733 on the Protection of Personal Data, https://www.gob.pe/institucion/congreso-de-la-republica/normas-legales/243470-29733 (Peru).

[169] *See* Law No. 31814, Ley que Promueve el Uso de la Inteligencia Artificial en Favor del Desarrollo Económico y Social del País, Julio 5, 2023 (Peru).

[170] *Access Alert: Peru's Congress Introduces Bill to Regulate AI*, Access Partnership (Feb. 22, 2024), https://accesspartnership.com/access-alert-perus-congress-introduces-bill-to-regulate-ai/.

8.5. Global Efforts to Regulate AI

Efforts to regulate AI have ramped up over the past eighteen months, with thirty-two countries now having passed AI-related legislation.[171] Of that group, Europe has emerged as the leader in setting forth a risk-based framework for addressing AI. Like the GDPR, the EU AI Act will have reverberations throughout the world. That said, major economic players across the globe are each examining how to strike the balance between innovation and the regulation of AI technologies.

171 *Artificial Intelligence Index Report 2024, supra* note 2.

9
Bias and Inequities in the Digital Realm

By Jon M. Garon

The digital world of cyberspace offers a wealth of opportunities for individuals to become whoever they wish to be online and shed their physical constraints in a manner limited only by imagination and social custom.[1] One can choose to adopt a digital replica, recreating one's exact identity in digital form, or choose to present oneself online as a very different person—or even nonhuman—avatar. There need be no limits.

At the same time, however, historical inequities pervade the online world. Algorithms are based on historical data, resource-intensive online activities require substantial funding for individuals and for community services, and intrusive tracking technologies can re-identify and categorize people without their meaningful consent.

This chapter identifies the key concerns regarding bias and inequities that impact data-driven systems and the digital environment. There are three primary ways in which these disparities present themselves. The term "digital divide" is used to describe the disparate access to resources needed to participate in the world of digital content. The phrase "algorithmic bias" reflects the presumptions and prejudices that pervade training data in artificial intelligence (AI) systems. The concept of "digital redlining" captures concerns about the use of refined behavioral and demographic targeting to disadvantage certain communities. Finally, the section of "cultural sensitivity" addresses digital blackface and online cultural representation, reflecting on the legal and ethical considerations for managing online identity in the workplace and in social settings. Each of these areas impacts the public in all aspects of their life, but most critical concerns involve employment, housing, healthcare, education, and decision making in the criminal justice system.

---

1 *See* Jess Kung, *Should Your Avatar's Skin Match Yours?* NPR Code Switch (Aug. 31, 2019), https://www.npr.org/sections/codeswitch/2019/08/31/430057317/should-your-avatars-skin-match-yours.

9.1. The Context of U.S. Antidiscrimination Law

U.S. antidiscrimination laws have their roots in the Fourteenth Amendment, providing that no State shall "deny to any person . . . the equal protection of the laws."[2] The enforcement of the Fourth Amendment, however, quickly waned during the reconstruction era. The country took nearly a century to treat this promise seriously, but it reemerged with force during the Civil Rights movement. Although significant work led up to the opinion, the seminal decision of *Brown v. Board of Education*[3] was the turning point, calling for an end to the legal fiction of "separate but equal accommodations."[4] With *Brown*, the Supreme Court "required schools to admit students 'on a racially nondiscriminatory basis.'"[5]

In the decades that followed, the Supreme Court also recognized that sex or gender discrimination also runs afoul of the Fourteenth Amendment, though the assessment of sex discrimination often falls under the "intermediate scrutiny" instead of the "strict scrutiny" standard.[6] Additional constitutional protections extend to national origin, legitimacy of birth, and other immutable characteristics. As a constitutional matter, these cases require the government itself to be involved in the discrimination.

To redress discrimination by private parties, Congress and state governments have enacted a range of antidiscrimination laws to protect the public from discrimination. These laws cover more forms of discrimination than those identified in the Constitution. These laws include Title VII of the Civil Rights Act of 1964 (Title VII), the American with Disabilities Act (ADA), the Fair Credit Reporting Act; the Rehabilitation Act of 1973, Title IX of the Education Amendment of 1972, the Age Discrimination in Employment Act (ADEA), and the Vietnam Era Veterans' Readjustment Assistance Act of 1974, among others.[7] As reflected in the titles of the federal laws, antidiscrimination laws generally prohibit discrimination in the fields of employment, education, housing, financial reporting, and healthcare. In many situations, state laws duplicate or expand upon the federal protections from discrimination, offering state as well as federal mechanisms for enforcement.

A significant portion of the antidiscrimination enforcement occurs to prevent employment discrimination. The employment example provides a model that generally extends into the other protected categories as well. "The federal government enforces employment discrimination laws. It does so through the U.S. Equal Employment Opportunity Commission (EEOC)."[8] The EEOC protects against discrimination in the decision-making

---

2 Students for Fair Admissions, Inc. v. Pres. and Fellows of Harvard College, 600 U.S. 181, 201–202 (2023) (quoting U.S. Const. amend. XIV, § 1).

3 Brown v. Board of Education, 347 U.S. 483, 491 (1954).

4 Students for Fair Admissions, Inc., 600 U.S. at 204 (2023) (quoting Brown v. Board of Education, 349 U.S. 294, 300–301 (1955) (Brown II)).

5 *Id.*

6 *See* United States v. Virginia, 518 U.S. 515 (1996).

7 *See, e.g.*, 42 U.S. Code §§ 2000e(c), 12111(7); 29 U.S. Code § 630(c); 15 U.S.C. § 1681. *See generally*, Summary of Federal and State Laws, Update Medical University, https://www.upstate.edu/diversityinclusion/policies-and-procedures/eeo/fedstatelaw.php (last visited Sept. 7, 2024).

8 Oni Harton, *Discrimination Overview*, FindLaw (Jul. 12, 2024), https://www.findlaw.com/employment/employment-discrimination/discrimination-overview.html.

process to hire, retain, and promote employees; to set the conditions of employment; and to determine the employment policies for the employer.

The EEOC "is responsible for enforcing federal laws that make it illegal to discriminate against a job applicant or an employee because of the person's race, color, religion, sex (including pregnancy, childbirth, or related conditions, gender identity, and sexual orientation), national origin, age (40 or older), disability or genetic information."[9] In most cases, EEOC enforcement applies to companies with fifteen or more workers, or in the case of age discrimination, to those with twenty or more workers.[10] If a business fails to stop harassment by its employees directed toward other employees, that failure may also create a discriminatory workplace.[11]

Title II of the Civil Rights Act of 1964 (Title II) prohibits discrimination in public accommodation, which includes hotels, restaurants, nightclubs, retail business establishments, theaters, and similar places of public accommodation. The Housing and Civil Enforcement Section of the Department of Justice Civil Rights Division provides enforcement for both the Fair Housing Act (FHA) and Title II because many rental properties will be governed by both.[12] Victims of domestic violence and military personnel on active duty have additional laws providing supplemental legal protections.[13] Congress has also extended statutory protection under the Religious Land Use and Institutionalized Persons Act to "prohibit[] local governments from adopting or enforcing land use regulations that discriminate against religious assemblies and institutions or which unjustifiably burden religious exercise."[14]

The FHA was first enacted in 1968, but the impact was not really felt until amendments in 1988 gave the government sufficient authority to enforcement law.[15] Since 1988, the government "has brought over 1,500 cases under the FHA, obtaining over $200 million in monetary relief and civil penalties, much of which has gone back to tens of thousands of victims, individuals, and communities that have experienced housing discrimination. These cases have had ripple effects on people, industries, and communities across the country."[16]

While each statute and regulation has its own requirements, the general standard for bringing a discrimination claim requires the plaintiff to prove either a discriminatory purpose or prove that as a result of the defendant's conduct, there is a discriminatory effect caused by their policies or decisions.[17] Housing regulations, for example, use a

---

9 *Overview*, Equal Employ. Opp. Comm'n, https://www.eeoc.gov/overview (last visited Sept. 7, 2024).

10 *Id.*

11 *See* Meritor Savings Bank, FSB v. Vinson, 477 U.S. 57 (1986).

12 *See Housing and Civil Enforcement Section Overview*, Civil Right Div., Dept. of Justice, https://www.justice.gov/crt/housing-and-civil-enforcement-section-overview (last visited Sept. 7, 2024).

13 *See id.* (discussing the Housing Rights Subpart of the Violence against Women Act Reauthorization Act of 2022 and the Servicemembers Civil Relief Act).

14 *Id.*

15 *See Opening the Door—Highlights in Fair Housing Act Enforcement*, Housing and Civil Enf. Sect., Civil Right Div., Dept. of Just., https://www.justice.gov/media/1219921/dl?inline.

16 *Id.* at 1.

17 *See* Texas Dept. of Hous. and Community Affairs v. Inclusive Communities Project, Inc., 576 U.S. 519, 527 (2015).

burden-shifting model of analysis to determine whether a practice giving rise to a disparate impact result is actionable discrimination. "Under the regulation, a plaintiff first must make a prima facie showing of disparate impact. That is, the plaintiff 'has the burden of proving that a challenged practice caused or predictably will cause a discriminatory effect.'"[18]

If the plaintiff can establish a prima facie case of disparate impact, the burden then shifts to the defendant. The defendant must "prov[e] that the challenged practice is necessary to achieve one or more substantial, legitimate, nondiscriminatory interests."[19]

As noted by the Supreme Court, a very similar burden-shifting approach is used in Title VII employment discrimination cases. Discrimination in the form of discriminatory purpose is never allowed. In addition, however, a disparate impact that results in lower access to opportunity for those in a protected class can only be permitted if the disparate impact is job related.[20]

The burden-shifting approach for housing and employment discrimination has a third step. Even if a defendant can justify the burden shifting by establishing a job-related purpose or a substantial nondiscriminatory purpose for housing, then the plaintiffs may still prevail "upon proving that the substantial, legitimate, nondiscriminatory interests supporting the challenged practice could be served by another practice that has a less discriminatory effect."[21]

Compliance with the ADA or Higher Education Act has more specialized tests for discriminatory purposes and discriminatory impacts, but the approach used in housing and employment provides a framework for those other fields as well. The three-step burden-shifting approach is particularly helpful in assessing each of the areas that are most significantly impacted by new technologies and the digital environment.

9.2. The Digital Divide

The digital divide represents the gap between those with ready access to modern information and communication technologies and those who do not have access to those resources.[22] "Well before the late 20th century, the digital divide referred chiefly to the division between those with and without telephone access. After the late 1990s, the term began to be used mainly to describe the split between those with and without internet access, however, particularly broadband."[23]

As more aspects of daily activities move online to access public information, engage with local governments, and conduct our daily lives, easy and efficient access to apps and

---

18 *Id.* (quoting 24 Code Fed. Reg. § 100.500(c)(1) (2014)).

19 *Id.* (quoting 24 Code Fed. Reg. § 100.500(c)(2) (2014)).

20 *Id.*

21 *Id.* (quoting 24 Code Fed. Reg. § 100.500(c)(3) (2014)).

22 *See* Katie Terrell Hanna, *Digital Divide*, TechTarget, https://www.techtarget.com/whatis/definition/digital-divide (last visited Sept. 7, 2024).

23 *Id.*

web-based services is essential. Those who do not have easy access to personal devices struggle to participate at the same level as those who are technologically connected. "The idea of the 'digital divide' refers to the growing gap between the underprivileged members of society . . ."[24] The digital divide disadvantages the disadvantaged, exacerbating preexisting inequities "especially [for] the poor, rural, elderly, and handicapped portion of the population who do not have access to computers or the internet; and the wealthy, middle-class, and young Americans living in urban and suburban areas who have access."[25]

Addressing the technology gap is not new but as more and more of our everyday activities have shifted online, the consequences of the gap are perhaps greater now than at any time in history. Retailers are shutting down locations as more shopping has moved online. Free, over-the-air radio and television broadcasting is being displaced with online streaming. Government office hours are being reduced because services are available online 24/7. These changes benefit many, but they leave those without access to technology behind.

"Public access to telecommunications has been a fundamental part of the U.S. communications policy since its early inception."[26] The 1934 Communications Act included an obligation to "make available, so far as possible, to all the people of the United States . . . a rapid, efficient, Nation-wide, and world-wide wire and radio communication service with adequate facilities at reasonable charges."[27] Still, it took until after World War II before three quarters of the public had home telephones.[28]

The statistics tell a clear story about who comprises the have-nots. "The digital divide disproportionately impacts Black Americans, with 62% having broadband internet access compared to 77% of White Americans."[29] The divide extends well past the penetration of broadband. "The racial gap persists on computer ownership, as well, with 69% of Black Americans owning a computer compared to 80% of White Americans."[30]

In 2019, the Pew Research Foundation reported that "only 57% of Hispanic adults own a desktop or laptop computer, compared to 82% of whites, and that a quarter of Hispanics surveyed rely on 'smartphone-only' access to the internet."[31] In a study from SOMOS Community Care's COVID-19 Crisis National Latino Survey, the data showed "[n]early

---

24 Digital Divide, STANFORD UNIV., https://cs.stanford.edu/people/eroberts/cs181/projects/digital-divide/start.html (last visited Sept. 8, 2024).

25 *Id.*

26 Jon M. Garon, *Dysregulating the Media: Digital Redlining, Privacy Erosion, and the Unintentional Deregulation of American Media*, 73 ME. L. REV. 45, 71 (2021), https://digitalcommons.mainelaw.maine.edu/mlr/vol73/iss1/3.

27 Monica Anderson et al., *10% of Americans Don't Use the Internet. Who Are They?* PEW RSCH. CTR. (Apr. 22, 2019), http://www.pewresearch.org/fact-tank/2019/04/22/some-americans-dont-use-the-internet-who-are-they.

28 *See* ROBERT D. PUTNAM, BOWLING ALONE: THE COLLAPSE AND REVIVAL OF AMERICAN COMMUNITY 167, 217 (2000).

29 Anna Merod, *Greater Commitment, Collaboration Key to Addressing Digital Divide for Black Communities*, K–12DIVE (Jan. 31, 2023), https://www.k12dive.com/news/addressing-digital-divide-black-communities/641618/ (citing study by McKinsey & Co.).

30 *Id.*

31 Omar L. Gallaga, *Coronavirus Has Increased the Digital Divide for Latino Students*, PULSO (Jul. 23, 2020), https://projectpulso.org/2020/07/23/coronavirus-has-increased-the-digital-divide-for-latino-students/.

40% of Latinos don't have broadband access at home."[32] Similar disparities impact rural Americans and the elderly, populations that are often left out of public and large-scale investments in new technologies.

The digital divide became starkly visible during the 2020 COVID-19 pandemic. The story of José Calix is illustrative.[33] José received a laptop distributed by Miami-Dade County Public Schools to participate in his online classes, but the school district provided only one laptop for each family. As a result, José had to share the computer with his two brothers, ages ten and eight, as they all tried to attend online classes at the same time throughout the pandemic.[34]

With the increased reliance on home computers, the digital divide has a direct impact on student learning and success. In more affluent families, parents could invest in a laptop for each of their children, but in poor families like that of José, all the children (as well as the working adults) had to compete for time on a single device. Nearly two years after the start of the pandemic, U.S. Secretary of Education Miguel Cardona stated, "[s]tudents without broadband access or only a cell phone have lower rates of homework completion, lower grade point averages . . . even lower college completion rates."[35]

Secretary Cardona supported the bipartisan efforts stemming from the 2022 Infrastructure Law to allocate "$2.75 billion under the Digital Equity Act to ensure that all people and communities can reap the full benefits of the digital economy."[36] Praising the investment, Secretary Cardona stated "[d]igital equity has never felt more urgent. But our opportunity to deliver digital equity has never felt more within reach. The pandemic turned equitable access to technology from an aspiration into an emergency."[37] Other projects are focusing on the expansion of broadband to rural communities, and the growth of satellite-based broadband may also help improve accessibility.

Internet access impacts far more than educational attainment (though that should be enough). "Internet access is increasingly recognized as a 'super determinant' of health. It plays a role in health care outcomes and influences more [than] traditionally recognized social determinants of health, such as education, employment, and healthcare access."[38] The digital divide in healthcare is well documented. "[T]he digital divide has contributed to the time and distance gap between doctors and patients, also known as the broadband health gap."[39]

---

32 *Id.*

33 Gallaga, *supra* note 31.

34 *Id.*

35 *U.S. Department of Education Communicates Vision to Advance Digital Equity for All Learners*, U.S. Dept. of Educ. (Sept. 22, 2022), https://www.ed.gov/news/press-releases/us-department-education-communicates-vision-advance-digital-equity-all-learners.

36 *Id.*

37 *Id.*

38 Yosselin Turcios, *Digital Access: A Super Determinant of Health*, Substance Abuse and Mental Health Services Admin (Mar. 22, 2023), https://www.samhsa.gov/blog/digital-access-super-determinant-health.

39 *Id. See* also *Advancing Broadband Connectivity as a Social Determinant of Health*, FCC (Feb. 7, 2022), https://www.fcc.gov/health/SDOH.

Despite the increased recognition of the importance for internet high-speed access, however, support services for those in need are being cut back. For example, effective June 1, 2024, the Affordable Connectivity Program has been suspended.[40] While in operation, the program "provided a discount of up to $30 per month toward internet service for eligible households and up to $75 per month for households on qualifying Tribal lands."[41] The program also provided a one-time discount to help with the purchase of a computer, laptop, or tablet. Participants were required to chip in with the purchase at an amount between $10-$50.[42]

Although a small public investment, these funds created the opportunity for in-home access, essential for "work, school, healthcare and more."[43] During the program's short operation, more than 20 million households enrolled for the financial assistance.[44]

The digital divide goes beyond ownership of a personal laptop. "Digital redlining has led to a lack of large-scale broadband infrastructure, which can happen when internet service providers invest in developing fiber infrastructure in wealthier communities while low-income households go unserved . . . This can ultimately lead to low-income families having access to slower but more expensive broadband services."[45]

There are also digital divides in:

- Inequalities in internet access for socioeconomic reasons.
- Geographical differences in internet speed and access.
- Unequal access to 4G/5G networks for mobile internet.
- Unequal access to computers/mobile devices.
- Gaps in digital literacy, due to generation and/or education gaps.[46]

"Many factors exacerbate the digital divide, from previous histories of discrimination to a lack of economic resources and poor infrastructure."[47] Urban planning and zoning decisions made over decades have resulted in neglected communities. Investment in new technologies tends to go to the wealthiest communities first, providing yet another advantage to the advantaged.

There are simple but costly solutions to the digital divide. "A major solution to reducing the digital divide is to increase connectivity in all communities. Providing widespread

---

40 *Affordable Connectivity Program*, FCC, https://www.fcc.gov/acp (last visited Sept. 7, 2024).

41 *Id.*

42 *Id.*

43 *Id.*

44 *More Than 20 Million Households Enroll in Nation's Largest Broadband Affordability Program*, FTC Factsheet (Aug. 14, 2023), https://docs.fcc.gov/public/attachments/DOC-395990A1.pdf.

45 Merod, *supra* note 29.

46 Kiara Taylor, *The Digital Divide: What It Is, and What's Being Done to Close It*, Investopedia (Apr. 28, 2024), https://www.investopedia.com/the-digital-divide-5116352.

47 *Solutions to the Digital Divide: Moving toward a More Equitable Future*, IEEE Connecting the Unconnected, https://ctu.ieee.org/solutions-to-the-digital-divide-moving-toward-a-more-equitable-future/ (last visited Sept. 8, 2024).

internet access can help previously unconnected users take advantage of economic and learning opportunities."[48]

Access to a free public education includes the books and materials needed to obtain that education, and it has been true for a long time that a laptop computer is a requirement for participation in school, at least starting in middle school. The laptop is no different than the textbooks and should be provided free of charge to each student.

Similarly, broadband access is a public service that should be provided, much like public roads. The analogy to roads is better than the frequent analogy to electricity, because as a metered service, all usage of electricity is paid based on consumption. Roads and internet access are generally ubiquitous but can be burdened by excessive use. Trucks, for example, do much greater damage to roads than normal sized cars and increase public maintenance. Truck companies and taxi services use the roads much more heavily than ordinary citizens. For the internet, heavy users of video streaming and downloading may place a greater load on the system than ordinary users.

Following this analogy, a public broadband system that includes some level of throttling to limit unreasonable loads would solve the problems of the access divide. Moreover, unlike the Affordable Connectivity Program, these suggestions are for universal access. Those who can currently pay for the service would also get it for free, and the tax base could be adjusted to allow for a more progressive, equitable tax system.

Both of these changes are actually quite modest in scope when compared to the current obligation for public education. As more and more government services move online, it is essential for the public sphere to provide access to those services for all. Like roads and other civic infrastructure, these are just part of maintaining a robust educated economy.

"However, reducing this gap is not as simple as handing a person a computer or a mobile phone. Users will also need to have the right infrastructure to connect to a device, the resources to keep it running, and knowledge of how to use it."[49]

Access to devices and public access to internet connectivity are two pieces of the puzzle, but the most important piece requires a public and private partnership to invest in digital literacy.[50]

By having strong knowledge of digital technologies, users can:

- Effectively control the physical components of a computer, including the keyboard, monitor, and mouse
- Access and utilize various software programs, such as word processors, internet browsers, and messaging applications
- Understand how to communicate in digital spaces, such as emails, social media sites, and other online forums

---

48 *Id.*
49 *Id.*
50 *See id.*

- Identify the elements of a credible source and effectively conduct online research
- Avoid scams, phishing schemes, and other malicious activities

With these skills, users can effectively engage with digital technologies and leverage these platforms to their benefit. For example, a person who understands how to find credible information online is more likely to obtain a research-based job than someone who struggles to navigate search engines.[51]

The benefits of closing the digital divide extend to every individual who gains additional access to information, education, employment opportunities, healthcare information, and civic engagement. By assisting poorer communities and rural communities, the divisions that undermine a healthy democratic society are narrowed and public engagement increases. The benefits extend well beyond just those who are directly benefited. Gains in educational outcomes increase economic success for every entire region.[52] The same is true for healthcare outcomes, crime rates, and other measures of regional health.[53]

9.3. Digital Redlining

Digital redlining was already mentioned above as a reflection of corporate and governmental failure to invest in infrastructure in economically disadvantaged communities. The failure to provide fiberoptic cable or 5G broadband in low-income and rural areas is a form of investment discrimination that reflects a decision to withhold resources from underserved communities. Redlining itself originated with the predecessor of the federal Fair Housing Authority, which segregated communities based on ethnic and racial status that it used to determine which home loans to guarantee.[54] Government agency "appraisers divided cities into neighborhoods and developed forms which were distributed to real estate professionals . . . [incorporating] 'notions of ethnic and racial worth' utilized by real estate appraisers."[55] This practice continued for decades as official government policy. The federal government ended its use of racial profiling when required to do so by the FHA, a chapter of the Civil Rights Act of 1968.[56] Still, even decades later, the legacy of these policies and continued failures to remediate these harms have left minority communities significantly underserved.[57]

Digital redlining highlights the modern iteration of these practices, extending the denial of access to services for low-income communities overrepresented by minority and

---

51 *Id.*

52 *See* Brent Radcliffe, *How Education and Training Affect the Economy*, Investopedia (Jun. 30, 2024), https://www.investopedia.com/articles/economics/09/education-training-advantages.asp ("An economy's productivity rises as the number of educated workers increases since skilled workers can perform tasks more efficiently.").

53 *See, e.g.*, Turcios, *supra* note 38.

54 *See* Denver D'Rozario & Jerome D. Williams, *Retail Redlining: Definition, Theory, Typology, and Measurement*, 25 J. Macromarketing 175, 175 (Dec. 2005); Garon, *Dysregulating the Media*, *supra* note 26 at 74.

55 Charles Lewis Nier III, *The Shadow of Credit: The Historical Origins of Racial Predatory Lending and Its Impact upon African American Wealth Accumulation*, 11 U. PA. J. L. & Soc. Change 131, 176–77 (2008).

56 *Id.*

57 *See id.*; D'Rozario & Williams, *supra* note 54.

ethnic populations. In the digital realm, the online activities include websites, apps, social media platforms, and other digital technologies. For example, there have been numerous claims that websites have facilitated racial discrimination in online housing markets.[58] Other examples include reduced access to employment opportunities, healthcare resources, education, and other essential services. Nonetheless, housing remains an excellent example of the potential problems and a leading area for federal enforcement efforts to combat discriminatory treatment.

In the context of rental housing, for example, the issue stems from the use of information gathered by online platforms to select whether or not to advertise a property to one of the platform's subscribers. "[D]iscriminatory housing advertisements that harm protected classes are illegal under the FHA."[59] Some of that information is wholly appropriate for use by the advertiser, but other data may be used to create a discriminatory purpose to the advertiser's housing practices or result in a discriminatory effect.[60] For example, some landlords refuse to rent to potential tenants who pay using Section 8 housing vouchers.[61] Others respond less frequently to inquiries from single parents, women, minorities, or potential tenants who fall into more than one of these categories.[62]

For the advertiser, accessing background information about prospective tenants is often difficult, given the lack of personal information that a person presents as part of the application. Using social media and content platforms, however, the advertisers can obtain a wealth of information about the background and characteristics of the applicants.[63] They can also steer their ads directly to the types of candidates they would most like to become new tenants and avoid categories of qualified potential tenants with characteristics disfavored by the property owners.[64] For example, Facebook "collects data from the on- and off-site activity of its users and allows advertisers to 'exclude' certain individuals from the audience of their advertisements on the basis of gender, familial status, and a litany of other categories created from this information."[65]

In 2019, the Federal Trade Commission (FTC) forced Facebook to settle claims that the company allowed "advertisers to unlawfully discriminate against minorities, women, and the elderly by using the platform's ad-targeting technology to exclude them from seeing ads for housing, jobs, and credit—three areas with legal protections for groups

---

58 *See, e.g.*, Chi. Laws'. Comm. for C.R. under Law, Inc. v. Craigslist, Inc., 519 F.3d 666 (7th Cir. 2008); Fair Hous. Council of San Fernando Valley v. Roommates.com, LLC, 521 F.3d 1157 (9th Cir. 2008); Adi Robertson, *What Happens Next in the Housing Discrimination Case against Facebook?* Verge (Apr. 2, 2019), http://www.theverge.com/2019/4/2/18286660/facebook-hud-housing-discrimination-case-section-230-legal-defense.

59 Chandler Nicholle Spinks, *Contemporary Housing Discrimination: Facebook, Targeted Advertising, and the Fair Housing Act*, 57 Hous. L. Rev. 925, 929 (2020).

60 *See* Jacob William Faber & Marie-Dumesle Mercier, *Multidimensional Discrimination in the Online Rental Housing Market: Implications for Families with Young Children*, Housing Policy Debate (2022), https://doi.org/10.1080/10511482.2021.2010118.

61 *Id.* at 2.

62 *Id.*

63 *See* Spinks, *supra* note 59 at 928–30.

64 *Id.*

65 *Id.* at 928.

that historically have been disenfranchised."[66] Evidently, however, the practices continued. Again in 2022, Meta—the renamed Facebook—entered into a consent decree with the FTC for similar activities.[67]

Private parties have made similar allegations. In May 2024, SafeRent Solutions, LLC (previously CoreLogic Rental Property Solutions, LLC) agreed to settle a lawsuit that had alleged the company relied upon discriminatory algorithms which disadvantaged Black and Hispanic rental applicants. The lawsuit alleged that SafeRent violated both the FHA and Massachusetts law.[68] In the lawsuit, which was settled without any admission of wrongdoing for $2.275 million, the plaintiffs alleged SafeRent and CoreLogic scoring methodology systematically undervalued Hispanic and Black applicant credit scores. "Black consumers have a median credit score of 612 and Hispanic consumers have a median credit score of 661, as compared to white consumers' median credit score of 725, leading to unfair bias in accepting an applicant's lease application."[69] Once the credit scores were assigned, the neutral use of credit scores to evaluate applicants would create an actionable disparate impact.

Another aspect of the digital redlining is the choice by the advertisers to offer opportunities to select customers while ignoring less desirable customers. This might seem an odd concept. After all, companies generally want as many customers as possible. But companies must decide where to spend their advertising budgets to maximize effectiveness and efficiency. Spending advertising dollars on affluent buyers, for example, makes strong business sense when promoting luxury goods. Companies advertising children's back to school products would prefer that their ads reach households with school-age children. Such decisions are economically sound and do not raise questions of bias or redlining.

On the other hand, if the targeting were undertaken by a nonprofit hospital that has an obligation to provide free and low-cost healthcare services in the community it serves, then intentionally avoiding any offer of services to the people that institution is required to help would raise serious ethical questions and may also constitute a violation of state or federal public accommodation laws.

Other examples involve advertisements for credit cards. In 2019, the public advocacy organization, the "Markup," "found examples of four different companies targeting ads for financial services to restricted age groups, a practice that violates Facebook's anti-discrimination policies and, in some cases, may violate federal or state civil rights laws."[70]

---

66 Emily Dreyfuss, *Facebook Changes Its Ad Tech to Stop Discrimination*, Wired (Mar. 19, 2019), https://www.wired.com/story/facebook-advertising-discrimination-settlement/.

67 U.S. v. Meta Platforms, Inc., No. 22 Civ. 5187 (S.D.N.Y. Jun. 21, 2022).

68 Louis v. SafeRent Solutions, LLC, Case 1:22-cv-10800 (D. Mass) (filed May 25, 2022) (citing 42 U.S. Code § 3604; Mass. Gen. Laws Ch. 151B, § 4 (6), § 4(10)).

69 Louis, et al. v. SafeRent Solutions, et al., CohenMilstein, https://www.cohenmilstein.com/case-study/louis-et-al-v-saferent-solutions-et-al/ (last visited Jun. 13, 2024) (data from a 2022 study conducted by the Urban Institute).

70 Corin Faife & Alfred Ng, *Credit Card Ads Were Targeted by Age, Violating Facebook's Anti-discrimination Policy*, The Markup (Apr. 29, 2021), https://themarkup.org/citizen-browser/2021/04/29/credit-card-ads-were-targeted-by-age-violating-facebooks-anti-discrimination-policy.

The provision of age-target services and accompanying advertising of those restricted offers may violate the Equal Credit Opportunity Act (ECOA).[71] Under the ECOA regulations, "'Disparate treatment' may be 'overt' (when the creditor openly discriminates on a prohibited basis) or it may be found through comparing the treatment of applicants who receive different treatment for no discernable reason other than a prohibited basis."[72]

Concerns over digital redlining have increased with the advent of AI screening systems. In April 2024, the Department of Housing and Urban Development (HUD) released new guidance to highlight these concerns. The release points out that "[a]n increasing number of tenant screening companies claim that they use advanced technologies, such as machine learning and other forms of artificial intelligence (AI)."[73] While these tools might improve the landlord's accuracy in selecting tenants who will pay their rent, they may have other purposes or effects. "These technologies can increase these companies' capacity to access and analyze information about applicants that has not been widely used for rental decisions until recently but may have little bearing on whether someone will comply with their lease."[74] In addition to using less relevant information to select the tenants, these tools also reduce the transparency of the rental process and obscure the decision making by the property owners.[75]

In understanding the challenge of digital redlining, it should also be noted that there are relatively few direct actions brought by those who faced discrimination. In part, this reflects the difficulty of any individual proving a case of systematic discrimination. The barrier to legal recourse is higher; however, because in many of the cases, the advertisements for tenants are posted by users of the service provider. At the dawn of the internet age, Congress gave broad immunity to interactive computer services from liability for third-party content under Section 230 of the Communications Decency Act.[76] This immunity extends far beyond the Internet Service Providers (ISPs) that host web services to include publishing platforms like YouTube and social media providers such as Meta, Craigslist, X (formerly Twitter), Instagram, or Pinterest.

Host sites can avoid civil liability for the content of their advertisers for many of the claims arising from the third-party content. Section 230 does not create the same limitation on federal agencies enforcing federal criminal law.[77]

---

71 *Id. See* 12 Code Fed. Reg. pt. 1002 (76 Fed. Reg. 79442) (Dec. 21, 2011).

72 12 Code Fed. Reg. pt. 1002 Supp. I, § 1002.4(a)-1.

73 *Guidance on Application of the Fair Housing Act to the Screening of Applicants for Rental Housing*, U.S. Dept. of Housing and Urban Dev. (Apr. 29, 2024), https://www.hud.gov/sites/dfiles/FHEO/documents/FHEO_Guidance_on_Screening_of_Applicants_for_Rental_Housing.pdf.

74 *Id.*

75 *Id.*

76 *See, e.g.*, Johnson v. Arden, 614 F.3d 785, 790–91 (8th Cir. 2010) ("The CDA states that '[n]o provider or user of an interactive computer service shall be treated as the publisher or speaker of any information provided by another information content provider,' 47 U.S.C. § 230(c)(1), and expressly preempts any state law to the contrary, *id.* § 230(e)(3)"); Fair Hous. Council of San Fernando Valley v. Roommates.com, LLC, 521 F.3d 1157, 1162–64 (9th Cir. 2008).

77 47 U.S.C. § 230(e)(1).

An open question remains regarding the interpretation by the courts of Section 230 in the context of content generated by a chatbot or large language model AI system. As the law evolves, "courts will likely find that ChatGPT and other [AI systems] are information content providers."[78] If a company utilizes an AI chatbot that steers some groups of prospective customers away from housing, financial services, employment, or healthcare in a manner that shows a discriminatory disparate impact, Section 230 is unlikely to provide a barrier to enforcement.

When dealing with digital content, AI has become pervasive, tracking the content and connecting that content to the demographics and psychographics of the content creator. Social media algorithms determine the next story in a person's social media feed, the next product or service to be advertised in online shopping, the next show to stream, book to read, or news item to digest. Mass media and mass marketing have been replaced with hyper-individualization. To accomplish this target, markets must be narrowly segmented.

"Segmentation allows marketers to identify distinct groups of customers whose behaviours significantly differ from others."[79] Demographic segmentation or targeting focuses on the external attributes, including Demographic segmentation variables include age, gender, family size, family life cycle, income, occupation, education, generation, ethnicity, nationality, religion, and social class.[80] Demographic segmentation is no longer considered sufficient as a driver of marketing effectiveness, so behavioral and psychographic targeting are increasingly used to individuate content.[81] Behavioral segmentation takes the next step. "[B]ehavioral segmentation groups consumers according to similar behaviors. . . . This is a powerful and lucrative tool for retailers, but it only uncovers what consumers are doing, not why they are doing it."[82]

"Psychographic segmentation is a market research method used to divide a market or customer group into segments based on their beliefs, values, lifestyle, social status, activities, interests and opinions and other psychological criteria."[83] Psychographic profiling goes beyond a person's demographic characteristics or their past behaviors. "Psychographic segmentation variables go deeper to uncover the why, and if one knows the why, one can customize messaging and media according to consumers' communication preferences and appeal to their motivations."[84]

Psychographic targeting offers marketers, political advocates, and other content providers to customize the audience in a very fine-grained manner and also to adjust their

---

78 Matt Perault, *Section 230 Won't Protect ChatGPT*, LAWFARE BLOG (Feb. 22, 2023), https://www.lawfareblog.com/section-230-wont-protect-chatgpt.

79 Sulekha Goyat, *The Basis of Market Segmentation: A Critical Review of Literature*, 3 EUROPEAN J. BUS. MAN. 45, 46 (2011).

80 *Id.* at 48.

81 *See id.*

82 Brent Walker, *The Importance of Psychographic Segmentation*, UPFRONT (Feb. 28, 2023), https://upfronthealthcare.com/resources/patient-activation/importance-psychographic-segmentation/.

83 Will Webster, *What Is Psychographic Segmentation? A Beginner's Guide*, QUALTRICS, https://www.qualtrics.com/experience-management/brand/psychographic-segmentation/ (last visited Jun. 14, 2024).

84 Walker, *supra* note 82.

messaging to use the types of advocacy that each different audience segment will find most compelling. "By understanding needs, wants, concerns, motivations and aspirations, businesses can tailor what they offer to better align with what their target audience cares about."[85]

As with any form of marketing, there is nothing categorically inappropriate to do with market segmentation and targeting. But the power to segment the marketplace so narrowly enables very detailed tracking of individuals and an almost limitless power to differentiate opportunities in the online environment. Without careful management of discriminatory effects in the datasets, design, and implementation of online markets, using psychographic targeting will invariably exacerbate the endemic biases in society. The digital environment has the potential to turn the chapter on historical discrimination, but by using demographic and psychographic market segmentation, companies are replicating historical disparities in the online world.

9.4. Algorithmic Discrimination and Bias

Another important consideration for understanding the bias that impacts the digital environment comes from the algorithms that power large language models AI systems and other decision-making AI.[86] "Algorithmic bias refers to the systemic and repeatable errors in a computer system that create unfair outcomes, such as privileging one arbitrary group of users over others. It's a prevalent concern today, with artificial intelligence (AI) and machine learning (ML) applications increasingly permeating every aspect of our lives."[87] "Examples of AI bias in the real world show us that when discriminatory data and algorithms are baked into AI models, the models deploy biases at scale and amplify the resulting negative effects."[88]

Algorithmic bias is similar to other forms of discrimination, in that some instances are triggered by an intentional discriminatory purpose, but more commonly, the discrimination results from an unintentional discriminatory effect resulting from the design choices made about the algorithms and the data selected on which to develop the patterns underlying system decision making.

Bias in the digital environment may be introduced in any of the three production steps: in the data, in the design, and in the deployment. There may be bias in the data because of the selection criteria used or because past practices included discriminatory practices that are reflected in the data.[89] There may be bias in the design because all humans

---

85 *Id.*

86 *See Shedding Light on AI Bias with Real World Examples*, IBM (Oct. 16, 2023), https://www.ibm.com/blog/shedding-light-on-ai-bias-with-real-world-examples/ ("As companies increase their use of artificial intelligence (AI), people are questioning the extent to which human biases have made their way into AI systems.").

87 Abid Ali Awan, *What Is Algorithmic Bias?*, Data Camp (Jul. 2023), https://www.datacamp.com/blog/what-is-algorithmic-bias.

88 *Id.*

89 *Id.* ("Data bias. If the data used to train an AI system doesn't represent the entire population, the algorithm's decisions may favor the group it was trained on.").

carry their cognitive and implicit biases with them when they go about their daily lives.[90] Finally, there may be bias in the deployment because of socio-technical factors.[91] "Socio-technical factors include the influence of social, economic, and cultural contexts on how AI systems are designed, deployed, and used, which may introduce bias."[92]

Biases, preferences, and learned responses are fundamental to human cognition.[93] Many of them are not consciously part of a person's decision making, even though they are quite influential.[94] "Implicit bias is defined as the set of attitudes or stereotypes that affect our cognition, affect and behavior in unconscious and automatic manner. . . . Implicit biases are pervasive; every individual is susceptible to them, including children and those with avowed commitments to impartiality."[95]

All systems designed by people necessarily incorporate the biases and preferences of the people who built them. "Implicit biases can be either positive or negative, and are activated involuntarily without an individual's intention, awareness, or control."[96] The important distinction between implicit bias and other cognitive shortcuts is that by making our biases explicit, thoughtful design can control for a demonstrated bias. When AI systems learn from historical data or from curated data, the results "reflect and perpetuate human biases within a society, including historical and current social inequality."[97]

Problems of facial recognition software provide a well-documented example. "AI facial recognition software has been notoriously poor in facial recognition for dark-skinned individuals as compared to Caucasian individuals."[98] "NIST's tests and other studies repeatedly have found that the algorithms have a harder time recognizing people with darker skin. . . . Many top performers in that report show . . . [a] 10-fold difference in error rate for black and white women."[99] Critics speculate that the lack of representation among women and African Americans in the tech communities building facial recognition software systems may have led to some of this disparity. Engineers tested early

---

[90] *See* Karen Steinhauser, *Everyone Is a Little Bit Biased*, Bus. L. Today (Mar 16, 2020), https://www.americanbar.org/groups/business_law/resources/business-law-today/2020-april/everyone-is-a-little-bit-biased/; Keith Payne et al., *How to Think about "Implicit Bias,"* Sci. Am. (Mar. 27, 2018), https://www.scientificamerican.com/article/how-to-think-about-implicit-bias/. *See also* Awan, *supra* note 87 ("Prejudice in design. If the AI designers have implicit biases, these can unknowingly be transferred into the system's behavior.").

[91] Awan, *supra* note 87.

[92] *Id.*

[93] *See* Xiaodan Hu & Ange-Marie Hancock, *State of the Science: Introduction to Implicit Bias Review 2018-2020*, Kirwan Inst. of The Ohio State U. (May 22, 2024), https://kirwaninstitute.osu.edu/research/state-science-introduction-implicit-bias-review-2018-2020.

[94] *See Cognitive Bias 101: What It Is and How to Overcome It*, Cleveland Clinic (May 2, 2023), https://health.clevelandclinic.org/cognitive-bias ("We all have cognitive biases, which happen as an attempt by our brains to simplify all the information it receives every second. It's a systematic error in our thinking that influences and affects how we make decisions and how we think about the world around us.").

[95] *Id.* (internal citations omitted).

[96] *Id.* (internal citations omitted).

[97] *Shedding light on AI Bias with Real World Examples*, *supra* note 86.

[98] Jon M. Garon, *Prometheus' Digital Fire: The Civic Responsibilities of Artificial Intelligence*, 20 Ohio State Tech. L. J. 225, 243 (2024). *See* Tom Simonite, *The Best Algorithms Struggle to Recognize Black Faces Equally*, Wired (Jul. 22, 2019), https://www.wired.com/story/best-algorithms-struggle-recognize-black-faces-equally/ ("US government tests find even top-performing facial recognition systems misidentify blacks at rates five to 10 times higher than they do whites.").

[99] Simonite, *supra* note 98.

prototypes on themselves and refined the designs based on the effectiveness with their colleagues.[100]

"Another key source of racial discrimination in face recognition lies in its utilization. . . . [F]ace recognition can potentially target other marginalized populations, such as undocumented immigrants by ICE, or Muslim citizens by the NYPD."[101] At the corporate level, the FTC brought and settled allegations against pharmacy chain Rite Aid over a decade-long misuse of facial recognition tools that resulted in false-positive reports that minority customers had committed shoplifting or other criminal activities.[102] "Rite Aid's actions disproportionately affected people of color, especially Black people, Asians and Latinos, all in the name of keeping 'persons of interest' out of hundreds of Rite Aid stores in cities including New York, Philadelphia and Sacramento."[103]

Increasingly, computer systems are not programmed to follow the logic of the engineer's hierarchical structure but instead "to learn through experience" through machine learning (ML) training.[104] To accomplish experience-based learning, ML systems require massive amounts of data.[105] The systems analyze the data, identify patterns, and increasingly develop predictions about the information.[106] Large language models that fuel chatbots and natural language systems like ChatGPT, Gemini, or Co-Pilot learn the patterns of language following a similar model.[107] "[I]f the data represents a single demographic, or lacks diversity, the outputs produced by the large language model will also lack diversity."[108]

---

100 *See id.*; Alex Najibi, *Racial Discrimination in Face Recognition Technology*, Harv. Sci. in the News (Oct. 24, 2020), https://sites.harvard.edu/sitn/2020/10/24/racial-discrimination-in-face-recognition-technology/.

101 Najibi, *supra* note 100.

102 *Rite Aid Banned from Using AI Facial Recognition after FTC Says Retailer Deployed Technology without Reasonable Safeguards*, Fed. Trade Comm'n (Dec. 19, 2023) (Rite Aid Press Release), https://www.ftc.gov/news-events/news/press-releases/2023/12/rite-aid-banned-using-ai-facial-recognition-after-ftc-says-retailer-deployed-technology-without. *See* FTC v. Rite Aid Corp., Case No. 2:23-cv-5023 (Dec. 19, 2023).

103 Eduardo Medina, *Rite Aid's A.I. Facial Recognition Wrongly Tagged People of Color as Shoplifters*, N.Y. Times (Dec. 21, 2023), https://www.nytimes.com/2023/12/21/business/rite-aid-ai-facial-recognition.html (quoting the FTC).

104 Sara Brown, *Machine Learning, Explained*, MIT (Apr. 21, 2021), https://mitsloan.mit.edu/ideas-made-to-matter/machine-learning-explained; Borgesius, *supra* note 387, at 13 (quoting Peter Donnelly et al., Machine learning: The Power and Promise of Computers that Learn by Example, Royal Society 19 (2017)), https://royalsociety.org/-/media/policy/projects/machine-learning/publications/machine-learning-report.pdf.
With machine learning, the knowledge in the system does not have to be provided by experts. "In contrast, machine learning systems are set a task and given a large amount of data to use as examples of how this task can be achieved or from which to detect patterns. The system then learns how best to achieve the desired output."

105 Brown, *supra* note 104.

106 *Id.*

107 *See What Is a Large Language Model (LLM)?* Elastic, https://www.elastic.co/what-is/large-language-models.
A large language model (LLM) is a deep learning algorithm that can perform a variety of natural language processing (NLP) tasks. Large language models use transformer models and are trained using massive datasets—hence, large. This enables them to recognize, translate, predict, or generate text or other content. LLMs are also referred to as neural networks (NNs), which are computing systems inspired by the human brain. These NNs work using a network of nodes that are layered, much like neurons.
See generally Zhengbao Jiang et al., *How Can We Know What Language Models Know?* 8 Transactions of the Ass'n for Comput. Linguistics 423 (2020), https://direct.mit.edu/tacl/article/doi/10.1162/tacl_a_00324/96460.

108 *What Is Large Language Models (LLM)?*, *supra* note 107.

Consider, hypothetically, if a large language model were trained on only books and publications that are currently in the public domain, primarily materials published prior to 1929 (or between 1929 and 1977 if published without a copyright notice). Much of the popular literature during the nineteenth and twentieth centuries promulgated a casual racism, incorporating Jim Crow segregation and a separate-but-equal mindset into descriptions of everyday discourse and description.[109] Even if one could postulate a world where all modern online communications and social media hubs were free of bias, racism, and harassment, the corpus of historical content creates a strong likelihood that the language available to large language models are replete with the biases of society.

"AI decision making often builds on these implicit biases. For example, Amazon attempted to use AI for its recruiting in 2014 but the AI learned to replicate the recommendations to the training data and reproduce the very hiring biases Amazon was hoping to eliminate."[110] The dataset Amazon used focused on the past ten years of the company's hiring practices. "Historical data contained biases against women since there was a male dominance across the tech industry and men were forming 60% of Amazon's employees. Therefore, Amazon's recruiting system incorrectly learnt that male candidates were preferable. It penalized resumes that included the word 'women's,' as in 'women's chess club captain.'"[111] Amazon tried and failed to excise the AI system's insistence on the pattern of gender discrimination. Ultimately, Amazon chose not to use the system at all since it could not overcome the discriminatory pattern recognition inherent in the design.[112]

At each step in the development of predictive and generative AI systems, developers must address the challenges of overcoming past discrimination and designing to avoid discrimination. Simply using historical data without thoughtful curation simply repeats the past without learning from it. Human interventions to assess the weighting of factors leading to predictions must address the challenge of unintended discriminatory effects. And the deployment of systems—particularly systems designed to restrict access to resources or services—must be carefully designed not to exclude people based on any status protected by law. Only by addressing discriminatory effects at each step of the project can the deployment of an AI system or the implementation of a digital environment be inclusive for all.

---

109 *See e.g.*, Anjali Enjeti, *On the Unbearable Whiteness of Mainstream, Canonical Southern Literature*, Literary Hub (Jun. 28, 2021), https://lithub.com/on-the-unbearable-on-the-unbearable-whiteness-of-mainstream-canonical-southern-literature-of-mainstream-southern-literature/ ("In the vast majority of white-authored southern novels I read, nostalgia served as a harbinger for racism, and southern pride was a stand-in for white fragility."). *Cf.* Russell Contreras, *Blackface, Other Insensitivities Ran Rampant in '80s Culture*, Denver Post (Feb. 10, 2019), https://www.denverpost.com/2019/02/10/blackface-virginia-politicians-racism/.

110 Garon, Prometheus Fire, *supra* note 98 at 250 citing Andrew Hundt et al., *Robots Enact Malignant Stereotypes*, Proceedings of the 2022 ACM Conference on Fairness, Accountability, and Transparency 743 (Jun. 2022), https://dl.acm.org/doi/10.1145/3531146.3533138 ("Stereotypes, bias, and discrimination have been extensively documented in Machine Learning (ML) methods such as Computer Vision (CV), Natural Language Processing (NLP), or both, in the case of large image and caption models such as OpenAI CLIP") (citations omitted).

111 Cem Dilmegani, *Bias in AI: Examples & 6 Ways to Fix It in 2025*, AIMultiple (Mar. 11, 2025), https://research.aimultiple.com/ai-bias/.

112 *Id.*

9.5. Cultural Sensitivity and Context in Online Personas

As noted in the introduction of the chapter, cyberspace enables users to shed their physical constraints, but that power is limited both by imagination and social custom.[113] With improvements in AI-based image generation, people can upload their own images to create digital replicas for use as avatars or select from a wide range of potential options. Although all choices are possible, however, not all choices might be ideal. These issues are wide-ranging, including the appropriateness of a person's online digital persona in the work environment, voice remodeling to change the listener's image of the speaker, the use of culturally appropriate memes in social media, and the types of avatars that might offend others even in social contexts.

Like any choice of personal representation, the first question is the extent to which the choices fit the environment in which the representation is being used. One can choose to adopt a digital replica, recreating one's exact identity in digital form or choose to present oneself online as a very different person—or even nonhuman—avatar. The choices one makes, however, will be dependent on the online environment.

As an initial matter, avatar users should be mindful of the social expectations of the environment in which they are participating.[114] "From decorative face filters, to the ability to appear as a Japanese anime-style figure, a glowy translucent StarWars-inspired hologram projected by your droid or an animoji fox, the avatar form you take should suit the type of conversation you hope to have in the workplace."[115] While these options may be interesting, they may not further the goals for a corporate planning meeting or build an appropriate customer relationship. "The issue of dress in the workplace is sensitive, layered, and nuanced."[116]

One consideration is who selects the avatar or other digital filter for working environments. "When using avatars in a working relationship, the employer can either propose its own avatar for staff, or allow employees to create their own. . . . If avatars are used to discriminate against employees on the basis of certain characteristics such as race, gender, religion, disability or age, this could lead to violations of discrimination laws."[117] Even if the avatars are selected by the individual employee, the selection must fall within accepted norms so that the choice does not create a hostile work environment or interfere with other employee's rights.

---

113 *See* Kung, *supra* note 1.

114 David Rose, *Which Avatar Will You Wear to Your Next Business Meeting?* Forbes (Jan. 9, 2022), https://www.forbes.com/sites/davidrose/2022/01/09/which-avatar-will-you-wear-to-your-next-business-meeting/.

115 *Id.*

116 *Id.*

117 Michel Maus, *The Use of Avatars in the Workplace. Legal Issues*, LinkedIn (May 17, 2023), https://www.linkedin.com/pulse/use-avatars-workplace-legal-issues-michel-maus/.

Another use of AI technology is for voice remodeling. AI services allow call centers to adjust or eliminate the accents of their workers.[118] A new entrant in the call center industry, Sanas, hopes to ease away the challenges accents place on the customer experience. "Using data about the sounds of different accents and how they correspond to each other, Sanas's AI engine can transform a speaker's accent into what passes for another one—and right now, the focus is on making non-Americans sound like white Americans."[119] In advocating for the use of the technology, Sanas points to the effort demanded by call center workers in India and the Philippines to reduce regional accents and drop British pronunciation of words as well as learn common American terms.[120] "They have to mimic the culture as well as neutralize their own culture . . ."[121] Reflecting on the practice, Dr. A. Aneesh noted that "artificially neutralizing accents represented a kind of 'indifference to difference,' which diminishes the humanity of the person on the other end of the phone."[122]

Other critics of accent neutralization point out that "[a]ccents can connect consumers to places, products and history in culturally nuanced ways that, at times, general 'neutral-accented standard American English' cannot. . . . Multicultural audiences are substantial across the country, and ignoring their presence does a brand no good."[123] Using AI and digital systems to erase differences is far different than respecting those differences. What is best for marketing may nonetheless have a corrosive effect on the broader society and a long-term reinforcement of normalcy driven by algorithm rather than society.

In 2000, Professor Jerry Kang noted that "race and racism are already in cyberspace."[124] He raised concerns that have largely gone unanswered over the past two decades: "Cyberspace enables new forms of social interaction. . . . As computing-communication technologies advance to engage more senses, those bodily characteristics that signal a person's race will increasingly appear in cyberspace. What should decisionmakers do to shape this architecture?"[125] The trends regarding the assimilation of race and gender valuation have already made their way into online communities. In markets for avatar skins, there are examples where female and darker-skinned options "tend to sell for less than avatars with male traits or fair skin . . ."[126]

---

118 *See* Wilfred Chan, *The AI Startup Erasing Call Center Worker Accents: Is It Fighting Bias—or Perpetuating It?* GUARDIAN (Aug. 24, 2022), https://www.theguardian.com/technology/2022/aug/23/voice-accent-technology-call-center-white-american.

119 *Id.*

120 *See id.*

121 *Id.* (quoting A Aneesh, a sociologist and the incoming director of the University of Oregon's School of Global Studies and Languages).

122 *Id.*

123 Antonio Francisco Lewis, *The Ethical Challenge of AI Accent Neutralization vs. Sonic Diversity*, ADWEEK, https://www.adweek.com/partner-articles/the-ethical-challenge-of-ai-accent-neutralization-vs-sonic-diversity/ (last visited Mar. 10, 2023) ("The Linguistic Society of America highlights a truth that is increasingly important to acknowledge: Everyone who speaks English does so with an accent.").

124 Jerry Kang, *Cyber-Race*, 113 HARV. L. REV. 1130, 1135 (2000).

125 *Id.*

126 Adriana Hamacher, *Zeroing in on NFT Diversity for a More Inclusive Metaverse*, DECRYPT (Jan. 4, 2022).

The simple answer would seem to be to ensure that tools to build avatars include a wide range of skin color, hair choices, body types, and as much customization as possible. Narrow forced choices will lead to consumer dissatisfaction and a sense that the community is unwelcoming.[127] At the same time, this is not a panacea. "[C]reating a perfect avatar to represent ourselves virtually could create its own problems. If Instagram is anything to go by, it's unlikely we'll rush to our avatars with features that society deems 'undesirable.'"[128]

There have been incidents of body shaming on many social platforms. Hurtful comments and online shaming portend issues that may likely emerge in other communities, particularly among adolescents for whom these issues are central to self-identity.[129] For example, when Second Life shifted avatar designs from animals to human, the switch led to changes in user behavior and expectations of beauty. "For those users whose avatars fall outside the norm, incidents of harassment still happen all the time . . . Anyone with a large avatar is going to get at least a few nasty comments."[130]

The norm setting for the environments should also recognize that the power to be "anyone" may be more culturally limited, if the choice to take on another identity could be viewed within the community as a form of "digital blackface."[131] "Digital blackface is a practice where White people co-opt online expressions of Black imagery, slang, catchphrases or culture to convey comic relief or express emotions. These expressions, what one commentator calls racialized reactions, are mainstays in Twitter feeds, TikTok videos and Instagram reels . . ."[132] As used in this definition, it reflects the posting of clips of minorities "expressing exaggerated emotions on social media."[133] When a person selects an exaggerated, decontextualized reaction featuring a minority of a different racial or ethnic background, the message includes derogatory reflections on the people represented by the clip.

This is not to say one cannot ever use a clip or an avatar that is not representative of oneself. First, these are social constraints not legal prohibitions. The law of the First Amendment does not apply to private speech, nor does it criminalize poor social choices. Nonetheless, social norms and values are essential to society, and norms should not be lightly dismissed.

---

[127] *See* Tayce Bandeira Marchesi, *Avatars, Skins, and Realistic Representations: The Impact of the Metaverse on Your Image*, LOOTVERSE GAZETTE (Jun. 21, 2022), https://gazette.lootverse.com/avatars-skins-realistic-representations-the-impacts-of-the-metaverse-on-your-image/; Maghan McDowell, Race, *Gender and Representation: The Grey Area of the Metaverse*, VOGUE BUSINESS (Sept. 28, 2021), https://www.voguebusiness.com/technology/race-gender-and-representation-the-grey-area-of-the-metaverse.

[128] Sophie Wilson, *In the Metaverse, Everyone Looks the Same*, DAZED BEAUTY (Apr. 13, 2022), https://www.dazeddigital.com/beauty/article/55818/1/in-the-metaverse-everyone-looks-the-same-beauty-insecure-social-media.

[129] *See* Oscar Holland, *Virtual Body-Shaming: Why the Metaverse Won't Fix Our IRL Beauty Standards*, CNN (Sept. 9, 2022), https://www.cnn.com/style/article/virtual-body-shaming-september-issues/index.html.

[130] *Id.* (quoting Wagner James Au.).

[131] John Blake, *What's "Digital Blackface?" And Why Is It Wrong When White People Use It?* CNN (Mar. 26, 2023), https://www.cnn.com/2023/03/26/us/digital-blackface-social-media-explainer-blake-cec/index.html.

[132] *Id.*

[133] *Id.*

Second, intent matters. For some online users, the ability to explore another identity using avatars might be quite freeing and revelatory.[134] In 1959, novelist John Howard Griffin medically darkened his skin as part of his research to understand the injustice in the Jim Crow South.[135] The resulting work, *Black Like Me*, became a best seller, selling more than 10 million copies and educating a generation of Americans.[136]

In the twenty-first century, individuals can explore their identity through digital personas and avatars. The digital environment has the potential to enable users to express themselves more fully and to explore who they might wish to become. At the same time, preset avatars are quite limiting in this regard. "We desperately need tech leadership to reflect people from all kinds of gender identities, sexual orientations, racial and ethnic backgrounds, religious identities, and levels of ability to eradicate toxic work environments and start creating diverse, inclusive digital identities."[137]

The choice to use a nonconforming avatar is about the intent and its impact on those to whom it communicates. Unless it is done with express, affirming purposes, however, the likely result is that it will simply reinforce the digital blackface narrative and demean both the wearer and the environment. Still, it creates a powerful resource, if the system design allows for enough customization. Whether users are trying to have their digital personas be more truly representative or using nonconforming personas to explore their own identity, the cultural effect will be determined by the users' intent and the cultural norms within the digital environment.

To make digital environments better suited for cultural respect, there are lessons that can be borrowed from the intentional design of educational spaces. These axioms include the need to foster a climate of belonging, to make any barriers explicit so that they can be addressed, to design with accessibility as a foundational requirement, and to promote community standards that emphasize self-awareness and respect for others.[138]

Ultimately, it takes a village to build a village. "Ensure as many types of identities, especially marginalized ones, are represented among creators during the entire life cycle of a product, from ideation to ongoing development. Ensure that people are in the room who you want to do right by, then listen to them. Better yet, step aside and let them lead."[139] By having an approach to design that starts with a broad, engaged team, it becomes easier to be mindful of other design choices. "[T]here are tantalizing glimpses of what may

---

[134] *See* Maghan McDowell, *Shaping Online Avatars: Why Our Digital Identities Differ*, Vogue Business (Oct. 19, 2021), https://www.voguebusiness.com/technology/shaping-online-avatars-why-our-digital-identities-differ.

[135] John Howard Griffin, Black Like Me (1959). *See* Bruce Watson, Black Like Me, 50 Years Later (Oct. 2011), https://www.smithsonianmag.com/arts-culture/black-like-me-50-years-later-74543463/; Helen Morgan et al., *The Role of the Avatar in Gaming for Trans and Gender Diverse Young People*, Int. J. Environ Res. Public Health (Nov. 20, 2020), https://www.ncbi.nlm.nih.gov/pmc/articles/PMC7699515/.

[136] *See id.*

[137] McDowell, *supra* note 134 (quoting Breanna Kilpack, a production coordinator at Daz Productions).

[138] *See Inclusive Teaching and Learning Online*, Columbia Center for Teaching and Learning, https://ctl.columbia.edu/resources-and-technology/teaching-with-technology/teaching-online/inclusive-teaching/.

[139] Justine Jones, *Meta-Clusivity: Building an Inclusive Metaverse*, Assembly (Apr. 7, 2022), https://www.assemblyglobal.com/insights/meta-clusivity-building-an-inclusive-metaverse (quoting Paul Freibott, Senior Director of Research at Assembly).

be achievable, such as data to suggest that taking on an alternate metaverse persona can lead to a reduction in implicit bias."[140]

9.6. Conclusion

As Professor Kang noted decades ago, race and racism followed the users of online communities into cyberspace. Although digital environments provide great opportunities to move past geographic limitations, they carry the demographic, behavioral, and psychographic backgrounds of the users. Even the geographic limitations are hard to overcome. Rural and inner-city urban access to online services are less robust than for other communities due to the digital divide. The lack of critical infrastructure creates a different experience for people in those communities rather than those in more affluent or accessible communities.

The digital divide also carries into the equipment available to users. Computers, laptops, up-to-date smartphones, and tablets are essential for engagement, but the devices are expensive. The promise of a level playing field cannot be fully met when cost creates differential barriers. The digital divide also extends beyond the physical to the content of the internet and the manner in which critical opportunities are advertised to the public. For ads about housing, employment, financial services, and healthcare, there have been some federal enforcement actions. Still, these are limited, and blanket immunity for ISPs makes more aggressive legal actions difficult. The reported cases likely represent only a tiny fraction of the choices being made by advertisers on how to spend their ad dollars and which members of the public to include or exclude in their campaigns.

Beyond the digital divide, there is also the replication of historical bias that comes from the use of historical data in algorithmic training, design, and deployment. The prejudices of the twentieth century simply cannot be left behind if the patterns of that century are used to train the decision-engines of the future. Only by making intentional choices to label and eradicate the discriminatory effects of past practices will the online world become a place that reduces and—someday—eliminates the structures of inequality that perpetuate a two-tiered nation.

Still, the digital environment holds the greatest promise for achieving these goals and empowering individuals to be whoever they choose to be. These are challenges, not immutable facts. As challenges, they can be overcome through intentional design choices and strategic investment in the future of the universal, inclusive digital realm.

---

[140] Hamacher, *supra* note 126.

10

The Development of Nonfungible Tokens

By Joshua H. Lida

10.1. Introduction

Apes,[1] Doodles,[2] Penguins,[3] and Squiggles[4]. These are some of the words people heard and associated with Nonfungible Tokens (NFTs) during the art and community-project fueled market boom in 2021.[5] This is the time that NFTs truly entered the mainstream in terms of the public consciousness in the United States. Interestingly, despite the rise in popularity of NFTs during 2021, a majority of consumers and potential users of the technology did not actually understand what they were or how the technology underlying the tokens worked.[6] Additionally, as NFTs are a more recent development in the technology space, and a technology the majority of potential users have not interacted with yet, the mechanism used to actually create, purchase, and sell NFTs is daunting for most people and likely is a prohibitive factor in the continual spread of NFTs, although this will likely change.[7]

---

1 *Bored Ape Yacht Club*, FORTUNE CRYPTO, https://fortune.com/crypto/crash-course/bored-ape-yacht-club/ (last visited Apr. 2024).

2 Incog, Happy & Langston Thomas, *The Ultimate Guide to Doodles: Everything You Need to Know*, NFT NOW (Aug. 11, 2024), https://nftnow.com/guides/doodles-guide/.

3 Jax Exmundo, *Pudgy Penguins NFTs: Everything You Need to Know*, NFT NOW (Dec. 28, 2022), https://nftnow.com/culture/the-rise-fall-and-redemption-of-pudgy-penguins-nfts/.

4 Jax Exmundo, *How Chromie Squiggles Pioneered Generative NFT Art*, NFT NOW (Nov. 28, 2022), http://nftnow.com/art/how-chromie-squiggles-pioneered-generative-nft-art/.

5 Peter Allen Clark, *Report: NFT Sales Exceeded $17B in 2021*, AXIOS (Mar. 10, 2022), https://www.axios.com/2022/03/10/nft-sales-17b-2021-report.

6 Julia Glum, *Only 1 in 4 People Actually Know What an NFT Is*, MONEY (Mar. 31, 2022), https://money.com/people-know-what-nft-is/.

7 David Senci, *The Future of NFTs Is Consumer Friendly*, THE BLOCK, https://www.theblock.co/post/173574/the-future-of-nfts-is-consumer-friendly (Oct. 1, 2022).

While the majority of consumers associate NFTs with art, community projects, and the concept of trading to make profit, the underlying technology for NFTs provides the potential to allow for simpler tracking of provenance of digital and physical assets, peer-to-peer transactions of digital and physical assets, simpler due diligence for purchases, and quicker transactions.[8] These use cases have been applied to various areas separate and apart from art such as music, real estate, and identity verification.[9] NFTs present an opportunity for disruption to these and additional areas as the technology becomes simpler to use for consumers and the usage becomes more widespread.

However, with disruption in various industries comes disruption to the law. While NFTs allow for quicker transactions and additional abilities for businesses and individuals to interact in a digital manner, this means developments will likewise continue to develop faster and faster. Accordingly, while laws which are already on the books can certainly be applied to NFTs, the fact that there is no legislation specifically governing NFTs, nor extensive case law providing guidance for practitioners, the law will struggle to keep up with the technology. In fact, we have already seen many large questions posed in various areas of the law and challenges in answering the same such as intellectual property (IP) and securities laws.[10] Thus, legal practitioners have an integral role to play in the development of the new standards and norms which will govern how the law is applied to NFTs. It is therefore essential that legal practitioners have, at a minimum, a basic understanding of the technology and the challenges that NFTs pose to the practice of law.

10.2. Basics of NFTs

Before we can discuss the development of NFTs and their origins, we must first have a basic understanding of what the technology is. An NFT is a digital record which can be used to represent an object of value whether a physical object (such as a painting, a sculpture, or a ticket to a concert) or a digital object (such as music, intellectual property rights, or digital art).[11] Similar to cryptocurrencies, NFTs rely on blockchain technology to function, but unlike cryptocurrencies, NFTs represent unique digital files with its own individual meaning and value.[12] Due to the "uniqueness" and ability to identify the ownership of each NFT, these tokens usually represent ownership of something other than just the token itself.[13] The immutable nature of blockchain technology, and the ability to track each transaction of an NFT, when it was created, what crypto wallet created it, and how it has been traded over its lifespan, makes it an ideal technology to use as a signifier of ownership. While NFTs were originally only able to be purchased using cryptocurrency,

---

8 Sasha Shilina, *A Comprehensive Study on Non-fungible Tokens (NFTs): Use Cases, Ecosystem, Benefits & Challenges*, MEDIUM (Jun. 6, 2022), https://medium.com/paradigm-research/a-comprehensive-study-on-non-fungible-tokens-nfts-use-cases-ecosystem-benefits-challenges-a4c20a932a.

9 Nathan Crooks, *Practical Use Cases of NFTs*, THE BLOCK (Sept. 20, 2023), https://www.theblock.co/learn/251481/practical-use-cases-of-non-fungible-tokens.

10 Marc Beckman, *The Business of Law: On the Verge of Disruption*, NYSBA (Oct. 24, 2022), https://nysba.org/the-business-of-law-on-the-verge-of-disruption/.

11 MAGNUS RESCH & TAM GRYN, HOW TO CREATE AND SELL NFTS 15 (2022).

12 *Id.*

13 Brian L. Frye, *A Brief History of NFTs* 1 (Sept.19, 2023), http://dx.doi.org/10.2139/ssrn.4577014.

their rise in popularity has led to technological solutions which allow for consumers to purchase with cash or credit card as well.[14]

As Professor Brian L. Frye explains, "an NFT can consist of any kind or amount of data and can represent literally anything or nothing."[15] However, they are not created solely from a blockchain itself. Rather, NFTs are issued or "minted" from smart contracts. Smart contracts are computer code stored on a blockchain designed to automatically execute when certain terms and conditions are met.[16] A useful analogy to explain a smart contract is to think of a vending machine. When I want to purchase something from a vending machine, I place the required amount of currency into the machine and push a combination of buttons to trigger the machine to provide me with the snack or item being purchased. The vending machine is not performing due diligence on me or my background, nor does the vending machine have any idea who I am. Rather, because I met the previously determined conditions necessary to purchase a snack, the snack is automatically provided to me. While this is an overly simplistic analogy, it provides a basic understanding of this technology which is essential for the issuance and trading of NFTs. Smart contracts allow decentralized and pseudonymous participants to conduct exchanges of crypto-based property through fair exchange without the need for a third party and allows for people to build applications to further enable these transactions.[17]

Usually, NFTs consist of the name of the NFT, the date it was created, the crypto wallet address of the creator, and a URL pointing to a media file of what the NFT represents.[18] Not all NFTs or the smart contracts which issue them are created equally, however. Depending on the blockchain itself, there are various types of smart contracts which issue different types of NFTs, each with their own unique use cases depending on the intention of the NFT.[19]

Currently, most NFTs are issued (what is known as "minted") on the Ethereum blockchain.[20] Other common blockchains which NFTs are minted on include Tezos and Solana.[21] For example, the ERC-20 is an Ethereum-based token which is fungible, or interchangeable, and is utilized for voting tokens or for cryptocurrencies.[22] ERC-721 is a token standard used for NFTs to represent deeds, songs, or artworks.[23] ERC-1155 is an Ethereum "multi-token" standard that allows for the creation of both fungible tokens, such as

---

14 *How to Buy an NFT: A Complete Guide*, Kraken (Aug. 14, 2023), https://www.kraken.com/learn/how-to-buy-nft; Raj Dhamodharan, *Mastercard Brings Its Payments Network to Web3 and NFTS*, Mastercard (Jun. 9, 2022), https://www.mastercard.com/news/perspectives/2022/simple-nft-purchasing-on-nft-marketplaces/; Onkar Singh, *How to buy NFTs without Owning Crypto*, Cointelegraph (Mar. 27, 2023), https://cointelegraph.com/news/how-to-buy-nfts-without-owning-crypto.

15 *Id.*

16 *What Are Smart Contracts on Blockchain*, IBM, https://www.ibm.com/topics/smart-contracts (last visited Apr. 2024).

17 Shilina, *supra* note 8.

18 Frye, *supra* note 13.

19 Shilina, *supra* note 8.

20 Nicholas Boey, *Top NFT Blockchains by Market Share & Trading Volume*, CoinGecko, https://www.coingecko.com/research/publications/market-share-nft-blockchains (Feb. 5, 2024).

21 Shilina, *supra* note 8.

22 Nico @nhsz, Ethereum (Aug.15, 2023), https://ethereum.org/en/developers/docs/standards/tokens/.

23 *Id.*

those created by ERC-20, and NFTs, such as those created by ERC-721. This allows for the creation of multiple token types under one contract providing for greater flexibility in creating an ecosystem depending on the creators' intentions.[24] The ERC-1155 contract was designed with games in mind, as the contract can create both an in-game currency as well as nonfungible item (represented by NFTs), which can be purchased and exchanged in game.[25] This further demonstrates the wide variety of uses and increasing complexity that can be built on top of the basic NFT framework.

10.3. The First NFTs

The first experiment where the use of cryptocurrency coupled with unique identifying metadata, which could represent something other than the underlying cryptocurrency itself, was created on Bitcoin in 2012 which were known as "colored coins."[26] Different bitcoins could be associated with various "colors" based on the metadata associated with the Bitcoin, and utilizing color-sensitive crypto wallets enabled users to trade Bitcoins based on their colors.[27]

While there is debate amongst crypto as to what the first NFT is, "Quantum" by the artists Jennifer and Kevin McCoy along with technologist Anil Dash is widely considered to be the first NFT on a blockchain in 2014.[28] Kevin McCoy had been looking for a way to utilize blockchain technology as a way to create provenance and ownership of digital images.[29] McCoy and Dash were partnered at Seven on Seven, an annual technology event designed to partner artists and technologist.[30] McCoy and Dash ultimately registered a video clip by McCoy and his wife, Jennifer, on the Namecoin blockchain (a bitcoin offshoot), which McCoy sold to Dash for $4.00 during a live presentation at Seven on Seven.[31]

From there, the first blockchain-based game was created which utilized NFTs. Spells of Genesis was the first blockchain-based game to utilize tokenized in-game assets.[32] Spells of Genesis was built on top of the Counterparty Protocol, which itself is built on the Bitcoin blockchain.[33] Counterparty is what is known as a decentralized exchange and token, which allowed users to create, buy, and sell unique digital assets on the Bitcoin

---

24 *A Definitive Guide to Buying and Selling ERC-1155 Tokens on Magic Eden*, Magic Den, https://help.magiceden.io/en/articles/8277047-a-definitive-guide-to-buying-and-selling-erc-1155-tokens-on-magic-eden (last visited Apr. 2024).

25 Shilina, *supra* note 8.

26 Frye, *supra* note 13 at 6.

27 *Id.*

28 Shilina, *supra* note 8.

29 Jex Exmundo, *Quantum: The Story behind the World's First NFT*, nft now (Mar. 21, 2023), https://nftnow.com/art/quantum-the-first-piece-of-nft-art-ever-created/.

30 *First NFT*, Guinness World Records, https://www.guinnessworldrecords.com/world-records/696336-first-nft (last visited Apr. 2024).

31 Exmundo, *supra* note 29.

32 *Spells of Genesis*, NFT History, https://www.nfthistory.org/wiki/Spells_of_Genesis (last visited Apr. 2024); Jolene Creighton, *NFT Timeline: The Beginnings and History of NFTs*, nft now (Dec. 15, 2022), https://nftnow.com/guides/nft-timeline-the-beginnings-and-history-of-nfts/.

33 *Spells of Genesis, supra* note 32.

blockchain.[34] Counterparty is generally recognized as being a precursor to the crypto art and collectibles movement which ultimately came about following Counterparty's introduction.[35]

Interestingly, the first "crypto art" and NFT movement to take hold and gain notoriety amongst consumers spawned from a frog meme, which originated in 2005. Pepe the Frog is a meme created by artist Matt Furie for his self-published zine.[36] Pepe has become ubiquitous with the internet with a peak in 2014, wherein multiple celebrities could even be seen posting frog memes.[37] During the height of the Pepe meme's popularity, users on message boards introduced the concept of rarity to their different frog memes, began adding watermarks to them, and dubbed them "Rare Pepes."[38] Internet users began trading the various memes like trading cards and the number of "Rare Pepes" quickly ballooned.[39]

In 2016, an anonymous user created three Pepe trading cards on Counterparty, which are technically not NFTs, because the cards were fungible, and are identified as some of the earliest NFTs and are hugely influential.[40] This ultimately led to the creation of the Rare Pepe Wallet, again built on top of Counterparty, which allowed for the Rare Pepe community to buy, sell, trade, destroy, and gift digital works of art as NFTs.[41] This allowed for more participants to create and mint their own crypto art NFTs and create a community around the same.[42] It should be noted that this aspect of "community" continues to be a vital component, and often a selling point, of crypto art NFT projects to this day with Rare Pepes and the Pepe meme generally providing as a huge influence in the space.[43] The historic significance of Rare Pepes has even been recognized by renowned auction houses, including a sale of a Rare Pepe, Pepenopoulos 2016, which sold at a Sotheby's 2021 sale "Natively Digital" for $3.6 million.[44]

10.4. 2021: NFT Boom

2021 was the year that saw the use of NFTs skyrocket in a big way. It is unknown if the global COVID pandemic played a role, but it is possible, as people were still mostly limited in where they could go in public and interact with other people. With people mostly confined inside, this may have inspired people to pay more attention to online

---

34 Mason Marcobello, *What Is Counterparty? Historical NFTs Built on Bitcoin*, Decrypt (Dec. 30, 2022), https://decrypt.co/resources/learn-counterparty-historical-nfts-built-bitcoin.

35 *Id.*

36 Martin Lukas Ostachowski, *A Brief History of Rare Pepe*, Right Click Save (Jan. 14, 2022), https://www.rightclicksave.com/article/a-brief-history-of-rare-pepe.

37 *Id.*

38 *Id.*

39 *Id.*

40 *Id.*

41 Jason Bailey, *Rare Pepe Wallet & The Birth of CryptoArt*, Artnome (Jan. 25, 2018), https://www.artnome.com/news/2018/1/23/rare-pepe-wallet-the-birth-of-cryptoart.

42 *Id.*

43 Ostachowski, *supra* note 36.

44 *Debut Sotheby's "Metaverse" Auction Sees Record-Breaking NFT Sales*, Coin Rivet (Oct. 27 2021), https://coinrivet.com/debut-sothebys-metaverse-auction-sees-record-breaking-nft-sales/.

interactions and transactions. This was not an insignificant jump. While the exact valuations in trading vary, the NFT trading surpassed tens of billions of dollars and increased at a tremendous rate percentage wise with some estimating a 21,000 percent increase.[45]

Many different NFT projects saw tremendous success. The success of these projects saw major businesses enter the market and begin experimenting with the technology. Some projects in particular had noticeable and outsized attention and success which drove subsequent entries into the NFT space.

CryptoPunks is one of the most successful NFT projects to date and is hugely inspirational to follow-up projects. CryptoPunks were minted in 2017, developed by developers and artists Matt Hall and John Watkinson, and is one of the first NFT projects minted on Ethereum.[46] CryptoPunks are collection of ten thousand unique 24 × 24 pixel art character headshots, which rose to the forefront of the push for digital personas in the online space.[47] Each CryptoPunk has its own unique attributes which means each one is completely different from the others.[48] Because the CryptoPunks are NFTs, each unique one can be tracked and the life cycle from creation to each subsequent transaction, as well as the number of traits each one has, can be tracked and researched.[49] These unique characteristics, limited number in existence, and ability to pinpoint specific CryptoPunks contributed to these tokens becoming highly sought after. CryptoPunks were initially available to mint for free; however, in 2021, as NFTs become associated with digital identities, CryptoPunks were viewed as the premier NFT to build this identity around.[50] The year 2021 saw multiple multi-million dollar sales of some of the rarest CryptoPunks as the market headed up.[51] As of the drafting of this chapter, there have been a total of $2.8 billion dollars in sales of CryptoPunks.[52]

Following the rise in popularity of CryptoPunks and this concept of digital identity fueled by known provenance as documented with NFTs, a new NFT project took the most notable portions of CryptoPunks and built its identity around it. The Bored Ape Yacht Club (BAYC) launched in May 2021 and brought in a wave of what is known as the "profile-picture" or PFP NFTs.[53] BAYC is a ten thousand NFT collection of stylized apes which, like CryptoPunks, had various hair colors, accessories, facial expressions, and other

---

45 Ryan Browne, *Trading in NFTs Spiked 21,000% to More than $17 Billion in 2021, Report Says*, CNBC (Mar. 10, 2022), https://www.cnbc.com/2022/03/10/trading-in-nfts-spiked-21000percent-to-top-17-billion-in-2021-report.html; Yogita Khatri, *NFT Trading Volume Surpassed $13 Billion in 2021*, The Block, https://www.theblock.co/linked/128676/nft-trading-volume-surpassed-13-billion-in-2021 (Dec. 28, 2021).

46 Abigail Miller, *How CryptoPunks NFTs Changed the Face of Digital Art*, Avant Arte (Oct. 12, 2023), https://avantarte.com/insights/avant-essay/how-cryptopunks-nfts-changed-the-face-of-digital-art.

47 *Id.*

48 *Id.*

49 *Id.*

50 *Id.*; NFT Now Staff, *The Ultimate Guide to CryptoPunks: Everything You Need to Know*, nft now (Feb. 9, 2024), https://nftnow.com/guides/cryptopunks-guide/.

51 NFT Now Staff, *supra* note 55.

52 CryptoPunks, https://cryptopunks.app/ (last visited Apr. 2024); A reminder, the value of total sales for CryptoPunks and other NFTs is affected by the current value of the underlying cryptocurrency it is bought and sold in.

53 Shanti Escalante-De Mattei, *The Year of the NFT: How an Emerging Medium Went Mainstream in 2021*, ARTnews (Dec. 21, 2021), https://www.artnews.com/list/art-news/artists/2021-year-of-the-nft-1234614022/bored-ape-yacht-club-jpeg-summer-and-rise-of-the-pfp/.

characteristics, which were unique to each ape.[54] The creators of BAYC, Yuga Labs, took things a step further and built exclusivity and a sense of community into the project. Because NFTs are immutable provenance of who owns a particular token, this allowed Yuga Labs to host exclusive festivals, events, and merch drops to holders of the NFTs.[55] Yuga Labs included something unique in their Terms of Service. Yuga Labs grants users a license to use their Ape for commercial purposes. Traditionally, businesses do not allow use of their product or offering to take intellectual property and repurpose it for its own use.[56] Here, it has become a feature in the NFT collectible space. There have been examples of this usage, including in the restaurant industry.[57] This concept has caused new discussions about IP, strategies to leverage the same, and how to properly license or assign such IP leveraging through NFT technologies.

While CryptoPunks and BAYC laid the groundwork for much of the NFT community and collectible projects which have followed, NFTs have also had a major impact on the visual art and the way art is sold. Digital art for many years had a provenance problem. It was difficult to sell and difficult to track. This created a void where many digital artists struggled to sell their work or keep track of their art regarding potential infringers. However, as discussed previously, NFTs allow for simple and immutable provenance tracking for items. Artists latched onto this concept early and have leveraged the technology to develop new and innovative ways to sell art while also allowing for effective attribution and provenance. Generative art is such an example. Generative art, generally, is art that has been created with the use of an autonomous system, such as an algorithm, to determine characteristics without direct input from a human.[58]

While generative art does not have to be digital, we will be discussing digital generative art specifically. Art Blocks, a generative art NFT marketplace and platform, has become synonymous with generative art. Erick Calderon is the creator of Artblocks and an artist interested in blockchain and smart contracts.[59] Inspired by CryptoPunks, Calderon wanted to create a project where the purchaser of the art does not choose the work, but rather when the NFT is minted onto the blockchain, the output or image is created randomly.[60] The project Calderon created is known as Chromie Squiggles. A unique characteristic about Chromie Squiggles, and some other projects which leverage NFTs, is that the Chromie Squiggles exist entirely on the blockchain.[61] Typically, NFTs contain a "pointer" which directs the viewer of the NFT to an image or file stored on a storage database.[62] However, Chromie Squiggles, and some other projects, actually built a computer script into the smart contract which runs a process that sets code for the token which is

---

54 *Id.*

55 *About Yuga*, Yuga, https://yuga.com/about (last visited Apr. 2024).

56 *Licenses*, Bored Ape Yacht Club, https://boredapeyachtclub.com/licenses/bayc (last visited Apr. 2024).

57 Martin Vassolo, *NFT-Themed Cuban Restaurant Opens*, AXIOS (Feb. 16, 2024), https://www.axios.com/local/miami/2024/02/16/bored-ape-nft-cuban-restaurant.

58 *What Is Generative Art*, Avant Arte (Sept.17, 2023), https://avantarte.com/insights/avant-advisory/what-is-generative-art.

59 *The Chromie Squiggle*, https://www.squiggledao.com/learn (last visited Apr. 2024).

60 *Id.*

61 *Chromie Squiggles Explorer*, https://chromie-squiggles.com/ (last visited Apr.2024).

62 *Id.*

stored there and remains as long as the blockchain exists.[63] This is truly unique in art, including digital art, where storage and maintenance are major issues particularly as works age.[64] Additionally, the number of outputs is limited by the artist who creates the code.[65] Chromie Squiggles were actually released in 2020, as a proof of concept, a collection of varying types of generative squiggle image designs in various colors and digital textures with each squiggle being unite.[66] However, similar to CryptoPunks, during the 2021 boom, Chromie Squiggles became identified as a premier NFT to collect and have seen large sales with a strong collector base.[67]

Since the release of Chromie Squiggles and the creation of the Art Blocks platform, this method of creating and selling generative art, where it is minted on command by the purchaser, has had a major impact on art and how art is collected. Even the traditional art world has taken notice. A prime example of the impact that NFTs generally, and Chromie Squiggles in particular, had on digital and generative art occurred in 2023, almost three years after Chromie Squiggles were introduced.

Vera Molnar was a Hungarian-Born generative artist who had been using computers since 1968 to create art and is referred to as the godmother of generative art.[68] On July 26, 2023, a collection of five hundred generative art NFTs created by the then ninety-nine-year-old Molnar, with the assistance of artist Martin Grasser, sold out in less than an hour during a sale at Sotheby's auction totaling 631 Eth (Ethereum) at the time $1.2 million.[69] Not only was the sale recognition for a historically important, but often overlooked artist, but it represented a change in the way one of the top auction houses, Sotheby's, sold art. For the first time in its three-hundred-year history, the auction house conducted a sale in the Dutch Auction format, where pieces start at the highest price and decrease in increments.[70] Likewise, in March 2024, Christie's held its first auction of generative art by the artist, Robert Alice, and also employed the Dutch Auction method for the auction.[71]

While the Dutch Auction method for art sales was not created by NFT platforms, the method for sales has nevertheless become an integral part of the ecosystem. In fact, the previously discussed Art Blocks built the auction system leveraged by Sotheby's and is credited by the auction house with experimenting with the Dutch Auction model and

---

63 *Id.*

64 It should be noted, however, that storing all art on chain is not necessarily feasible or cost-effective at this time. *See What Does "On-Chain" Really Mean*, Right Click Save (Jun. 23, 2023), https://www.rightclicksave.com/article/what-does-on-chain-really-mean.

65 *Id.*

66 Chromie Squiggles Explorer, *supra* note 61.

67 Exmundo, *supra* note 29.

68 Alex Williams, *Ver Molnar, Pioneer of Computer Art, Dies at 99*, N.Y. Times, https://www.nytimes.com/2023/12/15/arts/vera-molnar-dead.html (Dec.19, 2023).

69 Shanti Escalante-De Mattei, *Vera Molnar NFT Auction at Sotheby's Generates $1.2M. Total*, ARTnews (Jul. 26, 2023), https://www.artnews.com/art-news/news/vera-molnar-nft-auction-at-sothebys-realizes-1-2-million-total-1234675618/.

70 *Id.*

71 Louis Jebb, *Robert Alice Breaks New Ground with Auction of Generative Art NFTs on Christie's 3.0*, The Art Newspaper (Mar. 29, 2024), https://www.theartnewspaper.com/2024/03/29/robert-alice-generative-art-nfts-auction-christies.

creating a whole new ecosystem for both the sale of art and new collectors.[72] This development in the art auction world was made possible by the NFT technology. NFTs allowed for a system to be created where generative art could be easily accessible by collectors, purchased in an innovative and enticing way, and brought new energy to the art world. The power of the blockchain and the NFTs allowing for simple provenance review and quick purchases to be made has changed art within a matter of a few years.

One could make the argument that the adoption of both NFTs and blockchain technology by auction houses is not necessarily a tide change for the art world. Art is a business after all, and the massive amount of sales volume in 2021 and continued interest in the space allows for an opportunity for more sales for the auction houses and lower costs associated with the same due to the digital nature of the art and NFTs. However, it is not just auction houses leveraging NFTs. Art museums globally have also embraced NFTs as a new frontier for art providing different dynamics than before. For example, in 2023, the Los Angeles County Museum of Art (LACMA) acquired twenty-two NFTs of generative artworks donated by a well-known pseudonymous collector, "Cozomo de' Medici."[73] LACMA is not alone, however. Paris' renowned Centre Pompidou acquired eighteen NFTs in 2023 to be included in France's national collection of modern and contemporary art.[74]

The recognition by both auction houses and art museums of NFTs and blockchain-based art is crucial and demonstrates the significance of change NFTs represent for the art world and is potentially an indication of the impact it will have on other industries. As discussed, the technology behind NFTs allows for easily creating immutable provenance, something essential for the collection of art. NFTs also allow for easily transferring the ownership of works of art from one collector to another as blockchain technology allows for almost instantaneous transactions. Additionally, while this chapter is not solely about art, it should also be noted that the unique characteristics of smart contracts and the way code is an integral part of the same, allows for truly new and unique ways artists can sell work to collectors as well. NFTs have already changed the art world in a substantial and meaningful way, not because of the hype or money involved, but because of the technology and ideas fueled by the same. However, art is not the only industry to latch onto NFT technology during the halcyon boom of 2021.

Similar to art where a tight knit community values uniqueness, provenance, and authenticity, fashion and NFTs appear to be well suited to mesh together. A prime, and possibly the most well-known example of this, is RTFKT (pronounced artifact).[75] RTFKT describes

---

72 Shanti Escalante-De Mattei, *Sotheby's Attempts a New Auction Model amid Economic Downtown*, ARTNEWS (Jun. 29, 2023), https://www.artnews.com/art-news/news/sothebys-new-auction-model-vera-molnar-dutch-1234672950/.

73 Shanti Escalante-De Mattei, *LACMA Has Acquired a Who's Who of Blockchain Art by Important Generative Artists*, ARTNEWS (Feb. 13, 2023), https://www.artnews.com/art-news/news/lacma-acquires-generative-art-nfts-art-blocks-1234657137/; Interestingly, the last Chromie Squiggle which will be minted will be donated to LACMA by Calderon.

74 Dorian Batycka, *Paris's Centre Pompidou Breaks New Ground by Acquiring 18 NFTs*, THE ART NEWSPAPER (Feb. 14, 2023), https://www.theartnewspaper.com/2023/02/14/pariss-centre-pompidou-breaks-new-ground-by-acquiring-18-nfts.

75 One37pm Editors, *Get to Know RTFKT Studios, the Innovative Brand Changing Digital Fashion*, Y!ENTERTAINMENT (Jan. 19, 2023), https://www.yahoo.com/entertainment/know-rtfkt-studios-innovative-brand-043853112.html.

itself as an "eclectic, future-focused, creator-led organization," which uses technology to create unique experiences with physical and digital fashion, sneakers, and products.[76] RTFKT was founded in 2020 and has leveraged NFTs to try to combine users digital and physical experiences into a unified brand and community centered around fashion.[77] In March 2021, RTFKT teamed up with teenage NFT artist Fewocious for a digital sneaker sold as an NFT which raised over $3.1 million.[78] The NFTs were redeemable for physical real-life pairs of sneakers.[79] This is another example of the use of the immutable nature of the provenance tracked by blockchain. NFTs can be used to provide for redeemable purchases of physical items. Not only does this allow to know who initially purchased the item, it allows for the creation of a secondary market for the same. This is ideal for sneakers and fashion as it is a community which thrives on secondary markets. RTFKT's success in the space was recognized by one of the largest brands in the world. In December 2021, Nike purchased RTFKT to work toward the next generation of its brand as it seeks to incorporate digital culture and technology.[80] Since then, RTFKT and Nike have continued to leverage NFTs and merge physical and digital limited-edition items.[81] Since the original drafting of this chapter, Nike announced in December of 2024 that they will be shutting down RTFKT production.[82]

However, it is not just sneakers and sportswear which have adopted NFTs. Luxury brands entered the NFT space in a big way following the initial boom of early 2021.[83] In May 2021, Gucci launched its debut into the NFT world by offering a short film inspired by one of its clothing collections as part of a curated NFT auction at Christie's auction house which was directed by Gucci's creative director.[84] This was not a one-time affair. Gucci has since released additional projects including a ten thousand (this number is significant in NFTs as demonstrated by CryptoPunks showing the influence) piece drop called SUPERGUCCI; in 2022 followed by another collection called 10KTF: Gucci Grail Mint Pass.[85] Later in 2021, Dolce and Gabbana launched an a physical/digital NFT collection where one called the Glass Suit sold for over $1 million.[86] Since Gucci's initial dabble into the space, numerous other brands have experimented as well such as Yves Saint Laurent, Givenchy, Prada, and Louis Vuitton.[87] It is clear that clothing luxury brands

---

[76] *What We do?* RTFKT, https://101.rtfkt.com/rtfkt/what-we-do (last visited Apr. 2024).

[77] Philip Maughan, *RTFKT Is the Creator-Led Studio Bringing Art, Fashion, & Nike into the Metaverse*, HIGHSNOBIETY, https://www.highsnobiety.com/p/rtfkt-interview/ (last visited Apr. 2024).

[78] Rob Nowill, *A Sale of Virtual Sneakers Raised $3.1 Million USD in Seven Minutes*, HYPEBEAST, https://hypebeast.com/2021/3/rtfkt-studios-fewocious-sale-nfts (last visited Apr. 2024).

[79] *Id.*

[80] One37pm Editors, *supra* note 82.

[81] *What Are Forging Events*, RTFKT, https://101.rtfkt.com/rtfkt/what-are-forging-events (last visited Apr. 2024).

[82] Joyce Li, *Nike Shuts Down Virtual Sneaker Brand RTFKT*, HYPEBEAST (December 3, 2024), https://hypebeast.com/2024/12/nike-shuts-down-virtual-sneaker-brand-rtfkt-news.

[83] Eric James Beyer, *Luxury Brands Are a Great Example of Web3 Adaptation*, NFT NOW (Jul. 12, 2022), https://nftnow.com/culture/luxury-brands-are-a-great-example-of-web3-adaptation/.

[84] Joyce Li, *Gucci Launches First NFT, a Film Inspired by Recent Aria Collection*, HYPEBEAST (May 27, 2021), https://hypebeast.com/2021/5/gucci-nft-debut-film-aria-collection-inspired-announcement.

[85] Beyer, *supra* note 89.

[86] *Dolce & Gabbana's NFT Experiment Is a Million-Dollar Success Story*, VOGUE (Sept. 30 2021), https://www.vogue.co.uk/news/article/fashion-nft-dolce-and-gabbana.

[87] *Top Global Fashion Brands with NFTs*, COINGECKO (Jan. 15, 2024), https://www.coingecko.com/research/publications/top-fashion-brand-nfts.

view NFTs and the underlying technology as a new way to engage fans and expand their outreach outside their traditional business.

10.5. Other Uses for NFTs

Based on what has been discussed in this chapter regarding the immutable provenance of NFTs, the ability to perform due diligence in a quicker streamlined fashion, and the speed of transactions powered by blockchain, it is logical that real estate transactions are an area primed for NFT usage. In the United States, as of the time of writing, your author is not aware of a local recording office which has incorporated blockchain or NFT technology into its land sale recording process.[88] However, there are companies seeking to take matters into their own hands and leverage the technology for such sales.

Propy describes itself as a company which is automating the real property closing process, making it "faster, easier, and more secure" by leveraging technology to migrate closings to the blockchain.[89] In February 2022, Propy sold its first NFT backed property in the United States—a 2,164 square foot home in Gulfport, Florida, sold for $653,000.00 as an NFT.[90] Considering there was no way to sell the property as an NFT and properly record the title in the local recording office seamlessly, Propy transferred the property rights to an LLC.[91] The ownership rights of the LLC were then incorporated into the NFT when minted allowing the rights to transfer to the new recipient of the NFT.[92] Accordingly, the purchaser of the NFT receives the ownership rights to the LLC, which in turn owns the real property pursuant to the local property records, thereby transferring ownership to the new purchaser.[93] While a clever method to effectuate the transfer of ownership, there very well could be issues down the road, not only with ensuring all title requirements are fulfilled but also with potentially limiting such purchases to cash buyers as it is unclear how a mortgage lender would respond to this type of transaction. Further, it may have an impact on purchaser's ability to receive homestead or other property-based exemptions.[94] Other companies are seeking to impact the real estate mortgage market. For example, LoanSnap introduced NFT mortgages via their Bacon Protocol.[95] At the moment, it appears real estate NFTs are in their early development with some

---

88 That being said, the city of South Burlington, Vermont, entered into a partnership with Propy to test blockchain as a recording system in 2018 and even received a paper deed recorded in the city's land records which contained a blockchain address and QR code identifying the deed's location on the Ethereum blockchain. Juliet M. Moringiello & Christopher K. Odinet, *Blockchain Real Estate and NFTs*, 64 WM. & MARY L. REV. 1131, 1171 (2023).

89 *Our Story*, PROPY, https://propy.com/browse/about/ (last visited Apr. 2024).

90 Eli Tan, *NFT-Linked House Sells for $650K in Propy's First US Sale*, COINDESK (Feb. 11, 2022), https://www.coindesk.com/business/2022/02/11/nft-linked-house-sells-for-650k-in-propys-first-us-sale/.

91 TRD Staff, *Tampa-Area Home Billed as First in US to Be Sold as NFT*, THEREALDEAL (Feb. 19, 2022), https://therealdeal.com/miami/2022/02/19/tampa-area-home-billed-as-first-in-us-to-be-sold-as-an-nft/.

92 *Id.*

93 *Id.*

94 Robert C. Meyer, *Florida Exemptions and How the Same May Be Lost*, FLA. BAR J. (Sept.–Oct. 2021), at 18.

95 Moringiello & Odinet, *supra* note 94 at 1170; at the time of writing, it is unclear what the current status of the Bacon Protocol is or if it is still functioning.

severe roadblocks which must be overcome. There are some commentators who think such roadblock cannot be overcome.[96] The reality remains to be seen.

For similar reasons that real estate may be well suited for the usage of NFTs and blockchain technology, car title appears to be another area NFTs may disrupt. The California Department of Motor Vehicles is piloting a blockchain-based solution leveraging NFTs to simplify transfer and tracking of car titles.[97] The idea is to tokenize more than 14 million car titles, which are registered to the state and issue them as NFTs on a private version of the Tezos blockchain.[98]

A potentially obvious use for NFTs would be ownership of video game items. Many video games contain in-world virtual items that are purchasable and tradeable within the game itself.[99] Historically, the ownership of these in-game items remains solely with the creator of the game, and end user has no actual ownership rights in the item itself.[100] Despite this face, in-game items manage to accrue expensive value with some in-game items selling anywhere from $4,500.00 to $6 million.[101] Typically, it is the End User License Agreement (EULA), which governs the rights of games in-game activity and item ownership.[102] EULA grants game creators rights over the world and can control the access to the game such as preventing user access or restricting the use of certain game features.[103] Accordingly, game users can accrue value and lose it all at the decision of a game creator. NFTs provide an opportunity to change this moving forward.[104] NFTs allow for the possibility for the end users to not only play the game and accrue value but to actually own the individual items. This presents a potentially new paradigm for video games with multiple options such as allowing the NFTs to live solely within the one game, or, potentially in the future, be transferrable among multiple games or metaverses.

Additionally, NFTs have fueled a new entry called Play-to-Earn games where players can earn rewards for in-game accomplishments such as cryptocurrency, own in-game items powered by NFTs, and build communities around the same.[105] Probably, the most well-known NFT-based Play-to-Earn game is Axie Infinity, which allows players to collect,

---

96 *Id.* at 1181.

97 Will Canny, *California Leads the Way as U.S. Federal, State Agencies Consider Blockchain's Applications: Bank of America*, CoinDesk (Mar. 24, 2023), https://www.coindesk.com/business/2023/03/24/california-leads-the-way-as-us-federal-state-agencies-consider-blockchains-applications-bank-of-america/.

98 *Id.*; at the time of writing, it is unclear what the current state of this pilot project is.

99 Oliver Herzfeld, *What Is the Legal status of Virtual Goods*, Forbes (Dec. 4, 2012), https://www.forbes.com/sites/oliverherzfeld/2012/12/04/what-is-the-legal-status-of-virtual-goods/?sh=3a2b3212108a.

100 *Id.*

101 Michael Fernandez, *10 Most Expensive In-Game Items Ever Sold*, TheGamer (Jul. 10, 2023), https://www.thegamer.com/most-expensive-in-game-items-ever-sold/.

102 Christopher J. Cifrino, *Virtual Property, Virtual Rights: Why Contract Law, Not Property Law, Must Be the Governing Paradigm in the Law of Virtual Worlds*, 55 BC L. Rev. 235, 243 (2014).

103 *Id.*

104 *How NFTs Will Impact Ownership of Virtual Items in Videogames*, Winston & Strawn LLP (Oct. 18, 2021), https://www.winston.com/en/blogs-and-podcasts/the-playbook/how-nfts-will-impact-ownership-of-virtual-items-in-videogames#_ftnref9.

105 *What Are Play-to-Earn Crypto Games*, kraken, https://www.kraken.com/learn/what-play-to-earn-crypto-games (last visited Apr. 2024).

breed, and mint (as NFTs) creatures called Axies and battle them.[106] The game runs on the Ethereum blockchain.[107] It is not just the Axies that can be purchased as NFTs, but players can purchase land as well.[108] In November 2021, a plot of land sold for $2.48 million.[109]

There is a myriad of other uses for NFTs still in their infancy stages which can potentially have a major impact on both digital and physical assets. For example, NFTs allow for the fractionalization of assets where the ownership of one item is split into smaller pieces of ownership.[110] This could potentially be applied to any real-world or digital asset with the idea that it can allow greater access to more people and allow for greater potential liquidity for asset markets.[111] While this does exist in the form of securitized assets, such as what Masterworks offers for blue chip art, the concept coupled with NFTs can potentially speed up the transactions and allow for easier access to more people, thanks to the technology.[112] However, users of fractionalized NFTs should be cognizant of the potential for them to be considered unregistered securities.[113]

NFTs can also be used to secure and provide for various types of loans. There is Peer-to-Peer NFT lending where users can use a platform to list NFTs as collateral and receive offers from other users; Peer-to-Protocol NFT lending where an NFT is sent to a platform or protocol where the NFTs are collateralized and locked into a smart contract pending the execution of the terms of the loan; and nonfungible debt position where a unique NFT asset is minted on the blockchain representing a debt position as a record of a loan agreement.[114] For example, NFTfi allows users to utilize their NFTs to get a cryptoloan with fixed terms and no liquidations.[115] While these methods refer to lending protocols for NFTs specifically, as NFTs can represent real-world assets, these types of loans can again offer more opportunities for users to access capital and loans from more sources by leveraging NFTs and the blockchain. We may potentially see real-world ownership of items being minted as NFTs to be treated as security for loans.

NFTs are also an ideal mechanism for the ticketing of events as it can assure users that the tickets being purchased are legitimate. NFT tickets are, as they sound, digital tickets which are stored and managed on the blockchain which allows the provenance of the tickets to be verified securely and limits issues from traditional ticketing models,

---

106 Jex Exmundo, *The Dawn of P2E Giants? An Inside Look at Axie Infinity*, NFT NOW (Aug. 17, 2022), https://nftnow.com/guides/inside-axie-infinity-a-deep-dive-into-the-worlds-largest-p2e-game/.

107 *Id.*

108 *Id.*

109 *Id.*

110 Anthony Clarke, *Fractional NFTs and What They Mean for Investing in Real-World Assets*, COINTELEGRAPH (Nov. 9, 2022), https://cointelegraph.com/news/fractional-nfts-and-what-they-mean-for-investing-in-real-world-assets.

111 *Id.*

112 *A Complete Platform for Investing in Art*, MASTERWORKS, https://www.masterworks.com/about/how-it-works (last visited Apr. 2024).

113 *Fractional NFTs Boost Accessibility and Liquidity of Crypto Assets*, HEDERA, https://hedera.com/learning/nfts/fractional-nft (last visited Apr. 2024).

114 Michael Deer, *What Is NFT Lending, and How Does It Work?* COINTELEGRAPH (Apr. 3, 2024), https://cointelegraph.com/explained/what-is-nft-lending-and-how-does-it-work.

115 *How NFT Lending Works*, NFTFI, https://nftfi.com/how-it-works/ (last visited Apr. 2024).

including double-booking.[116] Additionally, by leveraging a process called "token-gating," event organizers can have additional security and fraud protection.[117] Token-gating is the process where access to a particular service or resource on the internet is restricted by using an NFT; to gain entry, the entrant must present the appropriate NFT, which is stored on a blockchain.[118] For example, token gates can be used to allow for an in-world event access or limiting access to message boards.[119] As an example, an event can be limited solely to owners of BAYC NFTs.[120]

Please be aware that this is only a sample of current uses of NFT technology. There are examples that the limited space in this chapter does not allow for us to discuss. Additionally, while NFTs have been around since at least 2017, they have only been in the public consciousness in a more mainstream way since 2021. Despite the billions of dollars that have been spent on NFTs and that have flowed into investment in companies experimenting with the same, the usage is still not quite an everyday occurrence. Accordingly, expect many more experiments and products, not only in the above categories but in many other industries as the technology spreads and becomes easier to use. It will not be slowing down.

10.6. Overall Takeaways and Potential Implications on the Law

This chapter has sought to provide a brief and simplified overview of the development of NFTs. If it may feel like a large part of the chapter was heavily focused on collectible and art-based NFTs, that is because it did. The reality of the development of NFTs is that the first use case which really caught on and began leveraging the technology for its various benefits are artists and internet/crypto culture projects. It makes sense when one thinks about it. Not only are artists often times closely tied to technology and operate at the cutting edge consistently looking for new ways to provide expression or distribute their art, but NFTs are really an ideal mechanism to document the provenance of art as well as transfer art. This is particularly true for digital art. This chapter only scratched the surface. While the basic transfer of art and collectibles is all that is necessary to provide information for practitioners to have an understanding and apply to their practice, artists have utilized the technology to tell stories in truly unique ways and find new ways to engage collectors. The power of this movement has been demonstrated by the quick adoption of both traditional art auction houses and art museums.

However, just because art is a natural fit for NFTs does not mean it is the sole use for the technology. As has been discussed in this chapter, many businesses are hard at work either developing new use cases for other industries or have already established new

---

116 Sankrit K., *What Are NFT Tickets? How NFT Ticketing Could Disrupt Entertainment*, MoonPay (Jan. 9, 2024), https://www.moonpay.com/learn/nft/nft-ticketing.

117 *Id.*

118 *Id.*

119 *FAQs*, tokenproof.xyz, https://docs.tokenproof.xyz/documentation/misc/faqs (last visited Apr. 2024).

120 *Id.*

mechanisms to leverage the same. For example, token-gating provides a powerful tool to simplify event entry as well as providing tools to businesses to reward their customers by offering unique NFTs both as collectibles which can then be utilized for exclusive events. Additionally, the use of smart contract protocols for various financial arrangements provides an opportunity for additional capital to be provided to more people as well as offering people and opportunity to develop a lending portfolio. We are witnessing, in real time, the development of a brand-new financial market, which does not simply create a new asset but allows individuals to interact with already existing assets in new and unique ways. This is an exciting time and provides practitioners with an opportunity to learn about new business models, interact with new potential clients, and establish a name for themselves in a developing area of law.

It is important to note that it is not just businesses that will be impacted by this, but the practice of law will be too. For example, at least two Federal District Courts in the United States have authorized service of a lawsuit seeking recovery of digital assets via NFTs containing the complaint, the summons, and a website created by the Plaintiff containing the pleadings.[121] The NFT was then sent to a digital wallet maintained by the defendants.[122] Additionally, the technology very well may be applied in creative ways going forward. We could potentially see court dockets for individual judges turned into private blockchains with court documents issued as NFTs. This could simplify the legal research into a judge's decisions or ensure that records are maintained in an immutable manner. Or maybe the rights to an asset need to be maintained as collateral between two parties for which the attorney is working on the matter. The rights to the asset, whether tangible or intangible, can be minted into an NFT and locked in a smart contract unless and until certain preconditions are met. The attorney can serve as a third party and trigger the smart contract to automatically transfer the rights to the appropriate party pursuant to the underlying agreement. Perhaps law firms will have their own private blockchains to store all their executed documents rather than a traditional cloud storage system. We are far too early into the process to know where the technology is going to go or what its uses are going to be. However, we do know that the uses will continue to grow at a quick pace and attorneys need to be prepared.

Finally, while the potential legal implications of these technologies will be discussed in other chapters of this book, it should be clear to practitioners that as new experiments and ideas for uses of the technology develop, new legal issues will arise. For example, regarding art and collectible NFTs alone, so many questions are raised. Can NFT projects effectively transfer NFT licenses to purchasers via terms of service? Is there a particular way this needs to be done? Can that user then effectively transfer those rights to a secondary user? Can creators of NFTs effectively waive their IP rights by simply declaring it on a website? If an agreement programmed into a smart contract and there is somehow an alleged breached will that smart contract be deemed enforceable? If title to property

---

121 Matthew Miller, *Florida Court Allows Service of Lawsuit upon Foreign Crypto Scammers by NFT*, DLA Piper (Dec. 19, 2022), https://www.dlapiper.com/en/insights/publications/2022/12/florida-court-allows-service-of-lawsuit-crypto-scammers.

122 *Id.*

is consistently transferred via blockchain but no additional information of the equitable owner is ever provided to the local governing authority, does that create additional legal concerns? These questions merely scratch the surface, and as more use cases develop, more questions will arise.

While there is a dearth of NFT litigation at the moment, and no specific legislation in the United States, that will not always be the case. It is absolutely essential that attorneys understand the base mechanisms of NFTs and how they operate on blockchains. They should also understand the value proposition and what potential benefits there are if they are going to effectively and ethically advise their clients on the same. This author thinks it is also important to understand that the origins of the use which has driven this adoption is the collectible and art community. It is important to recognize where these innovations came from as there is, currently at least, an NFT "culture" and "ethos" that has been driving the push for the technology. Finally, it is important for practitioners to realize that for all of the serious implications of NFTs and their uses, as a result of their newness and lack of precedent, NFTs can present fun new issues for practitioners to help develop new law and legal standards.

11 Digital Money Transfer, Anti-money Laundering, and Related Laws and Regulations

By Susan H. Stephan

11.1. Introduction

Transformative advances in the financial sector are serving to disrupt and reshape the transfer of value for consumers and business clients. As opportunities for frictionless transactions relying on digital, often blockchain-based, currencies flow into mainstream marketplaces, traditional banking will continue to evolve. However, regulatory challenges associated with digital assets and blockchain technology are significant, particularly in the financial world. Most laws that address financial compliance, fraud, and crime focus on centralized services and fail to encompass technology-enhanced or decentralized finance (DeFi) providers. As U.S. lawmakers struggle to pass a comprehensive framework for digital asset regulation amid rapid technological change, enforcement activities in the digital sector have largely relied on preexisting financial laws and regulations.

Major U.S. regulation and oversight of the digital financial space is led by the Securities and Exchange Commission (SEC), Commodity Futures Trading Commission (CFTC), Internal Revenue Service (IRS), Financial Crimes Enforcement Network (FinCEN), Federal Reserve Board (the Fed), Office of Foreign Assets Control (OFAC), Office of Financial Research (OFR), Federal Deposit Insurance Corporation (FDIC), Office of the Comptroller of the Currency (OCC), and state-level regulators. A March 2022 Executive Order (EO) issued by President Biden titled, "Ensuring Responsible Development of Digital Assets," sought coordination by federal agencies to recommend legislative and regulatory proposals to address risks and opportunities related to the development of digital assets. Although several agencies, the Attorney General's Office, and the Fed issued a total of nine reports addressing the need for further study and support for a framework, the White House did not take specific actions based on the recommendations. The 2022 Biden EO was revoked in January 2025 by the Trump EO titled "Strengthening American Leadership in Digital Financial Technology, " which set forth the stated goal of "to support the responsible growth and use of digital assets, blockchain technology, and related technologies across all sectors of the economy." Some agencies have focused on nonbinding guidelines and the anticipation of rulemaking, but a concrete regulatory framework has not yet emerged.

From the legislative standpoint, scores of proposed bills since 2020 have focused on digital assets, including cryptocurrency regulation, stablecoin[1] limitations, and the possibility of a Central Bank Digital Currency (CBDC).[2] The prevailing themes of the numerous pieces of proposed legislation are clarifying rules and the roles of regulators, supporting additional study and definitions of certain aspects of the digital economy, stemming terrorism, maintaining national financial stability, and remaining competitive in the global market. Although some proposals for digital asset regulation advanced through committee and even the full U.S. House of Representatives with bipartisan support, existing laws addressing financial transaction in the United States have remained largely unchanged.

This chapter reviews current laws and regulations addressing banking, money transfer, and anti-money laundering (AML) concerns related to clients transacting in the digital economy. Other chapters focus on significant regulation of digital assets by the SEC, the CFTC, and the IRS; this chapter centers on the jurisdiction of FinCEN and related financial regulators under the Bank Secrecy Act (BSA).[3]

11.2. FinCEN and the Bank Secrecy Act

The FinCEN,[4] a bureau of the U.S. Department of the Treasury, is tasked with enforcing AML regulations, including compliance with the BSA. In the United States, cryptocurrency exchanges are subject to the BSA, which includes a requirement to register with FinCEN and to comply with AML requirements. Although it was not initially clear that virtual currency businesses were subject to FinCEN jurisdiction, FinCEN issued guidance in 2013 confirming its intent to treat "real" currency and convertible virtual currency

---

1 Stablecoins are digital currencies designed to maintain a stable value by pegging them to an underlying asset, such as a fiat currency like the U.S. dollar or a commodity like gold. *See* President's Working Group on Financial Markets, the Federal Deposit Insurance Corporation, and the Office of the Comptroller of the Currency, *Report on Stablecoins* Dept. of Treasury (Nov. 2021), https://home.treasury.gov/system/files/136/StableCoinReport_Nov1_508.pdf.

2 A Central Bank Digital Currency (CBDC) is a digital form of a country's fiat currency issued by the central bank. CBDC development varies by country. Some countries have active CBDC projects, while others like the United States are still in the exploration phase. *See* Tobias Adrian et al., *Central Bank Digital Currency Development Enters the Next Phase*; Int'l Monetary Fund Blog (Nov. 20, 2023), https://www.imf.org/en/Blogs/Articles/2023/11/20/-central-bank-digital-currency-development-enters-the-next-phase.

3 The Bank Secrecy Act of 1970, 31 U.S.C. § 5311 *et seq.* (2021).

4 *Financial Crimes Enforcement Network*, FinCEN, https://www.fincen.gov (last visited Jun. 20, 2024).

(CVC)—centralized and decentralized—the same.[5] FinCEN's 2019 guidance confirmed that registration with FinCEN would be required by virtual currency businesses that qualify as money transmitters.[6] This aspect of the 2019 guidance was codified by the Anti-Money Laundering Act of 2020 (AMLA),[7] which expanded the prior BSA definition of currency,[8] as is discussed in more detail in Section 11.2.5.

11.2.1. Federal Regulations and Virtual Currency

The BSA establishes program, recordkeeping, and reporting requirements for financial institutions, including currency exchanges and money transfer systems. Originally passed in 1970, the BSA was amended by the Uniting and Strengthening America by Providing Appropriate Tools Required to Intercept and Obstruct Terrorism Act (USA PATRIOT Act) of 2001[9] and the AMLA[10] in 2020. The primary purpose of the BSA is to address money laundering and to combat the financing of terrorism (CFT).[11]

FinCEN's 2019 Guidelines define "virtual currency" as a medium of exchange that can operate like currency but does not have all the attributes of "real" currency, as defined in 31 CFR § 1010.100(m), including legal tender status.[12] Virtual currency can be seen more broadly as "digital assets used as a medium of exchange." [13] A CBDC, a digital form of a country's fiat currency issued by the central bank, is an example of a virtual currency.[14] By comparison, "convertible virtual currency" (CVC) is seen as a type of virtual currency that either has an equivalent value as currency or acts as a substitute for currency, and is therefore a type of "value that substitutes for currency."[15] Cryptocurrency, a digital

---

5 Department of the Treasury, Financial Crimes Enforcement Network, Application of FinCEN's Regulations to Certain Business Models Involving Convertible Virtual Currencies, FIN-2013-G001 (Mar. 18, 2013), https://fincen.gov/statutes_regs/guidance/pdf/FIN-2013-G001.pdf; *See also* Daniel T. Stabile et al., Digital Assets and Blockchain Technology: US Law and Regulation 30 (2020).

6 FinCEN's 2019 guidance "reminded" those who are subject to the BSA that convertible virtual currencies (CVCs) involving money transmission denominated in value that substitutes for currency invoke rules for Money Services Businesses (MSBs) for purposes of FinCEN jurisdiction. *Financial Crimes Enforcement Network*, Dept. of Treasury, FIN-2019-G001 (May 9, 2019), https://www.fincen.gov/sites/default/files/2019-05/FinCEN Guidance CVC FINAL 508.pdf.

7 William M. (Mac) Thornberry National Defense Authorization Act for Fiscal Year 2021, Pub. L. 116-283 134 Stat. 3388 (2021), 31 U.S.C. § 6101 *et seq.* (2021).

8 *Id.* at § 6102 (d), amending BSA, 31 USC § 5312(a) (2021).

9 Uniting and Strengthening America by Providing Appropriate Tools Required to Intercept and Obstruct Terrorism Act (USA PATRIOT Act) of 2001, Pub. L. 107-56 (Oct. 26, 2001).

10 *Supra* note 7. *See also* Section 11.2.5.

11 "Combatting the financing of terrorism," or CFT, is also known as counter terrorist financing (CTF).

12 *Financial Crimes Enforcement Network*, Dept. of Treasury, FIN-2019-G001 (May 9, 2019), https://www.fincen.gov/sites/default/files/2019-05/FinCEN Guidance CVC FINAL 508.pdf. By comparison, the IRS defines virtual currency as "any digital representation of value recorded on a cryptographically secured, distributed ledger (blockchain) or similar technology." *Digital Assets*, IRS, https://www.irs.gov/businesses/small-businesses-self-employed/digital-assets, *citing* Infrastructure Investment and Jobs Act, Pub. L. 117-58 (Nov. 15, 2021).

13 CFTC v. McDonnell, 287 F. Supp. 3d 213, 228 (E.D.N.Y. 2018). The CFTC and the court distinguish virtual currencies from "goods exchanged in a market for a uniform quality and value," which would be commodities.

14 For more detailed information, *see CBDC Virtual Handbook*, Int'l Monetary Fund, https://www.imf.org/en/Topics/fintech/central-bank-digital-currency/virtual-handbook.

15 *Supra* note 12.

currency like Bitcoin[16] that operates in a decentralized blockchain environment,[17] is seen as a CVC for purposes of the BSA.

11.2.2. Money Transfer Systems as Defined by the BSA

A Money Services Business (MSB) is defined by the BSA as an individual or entity doing business as a (1) currency dealer or exchanger; (2) check casher; (3) issuer of traveler's checks, money orders, or stored value; (4) seller or redeemer of traveler's checks, money orders, or stored value; (5) money transmitter; and (6) the U.S. Postal Service.[18]

MSBs include those providing "money transmission services," which means the acceptance of currency, funds, or other value that substitutes for currency from one person and the transmission of currency, funds, or other value that substitutes for currency to another location or person by any means.[19] MSBs do not include (1) a bank or foreign bank; (2) a person registered with and functionally regulated or examined by the SEC or CFTC, or a foreign financial agency that engages in financial activities that, if conducted in the United States, would require the foreign financial agency to be registered with the SEC or CFTC; or (3) a natural person who engages in certain identified MSB activity.[20] MSB status is determined on a case-by-case basis but is generally seen to include trade in virtual currencies and CVCs. "Mixers," also known as "tumblers," are programs that comingle cryptocurrency before transferring it to its recipients, so no one knows who sent what to whom.[21] Mixers are classified as "money transmitters" by FinCEN, so they are required to register as MSBs.[22]

---

16 Bitcoin is the first cryptocurrency, created in 2009 after the pseudonymous "Satoshi Nakamoto" proposed a decentralized distributed ledger technology to support an "electronic payment system based on cryptographic proof instead of trust" named "Bitcoin." Satoshi Nakamoto, *Bitcoin: A Peer-to-Peer Electronic Cash System* (2008), https://bitcoin.org/bitcoin.pdf.

17 A blockchain is the result of digital transactions that are encrypted and stored in "blocks," connected by the fact that each block contains identifying information (or the "hash digest") from the previous block. Robby Houben & Alexander Snyers, *Crypto-Assets: Key Developments, Regulatory Concerns and Responses*, European Parliament's Pol'y Dept. Econ., Sci. and Quality of Life Pol'y, PE 648.779 (Apr. 2020), 17. Blockchain technology uses "asymmetric" or "public" key cryptography, by which a public key and a private key (that remains undisclosed) work together to ensure cryptographic security. This process provides a way for parties to a transaction to verify the integrity and authenticity of public transactions on a blockchain through a digital signature. The keys are based on a digital signature, which involves a private key being used to encrypt a transaction that anyone with the public key can decrypt, or a public key being used to encrypt data that only users with the private key can decrypt. *See* Dylan Yaga et al., *Blockchain Technology Overview*, National Institute of Standards and Technology Interagency or Internal Report (IR) 8202 (2018), 1, 10–11, https://doi.org/10.6028/NIST.IR.8202.

18 31 CFR §§ 1010, 1021, and § 1022.

19 31 CFR § 1010.100 (ff).

20 *Id.*

21 *See* Department of the Treasury, Financial Crimes Enforcement Network, *Proposal of Special Measure Regarding Convertible Virtual Currency Mixing, as a Class of Transactions of Primary Money Laundering Concern*, Docket No. FINCEN-2023-0016, § II (Oct. 22, 2023). (FinCEN issued this notice of proposed rulemaking pursuant to Section 311 of the USA PATRIOT Act, proposing the requirement that in addition to registration as MSBs, domestic financial institutions and domestic financial agencies implement certain recordkeeping and reporting requirements relating to transactions involving CVC mixing.)

22 Mixers also generally must apply for a state-by-state license to operate.

Pursuant to the BSA, MSBs and other financial institutions must register with FinCEN, keep transactional records, and file reports. One significant reporting requirement is the filing of a Suspicious Activity Report (SAR), which must include detailed information about transactions that are suspicious from a potential money laundering or terrorism perspective. MSBs also are required to notify the OFAC of any SARs where there is a suspected sanctions connection, as discussed in Section 11.2.3.

11.2.3. Know Your Customer Pursuant to PATRIOT Act Amendments to the BSA

In 2001, the PATRIOT Act established a Know Your Customer (KYC) requirement for financial institutions, which requires the implementation of rules for customer due diligence, verification of legal identity and ownership of all customers, and conduct-screening through the Specially Designated Nationals and Blocked Persons list (the SDN), which is maintained by the OFAC.[23] Additionally, the BSA requires that financial institutions report suspicious activities through SARs and maintain and regularly update customer information.[24]

11.2.4. The Funds Travel Rule

The Funds Travel Rule[25] within the BSA requires financial institutions to share some information with other financial institutions, with regard to certain funds transmittals involving more than one financial institution. In its 2019 regulatory guidance, FinCEN announced its determination that the travel rule also applies to virtual currency businesses.[26] Therefore, in the United States, if the value of a cryptocurrency transaction is $3,000 or more, Virtual Asset Service Providers (VASPs) are required to exchange information, including the date and amount of the transaction, the identity of the VASP, and the transmitter's name, address, and account number. VASPs might include clients that control crypto exchanges, wallet services, initial coin offering (ICO) finance providers, and crypto custodial solutions.

The travel rule originally applied to bank transfers, when the information required under the rule was substantially the same as the information already required to complete the transfer itself; applying the travel rule to cryptocurrency exchanges and other VASPs requires the collection and retention of information that is not required for the underlying transfer. Although the application of the travel rule has been unpopular in the DeFi community, it has also been possible to circumvent application of the rule by either (1) transferring from a VASP to an individual account, and then from that individual account to a second VASP, or (2) using a purely peer-to peer transaction, avoiding the participation of a VASP altogether.

---

23 PATRIOT Act, *supra* note 9, § 5318A(b)(3).

24 *Supra* note 3, § 103.33(g).

25 *Id.*

26 *Supra* note 12.

11.2.5. The Anti-Money Laundering Act of 2020

As discussed briefly above, part of the William M. (Mac) Thornberry National Defense Authorization Act for Fiscal Year 2021,[27] the Anti-Money Laundering Act of 2020 (AMLA),[28] states that businesses involved in crypto exchanges or any individual or entity engaging in crypto transmission might be categorized as a "money transmitter" subject to the laws and regulations governing MSBs, including the BSA. The AMLA expands upon the BSA's focus on AML and CFT, requiring that MSBs enact programs that are (1) reasonably designed to assure and monitor compliance with the BSA and (2) risk-based, including ensuring that more attention and resources of financial institutions are directed toward higher risk customers and activities, consistent with the financial institution's risk profile.[29]

Significantly, the AMLA expanded the prior BSA definition of "currency" to specifically encompass "value that substitutes for currency," including those pertaining to "financial agency," "financial institution," "money transmitting business," and "money transmitting service."[30] Thus, virtual currency businesses that qualify as money transmitters must register with FinCEN, codifying existing FinCEN guidance from 2013 to 2019.[31]

11.3. Additional Federal Oversight

In addition to FinCEN and its jurisdiction pursuant to the BSA, other agencies under the Department of the Treasury oversee financial stability in the United States and are therefore relevant to the digital financial sector. These include the Fed, the OFAC, the OFR, the OCC, and the FDIC. Each of these federal entities plays a role in the consideration of current compliance in the digital asset market.

11.3.1. The Federal Reserve Board and DeFi

As the central bank of the United States, the Fed is tasked with promoting "the effective operation of the U.S. economy and, more generally, the public interest."[32] In August 2023, the Fed implemented its Novel Activities Supervision Program,[33] which focuses on novel and nonbank activities related to crypto-assets and distributed ledger technology (DLT). Through this program, the Fed provides written notification to supervised banking organizations whose "novel activities"[34] will be subject to examination. The Fed's program

---

27 *Supra* note 7.

28 *Supra* note 8.

29 *Supra* note 7, § 6101 (b)(2)(B)(iv)(1) and (2).

30 *Supra* note 8.

31 *Supra* note 12.

32 *About the Fed*, FED.RSRV. BD. , https://www.federalreserve.gov/aboutthefed.htm.

33 Board of Governors of the Federal Reserve System, *Creation of Novel Activities Supervision Program*, FED. RSRV. SR 23-7 (Aug. 8, 2023), https://www.federalreserve.gov/supervisionreg/srletters/SR2307.htm.

34 The Fed's initial focus on novel activities included "Complex, technology-driven partnerships with non-banks to provide banking services . . . Crypto-asset related activities . . . Projects that use DLT with the potential for significant impact on the financial system . . . [and] Concentrated provision of banking services to crypto-asset-related entities and fintechs." *Id.*

also includes the charge to routinely monitor all supervised financial institutions looking into novel activities.[35]

11.3.2. The Role of OFAC, OFR, OCC, and the FDIC

The OFAC has jurisdiction over "blocked property"[36] and rejected financial transactions.[37] Financial institutions are required to submit an annual report by September 30 regarding all blocked property, as well as a report on any rejected financial transaction within ten business days of the rejection.[38] The electronic OFAC reporting system accepts these required reports from financial institutions as well as the required submission by MSBs of any SAR in which there is a suspected sanctions connection.[39]

Although the Office of Financial Research (OFR) does not directly regulate DeFi, it can serve as an important resource for spotting emerging legal and regulatory issues for the digital economy. The OFR is tasked by the Dodd–Frank Wall Street Reform and Consumer Protection Act[40] with identifying and monitoring potential risks to financial stability and submitting an annual report to Congress addressing the state of the U.S. financial system.[41] In its recent annual reports, the OFR consistently cites to the interconnected nature of digital assets markets with traditional financial markets and the need for regulations to address new risks.[42] A recent OFR presentation specifically addressed risks and proposed strategies for the DeFi and cryptocurrency space, highlighting the perceived need for targeted updates to current regulatory requirements to protect the public and the economy from systemic risk.[43]

The OCC supervises and charters national banks and savings associations, with the mission of ensuing a sound U.S. federal banking system. Originating with the National Currency Act of 1863,[44] the OCC "prescribes regulations, conducts supervisory activities and, when necessary, takes enforcement actions to ensure that national banks have the necessary controls in place and provide the requisite notices to law enforcement to deter and detect money laundering, terrorist financing and other criminal acts and the misuse of our nation's financial institutions."[45]

---

35 *Id.*

36 OFAC's reference to "blocked property" generally refers to frozen assets, such as bank accounts or other funds of Specially Designated Nationals or sanctioned governments. *Basic Information on OFAC and Sanctions*, FAQ 9, Off. of Foreign Assets Control, https://ofac.treasury.gov/faqs/9.

37 31 C.F.R. § 501.

38 *OFAC Reporting System*, Off. of Foreign Assets Control, https://ofac.treasury.gov/ofac-reporting-system.

39 *Id.*

40 Dodd–Frank Wall Street Reform and Consumer Protection Act, 124 Stat. 1376, Pub. L. 111-203 (Jul. 21, 2010).

41 *Id.* at § 154(d).

42 *See, e.g.*, *Annual Reports*, Off. Fin. Rsch. https://www.financialresearch.gov/annual-reports/.

43 Greg Hopper, *Presentation to Office of Financial Research Advisory Committee*, Off. Fin. Rsch (Nov. 8, 2022), https://www.financialresearch.gov/frac/files/OFR_FRAC_DeFi-Hopper.pdf.

44 12 CFR § 21.11 and 12 CFR § 21.21.

45 *Bank Secrecy Act*, Off. Comptroller Currency, https://www.occ.treas.gov/topics/supervision-and-examination/bsa/index-bsa.html.

Established by the Glass–Steagall Act of 1933, the FDIC was created to ensure the financial stability of the U.S. banking system and the protection of depositors by insuring deposits in traditional financial institutions.[46] The FDIC does not insure assets issued by nonbank entities, including cryptocurrencies and other digital tokens. CBDCs, including a potential U.S. CBDC, are not currently covered by the FDIC; however, as a liability of central banks, the CBDC might garner such status in the future.

11.4. State-Level Regulations for Money Transmitters

In addition to compliance with BSA provisions, virtual currency businesses that qualify as money transmitters also must consider state-level requirements. With increasingly clear guidance in terms of existing financial regulation but no comprehensive federal policy specifically addressing digital assets in place, states have been enacting their own cryptocurrency regulation. This patchwork of rules ranges from the less-than-friendly approach to crypto by New York and California, to Texas' middle ground, and Wyoming's welcome with open arms. A few examples of state's efforts are set forth below, but it is important to research each state in which a digital asset or DeFi client is conducting business for a comprehensive view of the various regulations.[47]

Applying a more restrictive state-level approach to virtual currency, New York's Department of Financial Services (NYDFS) passed a "BitLicense" statute in 2015 to address virtual currency businesses operating in New York. This rule has resulted in a lengthy and complicated licensure process to operate "any virtual currency business activity."[48] California adopted the Digital Financial Assets Law[49] with an effective date of January 2025, which takes a similar approach to New York's BitLicense.[50]

In 2014, the Texas Department of Banking was the first state bank regulator in the United States to release regulatory guidance for virtual currency businesses, which it updated in 2019.[51] According to Texas' guidance, virtual currency is not money for purposes of the Texas Money Services Act, so state-level money transmission requirements do not need to be followed unless a third-party exchanger or escrow-like intermediary is involved, or

---

[46] The FDIC protects up to $250,000 per depositor and $1.25 million for trust accounts as of April 1, 2024. *What We Do*, FDIC, https://www.fdic.gov/about/what-we-do/.

[47] Individual state legislatures will be key resources, but the National Conference of State Legislatures regularly updates state-level legislative proposals. Survey information can be found at the NAT'L CONF. OF STATE LEGISLATURES, https://www.ncsl.org.

[48] 23 NYCRR Part 200.3(a) states that: License required. No person shall, without a license obtained from the superintendent as provided in this Part, engage in any virtual currency business activity . . . (b) Unlicensed agents prohibited. Each licensee is prohibited from conducting any virtual currency business activity through an agent or agency arrangement when the agent is not a licensee. The full regulatory framework is found at N.Y. Comp. Codes R. & Regs. Tit. 23 § 200.1 *et seq.* (2015).

[49] CA Fin. Code § 3101 *et seq.* (2023).

[50] *See Digital Assets Finance Law*, CALIFORNIA DEPT.OF FIN. PROTECTION AND INNOVATION, https://dfpi.ca.gov/dfal/.

[51] Nelson S. Ebaugh, *Texas Cryptocurrency Jurisprudence: Examining the Current Legal Framework*, STATE BAR TEXAS, https://www.texasbar.com/AM/Template.cfm?Section=articles&ContentID=60081&Template=/CM/HTMLDisplay.cfm.

if the transaction involves a stablecoin.[52] Virtual currency businesses also are required to demonstrate "secure operations."[53] In addition to its virtual currency guidance, Texas amended its Penal Code in 2015 to include a digital currency in the definition of "funds" for purposes of the offense of money laundering.[54]

Wyoming has passed significant legislation that is seen as creating an environment that is more welcoming to virtual currency businesses. For instance, Wyoming exempts virtual currency to virtual currency transmission from state money transmission laws[55]; provides that a person who develops, sells, or facilitates the exchange of an open blockchain token (utility token) is not subject to specified securities and money transmission laws, if certain requirements are met[56]; exempts virtual currencies from property taxation[57]; and amends the definition of digital asset, provisions relating to the nature of digital assets under commercial law, and security interest provisions relating to digital assets.[58] Wyoming law also directs the application of commercial law to specific types of digital assets, clarifies provisions relating to custody of digital assets by banks, and establishes that certain digital asset provisions are consumer protection statutes for commercial law purposes.[59] In addition, Wyoming amended its Uniform Commercial Code (UCC) provisions in 2019 to address some of the issues related to digital assets, which included the addition of subcategories such as digital consumer assets, digital securities, and virtual currency.[60]

11.5. Criminal Regulations in the Digital Financial Sector

As technology continues to advance, crimes that implicate technology are likely to become more frequent and increasingly complex. However, for the past several years, digital-asset-related crime, including theft and fraud in crypto exchanges, has remained on average less than one percent of the total volume of reported criminal activity across all sectors.[61] Although money laundering implicating digital assets totaling double-digit billions of U.S. dollars annually has been a significant concern for regulators and the Department of Justice (DOJ), the UN Office of Drugs and Crime estimated that, by comparison, between $800 billion and $2 trillion in fiat currency is laundered every year offline.[62]

---

52 *Id.*

53 *Id.*

54 Tex. Pen. Code § 34.01 D. (2023).

55 Wyo. Stat. § 40-22-104(a)(vi) (2022).

56 Wyo. Stat. § 17-4-206 (2018).

57 Wyo. Stat.§ 39-11-105 (b)(vi)(A) (2018).

58 Wyo. Stat. §§ 40-29-101 through 40-29-109 (2022); 021.0008.1 Wyo. Code R. §§ 1 to 8; Wyo. Stat. § 40-22-104(b) (2022).

59 *Id.*

60 Wyo. U. Com. Code, Wyo. Stat. Section 34-29-101-106 (2022).

61 *See 2024 Crypto Crime Trends: Illicit Activity Down as Scamming and Stolen Funds Fall, but Ransomware and Darknet Markets*, Chainalysis (Jan. 18, 2024), https://www.chainalysis.com/blog/2024-crypto-crime-report-introduction/. Growth, for example: Chainalysis estimated that the share of all crypto transaction volume associated with illicit activity fell to 0.34 percent in 2023 from 0.42 percent in 2022.

62 *Money Laundering*, UN Off. Drugs & Crime, https://www.unodc.org/unodc/en/money-laundering/overview.html.

Nonetheless, coverage of digital financial crime has been high profile, and criminal enforcement is a true threat to individuals and entities on the wrong side of the law. As with financial regulations focused on administrative requirements, crime that is connected to cryptocurrency and other digital assets comprises broad regulatory issues.[63] Like civil financial regulation in the United States, criminal enforcement related to digital assets also has primarily relied upon laws and regulations that pre-date the use of cryptocurrency.

11.5.1. The BSA's Criminal Side

As discussed in Section 11.2, the BSA requires that financial institutions establish AML programs, report large currency transactions and suspicious activity to FinCEN, and maintain records related to large transactions involving foreign banks. This includes the requirement that MSBs, including money transmitters, register with FinCEN and abide by AML requirements. In addition to the potential for civil penalties issued by FinCEN for a lack of compliance with the BSA, FinCEN also has the authority to refer violative conduct to the DOJ for criminal prosecution.

The BSA includes the provision that any person willfully violating the recordkeeping requirements of the BSA may be fined up to $1,000 and/or imprisoned up to one year for each violation, with the fine increasing up to $10,000 and/or five years in prison if the violation is committed in conjunction with another Federal law punishable by imprisonment for more than one year.[64] In addition, any person willfully violating the currency and foreign transactions reporting requirements of the BSA may be fined up to $250,000 and/or imprisoned up to five years.[65] If a willful violation is committed while violating another Federal law or as a "pattern of illegal activity" involving transactions exceeding $100,000 in any twelve-month period, fine is increased up to $500,000 and/or ten years' imprisonment.[66]

11.5.2. Additional Criminal Penalties and Actions

Under the U.S. Code's Racketeering Chapter, it is unlawful to conduct transactions using funds known to be proceeds from unlawful activity for illegal purposes, to conceal the source of those funds, or to avoid reporting requirements.[67] It is also criminally unlawful

63 Evidentiary issues also are significant. Legal requirements of the relevant jurisdiction(s) in a digital investigation will always be crucial considerations in terms of the ability to use evidence obtained in the prosecution and conviction of criminals. Authentication and admissibility of evidence depend on forensic processes that comply with the relevant laws, but the applicability of the law of the land can be opaque in the context of a crime committed through a technology that did not exist at the time that the law was drafted. In addition, permissionless blockchain networks, such as Bitcoin, can be accessed from any jurisdiction, making the legal requirements even murkier.

64 31 CFR § 1010.840(a) (2022).

65 31 CFR § 1010.840(b) (2022).

66 31 CFR § 1010.840(c) (2022). Additionally, any person who knowingly makes a false, fictitious, or fraudulent statement or representation in any report may be fined up to $10,000 and/or imprisoned up to five years. 31 CFR 1010.840(d). Also, the AMLA of 2020 provides more standards for reporting, plus expands BSA requirements and obligations to persons engaged in the trade of antiquities (and requiring a study on the potential expansion of BSA requirements to persons engaged in the art trade). 31 CFR § 6110 (2021).

67 18 U.S.C. § 1956(a)(1) (2022).

to knowingly spend proceeds from unlawful activity[68] and to operate an unlicensed money transmitting business.[69] In addition to criminal charges related to Racketeering and referrals to FinCEN pursuant to the BSA, statutory guidance for the SEC, CFTC, and IRS provides the authority to support both civil and criminal investigations and to refer cases to the DOJ for criminal prosecution.

In 2022, the DOJ created the National Cryptocurrency Enforcement Team (NCET) to focus on investigations and prosecutions involving the criminal misuse of cryptocurrency. U.S. Attorneys General take the prosecutorial lead for prosecutions recommended by NCET. Additionally, other agencies, including OFAC, the Federal Bureau of Investigation (FBI), the Department of Homeland Security (DHS), as well as state agencies and attorneys general, have the authority to investigate and support criminal prosecutions related to unlawful digital asset activity.

11.6. U.S. Legislative Activity and Framework Goals

Particularly since 2020, the U.S. Congress has seen scores of proposals related to decentralized finance, cryptocurrencies, digital or virtual currencies, and other digital assets.[70] Most proposed bills have been bipartisan, with varying levels of detail and comprehensiveness. Many have focused on cryptocurrency regulation and oversight, with some more narrowly targeting the possibility of a U.S. CBDC[71] or controls on the issuance of stablecoins.[72] The prevailing themes of past proposed legislation concerning the crypto economy center on the need for clarity of rules and the roles of regulators. Additionally, they emphasize the importance of further study and definitions for certain aspects of the crypto economy. The overarching goals remain consistent: to catch terrorists and other criminal actors, to remain competitive in the global market, and to ensure overall financial stability.

An example of a relatively successful digital assets bill is the bipartisan Financial Innovation and Technology for the 21st Century Act (FIT21),[73] which was introduced in 2024. FIT21 explicitly addressed the treatment of digital assets under U.S. law, providing

---

68 18 U.S.C. § 1957(a) (2022).

69 18 U.S.C. § 1960 (2022).

70 A few examples include the Digital Commodities Consumer Protection Act of 2022, which sought to give the CFTC regulatory authority to make rules for digital commodity platforms; the Blockchain Regulatory Certainty Act, which was introduced in 2023 and sought to legislate that blockchain developers and service providers that do not custody consumer funds are not "money transmitters"; and the Lummis Gillibrand Responsible Financial Innovation Act, which was introduced in 2022 and sought to establish a regulatory framework addressing innovation; clarify standards, jurisdictional boundaries, and consumer protection; clarify CFTC and SEC jurisdiction; and create interagency coordination on stablecoin regulation and banking and tax treatment of digital assets.

71 CBDC-related bills have included proposed amendment to the Federal Reserve Act at 12 U.S.C. 347d to prohibit the Fed from developing a CBDC, as well as supporting the consideration of a U.S. CBDC for various reasons, including financial inclusion, efficiency, and payment system resilience.

72 Stablecoin Trust Act in 2022 sought to create a framework to regulate stablecoins; the Clarity for Payment Stablecoins Act of 2023 had similar goals. Although stablecoins operate in a regulatory gray area, ongoing efforts to establish clearer rules for their issuance and use have not yet progressed.

73 H.R.4763, Financial Innovation and Technology for the 21st Century Act, https://www.congress.gov/bill/118th-congress/house-bill/4763/all-actions.

a fairly comprehensive regulatory framework for digital assets. It also defined responsibilities of various U.S. agencies, notably the CFTC for digital commodities and the SEC for securities and related entities. The goal was to provide regulatory clarity and strong consumer safeguards for digital assets in the United States. FIT21 also set forth requirements for primary and secondary market transactions related to digital assets. Overall, FIT21 aimed to provide regulatory clarity, protect consumers, and foster innovation in the digital asset space by defining roles for regulatory agencies and addressing the unique structure of U.S. digital asset markets. In May 2024, FIT21 became the first comprehensive digital assets bill that passed by the U.S. House of Representatives, but it stalled with the Senate. However, it is likely that the core themes of this bill will continue to surface in future proposed frameworks. Regardless of the final disposition of FIT21, reviewing this proposed legislation might assist with the navigation of the evolving landscape of digital assets regulation in the United States.

11.7. The Global Perspective

The Financial Action Task Force (FATF) is the self-proclaimed "global watchdog" for money laundering and terrorist financing.[74] With forty member countries and blocs, including the United States, plus associate members and observer organizations, more than two hundred jurisdictions are involved.[75] In October 2021, the FATF issued guidelines titled, *Updated Guidance for a Risk-Based Approach to Virtual Assets and Virtual Asset Service Providers*, which covers the obligations applicable to VASPs under the FATF Recommendations.[76] Although all of the FATF guidance is in the form of recommendations, therefore not binding on even the member countries, it nonetheless is worth considering due to the global nature of many crypto transactions and the increasing need for international cooperation in the DeFi realm.

On the nation-state level, regulators globally are grappling with the regulation of digital assets. El Salvador made Bitcoin a legal currency in 2021.[77] At the other extreme, more than twenty jurisdictions have banned the use of cryptocurrencies altogether.[78] Most other countries, including the United States, are still working on creating a comprehensive framework for digital assets. In some jurisdictions, cryptocurrencies are legal and treated as property, thus being subject to capital gains tax[79]; many others have determined that cryptocurrency and exchanges are legal but subject to registration, AML laws, and various levels of taxation. Notable progress on national frameworks has been made in the European Union (EU) and the United Kingdom, both of which will likely continue to see evolution as political, regulatory, and technology environments transform.

---

74 Financial Action Task Force Website, https://www.fatf-gafi.org.

75 *Id.*

76 *Updated Guidance for a Risk-Based Approach to Virtual Assets and Virtual Asset Service Providers*, FATF (Oct. 2021), https://www.fatf-gafi.org/publications/fatfrecommendations/documents/guidance-rba-virtual-assets-2021.html.

77 The Central African Republic followed suit in 2022 but reversed its decision in 2023.

78 *E.g.*, China, Egypt, and Turkey.

79 *E.g.*, Australia, Japan, and Switzerland.

In the EU, the European Council presidency and the European Parliament passed the Markets in Crypto Assets (MiCA)[80] legislation, which received a formal vote by the EU Parliament in April 2023, and was subsequently passed in its final form on June 13, 2024. As the first comprehensive national framework for digital assets regulation,[81] MiCA covers exchanges, issuers of cryptocurrencies, and digital asset wallets that are not classified as "financial instruments," including stablecoins and utility tokens.[82] Under MiCA, Crypto-Assets Service Providers (CASPs) must comply with MiCA to be granted a license to operate in the EU. In the United Kingdom, the Financial Services and Markets Act 2023[83] classifies crypto as a regulated financial activity, and its Financial Conduct Authority (FCA) continues to consult on an authorization regime for crypto companies as it works to bring digital assets within the fold of traditional financial service oversight.

11.8. Conclusion

As U.S. regulators join the global push to address the regulatory challenges posed by technological advancements and the rapid growth of digital assets, continuing education for attorneys and clients will be vital. DeFi and other nontraditional providers, along with their customers, will need to understand current enforcement trends as legislators and regulators pursue a comprehensive regulatory framework that balances myriad competing interests. Striking a balance between consumer protection, economic stability, and global leadership in innovation is essential in charting a sensible path forward.

Currently, regulators continue to operate within the bounds of existing authority. The SEC, CFTC, and IRS often join FinCEN and its Treasury Department colleagues in applying the rules and oversight that seem most appropriate in an effort to avoid a financial industry meltdown, as Congress struggles with establishing suitable limits. Anticipating the enforcement of the amended BSA, criminal statues, and state-level financial regulations is critical in this evolving landscape. Additionally, the global nature of DeFi and the jurisdictional complexities of digital asset creation and transfer introduce further challenges that must be addressed.

While the exact nature of the forthcoming digital asset framework remains uncertain, meaningful roadmaps are emerging through global progress and increasingly focused proposals in the United States. In the short term, time and patience will be crucial as regulatory developments unfold, paving the way for more stable long-term solutions.

---

80 Markets in Crypto Asset Regulation, *Regulation (EU) 2023/1114 of the European Parliament and of the Council of 31 May 2023 on Markets in Crypto-assets, and Amending Regulations (EU) No 1093/2010 and (EU) No 1095/2010 and Directives 2013/36/EU and (EU) 2019/1937.*

81 *See* Ryan Browne, *EU Lawmakers Approve World's First Comprehensive Framework for Crypto Regulation*, CNBC (Apr. 20, 2023), https://www.cnbc.com/2023/04/20/eu-lawmakers-approve-worlds-first-comprehensive-crypto-regulation.html.

82 *Supra* note 80.

83 Financial Services and Markets Act 2023, UK Public General Acts 2023, Chapter 29.

12 Securities and Commodities Regulation for Crypto and Other Digital Assets

By Susan H. Stephan

12.1. Introduction

The application of U.S. securities and commodities laws to digital assets is a complex and evolving area. Although Congress has reviewed numerous proposals related to digital asset regulation, legislators have not passed a comprehensive framework to date.[1] In the absence of clear legislative guidance, enforcement activity in the digital sector predominantly has been under the purview of federal agencies. Regulators determine whether a digital asset is a security or commodity under U.S. law based on the specific characteristics of the asset and how it is used. The Securities and Exchange Commission (SEC) is actively involved in determining which digital assets are considered securities and ensuring compliance with applicable laws. The Commodity Futures Trading Commission (CFTC) regulates aspects of digital assets that are viewed as commodities. The Financial Industry Regulatory Authority, Inc. (FINRA) is a self-regulatory nonprofit authorized by Congress that oversees U.S. broker-dealers.[2] In addition to security

[1] One ultimately unsuccessful proposal, H.R.4763, "Financial Innovation and Technology for the 21st Century Act" (FIT21) was a bipartisan bill passed by the House Financial Services Committee and the full House of Representatives that sought to clarify when cryptocurrency is a security or a commodity, expand CFTC oversight, and clarify SEC jurisdiction. H.R.4763, Financial Innovation and Technology for the 21st Century Act, https://www.congress.gov/bill/118th-congress/house-bill/4763/all-actions (last visited Nov. 10, 2024). FIT21 is briefly discussed in Section 12.5.

[2] About FINRA, Fin. Ind. Regul. Auth., https://www.finra.org/about (last visited Nov. 10, 2024).

broker-dealers, FINRA also has some jurisdiction relating to commodity traders.[3] Although many other agencies are involved in the regulation of digital assets, this chapter reviews the current regulatory environment for securities and commodities involving the SEC, the CFTC, and FINRA.

12.2. U.S. Securities Laws and the SEC

In the United States, securities laws are designed to protect investors and ensure fair and efficient markets.[4] The SEC has jurisdiction over securities, including digital assets that are characterized as securities. According to the SEC's website, it is "the agency that protects investors from misconduct, promotes fairness & efficiency in the securities markets, and facilitates capital formation for those looking to hire, innovate, and grow."[5] The primary securities legislation includes the Securities Act of 1933 (Securities Act)[6] and the Securities Exchange Act of 1934 (Exchange Act),[7] in addition to the Trust Indenture Act of 1939,[8] the Investment Company Act of 1940,[9] the Investment Advisers Act of 1940 (Advisers Act),[10] the Sarbanes–Oxley Act of 2002 (SOX),[11] the Dodd–Frank Wall Street Reform & Consumer Protection Act of 2010 (Dodd–Frank),[12] and the Jumpstart Our Business Startups Act of 2012 (JOBS Act).[13] The SEC, which was established by the Exchange Act, also may supplement the statutes with regulations through rulemaking and nonbinding guidelines.

Under Section 5(c) of the Securities Act, the offer and sale of securities must be registered unless an exemption from registration is available. According to the Exchange Act, a broker-dealer must be registered with the SEC to assist with any transactions involving the purchase or sale of securities; the Exchange Act also prohibits insider trading or market manipulation under Rule 10(b)(5), subjecting these activities to criminal penalties.[14] The Securities Act prohibits deceit, misrepresentation, and other fraud in connection with the sale of securities; it also requires disclosure of financial and other material information to allow investors to make an informed judgment on whether to purchase securities.

The Securities Act allows certain exemptions from registration requirements to facilitate capital formation while reducing the regulatory burden on smaller or more localized offerings. Exemptions include sales to accredited investors where no public solicitation or advertising is made under Rule 506(b) for private placements[15]; smaller offerings up

---

3 For example, FINRA issues the National Commodities Futures ("Series 3") Examination, which is required for individuals who want to trade commodity futures and options. *Id.*

4 The impetus for the securities laws was the stock market crash of 1929 and the resulting Great Depression. Before the crash, companies issued stock and enthusiastically promoted the value of their company without oversight.

5 Crypto Assets, Sec. Exch. Comm'n, https://www.sec.gov/securities-topics/crypto-assets (last visited Nov. 10, 2024).

6 Securities Act of 1933, 15 U.S. Code § 77 *et seq.* (2021).

7 Securities Exchange Act of 1934, 15 U.S. Code § 78 *et seq.* (2021).

8 Trust Indenture Act of 1939, 15 U.S.C. §§ 77aaa–77bbbb (2021).

9 Investment Company Act of 1940, 15 U.S. Code § 80a-64 (2021).

10 Investment Advisers Act of 1940, 15 U.S.C. §§ 80b-1-80b-21 (2021).

11 Sarbanes–Oxley Act of 2002, 116 Stat. 745, Pub. L. 107-204 (Jul. 30, 2002).

12 Dodd–Frank Wall Street Reform and Consumer Protection Act, 124 Stat. 1376, Pub. L. 111-203 (Jul. 21, 2010).

13 Jumpstart Our Business Startups Act of 2012 (JOBS Act), 126 Stat. 306, Pub. L. 112-10 (Apr. 5, 2012).

14 17 CFR § 240.10b-5 (2024).

15 Securities Act, 17 CFR § 230.506, Section 4(a)(2) (2024).

to $10 million under Rule 504, generally involving investors with whom the offeror has a relationship[16]; offerings under Rule 506(c) allowing companies to raise unlimited capital by broadly soliciting investors who meet certain wealth thresholds or have certain professional credentials[17]; offerings eligible under Title IV of the JOBS Act and Regulation A+, also known as "mini-IPOs"[18]; intrastate offerings of securities offered and sold only within one state under "blue sky laws"[19]; crowd-funded offerings of up to $5 million through a FINRA-registered online portal[20]; and securities issued as part of employee compensation plans.[21]

12.2.1. Digital Assets as Securities—The Howey Test

Section 2(a)(1) of the Securities Act broadly defines a "security" as "any note, stock, treasury stock, security future . . . investment contract . . . any interest or instrument commonly known as a 'security,' or any certificate of interest or participation in, temporary or interim certificate for, receipt for, guarantee of, or warrant or right to subscribe to or purchase, any of the foregoing." It is the "investment contract" designation that serves as the basis for the SEC's jurisdiction over some digital assets. Whether or not a digital asset is an investment contract, and therefore a security, depends on various factors, including how the asset is promoted and used. Currently, the SEC and the courts primarily use the "*Howey* test," from the 1946 case *SEC v. W.J. Howey Co.*,[22] to determine the status of an asset as a security.[23] The *Howey* test requires an affirmative response to the following prongs:

- an investment of money or other value,
- in a common enterprise,
- with an expectation of profits primarily based on the efforts of others.[24]

---

16 17 CFR § 230.504 (2024).

17 17 CFR § 230.506 (2024).

18 Under Title IV of the JOBS Act and Regulation A+, eligible entities can raise up to $20 (Tier 1)/$75 (Tier 2) million in any twelve-month period with much more SEC involvement regarding qualification, two-year audits, and so on. This is often referred to as a "Mini-IPO." JOBS Act, *supra* note 13.

19 17 CFR § 230.147 (2024). "Blue Sky" law refers to state-level statutes, rules, and regulations regarding the supervision and regulation of offers and sales of securities. Blue sky laws typically require registration prior to offering and selling securities in a particular state, absent an available exemption.

20 17 CFR § 227 *et seq.* (2024). The sale of equity interest in a business to raise capital might be permitted without SEC registration for small offerings and investors that qualify under Title III of the JOBS Act. Title III is also known as the Capital Raising Online While Deterring Fraud and Unethical Non-Disclosure (CROWDFUND) Act of 2012. Offerors may raise up to $5 million in a twelve-month period (amount adjusted for inflation). Securities must be offered through an SEC-registered funding portal (or broker-dealer). FINRA maintains a list of registered funding portals. The SEC's *Regulation Crowdfunding: A Small Entity Compliance Guide for Issuers* provides a helpful resource relating to Regulation Crowdfunding.

21 17 CFR § 230.701 (2024).

22 SEC v. W.J. Howey Co., 328 U.S. 293 (1946).

23 When a promissory note is involved, courts look to Reves v. Ernst & Young, 494 U.S. 56 (1990), to apply a "family resemblance" test to determine whether a note is a security. The Reves analysis begins with the rebuttable presumption that a note is a security; rebutted if the note bears a resemblance to one of the enumerated categories on a judicially developed list of exceptions (e.g., a note secured by an assignment of accounts receivable or a standard business debt). If not rebutted, then a four-factor test is implemented.

24 SEC v. W.J. Howey Co., 328 U.S. at 300-302. For clarification of the first prong as it relates to digital assets, *See* SEC, *Report of Investigation Pursuant to Section 21(a) of the Securities Exchange Act of 1934: The DAO*, Release No.

For several years after the introduction of the cryptocurrency Bitcoin and its blockchain[25] platform in 2009,[26] the regulatory environment for completing and recording online transactions was unclear. Since Bitcoin is seen as a peer-to-peer electronic payment system as opposed to an investment opportunity, the SEC has not exercised jurisdiction over Bitcoin transactions. Bitcoin and other cryptocurrencies that rely on decentralized platforms do not meet the definition of an investment contract pursuant to *Howey*. Although cryptocurrency transactions involve investments that might be profitable, a decentralized platform generally is not seen as a common enterprise, and any anticipated profit would be determined by the market as opposed to the efforts of a specific individual or entity. Therefore, Bitcoin does not meet all the *Howey* prongs, particularly the "common enterprise" and "efforts of others" criteria. Bitcoin and other cryptocurrencies operating in a decentralized environment are unlikely to be considered securities.

In 2015, Ethereum launched as the first major "smart contract"[27] platform for building decentralized applications (or "DApps") using blockchain technology.[28] Ethereum offers its own cryptocurrency called Ether (ETH), and it promotes the opportunity for developers to build DApps that can do anything from creating new digital assets to building collectively governed virtual worlds.[29] The expanded opportunity to create digital assets that function in ways beyond a decentralized payment system has piqued the SEC's interest, particularly after the "merge"[30] in 2022, which transitioned the consensus mechanism to

81207 (Jul. 25, 2017), *infra* note 35, in which the SEC states, "In determining whether an investment contract exists, the investment of 'money' need not take the form of cash." *See, e.g.*, Uselton v. Comm. Lovelace Motor Freight, Inc., 940 F.2d 564, 574 (10th Cir. 1991) ("[I]n spite of Howey's reference to an 'investment of money,' it is well established that cash is not the only form of contribution or investment that will create an investment contract."). In applying the *Howey* test to any potential security under the second prong, courts recognize three types of commonality: (1) Horizontal, which requires a pooling of investors' funds and/or a *pro rata* distribution of profits among more than one investor (the D.C., First, Second, Third, Fourth, Sixth, and Seventh Circuits all apply the horizontal approach); (2) Broad Vertical, wherein the requisite commonality exists if the success or failure of the investment is dependent upon the expertise of the promoter (the Fifth and the Eleventh Circuits follow this approach); and (3) Strict/Narrow Vertical, which requires that the economic successes or losses of the investor and promoter be mutually dependent (only the Ninth Circuit follows this approach). Additionally, to fulfill the expectation of profits prong, the *Howey* Court required that the expectation of profits be "solely" due to the efforts of others, but that requirement has been relaxed and clarified.

25 Blockchains have been described more concisely as "distributed digital ledgers of cryptographically signed transactions that are grouped into blocks." Dylan Yaga et al., *Blockchain Technology Overview*, National Institute of Standards and Technology Interagency or Internal Report (IR) 8202 (2018), 1, 10–11, https://doi.org/10.6028/NIST.IR.8202. According to blockchain's pseudonymous creator Satoshi Nakamoto, the digital ledger "timestamps transactions by hashing them into an ongoing chain of hash-based proof of work, forming a record that cannot be changed without redoing the proof of work." Satoshi Nakamoto, *Bitcoin: A Peer-to-Peer Electronic Cash System*, Bitcoin (2008), https://bitcoin.org/bitcoin.pdf (last visited Nov. 10, 2024).

26 Dylan Yaga et al., *Blockchain Technology Overview*, National Institute of Standards and Technology Interagency or Internal Report (IR) 8202 (2018), 1, 10–11, https://doi.org/10.6028/NIST.IR.8202.

27 Sometimes, self-executing, smart contracts put together code and data recorded on a blockchain that is accessible by the parties involved. Tom Lyons et al., *Legal and Regulatory Framework of Blockchains and Smart Contracts*, The European Union Blockchain Observatory & Forum, Thematic Report (Sept. 27, 2019), 22. They tend to be more like programs than actual contracts, and they can be used to automate processes as well as agreements. *Id.*

28 *Ethereum*, Ethereum, https://ethereum.org/en/ (last visited Nov.10, 2024).

29 *Id.*

30 For a detailed description of the 2022 merge, *see The Merge*, Ethereum (Jul. 2024), https://ethereum.org/en/roadmap/merge (last visited Nov. 10, 2024).

add transactions to the Ethereum blockchain from "proof of work"[31] to "proof of stake."[32] Although SEC representatives have hinted that this increased involvement of Ethereum developers in maintaining and supporting the blockchain might decrease decentralization enough to warrant additional scrutiny,[33] in 2023, the SEC approved several ETH-based Exchange Traded Funds (ETFs) tracking the ETH commodity futures market, which is overseen by the CFTC.[34] The SEC has not yet undertaken an enforcement action regarding ETH, although it has pursued investigations.[35] The current regulatory landscape regarding ETH and other tokens is subject to change at any point, as the agencies and Congress continue to explore the functioning of blockchain environments.

12.2.2. The Decentralized Autonomous Organization Report and SEC Guidelines

The history of SEC enforcement involving digital assets has evolved significantly since 2015, reflecting the increasing complexity of the digital asset market. The SEC's first major activity in the digital asset space was the publication of its *DAO Report*[36] in July 2017. The Decentralized Autonomous Organization (DAO) was a digital investment business launched in early 2016 on the Ethereum blockchain. It was designed to function without a central authority, relying instead on smart contracts to manage its fundraising operations and decision making.[37] In June 2016, the DAO experienced a significant attack,

---

[31] According to blockchain's pseudonymous creator Satoshi Nakamoto, proof of work on the blockchain involves timestamping transactions "by hashing them into an ongoing chain of hash-based proof of work, forming a record that cannot be changed without redoing the proof of work." Satoshi Nakamoto, *Bitcoin: A Peer-to-Peer Electronic Cash System* (2008), https://bitcoin.org/bitcoin.pdf (last visited Nov. 10, 2024). Once it is verified by a "miner" who solves the complex mathematical problem to connect a new transaction to the chain in exchange for compensation in cryptocurrency, the transaction is immediately visible to all blockchain users on the relevant network. Yaga, *supra* note 26 at 10–11. When miners solve a problem, the publication of the solution is the "proof of the work" performed. The problems are adjusted and made increasingly complicated to keep the network secure. *Id.*

[32] The proof of stake consensus model involves validators with a stake in the outcome of transaction validation; potential validators lock up, or "stake," cryptocurrency on the platform and typically are selected to perform block validation through a random process with chances weighted by the amount staked and the length of time the cryptocurrency has been held. Yaga, *supra* note 26 at 21.

[33] *See* Paul Kiernan & Vicky Ge Huang, *Ether's New "Staking" Model Could Draw SEC Attention*, W.S.J. (Sept. 15, 2022), https://www.wsj.com/articles/ethers-new-staking-model-could-draw-sec-attention-11663266224; *See also* Securities Exchange Comm'n v. Ian Balina, Civil Action No. 1:22-CV-950 (filed Sept. 19, 2022) (The SEC's complaint against Balina includes the concern that contributions to Balina's pool were validated on the Ethereum blockchain nodes that "are clustered more densely" in the United States, and thus "took place in" the United States, implying that the SEC might seek jurisdiction to police all Ethereum network-based projects as potential securities.).

[34] *See* Lucy Brewster, *SEC Approves 9 Ether Futures ETFs*, ETF.com (Oct. 2, 2023), https://www.etf.com/sections/news/-sec-approves-9-ether-futures-etfs (last visited Nov. 10, 2024).

[35] In 2024, blockchain technology company Consensys filed a preemptive lawsuit against the SEC in a Texas federal district court after the SEC issued a "Wells Notice" (a formal letter from the SEC notifying a party of an investigation and intent to sue) based on Consensys' ETH-related activity. The lawsuit sought the court's determination that ETH is not a security. The SEC dropped its ETH investigation contemplated in the Wells Notice, at least temporarily, and the court dismissed the Consensys lawsuit on procedural grounds. *See* Consensys Software, Inc. v. Securities Exchange Comm'n, Case No. 4:24-cv-00369-O (N.D. Tex filed Sept. 19, 2024), https://storage.courtlistener.com/recap/gov.uscourts.txnd.389154/gov.uscourts.txnd.389154.57.0.pdf (last visited Nov. 10, 2024).

[36] *Report of Investigation Pursuant to Section 21(a) of the Securities Exchange Act of 1934: The DAO*, SEC, Release No. 81207 (Jul. 25, 2017).

[37] *Id.*

where a hacker exploited a vulnerability in its code, leading to the loss of a substantial portion of the $150 million that it had raised.[38] The attack and subsequent compromise of investor funds caught the attention of the SEC, which issued its 2017 report concluding that the DAO's "tokens" were securities and therefore subject to federal securities laws.[39] The report made clear its position that a platform offering digital asset securities trading and operating as an exchange needs to register with the SEC as a national securities exchange or be exempt from registration.[40]

Following the DAO Report, the SEC began targeting unregistered offerings of digital tokens, or "Initial Coin Offerings" (ICOs) in earnest, bringing enforcement actions against unregistered token issuers, exchanges trading in virtual currencies that it viewed as securities, and broker-dealers facilitating the issuance, purchase, or sale of digital securities.[41] The SEC sees ICOs as "distributed ledger or blockchain-enabled means for capital raising,"[42] which it specifically describes as activities involving securities in the DAO Report, due to the expectations of profits "based on the efforts of others" prong of the *Howey* test. To further clarify its treatment of digital assets under U.S. securities laws, the SEC provided nonbinding guidelines in 2019. In its *Framework for "Investment Contract" Analysis of Digital Assets*,[43] the SEC's Strategic Hub for Innovation and Financial Technology (FinHub) confirmed that the *Howey* test is the standard for a digital asset to qualify as a security.[44] The guidelines emphasize that an asset's characterization under *Howey* depends on the specific "facts and circumstances" and "economic realities" of each digital asset.[45] For example, in determining whether the offering in question meets the "based on the efforts of others" prong in *Howey*, in *United Housing Foundation, Inc. v. Forman*[46]—to which it cites in the DAO Report—the Court focuses on substance over description or form of an offering, and considers advertising bulletins and any representations that "seek to attract investors by the prospect of profits resulting from the efforts of the promoters or third parties."[47] The SEC continues to review all public representations regarding an expectation of profit, including social media posts,[48] to determine the economic reality behind a specific digital asset transaction. According to the

---

38 This event had a major impact on the Ethereum community and led to a hard fork in the Ethereum blockchain, resulting in the creation of Ethereum (ETH) and Ethereum Classic (ETC). *Id.* at 9, n. 32.

39 *Id.* at 1.

40 *Id.* at 16.

41 *See, e.g., In the Matter of Zachary Coburn*, No. 3-18888 (SEC) (Nov. 8, 2018) at 58. (EtherDelta, an unregistered and nonexempt decentralized trading platform for Ether and "ERC20" protocol tokens [generally used in ICOs], was launched by Coburn in 2016, facilitating 3.3 million trades after the DAO Report); *In the Matter of Tokenlot, LLC, Lenny Kugel, and Andeli L. Lewitt*, No. 3-18739 (SEC) (Sept. 11, 2018) at 64 (An unregistered broker-dealer advertised and sold digital tokens, including securities, online to investors through ICOs and on the secondary market; the administrators were also unregistered, without securities licenses.).

42 *Report of Investigation Pursuant to Section 21(a) of the Securities Exchange Act of 1934: The DAO*, *supra* note 36 at 2.

43 *Framework for "Investment Contract" Analysis of Digital Assets*, SEC - Strategic Hub for Innovation & Fin. Tech., (2019), https://www.sec.gov/about/divisions-offices/division-corporation-finance/framework-investment-contract-analysis-digital-assets (last visited Nov. 10, 2024).

44 *Id.*

45 *Id.*

46 421 U.S. at 849 (1975).

47 *Id.* at 854.

48 *See, e.g., In re* Stoner Cats 2 LLC, *infra* note 124.

guidelines, when a digital asset is deemed to be a security, it must comply with federal securities laws, including somewhat onerous registration requirements,[49] or qualify for an exemption.

The SEC's 2019 digital asset guidelines have been criticized as still not providing sufficient clarity regarding the classification and regulation of digital assets.[50] A primary concern with the lack of clarity is the perceived difficulty for entities to actually comply, potentially resulting in the stifling of innovation due to the fear of SEC enforcement actions.[51] The guidelines are also nonbinding when it comes to judicial enforcement, should an SEC decision be challenged in court. In addition, the SEC frequently has been condemned for its approach of regulating through enforcement actions rather than engaging in rulemaking—or at least providing clearer, proactive guidance. The lack of clarity and the resulting uncertainty might create instability among market participants, driving innovation to more crypto-friendly jurisdictions. These points contribute to an ongoing debate regarding how best to regulate digital assets while fostering innovation and protecting investors.

12.2.3. SEC Enforcement Insights and Early Litigation Results

Despite regulatory uncertainties, the SEC continues to pursue enforcement actions against entities and individuals to ensure compliance with securities laws, including civil and criminal cases of fraud and failure to register digital asset offerings. Although the SEC actively pursued enforcement actions after its 2017 DAO Report, it became even less friendly with the digital asset community beginning in 2022, primarily due to alleged fraud, following the collapse of significant economic interests tied to platforms such as Terraform Labs[52] and FTX Trading, Ltd.[53] It also pursued celebrity endorsers touting[54]

---

[49] The registration process under Securities Act 5(a) involves extensive SEC filing requirements through the Electronic Data Gathering Analysis and Retrieval (EDGAR) system. File with SEC prior to any offering. *See* 15 U.S. Code § 78l *et seq.* (2024).

[50] Note, *SEC, Framework for "Investment Contract" Analysis of Digital Assets*, 132 Harv. L. Rev. 2418 (2019).

[51] *Id.* at 2426.

[52] Terraform Labs, co-founded by Do Kwon and Daniel Shin in 2018, developed Terra (LUNA), a stablecoin ecosystem that was promoted as combining the stability of fiat currencies with the benefits of blockchain technology. In 2023, the SEC charged Terraform Labs and founder Do Kwon with fraud and unregistered securities offerings related to the TerraUSD (UST) stablecoin and the LUNA token. Do Kwon, awaiting extradition to the United States, was tried and convicted *in absentia* of crypto asset securities fraud. In a settlement with the SEC, Terraform agreed to pay more than $3.5 million in disgorgement, more than $466 million in prejudgment interest, and a $420 million civil penalty. Kwon agreed to pay $110 million in disgorgement and more than $14 million in prejudgment interest, plus a $80 million civil penalty. *See SEC, Terraform and Kwon to Pay $4.5 Billion following Fraud Verdict*, SEC, https://www.sec.gov/newsroom/press-releases/2024-73 (last visited Nov. 10, 2024).

[53] FTX Trading Ltd. was a prominent cryptocurrency exchange founded in 2019 by Sam Bankman-Fried and Gary Wang. In November 2022, FTX filed for Chapter 11 bankruptcy following revelations of significant financial misconduct. The collapse resulted in the arrest of Sam Bankman-Fried and substantial negative publicity for cryptocurrency industry. Bankman-Fried eventually was convicted of seven counts of fraud and sentenced to twenty-five years in federal prison and the payment of $11 billion in forfeiture. *See DOJ, Samuel Bankman-Fried Sentenced to 25 Years for His Orchestration of Multiple Fraudulent Schemes*, Dept. of Justice, https://www.justice.gov/opa/pr/-samuel-bankman-fried-sentenced-25-years-his-orchestration-multiple-fraudulent-schemes (last visited Nov. 10, 2024).

[54] Securities touting refers to the practice of promoting or endorsing a security for financial gain, without disclosing compensation for the endorsement. Securities Act of 1933, Section 17(b).

digital asset investment opportunities, including Floyd Mayweather,[55] Kim Kardashian,[56] and Lindsey Lohan.[57] In response to its increasing attention to digital asset cases, the SEC nearly doubled the size of its Crypto Assets and Cyber Unit in 2022.[58]

Also in 2022, Coinbase, the largest U.S.-based cryptocurrency exchange, filed a petition to try to force the SEC to engage in rulemaking for digital assets. The SEC refused to propose new rules, maintaining that the current federal securities laws apply to crypto securities markets.[59] The following year, the SEC charged Coinbase in the U.S. District Court for the Southern District of New York (SDNY) with operating its crypto asset trading platform as an unregistered securities exchange, broker, and clearing agency.[60] Additionally, the SEC alleged that Coinbase failed to register the offer and sale of its "staking-as-a-service" program, by which customers can earn profits from the "proof of stake" mechanisms of certain blockchains.[61] In March 2024, the court ruled in favor of the SEC on all but one argument raised in Coinbase's motion for judgment on the pleadings,[62] finding that the SEC adequately alleged the tokens at issue and Coinbase's staking services are securities, and that Coinbase has been operating as an unregistered broker, exchange, and clearing agency.[63] The court also found that thirteen third-party tokens and Coinbase's staking program were sufficiently pled to be "investment contracts" under *Howey*, leaving the final disposition of the claims to the jury.[64]

---

55 *In the Matter of Floyd Mayweather Jr.*, Release No. 10578 (Nov. 29, 2018), https://www.sec.gov/files/litigation/admin/2018/33-10578.pdf (The SEC found that Mayweather failed to disclose promotional payments from three ICO issuers in return for his social media touting of the tokens to his 21 million Instagram followers, 7.8 million Twitter followers, and 13.4 million Facebook followers. Mayweather agreed to pay $300,000 in disgorgement, a $300,000 penalty, and $14,775 in prejudgment interest.).

56 *In the Matter of Kimberly Kardashian*, Release No. 11116 (Oct. 3, 2022), https://www.sec.gov/files/litigation/admin/2022/33-11116.pdf (Kim Kardashian allegedly touted on social media an EthereumMax crypto asset security without disclosing the payment she received and agreed to settle for $1.26 million in penalties, disgorgement, and interest.).

57 *In the Matter of Lindsey Dee Lohan*, Release No. 11173 (Mar. 22, 2023), https://www.sec.gov/files/litigation/admin/2023/33-11173.pdf (Lohan failed to disclose that she was paid $10,000 for promoting a TRX offering on social media. Lohan settled with the SEC for disgorgement, prejudgment interest, and civil money penalties in the amount of $40,670.).

58 Sec. Exch. Comm'n, https://www.sec.gov/newsroom/press-releases/2022-78 (last visited Nov. 10, 2024).

59 *See Statement on the Denial of a Rulemaking Petition Submitted on Behalf of Coinbase Global, Inc.*, SEC (Dec. 15, 2023), https://www.sec.gov/newsroom/speeches-statements/gensler-coinbase-petition-121523 (last visited Nov. 10, 2024). Coinbase's petition is available at https://www.sec.gov/files/rules/petitions/2022/petn4-789.pdf (last visited Nov. 10, 2024). Coinbase appealed the SEC's refusal to the Third Circuit Court of Appeals.

60 *See SEC Charges Coinbase for Operating as an Unregistered Securities Exchange, Broker, and Clearing Agency*, SEC (Dec. 13, 2023), https://www.sec.gov/newsroom/press-releases/2023-102 (last visited Nov. 10, 2024). Public Filings in the case are available at https://www.coinbase.com/legal/sec-enforcement-docket (last visited Nov. 10, 2024).

61 *Id.* In February 2023, Kraken had agreed to pay a $30 million settlement to the SEC and cease its staking-as-a-service program, which the SEC claimed was an unregistered securities offering. *See SEC Charges Kraken for Operating as an Unregistered Securities Exchange, Broker, Dealer, and Clearing Agency*, SEC (Nov. 20, 2023), https://www.sec.gov/newsroom/press-releases/2023-237 (last visited Nov. 10, 2024).

62 Securities Exchange Comm'n v. Coinbase, Inc., Case 1:23-cv-04738-KPF Document 105 (S.D.N.Y. filed Mar. 27, 2024), https://storage.courtlistener.com/recap/gov.uscourts.nysd.599908/gov.uscourts.nysd.599908.105.0.pdf (last visited Nov. 10, 2024). The court rejected the SEC's allegations that Coinbase acted as a broker through its wallet software.

63 *Id.*

64 *Id.*

Also in 2024, the SDNY ordered technology company Ripple to pay $125 million in civil penalties[65] and imposed an injunction against future securities law violations, after a 2023 ruling that Ripple violated federal securities laws through its direct sale of its native token, XRP, to institutional clients.[66] The court applied the *Howey* test and agreed with the SEC that reasonable investors situated in the position of the institutional buyers would have purchased Ripple's XRP tokens with the expectation that they would derive profits from Ripple's efforts, primarily due to Ripple's communications, marketing campaign, and the nature of the sales.[67] The court determined that these investors would understand that Ripple would use the capital received from its institutional sales to improve the market for XRP and develop uses for the XRP platform, thereby increasing the value of XRP.[68]

These court-tested SEC actions against Coinbase and Ripple serve to establish at least some support for the SEC's approach to regulatory policies. Additionally, in 2023, the SEC filed a lawsuit against Binance, the world's largest cryptocurrency exchange by trading volume,[69] as well as its U.S. affiliate BAM Trading Services, and its founder Changpeng Zhao. The lawsuit alleged multiple violations of securities laws,[70] including operating unregistered exchanges, broker-dealers, and clearing agencies; misleading investors about controls and oversight; commingling customer assets; and manipulative trading practices.[71] Binance and Zhao ultimately agreed to pay $4.3 billion in fines based on a separate Department of Justice (DOJ) criminal action for money laundering, unlicensed money transmitting, and sanctions violations; Zhao also spent four months in prison in the United States related to the criminal charges,[72] but he and Binance continue to contest the SEC litigation.[73]

---

65 *Id.* The fine is well below the $1 billion in disgorgement and prejudgment interest and $900 million in civil penalties the SEC sought.

66 Securities Exchange Comm'm v. Ripple Labs, Case 1:20-cv-10832-AT-SN (S.D.N.Y. filed Jul. 13, 2023), https://www.nysd.uscourts.gov/sites/default/files/2023-07/SEC%20vs%20Ripple%207-13-23.pdf (last visited Nov. 10, 2024). The court also ruled that Ripple's programmatic sales of XRP to retail clients through exchanges did not violate any securities laws, a decision that the SEC tried unsuccessfully to appeal while the case was ongoing. The SEC appealed the case in November 2024 after a judge imposed a sentence in July 2023.

67 *Id.*

68 *Id.*

69 *See SEC Files 13 Charges against Binance Entities and Founder Changpeng Zhao*, SEC (Jun. 5, 2023), https://www.sec.gov/newsroom/press-releases/2023-101 (last visited Nov. 19, 2024).

70 *Id.* Binance filed a motion to dismiss the SEC's charges in November 2024. *See* Callan Quinn, Binance, CZ's Lawyers File Motion to Dismiss Amended Complaint in SEC Lawsuit, CoinDesk (Nov. 5, 2024), https://www.coindesk.com/policy/2024/11/05/binance-czs-lawyers-file-motion-to-dismiss-amended-complaint-in-sec-lawsuit/ (last visited Nov. 10, 2024).

71 *SEC Files 13 Charges against Binance Entities and Founder Changpeng Zhao, supra* note 69.

72 *See* Chris Strohm, *CEO of World's Largest Crypto Exchange Pleads Guilty and Agrees to $50-Million Fine*, L.A. Times (Nov. 21, 2023), https://www.latimes.com/business/story/2023-11-21/binance-ceo-zhao-to-plead-guilty-to--criminal-charges-pay-4-3-billion-fine#:~:text=In%20a%20document%20unsealed%20Tuesday%2C%20Binance%20was%20charged,forfeiting%20%242.5%20billion%2C%20according%20to%20the%20court%20filing (last visited Nov. 10, 2024).

73 SEC, *SEC Files 13 Charges against Binance Entities and Founder Changpeng Zhao, supra* note 69.

12.3. Commodities and the CFTC

While the SEC focuses on securities, the CFTC focuses on commodities and derivatives. In the United States, commodities are generally defined as goods or raw materials traded on commodity markets, such as oil, gold, or wheat.[74] More specifically, the Commodity Exchange Act (CEA) defines commodity broadly, as "physical like an agricultural product or natural resource (gold); or a currency or interest rate"; or "all services, rights, and interests . . . in which contracts for future delivery are presently or in the future dealt in."[75] U.S. laws regarding commodities apply to digital assets primarily through the CFTC, which regulates derivatives[76] and futures[77] markets and addresses fraud and manipulation related to digital assets. Although proposed legislation has attempted to define "digital commodities" specifically,[78] nothing yet has advanced through Congress.

The CFTC's oversight is designed to ensure that digital assets treated as commodities are traded fairly and transparently.[79] For example, Bitcoin futures are traded on regulated exchanges, and the CFTC mandates that these markets implement real-time trade monitoring and reporting to detect and prevent price manipulation. While the CFTC does not directly regulate spot markets where digital assets are purchased and delivered right away, it does have jurisdiction over fraud and manipulation related to these markets. This means that when individuals or entities attempt to manipulate the price of a digital token or engage in fraud, the CFTC has jurisdiction. Commodities as digital assets, then, are often subject to CFTC oversight, particularly when it comes to derivatives and futures contracts, as well as fraud and manipulation. In one digital commodities action brought in 2021, the CFTC charged John McAfee and his business partner with a "pump-and-dump" scheme, through which they bought cryptocurrencies, hyped them to McAfee's 784,000

---

74 Commodities Futures Trading Commission, cftc.gov (last visited Nov. 10, 2024).

75 7 U.S.C. § 1(a)(9).

76 Derivatives include financial contract between or among parties where the derivative value is based on an underlying asset. Examples of derivatives are call options, forwards, swaps, and futures.

77 Futures are a type of derivatives contract by which one buys or sells at a predetermined price at a particular time in the future.

78 For example, the proposed, but not advanced, "Digital Commodities Consumer Protection Act of 2022" would have defined "digital commodity" as follows: "(A) . . . a fungible digital form of personal property that can be possessed and transferred person-to-person without necessary reliance on an intermediary. (B) INCLUSIONS.—The term 'digital commodity' includes property commonly known as cryptocurrency or virtual currency, such as Bitcoin and Ether." The bill excluded certain financial instruments, including securities, and amended the definition of "commodity" in the Commodity Exchange Act ("Act") to include "digital commodity." It also introduced new categories of registration, including "digital commodity broker," "digital commodity custodian," "digital commodity dealer," "digital commodity trading facility" (collectively, "digital commodity platforms"), and associated persons of digital commodity brokers and digital commodity dealers. Said mining activity, alone, is not sufficient to trigger registration as a digital commodity platform. In addition, it granted the Commodity Futures Trading Commission ("Commission") exclusive jurisdiction over digital commodity trades, except for transactions in which a merchant or consumer is using a digital commodity solely for the purchase or sale of a good or service and prohibited fraud with respect to any digital commodity trade. *See* S.4760 Digital Commodities Consumer Protection Act of 2022 (Sept. 3, 2022), https://www.congress.gov/bill/117th-congress/senate-bill/4760/text (last visited Nov. 10, 2024).

79 *Report of Investigation Pursuant to Section 21(a) of the Securities Exchange Act of 1934: The DAO, supra* note 36.

Twitter followers, then sold them for a profit of more than $2 million.[80] More recently, the CFTC charged Alexander Mashinsky[81] and Celsius Network, LLC, with fraud and material misrepresentations in a commodity pooling scheme involving digital asset commodities. The complaint alleged that over a four-year period, Mashinsky and Celsius misrepresented the safety and profitability of their digital-asset-based finance platform, leading customers to deposit approximately $20 billion.[82]

The CFTC has formally exercised jurisdiction over cryptocurrency since 2015, when it undertook an enforcement action regarding a Bitcoin derivative contract, as set forth in *In the Matter of Coinflip, Inc.*[83] Since *Coinflip*, the CFTC has classified certain cryptocurrencies such as Bitcoin and Ethereum as commodities. In 2018, the CFTC took on the alleged misappropriation of investor funds through a fraudulent virtual currency scheme in *CFTC v. McDonnell, et al.*,[84] also establishing CFTC jurisdiction over fraud allegations not involving futures or derivative contracts when the CEA is invoked. Since the CEA prohibits (1) manipulative or deceptive devices in conjunction with a contract of sale of any commodity in interstate commerce[85] and (2) fraudulent or misleading actions in connection with commodity sales or contracts for future delivery,[86] the *McDonald* proceeding confirmed CFTC jurisdiction. In addition to futures and derivative markets, then, the CFTC also will pursue actions involving spot market fraud, the rationale being that fraud in spot markets can generate profits in derivative markets.[87]

---

80 *See* Commodity Futures Trading Comm'n v. John David McAfee and Jimmy Gale Watson, Jr., No. 21-cv-138 (S.D.N.Y. filed Mar. 5, 2021), https://www.cftc.gov/PressRoom/PressReleases/8366-21. The same day as the CFTC action, the DOJ unsealed a criminal indictment against McAfee for the pump-and-dump scheme, for promoting cryptocurrency offerings without disclosing payments received, and for tax evasion. United States v. John David McAfee (S.D.N.Y. filed Mar. 5, 2021), https://www.justice.gov/d9/press-releases/attachments/2021/03/05/mcafee_complaint_-_21_mag_1600_0.pdf (last visited Nov. 10, 2024). The SEC also sued McAfee and his business partner for securities fraud, *see* Securities and Exchange Commission v. McAfee et al., No. 20-cv-08281 (S.D.N.Y. Oct. 5, 2020), https://www.sec.gov/files/litigation/litreleases/2022/judg25445.pdf (last visited Nov. 10, 2024). McAfee faced a thirty-year prison sentence related to the criminal action but died by suicide in a Spanish prison while awaiting extradition to the United States.

81 Alexander Mashinsky, the (now-former) CEO of Celsius Network, has faced multiple lawsuits related to alleged digital asset fraud. In addition to the CFTC action, the SEC charged Mashinsky and Celsius with fraud and unregistered offers and sales of securities in Securities Exchange Commission v. Celsius Network Limited and Alexander "Alex" Mashinsky, Case 1:23-cv-06005 (Jul. 13, 2023), Complaint is available at https://www.sec.gov/files/litigation/complaints/2023/comp-pr2023-133.pdf (last visited Nov. 10, 2024); the New York Attorney General filed a lawsuit against Mashinsky for defrauding investors out of billions of dollars' worth of cryptocurrency in the People of New York v. Alex Mashinsky (Jan. 1, 2023), and the U.S. Department of Justice charged him with fraud related to commodities, securities, and wire fraud.

82 *Id.*

83 *In the Matter of Coinflip, Inc.*, CFTC Docket No. 15-29 (2015).

84 CFTC v. McDonnell, et al., No. 1:18-cv-00361-JBW-RLM (E.D.N.Y. Mar. 6, 2018).

85 7 U.S.C. § 9(1).

86 17 C.F.R. § 180.1.

87 *Also see* Inv. Co. Inst. v. Commodity Futures Trading Comm'n, 720 F.3d 370, 372 (D.C. Cir. 2013) (CFTC has regulatory jurisdiction over a wide variety of markets in futures and derivatives); CFTC v. Gelfman Blueprint, Inc., Case No. 17-7181, 2017, WL 4228737 (S.D.N.Y. filed Sept. 21, 2017) (CFTC has broad jurisdiction over fraudulent contracts of sale of commodities).

12.3.1. Increased CFTC Enforcement and a New Theory

Before 2022, the CFTC brought more than fifty enforcement actions related to digital assets.[88] In 2023, more than half of the CFTC's actions involved digital assets.[89] By 2024, the CFTC was even more firmly established in the digital asset space, as it continued to pursue a relatively new theory of liability for "facilitating" the use of margin, leverage, or financing in the trading of digital asset commodities, as discussed below. As the CFTC continues to classify certain cryptocurrencies as commodities warranting CFTC oversight, it also has been increasing enforcement activity and expanding its view of leverage to include "facilitation," while continuing to pursue perpetrators of fraud as well as unregistered commodities dealers.

In 2010, the Dodd–Frank Wall Street Reform and Consumer Protection Act of 2010 (Dodd–Frank) amended the CEA to include offers of leveraged, margined, or financed retail commodity transactions.[90] Neither "facilitate" nor "facilitation" appears in the text of the amended CEA, but beginning in 2023, the CFTC added as a cause of action the "facilitation" of leveraged commodity transactions to its stated jurisdiction. This new category is somewhat controversial, as the addition of a facilitation claim is based on CFTC's nonbinding 2020 *Interpretive Guidance on Actual Delivery for Digital Assets* (2020 Interpretive Guidance)[91] as opposed to the CEA. In the 2020 Interpretive Guidance, the CFTC indicates that when evaluating potential retail commodity transactions, it will consider the word "offeror" broadly to include "any persons presenting, soliciting, or otherwise facilitating 'retail commodity transactions,' including by way of a participation interest in a foundation, consensus, or other collective that controls operational decisions on the protocol."[92]

In 2023, building on its expanded interpretation of "offeror" from the 2020 Interpretive Guidance, the CFTC took action against several blockchain infrastructure projects, including Uniswap,[93] claiming that the Uniswap protocol facilitated regulated transactions by enabling peer-to-peer token swaps and therefore allegedly facilitated unregistered regulated transactions. The platform did not sell, offer, or market leveraged tokens, nor was it designed to allow traders to speculate on leverage. Despite Uniswap's more passive role in leverage speculation, the CFTC found that Uniswap-traded tokens were "leveraged or margined retail commodity transactions"[94] that must only be offered on registered exchanges pursuant to CEA and CFTC regulations, including the requirement

---

88 *See Enforcement Actions*, Com. Futures Trading Comm'n, https://www.cftc.gov/LawRegulation/EnforcementActions/index.htm (last visited Nov. 10, 2024).

89 *Remarks of Enforcement Director Ian McGinley at the City Bar White Collar Institute: "Trends in the CFTC's Recent Crypto Enforcement Actions,"* Com. Futures Trading Comm'n, https://www.cftc.gov/PressRoom/SpeechesTestimony/opamcginley4 (last visited Nov. 10, 2024).

90 Dodd–Frank Wall Street Reform and Consumer Protection Act, *supra* note 12.

91 *2020 Interpretive Guidance on Actual Delivery for Digital Assets*, Com. Futures Trading Comm'n, 85 Fed. Reg. 37,734-01, at 37,737 n.63, 37,742 n.164 (Jun. 24, 2020).

92 *Id.* at 63.

93 *CFTC Issues Order against Uniswap Labs for Offering Illegal Digital Asset Derivatives Trading*, Com. Futures Trading Comm'n, Release Number 8961-24 (Sept. 4, 2023), https://www.cftc.gov/PressRoom/PressReleases/8961-24 (last visited Nov. 10, 2024).

94 *In the Matter of Universal Navigation, Inc. d/b/a Uniswap Labs*, CFTC Docket No. 24-25 (Sept. 4, 2024).

that leveraged transactions must result in actual delivery of the relevant commodities within twenty-eight days.[95] Ultimately, Uniswap agreed to a $175,000 civil penalty in settlement of the CFTC's claim.[96]

Two dissenting CFTC Commissioners in the Uniswap action criticized the enforcement claim, challenging the lack of evidence regarding the specific terms and characteristics of the leveraged tokens[97] and expressing concern that enforcement such as the Uniswap action could stifle innovation in the decentralized finance (DeFi) space.[98] Both dissenting Commissioners highlighted the need for clearer regulatory guidance for DeFi protocols in the form of formal rulemaking.[99] Calls for clearer guidance in the form of rulemaking as opposed to regulation by enforcement have been common in the securities as well as the commodities space.[100]

12.4. FINRA Jurisdiction and Digital Assets

FINRA regulates broker-dealers who trade various financial instruments, including equities, corporate bonds, securities futures, and options. Its primary role is to protect investors by ensuring that broker-dealers comply with industry standards and federal securities laws.[101] FINRA conducts regular examinations of its member firms to ensure compliance with regulations, and it has an enforcement program to discipline firms and individuals who violate the rules. In addition, FINRA operates the largest securities dispute resolution forum in the United States, providing arbitration and mediation services to resolve conflicts between investors and brokers.

FINRA also plays a significant role in regulating Alternative Trading Systems (ATSs). An ATS is a trading venue that matches buyers and sellers of securities but does not set rules for subscribers other than the conduct of trading. Unlike traditional exchanges, ATSs are not required to register as national securities exchanges but must comply with specific regulatory requirements. They also must adhere to antifraud and antimanipulation provisions of federal securities laws.[102] Any ATS that registers as a broker-dealer must

---

95 *See* 28-Day Actual Delivery rule, *supra* note 91 at § 2 (C) 2(d).

96 *CFTC Issues Order against Uniswap Labs for Offering Illegal Digital Asset Derivatives Trading*, *supra* note 93.

97 *Dissenting Statement of Commissioner Caroline D. Pham on DeFi Enforcement Action Involving Uniswap Protocol*, Com. Futures Trading Comm'n (Sept. 4, 2024), https://www.cftc.gov/PressRoom/SpeechesTestimony/phamstatement090424.

98 *Dissenting Statement of Commissioner Summer K. Mersinger Regarding Settlement with Uniswap Labs*, Com. Futures Trading Comm'n (Sept. 4, 2024), https://www.cftc.gov/PressRoom/SpeechesTestimony/mersingerstatement090424 (last visited Nov. 10, 2024).

99 *See id.* at 28.

100 In addition to calls for clearer regulation from within the crypto industry, then-President Biden issued an executive order in March 2022 aimed at establishing a comprehensive framework for digital asset regulation. This order emphasized the need for coordinated efforts among various federal agencies to address the regulatory challenges posed by digital assets. White House, "Executive Order on Ensuring Responsible Development of Digital Assets" (Mar. 9, 2022), https://www.whitehouse.gov/briefing-room/presidential-actions/2022/03/09/executive-order-on-ensuring-responsible-development-of-digital-assets/ (last visited Nov. 10, 2024).

101 *See Dissenting Statement of Commissioner Summer K. Mersinger Regarding Settlement with Uniswap Labs*, *supra* note 98.

102 17 C.F.R. § 242.300 through 242.303.

also become a member of FINRA and comply with its rules.[103] This includes adhering to FINRA's standards for conduct, reporting, and transparency.[104] FINRA requires ATSs to report their trades to its equity trade reporting facilities. This has the stated goal of ensuring transparency and allowing FINRA to monitor trading activities for compliance with regulations.[105] By overseeing ATSs, FINRA seeks to maintain the integrity of the securities markets and protects investors from potential abuses.

FINRA has jurisdiction over digital assets that are classified as securities that involve FINRA member firms and their "associated persons."[106] If a digital asset is classified as a security, member firms and associated persons must comply with applicable federal securities laws and FINRA rules, resulting in concurrent jurisdiction with the SEC. Even if a digital asset is not a security, certain FINRA rules might still apply to the activities of member firms and their associated persons.[107] Through Regulatory Notices, FINRA has encouraged member entities to notify FINRA if they or their affiliates engage in, or plan to engage in, activities related to crypto assets, including crypto assets that are not securities.[108] FINRA members engaging in or at the periphery of crypto-asset-related activities[109] must comply with securities laws and FINRA rules, in addition to CFTC regulations related to commodities when dealing with nonsecurity digital assets. As might be expected, a prospective FINRA member firm intending to engage in digital asset activities needs prior approval for crypto-related activities,[110] as does an existing member considering a material crypto-related change in business operations.[111]

FINRA has been actively involved in regulating digital assets involving its members, and it has brought several related actions. In 2018, FINRA's first disciplinary action involving digital assets was *FINRA Dep't of Enforcement v. Timothy Tilton Ayre*,[112] in which broker-dealer Ayre was charged with securities fraud and the unlawful distribution of an unregistered cryptocurrency security called HempCoin. FINRA sanctioned and fined Ayre for having made fraudulent statements about his company to lure public investment, including the statement that HempCoin was a security backed common stock, despite never having

---

103 *Guidance for Alternative Trading Systems*, Com. Futures Trading Comm'n, https://www.finra.org/compliance-tools/-map-tools/alternative-trading-systems-guidance (last visited Nov. 10, 2024).

104 *Id.*

105 *See id.*

106 *See FINRA Provides Update on Member Firms' Crypto Asset Activities*, FINRA, https://www.finra.org/rules-guidance/guidance/crypto-assets-update (last visited Nov. 10, 2024).

107 *Id.*

108 FINRA Notice 20–23 (Jul. 2020) and FINRA Notice 21–25 (Jul. 2021).

109 FINRA includes as examples of these members: firms engaged in private trading in and placements of crypto asset securities, firms operating Alternative Trading Systems (ATSs) for crypto asset securities, those functioning as Special Purpose Broker-Dealers (SPBDs), users of distributed ledger technology, and persons engaging in crypto-asset-related activities through outside business activities (OBAs) or private securities transactions (PSTs). *See Guidance for Alternative Trading Systems*, *supra* note 103.

110 Prospective members must seek approval for new FINRA membership through the submission of a New Membership Application under FINRA Rule 1013. *Id.*

111 Existing members contemplating a change with the way that it interacts with digital assets must submit a Continuing Membership Application (CMA) pursuant to FINRA Rule 1017. *Id.*

112 Disciplinary Proceeding No. 2016049307801 (Sept. 2018), FINRA, https://www.finra.org/sites/default/files/Ayre_Complaint_091118.pdf (last visited Nov. 10, 2024).

registered HempCoin as a security or qualifying for an exemption from registration.[113] FINRA also has fined a member firm for failing to comply with anti-money laundering (AML) requirements in relation to its digital asset business.[114]

In addition to establishing specialized units to focus on complex investigations related to crypto asset fraud, including the Crypto Asset Investigations (CAI) team, the Blockchain Lab, and the Crypto Asset Surveillance Team (CAST), FINRA also routinely conducts risk-based examinations of firms' compliance with FINRA rules and federal securities laws.[115] FINRA compliance will continue to be a key consideration for broker-dealers involved with digital assets, as it considers its efforts to be "part of a broader initiative to address the unique regulatory challenges presented by digital assets and to protect investors from potential fraud and misconduct in the rapidly evolving crypto market."[116] Broker-dealers and their attorneys need to be aware of continuing adjustments to regulatory requirements related to all regulators as digital asset markets evolve, including updates to FINRA's Regulatory Notices.[117]

12.5. Practical Challenges with the Classification of Digital Assets

In addition to cryptocurrencies and ICO-issued tokens as discussed above, a third blockchain-based digital asset category that warrants consideration related to regulatory classification is the nonfungible token (NFT). An NFT is a digital asset that comprises smart contract code using blockchain technology to identify an original digital work, with a pointer to an off-chain location where the work is stored.[118] NFTs might be used as assets, including collectibles,[119] in-game assets,[120] art,[121] music,[122] or securitized

---

113 *Id.*

114 Re: Aegis Investments, Inc., FINRA Case #2021069363301 (Mar. 11, 2022).

115 Jaron Foye, *An Inside Look into FINRA's Crypto Asset Work*, FINRA (Aug. 3, 2023), https://www.finra.org/media-center/blog/inside-look-finras-crypto-asset-work.

116 *Id.*

117 *Id.*

118 *Ethereum*, Ethereum, https://ethereum.org/en/nft/ (last visited Nov. 10, 2024).

119 Examples of NFT collectibles are CryptoKitties and the Bored Ape Yacht Club. CryptoKitties were developed in 2017 by Dapper Labs and launched on the Ethereum blockchain. Buyers can collect, breed, and trade virtual cats, each represented as an NFT. *What Are CryptoKitties*, Kraken, https://www.kraken.com/learn/what-are-cryptokitties-nft (last visited Nov. 10, 2024). The Bored Ape collection consists of ten thousand unique, algorithmically generated cartoon apes, each with distinct traits and accessories. *See Bored Ape Yacht Club*, OpenSea, https://opensea.io/collection/boredapeyachtclub (last visited Nov. 10, 2024). Collectible NFTs are popular for their artistic value as well as exclusive benefits they might offer, such as access to special events and communities.

120 Examples of in-game NFTs are Axie Infinity creatures. In the blockchain-based Axie Infinity game, players collect, breed, and battle digital pets called Axies, each of which is an NFT. These Axies have unique traits and can be traded or sold on various marketplaces. *Axie Infinity*, Axie Infinity, https://axieinfinity.com/ (last visited Nov. 10, 2024).

121 A notable example of an NFT that is considered art is Beeple's "Everydays: The First 5000 Days." This digital artwork is a collage of five thousand individual images created by the artist Beeple (Mike Winkelmann) over a thirteen-year period. It was sold at a Christie's auction for $69 million in 2021. Beeple, https://www.beeple-crap.com/everydays (last visited Nov. 10, 2024).

122 Several musicians have released NFTs as media to allow fans to own and interact with their music. Musical artist Snoop Dogg (Calvin Broadus, Jr.) has been an avid NFT collector, and he released an NFT collection in 2021 that included an original song called "NFT." He also made his 2022 album *B.O.D.R.* available on the blockchain, and he

investment opportunities.[123] As with any digital asset, the classification of an NFT as either a commodity or a security depends on the token's characteristics and the context in which it is sold and used. The potential complexities associated with NFT classification demonstrate many of the challenges and risks inherent in the overall digital asset market.

An NFT might be classified as a security if it meets the criteria of the *Howey* test, which is used to determine whether a transaction qualifies as an "investment contract," as discussed above. Because NFTs are unique, it is possible to use them to create new forms of investment; by tokenizing a property or a work of art, it is possible to sell uniquely identifiable fractional shares, or "shards," of those assets, potentially increasing their value. If an NFT shard is sold with the offeror's promise that its value will increase based on the efforts of a third party, it likely will be viewed as a security that falls under the jurisdiction of SEC and requires compliance with federal securities laws.

Alternatively, an NFT might be seen as a commodity if it is traded primarily as a good, without the expectation of profit based on the efforts of others. Commodities are typically physical goods, but digital assets like NFTs can also be classified as commodities if they are used or traded in a similar manner to "traditional" commodities. For example, an NFT that represents a digital collectible, musical release, or a work of art that is acquired because of its inherent value as opposed to the expectation of profit, is more likely to be seen as a commodity. In this case, the NFT would not be marketed with promises of increased future value or returns from the efforts of a third party. Instead, it would be viewed similarly to a traditional collectible or memento. However, if that same NFT were marketed as part of an investment opportunity or with assurances that its value will rise due to ongoing actions by the creator or platform, it might be classified as a security and subject to SEC oversight. An NFT classified as a commodity might be regulated by the CFTC, then, particularly if it involves futures contracts or other derivatives—or fraud.

As with all digital assets, NFT classification has significant regulatory implications, affecting how NFTs are issued, traded, and marketed. An enforcement action that offers insight into some of the complex digital asset classification issues is the SEC's 2023 order in *In the Matter of Stoner Cats 2, LLC*.[124] The SEC charged the entity in *Stoner Cats* with conducting an unregistered offering of securities in the form of NFTs. The entity, *Stoner Cats 2, LLC*, sold more than ten thousand tokens to fund an animated online series called "Stoner Cats,"[125] raising approximately $8 million.[126] Each token uniquely represented a character in the

---

released a limited-edition package that includes exclusive content featuring an NFT of one of the album's songs. Chris Morris, *Snoop Dogg Is converting Death Row Records into the First NFT Music Label*, FORTUNE (Feb. 16, 2022), https://fortune.com/2022/02/16/snoop-dogg-death-row-records-nfts/ (last visited Nov. 10, 2024).

123 A securitized investment opportunity would include fractionalized real estate NFTs, wherein a property is divided into multiple shares, each represented by an NFT. Investors can purchase these NFTs, effectively owning a securitized fraction of the property. *See* REALT, https://realtusa.pulse.is/ (last visited Nov. 23, 2024).

124 *In the Matter of Stoner Cats 2 LLC*, SEC Release No. 11233 (Sept. 13, 2023), https://www.sec.gov/files/litigation/admin/2023/33-11233.pdf (last visited Nov. 10, 2024).

125 The premise of the animated *Stoner Cats* series centers on house cats that become sentient after being exposed to their owner's medical marijuana that she is using for the treatment of early onset Alzheimer's disease. STONER CATS, https://stonercats.com (last visited Nov. 10, 2024).

126 *See id.*

series and offered purchasers access to the six episodes to be produced.[127] Although the issuers alleged that the NFTs were digital collectibles as opposed to securities,[128] the SEC argued that these NFTs were marketed in a way that led investors to expect profits based on the issuer's efforts.[129] Of particular concern to the SEC was website and social media content that highlighted the expertise that the *Stoner Cats* team brought to the project, including experience as Hollywood producers, animators, writers, and editors, as well as specific knowledge of NFTs. Promotional content also encouraged the resale of the NFTs, focusing on a potential increase in value. Considering the expectation of profit based on the "efforts of others" prong of the *Howey* test, the SEC found that the marketing of the *Stoner Cats* web series "led investors to expect profits from their entrepreneurial and managerial efforts, because a successful web series could cause the resale value of the Stoner Cats NFTs to rise in the secondary market."[130]

The *Stoner Cats* proceeding resulted in a cease and desist order and settlement agreement, including destruction of any remaining *Stoner Cats* NFTs, the publication of notice of the SEC's Order on the entity's website and social media channels, and the payment of a civil money penalty in the amount of $1,000,000.[131] Notably, two dissenting Commissioners questioned the SEC's application of the *Howey* test in this case, arguing that the NFTs at issue were more similar to collectibles than securities and expressing concern that the *Stoner Cats* enforcement action might stifle creativity and innovation among artists and content creators.[132] The dissenters emphasized the need for clear guidelines for artists and creators who use NFTs to support their work and engage with their fan communities, rather than potentially arbitrary enforcement actions.[133]

To understand the potential regulatory requirements and pitfalls of any digital asset, it is important to address the asset's characterization promptly. A platform that offers NFTs, cryptocurrency, and/or any token sold with the expectation of profits likely will face inconsistent regulatory guidance and unclear defining characteristics, leading to uncertain agency jurisdiction. Particularly in the case of centralized cryptocurrency exchanges, platforms are likely to offer some tokens that will be seen as commodities and others that will be classified as securities pursuant to *Howey*. For example, Coinbase—which the SEC has alleged serves as an unregistered securities broker, exchange, and clearing agency as discussed above—also offers tokens such as Bitcoin that are viewed as commodities. The now-defunct FTX Trading Ltd. exchange, founded in 2019 by convicted offender Sam Bankman-Fried, specialized in derivatives and leveraged products subject

---

[127] *SEC Charges Creator of Stoner Cats Web Series for Unregistered Offering of NFTs*, SEC (Sept. 13, 2023), https://www.sec.gov/newsroom/press-releases/2023-178.

[128] *Id.*

[129] *In the Matter of Stoner Cats 2 LLC*, Release No. 11233, *supra* note 124 at 1, 4–6.

[130] *Id.* at 5.

[131] *Id.* at 7–8.

[132] The dissenters compared the *Stoner Cats* NFTs to Star Wars collectibles from the 1970s, suggesting that applying the same logic would have led to similar enforcement actions against those collectibles. Commissioners Hester M. Peirce & Mark T. Uyeda, "Collecting Enforcement Actions: Statement on Stoner Cats 2, LLC" (Sept. 13, 2023), https://www.sec.gov/newsroom/speeches-statements/peirce-uyeda-statement-stonercats-091323 (last visited Nov. 10, 2024).

[133] *Id.*

to CFTC oversight, offered support for various cryptocurrencies, and also was charged by the SEC for defrauding equity investors with security interest in FTX.[134] Similarly, NFT marketplace OpenSea[135] has seen SEC and DOJ scrutiny related to the listing of NFTs that are investment contracts and therefore securities,[136] while other OpenSea offerings are not subject to classification as securities.

Issuers of digital assets face a heavy compliance burden when looking to balance unclear regulatory standards. While there has been some Congressional activity, such as the 2024 initial passage of the bipartisan Financial Innovation and Technology for the 21st Century Act (FIT21) by the House of Representatives,[137] no comprehensive digital asset legislation has been enacted into law. The proposed FIT21 Act would have established three primary categories for digital asset classification, including (1) restricted digital assets to be regulated by the SEC, (2) digital commodities to be regulated by the CFTC, and (3) permitted payment stablecoins,[138] which would be regulated by either the SEC or the CFTC, depending on context. FIT21 also set forth requirements for primary and secondary market transactions related to digital assets and allowed for certification of digital assets classified as "digital commodities," under certain circumstances.[139] A comprehensive framework such as that proposed by FIT21 and some of its predecessor bills[140] could provide consumer protections while offering the digital asset community increased regulatory and jurisdictional clarity. A codified regulatory framework supporting digital asset characterization and sustainable growth is an important legislative priority; Congress continues to face pressure to revisit previous proposals' main goals of protecting consumers, supporting innovation, and streamlining regulatory oversight for digital assets through future legislation.

---

134 *DOJ, Samuel Bankman-Fried Sentenced to 25 Years for His Orchestration of Multiple Fraudulent Schemes, supra* note 53.

135 *OpenSea*, opensea.io (last visited Nov. 10, 2024).

136 Nathanial Chastain, a former OpenSea product manager, was sentenced to three months in prison for insider trading in NFTs after he used confidential information regarding NFTs for personal financial gain. *See Former Employee of NFT Marketplace Sentenced to Prison in First-Ever Digital Asset Insider Trading Scheme*, Dept. of Justice (Aug. 22, 2023), https://www.justice.gov/usao-sdny/pr/former-employee-nft-marketplace-sentenced-prison-first-ever-digital-asset-insider.

137 H.R.4763—Financial Innovation and Technology for the 21st Century Act, https://www.congress.gov/bill/118-th-congress/house-bill/4763/all-actions (last visited Nov. 10, 2024).

138 Stablecoins are digital currencies pegged to an underlying asset such as a fiat currency or a commodity such as gold. *See President's Working Group on Financial Markets, the Federal Deposit Insurance Corporation, and the Office of the Comptroller of the Currency, Report on Stablecoins*, Dept. of Treasury (Nov. 2021), https://home.treasury.gov/news/press-releases/jy0454.

139 H.R.4763—Financial Innovation and Technology for the 21st Century Act, *supra* note 137 at § 503.

140 *See, e.g.*, Digital Commodities Consumer Protection Act of 2022 would have given the CFTC jurisdiction over digital commodity platforms. S.4760 Digital Commodities Consumer Protection Act of 2022, https://www.congress.gov/bill/117th-congress/senate-bill/4760 (last visited Nov. 10, 2024); and the 2022 Lummis-Gillibrand Responsible Financial Innovation Act would have established a regulatory framework for innovation; clarified standards, jurisdictional boundaries, and consumer protection; clarified CFTC and SEC jurisdiction; and created interagency coordination on stablecoin regulation and banking and tax treatment of digital assets. S.4356—Lummis-Gillibrand Responsible Financial Innovation Act, https://www.congress.gov/bill/117th-congress/senate-bill/4356/text (last visited Nov. 10, 2024).

12.6. Conclusion

Most cryptocurrencies, including Bitcoin, are not characterized as securities because they function more as digital currencies, or as commodities that are overseen by the CFTC if they involve derivatives, futures, or fraud. Generally, cryptocurrencies are decentralized and not sold as investments in a company or project. However, tokens sold as investment tokens during ICOs and as NFTs might be characterized as securities, primarily if they meet the *Howey* test criteria. These tokens might be sold as investments with the promise of future profits, and their classification can lead to security-related regulatory requirements, such as registration and disclosure obligations. The SEC, and occasionally FINRA, has provided guidance and taken enforcement actions in cases where digital assets are deemed securities. This means that entities issuing investment tokens or conducting ICOs must comply with securities laws, including registration with the relevant securities authorities, or fit into an exemption category.

The regulatory landscape for digital assets continues to evolve. As technology and market practices develop, regulatory agencies will adapt, and hopefully they also will clarify the application of existing laws. In addition to clarification, there also have been calls for agencies to further engage in the rulemaking process to create binding guidance, and a call for an as-yet elusive comprehensive digital asset legislative framework. Since the regulatory environment surrounding the characterization of digital assets might change at any point with potential legislative or rulemaking updates, it is vital that individuals and businesses engaged with digital assets seek out the most current legal guidance. Rapid changes in guidance and enforcement create ongoing legal risks that require ongoing compliance protocols to protect clients from significant liability.

13

A Northern Perspective: Comparative Regulation of Digital Content and Technology in Canada

By Lisa R. Lifshitz and Laura Crimi

Canada has embraced the use of technology in its economy. However, due to different legislative structures and historical perspectives, Canada's approach to the regulation of technology often diverges from that of the United States. Canada skews toward having a more centralized regulation of technology (including digital content), whereas the United States, in contrast, relies on state-level initiatives, resulting in a more fragmented landscape. Understanding the similarities and differences between the two regimes is critical for legal professionals practicing in either jurisdiction, especially when undertaking cross-border transactions and representing clients operating across North America.

This chapter provides a high-level and practical overview of Canadian law and regulations with respect to digital content (including content generated by artificial intelligence "AI" and technology). Specifically, we aim to provide a succinct, comparative text that will assist an American attorney seeking to navigate the Canadian legal system while highlighting key points for consideration when dealing with both novel technologies in Canada and the applicable emerging regulatory environments. We focus on the Canadian regulation of digital content and technology in four (4) key areas and provide a basic overview of the following: (1) Digital Content and AI in Canada; (2) Intellectual Property, AI, and Digital Content; (3) Privacy and Technology; and (4) Canadian Consumer Protection Laws. Through this examination, we endeavor to provide a clear understanding of how Canada is presently navigating, at the domestic level, the complex and rapidly evolving regulatory landscape of digital content and emerging technology.

13.1. Digital Content and AI in Canada

At present, Canada lacks comprehensive legislation specifically governing the use of digital content and AI technology. Instead, Canada currently employs a patchwork approach where digital content and AI technology are subject to various applicable provincial and federal privacy laws governing the collection, use, and disclosure of personal information used by generative AI systems as well as other sector-specific laws.

13.1.1. AI Legislation

Disappointingly, draft legislation introduced at the Canadian federal level, through Bill C-27, An Act to enact the Consumer Privacy Protection Act, the Personal Information and Data Protection Tribunal Act, and the Artificial Intelligence and Data Act, stalled and died due to the prorogation of the Canadian Parliament at the request of the then-Prime Minister, Justin Trudeau, on January 6, 2025 pending a looming federal election.[1] In the absence of formal federal legislation, Canadians have been forced to make do with a variety of federal directives and voluntary codes of conduct as well as guidance from various regulators.[2]

For example, Innovation, Science and Economic Development Canada, a federal department, launched a voluntary AI code of practice in 2023, called the Voluntary Code of Conduct on the Responsible Development and Management of Advanced Generative AI Systems ("Voluntary AI Code of Conduct").[3] The Voluntary AI Code of Conduct calls on Canadian organizations to achieve the following outcomes when employing the use of generative AI in business: (a) accountability, (b) safety, (c) fairness and equity, (d) transparency, (e) human oversight and monitoring, and (f) validity and robustness. As of the publication date of this text, there are forty-six ("4C") signatories to the Voluntary AI Code of Conduct, including Blackberry, Cohere, Ada, IBM, Mastercard, and Salesforce.[4] Compliance with the Voluntary AI Code of Conduct should be considered by any U.S. business moving into the Canadian market that is using AI technology in the provision of products or services to consumers, or anticipates doing so in the near future.

Additionally, various Canadian provinces have moved ahead with legislation that imposes requirements on the use of AI by the public sector. On November 25, 2024, the provincial government of Ontario passed Bill 194, "An Act to enact the Enhancing Digital Security and Trust Act, 2024 and to make amendments to the Freedom of Information

---

1 Bill C-27, An Act to enact the Consumer Privacy Protection Act, the Personal Information and Data Protection Tribunal Act, and the Artificial Intelligence and Data Act and to make consequential and related amendments to other Acts, 1st Sess, 44th Parl, 2022 ["Digital Charter Implementation Act"] (Can.).

2 See: *Principles for the Development, Provision and Use of Generative AI Systems*, Office of the Privacy Commissioner of Canada (Dec. 2023), https://www.priv.gc.ca/en/privacy-topics/technology/artificial-intelligence/gd_principles_ai/; and *OSFI-FCAC Risk Report - AI Uses and Risks at Federally Regulated Financial Institutions*, The Office of the Superintendent of Financial Institutions (Sept. 2024), https://www.osfi-bsif.gc.ca/en/about-osfi/reports-publications/-osfi-fcac-risk-report-ai-uses-risks-federally-regulated-financial-institutions.

3 *Voluntary Code of Conduct on the Responsible Development and Management of Advanced Generative AI Systems*, Gov't of Canada (Sept. 2023), https://ised-isde.canada.ca/site/ised/en/voluntary-code-conduct-responsible-development-and-management-advanced-generative-ai-systems.

4 Id.

and Protection of Privacy Act respecting privacy and protection measures" ("Ontario Cyber Act"). The Ontario Cyber Act's objective is to enhance digital security in the public sector and will be applicable to any organizations doing business with the public sector in Ontario. Ontario public sector entities will be required to provide information to the public about their use of an AI system, develop and implement an accountability framework with resect to their use of an AI system, and take steps as may be prescribed to manage risks associated with their use of an AI system. Regulations may be made respecting cybersecurity and public sector entities, including regulations requiring the public sector to develop and implement programs. Regulations may also prohibit certain uses of AI systems by public sector entities and set technical standards respecting AI systems for public sector entities. Additionally, regulations may be made specifically respecting children's aid societies and school boards related to digital technology and the collection, use, retention and disclosure of digital information affecting individuals under the age of 18. Further, under Bill 194, public sector entities may be required to comply with requirements respecting their use of AI. For example, in certain prescribed circumstances, public sector entities may be required to disclose certain information to the public about their use of an AI system and ensure an individual can exercise oversight of the use of an AI system by the public sector entity.[5]

As well, on December 5, 2025, both Alberta's Bill 33, the *Protection of Privacy Act*, and Bill 34, the *Access to Information Act*, received royal assent. This represents major updates to Alberta's public sector privacy legislation. Bill 33 represents some of the strongest privacy protections in Canada and includes a prohibition on selling personal information, mandatory breach obligation requirements, a requirement of transparency when using automated decision-making and an obligation to implement privacy management programs. Bill 33 introduces a requirement that where an individual's personal information will be used by a public body to make a decision that directly affects the individual, including a decision using an automated system, the public body must: (i) make every reasonable effort to ensure that the information is accurate and complete; and (ii) retain the information for at least one year after using it.[6] Updates to privacy legislation stemming from Bill 34 aim to modernize Alberta's access to information laws to recognize electronic records, strengthen workplace investigation records, and prohibit public bodies from submitting an access request for information to another public body.

American attorneys should be aware of the Ontario Cyber Act and recent changes to Alberta public sector privacy legislation in order to provide clients providing services to the public sector in Ontario with current and accurate advice.[7]

At the private sector provincial level, recent amendments to Quebec's *Act respecting the protection of personal information in the private sector* ("Quebec's Private Sector Privacy

---

5 Bill 194, An Act to enact the Enhancing Digital Security and Trust Act, 2024 and to make amendments to the Freedom of Information and Protection of Privacy Act respecting privacy and protection measures, 2024 ["Bill 194"] (Can.).

6 *See* Bill 33, Protection of Privacy Act, First Session, 31st Legislature, 3 Charles III, 2024 ["Bill 33"] (Can. Alb.).

7 *See* Bill 34, Access to Information Act, First Session, 31st Legislature, 3 Charles III, 2024 ["Bill 34"] (Can. Alb.).

Act")[8] though the passage of the *An Act to modernize legislative provisions as regards the protection of personal information* ("Law 25")[9] did impact Quebec-based organization's use of automated decision-making/AI tools, and personal information. While we will discuss the impact of Law 25 in greater detail further on in this chapter, Law 25 now requires any person carrying on an enterprise who uses personal information to render a decision based exclusively on an automated processing of such information must inform the person concerned accordingly not later than at the time it informs the person of the decision. Additionally, any person carrying on an enterprise who uses personal information to render a decision based exclusively on automated processing must also inform the person concerned, at their request, of the following: (i) of the personal information used to render the decision; (ii) of the reasons and principal factors and parameters that led to the decision; and (iii) of the right of the person concerned to have the personal information used to render the decision concerned.[10] The person concerned must be given the opportunity to submit observations to a person in the enterprise who is in a position to review the decision. An administrative monetary penalty may be imposed on anyone who does not inform the person concerned by a decision based exclusively on an automated process or does not give the person an opportunity to submit observations. Law 25 establishes significant new monetary penalties for non-compliance. Directors and officers of corporations may also be liable. Under Law 25, provincial regulators in the province of Quebec can impose penalties for breaching various sections of Quebec's Private Sector Privacy Act, including: (a) administrative monetary penalties of $10 million CAD or 2 percent of worldwide turnover for the preceding fiscal year, whichever is greater; or (b) fines of up to $25 million CAD or 4 percent of worldwide turnover for the preceding fiscal year, whichever is greater.

Without any overarching legislation or regulation explicitly governing the use of data by AI technology, businesses must navigate and comply with a patchwork of privacy and sector-specific laws in Canada. It is critical that the use and ownership of data are adequately addressed in all business and consumer-facing contracts to ensure compliance with applicable Canadian laws. This is further discussed below.[11]

13.1.2. AI in Legal Practice

Canadian courts have issued notices regarding the use of generative AI in proceedings. Specifically, the Federal Court of Canada requires a party to inform the Court in writing if AI has been used to prepare a document filed with the Court. The declaration is required to be in the first paragraph of the document submitted to the Court. The Federal Court of Canada also encourages parties to verify any AI-generated content used in those court documents.[12]

---

[8] Act respecting the protection of personal information in the privacy sector, chapter P-39.1 ["Quebe's Private Sector Privacy Act"] (Can. Que.).

[9] An Act to modernize legislative provisions as regards the protection of personal information, SQ 2021, c 25 ["Law 25"] (Can. Que.).

[10] *See* Quebec's Private Sector Privacy Act §§ 12.1.

[11] *See* discussion *infra* Section 13.2.2, "Protection of Data."

[12] Notice to the Parties and the Profession: The Use of Artificial Intelligence in Court Proceedings, Fed. Ct (Dec. 20, 2023) (Can.). *See also* Intelligence: Interim Principles and Guidelines of the Court's Use of Artificial Intelligence, Fed.

AI can be broadly characterized as a machine-based system that is able to predict and automatically generate outputs or decisions based on data provided. An ad hoc generative AI panel of external experts funded by the government of Canada[13] has put forward a formal definition of generative AI, which is defined as systems that have the following four characteristics: (i) they present a straightforward, often conversational, interface that makes deploying the power system accessible to a broad range of nonexpert users; (ii) they intrinsically enable iterative design and improvement processes; (iii) they make available information extracted from enormous amounts of data, by systems using enormous amounts of computing power; and (iv) the output of the system approaches a level of sophistication that may cause nonexperts to erroneously identify the output as having been human created.[14]

Similar to the United States, the use of AI in the Canadian courtroom has been reprimanded by both the judiciary and the media. In *Zhang v. Chen*, the Honorable Justice Masuhara was highly critical of counsel that used generative AI to draft submissions, stating, "As this case has unfortunately made clear, generative AI is still no substitute for the professional expertise that the justice requires of lawyers. Competence in the selection and use of any technology tools, including those powered by AI, is critical. The integrity of the justice system requires no less."[15] Counsel in *Zhang v. Chen* submitted an application to the Court that cited two cases that were "discovered subsequently to have been invented by ChatGPT." Ultimately, the fabricated cases were withdrawn by counsel before the hearing of the application. The cases cited can be classified as "hallucinations" that were generated by AI and contain false information presented as fact. Misleading information may be produced by generative AI as a result of a number of factors, including biases in the training data used in the model itself or insufficient training data used to create the model.

In the *Pacific Smoke International Inc. v Monster Energy Company* decision,[16] the Applicant relied on a case as a ground of opposition that did not exist. The Trademark Opposition Board commented that the citation appeared to be an AI "hallucination" and disregarded that portion of the submission. The Trademark Opposition Board reminded the Applicant that "even if accidental, reliance on a false citation, AI hallucination or otherwise, is a serious matter."[17]

Further, a study published in June 2024 in the *Journal of Legal Analysis* found that "hallucinations" generated by AI may be extremely prevalent in any output produced by an AI system.[18] Though AI trained on large language models has the potential to reshape

---

Ct. (Dec. 20, 2023) (Can.).

13 The ad hoc generative AI panel of external experts was established by the Canadian Institutes of Health Research (CIHR), the National Sciences and Engineering Research Council of Canada (NSERC), the Social Sciences and Humanities Research Council of Canada (SSHRC), and the Canada Foundation for Innovation (CFI).

14 *Advice from the Ad Hoc Generative AI Panel of External Experts*, Gov't of Canada, https://science.gc.ca/site/science/en/-interagency-research-funding/policies-and-guidelines/use-generative-artificial-intelligence-development-and-review-research-proposals/advice-ad-hoc-generative-ai-panel-external-experts (Jan. 12, 2024) (Can.).

15 Zhang v. Chen, 2024 BCSC CanLII 285, para. 46 (Can.).

16 Pacific Smoke International Inc. v Monster Energy Company, 2024 TMOB 211 (Can.).

17 *Id* at 16.

18 Matthew Dahl et al., *Large Legal Fictions: Profiling Legal Hallucinations in Large Language Models*, 16 J. OF LEGAL ANALYSIS 1, 64 (2024).

the practice of law, the problem of "hallucinations" remains a serious obstacle to widespread adoption as AI is proficient at internalizing legal knowledge but is not considered to be a reliable source of legal information.[19] It is of utmost importance that legal professionals exercise extreme caution when utilizing AI tools in Canada or, as a best practice, refrain from using them at all.[20]

13.1.3. OpenAI and ChatGPT in Canada

ChatGPT, a generative AI chatbot, was launched by OpenAI to create great global fanfare in November 2022. The Office of the Privacy Commissioner (OPC), a federal regulatory body in Canada, along with the equivalent provincial privacy authorities in Alberta, Quebec, and British Columbia, announced on May 25, 2023, that there would be a collective investigation of OpenAI across Canada as a response to a complaint brought forward alleging that OpenAI is collecting, using, and disclosing personal information without consent. The investigation will determine whether OpenAI has

1. obtained valid and meaningful consent for the collection, use, and disclosure of the personal information of individuals based in Canada via ChatGPT;
2. respected its obligations with respect to openness and transparency, access, accuracy, and accountability; and
3. collected, used, and/or disclosed personal information for purposes that a reasonable person would consider appropriate, reasonable, or legitimate in the circumstances, and whether this collection is limited to information that is necessary for these purposes.[21]

Other jurisdictions, including the United States and Italy, have initiated similar investigations into OpenAI's use of personal information. On March 31, 2023, Italy was the first Western country to ban the use of ChatGPT during the Italian Data Protection Authority's investigation into ChatGPT's compliance with the applicable European Union General Data Protection Regulation (GDPR). The outcome of the Canadian investigation into OpenAI is one to watch. It will likely be a precedent setting decision that will outline how

---

[19] *Id.* at 87.

[20] The authors of this chapter would like to draw the reader's attention to a pair of family law decisions, released at the time of publication of this book, that together dealt with the use of AI in the Canadian courtroom, specifically *Ko v Li*, 2025 ONSC 2766 (Can.) and *Ko v Li*, 2025 ONSC 2965 (Can.). Counsel for the applicant in the family law matter relied on two fictious cases to support her argument during oral submissions. The fabricated cases were also cited in the applicant's factum. The Motion Judge ordered that the applicant's counsel "show cause why she should not be held in contempt of court" for her use of AI in generating the applicant's materials that resulted in producing sham cases. Ultimately, the applicant's counsel admitted to using AI to prepare the materials, apologized and proposed positive steps to address the issue. The order for the show cause hearing was dismissed on the condition that the applicant's counsel fulfill her commitment to taking continuing education courses on the proper use of AI and that she not bill her client for the time spent preparing and attending the motion. Please see Lisa R. Lifshitz and Laura Crimi, *AI Gone Awry: The Unauthorized of Use of Ai in Court*, Torkin Manes Legalpoint (May 26, 2025), available at https://www.torkin.com/insights/publication/ai-gone-awry--the-unauthorized-use-of-ai-in-courts.

[21] Office of the Privacy Commissioner, *OPC to investigate ChatGPT Jointly with Provincial Privacy Authorities*, Off. of the Privacy Comm'r of Can. (May 23, 2023), https://www.priv.gc.ca/en/opc-news/news-and-announcements/2023/an_230525-2/.

businesses can best employ the use of AI technology in Canada and is expected to have a subsequent ripple effect on future policy and regulation provincially and nationwide.

While not directly related to ChatGPT, Canadian courts are beginning to consider issues relating model training and data scraping that will impact generative AI products such as ChatGPT. For example, on November 4, 2024, the Canadian Legal Information Institute ("CanLII") filed a Notice of Claim with the Supreme Court of British Columbia as against 134 BC Ltd et al, including Caseway AI Legal Ltd. ("Caseway.ai," collectively the "Defendants").[22] CanLII is a non-profit that owns and operates a proprietary search engine and database containing court decisions, legislation and secondary sources (the "CanLII works"). CanLII's mandate is to provide efficient and open online access to judicial decisions and legislative documents and to support members of the legal profession. Caseway.ai operates a for-profit AI platform trained on Canadian court decisions that aims to improve access to justice by providing enhanced legal research tools. The platform is available for a monthly subscription fee. Caseway.ai does not disclose the source of its catalogue of legal documents but has suggested, in public promotional materials and public articles, that the database is based on data scraped from the CanLII website. In the Notice of Claim, CanLII alleges, amongst other things, that the Defendants violated the CanLII website terms of use, which expressly prohibits the bulk downloading and web scraping of the CanLII website without permission or a license or any form of compensation to CanLII. CanLII also asserts that Caseway.ai infringed its copyright in the CanLII Works. CanLII seeks injunctive relief, damages and disgorgement of the Defendant's profits.[23]

Additionally, Canadian courts are poised to make another ruling on using AI to scrape data from websites. On November 29, 2024, Canada's leading news companies, including the Toronto Star Newspapers Limited, Postmedia Network Inc., The Globe and Mail Inc., and Canadian Broadcasting Corporation (the "Plaintiffs") brought forward a notice of claim in the Ontario Superior Court against OpenAI and its related companies that work to develop, commercialize and fund OpenAI's products (the "Defendants") for the alleged data scraping of the Plaintiffs' copyrighted content. The Plaintiffs allege that the Defendants have used their intellectual property without proper authorization as a means of building a commercially successful business. The legal basis of the Plaintiffs' claim is rooted in copyright infringement and breach of contract, specifically alleging that the Defendants' use of the Plaintiffs' works violates section 3(1) and 27(2) of the *Copyright Act* and breaches the terms and conditions of the Plaintiffs' websites. The Plaintiffs also allege that the Defendants are liable for the alleged circumvention of technological

---

22 *Canadian Legal Information Institute v 1345750 B.C. Ltd. et al* (4 November 2024) Vancouver, VLC-S-S-247574 (Supreme Court of British Columbia) (see https://www.lawnext.com/wp-content/uploads/2024/11/Notice-of-civil-claim.pdf to Notice of Civil Claim).

23 On December 11, 2024 the CEO of Caseway.ai stated in an article that "Caseway trains its ai using public court decisions, not CanLII's enhancements or proprietary metadata. Many of these AI lawsuits are about monopolizing access to publicly available data under the guise of copyright and restrictive terms of use. When we approached CanLII to collaborate, they said no. We had to develop other expensive web crawling technology that pulls cases directly from the courts, tribunals, and boards. We don't scrape any websites. Traditional companies argue that AI companies exploit creators by using their data without compensation. But this narrative oversimplifies the issue. Caseway and other AI firms are not stealing value but creating it." See: https://techcouver.com/2024/12/11/dont-scare-ai-companies-away-canada-theyre-building-the-future/

protection measures used by the Plaintiffs to prevent unauthorized copying and access to its works, specifically in violation of sections 41 and 41.1 of the *Copyright Act* and that the Defendants were unjustly enriched by the misappropriation of the Plaintiffs' intellectual property. The Plaintiffs are seeking substantial compensation from the Defendants. The order for compensation requested by the Plaintiffs includes a portion of the profits earned by the Defendants from the alleged infringement of the Plaintiffs' copyright works and circumventing protections; statutory damages set at CAD 20,000 per work; damages for unjust enrichment; and, further, punitive damages for the Defendants' willful misconduct. In addition to the damages sought, the Plaintiffs are requesting both prejudgment and post judgment interest, along with the costs of the legal proceedings.[24] The claim brought forward by the Plaintiffs against the defendants, amongst others, has generated considerable public interest in Canada as we await further guidance from the Ontario Superior Court of Justice regarding the legality of mass data scaping by AI systems.[25]

13.2. Intellectual Property Rights, AI, and Digital Content

The core principles of intellectual property law in Canada promote innovation. The subsequent regulation of AI technology is aimed at furthering innovation while simultaneously protecting the public from its potential harm. The advent of generative AI has raised issues surrounding the rights to the intellectual property ownership of AI-generated works, the protection of data in light of AI, and the protection of trade secrets. These issues challenge traditional Canadian legal intellectual property protection and the accompanying norms of intellectual property ownership.

13.2.1. Intellectual Property and AI-Authored Works

Traditional copyright law in Canada is a statutory right. The *Copyright Act* provides that no person is entitled to copyright or any similar right in any literary, dramatic, musical, or artistic work other than under and in accordance with the *Copyright Act*.[26] Further, the *Copyright Act* does not require that a copyright owner register the work, rather, it confers rights in unpublished, as well as published, works upon creation. A formal copyright registration in Canada is merely a certificate of ownership that easily provides proof of authorship of a work.

One of the central problems of generative AI is that it challenges the Canadian copyright regime and its traditional notion of authorship. Is AI capable of authoring and owning a specific work? If not, who would be the appropriate owner of a work authored solely by

---

24 *Torstar et al v OpenAI, Inc. et al* (28 November 2024), Toronto CV-24-00732231-00CL (Ontario Superior Court of Justice) (see https://litigate.com/assets/uploads/Canadian-News-Media-Companies-v-OpenAI.pdf to Notice of Claim).

25 *See* L. Lifshitz and L. Crimi, "Scraping the Surface: OpenAI Sued for Data Scraping in Canada," ABA Business Law Today (February 12, 2025) at https://businesslawtoday.org/2025/02/scraping-the-surface-openai-sued-for-data-scraping-in-canada/.

26 Copyright Act, R.S.C. 1985, c C-42, § 5 (Can.).

AI, or a work authored by AI in conjunction with a natural person? Would it be appropriate to assign rights to the developer of the AI itself or to the individual who may have directed or prompted the AI program to create the work? Current Canadian legal frameworks do not provide an easy answer to these questions, which results in an undeniable legal gray area. Up until this point, no Canadian legal decision has addressed the problem of authorship solely by a computer program, generative AI, or otherwise.

Patent protection is generally afforded to inventive ideas by those inventors who have contributed to the patentable idea. In *Apotex Inc. v. Wellcome Foundation Ltd.*, the Supreme Court of Canada stated, "Of course, in the steps leading from conception to patentability, the inventor(s) may utilize the services of others, who may be highly skilled, but those others will not be co-inventors unless they participated in the conception as opposed to its verification."[27] This provides some insight or inference into how AI authorship may be treated by the Courts in Canada, but the Canadian Government has yet to officially legislate on the issue of generative AI and authorship.

In 2021, the Government of Canada launched a public consultation titled the "Consultation on Modern Copyright Framework for Artificial Intelligence and the Internet of Things." This consultation focused on obtaining insights from key stakeholders as to how to best adapt the current Canadian copyright framework for the digital age.[28] Following this initial consultation, and in light of the rapid onset of AI systems, specifically ChatGPT, the Government of Canada undertook a second round of public consultation titled "Consultation on Copyright in the Age of Generative Artificial Intelligence."[29] Each of these consultations has resulted in a wide range of submissions put forward by various stakeholders, but collectively they have yet to result in any tangible Canadian legislative reform regulating the use of AI systems.

On December 1, 2021, copyright in the artistic work *Suryast*[30] was registered with the Canadian Intellectual Property Office (CIPO). *Suryast* is registered as having two coauthors, one being Ankit Sahni and the other being RAGHAV Artificial Intelligence Painting App, which is an AI system. It is important to reiterate that CIPO does not verify authorship upon application for copyright registration and simply grants copyright registrations instantaneously following the completion of the online form and payment of the applicable fee.

On July 8, 2024, the Samuelson-Glushko Canadian Interest Policy and Public Interest Clinic (CIPPIC) filed an application under Section 57(4) of the *Copyright Act* with the Federal Court of Canada seeking a declaration that there is no copyright in the artistic

---

27 Apotex Inc. v. Wellcome Foundation Ltd., 2002 SCC 77, para. 97 (Can. S.C.C.).

28 Canada, Innovation, Science and Economic Development Canada, *Consultation on a Modern Copyright Framework for Artificial Intelligence and the Internet of Things*, Gov't of Canada, https://ised-isde.canada.ca/site/strategic-policy-sector/en/marketplace-framework-policy/copyright-policy/consultation-modern-copyright-framework-artificial-intelligence-and-internet-things (Feb. 15, 2022).

29 Canada, Innovation, Science and Economic Development Canada, *Consultation on Copyright in the Age of Generative Artificial Intelligence,* Gov't of Canada, https://ised-isde.canada.ca/site/strategic-policy-sector/en/marketplace-framework-policy/consultation-copyright-age-generative-artificial-intelligence (Jun. 19, 2024).

30 SURYAST, Registration No. 1188619 (Dec 1, 2023) (Can.).

work *Suryast*, or, in the alternative, that if there is copyright in the artistic work *Suryast*, that Ankit Sahni is the sole author of the work. The application brought forward by CIPPIC, Canada's first and only public interest technology law clinic, raises crucial public policy issues with respect to the ownership of AI-generated works, and whether or not an AI system can in fact hold copyright ownership in an artistic work.

It is worth noting that Ankit Sahni has attempted to register copyright in *Suryast* in multiple jurisdictions around the world, including in India and the United States, among others. In December 2023, the United States Copyright Review Board refused to register copyright in the artistic work *Suryast*. Despite several appeals by Ankit Sahni, the United States Copyright Review Board found that the work was not a product of human authorship, denied authorship to the RAGHAV Artificial Intelligence Painting App, and denied that copyright subsisted in the work itself.[31]

The Canadian Federal Court's decision on the ownership of works coauthored by generative AI is highly anticipated by numerous stakeholders, including legal professionals, AI developers, users of AI tools, and policymakers alike. The ruling has the potential to have far-reaching implications with respect to AI ownership in Canada and the application of traditional norms with respect to the ownership of artistic works in light of novel AI technology.

It is clear that AI challenges the traditional notion of copyright law in Canada. AI, specifically generative AI, presents a unique challenge to the Canadian intellectual property regime. It is key that American attorneys stay current with respect to Canadian regulation or critical decisions from the Canadian courts or regulatory bodies with respect to intellectual property law applying to AI-authored works in order to best advise their clients. While lawyers can look to patent law in Canada for clues as to how the Federal Court of Canada may rule on the question of authorship or ownership of works or inventions created by AI, overall, the issue remains unresolved.

13.2.2. Protection of Data

Data has become increasingly valuable in the information age, especially considering that AI systems are trained on large datasets. However, there are no *sui generis* rights to a dataset in Canada. In order to adequately protect a dataset, Canadian data-owners must employ a patchwork of legal protection. There are four primary sources of legal rights that together can work to protect the rights in and to a dataset: (i) intellectual property rights, (ii) contractual rights, (iii) common law rights, and (iv) statutory rights.

1. **Intellectual Property Rights:** The only right that arises in and to a dataset under the *Copyright Act* is the copyright in the original expression or arrangement of data. The rights to the underlying data points are not afforded any protection in Canada. A patent may be able to protect a specific methodology of analyzing data, but, similar to

[31] Second Request for Reconsideration for Refusal to Register SURYAST (U.S. Copyright Off. Rev. Bd., Dec. 11, 2023).

copyright protection, a patent is unable to protect the dataset itself. Trademark protection is not applicable to a dataset.

2. **Contractual Rights:** The most practical means of protecting a dataset in Canada is by way of contract. Ensuring that a dataset is protected with the appropriate safeguards and security protection is the first line of defense to protect the dataset. Employing a multifaceted approach, which includes using contractual clauses, nondisclosure agreements, and imposing security obligations on users, is critical to ensuring that a dataset remains proprietary and confidential. Careful legal drafting can ensure datasets are adequately protected in Canada.
3. **Common Law Rights:** Common law principles, like breach of confidence, misappropriation, and unjust enrichment, are capable of protecting datasets in Canada. Organizations must take adequate measures to ensure the confidentiality of a dataset, including proper labeling of confidential information and restricting access to only those that have a need to know the information. Unfair competition laws may also be applicable where a party's actions in using a dataset amount to unfair business practices.
4. **Statutory Rights:** In addition to the statutory protection afforded to the expression of a dataset under the *Copyright Act* in Canada, there are other statutory regimes that can further safeguard a dataset. The *Personal Information Protection and Electronic Documents Act* ("PIPEDA") is a federal statute that, while not specifically designed to protect a dataset, provides protection for personal data in a dataset and governs how commercial entities can collect, use, and disclose personal information.[32] This means that any entity collecting personal information is required to comply with PIPEDA. There are further statutory regimes that offer protection for business-specific data collected, including the provincial *Personal Health Information Protection Act* ("PHIPA"),[33] which governs the collection of personal health information in Ontario, and the federal *Bank Act*,[34] along with associated banking regulations, that regulate how financial information is handled and disclosed.

American companies entering the Canadian market that collect data should leverage each of the above protections and ensure compliance with sector-specific laws and regulations in order to appropriately safeguard their datasets.

13.2.3. Protection of Trade Secrets

In Canada, the protection of trade secrets is not ruled by a specific statutory regime and is instead entirely governed by common law principles, like breach of confidence. Where an entity employs the use of AI in day-to-day business operations, there is potential for company trade secrets to be disclosed through an AI platform by an uninformed employee.

---

32 The Personal Information Protection and Electronic Documents Act, S.C. 2000 c. 5 ["PIPEDA"] (Can.).

33 The Personal Health Information Protection Act, 2004, S.O. 2004, c 3, Schedule A (Can.).

34 The Bank Act, S.C. 1991, c 46 (Can.).

Further, there is a risk that an AI system inadvertently uses information entered by a user in the output provided to another user. Considering the lack of statutory protection of trade secrets in Canada, it is critical that technology companies entering the Canadian market adequately protect all of their proprietary information and properly inform their employees on the risks of using AI in day-to-day business operations.

The test for failure to protect a trade secret falls under the test for breach of confidence. The following three elements must be established by a plaintiff in an action for breach of confidence: (1) the information conveyed was confidential and had economic value, (2) the confidential information was communicated in confidence, and (3) the confidential information was misused by the party to whom it was communicated.[35]

It is critical to ensure all Canadian contracts, including employment and vendor contracts, adequately protect trade secrets and confidential information. When a trade secret is breached, the Court has jurisdiction to grant a remedy that is highly fact specific. A successful plaintiff in a breach of confidence action may seek the following types of remedies: (1) injunctions, either on an interlocutory[36] or permanent basis[37]; (2) damages[38]; (3) accounting of profits; and (4) imposition of a constructive trust.[39]

Please note that criminal penalties may also apply under the *Criminal Code* for theft of trade secrets in Canada.[40] Any person who knowingly obtains a trade secret or communicates or makes available a trade secret, knowing that it was obtained by the commission of an offense, is guilty of an indictable offense and is liable to imprisonment for a term not exceeding fourteen years, or is guilty of an offense punishable on summary conviction.[41]

American attorneys should advise all technology clients operating in Canada, or those considering moving into the Canadian market, to adequately protect their data, intellectual property, and other proprietary information, including trade secrets, in the manners described above.

13.3 Privacy and Technology

The rapid onset of technology, the accessibility of digital devices, the use of big data analytics, and the broad application of AI systems have revolutionized both business and the day-to-day life of consumers. These great advancements come with significant concerns regarding data privacy, which have generated a serious proposed reform of the regulatory landscape of data and the advancement of privacy law in Canada.

---

35 Lac Minerals Ltd. v. International Corona Resources Ltd. (1989) 2 S.C.R. 574, 576 (Can. S.C.C.).

36 Altam Holdings Ltd. v. Lazette (2009), 479 A.R. 89 (Can. Alta. Q.B.).

37 Cadbury Schweppes, Inc. v. FBI Foods Ltd. (1999), 1 S.C.R. 142 (Can. S.C.C.).

38 *Id.*

39 *Lac Minerals Ltd.*, 2 S.C.R. at 579.

40 Criminal Code, R.S.C. 1985, c C-46 (Can.).

41 *Id.* §§ 391(1)-(3).

13.3.1 Federal Privacy Legislation

Canada's PIPEDA is a federal data protection statute that governs the collection, use, and disclosure of personal information by federal works, undertakings and businesses (FWUBs)[42] as well to all private sector organizations regulated by provinces that do not have substantially similar private sector privacy legislation that collect, use or disclose personal information in the course of their commercial activities. It is worth noting that business information is not regulated by PIPEDA,[43] and the *Privacy Act*[44] governs the personal information held by federally regulated government institutions.[45] PIPEDA applies in all provinces and territories that have not enacted substantially private-sector data protection laws. Only three provinces, being Quebec,[46] British Columbia,[47] and Alberta,[48] currently have PIPEDA-equivalent private-sector data protection regulations. These laws will apply, in addition to PIPEDA, to businesses transferring personal information across national, provincial and territorial borders.

Under PIPEDA, personal information is defined as any information about an identifiable individual. The OPC administers and enforces PIPEDA and has provided guidance clarifying what constitutes personal information, stating that it includes "age, name, ID numbers, income, ethnic origin or blood type; opinions, evaluations, social status or disciplinary actions; and employee files, credit records, loan records, medical records, evidence of a dispute between a consumer and a merchant, and intentions (for example, to acquire goods or services, or to change jobs)."[49]

PIPEDA dictates that personal information may only be collected, used, and disclosed for purposes that a reasonable person would consider appropriate in the circumstances.[50] PIPEDA is founded on ten principles that outline a private-sector business's obligation when collecting, using, and disclosing personal information. Schedule 1 of PIPEDA lists these fair information principles, which are further described below.

---

42 Examples of FWUBs in Canada include airlines, banks, ferries, broadcasting, inter-provincial railways, interprovincial or international trucking, shipping or other transportation, aviation, banking, nuclear energy, activities related to maritime navigation, and radio stations.

43 *See, e.g.*, business information includes individuals' business contact information, which is defined under Section 2(1) of PIPEDA as any information that is used for the purpose of communicating or facilitating communication with an individual in relation to their employment, business, or professions such as the individual's name, position name or title, work address, work telephone number, work fax number, or work email address.

44 Privacy Act, R.S.C., 1985, c P-21 (Can.).

45 The *Privacy Act* protects the privacy of individuals with respect to personal information held by a government institution and broadly defines personal information to include, among other criteria, information about an identifiable individual that is recorded in any form, including, without restricting the generality of the foregoing: (a) information relating to the race, national or ethnic origin, color, religion, age, or marital status of the individual; (b) information relating to the education or the medical, criminal, or employment history of the individual or information relating to financial transactions in which the individual has been involved; (c) any identifying number, symbol, or other particular assigned to the individual; and (d) the address, fingerprints, or blood type of the individual.

46 Act respecting the protection of personal information in the private sector, CQLR, c P-39.1 (Can. Que.).

47 Personal Information Protection Act, S.B.C. 2003, c 63 (Can. B.C.).

48 Personal Information Protection Act, S.A. 2003, c P-6.5 (Can. Alta.).

49 Office of the Privacy Commissioner of Canada, *Privacy Guide for Businesses,* Off. of the Privacy Comm'r of Can., https://www.priv.gc.ca/media/2038/guide_org_e.pdf (Sept. 2020).

50 Personal Information Protection and Electronic Documents Act, S.C. 2000 c. 5, § 5(3) ["PIPEDA"] (Can.).

1. **Accountability:** An organization is responsible for the personal information in its control and must designate individuals who are accountable for the organization's compliance with PIPEDA; generally, the appointed role is that of a Privacy Officer.[51] Adhering to the principle of accountability also requires an organization to implement procedures to protect personal information in its possession, establish procedures to receive and respond to complaints, adequately training staff and developing information, like a privacy policy, to explain the organization's policies and procedures.[52]

2. **Identifying Purpose:** PIPEDA requires that a business collecting personal information shall identify the purpose of collection at or before the time the information was collected.[53] This may be done either orally or in writing.[54] It is also critical for a business to notify users of any new use of personal information already collected. Unless the new purpose is required by law, the individual must provide consent before the personal information can be used for that new purpose.[55]

3. **Consent:** Knowledge and consent of the data subject are required for the collection, use, or disclosure of information, except where it is inappropriate. Organizations are required to undertake reasonable efforts to ensure the individual is actually advised of the purpose of collection and when it will actually be used. In order to make consent meaningful, the purpose of collection must be relayed to the individual in a manner so that they can reasonably understand how the information may be used or disclosed.[56]

4. **Limiting Collection:** An organization subject to PIPEDA is required to limit collection of personal information only to that which is necessary for the identified purpose.[57]

5. **Limiting Use, Disclosure, and Retention:** Personal information should not be used or disclosed for other than the original purpose of collection. Furthermore, information should only be retained for as long as necessary for the fulfillment of the purpose for which it was collected.[58]

6. **Accuracy:** Personal information collected should be accurate, complete, and up to date as is necessary for the purposes for which it is to be used. Information should be sufficiently accurate to minimize the possibility that inappropriate information may be used to make a decision about the individual.[59]

7. **Safeguards:** Personal information collected by a business must be protected by security safeguards that are proportional and appropriate for the sensitivity of the information. More sensitive information should be safeguarded by a higher level of protection and include physical, organizational, and technological measures of protection.[60]

---

51 *Id.* Schedule 1, Principle 1, § 4.1.2.
52 *Id.* § 4.1.4 (a)-(d).
53 *Id.* Schedule 1, Principle 2.
54 *Id.* § 4.2.3.
55 *Id.*
56 *Id.* Schedule 1, Principle 3.
57 *Id.* Schedule 1, Principle 4.
58 *Id.* Schedule 1, Principle 5.
59 *Id.* Schedule 1, Principle 6.
60 *Id.* Schedule 1, Principle 7.

8. **Openness:** An organization collecting personal information is required to make available to the individuals that they have collected the personal information from the details about the organization's policies and practices related to its collection, management, and retention of personal information.[61]

9. **Individual Access:** Organizations collecting personal information must allow individuals who they have collected personal information from to be informed about the existence, use and disclosure of their personal information and further, be provided with the ability to access their personal information, challenge its accuracy and have it amended, where appropriate.[62]

10. **Compliance:** Organizations collecting personal information are required to have procedures in place to receive and respond to complaints from individuals. Individuals must be able to challenge an organization's compliance with PIPEDA principles with a designated individual, usually being the Privacy Officer of the organization.[63]

Any U.S. business moving into Canada is obligated to comply with applicable Canadian federal and provincial legislation with respect to processing and collecting of personal information, which also includes any cross-border sharing of personal information. Failure to comply with applicable Canadian law will subject a business to significant risk and cause it to be open to regulatory fines and potential lawsuits. An organization using third-party service providers to collect personal information on its behalf remains responsible for the collection of the personal information. It is critical for all entities engaging in business in Canada to ensure that they are adequately protected in contract with third-party service providers to minimize risk and ensure protection of any transferred personal information.[64]

There have been calls in Canada for reform of this fragmented privacy landscape that encompasses both federal and provincial legislation, depending on jurisdiction. Bill C-27, first introduced in 2022, proposed to overhaul Canada's private-sector data protection scheme with new enforcement powers, establish the implementation of a tribunal, and provide stronger rights to administer monetary penalties. Unfortunately, as briefly mentioned at the beginning of this chapter, Bill C-27 frustratingly died on its order paper upon the prorogation of Parliament in January, 2025. It is worth noting that urgency for privacy reform in Canada has been mitigated somewhat by the fact that the European Commission once again upheld Canada's adequacy status under the European Union's GDPR in its January 15, 2024 decision, which was first granted c under the *Data Protection Directive* (Directive 65/46/EC), the predecessor to the European Union's GDPR. Unlike the United States, personal data can flow into Canada from the European Union without the need for additional data protection mechanisms, including the use of data protection addenda or the use of model clauses, as long as the recipient of the personal information is subject to PIPEDA. The reaffirming of

---

61 *Id.* Schedule 1, Principle 8.
62 *Id.* Schedule 1, Principle 9.
63 *Id.* Schedule 1, Principle 10.
64 *Id.* Schedule 1, Principle 1, § 4.1.3.

Canada's data protection legislation's equivalency with the GDPR has cooled the legislature's urgent need to overhaul Canada's privacy scheme.

13.3.2 Privacy in Quebec

As briefly discussed above, in contrast to the federal stalemate regarding privacy reform, in September 2021, the province of Quebec passed Law 25, that significantly amended its provincial privacy legislation, including the Quebec's Private Sector Privacy Act, among others. The reform of the Quebec's Private Sector Privacy Act brought a multitude of changes that enhanced data protection requirements, modernized the protection of personal information, and brought Quebec in alignment with the gold standard of privacy protection, the European Union's GDPR. The changes were slowly rolled out in three phases, with the last of the amendments coming into force in September 2023. The notable changes brought forward by Law 25 include the following:

1. The individual bearing the highest authority in a corporation is by default deemed the Privacy Officer and is responsible for ensuring compliance with the *Private Sector Act*. Any delegation of the responsibility of a Privacy Officer to another individual must be in writing.
2. An enterprise is now required to establish internal regulation and governance policies with respect to the collection, use, and processing of personal information.
3. Akin to the GDPR, where an enterprise takes personal information outside of Quebec, it must conduct a privacy impact assessment.
4. Where an enterprise makes decisions that are automated, for example, using AI systems, it must notify the individuals affected by the decisions.
5. The collection of personal information from an individual that is over the age of fourteen does not require the consent of a parent or a guardian.
6. If there are any settings with respect to a user's privacy, the highest level of protection must be selected by default.
7. As stated above, Law 25 introduced significant administrative monetary penalties for noncompliance with the Quebec Private Sector Privacy Act of up to $10 million CAD or 2 percent of worldwide turnover and penal offenses that may result in fines of $25 million CAD or 4 percent of worldwide turnover for breaches of certain sections.

All entities entering Canada that are collecting personal information from individuals must be cognizant of the additional obligations required by Law 25 when providing goods or services in the province of Quebec.

13.3.3 Privacy Tort—Intrusion upon Seclusion

The tort of intrusion upon seclusion is now recognized in Ontario. Several Canadian provinces have recognized, either through statute or at common law, invasion of privacy torts, which may apply to the use and misuse of digital content, AI, and other technology. The provinces of British Columbia, Manitoba, and Saskatchewan each have their own provincial privacy legislation and have codified the tort of invasion of privacy.[65] Intrusion upon seclusion holds an individual liable who intrudes upon the seclusion, private affairs, or private concerns of another.[66] The act of the intrusion must be reckless and intentional, invading the private affairs or concerns of another, without lawful justification, where a reasonable person would regard the invasion as highly offensive causing distress, humiliation, or anguish. Establishing actual losses or harm is not required.

The scope of the tort of intrusion upon seclusion was recently narrowed for "database defendants" in the Province of Ontario, which have been characterized as collectors and custodians of personal information about individuals for a commercial purpose. In short, the Ontario Court of Appeal established, in a trilogy of decisions, that a claim for intrusion upon seclusion cannot succeed against "database defendants" where they are alleged to have acted recklessly in the storage of that information such that the information was accessed by a third party.[67] The Court has made clear that a claim for intrusion upon seclusion is no longer available where the intrusion arises when cyber criminals illegally access or steal information. This new development is welcome for "database defendants," which clarified that liability only attaches to a party that is an active participant in the wrongful and unauthorized access of personal information by another. However, database defendants could still remain liable in negligence where their failure to take adequate steps to protect personal information causes actual damages.

However, the British Columbia Court of Appeal has departed from the law set by the Ontario Court of Appeal outlined above. In 2024, in *G.D. v South Coast British Columbia Transportation Authority* and *Campbell v Capital One Financial Corporation*,[68] the British Columbia Court of Appeal found that "database defendants" that have been hacked may be liable for statutory breach of privacy under British Columbia's provincial privacy legislation. A "database defendant" in British Columbia that fails to adequately safeguard personal information may be liable for willful violation of privacy. Notably, the British Columbia Court of Appeal declined to specifically address whether the common law tort of intrusion upon seclusion is available in the province of British Columbia in light of the existence of the provincial statutory tort for willful violation of privacy.

13.4. Canadian Consumer Protection Laws

The purpose of consumer protection legislation is to safeguard consumers from unfair business practices and ensure businesses meet certain standards when supplying products and services to consumers. In Canada, consumer contractual protections are afforded to consumers, some of which cannot be waived. For example, Ontario's Bill 142 has received royal assent, and once in force will repeal Ontario's current *Consumer*

---

65 Privacy Act, R.S.B.C. 1996, c 373 (Can. B.C.); Privacy Act, R.S.M. 1987, c P125, C.C.S.M., c P125 (Can. Man.); Privacy Act, R.S.S. 1978. C. P-24 (Can. Sask.).

66 Jones v. Tsige, 2012 ONCA 32 (Can. Ont. C.A.).

67 *See* Owsianik v. Equifax Co., 2022 ONCA 813 (Can. Ont. C.A.); Obodo v. Trans Union of Canada, Inc., 2022 ONCA 814 (Can. Ont. C.A.); Winder v. Marriott International, Inc., 2022 ONCA 815 (Can. Ont. C.A.).

68 *See* G.D. v South Coast British Columbia Transportation Authority, 2024 BCCA 252 (Can. B.C. C.A.) and Campbell v Capital One Financial Corporation, 2024 BCCA 253 (Can B.C. C.A.)

Protection Act ("Current Consumer Protection Act")[69] and replace it with a new *Consumer Protection Act* ("Consumer Protection Act 2023")[70] while also amending the *Consumer Reporting Act*.[71] The Consumer Protection Act 2023 expands the prohibited terms in consumer contracts and specifically restricts clauses that require arbitration, prohibits participation in class actions, negates implied warranties, or prohibit a consumer from communicating a review of a supplier.

While both Canada and the United States each have robust consumer protection frameworks, the approach of each varies. Canada relies on federal legislation, like PIPEDA and Canada's Anti-Spam Law (CASL), described below, in conjunction with provincial and territorial consumer protection legislation to protect consumers. Similarly, the United States has a patchwork quilt of various sector-specific laws and state-specific legislation. Canada affords consumers protection through (a) express consumer protection legislation, (b) consumer privacy protection, (c) antispam legislation, (d) online harms frameworks, and (e) tort law.

13.4.1. Consumer Protection Legislation

Canadian consumer protection legislation is generally governed at the provincial and territorial levels. Though there is federal law, like the *Competition Act*[72] and the *Consumer Packaging and Labeling Act*,[73] each province and territory in Canada has enacted its own consumer protection statutes.

Ontario's Current Consumer Protection Act defines a consumer as "an individual acting for personal, family or household purposes and does not include a person who is acting for business purposes."[74] Quebec's provincial consumer protection legislation has a similar definition of a consumer, which is defined as "a natural person, except a merchant who obtains goods or services for the purposes of business."[75] This further solidifies that a business entity is not afforded contractual consumer protection when contracting in the ordinary course of business. In *Hatcher v. Sheikhan*, Justice Fowler Byrne, for the Ontario Superior Court of Justice, found that Ontario's Current Consumer Protection Act is focused on protecting the consumer when dealing with a business and does not apply to a transaction to two private individuals.[76]

Canadian consumer protection legislation is notably reflexive and highly responsive to public concerns of consumers. By way of example, Alberta and Ontario, in 2017 and 2018, respectively, introduced amendments to their provincial consumer protection legislation to address public worries. Alberta enacted the Consumer Bill of Rights that ensures consumers are adequately informed about specific products and services and

---

[69] Consumer Protection Act, 2002, S.O. 2002, c 30, Schedule. A (Can. Ont.).
[70] Consumer Protection Act, 2023, S.O. 2023, c 23, Schedule 1 (Can. Ont.).
[71] Consumer Reporting Act, 1990, R.S.O. 1990, c C.33 (Can. Ont.).
[72] Competition Act, 1985, R.S.C., c. C-34 (Can.).
[73] Consumer Packaging and Labelling Act, 1985, R.S.C., c. C-38 (Can.).
[74] S.O. 2023, c 23, Sched 1, at Part I, § 1 (Can.).
[75] Consumer Protection Act, CQLR, c. P-40.1 (Can. Que.).
[76] Hatcher v. Sheikhan, 2019 ONSC 3890 (Can. Ont. C.A.).

protect against unfair business practices, and specifically prohibits the prevention of consumers posting negative reviews.[77] Alternatively, Ontario banned unsolicited door-to-door sales, created rules protecting consumers against the resale of tickets, prohibited the expiry of consumer reward points, and created an administrative monetary penalty scheme for noncompliance.

Ontario's Consumer Protection Act 2023 is expected to further enhance consumer protection in Ontario and strengthen prohibitions on businesses using unfair practices like price gauging, misleading consumers, subjecting a consumer to undue pressure, and will provide consumers with further protections to limit automatic renewals and make it easier to cancel subscriptions.

Though provincial and territorial consumer protection laws can be extremely similar, there are many material differences that can make broad compliance challenging for companies entering the Canadian market. American counsel should seek guidance from Canadian lawyers as soon as possible to ensure that any U.S. client moving into the Canadian market adequately understands and complies with each applicable piece of provincial or territorial legislation and implements deal flow documents, including sales terms and end user license agreements, which are compliant with the consumer protection legislation in relevant jurisdictions.

Finally, we would like to highlight to our American friends that certain sectors, like financial services, product packaging, and pharmaceuticals, are subject to additional industry-specific Canadian regulations that have not been reviewed in this text. It is critical that any entity engaging in cross-border transactions or moving into the Canadian market understands and complies with ever-changing regulatory environment.

13.4.2. Consumer Privacy Protection

One aspect of Canadian law that differs from the regime in the United States is antispam legislation. Canada's anti spam legislation ("CASL") governs the delivery of commercial electronic messages in Canada, which is one of the world's most onerous antispam statutes.[78] The *Controlling the Assault of Non-solicited Pornography and Marketing Act* ("CAN-SPAM Act") provides U.S. entities with guidance on commercial electronic messaging. Despite the fact that both CASL and CAN-SPAM Act regulate electronic correspondence, CASL is significantly broader in scope, containing both form and consent requirements, and has much more significant penalties than the CAN-SPAM Act. CASL regulates a wider range of commercial electronic messages, and violation of CASL could result in administrative monetary penalties of up to $10 million for corporations and $1 million for individuals, and potential criminal sanctions under the *Competition Act*.[79]

---

[77] Consumer Protection Act, RSA 2000, c C-26.3 at s. 183.1 (Can. Alta.).

[78] *An Act to promote the efficiency and adaptability of the Canadian economy by regulating certain activities that discourage reliance on electronic means of carrying out commercial activities, and to amend the Canadian Radio-television and Telecommunications Commission Act, the Competition Act, the Personal Information Protection and Electronic Documents Act and the Telecommunications Act* (S.C. 2010, c. 23) ["CASL"] (Can.)

[79] Competition Act, 1985, R.S.C., c. C-34 (Can.).

Additionally, CASL deems that any director, officer, or agent that acquiesces or participates in an entity's violation of CASL can be held personally liable. It is highly advisable that American attorneys advise clients engaging in business in Canada to confirm that the company's director's liability insurance policy covers administrative actions for non-compliance with CASL.

Under CASL, commercial electronic messages are defined as messages that encourage participation in commercial activities, regardless of an expectation of profit. Unlike the CAN-SPAM Act, CASL requires senders of commercial electronic messages to obtain explicit consent from an individual before sending a commercial electronic message, provide identification information, and abide by any unsubscribe requests. In contrast, CAN-SPAM Act's consent model operates on opt-out consent where organizations can rely on implied consent from an individual to receive commercial electronic messages unless the individual explicitly opts out. U.S. entities moving into the Canadian market should use extreme caution before sending promotional emails to Canadian contacts.

CASL has an extremely broad scope and extends to any commercial electronic messages sent from or accessed by a computer located in, but not routed through, Canada. Any entity operating in Canada, or sending commercial electronic messaging to Canadians, must comply with CASL requirements and ensure that any third-party service provider that is engaged to send commercial electronic messages on its behalf must also be compliant.

It is critical that American companies marketing to, or operating in, the Canadian market adhere to the strict CASL regulations to avoid extremely onerous monetary penalties or personal liability of its directors, officers, or agents. The discrete differences between CASL and the CAN-SPAM Act listed above, among others, reinforce that U.S. businesses should use extreme diligence when sending out promotional electronic messaging for commercial purposes in Canada, as a breach of CASL may come with severe penalties.

13.4.3. Tort Law and Technology

Presently, as noted above, there are no specific rules, laws, or causes of action in Canada that would give rise to a claim for damages caused by digital content or AI technology. Any claim for damages caused by digital content or AI would have to be rooted in existing legal frameworks, including intellectual property law, privacy laws, strict liability torts, or negligence.

In order to succeed with a claim for negligence in Canada, the Court must first find that a plaintiff was owed a duty of reasonable care, and that duty was not exercised by the defendant, and second, the individual must establish that damages were in fact suffered as a direct result of the defendant's failure to exercise that duty of care.

In *Moffat v. Air Canada*, the applicant brought a small claim under the *Civil Resolution Tribunal Act* against the respondent, Air Canada, for negligent misrepresentation of its chatbot. In November 2022, Jake Moffat (the "Applicant") booked a flight with Air Canada following the death of his grandmother. While researching flights, the Applicant used a chatbot on Air Canada's website that stated Mr. Moffat could apply for bereavement fares retroactively, after travel. Later, Mr. Moffat was advised by Air Canada employees that Air Canada did not permit retroactive applications for bereavement fares. The Mr. Moffat applied to the Civil Resolution Tribunal of British Columbia, claiming the difference in price between the regular and the alleged bereavement fares. Air Canada argued that it "cannot be held liable for information provided by one of its agents, servants, or representatives—including a chat bot." The Civil Resolution Tribunal of British Columbia noted that Air Canada failed to explain why it should not be responsible for a chat bot, finding that "While a chatbot has an interactive component, it is still just a part of Air Canada's website. It should be obvious to Air Canada that it is responsible for all the information on its website. It makes no difference whether the information comes from a static page or chatbot."[80] The Civil Resolution Tribunal of British Columbia, which had jurisdiction over this matter, found that the Applicant was entitled to damages as a result of Air Canada's negligent misrepresentation through the chatbot. This decision provides that there is some level of a reasonable duty of care required of a company in Canada to ensure its chatbot, and its output, is accurate and not misleading. While the reach of this decision is limited, it is interesting in that this is the first case in Canada to affirm the principle that companies are liable for acts and omissions of an AI chatbot. Air Canada was ordered to pay Moffat $812.02 but as the decision generated headlines in the BBC, *The Washington Post,* and many other media outlets, the reputational damage to Air Canada was more costly. If nothing more, this decision out of the Civil Resolution Tribunal of British Columbia provides us with the notion to exercise caution when using AI technology in a customer facing manner in Canada.

13.5. Conclusion

In Canada, the scope and use of digital content, including content generated by AI systems in day-to-day business operations, has rapidly accelerated in recent years. This has continued to challenge the application of traditional legal norms to novel technology. Regrettably, Canada has lagged behind other jurisdictions in creating digital content and AI-specific legislation, with attempts at reform of its existing legislative landscape at an impasse. If the trajectory of use of AI in Canadian society continues, it will become increasingly important for Canada to legislate its use while promoting innovation. In the meantime, it is status quo, with old laws being pressed into usage for newer technologies and for now lawyers doing business in Canada must rely on a patchwork approach applying existing (however outdated) legislation to the protection and commercial use of digital content and novel use of AI technologies. The strongest protections for both digital content and use of artificial intelligence technology would arise from contract. It is critical for American businesses moving into the Canadian market to be cognizant of the existing and emerging regulatory environment and ensure compliance to minimize potential risks.

---

[80] Moffat v. Air Canada, 2024 BCCRT 149, para. 27 (Can. B.C. C.R.T). Air Canada also seemed to assert that its chatbot should be considered a separate entity and that Air Canada was not liable for its actions.

The below points summarize the key takeaways from this chapter and provide practical advice for American legal professionals on Canada's approach to technology governance:

- **Understand the centralized nature of Canadian technology regulation:** Canada's technology regulation is more centralized than the comparative American regime. U.S. attorneys advising technology companies expanding into Canada should familiarize themselves with the applicable, industry-dependent, federal and provincial laws and regulations.
- **Stay updated on Canada's emerging technology regulations:** While recent efforts at achieving federal AI legislation have failed, there has nonetheless been movement in various provincial sector environments. There is no doubt that federal reform efforts will occur again, and it is essential that American attorneys stay current on new developments to provide accurate and timely advice to technology clients seeking to enter or currently operating in Canada.
- **Copyright law is critical to the regulation of digital content, including AI-generated content in Canada:** There is a growing importance of understanding Canadian copyright law in the context of AI use and development. U.S. attorneys should again stay current with upcoming Canadian legislative copyright reform and adapt strategies for protecting clients' intellectual property rights.
- **Comply with applicable provincial and territorial consumer protection legislation:** Consumer protection legislation in Canada is a patchwork that requires expert attention for entities providing goods, services, or marketing across North America. U.S. attorneys should flag these issues to their clients and engage with Canadian counsel to ensure compliance with applicable statutes.

14 Intersection with Other Law and Regulation—The European Union and the United Kingdom

By David Flint

14.1. Comparative Regulation with the European Union

14.1.1. Introduction

The European Union (EU) is comprised of twenty-seven Member States in Europe. The United Kingdom is not a member of the EU; accordingly, much of the following will not apply to interactions with the United Kingdom. Post-Brexit, the United Kingdom is revising its data protection laws,[1] which may weaken, and will certainly change, many previous protections for personal data. The impact of that is, as yet, unclear. Most of the data laws which existed when the United Kingdom left the EU remain in force, but those enacted since January 30, 2020, will not apply in the United Kingdom.

In the EU, laws are passed by a process involving the Council of Ministers, the European Commission, and the European Parliament.

Insofar as this chapter is concerned, the relevant types of legislation are Directives and Regulations. Directives are binding on Member States as to the outcome to be achieved (which will be achieved through the Member States passing implementing national

---

1 Data (Use and Access) (DUA) Bill—*see* discussion *infra* Section 14.2.3.

legislation). In contrast, Regulations are binding on Member States in accordance with their terms without any further action being required by the Member States.

This chapter will consider the rules relating to digital content and, separately, those relating to digital services. While it is possible to distinguish these two concepts in various ways, the way in which the distinction is made here is that digital content is directed toward the end user whether consumer or business. In contrast, digital services are directed toward service providers, who must provide ongoing interaction or involvement with the user.

In relation to data, particularly personal data, the EU has taken a very different approach to that in the United States; there are some possible reasons for this, and a recognition of these potential reasons (none of which is of itself either definitive or exclusive) is essential for a proper understanding of why the law is different.

First, within the EU, personal data is treated differently from how it is handled in the United States; personal data is treated as the individual's property, and its processing requires compliance with the EU's General Data Protection Regulation (GDPR).[2] The individual ("data subject") is able to control the processing of his or her data, and the entity that is carrying out such processing (either as controller or processor, or a combination thereof) can only do so within the confines of the GDPR.

Second, in addition to the strictures put in place by the GDPR, the EU Member States are also subject to the provisions of Council of Europe Convention 108,[3] the EU Charter of Fundamental Rights,[4] and the European Convention on Human Rights (ECHR).[5] These three pieces of legislation are, in some way, akin to the Constitution of the United States in that all laws of the EU must be compliant with all three. This has and will in the future inevitably make it difficult for the EU to find that the laws of a third country provide equivalent protection to that in EU law as the EU cannot enact or amend its rules in a manner that would mean a lesser standard of protection than in the Convention, the Charter, and the ECHR.

Third, the psyche of the population in the EU is perhaps different from that of the U.S. population; in the EU, the citizens are generally more trusting of government concerning the handling of their data and less trusting of big business. The U.S. position historically may be the opposite.

Finally, the enforcement of data privacy legislation is perhaps less partisan in Europe, and the enforcement authorities are generally less political, which may mean a longer term, more consistent approach to the subject. Ultimately, only one court of last resort—the

---

2 Regulation (EU) 2016/679 of the European Parliament and of the Council of April 27, 2016, on the protection of natural persons with regard to the processing of personal data and on the free movement of such data, and repealing Directive 95/46/EC (General Data Protection Regulation), 2016 O.J. L 119, 1 [hereinafter GDPR].

3 Council of Europe, Convention for the Protection of Individuals with Regard to Automatic Processing of Personal Data, Jan. 28, 1981, ETS No. 108.

4 Charter of Fundamental Rights of the European Union, 2016 O.J. (C 202), 389.

5 Convention for the Protection of Human Rights and Fundamental Freedoms (Nov. 4, 1950).

Court of Justice of the European Union—can issue binding interpretations of the relevant law, even if the national data protection authorities are unwilling or disinclined to act. The European Data Protection Board's oversight of the decisions of national data protection authorities means more consistent, or at least more consensual, enforcement across the EU.

Although the last few years have seen a flurry of new legislation, the activities of the EU Commission (as the instigator of laws in the EU) have been going on for some considerable time in this area, and a brief overview is offered below.[6]

14.1.2. Digital Content

14.1.2.1. Open Data Directive

The Open Data Directive[7]—Directive (EU) 2019/1024—on open data and the reuse of public-sector information, also known as the "Open Data Directive," lays down the legal framework for reusing public-sector information. This includes information such as geographical, land registry, statistical, or legal information held by public-sector bodies or public undertakings, and publicly funded research data.

The Directive is based on the principle that public and publicly funded data should be reusable for commercial or noncommercial purposes. It promotes the use of open data, which are data presented in open formats that individuals can use freely and share for any purpose. Public-sector bodies and public undertakings must make their documents available in any preexisting format or language and, where appropriate, by electronic means, in formats that are open, machine-readable, accessible, findable, and reusable, complete with their metadata.

The Directive aims to boost the socioeconomic potential of public-sector information, for example, by making it more easily available for startups and small and medium-sized enterprises (SMEs), by increasing the supply of dynamic data and datasets with a particularly high-economic impact, and by promoting competition and transparency in the information market. It is part of a package of measures designed to reinforce the EU's data economy, including the development of artificial intelligence (AI).

14.1.2.2. Digital Content Directive

The EU's Digital Content Directive—Directive (EU) 2019/770[8]—deals with certain aspects concerning contracts for the supply of digital content and services. It was adopted in May 2019 and required Member States to transpose it into their national laws by January 1, 2022.

---

6 *See* discussion *infra* Sections 14.1.9.2–14.1.10.3.

7 Directive (EU) 2019/1024 of the European Parliament and of the Council of June 20, 2019, on Open Data and the Re-use of Public Sector Information, 2019 O.J. (L 172), 56.

8 Directive (EU) 2019/770 of the European Parliament and of the Council of May 20, 2019, on Certain Aspects Concerning Contracts for the Supply of Digital Content and Digital Services, 2019 O.J. (L 136), 1.

It includes both digital content and digital services. It aims to ensure consumer protection, harmonization of rules across the EU, and fairness to address imbalances in power between consumers and businesses in the digital space.

Key Provisions

- **Clear information:** Businesses must provide clear and accessible information about the digital content or service before purchase, including functionality, compatibility, and duration of access.
- **Conformity:** The content or service must be as described and fit for its intended purpose.
- **Remedies:** Consumers have the right to a remedy if the content or service is faulty, including repair, replacement, price reduction, or contract termination.
- **Right of withdrawal:** Consumers can withdraw from a contract within a certain time frame, usually fourteen days.
- **Transparency:** Businesses must be transparent about how they use personal data collected from consumers.

14.1.3. Digital Services under the Digital Services Act (DSA)

The Digital Services Act—Regulation (EU) 2022/2065[9]—entered into force on November 7, 2022. It applies from February 17, 2024.

The DSA is part of the European Union's digital strategy and aims to create a safer and fairer digital space. It applies to all digital services connecting consumers to goods, services, or content, including social media, online marketplaces, and other platforms.

The DSA aims to contribute to the proper functioning of the internal market for intermediary services by setting out harmonized rules for a safe, predictable, and trusted online environment that facilitates innovation and in which fundamental rights enshrined in the EU Charter of Fundamental Rights,[10] including the principle of consumer protection, are effectively protected.[11]

The DSA lays down[12] harmonized rules on the provision of intermediary services[13] in the internal market. In particular, it establishes:

(a) a framework for the conditional exemption from liability of providers of intermediary services;[14]

---

9 Regulation (EU) 2022/2065 of the European Parliament and of the Council of October 19, 2022, on a Single Market for Digital Services and amending Directive 2000/31/EC (Digital Services Act), 2022 O.J. (L 277), 1 [hereinafter DSA].

10 Charter of Fundamental Rights of the European Union, 2016 O.J. (C 202) 389.

11 DSA, *supra* note 9, art. 1(1).

12 *Id.* art. 1(2).

13 *Id.* art. 3(g).

14 *Id.* arts. 4(1), 5(1), 6(1).

(b) rules on specific due diligence obligations tailored to certain specific categories of providers of intermediary services; and

(c) rules on implementing and enforcing the DSA, including cooperation and coordination between the competent authorities.[15]

Definitions of "mere conduit," "caching," and "hosting" are set out in the DSA.[16] Here are some key provisions of the DSA:

Scope: The DSA applies to intermediary services[17] offered to recipients of that service who have their place of establishment or are located in the EU, irrespective of where the providers are located.[18]

For online platforms, the first step to understanding what is required is establishing whether they offer intermediary services within the scope of the Act. The next step is understanding into which category of intermediary service they fall.

While there are exceptions for microenterprises and small and medium-sized enterprises, categorization is generally as follows:

- All in-scope intermediary services are subject to due diligence and transparency obligations.[19]
- Further requirements with which hosting service providers, including online platforms, must comply.[20]
- Additional provisions specific to online platforms.[21]
- Further rules again for online platforms which allow consumers to conclude distance contracts with traders.[22]
- Additional obligations with which only providers of very large online platforms (VLOPs) and very large online search engines (VLOSEs)[23] must comply.[24]

---

15 *Id.* arts. 56–60.

16 *Id.* arts. 4–6.

17 (g) "intermediary service" means one of the following information society services:

(i) a "mere conduit" service, consisting of the transmission in a communication network of information provided by a recipient of the service, or the provision of access to a communication network;

(ii) a "caching" service, consisting of the transmission in a communication network of information provided by a recipient of the service, involving the automatic, intermediate and temporary storage of that information, performed for the sole purpose of making more efficient the information's onward transmission to other recipients upon their request;

(iii) a "hosting" service, consisting of the storage of information provided by, and at the request of, a recipient of the service.

Id. art. 3(g).

18 *Id.* art. 2(1).

19 *Id.* ch. III, § 1, arts. 11–15.

20 *Id.* ch. III, § 2, arts. 16–18.

21 *Id.* ch. III, § 3, arts. 19–28.

22 *Id.* ch. III, § 4, arts. 29–32.

23 Very large online platforms and search engines are those with over 45 million users in the EU. These are designated by the Commission under the Digital Services Act, and a list is maintained at https://digital-strategy.ec.europa.eu/en/policies/list-designated-vlops-and-vloses.

24 DSA, *supra* note 9, ch. III, § 5, arts. 33–43.

Uniform rules for removal of illegal content: The DSA sets out clear procedures and safeguards for the removal of illegal content by online platforms.[25] It also provides for the establishment of an external audit mechanism. There is no general obligation under the DSA to monitor the information which the providers of intermediary services transmit or store.[26]

Platforms are mandated to establish and deploy effective measures for the expeditious detection and removal of illegal content, encompassing a range of offenses such as hate speech, terrorism, and child sexual abuse material.[27]

The fact that the intermediary carries out voluntary own-initiative investigations into and removes or disables access to illegal content will not remove the exemptions from liability in Articles 4, 5, and 6 of the DSA.

A new group, "trusted flaggers," is introduced by the DSA. These entities are granted that status by the Digital Services Coordinator of a Member State to any entity which has met various conditions, including "particular expertise for the purposes of detecting, identifying and notifying illegal content."[28] Notifications from trusted flaggers are to be given priority and processed without delay. Presumably, this system is designed to mimic the procedures under the US Digital Millennium Copyright Act.[29]

Transparency obligations: VLOPs[30] are required to conduct annual assessments of the systemic risks posed by their services and to take mitigating measures. They must also provide researchers with access to data. Article 15 requires providers of intermediary services to make publicly available, in a machine-readable format and an easily accessible manner, at least once a year, clear, easily comprehensible reports on any content moderation in which they engaged during the relevant period. That Article sets out the information which is to be provided. In March 2024, the European Commission requested information from nine big tech platforms[31] on their use of targeted ads and generative AI to gauge compliance with the DSA.

New supervisory structure: The DSA establishes a new cooperation process among national supervisory authorities and the Commission. A new European Board for Digital Services has been created to facilitate this cooperation.

Users' rights: The DSA strengthens users' rights, giving them effective means to contest the decisions taken by the platforms, particularly regarding content moderation. Where

---

[25] "Illegal content" means any information that, in itself or in relation to an activity, including the sale of products or the provision of services, is not in compliance with Union law or the law of any Member State, which is in compliance with Union law, irrespective of the precise subject matter or nature of that law.
Id. art. 3(h).

[26] *Id.* art. 8.

[27] *Id.* at art. 9.

[28] *Id.* at art. 22.

[29] 17 U.S.C. 512(c)(3).

[30] *See supra* note 23.

[31] The Commission asked Bing, Google Search, Facebook, Instagram, Snapchat, TikTok, YouTube, and X to provide details regarding their strategies to address risks associated with generative AI, including on elections. It also asked LinkedIn to clarify how it complies with a prohibition not to target ads based on sensitive personal data.

data cannot be directly accessed by the user from the connected product or related service, data holders must make data readily available, together with the relevant metadata necessary to interpret and use those data, accessible to the user without undue delay, of the same quality as is available to the data holder, easily, securely, free of charge, in a comprehensive, structured, commonly used, and machine-readable format, and, where relevant and technically feasible, continuously and in real time.

As with other EU Data laws, including the GDPR,[32] providers of intermediary services which do not have an establishment in the EU are required to designate in writing a legal or natural person to act as their legal representative in one of the Member States where the provider offers its services.[33]

Liability regime: The DSA maintains the existing liability regime established by the E-Commerce Directive,[34] which does not hold platforms liable for illegal content of which they are unaware. They are, however, required to take action to remove illegal content once they become aware of it.[35]

There are provisions in the DSA that deal with dispute resolution arising from any complaint relative to material, including decisions on access to information, account suspension, and service provision.[36]

Very large online platforms and very large online search engines: There are separate and additional obligations imposed by the DSA on very large online platforms (VLOPs) and very large online search engines (VLOSSs), which are entities that have at least 45 million active monthly recipients of the service in the EU and have been designated as a VLOP or a VLOSS under the DSA.[37] These entities are required to carry out risk assessments in relation to any systemic risks in the EU stemming from the design or functioning of their service and its related systems, including algorithmic systems, or from the use of their services.[38] The VLOP or VLOSS must put mitigation measures in place concerning these systemic risks and conduct an annual independent audit to assess compliance with their obligations under the DSA.[39]

Enforcement and penalties: The DSA outlines enforcement mechanisms and potential penalties for noncompliance. Penalties may include fines and other measures to ensure

---

32 GDPR, *supra* note 2.

33 DSA, *supra* note 9, art. 13.

34 Directive 2000/31/EC of the European Parliament and of the Council of June 8, 2000, on certain legal aspects of information society services, in particular electronic commerce, in the Internal Market ("Directive on electronic commerce"), 2000 O.J. (L 178), 1; *See infra* Section 14.1.9.2.

35 DSA, *supra* note 9, art. 6(1)(b).

36 *Id.* art. 20–21

37 *Id.* art. 33.

38 *Id.* art. 34.

39 *Id.* art. 37.

adherence to the rules.[40] Fines on intermediary service providers,[41] VLOPs, and VLOSEs[42] may reach 6 percent of worldwide turnover.

On December 18, 2023, the European Commission opened formal proceedings to assess whether X had breached the DSA in areas linked to risk management, content moderation, dark patterns, advertising transparency, and data access for researchers.[43]

On February 19, 2024, the European Commission opened formal proceedings to assess whether TikTok had breached the DSA in areas linked to the protection of minors, advertising transparency, and data access for researchers, as well as the risk management of addictive design and harmful content.[44]

On March 14, 2024, the European Commission opened formal proceedings to assess whether AliExpress had breached the DSA in areas linked to the assessment and mitigation of the systemic risks of dissemination of illegal content, transparency, data access for researchers, and notification systems for illegal content.[45]

On October 31, 2024, the European Commission opened formal proceedings against Chinese e-commerce company Temu under the DSA in areas linked to the sale of illegal products, the potentially addictive design of the service, the systems used to recommend purchases to users, as well as data access for researchers.[46]

The DSA envisages compensation being payable to service recipients,[47] although there is no guidance on how this is to be calculated.

14.1.4. Data under the EU Data Act

The EU Data Act—Regulation (EU) 2023/2854—was enacted on December 13, 2023, and came into force on January 11, 2024, following its publication in the *Official Journal of the European Union*.[48]

---

40 *Id.* art. 52, 74.

41 *Id.* art. 52.

42 *Id.* art. 74.

43 European Commission Press Release, Commission opens formal proceedings against X under the Digital Services Act (Dec. 18, 2023), https://ec.europa.eu/commission/presscorner/api/files/document/print/en/ip_23_6709/IP_23_6709_EN.pdf.

44 European Commission Press Release, Commission Opens Formal Proceedings against TikTok under the Digital Services Act (Feb. 19, 2024), https://ec.europa.eu/commission/presscorner/api/files/document/print/en/ip_24_926/IP_24_926_EN.pdf.

45 European Commission Press Release, Commission Opens Formal Proceedings against AliExpress under the Digital Services Act (Mar. 14, 2024), https://ec.europa.eu/commission/presscorner/api/files/document/print/en/ip_24_1485/IP_24_1485_EN.pdf.

46 European Commission Press Release, Commission Opens Formal Proceedings against Temu under the Digital Services Act (Oct. 31, 2024), https://ec.europa.eu/commission/presscorner/detail/en/ip_24_5622.

47 DSA, *supra* note 9, art. 54.

48 Regulation (EU) 2023/2854 of the European Parliament and of the Council of December 13, 2023, on harmonized rules on fair access to and use of data and amending Regulation (EU) 2017/2394 and Directive (EU) 2020/1828 (Data Act), 2023 O.J. (L 2023/2854), 1 [hereinafter Data Act].

The Data Act aims not just to protect data but also to ensure and promote its accessibility and interoperability. It covers personal and nonpersonal data relating to connected products' performance, usage, and environment.[49] However, the processing of personal data will continue to require compliance with the GDPR.[50]

The Data Act will apply generally from September 12, 2025, although the specific provisions[51] for connected products and related services will not apply until September 12, 2026, and for unfair contractual terms[52] until September 12, 2027. The Data Act applies to manufacturers of connected products sold in the EU and providers of related services, irrespective of their place of establishment.

Most importantly for businesses, manufacturers of connected products can only use any data they obtain from a connected device (such as an Internet of Things [IoT] device or connected vehicle) based on a contractual agreement with the user. It remains to be seen how such an agreement will be evidenced, given the reluctance of the European Court of Justice to accept that consumers, in particular, can be bound by a standard form of contract which they could not influence. How such an obligation can be imposed and enforced against an enterprise outside the EU also remains to be seen.

The Data Act introduces several new actors in relation to the processing of data. In addition to the controllers and processors mentioned in the GDPR, we now have the addition of data holders and data recipients.

A data holder is a natural or legal person that has the right or obligation, under the Data Act,[53] applicable Union law, or national legislation adopted under Union law, to use and make available data, including, where contractually agreed, product data or related service data which it has retrieved or generated during the provision of a related service.

A data recipient is a natural or legal person acting for purposes, which are related to that person's trade, business, craft, or profession, other than the user of a connected product or related service to whom the data holder makes data available, including a third party following a request by the user to the data holder or under a legal obligation under Union law or national legislation adopted per Union law.[54]

Here are some of the key provisions of the Data Act:

Data-driven technologies: The Data Act acknowledges the transformative effects of data-driven technologies on all sectors of the economy. It recognizes the increased volume and

---

[49] Defined as an item that obtains, generates, or collects data concerning its use or environment and that is able to communicate product data via an electronic communications service, physical connection or on-device access, and whose primary function is not the storing, processing, or transmission of data on behalf of any party other than the user.
Id. art. 2(5). This would include, but not be limited to, IOT devices, connected vehicles, and fitness trackers.

[50] GDPR, *supra* note 2.

[51] Data Act, *supra* note 48 art. 3(1).

[52] *Id.* art. 13.

[53] *Id.* art. 2(13).

[54] *Id.* art. 2(14).

potential value of data for consumers, businesses, and society due to the proliferation of internet-connected products.

Before a user enters into a contract for a connected product, or a related service, the seller/rentor/lessor/provider (who may be the manufacturer) must provide clear information about the type, format, volume, and manner of data generation; whether the generation is continuous or real-time, storage capabilities on the device or a remote server (including where applicable the intended duration or retention); and intended access by third parties. The user must also be given information about how to access, retrieve, or, where relevant, erase the data.[55]

Barriers to data sharing: The Data Act identifies obstacles to data sharing that prevent optimal data allocation for societal benefit. These barriers include a lack of incentives for data holders to enter voluntarily into data-sharing agreements, uncertainty about rights and obligations concerning data, costs of contracting and implementing technical interfaces, high level of fragmentation of information in data silos, poor metadata management, absence of standards for semantic and technical interoperability, bottlenecks impeding data access, lack of common data-sharing practices, and abuse of contractual imbalances concerning data access and use. The Data Act seeks to eliminate or, at least, minimize these barriers.

Data holders are entitled to receive compensation for making data available in business-to-business relationships, and such compensation is required to be nondiscriminatory and reasonable. It may include a margin,[56] considering costs and investment in making the data available and in its collection and production. For stand-alone data recipients, which are SMEs or not-for-profit research organizations, only direct costs of making data available may be recovered. The Commission is to adopt guidelines[57] on calculating such reasonable compensation, but these are not yet available.

SMEs and data access: The Data Act notes that in sectors characterized by the presence of microenterprises and SMEs, there is often a lack of digital capacities and skills to collect, analyze, and use data. Access is frequently restricted where one actor holds them in the system or due to a lack of interoperability between data, between data services, or across borders. Many obligations on data sharing concerning connected products and related services will not apply to microenterprises and small enterprises, provided they are not linked to larger enterprises.[58] The Data Act facilitates switching between cloud service providers to promote consumer choice and competition.

Harmonized framework: The Data Act aims to lay down a harmonized framework specifying who is entitled to use product or related service data, under which conditions, and on what basis. The Data Act also seeks to improve data interoperability[59] and remove obstacles to switching between data processing services. Unfair contract terms and switching fees are to be removed.

---

55 *Id.* arts. 3(2), 3(3).
56 *Id.* art. 9.
57 *Id.* art. 9(5).
58 *Id.* art. 7.
59 *Id.* art. 35.

The Data Act also provides that any "unfair contractual term" unilaterally imposed by an enterprise on another enterprise shall not be binding.[60] While the Data Act gives some examples of what it considers to be "unfair," it also includes a general statement that "A contractual term is unfair if it is of such a nature that its use grossly deviates from good commercial practice in data access and use, contrary to good faith and fair dealing."[61] Presumably, it will be for the courts to decide what that means in practice.

Dispute settlement: The Data Act envisages some form of dispute resolution body, which will be certified by the Member States, to settle disputes about a Data Holder's decision to refuse, withhold, or suspend data sharing or impose conditions for such sharing.[62] As of today's date, no such body has been certified.

14.1.5. Digital Markets

14.1.5.1. Digital Markets Act

The EU Digital Markets Act (DMA)[63]—Regulation (EU) 2022/1925—was enacted on September 14, 2022, and came into force in November 2022, following its publication in the *Official Journal of the European Union*. It applies from May 2, 2023. It applies to all platforms, which have a significant impact on the European digital market, irrespective of their place of establishment.

The DMA aims to ensure fair and open digital markets. It primarily targets large online platforms, called "gatekeepers," whose activities significantly impact the market.[64]

Although the DMA is included in the EU's data package, it has as much to do with antitrust as it does with data. The EU has decided that the market power of the gatekeepers in the digital space is so great that, without reaching the levels at which it could necessarily be regulated successfully under the provisions of Article 102 of the Treaty on the Functioning of the EU[65]—abuse of a dominant position—the designated gatekeepers need to be subject to additional controls. The EU is moving from an *ex post facto* regulation system to one of *ex-ante* control.

---

60 *Id.* art. 13.

61 *Id.* art. 13(3).

62 *Id.* art. 10.

63 Regulation (EU) 2022/1925 of the European Parliament and of the Council of September 14, 2022, on contestable and fair markets in the digital sector and amending Directives (EU) 2019/1937 and (EU) 2020/1828 (Digital Markets Act), 2022 O.J. (L 265), 1 [hereinafter DMA].

64 *Id.* recital 1.

65 Any abuse by one or more undertakings of a dominant position within the internal market or in a substantial part of it shall be prohibited as incompatible with the internal market insofar as it may affect trade between Member States.

Such abuse may, in particular, consist in:

(a) directly or indirectly imposing unfair purchase or selling prices or other unfair trading conditions;
(b) limiting production, markets, or technical development to the prejudice of consumers;
(c) applying dissimilar conditions to equivalent transactions with other trading parties, thereby placing them at a competitive disadvantage;
(d) making the conclusion of contracts subject to acceptance by the other parties of supplementary obligations which, by their nature or according to commercial usage, have no connection with the subject of such contracts.

Consolidated Version of the Treaty on the Functioning of the European Union, art. 102, May 9, 2008, 2008 O.J. (C 115) 47, 89 [hereinafter TFEU].

Within the DMA, the obligations incumbent on gatekeepers and the related prohibitions are set out clearly so that the gatekeepers (whose designation as such will have been set out in advance) are given greater legal certainty as to what is not permitted. This is in accordance with the EU's general approach to antitrust; EU antitrust seeks to protect consumer and competitor competition by aiming to facilitate an environment where competition can thrive and consumers benefit.

Here are some of the key provisions of the DMA:

Definition of gatekeepers: The DMA establishes a set of narrowly defined objective criteria for qualifying a large online platform as a "gatekeeper."

A gatekeeper is an undertaking providing core platform services, which has been designated according to the criteria set out in Article 3.[66]

An undertaking is to be designated under Article 3(1) of the DMA as a gatekeeper if:

(a) it has a significant impact on the internal market;

(b) it provides a core platform service, which is an important means for business users to reach end users; and

(c) it enjoys an entrenched and durable position in its operations, or it is foreseeable that it will enjoy such a position in the near future.[67]

An undertaking shall be presumed to satisfy the respective requirements in Article 3(1):

(a) as regards paragraph 1, point (a) *[significant impact]*, where it achieves an annual Union turnover equal to or above EUR 7.5 billion in each of the three previous financial years, or where its average market capitalization or its equivalent fair market value amounted to at least EUR 75 billion in the previous financial year, and it provides the same core platform service in at least three Member States;

(b) as regards paragraph 1, point (b), *[important gateway for business users]* where it provides a core platform service that in the previous financial year has at least 45 million monthly active end users established or located in the Union and at least 10,000 yearly active business users established in the Union;

(c) as regards paragraph 1, point (c), *[entrenched and durable position]*, where the thresholds in point (b) of this paragraph were met in each of the last three financial years.[68]

Where an undertaking meets the requirements of Article 3, it must advise the Commission of this fact and of the core platform services it provides within two months of meeting the criteria,[69] and the Commission has then to designate such an enterprise as a gatekeeper

---

66 DMA, *supra* note 63, art. 2(1).
67 DMA, *supra* note 63, art. 3(1).
68 *Id.* art. 3(2).
69 *Id.* art. 3(3).

within forty-five working days.[70] In addition to those core platform services which were notified, the Commission has opened a market investigation to assess further whether Apple should be designated as a gatekeeper in relation to iPadOS.[71]

An undertaking can provide sufficiently substantiated information to the Commission to show why, although it meets the thresholds of Article 3(2), it should not be designated as a gatekeeper regarding a particular core platform service under Article 3(1).[72]

Where insufficient evidence is produced or the evidence is not accepted, the provisions of Articles 3(5) and 17(3) apply, which may involve a market analysis in the case of the latter.[73]

By the initial notification deadline of July 4, 2023, the Commission had received notifications from seven technology companies and, subsequently, the Commission designated six gatekeepers[74] (Alphabet,[75] Amazon,[76] Apple,[77] ByteDance,[78] Meta,[79] and Microsoft[80])—the seventh original notification was from Samsung—and twenty-two core

---

[70] *Id.* art. 3(4).

[71] Summary of Commission Decision of April 29, 2024, relating to a decision pursuant to Article 17 of Regulation (EU) 2022|1925 (Case DMA.100047—Apple—iPadOS), 2024 O.J. (C. 437), 1.

[72] DMA, *supra* note 63, art. 3(5); the Commission opened four market investigations to further assess Microsoft's and Apple's submissions, arguing that, despite meeting the thresholds, some of their core platform services do not qualify as gateways:

Microsoft: Bing, Edge, and Microsoft Advertising.
Apple: iMessage.

On February 7, 2024, the Commission accepted the parties' submissions that iMessage, Bing, Edge, and Microsoft Advertising were not gateways to reach end users and were therefore not included in the DMA as gatekeeper services.

[73] The Commission has concluded that, although Gmail, Outlook.com, and Samsung Internet Browser meet the thresholds under the DMA to qualify as a gatekeeper, Alphabet, Microsoft, and Samsung provided sufficiently justified arguments showing that these services do not qualify as gateways for the respective core platform services. Therefore, the Commission decided not to designate Gmail, Outlook.com, and Samsung Internet Browser as core platform services. *See* European Commission Press Release, Digital Markets Act: Commission designates six gatekeepers (Sept. 6, 2023), https://ec.europa.eu/commission/presscorner/api/files/document/print/en/ip_23_4328/IP_23_4328_EN.pdf.

[74] European Commission, *Commission designated six gatekeepers under the Digital Markets Act*, Eur. Comm'n (Sept. 6, 2023), https://digital-markets-act.ec.europa.eu/commission-designates-six-gatekeepers-under-digital-markets-act-2023-09-06_en; on March 1, 2024, the European Commission advised that it had received notifications from Booking, ByteDance, and X, about their services potentially meeting the DMA thresholds, which could make them subject to the EU rules on gatekeeper platforms.

[75] Summary of Commission Decision of September 5, 2023, Relating to a Decision Pursuant to Article 3 of Regulation (EU) 2022/1925, 2023 O.J. (C 549).

[76] Commission Decision of September 5, 2023, Designating Amazon as a Gatekeeper Pursuant to Article 3 of Regulation (EU) 2022/1925 of the European Parliament and of the Council on Contestable and Fair Markets in the Digital Sector, 2023 O.J. (C 6104).

[77] Summary of Commission Decision of September 5, 2023, Designating Apple as a Gatekeeper Pursuant to Article 3 of Regulation (EU) 2022/1925 of the European Parliament and of the Council on Contestable and Fair Markets in the Digital Sector, 2023 O.J. (C 548).

[78] Commission Decision of September 5, 2023, Designating ByteDance as a Gatekeeper Pursuant to Article 3 of Regulation (EU) 2022/1925 of the European Parliament and of the Council on Contestable and Fair Markets in the Digital Sector, 2023 O.J. (C 549).

[79] Summary of Commission Decision of September 5, 2023, Relating to a Decision Pursuant to Article 3 of Regulation (EU) 2022|1925, 2023 O.J. (C 1092).

[80] Commission Decision of September 5, 2023, Designating Microsoft as a Gatekeeper Pursuant to Article 3 of Regulation (EU) 2022/1925 of the European Parliament and of the Council on Contestable and Fair Markets in the Digital Sector, 2023 O.J. (C 6106).

platform services.[81] Booking.com was designated as a gatekeeper in May 2024[82] and also in that month, the Commission opened a market investigation into X,[83] but decided in October that the online social networking service of X should not be designated under the DMA.[84]

Initial Designations by the Commission

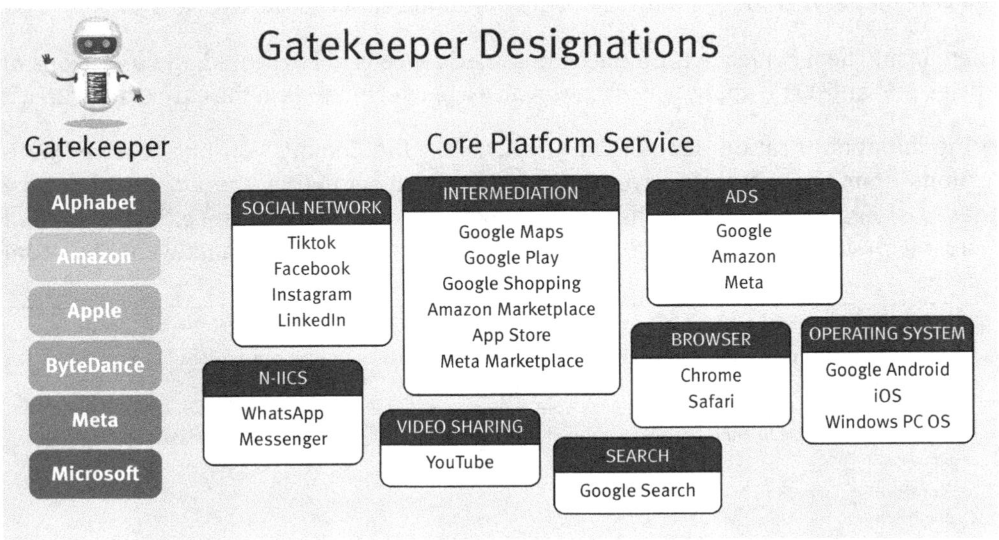

Undertakings had until March 2024 to comply with their obligations under the DMA[85] and produce a compliance report to that effect.[86]

Appeals against the Commission Decisions designating the undertaking as a gatekeeper have been lodged with the General Court by Apple, Meta (regarding Messenger and Marketplace services), TikTok, and Microsoft. On February 7, 2024, the Commission accepted the parties' submissions that iMessage, Bing, Edge, and Microsoft Advertising were not gateways to reach end users and were, therefore, not included in the DMA as gatekeeper services.

On November 22, 2023, Microsoft announced it was testing Windows updates to comply with the DMA.[87]

---

[81] Image from European Commission, *Digital Markets Act: Commission Designated Six Gatekeepers under the Digital Markets Act* , Eur. Comm'n (Sept. 5, 2023), https://ec.europa.eu/commission/presscorner/detail/en/ip_23_4328.

[82] European Commission Press Release, *Commission Designates Booking as a Gatekeeper and Opens a Market Investigation into X*, https://ec.europa.eu/commission/presscorner/detail/en/ip_24_2561.

[83] European Commission Press Release, *Decision to Open a Market Investigation Based on Art.3(8) and Art.17(1)*, https://ec.europa.eu/commission/presscorner/detail/en/ip_24_2561.

[84] European Commission Press Release, *Commission Concludes that Online Social Networking Service of X Should Not Be Designated under the Digital Markets Act*, https://ec.europa.eu/commission/presscorner/detail/en/mex_24_5324.

[85] *See* DMA, *supra* note 63, art. 11(1).

[86] Initial Compliance Reports have been made by all six gatekeepers. *Compliance Reports*, Eur. Comm'n https://digital-markets-act-cases.ec.europa.eu/reports/compliance-reports (last visited Oct. 23, 2024).

[87] Rima Alaily & Nanna-Louise Linde, *Microsoft Testing Windows Updates to Comply with the DMA and Beyond*, MICROSOFT (Nov. 22, 2023), https://blogs.microsoft.com/eupolicy/2023/11/22/windows-updates-comply-dma-edge/.

On January 25, 2024, Apple announced changes to iOS, Safari, and the App Store concerning developers' apps in the EU to comply with the DMA.[88] However, on June 24, 2024, the Commission sent its preliminary findings to Apple with respect to the App Store and opened an additional noncompliance investigation under the DMA.[89]

On July 1, 2024, the Commission sent its preliminary findings to Meta over its "Pay or Consent" model for breach of the DMA.[90] The Commission took the preliminary view that Meta's "pay or consent" advertising model is not compliant with the DMA as it does not meet the necessary requirements set out under Article 5(2). In particular, Meta's model:

- Did not allow users to opt for a service that uses less of their personal data but is otherwise equivalent to the "personalized ads"-based service, and
- Did not allow users to exercise their right to consent freely to the combination of their personal data.

On September 19, 2024, the Commission started its first proceedings to specify Apple's interoperability obligations under the DMA.[91]

Benefits of the DMA: The DMA aims to create a fairer business environment for business users who depend on gatekeepers. It also seeks to provide new opportunities for innovators and technology startups, more and better consumer services, and fairer prices.[92]

Obligations for gatekeepers: The DMA establishes obligations for gatekeepers to comply with in their daily operations. These obligations are designed to ensure that gatekeepers operate in a way that is fair, transparent, and beneficial to consumers and businesses. Article 5 of the DMA[93] is captioned "Obligations for gatekeepers," but other than a general statement in Article 5(1) requiring the gatekeeper to comply with the obligations in Article 5, most of that Article is, in fact, things that the gatekeeper must not do. These prohibitions are discussed below. There are, however, several positive obligations as follows:

1. **Fair Practices:** The DMA aims to prevent unfair practices by companies providing core platform services.
   i. The gatekeeper must allow business users, free of charge, to communicate and promote offers, including under different conditions, to end users acquired via its core platform service or through other channels and to conclude contracts with

---

[88] Press Release, Apple, *Apple Announces Changes to iOS, Safari, and the App Store in the European Union* (Jan. 25, 2024), https://www.apple.com/newsroom/2024/01/apple-announces-changes-to-ios-safari-and-the-app-store-in-the-european-union/.

[89] *Case DMA. 100206—Apple—New Business Terms. Commission Decision Opening a Proceeding Pursuant to Article 20(1) of Regulation (EU) 2022/1925 (1) of the European Parliament and of the Council on Contestable and Fair Markets in the Digital Sector.* https://ec.europa.eu/competition/digital_markets_act/cases/202431/DMA_100206_50.pdf.

[90] European Commission Press Release, Meta "Pay or Consent," https://ec.europa.eu/commission/presscorner/detail/en/ip_24_3582.

[91] *CASE DMA.100203—Apple—Operating systems—iOS—Article 6(7)—SP—Features for Connected Physical Devices*, https://ec.europa.eu/competition/digital_markets_act/cases/202440/DMA_100203_76.pdf.

[92] DMA, *supra* note 63, recital 25.

[93] *Id.* art. 5.

those end users, regardless of whether, for that purpose, they use the core platform services of the gatekeeper.[94]

ii. The gatekeeper must allow end users to access and use, through its core platform services, content, subscriptions, features, or other items, by using the software application of a business user, including where those end users acquired such items from the relevant business user without using the core platform services of the gatekeeper.[95]

iii. The gatekeeper must provide each advertiser to which it supplies online advertising services or third parties authorized by advertisers, upon the advertiser's request, with information daily, free of charge, concerning each advertisement placed by the advertiser regarding:

(a) the price and fees paid by that advertiser, including any deductions and surcharges, for each of the relevant online advertising services provided by the gatekeeper;

(b) the remuneration received by the publisher, including any deductions and surcharges, subject to the publisher's consent; and

(c) the metrics on which each price, fee, and remuneration are calculated.

iv. The gatekeeper must provide each publisher to which it supplies online advertising services, or third parties authorized by publishers, upon the publisher's request, with free-of-charge information daily concerning each advertisement displayed on the publisher's inventory regarding:

(a) the remuneration received and the fees paid by that publisher, including any deductions and surcharges, for each of the relevant online advertising services provided by the gatekeeper;

(b) the price paid by the advertiser, including any deductions and surcharges, subject to the advertiser's consent; and

(c) the metrics on which each of the prices and remunerations are calculated.

Article 6 of the DMA lists further obligations imposed on a gatekeeper, which relate primarily to using nonpublic data the gatekeeper may hold. In short, these prevent discrimination by the gatekeeper against third parties who do not have access to the specified data.[96]

2. **Interoperability:** Gatekeepers must allow third parties to interoperate with the gatekeeper's services in certain specific situations.[97]

3. **Data Access:** Gatekeepers must allow business users to access the data they generate using the gatekeeper's platform.[98]

---

94 *Id.* art. 5(4).
95 *Id.* art. 5(5).
96 *Id.* art. 6.
97 *See Id.* arts. 5(7), 6.
98 *See Id.* arts. 5, 6.

4. **Advertising Transparency:** Gatekeepers must provide companies advertising on their platform with the tools and information necessary for advertisers and publishers to verify independently their advertisements hosted by the gatekeeper.[99]

5. **Nondiscrimination:** Gatekeepers are prohibited from treating services and products offered by the gatekeeper itself more favorably in ranking than similar services or products offered by third parties on the gatekeeper's platform.[100]

These provisions allow third parties to interoperate with the gatekeeper's services in certain situations.[101]

6. **Prohibitions for Gatekeepers:** The DMA also establishes prohibitions for gatekeepers. For example, gatekeeper platforms may no longer treat services and products offered by the gatekeeper itself more favorably in ranking than similar services or products offered by third parties on the gatekeeper's platform.[102] Other prohibitions in Article 5(2) stipulate that the gatekeeper must not do any of the following:
   (a) process, for the purpose of providing online advertising services, personal data of end users using services of third parties that make use of core platform services of the gatekeeper;
   (b) combine personal data from the relevant core platform service with personal data from any further core platform services or from any other services provided by the gatekeeper or with personal data from third-party services;
   (c) cross-use personal data from the relevant core platform service in other services offered separately by the gatekeeper, including other core platform services, and vice versa; and
   (d) sign in end users to other services of the gatekeeper to combine personal data, unless the end user has been presented with the specific choice and consented.[103]

The gatekeeper must not prevent business users from offering the same products or services to end users through third-party online intermediation services or their own direct online sales channels and prices or conditions different from those offered through the gatekeeper's intermediation services.[104]

This is perceived as essential because it helps ensure that the digital market remains competitive, leading to better products and services for consumers.

---

99 *Id.* arts. 5(9), 5(10).

100 *Id.* arts. 6, 7.

101 *Id.* arts. 5, 6, 7.

102 *Id.* art. 5(3).

103 According to the GDPR, consent is defined as "Any freely given, specific, informed, and unambiguous indication of a data subject's wishes by which they, through a statement or clear affirmative action, signify agreement to the processing of personal data related to them." GDPR, *supra* note 2, art. 4.

104 DMA, *supra* note 63, art. 5(3).

14.1.5.2. Compliance Powers and Remedies under the DMA

Investigations: The Commission can conduct investigations into suspected infringements of the DMA.[105] It has broad powers to gather information, including performing inspections[106] and requesting information from gatekeepers and other relevant undertakings.[107] It may conduct interviews and take statements from any natural or legal person.[108]

On March 25, 2024, the Commission opened noncompliance investigations[109] against Alphabet,[110] Apple,[111] and Meta.[112] The Commission is also gathering information to clarify whether Amazon may be preferencing its own brand products in the Amazon Store in contravention of Article 6(5) and whether Apple's new fee structure and other terms and conditions for alternative app stores and distribution of apps from the web (sideloading) may be defeating the purpose of its obligations under Article 6(4).

Interim measures: The Commission can order interim measures to prevent imminent harm to consumers or to ensure the effectiveness of its investigation.[113] On March 25, 2024, the Commission adopted five retention orders addressed to Alphabet, Amazon, Apple, Meta, and Microsoft, asking them to retain documents, which might be used to assess their compliance with the DMA obligations so as to preserve available evidence and ensure effective enforcement.

Decisions: The Commission can adopt decisions prohibiting infringements of the DMA and imposing fines of up to 10 percent of the gatekeeper's total annual worldwide turnover in the preceding financial year, or up to €20 million, whichever is higher.[114] The Commission can accept commitments offered by a gatekeeper to ensure compliance with any obligations in the DMA where it considers this sufficient and the Commission is required[115] to monitor the effective implementation and compliance with the obligations in the DMA and any decision taken.

Each gatekeeper must have a separate compliance function independent from the gatekeeper's operational functions. The tasks of the head of such compliance function are set out in the DMA.[116]

---

105 *Id.* arts. 16–19.

106 *Id.* art. 23.

107 *Id.* arts. 21, 22

108 *Id.* art. 22.

109 European Commission Press Release, *Commission Opens Non-compliance Investigations against Alphabet, Apple and Meta under the Digital Markets Act* (Mar. 24, 2024), https://ec.europa.eu/commission/presscorner/detail/en/ip_24_1689.

110 For Alphabet's rules on steering in Google Play and self-preferencing on Google Search *contra* DMA, *supra* note 63, arts. 5(4), 6(5).

111 In relation to Apple's rules on steering in the App Store and the choice screen for Safari *contra Id.* arts. 5(4), 6(3).

112 In relation to Meta's "pay or consent" model *contra Id.* art. 5(2).

113 *Id.* art. 24.

114 *Id.* art. 30.

115 *Id.* art. 26.

116 *Id.* art. 28(5).

Structural remedies: The Commission can impose structural remedies, such as requiring the gatekeeper to divest certain assets or businesses[117] as are proportionate and necessary to ensure effective compliance with the DMA. The Commission may impose structural remedies where there is no equally effective behavioral remedy or where any equally effective behavioral remedy would be more burdensome for the gatekeeper concerned than the structural remedy.

Behavioral remedies: The Commission can impose behavioral remedies, requiring the gatekeeper to change its practices.[118]

Market investigations: The Commission can conduct market investigations to assess whether there are systemic competition problems in a particular digital market.

Chapter IV of the DMA[119] provides the mechanism for the conduct of market investigations, which the Commission is required to carry out before it takes a decision:

- For the purpose of examining whether an undertaking providing core platform services should be designated as a gatekeeper under Article 3(8) or to identify the core platform services to be listed in the designation decision under Article 3(9).[120]
- For the purpose of examining whether a gatekeeper has engaged in systematic noncompliance.[121]
- For the purpose of examining whether one or more services within the digital sector should be added to the list of core platform services laid down in Article 2(2) or for the purpose of detecting practices that limit the contestability of core platform services or that are unfair and which are not effectively addressed by [the DMA].[122]

Penalties: The Commission can adopt decisions prohibiting infringements of the DMA and imposing fines.[123] The DMA also allows for the imposition of periodic penalty payments, not exceeding 5 percent of the average daily worldwide turnover in the preceding financial year per day, to compel the gatekeeper to comply with its various obligations under the DMA as set out in that Article.[124]

There is a five-year-limitation period for action by the Commission.

National enforcement authorities: National enforcement authorities have concurrent powers to enforce the DMA,[125] and national courts may ask the Commission for information in its possession where there are national proceedings for applying the DMA.

---

[117] *Id.* art. 18(1).
[118] *Id.* art. 18(1).
[119] *Id.* arts. 16–19.
[120] *Id.* art. 17.
[121] *Id.* art. 18.
[122] *Id.* art. 19.
[123] *Id.* art. 30.
[124] *Id.* art. 31.
[125] *Id.* arts. 37, 41.

14.1.6. Data Governance

14.1.6.1. Data Governance Act

The EU Data Governance Act (DGA) Regulation (EU) 2022/868[126]—was enacted on May 30, 2022, amending the earlier Regulation (EU) 2018/1724[127] and came into force on June 23, 2022, following its publication in the Official Journal of the European Union and applied from September 24, 2023.

The DGA is a legislative framework at the Union level that facilitates the reuse of public-sector data and establishes a single Union-wide market for providing data mediation services and processing data for altruistic purposes. Key aspects of the DGA include:

Increasing trust in data sharing: The DGA seeks to strengthen mechanisms to increase data availability and overcome technical obstacles to the reuse of data. The DGA sets conditions for the wider use/reuse of public-sector data, even if it is protected by commercial confidentiality, intellectual property, or privacy laws.

The DGA provides a framework to enhance trust in voluntary data sharing. It regulates the reuse of publicly held, protected data; boosts data sharing by regulating data intermediaries; and encourages data sharing for altruistic purposes. The DGA contains rules on these intermediaries' establishment, supervision, and practices, including neutrality and transparency.[128] Data intermediaries are not permitted to make money from data transfers, and the overriding aim seems to be to counter the power of very large technology platforms with a preeminent market position due to the volume of data they hold.

Data intermediaries must be independent, and if they provide other services, the data intermediation services must be strictly segregated legally and economically from the other services.[129] Data intermediaries have to comply with notification requirements and notify their intention to provide data intermediation services to the competent authority designated by each Member State to carry out the tasks related to the notification framework[130]; the principal task is to make sure that the service is nondiscriminatory and does not distort competition.

Personal and nonpersonal data are within the scope of the DGA, although the GDPR applies wherever personal data are concerned.[131]

The DGA includes provisions to make it easier for citizens and undertakings to make their data available for the good of society. The rules for such data altruism are complex and

[126] Regulation (EU) 2022/868 of the European Parliament and of the Council of May 30, 2022, on European data governance and amending Regulation (EU) 2018/1724 (Data Governance Act), 2022 O.J. (L 152), 1. [hereinafter DGA].

[127] Regulation (EU) 2018/1724 of the European Parliament and of the Council of October 2, 2018, establishing a single digital gateway to provide access to information, to procedures, and to assistance and problem-solving services and amending Regulation (EU) No 1024/2012, 2018 O.J. (L 295), 1.

[128] DGA, *supra* note 126, recitals 2, 33.

[129] *Id.* art. 18(c).

[130] *Id.* recital 38.

[131] GDPR, *supra* note 2.

include requirements for registering such undertakings, which must be nonprofit and meet transparency requirements.[132]

Establishment of common European data spaces: The DGA supports the setup and development of common European data spaces. European data spaces are part of the European strategy for data, which aims to create a single market for data that ensures Europe's global competitiveness and data sovereignty. They are data infrastructures and governance frameworks, which facilitate data pooling and sharing.

The vision is to establish common European data spaces in all strategic societal sectors and domains of public interest.[133] These data spaces are envisioned as sovereign, trustworthy, and interoperable data-sharing environments where data can flow within and across sectors while respecting the rights and control of the companies and individuals who generate the data.

As for its data strategy in 2020,[134] the European Commission announced ten common data spaces in sectors and domains of public interest, and more have been added since, bringing the current number to a total of fourteen. These include areas such as agriculture, cultural heritage, energy, finance, health,[135] manufacturing, media, mobility, research and innovation, public administration, skills, and tourism.

The EU is funding several initiatives related to common European data spaces for sector and domain-specific initiatives, such as the Data Spaces Support Centre and Smart Open-source Middleware (SIMPL) under the Digital Europe program and Horizon Europe. The goal is to make more data available for use in the economy and society while keeping the companies and individuals who generate the data in control.

The DGA does not make clear the circumstances in which it might apply to organizations outside the EU. However, some of its provisions and recitals indicate that it is intended to have extraterritorial application. In particular, any business not established in the EU but that offers services within the EU and meets the requirements to qualify as a data altruism organization or a data intermediary under the DGA will require to appoint a legal representative in one of the Member States in which it offers services.[136]

As provided by the DGA,[137] the European Commission established the European Data Innovation Board[138] to facilitate the sharing of best practices, in particular on data

---

[132] *See infra* Section 14.1.6.2.

[133] DGA, *supra* note 126, art. 11.

[134] *European Data Strategy*, Eur. Comm'n, https://commission.europa.eu/strategy-and-policy/priorities-2019-2024/-europe-fit-digital-age/european-data-strategy_en (last visited Oct. 24, 2024).

[135] A provisional deal was reached between the Council and the European Parliament on March 15, 2024. Council of the EU Press Release, European Health Data Space: Council and Parliament Strike Deal, https://www.consilium.europa.eu/en/press/press-releases/2024/03/15/european-health-data-space-council-and-parliament-strike-provisional-deal/ (last updated Mar. 22, 2024).

[136] DGA, *supra* note 126, art. 37(11).

[137] *Id.* recital 53, ch. VI.

[138] *Register of Commission Expert Groups and Other Similar Entities: European Dara Innovation Board (E03903)*, Eur. Comm'n, https://ec.europa.eu/transparency/expert-groups-register/screen/expert-groups/consult?lang=en&groupID=3903 (Oct. 10, 2024).

intermediation, data altruism, and the use of public data that cannot be made available as open data as well as prioritization of cross-sectoral interoperability standards.

Benefits for EU citizens and businesses: The DGA aims to make more data available and facilitate data sharing across sectors and EU countries to leverage the potential of data for the benefit of European citizens and businesses. The DGA provides for rules and safeguards to facilitate the reuse of public-sector data and imposes several preconditions to enable this.

- Member States will need to be technically equipped to ensure that the privacy and confidentiality of data are respected in use, whether by technical means (anonymization, pseudonymization, or secure processing environments such as access through data rooms or contractual solutions such as confidentiality agreements with the reuser).[139]
- If the public-sector body cannot grant access for reuse, it is to assist the potential reuser in seeking the individual's consent to such reuse.[140]
- The DGA limits reliance on exclusive data reuse agreements, which, while possibly making more data available for reuse, may also restrict its value.[141]
- The only fees the public-sector body may charge for reuse are those that do not exceed the costs incurred. The DGA does not indicate how these "costs" should be calculated.[142]

Decisions on data reuse must be taken within two months of request.[143]

To help potential reusers find relevant information on what data is held by which public-sector authorities, Member States must set up a single information point, and a list of national single information points has been established.[144]

Development of trustworthy data-sharing systems: The EU aims to boost the development of these systems through measures such as facilitating the reuse of certain public-sector data that cannot be made available as open data.

Data transfers to third countries: For personal data, the GDPR[145] will apply to any such transfers. For other protected data categories, the DGA introduces provisions to safeguard

---

139 DGA, *supra* note 126, art. 7(4)(c).

140 *Id.* art. 7(4)(d).

141 *Id.* art. 4.

142 *Id.* art. 6.

143 *Id.* art. 9.

144 The European Register for Protected Data (ERPD) held by the public sector provides relevant information on what data are held by public authorities in the Member States, according to Art. 8.2 of the DGA. Any user, such as citizens, entrepreneurs, or researchers, can therefore search for and find information about public-sector data in the EU Member States, including information on protected data that cannot be made available under the general open data rules (e.g., health or mobility data). *European Data*, Eur. Union, https://data.europa.eu/data/datasets?superCatalogue=erpd&locale=en (last visited Oct. 24, 2024).

145 GDPR, *supra* note 2.

data flow to third countries,[146] including the Commission's ability to adopt delegated legislation setting out the criteria for such transfers, any limitations on use, and other similar aspects. These criteria may include restrictions on reusing such transferred data in the third countries and who may make such transfers. The DGA also requires that a natural or legal person who is reusing data under the DGA must, at the time of requesting the reuse of the data, inform the public-sector body from which he seeks to obtain the data of the intention to transfer the data and the purpose of the transfer.[147]

The public-sector body may only transfer confidential nonpersonal data or data protected by intellectual property rights to a reuser intending to transfer the data to a third country if the reuser contractually commits to complying with certain obligations and accepts the jurisdiction of the courts of the Member State in which the transferring public-sector body is located or if the EU has declared that the relevant third country ensures protection of trade secrets and intellectual property in a way that is essentially equivalent to that in the EU, has legal or other enforcement arrangements to ensure that such protections are effectively applied and protected, and provides judicial redress.[148] This seems to be an adequacy, separate, and distinct from the adequacy requirements of the GDPR.[149]

In terms of the DGA, some entities cannot be considered data services providers under the Regulation:

- Cloud service providers;
- Data brokers;
- Social network companies, search engines, and other entities with services that focus on the intermediation of content;
- Data exchange platforms;
- IoT platforms;
- Data-sharing services meant to be used by a closed group of data holders and users.

Non-EU entities must register with a regulatory authority and put their data-sharing services in a separate legal entity.[150]

14.1.6.2. Data Altruism under the DGA

Data altruism is about individuals and companies giving their consent or permission to make available data that they generate—voluntarily and without reward—to be used in the public interest. The DGA provides several trusted tools that will allow data to be shared easily for the benefit of society.

---

[146] DGA, *supra* note 126, recital 101, arts. 28, 32.
[147] *Id.* art. 5(9).
[148] *Id.* art. 5(10).
[149] GDPR, *supra* note 2.
[150] DGA, *supra* note 126, art. 14(5).

Entities which make available relevant data based on data altruism will be able to register as "data altruism organizations recognized in the Union."[151] These entities must have a not-for-profit character, meet transparency requirements, and offer specific safeguards to protect the rights and interests of citizens and companies who share their data. In addition, they must comply with the rulebook (at the latest eighteen months after it comes into force), which will lay down information requirements, technical and security requirements, communication roadmaps, and recommendations on interoperability standards. The Commission is developing the rulebook in close cooperation with data altruism organizations and other relevant stakeholders.[152]

Data altruism organizations will be able to use a common logo[153] and may choose to be included in the public register of data altruism organizations.[154] As of April 7, 2025, that register had one entry.

14.1.7. Cybersecurity

14.1.7.1. NIS Directive and NIS2 Directive

In July 2016, the Directive on the Security of Network and Information Systems[155]—Directive (EU) 2016/1148—(NIS Directive) entered into force. This Directive was an EU-wide cybersecurity-related legislation established to increase cyber resilience across the whole EU through specific regulatory measures. More specifically, the Directive strengthened the cybersecurity capabilities on a national level, enhanced collaboration between states, and implemented cybersecurity in the organization by default.

On January 16, 2023, the NIS2 Directive[156] entered into force. This is a successor to the NIS Directive. The objective of the NIS2 Directive is to boost cybersecurity in the EU, keep up with evolving digitalization, and address the threats posed on the cybersecurity landscape more effectively.

The NIS2 Directive aims to establish a high common level of cybersecurity throughout the EU.

It builds upon the foundation laid by the NIS Directive, which focused on cybersecurity capabilities, threat mitigation, and continuity of essential services. The NIS2 Directive extends its reach to various sectors, including energy, transportation, health, and digital

---

151 *Id.* art. 17.

152 *Id.* recitals 46, 58, art. 22.

153 *Logos for Data Intermediaries and data Altruism Organisations Recognised in the Union*, Eur. Comm'n, https://digital-strategy.ec.europa.eu/en/library/logos-data-intermediaries-and-data-altruism-organisations-recognised-union (Jan. 10, 2024).

154 *EU Register of Recognized Data Altruism Organisations*, Eur. Comm'n, https://digital-strategy.ec.europa.eu/en/policies/data-altruism-organisations (Oct. 23, 2024).

155 Directive (EU) 2016/1148 of the European Parliament and of the Council of July 6, 2016, concerning measures for a high common level of security of network and information systems across the Union (2016), O.J. (L 194), 1.

156 Directive (EU) 2022/2555 of the European Parliament and of the Council of December 14, 2022, on measures for a high common level of cybersecurity across the Union, amending Regulation (EU) No 910/2014 and Directive (EU) 2018/1972, and repealing Directive (EU) 2016/1148 (NIS2 Directive), 2022 O.J. (L 333), 80.

infrastructure. Organizations within the EU are subject to stricter requirements for risk management. This includes measures to prevent, detect, and respond to cybersecurity incidents. The Directive mandates timely reporting of cyber incidents to relevant authorities. The NIS2 Directive establishes mechanisms for effective cooperation across EU member states. It creates the Cyber Crisis Management Structure (CyCLONe), enhancing the Union's ability to respond to cyber threats.

Member States have until October 17, 2024, to adopt and publish the measures to comply with and transpose the NIS2 Directive. The measures must be applied by October 18, 2024, and the NIS Directive will be repealed on the same day.

NIS2 applies to all operators of essential and important services in the relevant sectors, irrespective of their place of establishment.

14.1.7.2. The Digital Operational Resilience Act

The Digital Operational Resilience Act (DORA)—Regulation 2022/2554[157]—is legislation for the financial sector within the EU, aiming to bolster the information and communication technology (ICT) security of financial entities.

The Regulation aims to enhance financial entities' digital resilience within the EU. It recognizes the critical role of ICT in financial services and the need to address ICT risks effectively.

The Regulation covers various financial activities, including payments, securities clearing, algorithmic trading, lending, and insurance. It applies both to financial institutions in the EU and other financial entities which provide services in the EU, irrespective of their place of establishment.

It emphasizes the importance of digital resilience in maintaining financial stability.

DORA establishes a robust governance framework that necessitates the implementation of an ICT risk management framework within financial entities. Monitoring third-party risk providers is a critical component of DORA. Businesses must ensure that key contractual provisions are in place to maintain oversight and control over third-party providers, especially those deemed critical. There will be significant penalties for noncompliance with the requirements of DORA.

The oversight framework for critical ICT third-party providers requires financial entities to manage and monitor these relationships diligently, ensuring that the risks associated with outsourcing are mitigated. DORA mandates both basic and advanced digital operational resilience testing. DORA sets out general requirements for ICT-related incident management, including establishing a clear process for classifying and reporting major incidents to competent authorities.

---

157 Regulation (EU) 2022/2554 of the European Parliament and of the Council of December 14, 2022, on digital operational resilience for the financial sector and amending Regulations (EC) No 1060/2009, (EU) No 648/2012, (EU) No 600/2014, (EU) No 909/2014, and (EU) No 2016/1011, 2022 O.J. (L 333), 1.

Finally, DORA encourages the exchange of information and intelligence on cyber threats within the financial sector.

DORA applied from January 17, 2025.

14.1.7.3. Cyber Resilience Act

On October 23, 2024, the Cyber Resilience Act (CRA) was adopted and is set to take effect on December 11, 2027.[158]

The CRA seeks to address existing regulatory gaps in cybersecurity and bolster the security of products with digital elements (such as connected devices and software) throughout their life cycle.

It aims to protect consumers and businesses by ensuring that digital products meet adequate security standards.

Scope

- The CRA covers both tangible and nontangible digital products.
- Tangible digital products include connected devices (like IoT devices), while nontangible ones include software embedded into connected devices.
- The Regulation applies to products directly or indirectly connected to other devices or networks, except for specified exclusions (e.g., open-source software, medical devices, aviation, and cars).

Mandatory cybersecurity requirements

- Manufacturers and retailers of digital products must adhere to mandatory cybersecurity requirements.
- These requirements apply at every value chain stage, from planning and design to development and maintenance.
- The goal is to eliminate inadequate security features and ensure better protection for consumers and businesses.

CE marking: When the Regulation comes into force, digital products connected to the internet will bear the CE marking, indicating compliance with the new standards.

This empowers customers and businesses to make informed choices based on the cybersecurity credentials of CE-marked products.

The Council adopted the CRA on October 10, 2024, and it will enter into force on December 11, 2027.

---

[158] Regulation (EU) 2024/2847 of the European Parliament and of the Council of October 23, 2024, on horizontal cybersecurity requirements for products with digital elements and amending Regulations (EU) No 168/2013 and (EU) 2019/1020 and Directive (EU) 2020/1828 (Cyber Resilience Act), OJ L, 2024/2847, November 20, 2024.

Manufacturers will have thirty-six months after it enters into force to comply with the rules.

The CRA will apply to products with digital elements sold in the EU, irrespective of where the manufacturers are established or where the products are manufactured.

14.1.7.4. EU Cyber Solidarity Act

The EU Cyber Solidarity Act entered into force on February 4, 2025.[159]

The EU Cyber Solidarity Act will improve the preparedness, detection, and response to cybersecurity incidents across the EU.

The EU Cyber Solidarity Act aims to strengthen the EU's capacity to detect, prepare for, and respond to significant and large-scale cybersecurity threats and attacks. The Act includes a European Cybersecurity Alert System comprising Security Operation Centers interconnected across the EU and a comprehensive Cybersecurity Emergency Mechanism to improve the EU's cyber resilience.

14.1.8. Artificial Intelligence under the EU AI Act

The EU's Artificial Intelligence Act (AI Act)[160] is legislation aimed at regulating the development and use of artificial intelligence within the EU.

It will be fully applicable on August 2, 2026,[161] except bans on prohibited practices (which will apply from February 2, 2025); codes of practice (nine months after entry into force); general-purpose AI (GPAI) rules, including governance (August 2, 2025); and obligations for high-risk systems (August 2, 2027).

The AI Act applies[162] to:

(a) Providers placing on the market or putting into service AI systems or placing on the market general-purpose AI models in the Union, irrespective of whether those providers are established or who are located within the Union or in a third country;

(b) Deployers of AI systems that have their place of establishment or are located within the Union;

(c) Providers and deployers of AI systems that have their place of establishment or who are located in a third country, where the output produced by the system is used in the Union;

---

[159] Regulation (EU) 2025/38 of the European Parliament and of the Council of 19 December 2024 laying down measures to strengthen solidarity and capacities in the Union to detect, prepare for and respond to cyber threats and incidents and amending Regulation (EU) 2021/694 (Cyber Solidarity Act), 2025 O.J. L 038 15.1.2025, p. 1.

[160] Regulation (EU) 2024/1689 of The European Parliament and of the Council of June 13, 2024, Laying Down Harmonised Rules on Artificial Intelligence and Amending Regulations (EC) No 300/2008, (EU) No 167/2013, (EU) No 168/2013, (EU) No 2018/858, (EU) No 2018/1139 and (EU) No 2019/2144, and Directives 2014/90/EU, (EU) 2016/797, and (EU) 2020/1828 (Artificial Intelligence Act), 2024 O.J. (L 1689), 1 [hereinafter AIA].

[161] The AI Regulation will enter into force on the twentieth day following its publication in the Official Journal of the European Union. AIA, *supra* note 160, art. 113.

[162] *Id.* art. 2(1).

(d) Importers and distributors of AI systems;

(e) Product manufacturers placing on the market or putting into service an AI system together with their product and under their own name or trademark;

(f) Authorized representatives of providers who are not established in the Union;

(g) Affected persons that are located in the Union.

Here are some key points about the AI Act:

Risk classification: The AI Act classifies AI systems into three risk categories based on their potential impact.

1. **Unacceptable risk:** Certain applications and systems, such as government-run social scoring, are banned due to their high risk. The AI Act bans certain AI applications that threaten citizens' rights, including biometric categorization systems based on sensitive characteristics, untargeted scraping of facial images from the internet or CCTV footage for facial recognition databases, emotion recognition in workplaces and schools, social scoring, predictive policing based solely on profiling a person or assessing their characteristics, and AI that manipulates human behavior or exploits people's vulnerabilities.[163]

2. **High risk:** AI systems that pose significant risks to health, safety, or fundamental rights fall into this category.[164] These systems are subject to stringent requirements. Clear obligations are established for other high-risk AI systems, which could significantly impact health, safety, fundamental rights, the environment, democracy, and the rule of law. High-risk uses include those in critical infrastructure management, medical devices, vehicles, education, vocational training, recruitment, HR and worker management, biometric identification, employment, essential services (e.g., health care, banking), certain systems in law enforcement, emotion recognition systems, migration, and border management, justice, and democratic processes (e.g., influencing elections). Citizens will have a right to complain about AI systems and receive explanations about decisions based on high-risk AI systems affecting their rights.

   There needs to be a fundamental rights impact assessment and conformity assessment; high-risk AI systems must be registered in a public EU database; businesses must implement risk management and quality management systems. Data governance is required in areas such as bias mitigation. Importantly, there must be human oversight—explainability, auditable logs, human-in-the-loop—in high-risk AI systems.[165]

---

[163] *Id.* art. 5(1).
[164] *Id.* art. 6.
[165] *Id.* art. 14.

3. **Limited risk:** AI systems with lower risks are subject to fewer regulatory obligations.[166]

The AI Act also imposes distinct requirements for GPAI[167] in addition to the higher standards imposed on high-risk systems. Some of these are as follows:

(a) **Data quality:** The AI Act emphasizes rules around data quality to ensure reliable and unbiased AI.[168]

(b) **Transparency:** It promotes transparency by requiring clear explanations of AI decisions. GPAI systems and the models they are based on must meet certain transparency requirements and comply with EU copyright law during their training. (It remains unclear to what extent the training of AI models is permitted under EU copyright law.) More powerful GPAI models that could pose systemic risks face additional requirements, including performing model evaluation, risk assessment, and reporting on incidents. Additionally, artificial or manipulated images, audio, or video content ("deepfakes") need to be clearly labeled as such.[169]

(c) **Accountability:** Developers and users must be accountable for AI system behavior and ensure that AI respects EU values, ethical standards, and fundamental rights.[170]

(d) **Penalties:** The AI Act sets out some potential penalties and enforcement possibilities:

- Up to 7 percent of global annual turnover or €35m for prohibited AI violations;[171]
- Up to 3 percent of global annual turnover or €15m for most other violations;[172]
- Up to 1.5 percent of global annual turnover or €7.5m for supplying incorrect information;[173]
- There are caps on fines for SMEs and startups;[174]
- A European AI Office and AI Board will be established centrally at an EU level;[175]
- There will be a Market Surveillance Authority in EU countries to enforce the AIAct;[176]
- Any individual can make complaints about noncompliance.[177]

---

166 *Id.* recital 53.
167 *Id.* art. 53.
168 *Id.* art. 10.
169 *Id.* art. 50.
170 *Id.* recital 27.
171 *Id.* art. 99(3).
172 *Id.* art. 99(4).
173 *Id.* art. 99(5).
174 *Id.* art. 99(6).
175 *Id.* arts. 64, 65.
176 *Id.* art. 70.
177 *Id.* art. 85.

14.1.9. Data Protection

14.1.9.1. General Data Protection Regulation

The EU's GDPR[178] is a comprehensive privacy law enacted by the EU that governs how personal data of individuals in the EU may be processed. It has been in effect since May 25, 2018.

This section will offer a brief overview of the GDPR; more detailed analyses are available.

The GDPR sets out mandatory rules for how organizations and companies must use personal data in an integrity-friendly way. Personal data refer to any information which, directly or indirectly, could identify a living person. This would include name, phone number, address, interests, information about past purchases, health, and online behavior, but there is no definitive list as it is the nature of the data rather than its form that matters.

There is an additional subcategorization of personal data—special category data—personal data revealing racial or ethnic origin, political opinions, religious or philosophical beliefs, trade union membership, genetic data, biometric data to uniquely identify a natural person, data concerning health or data concerning a natural person's sex life or sexual orientation, the processing of which is prohibited, absent explicit consent by the data subject or one of the conditions in Article 9,[179] which will be interpreted strictly, and in all cases the necessity for the data processing must be substantial.

Processing data involves collecting, structuring, organizing, using, storing, sharing, disclosing, erasing, and destruction of data. Every organization that processes personal data must ensure that the personal data it uses fulfills the requirements of the GDPR. Unlike many privacy laws in other jurisdictions, there is no size threshold in the GDPR (although processing by a natural person during a purely personal or household activity is excluded), and it applies to all types of business entities, including public-sector and third-sector organizations.[180]

The main requirements of the GDPR are as follows:

- The GDPR applies to all EU Member States and to all data subjects in a Member State, irrespective of nationality. To be caught by the GDPR, the processing must be by a controller or a processor in the Union, regardless of whether the processing takes place in the Union or not or the processing of personal data of data subjects who are in the Union by a controller or processor not established in the Union, where the processing activities are related to:

  (a) the offering of goods or services, irrespective of whether a payment of the data subject is required, to such data subjects in the Union;[181] or

---

[178] GDPR, *supra* note 2.
[179] *Id.* art. 9(1).
[180] *Id.* arts. 2(1), 4(7).
[181] *Id.* art. 3(2)(a).

(b) the monitoring of their behavior as far as their behavior takes place within the Union.[182]

- Processing must have a defined purpose.[183] Thus, you cannot collect personal information "just in case" you might need it later.[184] That purpose must be made known to the data subject when the data is collected; should the desired use change at a later date, that new use must be approved by the data subject or covered by one of the permitted uses in the GDPR.
- Individuals have a right to know how their data is being used and must have a say in this matter.[185]
- Personal information must be kept in a form which permits identification of data subjects for no longer than is necessary for the purposes for which the personal data are processed.[186]
- Organizations must handle personal data in a way that ensures its security. This includes preventing unauthorized access, unlawful processing, and accidental loss, destruction, or damage. It also means that organizations must use appropriate security measures to protect the data.[187] A recent case held that hackers' unauthorized access to personal data was a GDPR breach.[188]

Article 5(2) of the GDPR is about the "accountability" principle. It states that: "The controller shall be responsible for, and be able to demonstrate compliance with, [*Article 5(1)*]."[189]

This principle requires data controllers to demonstrate that they comply with the other principles in Article 5(1). This includes lawfulness, fairness, transparency, purpose limitation, data minimization, accuracy, storage limitation, integrity, and confidentiality.

This means that organizations not only have to comply with the GDPR, but they also have to be able to prove that they comply with it. This could involve implementing and maintaining data protection policies, conducting data protection impact assessments, appointing a data protection officer (if required), and implementing measures to ensure data security.[190]

---

182 *Id.* art. 3(2)(b).
183 *Id.* art. 5(1)(b).
184 *Id.* art. 5(1)(c).
185 *Id.* recital 60.
186 *Id.* art. 5(1)(e).
187 *Id.* art. 5(1)(f).
188 Case C-340/21, VB v. Natsionalna Agentsia za Prihodite, ECLI:EU:C:2023:986 (Dec. 12, 2023).
189 GDPR, *supra* note 2, art. 5(2).
190 *Id.* art. 5(2).

The use of personal data must have a legal basis in terms of the GDPR. The GDPR sets out six alternatives for the legal basis. These alternatives are:

(a) The data subject has given consent[191] to processing his or her personal data for one or more specific purposes.[192]

(b) Processing is necessary for the performance of a contract to which the data subject is party or to take steps at the data subject's request before entering into a contract—for example, to deliver an order from an online supplier.[193]

(c) Processing is necessary to comply with a legal obligation to which the controller is subject—for example, to process payroll taxes or deductions.[194]

(d) Processing is necessary in order to protect the vital interests of the data subject or another natural person—for example, to record some health issue which the data subject may have, which might need to be dealt with.[195]

(e) Processing is necessary to perform a task in the public interest or in the exercise of official authority vested in the controller.[196]

(f) Processing is necessary for the legitimate interests pursued by the controller or by a third party, except where such interests are overridden by the interests or fundamental rights and freedoms of the data subject, which require personal data protection, particularly where the data subject is a child. Use of client or employee data for regular business operations is likely to be a permitted legitimate interest. However, using personal data for direct marketing is more problematic as this will only be allowed provided it does not infringe on the rights and freedoms of data subjects. Legitimate interests must be balanced against the interests or fundamental rights and freedoms of the data subject. If there is a less intrusive way to achieve the same end, legitimate interests cannot be relied upon as the legal reason for data processing.[197] Point (f) does not apply to processing carried out by public authorities in the performance of their tasks.

- Personal data breaches must be reported within seventy-two hours.[198] If personal data is disclosed, accessed, changed (other than by the controller or authorized by him), or stolen, the controller is responsible for acting. This is the case even if the breach happened at a processor. It is probably not an event that must be reported if it can be determined that no personal data were risked.

---

[191] *Id.* art. 6(1)(a). Consent as a legal basis is problematic for a controller as consent may be withdrawn at any time and the removal of consent must be as simple to achieve as granting it. Furthermore, the courts have held that the consent must be freely given which will make it very difficult to obtain in an employment context or any similar context in which there is a disparity between the relative bargaining strengths of the parties.

[192] *Id.* art. 7.

[193] *Id.* art. 6(1)(b).

[194] *Id.* art. 6(1)(c).

[195] *Id.* art. 6(1)(d).

[196] *Id.* art. 6(1)(e).

[197] *Id.* art. 6(1)(f).

[198] *Id.* art. 33.

In the event of loss of sensitive data, such as health data, the incident must be reported to the supervisory authority and each affected individual without delay.[199]

- Controllers are responsible for the handling of personal data by their processors and suppliers or anyone else with whom they have shared the data.[200]
- The GDPR strengthens existing rights, provides new rights, and gives individuals more control over their personal data. It includes easier access to an individual's data, a new right to data portability, a clearer right to erasure (right to be forgotten), and the right to know when their data have been breached.
- The GDPR creates a level playing field for all companies operating in the European Economic Area (EEA—the EU plus Iceland, Liechtenstein, and Norway), adopts a technology-neutral approach, and stimulates innovation. It establishes a system of completely independent supervisory authorities in charge of monitoring and enforcing compliance.[201]

It is important to note that GDPR lays out responsibilities for organizations to ensure the privacy and protection of personal data, provides data subjects with certain rights, and assigns powers to regulators to ask for demonstrations of accountability or even impose fines in cases where an organization is not complying with GDPR requirements. An organization can also be ordered to cease processing personal data where there is a breach of the GDPR.[202]

There is a set of Six Principles under Article 5 of the GDPR:

- **Principle 1: Lawfulness, fairness, and transparency.** Personal data must be processed lawfully, fairly, and transparently in relation to the data subject. The specific requirements for lawful processing are set out in Article 6 (these are the lawful conditions for processing).
- **Principle 2: Purpose limitation.** Personal data must be collected only for specified, explicit, and legitimate purposes. It must not be further processed in any manner incompatible with those purposes.
- **Principle 3: Data minimization.** Personal data must be adequate, relevant, and limited to what is necessary in relation to the purposes for which it is processed. The inclusion of the word "necessary" is important here as this places a further restriction on future possibilities for processing.
- **Principle 4: Accuracy.** Personal data must be accurate and, where necessary, kept up to date. Every reasonable step must be taken to ensure that data which is inaccurate, with regard to the purposes for which it is processed, is erased, or rectified without delay.

---

199 *Id.* art. 34,
200 *Id.* art. 82.
201 *Id.* art. 51.
202 *Id.* art. 58(2)(f).

- **Principle 5: Storage limitation.** Personal data must not be kept in a form, which permits identification of data subjects for longer than is necessary for the purposes for which the data is processed. Personal data may be stored for longer periods provided it is processed solely for archiving purposes in the public interest, scientific or historical research purposes, or statistical purposes. This is subject to the implementation of appropriate data security measures designed to safeguard the rights and freedoms of data subjects.
- **Principle 6: Integrity and confidentiality.** Personal data must be processed in a manner that ensures its appropriate security. This includes protection against unauthorized or unlawful processing and against accidental loss, destruction, or damage. In this regard, data controllers and processors must use appropriate technical or organizational security measures.

Finally, Article 5(2) introduces the principle of accountability. Here, the data controller is responsible for and must be able to demonstrate compliance with the other data protection principles. While the principles of accountability and transparency have previously been implicit requirements of data protection law, the GDPR's emphasis elevates their significance, and organizations will be expected to put into place comprehensive but proportionate governance measures to be able to demonstrate their compliance.

The GDPR limits the transfer of personal data to countries outside the EEA[203] unless the European Commission has taken a Decision[204] that the third country provides adequate[205] protection for the personal data. Adequacy decisions[206] have been made in respect of Andorra,[207] Argentina,[208] Canada (commercial organizations),[209] Faroe Islands,[210]

---

203 *Id.* arts. 44–50.

204 *Adequacy Decisions: How the EU Determines if a Non-EU Country Has an Adequate Level of Data Protection*, Eur. Comm'n, https://commission.europa.eu/law/law-topic/data-protection/international-dimension-data-protection/adequacy-decisions_en (last visited Oct. 24, 2023).

205 In this context, "adequate" means no less than is afforded by the GDPR. The effect of such a decision is that personal data can flow from the EU (and Norway, Liechtenstein, and Iceland) to that third country without any further safeguard being necessary. In other words, transfers to the country in question will be assimilated to intra-EU transmissions of data.

206 GDPR, *supra* note 2, art. 45.

207 2010/625/EU: Commission Decision of October 19, 2010, pursuant to Directive 95/46/EC of the European Parliament and of the Council on the adequate protection of personal data in Andorra 2010 O.J. (L 277), 27.

208 2003/490/EC: Commission Decision of June 30, 2003, pursuant to Directive 95/46/EC of the European Parliament and of the Council on the adequate protection of personal data in Argentina, 2003 O.J. (L 168), 19.

209 2002/2/EC: Commission Decision of December 20, 2001, pursuant to Directive 95/46/EC of the European Parliament and of the Council on the adequate protection of personal data provided by the Canadian Personal Information Protection and Electronic Documents Act, 2002 O.J. (L 2), 13.

210 2010/146/: Commission Decision of March 5, 2010, pursuant to Directive 95/46/EC of the European Parliament and of the Council on the adequate protection provided by the Faroese Act on Processing of Personal Data, 2010 O.J. (L 58), 17.

Guernsey,[211] Israel,[212] Isle of Man,[213] Japan,[214] Jersey,[215] New Zealand,[216] Republic of Korea,[217] Switzerland,[218] the United Kingdom under the GDPR,[219] the Law Enforcement Directive[220] (LED),[221] the United States (commercial organizations participating in the EU–US Data Privacy Framework),[222] and Uruguay.[223]

The GDPR brings new protection to children's data in the context of internet services (such as social media). Organizations that collect personal data about children below sixteen years under the GDPR need to obtain consent for the processing from the child's parents/guardian and ensure that privacy notices are in a language understood by children.

Organizations (whether acting as data controller or data processor) must determine if they must appoint a mandatory Data Protection Officer.[224] Organizations that are required to appoint a mandatory Data Protection Officer are:

- public bodies,
- organizations that carry out regular and systematic monitoring of data subjects on a large scale, or

---

211 003/821/EC: Commission Decision of November 21, 2003, on the adequate protection of personal data in Guernsey 2003, O.J. (L 308), 27.

212 2011/61/EU: Commission Decision of January 31, 2011, pursuant to Directive 95/46/EC of the European Parliament and of the Council on the adequate protection of personal data by the State of Israel with regard to automated processing of personal data, 2011 O.J. (L 27), 39.

213 2004/411/EC: Commission Decision of April 28, 2004, on the adequate protection of personal data in the Isle of Man, O.J. L 151, April 30, 2004, pp. 48–51, http://data.europa.eu/eli/dec/2004/411/2016-12-17.

214 Commission Implementing Decision (EU) 2019/419 of January 23, 2019, pursuant to Regulation (EU) 2016/679 of the European Parliament and of the Council on the adequate protection of personal data by Japan under the Act on the Protection of Personal Information, 2019 O.J. (L 76), 1.

215 2008/393/EC: Commission Decision of May 8, 2008, pursuant to Directive 95/46/EC of the European Parliament and of the Council on the adequate protection of personal data in Jersey, 2008 O.J. (L 138), 21.

216 2013/65/EU: Commission Implementing Decision of December 19, 2012, pursuant to Directive 95/46/EC of the European Parliament and of the Council on the adequate protection of personal data by New Zealand, 2013 O.J. (L 28), 12.

217 Commission Implementing Decision (EU) 2022/254 of December 17, 2021, pursuant to Regulation (EU) 2016/679 of the European Parliament and of the Council on the adequate protection of personal data by the Republic of Korea under the Personal Information Protection Act, 2022 O.J. (L 44), 1.

218 2000/518/EC: Commission Decision of July 26, 2000, pursuant to Directive 95/46/EC of the European Parliament and of the Council on the adequate protection of personal data provided in Switzerland, 2000 O.J. (L 215), 1.

219 Commission Implementing Decision (EU) 2021/1772 of June 28, 2021, pursuant to Regulation (EU) 2016/679 of the European Parliament and of the Council on the adequate protection of personal data by the United Kingdom, 2021 O.J. (L 360), 1.

220 Directive (EU) 2016/680 of the European Parliament and of the Council of April 27, 2016, on the protection of natural persons with regard to the processing of personal data by competent authorities for the purposes of the prevention, investigation, detection, or prosecution of criminal offenses or the execution of criminal penalties, and on the free movement of such data, and repealing Council Framework Decision 2008/977/JHA, 2016 O.J. (L 119), 89.

221 Commission Implementing Decision (EU) 2021/1773 of June 28, 2021, pursuant to Directive (EU) 2016/680 of the European Parliament and of the Council on the adequate protection of personal data by the United Kingdom, 2016 O.J. (L 360), 69.

222 Commission Implementing Decision of July 10, 2023, pursuant to Regulation (EU) 2016/679 of the European Parliament and of the Council on the adequate level of protection of personal data under the EU–US Data Privacy Framework, 2023 O.J. (C 4745) final.

223 2012/484/EU: Commission Implementing Decision of August 21, 2012, pursuant to Directive 95/46/EC of the European Parliament and of the Council on the adequate protection of personal data by the Eastern Republic of Uruguay with regard to automated processing of personal data, 2012 O.J. (L 227), 11.

224 GDPR, *supra* note 2, arts. 37–39.

- organizations whose core activities consist of the processing on a large scale of special categories of data and personal data relating to criminal convictions and offenses.

Organizations which do not have a place of business in the EU but which offer goods or services, irrespective of whether a payment of the data subject is required, to data subjects in the EU may be required to appoint a representative in the EU.[225]

All organizations must notify supervisory authorities in the event of a data protection breach where an individual is likely to suffer damage (such as identity theft). For breaches of the GDPR, supervisory authorities can fine an organization up to 4 percent of its annual worldwide turnover or €20 million (whichever is higher).[226]

Organizations will also have to notify the individual concerned in certain circumstances (for example, if the breach may cause the individual financial loss). Individuals will also have the right to claim compensation for financial loss or distress resulting from a data breach.[227]

14.1.9.2. E-Commerce Directive

The EU E-Commerce Directive—Directive 2000/31—is the foundational legal framework for online services in the EU.[228] It aims to remove obstacles to cross-border online services.

The Directive establishes harmonized rules on issues such as

- transparency and information requirements for online service providers,
- commercial communications,
- electronic contracts and limitations of liability of intermediary service providers.

It also enhances administrative cooperation between the Member States and the role of self-regulation.

The Directive sets out basic requirements on mandatory consumer information, steps to follow in online contracting, and rules on commercial communications. This covers online advertisements, unsolicited commercial communications, and more. Providers of online services are subject to the law of the Member State in which they are established and not the law of the Member States where the service is accessible.[229]

The Directive exempts intermediaries from liability for the content they manage if they fulfill certain conditions. Service providers hosting illegal material must remove or

---

225 *Id.* arts. 3(2), 27.

226 *Id.* art. 83.

227 *Id.* art. 82.

228 Directive 2000/31/EC of the European Parliament and of the Council of June 8, 2000, on Certain Legal Aspects of Information Society Services, in Particular Electronic Commerce, in the Internal Market ("Directive on Electronic Commerce"), 2000 O.J. (L 178), 1 [hereinafter Directive on Electronic Commerce].

229 *Id.* art. 3, various recitals.

disable access to it as quickly as possible once they are aware of the illegal nature. The liability exemption only covers service providers who play a neutral, merely technical, and passive role toward the hosted content.[230]

Member States cannot force any general content monitoring obligation on intermediaries.[231]

14.1.9.3. E-Privacy Directive

The EU E-Privacy Directive[232]—Directive 2002/58/EC—the Privacy and Electronic Communications (PEC) Directive, also known as the EU Cookie Law—is a set of data protection and privacy rules in the EU.

This Directive was established to ensure confidentiality and privacy in electronic communication. It regulates important issues, such as information confidentiality, traffic data treatment, spam, and cookies.

The E-Privacy Directive has been amended by Directive 2009/136,[233] which introduces several changes, especially concerning cookies, that are now subject to prior consent. The E-Privacy Directive has been incorporated into each Member State's national laws as was required.

There are some interplays between the E-Privacy Directive and the GDPR, but each has its own characteristics.

The Directive was drafted specifically to address the requirements of new digital technologies and ease the advance of electronic communications services. It complements the GDPR and applies to all matters which are not specifically covered by that Regulation.

In particular, the subject of the Directive is the "right to privacy in the electronic communication sector" and free movement of data, communication equipment, and services.

Contrary to the GDPR, which specifically addresses only individuals, the E-Privacy Directive also applies to legal persons.[234]

The first general obligation in the Directive is to provide security of services.

---

230 *Id.* art. 12.

231 *Id.* recital 47, art. 15.

232 Directive 2002/58/EC of the European Parliament and of the Council of July 12, 2002, concerning the processing of personal data and the protection of privacy in the electronic communications sector (Directive on Privacy and Electronic Communications), 2002 O.J. (L 201), 37 [hereinafter Directive on Privacy and Electronic Communications].

233 Directive 2009/136/EC of the European Parliament and of the Council of November 25, 2009, amending Directive 2002/22/EC on universal service and users' rights relating to electronic communications networks and services, Directive 2002/58/EC, concerning the processing of personal data and the protection of privacy in the electronic communications sector and Regulation (EC) No 2006/2004 on cooperation between national authorities responsible for the enforcement of consumer protection laws, 2009 O.J. (L 337), 11 [hereinafter E-Privacy Directive].

234 *Id.* art. 1(2).

The EU E-Privacy Directive also addresses the issue of unsolicited communications,[235] where it opts for an opt-in solution. This means that unsolicited emails (spam) are strictly prohibited unless the user has given their prior consent.[236] The E-Privacy Directive specifies that people must opt-in before a company can communicate with them.[237] This applies not just to email marketing but also to calls, texts, and any other form of electronic communication. Unsolicited emails or calls are not allowed.

Also, emails must be from a legitimate address, and email mailshot senders must provide recipients with the option to unsubscribe.[238]

The Directive also covers the use of location data. It states that location data may only be processed when they are made anonymous or with the consent of the users. The users must also be allowed to withdraw their consent at any time.[239]

As for cookies, the Directive stipulates that cookies must be transparent, and the users must be allowed to refuse them.[240] The E-Privacy Directive requires that a website obtain a user's consent before storing cookies in the user's browser, except for strictly necessary cookies.[241] Users also have to be informed of the general purpose of the cookies before they consent. This applies to first-party and third-party cookies, although users do not have to be told about every cookie used. This is why you often see a banner asking for consent when you visit a website from the EU for the first time.

The EU Cookie Legislation requires four actions from website owners who use cookies:[242]

- When a user visits a website, they must be informed that the website uses cookies.
- Detailed information must be provided regarding how that cookie data will be utilized. Users must first be given clear and comprehensive information about the purposes of processing data (as well as information about storage, retention, and access) in order to give valid consent.
- Users must be given some means of accepting or refusing the use of cookies on a website. Websites must refrain from placing trackers and cookies on users' browsers until they consent.
- If users refuse to accept cookies, website operators must ensure that cookies will not be placed on their computer/device.

---

235 *Id.* art.13.
236 *Id.* art. 13(1).
237 *Id.* art. 13.
238 "The practice of sending electronic mail for purposes of direct marketing . . . without a valid address to which the recipient may send a request that such communications cease, shall be prohibited," *Id.* art. 13(4).
239 *Id.* art. 9.
240 *Id.* art. 13(2).
241 *Id.* art. 5(3).
242 *Id.* recital 25.

14.1.10. Other Relevant Legislative Proposals

14.1.10.1. Interoperable Europe Act

In March 2024, a Regulation was enacted laying down measures for a high level of public-sector interoperability.[243]

The initiative seeks to ensure a consistent, human-centric EU approach to interoperability, create an interoperability governance structure that helps public administrations and the private-sector work together, and establish an ecosystem of interoperability solutions for the EU's public sector. The Act should also cut red tape for citizens and businesses.

14.1.10.2. European Digital Identity Framework

The eIDAS Regulation—Regulation (EU) No 910/2014[244]—focuses on electronic identification and trust services for electronic transactions within the EU. It aims to enhance trust in electronic transactions by providing a common foundation for secure electronic interactions. The Regulation covers various aspects such as e-signatures, electronic seals, electronic time stamps, certified electronic delivery services, and website authentication. It establishes a legal framework for qualified trust service providers (TSPs) who play a crucial role in ensuring the security and validity of electronic documents and transactions. The eIDAS Regulation replaced the eSignature Directive (1999/93/EC)[245] and became mandatory in all EU Member States from July 1, 2016. It set standards for different types of electronic signatures, including advanced and qualified electronic signatures, ensuring their admissibility as evidence in EU courts. TSPs must meet European-Commission-recommended technical standards to be included on the EU Trusted List.[246]

eIDAS ensures that each form of electronic signature is admissible as evidence in EU courts and will not be denied legal effect solely because it is in electronic form.

The enforceability of a transaction concluded using electronic signatures will depend on various factors, including the type of signature used and the evidence embedded in it. For example, a typed name at the bottom of an email is more likely to be successfully challenged than a qualified electronic signature meeting multiple EU technical standards, including being backed by a TSP regulated by an EU Member State and containing significant embedded signer information.

---

243 Regulation (EU) 2024/903 of the European Parliament and of the Council of March 13, 2024, laying down measures for a high level of public-sector interoperability across the Union (Interoperable Europe Act), 2024 O.J. (L 903), 1 [hereinafter Interoperable Europe Act].

244 Regulation (EU) No 910/2014 of the European Parliament and of the Council of July 23, 2014, on electronic identification and trust services for electronic transactions in the internal market and repealing Directive 1999/93/EC, 2014 O.J. (L 257), 73 [hereinafter eIDAS Regulation].

245 Directive 1999/93/EC of the European Parliament and of the Council of December 13, 1999, on a community framework for electronic signatures, 2000 O.J. (L 13), 12.

246 The current list is available at *EU/EEA Trusted List Browser*, Eur. Comm'n, https://eidas.ec.europa.eu/efda/tl-browser/#/screen/home (last visited Oct. 25, 2024).

The eIDAS Regulation does not dictate when a signature is needed for a transaction or what type is necessary. This means that each EU Member State must specify in its laws when a particular transaction (i) cannot be signed electronically or (ii) needs a higher form of electronic signature, such as an advanced or qualified electronic signature.

A qualified electronic signature has the equivalent legal effect of a handwritten signature and enjoys mutual recognition in every EU Member State. However, it is uncommon for a Member State (or its courts) to use a qualified electronic signature to authenticate a transaction.

An amendment tothe eIDAS Regulation was published on April 30, 2024, and entered into force on May 20, 2024.[247]

The European Digital Identity Framework aims to establish a harmonized digital identity framework that allows Union citizens and residents to access public and private online and offline services throughout the Union. This framework includes a comprehensive technical architecture, common standards, guidelines, and best practices to enhance functionalities and interoperability across Member States.

The EU Digital Identity will give citizens control over their data, enabling them to share specific personal attributes like age without revealing full identity details. It will be used for various services such as public requests, banking, age verification, car rentals, and hotel check-ins. The initiative addresses shortcomings in current digital identification systems by offering a secure and widely usable digital ID for all EU citizens, residents, and businesses. Citizens will have access to a personal digital wallet that allows them to control the data they share, enabling them to prove specific personal attributes like age without revealing full identity details.[248]

The EU Digital Identity Wallet will undergo pilot projects before being rolled out in Member States to ensure practicality and effectiveness.[249]

By 2024, every EU Member State must make the Digital Identity Wallet available to all citizens who desire one, aiming to create a single cross-border EU Digital Identity Wallet. Member States will have to provide EU Digital Identity Wallets to their citizens twenty-four months after the adoption of Implementing Acts, setting out the technical specifications for the EU Digital Identity Wallet and the technical requirements for certification. These Implementing Acts—to be adopted six and twelve months after the adoption of the Regulation[250]—will draw on the specifications developed as part of the EU Digital Identity Toolbox,[251] setting harmonized conditions for implementing the wallets all across Europe.

---

[247] Regulation (EU) 2024/1183 of the European Parliament and of the Council of April 11, 2024, amending Regulation (EU) No 910/2014 as regards establishing the European Digital Identity Framework, 2024 O.J. (L 1183), 1 [hereinafter European Digital Identity Framework].

[248] *Id.* art. 6a.

[249] *A Digital ID and Personal Digital Wallet for EU Citizens, Residents and Businesses*, Eur. Comm'n, https://ec.europa.eu/digital-building-blocks/sites/display/EUDIGITALIDENTITYWALLET/ (last visited Oct. 25, 2024).

[250] European Digital Identity Framework, *supra* note 249, art. 1 5a (1).

[251] *Id.* recital 70; Commission Recommendation (EU) 2021/946 of June 3, 2021, on a common Union Toolbox for a coordinated approach toward a European Digital Identity Framework, 2021 O.J. (L 210), 51.

In addition to public services, VLOPs designated under the DSA[252] (including services such as Amazon, Booking.com, or Facebook) and private services that are legally required to authenticate their users will have to accept the EU Digital Identity Wallet for logging into their online services. The eIDAS 2 Regulation focuses on making cross-border e-ID a reality by providing a secure means of digital identification and authentication that enhances user experience while streamlining access to services for both citizens and enterprises.

14.1.10.3. European Media Freedom Act

The Media Freedom Act was formally enacted on April 11, 2024,[253] and applies completely from August 8, 2025, although some articles apply from earlier dates.[254]

The European Media Freedom Act implements new rules to protect media pluralism and independence in the EU. They will ensure that public and private media can operate more easily across borders in the EU internal market without undue pressure and taking into account the digital transformation of the media space.

Among others, the European Media Freedom Act will:[255]

- protect editorial independence;
- protect journalistic sources, including against the use of spyware;
- ensure the independent functioning of public service media;
- enhance transparency of media ownership;
- safeguard media against unjustified online content removal by VLOPs;
- introduce a right of customization of the media offering on devices and interfaces;
- enhance transparency in state advertising for media service providers and online platforms;
- ensure Member States assess the impact of key media market concentrations on media pluralism and editorial independence; and
- boost transparency in audience measurement for media service providers and advertisers.

A new independent European Board for Media Services will be set up, comprised of national media authorities, and assisted by a Commission secretariat. The Board will, among others, promote the effective and consistent application of the EU media law framework.

---

[252] *See supra* Section 14.1.3.

[253] Regulation (EU) 2024/1083 of the European Parliament and of the Council of April 11, 2024, establishing a common framework for media services in the internal market and amending Directive 2010/13/EU (European Media Freedom Act) O.J. (L 2024/1083), April 17, 2024.

[254] *Ibid.* art. 29.

[255] According to the European Commission, *European Media Freedom Act*, Eur. Comm'n, https://commission.europa.eu/strategy-and-policy/priorities-2019-2024/new-push-european-democracy/protecting-democracy/european-media-freedom-act_en (last visited Oct. 25, 2024).

14.2. Comparative Regulation with the United Kingdom

As indicated above,[256] the United Kingdom is not part of the EU. This section will consider some recent relevant legislation of the United Kingdom in the digital content sphere, which is in addition to or amends the EU law existing at the time of leaving the EU ("Brexit").

14.2.1. Online Safety Act 2023

The UK Online Safety Act 2023 was enacted on October 26, 2023.[257] According to its Introduction, "This Act provides for a new regulatory framework which has the general purpose of making the use of internet services regulated by this Act safer for individuals in the United Kingdom."[258] As the Online Safety Act deals with matters under discussion in Europe and the United States (at both State and Federal levels), its main points are set out here.

Here are some key points:

The Act aims to make social media companies and search engines more responsible for the content on their platforms.[259] The Act will force social media platforms to remove illegal content, stopping children and adults from seeing it.

The Act is also bringing in new offenses, including making content that promotes self-harm illegal for the first time.

Illegal content that platforms will need to remove includes

- child sexual abuse,
- controlling or coercive behavior,
- extreme sexual violence,
- fraud,
- hate crime,
- inciting violence,
- illegal immigration and people smuggling,
- promoting or facilitating suicide,
- promoting self-harm,
- revenge porn,

---

256 *See supra* Section 14.1.1.
257 Online Safety Act 2023, c. 50 (UK).
258 *Id.* § 1(1).
259 *Id.* § 56.

- selling illegal drugs or weapons,
- sexual exploitation, and
- terrorism.[260]

This is not just about removing existing illegal content but also about stopping it from appearing. It mandates companies to use various systems and processes to identify risks and harms.[261] Platforms are required to prevent and stop the proliferation of harmful content.[262] The Act mandates some content which is not illegal but could be harmful or age-inappropriate for children. Platforms will need to protect children from it.

The categories of harmful content that platforms will need to protect children from encountering are set out in the Act and include:

- pornographic content;
- content that does not meet a criminal threshold but which promotes, encourages, or provides instructions for suicide, self-harm, or eating disorders;
- content that depicts or encourages serious violence;
- bullying content.[263]

Ofcom is presently consulting on Codes of Practice concerning children. It is currently unclear how age verification of children can be done in a way that does not increase the risk to adults of having their privacy impacted.

The Act, as passed, also requires platforms, including end-to-end encrypted messengers, to scan for child pornography, despite warnings from experts that it is not possible to implement such a scanning mechanism without undermining users' privacy. The Act still includes the potential to order such scanning, but the government appears to have rowed back on that absolute obligation in a statement made during the passage of the Act.[264]

---

260 *Id.* § 49.

261 *Id.* § 9.

262 *Id.* § 12.

263 *Id.* § 16, 61.

264 In a ministerial statement in the House of Lords, where the bill was getting its third reading, Lord Parkinson of Whitley Bay said Ofcom could not be required to order scanning unless "appropriate technology" exists.

"When deciding whether to issue a notice [to scan for CSAM] Ofcom will work with the service to identify reasonable, technically feasible solutions to address the child sexual exploitation and abuse risk including drawing on evidence from a skilled person's report. If appropriate technology does not exist which meets these requirements Ofcom cannot require its use," he said. "That is why the powers include the ability for Ofcom to require companies to make best endeavours to develop or source a new solution."

"It is right that Ofcom should be able to require technology companies to be able to use their considerable resources and their expertise to develop the best possible protections for children in encrypted environments. That has been our long standing policy position. Our stance on tackling child sexual abuse online remains firm and we've always been clear that the bill takes a measured, evidence-based approach to doing so," he added.

Natasha Lomas, *Ministerial Statement on UK's Online Safety Bill Seen as Steering Out of Encryption Clash*, TechCrunch (Sept. 6, 2023), https://techcrunch.com/2023/09/06/osb-encryption-scanning-feasibility/.

Users must have explicit ways to report harm, and companies are required to maintain and enforce stricter age verification systems.[265] Critics have warned that the law may force companies to break end-to-end encryption to monitor content for illicit material.[266] The Act also includes a duty to consider users' rights to freedom of expression and privacy when implementing safety measures and policies.[267]

Implementing and enforcing the Online Safety Bill will be Ofcom's[268] responsibility.[269] Ofcom is presently consulting[270] on Codes of Practice under the Act, including on "Protecting people from illegal harms online."[271]

Internet companies that fail to comply with the new rules in the Online Safety Act 2023 could be fined up to £18 million or 10 percent of their annual turnover.[272]

14.2.2. Investigatory Powers Act 2016 and Amendments

The issue of the Investigatory Powers Act 2016,[273] regulations made thereunder, and amendments presently being discussed in parliament[274] fall largely outside the scope of this chapter. However, this legislation includes provisions dealing with data security; therefore, some coverage is included here. Reference should be made to the text of the Act, which is complex.

---

265 Online Safety Act § 12(4).

266 Technology companies have pointed out that what might be required is not possible given current technology. However, in a statement emailed to TechCrunch (https://techcrunch.com/2023/09/06/osb-encryption-scanning-feasibility/), a spokesperson for the Department for Science, Innovation and Technology said,

> Our position on this matter has not changed and it is wrong to suggest otherwise. Our stance on tackling child sexual abuse online remains firm, and we have always been clear that the Bill takes a measured, evidence-based approach to doing so.
>
> As has always been the case, as a last resort, on a case by case basis and only when stringent privacy safeguards have been met, it will enable Ofcom to direct companies to either use, or make best efforts to develop or source, technology to identify and remove illegal child sexual abuse content—which we know can be developed.
>
> Monday saw technology companies including TikTok, Meta, Microsoft and more come together to discuss the threats posed by sexual offenders exploiting our children. We all agreed to continue to work together to tackle these heinous crimes wherever they take place.

Lomas, *supra* note 264.

267 Online Safety Act §§ 1, 22.

268 The Office of Communications, commonly known as Ofcom, is the government-approved regulatory and competition authority for the broadcasting, telecommunications, and postal industries of the United Kingdom. Ofcom, https://www.ofcom.org.uk/ (last visited Oct. 25, 2024).

269 Online Safety Act §§ 130–151.

270 *Quick Guide to Illegal Content Codes of Practice*, Ofcom (Nov. 9, 2023), https://www.ofcom.org.uk/online-safety/-information-for-industry/guide-for-services/codes-of-practice.

271 *Protecting People from Illegal Harms Online*, Ofcom (Nov. 9, 2023), https://www.ofcom.org.uk/__data/assets/pdf_file/0030/270948/chapter-summaries-illegal-harms-consultation.pdf.

272 Online Safety Act, § 143, sched. 13, ¶ 4.

273 Investigatory Powers Act 2016, c. 25 (UK).

274 Investigatory Powers (Amendment) Bill 2023–4, HL Bill [157] (UK).

The specific area of discussion here relates to Technical Capability Regulations.[275] These regulations, made under Section 253 of the Investigatory Powers Act 2016, permit the Secretary of State to require a telecommunications operator:

> to provide and maintain the capability to carry out the interception of communications or the obtaining of secondary data and disclose anything obtained under a warrant to the person to whom the warrant was addressed, or any person acting on that person's behalf, within one working day, or such longer period as may be specified in the technical capability notice, of the service of a copy of the warrant.[276]

A Technical Capability Notice (TCN)[277] may be issued to a telecommunications operator requiring that operator to intercept communications and pass them to the government, to provide and maintain the ability to remove any encryption on data,[278] and to advise the government of any proposals to change telecommunications systems to which a TCN may relate before their launch. This last provision has been suggested to be to prevent the introduction of end-to-end encryption in messaging systems.

A company subject to a TCN is legally barred from discussing the specifics of the notice and disclosing whether the notice exists at all. Any employee of a company subject to a TCN who discloses its existence would be subject to criminal penalties for violating a gag order. The powers also appear to apply to the use of "warrant canaries."[279]In a judgment of April 7, 2025[280], the Investigatory Powers Tribunal ruled that the bare details of the case (the fact that Apple was the party concerned) could be disclosed. The Investigatory Powers Tribunal has now made it clear that the publication of the mere existence of the claim, the details or the identity of the parties does not jeopardize national security. The Home Office wanted to make even the fact that a hearing was taking place classified information, according to the tribunal's ruling.

The regulations further provide that a TCN can compel a service provider to remove electronic protections, including security standards such as encryption.[281]

---

[275] The Investigatory Powers (Technical Capability) Regulations 2018, SI 2018/353 (UK).

[276] *Id.*

[277] A technical capability notice imposes obligations on a relevant operator in order to ensure that the operator has the capability to provide assistance in relation to interception warrants, equipment interference warrants, or warrants or authorizations for the obtaining of communications data.

[278] SI 2018/353 sched. 1, ¶ 8 (UK).

[279] A warrant canary is a method by which a communications service provider aims to implicitly inform its users that the provider has been served with a government subpoena despite legal prohibitions on revealing the existence of the subpoena. The warrant canary typically informs users that there has not been a court-issued subpoena as of a particular date. If the canary is not updated for the period specified by the host or if the warning is removed, users might assume the host has been served with such a subpoena. The intention is for a provider passively to warn users of the existence of a subpoena, albeit violating the spirit of a court order not to do so, while not violating the letter of the order.
Warrant Canary, Wikipedia, https://en.wikipedia.org/wiki/Warrant_canary (last visited Oct. 25, 2024).

[280] Apple v Secretary of State for the Home Department, judgment of April 7, 2025. [2025] UKIPTrib 1; https://investigatorypowerstribunal.org.uk/wp-content/uploads/2025/04/IPT-25-68-CH-Judgment.pdf

[281] SI 2018/353 sched. 3, ¶10.

TCNs provide for the interception of communications data. TCNs are negotiated in secret and are not made public. Actual requests for data are made through further warrants signed off by a Judicial Commissioner. However, these warrants can be thematic, allowing for a general category of information or persons to be intercepted rather than against specific individuals or pieces of content.[282]

14.2.3. Data (Use and Access) Bill 2024

As was indicated at the beginning of this chapter,[283] the United Kingdom is no longer part of the EU. The U.K. government has stated an intention to diverge from many of the EU rules and introduced legislation—to alter the regime established by the GDPR in the sphere of data. According to the Explanatory Notes on Introduction of the Data (Use and Access) Bill[284] (DUA), "This Bill is intended to update and simplify the UK's data protection framework with a view to reducing burdens on organizations while maintaining high data protection standards." Organizations with activities outside the United Kingdom will, of course, require compliance with the rules of the GDPR, so the extent to which the new U.K. rules will achieve their stated aim is unclear. The DUA is at a very early stage of its parliamentary process and changes should be expected. Additionally, the changes proposed by the Bill appear as changes and replacements of existing legislation, so the DUA has to be cross-referenced with the Data Protection Act 2018, the UK GDPR, and the PEC Regulations[285] to determine the exact provisions.

Some of the changes brought about by the DUA are as follows:

- The definition of "legitimate interests" as a lawful ground for processing personal data is amended by the creation of a new lawful ground for processing personal data called "recognized legitimate interests." This means certain interests are predefined by law as legitimate, removing the need for data controllers to conduct a Legitimate Interest Assessment (LIA) for these specific purposes.[286] These would include national security, defense purposes, and responding to emergencies.[287]
- Data controllers may refuse Data Subject Access Requests in respect of information which the Data Controller is not able to provide based on a reasonable and proportionate search[288] (the GDPR test for refusal of a request is that it is "manifestly unfounded or excessive").[289]

---

282 *Id.* sched. 2.

283 *See supra* Section 14.1.1.

284 *Data (Use and Access) Bill [HL]: Explanatory Notes*, publications.parliament.uk (Oct. 23, 2024), https://bills.parliament.uk/publications/56554/documents/5227 (UK).

285 The Privacy and Electronic Communications (EC Directive) Regulations 2003, SI 2003/2426 (UK).

286 Article 6.9 of the UK GDPR. The "UK GDPR" means Regulation (EU) 2016/679 of the European Parliament and of the Council of April 27, 2016, on the protection of natural persons with regard to the processing of personal data and on the free movement of such data (United Kingdom General Data Protection Regulation), as it forms part of the law of England and Wales, Scotland, and Northern Ireland by virtue of Section 3 of the European Union (Withdrawal) Act 2018 (and see section 205(4)). European Union (Withdrawal) Act 2018, c. 16 (UK) [hereinafter UK GDPR].

287 *Data (Use and Access) Bill* 2024–25, HL Bill [40] sch. 4. (UK).

288 *Data (Use and Access) Bill* 2024–25, HL Bill [40] cl. 78 (UK).

289 UK GDPR art. 12A.

- It introduces a lawful basis that allows USA law enforcement authorities to obtain telecommunications data for its law enforcement purposes, as per a reciprocal Agreement with the United States (the "Access to Electronic Data for the Purpose of Countering Serious Crime").[290]
- It limits the right not to be subject to automated decision-making processing or profiling to a special category of personal data; this facilitates automated decision making or profiling using normal personal data.[291]
- The Secretary of State is allowed to add items of special category data so that the processing of newly defined categories of special category data would be prohibited.[292]
- Finally, new categories of "business data" and "customer data" are introduced, although the interaction of these with the existing categories is unclear.[293]

The Bill also changes the E-Privacy and Cookie Law rules by increasing penalties,[294] permitting the use of first-party cookies and similar technologies for website analytics without a requirement to collect consent, together with other changes.[295]

As the Bill progresses through the legislative process, there are likely to be other changes introduced or amended.

---

290 UK/USA: Agreement on Access to Electronic Data for the Purpose of Countering Serious Crime [CS USA No.6/2019].

291 HL [40] cl. 80 (UK).

292 HL [40] cl. 74 (UK).

293 HL [40] Part 1 (UK).

294 HL [40] sched.13, substituting a new Schedule 1 to The Privacy and Electronic Communications (EC Directive) Regulations 2003, SI 2003/2426 (UK).

295 HL [40] cl. 108–114, Sch. 12 and 13.

15 Media Regulation in the European Union

By Carla Pompa

15.1. Introduction

Mass media is defined as forms of communication designed to reach many people, such as newspapers, radio and television stations, websites, and other similar platforms, through which information is communicated to the public.[1] Independent, free media serve as vital watchdogs for democracy, essential in upholding the rule of law by scrutinizing those in power and public institutions.[2] A media landscape that fosters freedom and pluralism is crucial in preserving the public's right to information and ensuring accountability. Democracy flourishes when public *fora* are accessible, providing spaces for the exchange of ideas. These forums can be either physical or digital, such as various media platforms, as long as they offer meaningful information and ensure that people have adequate time to participate in the discussions.[3] Indeed, the concept of the forum as a place where people can exchange ideas traces back to ancient Rome, where members of the *Senatus* met in *fora* to discuss matters of the *res publica*.[4]

The digital revolution has profoundly transformed the way information is created, distributed, and exchanged. Communication methods have shifted from a point-to-point communication to a point-to-multipoint communication, typical of certain tools such as television and, more prominently today, the internet.[5] Through digital platforms, social

---

1 *Mass Media*, Merriam-Webster, https://www.merriam-webster.com/dictionary/mass%20media (Nov. 20, 2024).

2 *COMMUNICATION FROM THE COMMISSION TO THE EUROPEAN PARLIAMENT, THE COUNCIL, THE EUROPEAN ECONOMIC AND SOCIAL COMMITTEE AND THE COMMITTEE OF THE REGIONS 2022 Rule of Law Report The rule of law situation in the European Union*, at § 2.3, COM (2022) 500 final (Jul. 13, 2022).

3 Judit Bayer, Digital Media Regulation within the European Union: A Framework for a New Media Order 22 (Nomos ed. 2024).

4 The literal translation from Latin of *res publica* is "the public thing." This expression has been since used to refer to the republican form of government. This underscores the idea that democracy is fundamentally rooted in the public discussion about, and not limited to, political matters.

5 Stefano D'Alfonso, Mezzi di Comunicazione di Massa [Mass media], *in* Dizionario di Diritto Pubblico 3632 (Giuffrè ed., 2006) (It.).

media, and other innovative technologies, access to information has become faster and more widespread, breaking down geographical and temporal barriers. Indeed, the most authoritative sources of information have not changed with the shift to digitalization; what has changed is simply the tool through which they operate.[6] On the other hand, such a shift of perspective has exposed the cognitive limitations of individuals in selecting, evaluating, and delving into the overwhelming volume of information originating from diverse sources—commonly referred to as "infodemic."[7]

The borderless nature and unlimited access to the internet necessitate ensuring the neutrality of the media, particularly about the internet, and implementing appropriate responsibility frameworks for intermediaries, such as internet service providers.[8] Sharing platforms, owing to their central role, have amassed significant resources and power, enabling them to influence public opinion, political beliefs, and voting intentions, thereby undermining the functioning of democracy. However, as mere intermediaries, these platforms are not subject to the same editorial responsibilities and regulatory obligations imposed on traditional media. The influence these new digital actors bear has brought other important challenges regarding transparency, security, and consumer rights. The opacity of recommendation algorithms, the practices of collecting and processing personal data, and the lack of uniform standards for content moderation highlight the need for effective regulation.

In addition to these challenges, any political or governmental interference in the media sector threatens not only freedom of speech and expression but also the public's right to seek, receive, and share information.[9] In this context, the regulation is a crucial tool to rebalance the power dynamics between platforms, consumers, and governments.

Taking into account these serious risks to media freedom and independence, the European Commission, in its 2022 Rule of Law Report,[10] recognized the importance of free and pluralistic media, which has led to several recent initiatives at the European Union (EU) level.[11] These actions highlight the EU's commitment to safeguarding media freedom and fostering an environment where diverse voices and independent journalism

---

6 András Koltay, New Media and Freedom of Expression: Rethinking the Constitutional Foundations of the Public Sphere, 219 (2021).

7 Giuseppe Muto, *European Media Freedom Act: la Tutela Europea della Libertà dei Media* [*European Media Freedom Act: The European Protection of Media Freedom*], 3 Rivista di diritto dei media 209, 211 (2022), (It.); *see also* Michela Manetti, *Regolare internet* [*Regulate the Internet*], 2 Rivista di diritto dei media, 49 (2020), (It.) (explaining that we are now indeed facing a new form of scarcity, which today no longer concerns the nature and/or cost of the means used for dissemination, but rather the time and attention of users).

8 Muto, *supra* note 7, at 211.

9 COM (2022) 500 final, *supra* note 2, at § 2.3.

10 *Id.*

11 *See* Commission Recommendation on Ensuring the Protection, Safety and Empowerment of Journalists and Other Media Professionals in the European Union, 2021 O.J. (L 331), 8; *see also Commission Proposal for a Directive on Protecting Persons Who Engage in Public Participation from Manifestly Unfounded or Abusive Court Proceedings ("Strategic Lawsuits against Public Participation")*, COM (2022) 1772 (Apr. 4, 2022); *see also* Commission Recommendation Protecting Journalists and Human Rights Defenders Who Engage in Public Participation from Manifestly Unfounded or Abusive Court Proceedings ("Strategic Lawsuits against Public Participation"), 2022 O.J. (L 138), 30. The Commission is also implementing the Media and Audiovisual Action Plan, increasing EU funding support to media freedom and pluralism projects.

can flourish. Indeed, within the EU, Member States have a positive obligation to establish and protect an environment that enables journalistic work, ensures the safety of journalists, and promotes both media pluralism and freedom.[12] In the context of the EU, the need to regulate the digital sector aligns with a broader vision focused on protecting fundamental rights, promoting media pluralism, and safeguarding consumers.

This chapter provides a comprehensive overview of media regulation within the EU, with a particular emphasis on social media governance. It examines the key elements of the current legal framework, including the Audiovisual Media Services Directive (AVMSD),[13] the Digital Services Act (DSA),[14] and the Digital Markets Act (DMA).[15] Additionally, it analyzes the recently adopted European Media Freedom Act (EMFA).[16] The chapter also explores the influence of Directives 2019/770/EU,[17] 2019/771/EU,[18] and 2019/2161/EU[19] on consumer protection, as well as the data privacy obligations under the General Data Protection Regulation (GDPR).[20] Particular attention is given to the GDPR's interpretation by the Court of Justice of the European Union (CJEU), especially in light of the recent decision *Schrems v. Meta*.[21]

15.2. EU Media Regulatory Power

Freedom of expression can be understood in a twofold manner: as active freedom of expression, meaning the right of individuals to express their opinions, and as passive

---

12 COM (2022) 500 final, *supra* note 2, at § 2.3.

13 Directive (EU) 2018/1808 of the European Parliament and of the Council of November 14, 2018, Amending Directive 2010/13/EU on the Coordination of Certain Provisions Laid Down by Law, Regulation or Administrative Action in Member States Concerning the Provision of Audiovisual Media Services (Audiovisual Media Services Directive) in View of Changing Market Realities, 2018 O.J. (L 303), 69 [hereinafter AVMSD]; *see infra* Section 1.2.

14 Regulation (EU) 2022/2065 of the European Parliament and of the Council of October 19, 2022, on a Single Market for Digital Services and Amending Directive 2000/31/EC (Digital Services Act), 2022 O.J. (L 277), 1 [hereinafter DSA]; *see infra* Section 1.4.

15 Regulation (EU) 2022/1925 of the European Parliament and of the Council of September 14, 2022, on Contestable and Fair markets in the Digital Sector and Amending Directives (EU) 2019/1937 and (EU) 2020/1828 (Digital Markets Act), 2022 O.J. (L 265), 1 [hereinafter DMA]; *see infra* Section 1.5.

16 Regulation (EU) 2024/1083 of the European Parliament and of the Council of April 11, 2024, establishing a common framework for media services in the internal market and amending Directive 2010/13/EU (European Media Freedom Act), O.J. (L 2024/1083) [hereinafter EMFA]; *see infra* Section 1.6.

17 Directive (EU) 2019/770 of the European Parliament and of the Council of May 20, 2019, on certain aspects concerning contracts for the supply of digital content and digital services, 2019 O.J. (L 136) 1 [hereinafter Directive 2019/770]; *see infra* Section 1.8.1.

18 Directive (EU) 2019/771 of the European Parliament and of the Council of May 20, 2019, on certain aspects concerning contracts for the sale of goods, amending Regulation (EU) 2017/2394 and Directive 2009/22/EC, and repealing Directive 1999/44/EC, 2019 O.J. (L 136), 28 [hereinafter Directive 2019/771]; *see infra* Section 1.8.2.

19 Directive (EU) 2019/2161 of the European Parliament and of the Council of November 27, 2019, amending Council Directive 93/13/EEC and Directives 98/6/EC, 2005/29/EC, and 2011/83/EU of the European Parliament and of the Council as regards the Better Enforcement and Modernisation of Union Consumer Protection Rules, 2019 O.J. (L 328), 7 [hereinafter Directive 2019/2161]; *see infra* Section 1.8.3.

20 Regulation (EU) 2016/679 of the European Parliament and of the Council of April 27, 2016, on the Protection of Natural Persons with regard to the Processing of Personal Data and on the Free Movement of Such Data, and Repealing Directive 95/46/EC (General Data Protection Regulation), 2016 O.J. (L 119), 1 [hereinafter GDPR]; *see infra* Sections 1.7, 1.9 (about the obligations that social media bear under the GDPR).

21 Case C-446/21, Maximilian Schrems v. Meta Platforms Ireland Limited, ECLI:EU:C:2024:834 (Oct. 4, 2024); *see infra* Section 1.9.

freedom of expression, meaning the right to be adequately informed.[22] For the purposes of this work, the analysis will focus solely on the second dimension of freedom of expression.

Already recognized universally by the Universal Declaration of Human Rights, in Europe, Article 10 of the European Convention on Human Rights enshrines the right of everyone to freedom of expression.[23] This freedom also includes the right to receive and impart information without interference. The European Court of Human Rights (ECtHR) has clarified the scope of this provision, affirming that this freedom is not limited to the right itself but also extends to the medium that ensures the full enjoyment of the right—namely, the internet.[24]

This right has been incorporated into the *acquis communautaire* through Article 11 of the Charter of Nice, which additionally states, "The freedom of the media and their pluralism shall be respected."[25] This provision underscores once again the close connection between democracy and the freedom of information and the media. The importance of these principles is further underscored in Article 2 of the Treaty on the European Union (TEU), which identifies pluralism as a cornerstone of the rule of law.[26] This highlights the European Commission's emphasis on freedom of information and media independence, as reflected in its Annual Rule of Law Report.

Neither the Treaty of Rome nor the Treaty on the Functioning of the European Union (TFEU)[27] originally provided for direct competence in the field of audiovisual and media policy. Instead, the EU's jurisdiction in this area is derived from various provisions of the TFEU, aimed at formulating policies for the diverse sectors of media and communication technologies.[28] This reflects the dual nature of media goods and services, which serve both cultural and economic purposes. The legal foundation for EU media policy is grounded in multiple articles of the TFEU. These include provisions on the free movement of goods,[29] the free movement of persons, services, and capital,[30] and competition policy.[31] Additionally, Article 114 addresses technological harmonization and approximation of laws, Article 165 pertains to education, Article 166 covers vocational training, and Article 167 focuses on culture. Furthermore, Article 173 addresses industrial policy, while Article 207 outlines the common commercial policy. Articles 167 and 173 of the TFEU underscore the centrality of the single market and grant the EU authorities the

---

22 Muto, *supra* note 7, at 215.

23 Convention for the Protection of Human Rights and Fundamental Freedoms, art. 10 (Nov. 4, 1950).

24 Autronic AG V. Switzerland, App. No. 12726/87, ¶ 47 (May 22, 1990), https://hudoc.echr.coe.int/eng?i=001-57630.

25 Charter of Fundamental Rights of the European Union, art. 11, 2016 O.J. (C 202), 389.

26 Treaty on European Union, art. 2, February 7, 1992, O.J. (C 236), 17 [hereinafter TEU].

27 Consolidated Version of the Treaty on the Functioning of the European Union, May 9, 2008, 2008 O.J. (C 115) 47, 89 [hereinafter TFEU].

28 Agni Vourtsi & Lina Sasse, *Politica Audiovisiva e dei Media*, Eur. Parliament (Apr. 2024) https://www.europarl.europa.eu/factsheets/it/sheet/138/politica-audiovisiva-e-dei-media#:~:text=La%20politica%20audiovisiva%20nell'UE,oggetto%20di%20revisione%20nel%202018.

29 *See* TFEU arts. 28, 30, 34, 35.

30 *See* TFEU arts. 45–62.

31 *See* TFEU arts. 101–109.

regulatory power necessary to achieve this principle.[32] Specifically, these two articles aim to remove barriers to cross-border media services, ensure fair competition, and protect consumers within the internal market.[33]

15.3. Audiovisual Media Services Directive

The Audiovisual Media Services Directive (AVMSD) is one of the key regulatory instruments for media policy in the EU.[34] This Directive establishes a regulatory framework for both broadcasting and on-demand audiovisual media services across the EU. The AVMSD addresses various issues, including content standards, advertising, protection of minors, and media pluralism. Moreover, it ensures that media services uphold fundamental rights, promote cultural diversity, and contribute to fostering a competitive media environment.

The Directive 2010/13/EU entered into force on May 5, 2010, and on November 6, 2018, and the European Commission adopted Directive 2018/1808, known as the AVMSD 2.0, to amend it. Directive 2018/1808 was published on November 14, 2018, and Member States had to transpose it by September 19, 2020.

The AVMSD 2.0, as part of the Digital Single Market strategy, was published to extend certain audiovisual regulations to video-sharing platforms and audiovisual content shared on specific social media services.[35] It also introduced greater flexibility in the restrictions applicable to television broadcasts, strengthened the promotion of European content, enhanced the protection of minors, and addressed the issue of hate speech more effectively.[36] Lastly, it sought to ensure greater independence for national regulatory authorities.

The Directive's scope of application encompasses broadcasts delivered via terrestrial, cable, satellite, mobile networks, and the internet, adhering to the principles of platform and technology neutrality.[37] The Directive establishes a two-tier regulatory framework based on the distinction between traditional television channels and on-demand services.[38] It differentiates between linear services, which deliver content to viewers (such as traditional television, internet, or mobile broadcasts); nonlinear services, which allow users to access content on demand (e.g., video-on-demand platforms); and video-sharing platforms, which host programs and user-generated videos without assuming

---

32 Christopher Götz et al., *In Brief: Media Law and Regulation in European Union*, LEXOLOGY (Jun. 13, 2023), https://www.lexology.com/library/detail.aspx?g=d846dd0a-15de-4fa7-a9f7-0289cee0b42b.

33 TFEU art. 167, 173.

34 AVMSD, *supra* note 13.

35 *Summary of Audiovisual Media Services Directive (AVMSD)*, Eur. Union, https://eur-lex.europa.eu/IT/legal-content/summary/audiovisual-media-services-directive-avmsd.html (last updated May 17, 2019).

36 *Id.*

37 Götz et al., *supra* note 32.

38 *General Principles of the AVMSD*, Eur. Comm'n, https://digital-strategy.ec.europa.eu/en/policies/general-principles-avmsd (last visited Nov. 25, 2024).

editorial responsibility.[39] All three categories of services are subject to strict regulatory oversight under the framework.

All audiovisual media services are required to comply with fundamental obligations in key areas, including identification of media service providers, prohibition of incitement to hatred, accessibility for individuals with disabilities, quality standards for commercial communications, sponsorship guidelines, and regulations on product placement. Television broadcasts, however, are subject to stricter rules, particularly regarding advertising and the protection of minors, given their broader societal impact. By contrast, the Directive applies lighter regulation to on-demand services, recognizing the active role of users in selecting content and determining viewing times.

The AVMSD defines the content provided by audiovisual media services and specifies what is covered under the directive. This content is offered on a commercial basis, excluding content shared on private individuals' websites. Additionally, it is intended for the general public, thereby excluding private correspondence. Third, it is provided as a program that excludes websites that merely feature ancillary audiovisual elements, such as graphic content or short advertisements. Lastly, audiovisual content is provided under the editorial responsibility of a media service provider, which entails control over the selection and organization of the programs presented to the audience.[40]

Linear services entail television broadcasts that are defined as programs that are provided by a media service provider at a scheduled time and watched simultaneously by viewers.[41] The set of rules that specifically apply only to these media include obligations to cover *events of major importance* and ensure the public's access to *short news reporting* (Chapter V), thereby preserving the public's right to information. Additionally, broadcasters are required to adhere to *quotas for the promotion and distribution of European television programs* (Chapter VI), reflecting the EU's commitment to fostering cultural diversity and supporting local content creation. To safeguard viewers from excessive commercial exposure, broadcasters must comply with *time limits for TV advertising and teleshopping* (Chapter VII). Furthermore, *stricter protections for minors* are enforced (Chapter VIII), recognizing the influential role of television in shaping young audiences. Lastly, television broadcasters must uphold the *right of reply* (Chapter IX), ensuring that individuals have the opportunity to correct inaccurate or misleading information broadcasted about them. These measures collectively aim to balance commercial interests with the preservation of public interest values.[42]

By nonlinear services, the Directive refers to on-demand services that allow users to select and view programs from a catalog provided by the media service provider, offering flexibility to watch content at their convenience. The AVMSD establishes specific rules for these services, which are tailored to their unique nature. Chapter IV of the Directive outlines key provisions that apply solely to on-demand services, particularly focusing

---

[39] Götz et al., *supra* note 32.
[40] *General Principles of the AVMSD, supra* note 38.
[41] AVMSD, *supra* note 12, art. 1(e).
[42] *General Principles of the AVMSD, supra* note 38.

on the protection of minors,[43] ensuring that content harmful to younger audiences is properly regulated. Additionally, the Directive mandates the promotion and distribution of European works (Article 13), aiming to support and increase the visibility of European cultural content in the digital environment.

The AVMSD also establishes a set of common rules that apply to both television broadcasts and on-demand content, aiming to ensure consistency and protect viewers across different types of media services. These rules encompass several key areas. Article 4, paragraph 7, encourages the use of co-regulation and self-regulatory mechanisms, promoting industry-driven solutions alongside legal requirements. Articles 5 through 11 outline specific obligations, including the identification of media service providers,[44] the prohibition of incitement to hatred,[45] and ensuring accessibility for people with disabilities.[46] The Directive also sets requirements for the transmission of cinematographic works,[47] as well as regulations governing audiovisual commercial communications,[48] sponsoring,[49] and product placement.[50] These provisions ensure that media services operate within a framework that promotes transparency, inclusivity, and responsible content dissemination, regardless of the platform or delivery method.

Member States are prohibited from restricting broadcasts or retransmissions of programs from foreign broadcasters, provided these broadcasts comply with the Directive in the country of origin.[51] However, States are also granted flexibility to impose stricter or more detailed rules for media service providers under their jurisdiction, provided these measures align with EU law principles. This latitude is particularly relevant in areas such as television advertising, where Member States can introduce tailored regulations to ensure the protection of viewers' interests. In specific cases, national authorities

---

43 AVMSD, *supra* note 12, art. 12. With specific regard to minors, article 6(2)(2) prohibits the usage of minors' personal data for purposes of commercial, behaviorally target advertising. *See generally* AVMSD, *supra* note 12, recital 21:

> Regulation (EU) 2016/679 of the European Parliament and the Council recognises that children merit specific protection with regard to the processing of their personal data. The establishment of child protection mechanisms by media service providers inevitably leads to the processing of the personal data of minors. Given that such mechanisms aim at protecting children, personal data of minors processed in the framework of technical child protection measures should not be used for commercial purposes.

44 AVMSD, *supra* note 12, art. 5.

45 *Id.* art. 6.

46 *Id.* art. 7.

47 *Id.* art. 8.

48 *Id.* art. 9.

49 *Id.* art. 10.

50 *Id.* art. 11.

51 *Id.* art. 3 (1); *see also Id.* recital 10 (emphasis added):

> In accordance with the case-law of the Court of Justice of the European Union (the "Court"), it is possible to restrict the freedom to provide services guaranteed under the Treaty for overriding reasons in the general public interest, such as obtaining a high level of consumer protection, provided that such restrictions are justified, proportionate and necessary. Therefore, a Member State should be able to take certain measures to ensure respect for its consumer protection rules which do not fall in the fields coordinated by Directive 2010/13/EU. Measures taken by a Member State to enforce its national consumer protection regime, including in relation to gambling advertising, would need to be **justified**, **proportionate** to the objective pursued, and **necessary** as required under the Court's case-law. In any event, a receiving Member State must not take any measures which would prevent the re-transmission, in its territory, of television broadcasts coming from another Member State.

may establish differentiated conditions for television broadcasters operating within their jurisdiction, allowing for localized regulatory adjustments while adhering to the Directive's core framework.

Given this flexibility to Member States, disputes may arise when stricter rules are circumvented. The Directive outlines a two-step procedure to address such cases. When a Member State finds that a foreign television broadcast, wholly or primarily targeting its audience, violates its domestic rules, it may issue a *nonbinding request* to the authorities in the broadcaster's country of origin.[52] This request aims to encourage the broadcaster to voluntarily comply with the regulations of the targeted country.[53] The determination of whether a Member State is being "targeted" involves an analysis of various factors, including the origin of advertising or subscription revenues, the primary language of the broadcast, and the presence of targeted advertising directed at the local audience.

In cases where the broadcaster deliberately circumvents the rules of the targeted country despite the nonbinding request, the affected Member State can escalate its response by imposing *binding restrictions*.[54] Such measures require prior approval from the European Commission and must be strictly limited to addressing the circumvention of national rules.[55] Examples of binding restrictions include prohibiting the retransmission of the broadcaster's content via cable, terrestrial, or Internet Protocol Television (IPTV) networks; banning advertisements for the broadcasts or specific programs; restricting local companies under the jurisdiction of the targeted Member State from advertising on the broadcaster's platform; and limiting the broadcaster's presence in printed or electronic program guides. Additionally, the sale of subscriptions or smart cards for pay-TV services may be restricted as part of these binding measures. This two-tier mechanism ensures that Member States can safeguard their domestic regulatory frameworks while adhering to the overarching principles of the EU's AVMSD.

Furthermore, Member States are allowed to impose restrictions on the reception of specific content, such as incitement to hatred, which may not be prohibited in the broadcaster's country of origin but contravenes local laws.[56] Such restrictions, however, must adhere to strict conditions. First, any restriction must receive prior approval from the European Commission, following an established procedure. Second, restrictions are permissible only in exceptional circumstances:

- **For television broadcasts**, restrictions can be applied in cases of manifest and serious violations, such as incitement to hatred or content harmful to minors (e.g., gratuitous violence or pornography).[57]

---

52 *General Principles of the AVMSD, supra* note 38.
53 AVMSD, *supra* note 12, art. 4(2).
54 *General Principles of the AVMSD, supra* note 38.
55 AVMSD, *supra* note 12, art. 4(4).
56 *Id.* art. 3.
57 *Id.* art. 3(2)–(3).

- **For on-demand services,** restrictions are further justified when the content poses a significant risk to public order, public health, security, or consumer protection.[58]

All restrictions must be proportionate and limited to the Member State where the violation occurs.[59]Additionally, the Member State where the content originates must be given prior notification of the proposed measures.[60]

The AVMSD also imposes transparency obligations on media service providers, ensuring users have easy and continuous access to essential information about them, thereby enhancing accountability.[61] This includes the provider's name, physical address, electronic contact details or website, and the identity of the relevant regulatory or supervisory authority.[62]

Jurisdiction under the AVMSD is determined to ensure that all audiovisual media services adhere to consistent regulations across the EU. Each Member State is responsible for ensuring that services originating within its territory comply with the national rules implementing the Directive.[63] To prevent conflicts or gaps in jurisdiction, the Directive establishes clear criteria for assigning jurisdiction to a single Member State. The primary determinant is the location of the provider's central administration and the site where management decisions about programming and content selection are made.[64] Additional factors include the geographical presence of the workforce, satellite uplink facilities, and the use of a Member State's satellite capacity. Furthermore, the Directive extends its reach to include non-EU broadcasters that influence EU audiences via satellite uplinks or satellite capacity within EU territory.[65] According to the Country-of-Origin principle, a broadcaster needs to adhere only to the rules of its home member state rather than regulations of multiple states. This principle supports the development of cross-border business while maintaining regulatory clarity. However, stricter national rules adopted by individual Member States apply solely to providers within their jurisdiction.

By balancing regulatory flexibility with unified oversight, the AVMSD fosters a robust, transparent, and adaptable framework for audiovisual media services across the EU.

---

58 *Id.* art. 3(4)–(6).

59 *Id.* art. 3(2).

60 *Id.*

61 *See generally Id.* recitals 15, 16:

> Transparency of media ownership is directly linked to the freedom of expression, a cornerstone of democratic systems. Information concerning the ownership structure of media service providers, where such ownership results in the control of, or the exercise of a significant influence over, the content of the services provided, allows users to make an informed judgement about such content . . . Because of the specific nature of audiovisual media services, especially the impact of those services on the way people form opinions, users have a legitimate interest in knowing who is responsible for the content of those services. In order to strengthen freedom of expression, and, by extension, to promote media pluralism and avoid conflicts of interest, it is important for Member States to ensure that users have easy and direct access at any time to information about media service providers.

62 *Id.* art. 5(1).

63 *General Principles of the AVMSD, supra* note 38.

64 *Id.*

65 *Id.*

15.4. From the e-Commerce Directive to the Digital Services Act

When new media content did not qualify as an audiovisual media service, the Directive 2000/31/EC ("e-Commerce Directive") would apply.[66] For the e-Commerce Directive to apply, the service in question must have qualified as an information society service. As defined in Article 1, paragraph 1, of Directive 98/34/EC (the Information Society Services Directive), an information society service refers to any service typically provided for remuneration, delivered at a distance, by electronic means, and at the individual request of the recipient (e.g., web-based content, video platforms, e-commerce, and web-hosting services).[67]

Similar to the AVMSD, the e-Commerce Directive operated on the country-of-origin principle.[68] This means that providers of information society services were generally regulated by the EU Member State in which they are established. Notably, such providers are not required to obtain prior authorization under either the e-Commerce Directive or the AVMSD.[69]

The e-Commerce Directive categorizes intermediaries into three distinct roles: *mere conduits*, which simply transmit information; *caching providers*, which temporarily store information to facilitate more efficient transmission; and *hosting providers*, which store third-party content. A key objective of the Directive was to exempt these intermediaries from liability, thereby promoting the free flow of information and services across the internet. For hosting providers, however, this liability exemption is conditional on their lack of knowledge about the hosted content. If they become aware of illegal content, they are obligated to promptly remove it; failure to do so results in the loss of their immunity.

Platforms emerged in 2004 and rapidly transformed the internet economy and communication. They provided services that combined hosting and the transmitting and over time incorporated an increasing amount of content organizing through the use of algorithms. Because the literal interpretation of the e-Commerce Directive did not allow such a combination of services, platforms were not covered by the Directive. However, platforms have become the dominant channels for distributing information to the public, surpassing the market influence of traditional media service providers and outshining the role of television. Major platforms, in particular, have become emblematic of the disruptive transformation in the media landscape, fundamentally reshaping the information environment. In this context, platform liability has been a contentious topic, particularly concerning the interpretation of Article 14(1) of the E-Commerce Directive, which exempts

---

66 Directive 2000/31/EC of the European Parliament and of the Council of June 8, 2000, on Certain Legal Aspects of Information Society Services, in Particular Electronic Commerce, in the Internal Market ("Directive on Electronic Commerce"), 2000 O.J. (L 178), 1 [hereinafter e-Commerce Directive].

67 *Id.* art. 1(1).

68 Götz et al., *supra* note 32.

69 *Id.*

intermediaries from liability for hosted content if they lack knowledge of illegal activities or information and act expeditiously to remove such content upon becoming aware.[70]

In the landmark case of *L'Oréal v. eBay*,[71] the CJEU clarified that this exemption does not apply to service operators who play an active role in managing or optimizing stored content. The CJEU found that eBay's activities, such as optimizing the presentation of sale offers, constituted sufficient active involvement to strip it of immunity under Article 14(1).[72]

Another significant case arose with the Estonian online newspaper *Delfi*, which hosted a comment section that contained antisemitic hate speech targeting the head of a ferry company.[73] Although *Delfi* promptly removed the content upon notification, six weeks after its publication, the courts deemed it to be the publisher of the comments and thus responsible for them.[74] The ECtHR upheld this finding, ruling that *Delfi*'s liability did not violate Article 10 of the European Convention on Human Rights, as the hate speech in question did not merit protection.[75]

These cases highlighted the ambiguous status of platform services under existing regulations and underscored the lack of a unified monitoring obligation for intermediaries.[76] This regulatory gap became increasingly problematic as issues such as disinformation, hate speech, and political propaganda gained prominence, particularly in the mid-2010s. In response, several EU Member States enacted national laws to address these challenges, leading to fragmented regulations that created barriers within the internal market.

To address this lack of uniformity and prevent national divergences, the EU adopted the Digital Services Act (DSA).[77] The DSA provides a harmonized legal framework for platform liability and content moderation, ensuring consistency across Member States and reinforcing the principles of transparency, accountability, and user safety in the digital environment.[78] The choice of adopting a regulation instead of a directive ensures greater uniformity in implementation across Member States.

15.5. The Digital Services Act

The Digital Services Act became effective in November 2022, and it began applying to all online intermediaries on February 17, 2024. Its main objective is to provide a certain legal framework for digital platforms and to modernize the e-Commerce Directive adopted in 2000. Nevertheless, a second primary aim is outlined in the very first article,

---

70 BAYER, *supra* note 3, at 169.
71 Case C-324/09, L'Oréal SA and Others v. eBay International AG and Others, ECLI:EU:C:2011:474. (Jul. 12, 2011).
72 BAYER, *supra* note 3, at 169.
73 *Id.* at 170.
74 BAYER, supra note 3, at 170.
75 Delfi AS v. Estonia [GC], App. No. 64569/09 (Jun. 16, 2015), https://hudoc.echr.coe.int/eng?i=002-10636.
76 BAYER, supra note 3, at 172.
77 DSA, *supra* note 14.
78 *See Id.* recital 4.

and that is to provide "a safe, predictable, and trusted online environment that facilitates innovation and in which fundamental rights enshrined in the Charter, including the principle of consumer protection, are effectively protected."[79] For the purposes of this work, the analysis of the regulation will be limited to its impact on the media, particularly on how news is disseminated. The obligations of media outlets—especially online platforms—related to transparency and privacy will also be examined.

The DSA retains the foundational structure of its predecessor, the e-Commerce Directive. Similarly to the e-Commerce Directive, the personal scope of the regulation is limited to intermediary service providers.[80] To determine the scope more precisely, Article 1(1)(b) of Directive (EU) 2015/1535 defines "information society services." Article 3(g) of the Regulation, in contrast to the e-Commerce Directive, defines "mere conduit," "hosting," and "caching" services. However, the DSA preserves the key principle of liability exemptions for service providers engaged in mere conduit, caching, and hosting activities.[81]

Platforms are explicitly regulated as a subcategory of hosting providers. Article 3(i) defines an online platform:

> . . . as hosting service that, at the **request of a recipient** of the service, stores and **disseminates** information to the public, unless that activity is a minor and purely ancillary feature of another service or a minor functionality of the principal service and, for objective and technical reasons, cannot be used without that other service, and the integration of the feature or functionality into the other service is not a means to circumvent the applicability of this Regulation.[82]

By this definition, the core activity of the platforms seems to be the dissemination of the information to the public. However, this concept—as defined in the regulation[83]—inadequately captures the true nature of the governance performed by online platforms. Beyond merely hosting content, platforms play a pivotal role in ranking it, an activity that shapes the availability and prominence of information—be it goods, services, or news. This subtle yet powerful function, often referred to as the "invisible hand" of content ordering, has sparked significant policy concerns.[84] Indeed, criticism of platforms typically centers not on their role in disseminating content but on how they do so. While dissemination is defined as making information available to the public "at the request of the recipient of the service,"[85] ranking operates outside this scope. The ranking is not requested by users but is instead a platform-driven feature designed to enhance user engagement and, ultimately, profitability.

---

79 *Id.* art. 1(1).

80 *Id.* art. 2.

81 *Id.* arts. 1(2), 3(1) (combined reading). Indeed, the working of the liability exemption is almost the same as the e-Commerce Directive.

82 *Id.* art. 3(i) (emphasis added).

83 *Id.* art. 3(k).

84 BAYER, *supra* note 3, at 175.

85 DSA, *supra* note 14, art. 3(k).

This activity closely resembles that carried out by eBay, which led to the platform losing its immunity.[86] Nevertheless, the definition does not refer to a technical, passive, and automatic processing of the information, as was the case with the e-Commerce Directive. In addition, Recital 18 of the DSA[87] explicitly withdraws from the immunity those providers that play an active role that gives them knowledge of or control over that information.[88] Thus, a platform that ranks, fact-checks, or deprioritizes the post will likely not lose immunity for the content.

However, platforms will still be liable for the ranking. In this case, not even the newly added "Good Samaritan Clause"[89] would be of help for platforms in retaining the immunity. This clause allows intermediary services to retain their liability exemptions even when they voluntarily initiate investigations into illegal content.[90] Indeed, this provision provides an immunization when the provider investigates into illegal content, and it does not include the activities of optimizing, ranking, or recommending. By excluding the act of ranking from the definitional elements, the scope of the definition expands to include platforms that display content in a random, chronological, or user-specified order, rather than using ranking or organizing algorithms. Platforms that forgo ranking still qualify as platforms under this classification.[91] Regardless of whether they employ ranking, these platforms still meet the criteria for classification as platforms. The exclusion of content ranking from the definition clarifies that content governance is optional, meaning platforms undertake it voluntarily to increase their revenue. The way platforms manage the content they distribute, therefore, does not affect their immunity from liability for third-party content. Content moderation (i.e., the removal of illegal content) and content governance (i.e., optimization) should be treated as separate issues, each with its framework: liability and due diligence.[92]

The DSA regulates content moderation by partially retaining the e-commerce directive's framework while also introducing new elements. However, the same cannot be said for content governance. The legislator deliberately avoided imposing overly rigid rules on this complex issue for several reasons. First, the complexity of the phenomenon makes it difficult to regulate. Second, while platforms influence the content, the effects would not have been achieved without users' contributions through actions such as liking,

86 *See supra* Section 1.3.

87 *See DSA, supra note 14*, recital 18:

> The exemptions from liability established in this Regulation should not apply where, instead of confining itself to providing the services neutrally by a merely technical and automatic processing of the information provided by the recipient of the service, the provider of intermediary services plays an active role of such a kind as to give it knowledge of, or control over, that information . . .

88 Bayer, *supra* note 3, at 175.

89 DSA, *supra* note 14, art. 7.

90 *See Id.* arts. 4–6.

91 Bayer, *supra* note 3, at 176.

92 The due diligence obligations are diverse, with transparency being one of the most fundamental. These obligations apply to all types of intermediary service providers; however, a violation of these obligations does not lead to liability for the provider concerning third-party content. Nevertheless, violations are not without consequences. Any breach may result in a fine by the Commission (Art. 74 DSA) or a periodic penalty payment imposed by the Digital Services Coordinator, who can also issue orders and interim measures (Art. 51 DSA).

sharing, posting, and commenting. Third, imposing strict regulations on lawful content could limit freedom of expression. At the same time, excessive interference by platforms in their optimization processes could infringe on users' rights, including their freedom of expression.[93] This latter point is particularly important for our analysis.

In short, responsibility and freedom must go hand in hand. Reducing platforms' responsibilities helps maintain their role as neutral intermediaries focused on the technical transmission of third-party content. If platforms were held liable for third-party content due to failure to meet due diligence obligations, the consequences would be far from ideal. Platforms would effectively become publishers, with rights and obligations similar to traditional media outlets, including the right to freedom of expression and the ability to promote their agendas. This shift would make platforms the most powerful and influential content providers, diminishing the role of actual content creators and granting platforms significant power to manipulate the information shared.

Thus, the "relaxed" liability regime helps to keep platforms within defined boundaries, preventing them from entirely surpassing traditional media systems.[94] Even if platforms do not alter third-party content or assume responsibility for it, their role in organizing and presenting content still gives them unprecedented influence over public discourse. Intermediary service providers' obligations are further lightened by the retention of the absence of general monitoring or proactive fact-finding obligations.[95]

As for the territorial scope of application, the key factor for establishing EU jurisdiction is the residence or place of establishment of the service recipients, regardless of where the service providers are based.[96] Much like the GDPR's extraterritorial application, any service provider offering services to users residing in the EU falls under the law's purview and must comply with its requirements.

Among its several innovations, the DSA has adopted a risk-based approach that tailors obligations according to systemic risks posed by specific services. This differentiation is aimed at ensuring that larger platforms, or those with a greater social impact, bear adequate and proportionate responsibilities and are held accountable for the great power they hold. This approach is indeed grounded in the idea that when the number of active users of an online platform or marketplace represents a significant portion of the EU's population, systemic risks to freedom of expression and information can disproportionately affect the entire EU.[97] A platform is classified as "large" if its active users exceed 10 percent of the EU population (45 million users). These operators significantly impact

---

93 Kate Klonick, *The New Governors: The People, Rules, and Processes Governing Online Speech*, 131 HARV. L. REV. 1598, 1608 (2017) (discussing the collateral censorship that occurs when a private party has the power to control the speech of another private party).

94 BAYER, *supra* note 3, at 184.

95 DSA, *supra* note 14, art. 8.

96 *Id.* art. 2(1).

97 Diego Fulco, *Il Digital Services Act Tutela Davvero la Democrazia? I Problemi dell'Approccio Ue* [*Does the Digital Services Act Truly Protect Democracy? The Issues with the EU's Approach*], AGENDA DIGITALE EU (Jan 25, 2023), https://www.agendadigitale.eu/mercati-digitali/digital-service-act-unione-europea-democrazia/.

public and democratic discourse, necessitating stringent obligations to identify and mitigate risks arising from the operation and use of their services.

For this reason, the DSA mandates that these platforms conduct risk assessments focusing on four primary categories.[98] The first category involves the dissemination of illegal content, including hate speech. The second pertains to the impact on fundamental rights, such as freedom of expression and media pluralism. The third addresses risks to democratic processes and public security, encompassing civic and electoral debates. The fourth concerns consequences for public health and individual well-being, including risks to minors and the potential for manipulation. Furthermore, the DSA stipulates that platforms should also assess risks arising from content that, while not illegal, contributes to these systemic risks. These platforms must examine how their services are used to disseminate misleading or deceptive content, including misinformation.[99]

The DSA does not define disinformation, a gap that could be seen as a missed opportunity. However, in the European Commission's Communication on the European Democracy Plan (COM(2020) 790 final),[100] disinformation is described as "false or misleading content disseminated with the intent to deceive or secure economic or political gain, and which can cause public harm."[101] From an objective standpoint, the term "false" refers to content that is untrue and does not align with facts. Conversely, "misleading" refers to content that, while not misrepresenting facts, distorts the perception of the truth. While the application of the concept of "false" to information seems straightforward, the notion of "misleading" is more complex and ambiguous. On a subjective level, verifying the "intent to deceive or secure economic or political gain" appears less problematic compared to assessing the capacity of the content to "cause public harm." While we usually think of public harm as financial harm, here the European Commission refers to something different: collective harm, meaning harm to society as a whole. However, what the majority may perceive as "public harm" could be interpreted by minorities as "harm to the established order" or "harm to dominant power groups."

In line with the general direction established by the Commission in its communication,[102] the DSA mandates major platforms such as Meta, Twitter, and Google to assess the potential negative impacts of disinformation on society and democracy. Among the measures aimed at mitigating such risks, these large online platforms and search engines are required to consider the adoption of "awareness-raising actions," a category that remains somewhat undefined. Moreover, in the process of risk assessment and the development of mitigation measures, platforms must involve representatives of their service users, representatives of potentially affected groups, independent experts,

---

[98] DSA, *supra* note 14, § 5.

[99] Fulco, *supra* note 97.

[100] *Communication from the Commission to the European Parliament, the Council, the European Economic and Social Committee and the Committee of the Regions On the European democracy action plan*, COM (2020) 790 final (Dec. 13, 2020).

[101] *Id.* at ¶ 4.

[102] *See Id.* at ¶ 4.2: "In this context, very large platforms will also need to develop appropriate risk management tools and take measures to protect the integrity of their services against the use of manipulative techniques. The DSA will provide users with meaningful possibilities to challenge the platforms' decisions to remove or label content."

and civil society organizations. Finally, they are required to integrate such consultations into their risk assessment methodologies and the development of mitigation measures, using tools such as surveys, focus groups, roundtable discussions, and other methods of consultation and participatory design.

The DSA promotes co-regulation through mechanisms such as the Code of Practice on Disinformation, which was revised in 2022. Indeed, platforms adhering to the Code may benefit from reduced sanctions, a notable incentive given that fines for DSA violations can reach up to 6 percent of the provider's global annual turnover.

Among the innovations, the regulation establishes national authorities tasked with overseeing intermediary service providers, equipped with investigative and enforcement powers, and fosters coordination among these authorities and Member States in matters of digital services governance.[103]

Despite its comprehensive framework, the DSA presents certain challenges. Applying traditional tools such as risk analysis to the realm of information raises questions about their effectiveness in addressing complex issues such as manipulation and disinformation. Moreover, the obligation to consult intermediary bodies appears theoretical, given the difficulty of identifying entities that genuinely represent a global user base. Finally, the focus on user "awareness" initiatives lacks specificity, potentially undermining its practical impact. The DSA thus seeks to balance responsibility, freedom of expression, and pluralism. However, its success will depend on the platforms' ability to implement meaningful measures and the effectiveness of oversight by regulatory authorities.[104]

In conclusion, while the AVMSD remains intact and will persist as a *lex specialis*, the DSA, along with the e-Commerce Directive, will serve as a *lex generalis*. Thus, platforms such as YouTube will be subject to all three regulations.

15.6. Digital Markets Act

In line with the regulatory framework set by the Digital Services Act (DSA), the Digital Markets Act (DMA),[105] which came into force on May 2, 2023, imposes additional obligations on large online platforms to protect competition within the internal market. Specifically, the DMA aims to ensure the proper functioning of the internal market by establishing harmonized rules designed to guarantee fair and contestable digital markets, particularly where gatekeepers (access controllers) operate, benefiting both commercial users and end users across the EU.[106] Alongside the DSA, the DMA represents one of the most significant regulatory developments in the European digital landscape.

---

[103] DSA, *supra* note 14, arts. 49–55.

[104] Fulco, *supra* note 97.

[105] Regulation (EU) 2022/1925 of the European Parliament and of the Council of September 14, 2022, on Contestable and Fair Markets in the Digital Sector and Amending Directives (EU) 2019/1937 and (EU) 2020/1828 (Digital Markets Act), 2022 O.J. (L 265), 1 [hereinafter DMA].

[106] *Id.* art. 1(1).

For the purposes of this analysis, the focus will be on the provisions of the DMA concerning platforms as tools for information dissemination.

According to Article 2, Paragraph 1 of the DMA, a gatekeeper is defined as "an enterprise that provides core platform services, designated under Article 3."[107] This article provides both quantitative and qualitative criteria to identify a gatekeeper. The regulation targets entities listed in Article 2, Paragraph 2, which include online intermediation services, online search engines, social networking services, and video-sharing platform services. Gatekeepers are subject to a range of obligations aimed at ensuring fair competition in the digital services market and preventing the creation of unfair market conditions.[108] These obligations consist of both actions to be taken by the gatekeepers and actions they are required to refrain from. Gatekeepers, among other obligations, are required to allow third parties to interact with their services under specific circumstances, ensuring transparency and fair competition. For example, gatekeeper must ensure that fair, reasonable, and nondiscriminatory general conditions are applied to grant business users access to its software application stores, online search engines, and online social networking services.[109] Additionally, gatekeepers shall refrain from providing a more favorable treatment to its own services and products compared to similar services or products offered by third parties.[110] They must also grant business users access to data their customers generate while using the platform, promoting competition and preventing unfair advantages. Furthermore, advertisers and publishers must have free, real-time access to data related to their ads to optimize cost-effectiveness. Notably, gatekeepers must refrain from tracking end users outside of the gatekeeper's main platform service for targeted advertising purposes, unless they obtain explicit consent. This provision ensures that users' data is not exploited for marketing practices without their informed approval. Another important obligation requires gatekeepers to guarantee that users can transfer their data generated on devices or applications without incurring additional charges.

Furthermore, the DMA shifts the burden of proof, requiring gatekeepers to demonstrate their compliance with the regulations. In the event of noncompliance, penalties can reach up to 10 percent of the global annual turnover, with the possibility of increasing up to 20 percent in cases of repeated violations.[111] In cases of repeated violations, the Commission is also authorized to implement further measures, such as requiring a gatekeeper to divest a business or specific assets, or prohibiting the gatekeeper from acquiring additional services connected to the ongoing noncompliance.[112]

This regulatory framework is closely connected to the protection of freedom of expression online. Due to their dominant position, gatekeepers have the power to influence users by selecting which content to display based on their own interests, as seen with the

---

107 *Id.* art. 2(1).
108 *Id.* ch. III, arts. 5–15.
109 *Id.* art. 6(12).
110 *Id.* art. 6(5).
111 *Id.* arts. 30–33.
112 *Questions and Answers: Digital Markets Act: Ensuring Fair and Open Digital Markets*, EUR. COMM'N (Sept. 5, 2023), https://ec.europa.eu/commission/presscorner/detail/en/qanda_20_2349.

content shown on the feeds of major social media platforms. While the revised AVMSD emphasizes that video-sharing platforms do not bear editorial responsibility, they may still be subject to content-related obligations.[113] The Directive recognizes that such platforms organize (display, label, sequence) user content, and when required to intervene against illegal content, their role can be likened to that of an editor.[114] The importance of digital platforms in the realm of freedom of expression is highlighted by the 2016 Recommendation on Internet Freedom,[115] which stresses that, in accordance with Article 10 of the European Convention on Human Rights, these digital actors must respect the principles of legality, legitimacy, and proportionality when engaging in content blocking, filtering, and removal activities. In most cases, these activities are not carried out by individuals but by algorithms, which function as a sort of editor. These algorithms present content to users based on the decisions made by their developers and the data collected from the user's engagement with the platform or related services.[116] Furthermore, the role of algorithms goes beyond merely transmitting information; they also personalize the news flow for users. This inevitably leads to consequences for the polarization of public debate. Users, by nature, tend to consume content that aligns with their own beliefs, often excluding opposing viewpoints. This phenomenon is amplified by social media platforms, whose algorithms prioritize content from friends or individuals with similar opinions, thereby increasing the divide between individuals with conflicting views.[117] This fragmentation undermines social cohesion and strengthens extremist views. From this perspective, there is a clear opportunity to view algorithms as instruments through which freedom of expression is realized. This perspective also justifies the application of stringent constitutional and regulatory safeguards to ensure the protection of free speech, particularly in the context of automatic indexing services.[118]

15.7. The European Media Freedom Act

The European Media Freedom Act (EMFA)[119] entered into force on May 7, 2024, and it will fully apply as of August 8, 2025. The Media Freedom Act complements the DSA and DMA, which provide a harmonized framework for online services. This legislation focuses on addressing industry-specific challenges that are not comprehensively covered by the DSA and DMA.[120] The EMFA seeks to harmonize the diverse national regulatory frameworks governing media freedom, pluralism, and editorial independence. It aims to enhance the functioning of the internal market for media services while preventing barriers that

---

113 Koltay, *supra* note 6, at 92.

114 *Id.*

115 Committee of Ministers, Recommendation of the Committee of Ministers to Member States on Internet Freedom, CM/Rec (2016) 5 (Apr. 13, 2016).

116 Sue Halpern, *Mind Control & the Internet*, N.Y. Rev. of Books (Jun. 23, 2011).

117 Cass R. Sunstein, Republic.com: Cittadini Informati o Consumatori di Informazioni? [Republic.com: Informed Citizens or Consumers of Information?] (Mulino trans. 2003); *see also* Riccardo Montaldo, *La Tutela del Pluralismo Informativo nelle Piattaforme Online* [*The Protection of Media Pluralism on Online Platforms*], 1 Rivista di diritto dei media, 227 (2020).

118 Bayer, *supra* note 3, at 225.

119 EMFA, *supra* note 16.

120 *The European Media Freedom Act (EMFA)—Regulation (EU) 2024/1083*, Media Freedom Act, https://www.media-freedom-act.com/ (last visited Nov. 25, 2024).

could hinder the operations of media service providers across the EU.[121] This regulation was enacted to respond to the need to ensure informational pluralism and a healthy public debate. Microtargeting practices, which exploit users' personal data, enable the dissemination of polarizing political messages, thereby threatening democracy.[122] This legislation aims to protect media pluralism, counter the manipulation of public opinion, and guarantee citizens' right to form their own judgments.

It is noteworthy that the EU derives its legislative competence in the area of media freedom from Article 114 of the TFEU,[123] prioritizing the smooth functioning of the internal market over the direct protection of fundamental rights.[124] This choice is not accidental: the safeguarding of fundamental freedoms falls within the deeply rooted constitutional frameworks of each Member State—a domain where the EU lacks direct competence and where adopting a uniform regulatory framework across all twenty-seven Member States would be impractical.[125] Therefore, it becomes evident that the principle of a competitive market serves as the *Grundnorm* underpinning every legislative initiative at the European level.[126] In addition, linking the internal market to media freedom, while pragmatic, does not seem entirely artificial. The creation of monopolies or dominant positions within the information sector, which grant undue advantages to specific political leaders or parties, inevitably undermines the proper exercise of voting rights.[127]

The inherently cross-border nature of media content production and consumption, including news, underscores the necessity of a coordinated European approach to ensure legal certainty. For this reason, the Commission has opted for a regulation as the legislative instrument for the Media Freedom Act to ensure uniform implementation and avoid regulatory divergences or delays. Nevertheless, the EMFA includes several provisions that are abstract and principle-based, leaving room for Member States to interpret and fill in specific details. In this respect, it bears similarities to a directive, which sets overarching goals but delegates implementation to Member States. Unlike a directive, however, a regulation is directly and uniformly applicable not only to Member States but also to other legal and natural persons. The Act is further complemented by a Recommendation, which encourages voluntary measures, particularly in enhancing editorial independence and ensuring transparency in media ownership.

The legislator's decision to extend the proposal's scope to include all actions that could threaten media freedom, as well as all types of media services, both online and offline, is particularly commendable.[128] For instance, the proposal tackles both online and offline threats, including issues of algorithmic bias on social media platforms that may suppress certain viewpoints, the spread of fake news, as well as offline challenges such as

---

[121] *Id.*

[122] COM (2020) 790 final, *supra* note 100, at § 2.1.

[123] TFEU art. 114.

[124] *See generally* EMFA, *supra* note 16, recitals 1 to 7 (enhancing the importance of media freedom and pluralism, along with a harmonized set of rules, for the proper functioning of the internal market).

[125] Muto, *supra* note 7, at 225–26.

[126] *Id.*

[127] Roberto Mastroianni, *Freedom and Pluralism of the Media: An European Value Waiting to Be Discovered?*1 Rivista di Diritto dei Media, 109 (2022).

[128] Muto, *supra* note 7, at 227.

inappropriate political influence over print or broadcast media. By embracing a dynamic approach, the proposal is designed to address unforeseen challenges and evolving phenomena, minimizing the risk of future regulatory gaps. This forward-thinking framework ensures a comprehensive and adaptable safeguard for media freedom in a rapidly changing landscape.[129]

A key definitional element is that this activity is pursued with editorial responsibility. Indeed, under Article 3(2), a media service provider is defined as "a natural or legal person whose professional activity is to provide a media service and who has editorial responsibility for the choice of the content of the media service and determines the manner in which it is organized."[130] This definition aims to distinguish media service providers from platform providers, which, by contrast, do not exercise any type of editorial responsibility. Indeed, recital 11 of the EMFA recognizes that platforms "play a key role in organizing the content, including by automated means or by algorithms; however, they do not exercise any editorial control over the content to which they provide access."[131]

Article 3 of the proposed Regulation establishes that recipients of media services within the Union have the right to access a plurality of news and current affairs content produced in accordance with the editorial freedom of media service providers, thereby enriching public debate.[132] Complementing this, Article 4 enshrines the right of media service providers to conduct their economic activities without restrictions beyond those imposed by EU law.[133] Member States are therefore obligated to respect press freedom, refraining from interference in editorial decisions[134] or engaging in surveillance or interception activities targeting journalists, media service providers, or individuals connected to them, except in cases of overriding public interest, such as ensuring public safety, addressing national security threats, or preventing serious crimes.[135]

To ensure these protections, Member States must designate independent authorities competent to address complaints lodged by media service providers. The European Regulators Group for Audiovisual Media Services (ERGA) advocates for robust safeguards for media independence and the confidentiality of sources, including protection from national authorities. Additionally, ERGA stresses the importance of extending these protections to freelance journalists and balancing media independence against the need to achieve broader public interest goals, such as disseminating public health messages.[136] For instance, during the COVID-19 pandemic, media were required to diffuse to the public directives issued by the government regarding lockdown measures, physical distancing, and wearing masks. Additionally, to prevent misinformation about COVID-19, the EU strengthened its Code of Practice on Disinformation. This effort demonstrates the practical application of balancing the promotion of accurate public health information with the respect for media freedom and freedom of expression.

---

[129] *Id.*
[130] EMFA, *supra* note 16, art. 3(2).
[131] *Id.* recital 11.
[132] *Id.* art. 3.
[133] *Id.* art. 4(1).
[134] *Id.* art. 4(2).
[135] Muto, *supra* note 7, at 230.
[136] *Id.*

Publicly funded information services, in particular, must ensure that citizens have access to diverse and pluralistic information sources, upholding their role as watchdogs of democracy. This issue is particularly sensitive, given the limited legislative competence of the EU in this area, as outlined in Protocol 29, which leaves much of the authority over public broadcasting to individual Member States.[137] Consequently, regulatory efforts must remain confined to the definition of principles—such as independence, transparency, and plurality, that aim to promote democratic values while respecting national sovereignty—which appear reasonable and proportionate.[138] For instance, Article 5 further stipulates that public media providers must offer impartial and pluralistic information to their audience in line with their public service mission.[139] This objective relies on transparent and nondiscriminatory appointment procedures for management positions, adequate tenure to ensure effective independence, and the allocation of sufficient financial resources to carry out their mandate.

The proposal also imposes transparency obligations on private media entities, recognizing their public interest role. Media service providers must ensure that recipients have easy and direct access to up-to-date information, including their legal name and contact details, and the identity of direct or indirect owners with sufficient shareholdings to influence operational and strategic decisions—such as ownership by state entities or public authorities. They must also disclose the names of their beneficial owners, as defined by Article 3(6) of Directive (EU) 2015/849,[140] along with the total annual amounts of public funds received for state advertising and any advertising revenues originating from third-country public authorities or entities.[141]

Member States are required to task national regulatory or other competent authorities with the creation and maintenance of national media ownership databases that include this information.[142] Furthermore, media service providers offering news and current affairs content must take appropriate measures to guarantee the independence of their editorial decisions, ensuring that such decisions are made freely within the framework of the established editorial line and that any actual or potential conflicts of interest affecting the provision of news content are disclosed.[143] While preserving editorial independence, these measures aim to reinforce accountability and ensure the legitimacy of media in democratic processes.

The emphasis on media pluralism within the Regulation reflects its status as a corollary of media freedom. European history has demonstrated that media independence from powerful institutions, particularly the state, is essential for maintaining democratic legitimacy. Media outlets that fail to uphold this independence risk eroding public trust and undermining democracy, given their profound influence on public opinion. In this context, the activities of digital gatekeepers raise critical concerns about their potential

---

[137] Protocol No. 29, 2016 O.J. (C 202), 311.

[138] Position of the European Regulators Group for Audiovisual Media Services (ERGA), Proposal of the Commission for a European Media Freedom Act (Nov. 2022).

[139] EMFA, *supra* note 16, art. 5(1).

[140] *Id.* art. 6(1).

[141] *Id.*

[142] *Id.* art. 6(2).

[143] *Id.* art. 6(3).

to interfere directly with freedom of expression and media pluralism, underscoring the necessity of regulatory measures to mitigate these risks.

To address these issues, the Regulation requires large online platforms, as defined by the DSA, to declare their compliance with transparency obligations and their editorially independence from states, political parties, and third countries.[144] Annually, these platforms must publicly disclose how often they have restricted or suspended content provided by media service providers and provide reasons for such measures.[145] In the case of disputes with content providers, the Regulation mandates the resolution of such conflicts through Alternative Dispute Resolution (ADR) mechanisms, such as mediation under Article 12 of Regulation (EU) 2019/1150 or other out-of-court settlements provided for under Article 21 of the DSA.[146]

The Regulation also introduces the European Board for Media Services (Articles 8–13), which will replace the ERGA.[147] This new independent authority, with representatives from national regulators, will oversee the sector and facilitate dialogue between large platforms, media providers, and civil society. It will monitor compliance with self-regulation initiatives and promote best practices.[148] Moreover, recognizing the growing role of online platforms in news dissemination, Article 20 ensures that users can customize their media experiences by adjusting their default settings on platforms.[149]

Conclusively, it is noteworthy that in the United States, media diversity is safeguarded by the Federal Communications Commission (FCC), alongside antitrust regulations, to prevent media operators from becoming so dominant that they wield more power than state actors.

15.8. The GDPR 2016/679/EU, Consumer Rights Directive 2011/83/EU, and the Unfair Contract Terms Directive (UCTD) 93/13/EEC: Synergy and Complementarity

The immense market power of the large online platforms and marketplaces, as discussed, is largely attributable to the so-called "gratuitous contracts" that are entered into daily on the internet.[150] This type of "gratuitous" contract is one in which one party commits to providing a service (e.g., the use of a Social Network or simply a search engine), while the other party (knowingly or unknowingly) agrees to provide their data in exchange.

---

144 *Id.* art. 18(1).
145 *Id.* art. 18(8).
146 *Id.* art. 18(7).
147 *Id.* § 2.
148 *Id.* art. 19.
149 *Id.* art. 20(1).
150 Giorgio Resta, *I Dati Personali Oggetto del Contratto. Riflessioni sul Coordinamento tra la Direttiva (UE) 2019/770 e il Regolamento (UE) 2016/679* [*Personal Data as the Subject of the Contract: Reflections on the Coordination between Directive (EU) 2019/770 and Regulation (EU) 2016/679*], 2018 Annuario del Contratto, 127, 128 (2019).

The EU has enforced data protection regulations, first with Directive 46/1995 and later with the GDPR (2016/679/EU), to protect users' data and grant them control over it, as well as remedies in the event of a data breach. However, it has been proven insufficient to protect digital users merely through privacy regulations vis-à-vis the always growing amount of data collected. As a result, the EU has adopted an approach where data protection laws (GDPR), consumer protection laws (Consumer Rights Directive 2011/83/EU),[151] and unfair commercial practices laws (Unfair Commercial Practices Directive [UCPD] 2005/29/EC)[152] work together to provide safeguards for digital users and help create a more balanced market.

The GDPR and consumer protection regulations show some differences. However, it is in their differences that the complementarity nature of the regulations manifests itself.[153] First, personal data protection is acknowledged as a fundamental right, as recalled in the first recital of the GDPR[154] citing Articles 8(1) of the Charter of Fundamental Rights[155] and 16(1) of the TFEU.[156] On the contrary, no such qualification can be found for consumers' rights. The Charter of Fundamental Rights only guarantees consumers, in Article 38, the assurance of a high level of protection in EU policies.[157] Thus, while the right to protection of personal data opens the way to direct justiciability, consumer protection only provides grounds to challenge the invalidity of an EU legislative text that is not in accordance with the principle stated in Art. 38 of the Charter.

A foundation for a legitimate processing of personal data, according to the regulation, is the user's consent; other foundations may be found in context, public interest, etc., in accordance with the other objective of the regulation, which is the development of the digital economy.[158] However, the GDPR comes short of protecting consumers in specific contexts such as the imbalanced economic relationship. As previously demonstrated, the digital market can be the streambed in which power imbalances may even solidify.

Due to the technical complexity and opacity of the digital commercial environment, users' self-determination may be, and many times is, greatly influenced by the digital environment itself. In this situation, consumer law provisions can grant consumers/users rights that they could not invoke otherwise and protect the interests attached to their

---

[151] Directive 2011/83/EU of the European Parliament and of the Council of October 25, 2011, on Consumer Rights, Amending Council Directive 93/13/EEC and Directive 1999/44/EC of the European Parliament and of the Council and Repealing Council Directive 85/577/EEC and Directive 97/7/EC of the European Parliament and of the Council, 2011 O.J. (L 304), 64 [hereinafter Consumer Rights Directive].

[152] Directive 2005/29/EC of the European Parliament and of the Council of May 11, 2005, Concerning Unfair Business-to-Consumer Commercial Practices in the Internal Market and Amending Council Directive 84/450/EEC, Directives 97/7/EC, 98/27/EC, and 2002/65/EC of the European Parliament and of the Council and Regulation (EC) No 2006/2004 of the European Parliament and of the Council ("Unfair Commercial Practices Directive"), 2005 O.J. (L 149), 22 (EC) [hereinafter UCPD].

[153] TFEU art. 16(1); *see* Élise Poillot, *La protection des données personalles par le droit européen de la consommation* [*The Protection of Personal Data through European Consumer Law*], in LE DROIT EUROPÉEN DE LA CONSOMMATION AU XXIE SIÈCLE, 301, 309 (Larcier ed., 2022).

[154] GDPR, *supra* note 20, recital 1.

[155] Charter of Fundamental Rights of the European Union, *supra* note 25, art. 8(1).

[156] Poillot, *supra* note 15, at 309.

[157] *Id.*

[158] *Id.* at 311.

personal data.[159] A clear example of this is profiling for advertising.[160] Microtargeting, particularly through online profiling, represents a cornerstone of the digital economy. The objective is to predict user behavior and deliver personalized advertisements. While this approach drives significant technological and organizational innovations, it raises concerns over privacy and the potential for mass surveillance, as businesses and data brokers increasingly rely on personal data to optimize targeting. Data for such profiling is acquired through voluntary sharing, observation, statistical inference, or deterministic computations—often without user awareness. Methods such as cookies, web beacons, tracking walls, and device fingerprinting facilitate this process.

Although the GDPR introduces safeguards, its limitations are evident in addressing the challenges posed by microtargeting. Article 22 of the GDPR grants individuals the right not to be subject to decisions based solely on automated processing that significantly affects them. Profiling for targeted advertising typically falls outside the scope of this prohibition, as it does not usually produce significant effects on individuals. The Article 29 Working Party, however, has clarified that significant effects may arise depending on factors such as the intrusiveness of the profiling process, individuals' expectations, the delivery method of advertisements, and the exploitation of vulnerabilities.[161] For instance, an individual who is known to be or likely facing financial difficulties and is repeatedly targeted with advertisements for high-interest loans might be tempted to accept these offers, potentially leading to even greater debt. Automated decisions can have significant effects not only on the individual directly involved but also based on the actions of others.[162] For example, a credit card company might lower a customer's credit limit not based on their own repayment history but by analyzing nontraditional factors like the behavior of other customers in the same area.[163] In such cases, the processing must be lawful and based on explicit consent or other legal grounds under Article 22 of the GDPR. A critical issue with consent in the digital environment is its questionable authenticity. Often, data subjects are unable to distinguish consent for essential services from consent for data processing used in profiling and advertisements. This undermines the granularity requirement of the GDPR, which mandates that consent must be specific and freely given for each data usage.

To address gaps in the GDPR's enforcement, consumer protection laws, particularly the Unfair Contract Terms Directive (UCTD),[164] can provide complementary remedies. Recital 42 of the GDPR explicitly links the fairness of consent declarations to the standards of the UCTD. A contract term obliging users to collectively consent to all privacy terms, including data collection for targeted advertising, may create a significant imbalance between the parties' obligations. Such terms could be deemed unfair under Article 3(1)

---

159 *Id.* at 313.

160 *Id.*

161 *Art. 29 Data Protection Working Party, Guidelines on Automated Individual Decision Making and Profiling for the Purposes of Regulation 2016/679*, at 22, 17/EN WP251rev.01 (as last revised and adopted on Feb. 6, 2018).

162 *Id.*

163 *Id.*

164 Council Directive 93/13/EEC of April 5, 1993, on Unfair Terms in Consumer Contracts, 1993 O.J. (L 95), 29 [hereinafter UCTD].

of the UCTD.[165] Similarly, when large tech companies merge—such as Facebook's acquisition of Instagram—users may be forced to accept new, broader terms of service, including expanded data collection practices. These changes could create unfair imbalances in users' rights and expectations, leading to concerns about market dominance and privacy violations, which could also be challenged under the UCTD.

Furthermore, the UCTD's principles align with the GDPR's data minimization requirement.[166] If a digital service provider collects more data than necessary for its services, this practice violates the GDPR and may also constitute an unfair term under the UCTD. Consumers could invoke their right to refuse consent to such terms, and the terms would be deemed nonbinding. In cases where the term forms a core contractual obligation but is nontransparent, the entire contract could be invalidated, leaving consumers the option to object to its annulment and retain access to the service. This dual approach under the GDPR and UCTD enhances consumer protection in the face of exploitative practices, addressing the limitations of GDPR enforcement by allowing unfair terms to be challenged in contract law while enabling consumers to seek redress for excessive data collection.

The EU's legislative interventions for complementary protection for digital consumers have been Directives 2019/770/EU, 2019/771/EU, and 2019/2161/EU. Directive 2019/770/EU addresses contracts such as those involving streaming services (e.g., Netflix or Spotify), ensuring consumers have rights related to service quality, availability, and data protection. Directive 2019/771/EU applies to contracts for the sale of physical products with digital features, such as smart TVs or smartphones, guaranteeing consumer rights related to product functionality and updates. Directive 2019/2161/EU enforces consumer rights in the digital market by introducing transparency rules for online marketplaces, such as requiring platforms such as Amazon to disclose the identity of third-party sellers, thereby preventing unfair commercial practices and enhancing consumer confidence.

15.9. Directives 2019/770/EU, 2019/771/EU, and Omnibus Directive 2019/2161/EU

These directives were adopted as part of the "Digital Single Market Strategy" of the previous Commission.[167] The scope of innovation introduced by these legislative measures is significant, as they aim to adapt consumer protection to the continuous evolution of the digital world and market dynamics. For the purposes of this analysis, the focus will be on extending consumer protection to include so-called "gratuitous contracts," where

---

[165] "A contractual term which has not been individually negotiated shall be regarded as unfair if, contrary to the requirement of good faith, it causes a significant imbalance in the parties' rights and obligations arising under the contract, to the detriment of the consumer." *Id.* art. 3(1).

[166] *Id.* art. 5(1)(c).

[167] *COMMUNICATION FROM THE COMMISSION TO THE EUROPEAN PARLIAMENT, THE COUNCIL, THE EUROPEAN ECONOMIC AND SOCIAL COMMITTEE AND THE COMMITTEE OF THE REGIONS A Digital Single Market Strategy for Europe*, COM (2015) 0192 final (May 6, 2015).

data, rather than monetary compensation, is provided in exchange for digital content or services. Modern media and social media in particular exemplify this dynamic by offering users access to content in return for the provision of their personal data.

15.9.1. Directive 2019/770/EU

This directive provides a legal framework akin to that of conformity guarantees for physical goods but pertains to digital content and services not covered by a contract for the sale of goods.[168] Indeed, Article 1, captioned "subject matter and purpose," provides that the purpose of the Directive is to ensure the proper functioning of the EU internal market while at the same time granting consumers a high level of protection by laying down common rules about contracts for the supply of digital content or digital services.

This Directive safeguards, in particular, consumers' personal data because it broadens the scope of application to encompass digital content and digital service provided in exchange for personal data, with no necessity for a direct financial contribution from the consumers. The aim is to shield consumers from incorrect perceptions, as the notion of a gratuitous service can be deceptive. In this case, consumers may assume that they have no recourse against the provider if the digital service, offered without direct monetary payment, is not delivered correctly or is unsatisfactory. In determining the scope of application of the directive, Article 3(1) provides that the directive "shall also apply where the trader supplies or undertakes to supply digital content or a digital service to the consumer, and the consumer provides or undertakes to provide personal data to the trader."[169] For example, the directive will apply in any case where a user provides their data, such as their email address, to access a digital service or content.

The UCPD 2005/29/EC already offered consumers protection against misleading commercial practices in the context of business-to-consumer (B2C) transactions, including those involving the exchange of personal data for digital services.[170] Under the UCPD, practices are considered unfair if they mislead or omit material information that would otherwise inform the consumer's transactional decision, such as failing to disclose that a "free" service is effectively paid for with personal data. These protections also

---

[168] Poillot, *supra* note 15, at 316.

[169] Directive 2019/770, *supra* note 17, art. 3(1); *see also Id.* recital 24:

> While fully recognising that the protection of personal data is a fundamental right and that therefore personal data cannot be considered as a commodity, this Directive should ensure that consumers are, in the context of such business models, entitled to contractual remedies . . . For example, this Directive should apply where the consumer opens a social media account and provides a name and email address that are used for purposes other than solely supplying the digital content or digital service, or other than complying with legal requirements. It should equally apply where the consumer gives consent for any material that constitutes personal data, such as photographs or posts that the consumer uploads, to be processed by the trader for marketing purposes.

[170] UCPD, *supra* note 150, art. 2(d): "'business-to-consumer commercial practices' (hereinafter also referred to as commercial practices) means any act, omission, course of conduct or representation, commercial communication including advertising and marketing, by a trader, directly connected with the promotion, sale or supply of a product to consumers."

encompass the obligation to inform consumers about the purpose of data collection, as mandated by the GDPR, and remedies are available when such omissions occur.

However, the scope of the UCPD is limited to cases where the trader's behavior qualifies as unfair under the directive. By contrast, Directive 2019/770/EU offers broader safeguards by explicitly addressing contracts where personal data is exchanged for digital services or content, even in instances where the trader's actions do not constitute unfair commercial practices.

Article 3(8) of the Directive also reflects the complementary approach mentioned above. It provides that Union's law regarding data protection shall apply to any data processing and that in any case of conflict between the present directive and the GDPR, the latter will prevail.[171] Indeed, data protection Union laws will regulate, without any interference by directive 2019/770, all the aspects concerning the lawful processing of data, from the conditions for a freely given consent, to the right to data erasure and data portability. It follows that in any case of conflict, data protection laws will preempt the application of this directive.[172] Thus, while the GDPR, particularly its provisions on consent, governs the formation of contracts for the supply of digital content or services, this directive provides remedies for consumers who enter into such contracts.

Article 5 of Directive 2019/770/EU defines the obligations of traders in supplying digital content or services, emphasizing timely delivery and compliance with conformity requirements. Traders are required to provide the content or service without undue delay following the conclusion of the contract unless otherwise agreed by the parties. The obligation is considered fulfilled when the digital content or service, or the means to access it, is made available to the consumer or a designated facility. For example, when a consumer subscribes to a digital news platform like *The New York Times*, the trader must provide immediate access to the content or the means to access it, such as login credentials, once the subscription is confirmed.

The directive distinguishes between subjective and objective conformity requirements, which must both be satisfied.[173] Subjective conformity refers to compliance with the terms agreed in the contract, such as the description, quality, and functionality of the digital content or service. An example with regard to streaming services would be that if a consumer subscribes to Netflix for high-definition content but the service delivers lower quality, this would breach subjective conformity and entitle the consumer to a remedy, such as a refund. Subjective conformity also encompasses any specific purposes communicated by the consumer and accepted by the trader, as well as the provision of necessary accessories, instructions, or updates explicitly stipulated in the contract

Objective conformity, on the other hand, pertains to what consumers can reasonably expect based on the type of digital content or service. This includes its fitness for normal

---

[171] *See* Directive 2019/770, *supra* note 17, recitals 37, 38 (providing that any data processing involved in the contracts regulated by the directive should happen in respect to the GDPR and the E-privacy Directive (2002/58/EC)).

[172] Resta, *supra* note 148, at 132.

[173] Directive 2019/770, *supra* note 17, art. 7.

use, adherence to public statements or advertising made before the contract, and the provision of updates required to ensure the digital content or service remains functional and secure.[174] For example, a smartphone that fails to function properly or lacks timely security updates breaches objective conformity, as consumers expect devices to perform standard tasks reliably.

Directive 2019/770/EU mandates that traders provide updates, including security updates, to maintain conformity with the contract. Failure to comply results in noncompliance unless the consumer fails to install the updates within a reasonable time after being informed of their availability and the consequences of not doing so, or if installation issues arise due to inadequate instructions provided by the trader.[175] For example, if a consumer subscribes to a streaming service like Netflix and the service fails to provide promised software updates, which affects the functionality of the app, the consumer can seek remedies. In long-term contracts, this obligation extends for the duration of the contract. Additionally, traders must ensure that consumers can use the service without third-party claims, such as intellectual property, and provide remedies if such rights are violated.[176]

The Directive also operates in conjunction with data protection regulations, particularly the GDPR. Noncompliance with GDPR principles, such as data minimization or security obligations, may result in a lack of conformity under the directive. For instance, if a trader fails to secure personal data as required by the GDPR, leading to breaches such as exposure of credit card information, the service may be deemed nonconforming. In such cases, the trader's failure could violate both subjective and objective conformity requirements, depending on whether the obligation was explicitly agreed upon or reasonably expected.[177]Another example would be if a data breach occurs due to a provider's failure to secure personal data, such as in the case of *Yahoo!*,[178] it could constitute nonconformity under the Directive, entitling the consumer to compensation. This integration underscores the trader's dual responsibility to ensure the lawful processing of personal data and the delivery of a service that meets contractual and regulatory standards.

Under Article 14 of Directive 2019/770/EU, consumers are entitled to several remedies when a digital service or content fails to conform to the contract. First, the consumer has the right to request that the trader bring the digital content or service into conformity within a reasonable time, free of charge, and with minimal inconvenience. If the trader fails to meet this obligation, or if the defect persists despite efforts to fix it, the consumer may be entitled to a proportional reduction in the price in cases where the transaction

---

174 *See also Id.* recital 42 (providing that the service or content provided should comply with the requirements agreed by the parties. Some examples are given: number of music files that can be accessed, language and version agreed, picture resolution agreed in the contract).

175 *See also Id.* recitals 44 (providing that incomplete or defective updates should also be considered a lack of conformity, because this would mean the updates are not performed in the manner stipulated in the contracts), 47 (granting consumers the right to remain free to choose whether to install the updates provided, with the warning that the consumer should, however, not expect the digital content or digital service to remain in conformity).

176 *Id.* art. 10.

177 *Id.* art. 11.

178 *In re* Yahoo! Inc. Customer Data Sec. Breach Litig., No. 20-16633, 2022 WL 2304236 (9th Cir. Jun. 27, 2022).

involves a monetary payment.[179] In cases of serious defects, the consumer may also choose to terminate the contract. The remedy of contract termination is available even in the case of exchanges involving data, where the reduction of price is not applicable. For example, if Amazon sells an e-book with compatibility issues not disclosed upfront, it breaches subjective and objective conformity, and the consumer may seek a remedy like a replacement with a format that is compatible. In the case in which Amazon fails to cure such compatibility defect, the consumer may request a price reduction or a refund.

Upon termination of the contract, the trader must comply with *GDPR* obligations regarding the consumer's personal data. While the trader may continue to use the data in some limited circumstances (such as when it is aggregated or no longer identifiable), they must refrain from using any data that is specific to the consumer's usage of the product or service.[180] Moreover, the trader is required to make any content created by the consumer (excluding personal data) available post-termination. For example, if a consumer creates and uploads a playlist on music streaming platform such as Spotify, this latter would be required to make that playlist available to the consumer even after they cancel their subscription, as long as the content does not involve personal data. Finally, Article 17 mandates that the consumer must stop using the digital service or content and refrain from making it available to third parties after contract termination.

15.9.2. Directive 2019/771/EU

Directive 2019/771 complements Directive 2019/770 as it covers contracts for the sale of goods that are interconnected with or incorporate digital elements. This Directive modifies the Regulation 2017/2394/EU[181] and the Directive 2009/22/EC,[182] and it repeals the Directive 1999/44/EC, also known as the Sale of Goods Act.[183]

This Directive aims to provide a competitive and single EU digital market while also granting consumers rights. The twin directives are complementary and do not overlap, as provided by recitals 20 of Directive 2019/770, and 13 of Directive 2019/771. Understanding how these Directives interact with each other is indeed fundamental to make the legal framework of remedies available to the consumer more certain and will eventually benefit the digital market as well.[184]

Unlike its twin Directives, this will not apply to the exchange of service-for-data because it will encompass only monetary transactions.[185] Indeed, it will apply to digital services

---

179 *See also* Directive 2019/770, *supra* note 17, recital 65.

180 *See also Id.* recital 69.

181 Regulation (EU) 2017/2394 of the European Parliament and of the Council of December 12, 2017, on Cooperation between National Authorities Responsible for the Enforcement of Consumer Protection Laws and Repealing Regulation (EC) No 2006/2004, 2017 O.J. (L 345), 1.

182 Directive 2009/22/EC of the European Parliament and of the Council of April 23, 2009, on Injunctions for the Protection of Consumers' Interests (Codified version), 2009 O.J. (L 110), 30.

183 Directive 1999/44/EC of the European Parliament and of the Council of May 25, 1999, on Certain Aspects of the Sale of Consumer Goods and Associated Guarantees, 1999 O.J. (171), 12.

184 Jorge Morais Carvalho, *Sale of Goods and Supply of Digital Content and Digital Services—Overview of Directives 2019/770 and 2019/771*, 8 Issue no. 5 J. European Consumer & Market L., 194, 194 (2019).

185 Directive 2019/771, *supra* note 18, art. 3(3): "this directive shall not apply to contracts for the supply of digital content or digital services."

or contents that are incorporated in or interconnected with goods and are provided with goods under the sales contracts, even though the digital element or content is supplied by the seller itself or by a third party.[186] To clarify any ambiguity, *Article 3(3)* specifies that if there is doubt about whether the supply is part of the sales contract, the *Sales Directive* should apply. Once the different scope of application is clarified, the Directive shares many similarities with its counterpart, as both provide remedies for consumers when the seller breaches the contract. Whether the breach stems from a lack of conformity or a failure to supply, the requirements outlined in this Directive are largely consistent with those established in Directive 2019/770.

Goods that are incorporated or interconnected to digital content or digital services produce data. The Directive is silent about the regulatory framework applicable to this data. It can be inferred, however, that it will have to be processed in accordance with the GDPR.

15.9.3. Directive 2019/2161/EU

Directive 2019/2161/EU, also called the *omnibus* Directive, is the first pillar of the "New Deal for Consumers." The New Deal for Consumers was proposed by the Commission in its Communication to the European Parliament, the Council, and the European Economic and Social Committee in 2018.[187]

Directive 2019/2161 modernizes and strengthens consumer protection by amending four important European Directives: Directive 93/13/EEC on Unfair Contract Terms,[188] Directive 2005/29/EC on Unfair Commercial Practices,[189] Directive 98/6/EC on Product Pricing,[190] and Directive 2011/83/EU on Consumer Rights.[191] One of the areas of consumer protection most affected by these amendments is the Unfair Commercial Practices Directive. The purpose of the amendments is to adjust the legislative framework and to adequately address new challenges of new technologies to consumer law, including the emergence of online platforms and the increasing involvement of traders in new forms of unfair commercial practices typical of the digital market.[192] Accordingly, Directive 2019/2161 broadens the definition of "product" established by the UCPD to encompass digital services and digital content exchanged in digital markets.

The most significant innovations brought about by Directive 2019/2161 undoubtedly concern situations where consumer vulnerability could be exploited by professionals to the detriment of the consumer. First, additional information obligations were imposed

---

186 *Id.*

187 *COMMUNICATION FROM THE COMMISSION TO THE EUROPEAN PARLIAMENT, THE COUNCIL AND THE EUROPEAN ECONOMIC AND SOCIAL COMMITTEE A New Deal for Consumer*, COM (2018) 0183 final (Apr. 11, 2018).

188 UCTD, *supra* note 160.

189 UCPD, *supra* note 150.

190 Directive 98/6/EC of the European Parliament and of the Council of February 16, 1998, on consumer protection in the indication of the prices of products offered to consumers, 1998 O.J. (L 80), 27.

191 Consumer Rights Directive, *supra* note 149.

192 Mateja Đurović, *Adaptation of Consumer Law to the Digital Age: EU Directive 2019/2161 on Modernisation and Better Enforcement of Consumer Law*, 68, 2 Anali Pravnog Fakulteta U Beogradu 62, 64 (2020).

on professionals, with particular regard to price personalization resulting from profiling. Second, building on the principle outlined in Directive 2019/770, data was recognized as "consideration" for the supply of digital content or service. As a result, the scope of application of remedies set forth in Directive 2011/83 has been extended to encompass transactions involving the exchange of service-for-data. Moreover, the list of commercial practices that are inherently considered unfair provided by Annex I to the Directive 2005/29/EC (UCPD) was updated to include, among other things, nontransparent advertising and ranking of offers.

The major modification introduced by Directive 2019/2161, amending Directive 2011/83/EU, is the expanded scope of rights and remedies under Directive 2011/83/EU. In line with the principle in Article 3(1), second paragraph, of Directive 2019/770, Article 4(2)(b) broadens the scope to include the supply of digital services where the consumer provides or agrees to provide personal data—unless the data is processed solely for the purpose of supplying the digital product.[193]

The Directive introduces explicit obligations for traders to inform consumers about personalized pricing based on automated decision making.[194] This obligation is limited to the precontractual phase, even though price personalization may occur during the contract's duration, such as when tariff changes are allowed, or the contract is indefinite.[195] However, a regulatory gap remains, as penalties for noncompliance are only applied after the contract has been concluded, potentially leaving consumers already affected by unfair practices. Furthermore, the Directive does not harmonize the penalties for failing to inform consumers, leaving Member States to establish their own penalty regimes, which could result in fragmentation and inconsistent enforcement across the EU.

Another important obligation is for online platforms to inform consumers whether third-party sellers on their marketplace are professionals and to clarify that consumer rights under EU law will not apply if the third party is not a professional. Platforms must also disclose the parameters used to rank offers. Member States may impose additional information requirements.

The Omnibus Directive also bridges consumer protection and data protection by ensuring that traders comply with the GDPR, especially concerning data minimization and portability.

In terms of enforcement, the Directive strengthens penalties for breaches of consumer law. Member States are required to establish penalties that are effective, proportionate, and dissuasive.[196] These sanctions should take into account factors such as the nature, scale, and duration of the infringement; any remedial actions by the trader; and the trader's economic gains from the infringement. For the first time in EU consumer law, the

---

[193] *See also* Directive 2019/2161, *supra* note 19, recital 31 (stating that indeed Directive 2011/83/EU was already applicable to the exchange of digital content for the provision of data).

[194] *Id.* art. 4(4)(a): "Article 6 is amended as follows: (ii) the following point is inserted: "(ea) where applicable, that the price was personalised on the basis of automated decision-making."

[195] *See also* Poillot, *supra* note 15, at 336 (arguing about the informational requirements regarding price personalization).

[196] Directive 2019/2161, *supra* note 19, art. 4(13).

Directive introduces specific financial sanctions, allowing fines of at least 4 percent of the trader's annual turnover in the Member State concerned or a minimum of 2 million euros when turnover information is unavailable.[197] These penalties align more closely with those for breaches of competition and data protection law.[198]

In conclusion, the Omnibus Directive seeks to balance the information asymmetry between consumers and traders, especially in digital markets, by providing consumers with clearer information and stronger remedies, such as price reductions and contract termination. At the same time, it empowers national authorities to impose substantial fines on traders who breach consumer law, marking a significant step toward better enforcement and protection of digital consumers' rights in the EU.

15.10. Social Media and the GDPR

Social media, as previously mentioned, represents a means of communication and, as such, is subject to the regulations outlined above. Specifically, under the application of the DSA, the European Commission has designated nineteen platforms that meet the requirements outlined in the regulation. Among these platforms are Facebook, Instagram, X (formerly known as Twitter), and TikTok.[199] The role of these platforms as semiofficial communication channels used by political figures or as tools for disseminating electoral campaigns is widely recognized and uncontested.

It is beyond doubt that the primary activity of these platforms consists of processing a vast amount of personal data. Thus, this data processing must be carried out in accordance with the principles of the GDPR.

As previously mentioned,[200] the right to personal data protection is a fundamental right. This right encompasses a series of specific entitlements. First and foremost, any data processing must be carried out on a lawful basis, with consent being the most common, which must be explicit, freely given, and unambiguous. In addition, each data subject has the right to access, rectify, and erase their personal data held by companies. This is commonly referred to as the right to be forgotten. The right to data portability ensures that all data collected by a company can be transferred, at the request of the data subject, to another company, preventing situations of "lock-in." Moreover, in the event of a data breach, individuals have the right to be notified of the breach. Oversight of the application of the regulation is carried out by the European Data Protection Board (EDPB), which works in constant dialogue with the independent data protection authorities of each Member State.

---

[197] *Id.*

[198] Đurović, *supra* note 188, at 74.

[199] Ask EP, *Regulating Social Media: What Is the European Union Doing to Protect Social Media Users?* EPRS (Jun. 28, 2024), https://epthinktank.eu/2024/06/28/regulating-social-media-what-is-the-european-union-doing-to-protect-social-media-users/.

[200] *See supra* Section 1.7.

As a fundamental right, the GDPR provides that data subjects are entitled to the right to lodge a complaint with the competent supervisory authority and before the competent courts of the Member States.[201] Indeed, the volume of litigation in this area is substantial.

For the purposes of our analysis, and in light of the significant influence that profiling has on the dissemination of news and, consequently, on maintaining a robust public debate, a landmark case is *Schrems v. Meta*, decided on October 4, 2024.[202] In this case, the CJEU was called upon to rule following a preliminary reference from the Austrian Supreme Court. The referral asked the Court to interpret two key issues:

1. First, whether the principle of data minimization (Article 5(1)(c) GDPR) allows all personal data held by a platform to be aggregated, analyzed, and processed for targeted advertising purposes without any restrictions.
2. Second, whether Article 5(1)(b), read in conjunction with Article 9(2)(e) GDPR, permits a data controller to process additional data related to an individual's sexual orientation to offer personalized advertising, based on a statement made by that individual about their sexual orientation in a panel discussion.

On the first question, the CJEU clarified that Article 5(1)(c) GDPR does not permit a data controller, such as a social network platform, to process personal data collected both within and outside the platform for targeted advertising purposes in an unrestricted manner, either temporally or in terms of the types of data processed.

The Court drew on its previous rulings, notably the *Schufa*[203] and *Digi*[204] cases, which provide guidance on the interpretation of the data minimization principle. This principle mandates that personal data must be adequate, relevant, and limited to what is strictly necessary for the purposes of processing. Regarding the temporal aspect, the CJEU underscored that the data minimization principle requires controllers to limit the retention period of personal data to the time strictly necessary to achieve the processing objective. As for the indiscriminate collection, aggregation, and processing of personal data for targeted advertising, the Court held that a controller could not gather data in a generalized or unrestricted manner. It must exclude any data that are not strictly necessary for the stated processing purpose.

On the second question, the CJEU first recalled that under Article 9(1) of GDPR,

> the processing of personal data concerning, inter alia, a natural person's sex life or sexual orientation is to be prohibited, unless such processing falls within the scope of one of the exemptions provided for in Article 9(2) of that regulation. In particular, pursuant to Article 9(2)(e) of the GDPR, the prohibition on processing sensitive personal data does not apply if the

---

201 GDPR, *supra* note 20, ch. VII arts. 77–79.

202 Maximilian Schrems v. Meta Platforms Ireland Limited, ECLI:EU:C:2024:834 (2024).

203 *See Id.* ¶ 53; Joined Cases C-26/22 and C-64/22, UF and AB v. Land Hessen, ECLI:EU:C:2023:958, ¶ 53 (Dec. 7, 2023).

204 Schrems v. Meta Platforms, ¶ 51; *see* Case C-77/21, Digi Távközlési és Szolgáltató Kft. v. Nemzeti Adatvédelmi és Információszabadság Hatóság, ECLI:EU:C:2022:805, ¶ 39 (Oct. 20, 2022).

processing relates to personal data which are *manifestly made public* by the data subject.[205]

Therefore, the Court determined that the fact that an individual publicly disclosed their sexual orientation does not grant an online social network platform the right to process additional data related to that person's sexual orientation. Consequently, the exemption under Article 9(2)(e) GDPR does not apply in this context.

The Court, indeed, first noted that Meta processed data concerning the individual's sexual orientation before the individual publicly disclosed such information. Therefore, the exemption under Article 9(2)(e) GDPR could only apply to data processing occurring after the public disclosure. In its reasoning, the Court reiterated the need for a strict interpretation of Article 9(2) GDPR, as established in its prior rulings, including the *Meta* (C-252/21) case.[206] Specifically, for the exception under Article 9(2)(e) GDPR to apply, the data subject must have clearly intended to make their data publicly accessible.[207] While a disclosure of sexual orientation during a panel discussion open to the public may fall within the scope of Article 9(2)(e), this provision does not extend to the processing of other personal data related to the individual's sexual orientation. In addition, the CJEU stressed that an individual's public disclosure of their sexual orientation does not equate to consent for the processing of other data related to their sexual orientation by a social network platform under Article 9(2)(a) GDPR.

This interpretation underscores the narrow scope of the exceptions provided in Article 9 of GDPR and the importance of ensuring that data subjects retain control over their sensitive personal data.

15.11. Conclusion

In conclusion, the EU's regulatory framework for media governance demonstrates a comprehensive yet intricate approach to balancing media pluralism, consumer protection, and the promotion of freedom of expression. Legislative instruments such as the AVMSD, the DSA, the DMA, and the EMFA collectively provide an integrated framework to address the challenges posed by the digitalization and globalization of the media sector. These instruments aim not only to ensure transparency and accountability for digital platforms but also to foster a fair and competitive market while safeguarding citizens' fundamental rights, including the protection of personal data.

However, the effectiveness of these measures relies on their uniform implementation across Member States and their ability to adapt to rapid technological and societal

---

205 Schrems v. Meta Platforms, ¶¶ 34–35.

206 *Id.* ¶ 73 (citing to Case C-252/21, Meta Platforms, Inc. and Others v. Bundeskartellamt, ECLI:EU:C:2023:537, ¶ 90 (Jul. 4, 2023)).

207 *See also* Opinion of Advocate General Rantos, Case C-446/21, Maximilian Schrems v. Meta Platforms Ireland Limited, formerly Facebook Ireland Limited, ¶¶ 46–47 (delivered on Apr. 25, 2024) (making an interesting point by highlighting that when the protected data are made public by the data subject, these data become ordinary. As such, any processing of such data must be made in accordance with Articles 5, 6, and 7 of the GDPR).

changes. The profound influence of digital platforms on informational pluralism and democracy calls for continuous monitoring and constructive dialogue among regulators, service providers, and civil society. Only through collaborative efforts can the risks of informational power concentration be mitigated, ensuring that media continues to fulfill its vital role as a cornerstone of democracy and cultural diversity.

Index

Page numbers with fn indicate footnote.

C

D

E

G

H

N

O

P

Q

R

S

V

W

X

Y

Z

About the Editor

Jon M. Garon (Editor; Introduction to the Law of Digital Content; Chapter 1: The Transformation of the Internet from Protocol to Venue; Chapter 4: Publicity Rights in Digital Content; Chapter 9: Bias and Inequities in the Digital Realm) is Professor of Law, Director of the NSU Shepard Broad College of Law, Goodwin Program for Law and Society, and past dean of the College of Law. Professor Garon is a nationally recognized authority on technology law and intellectual property, particularly copyright law, entertainment, and information privacy. A Minnesota native, he received his bachelor's degree from the University of Minnesota in 1985 and his juris doctor degree from Columbia University School of Law in 1988. His recent books include *Artificial Intelligence Law and Regulation in a Nutshell* (West Academic 2025); *How AI, Metaverses, Crypto, and Cyber Will Upend the 21st Century* (Edward Elgar Pub. 2024); and *Parenting for the Digital Generation: The Parent's Guide to Digital Education and the Online Environment* (Rowman & Littlefield 2022).

About the Contributors

Reena R. Bajowala (Chapter 7: Privacy Regulation of Artificial Intelligence in the United States; Chapter 8: International Obligations for Privacy and Data Protection) is a Shareholder at Greenberg Traurig, LLP, in Chicago. She has deep experience with privacy, data protection, and AI laws, contributing significant insights on domestic U.S. and international regulatory frameworks. Her work emphasizes the intersection of these regulations with technology and digital content, showcasing her expertise in navigating complex compliance challenges while fostering innovation in the digital era. She is a Fellow of Information Privacy (through the International Association of Privacy Professionals).

Zachary L. Catanzaro (Chapter 3: Trademarks and Digital Assets) is an Assistant Professor of Law at St. Thomas University College of Law and is Director of the Intellectual Property Certificate Program. His research focuses on cutting-edge topics such as nonfungible tokens (NFTs) and generative AI, with recent publications in the *Harvard Journal of Sports and Entertainment Law* and the *NYU Journal of Intellectual Property and Entertainment Law*. Before academia, Catanzaro spent a decade in litigation and transactional practice, specializing in corporate cyberlaw, intellectual property, and digital assets. He also serves as Academic Chair for the Florida Bar's Blockchain & Digital Assets Committee and eDiscovery & Electronic Evidence Committee, contributing extensively to legal education and regulatory initiatives. In his spare time, he enjoys playing piano.

Laura Crimi (Chapter 13: A Northern Perspective: Comparative Regulation of Digital Content and Technology in Canada) is an associate in the Business Law Group at Torkin Manes LLP in Toronto. She focuses on corporate and commercial law, including mergers and acquisitions and preparing and advising on technology agreements. Crimi advises clients across diverse industries, offering tailored legal solutions for complex business matters. Her expertise and dedication make her a valuable contributor to discussions on the evolving regulation of digital content and technology in Canada.

Vicenç Feliú (Chapter 2: Copyright's Power and Limitation over Digital Assets) is a Professor of Law and Associate Dean for Library Services, NSU Shepard Broad College of Law. He oversees the Panza Maurer Law Library and contributes to the academic community with his expertise in intellectual property law. Feliú's scholarly work emphasizes the intersection of copyright law and digital assets, highlighting both the power and limitations of copyright in the evolving digital landscape. His dedication to legal education and research enriches the understanding of intellectual property in the digital age.

David Flint (Chapter 14: Intersection with Other Law and Regulation—The European Union and the United Kingdom) has over forty-five years of experience in commercial law, forty years of which were at a large Scottish law firm (latterly as Senior Partner), and is presently a Commercial Law Adviser at Inksters Solicitors, Scotland. He is the Chairman of the Glasgow Airport Consultative Committee. Before his recent (semi-)retirement, David was Chair of the American Bar Association Cyberspace Committee Non-US Cyberlaw Sub-Committee and was a Visiting Professor at Creighton University School of Law. He has published and lectured widely on corporate bankruptcy, antitrust, intellectual property, data protection, and privacy, including contributions to several ABA publications, panels, and programs.

Candace M. Jones (Chapter 5: Data: Building Blocks of Digital Assets) retired in 2022 from the Federal Reserve Bank of New York, where she served as a Vice President in the Legal Group, managing legal support for technology, security, and procurement matters. Since retiring, Ms. Jones has undertaken consulting legal roles and writing projects focusing on artificial intelligence, information technology, and cybersecurity. Ms. Jones is co-editing the American Bar Association's *Cybersecurity Handbook*, 4th Edition (forthcoming 2025), as a member of the ABA's Cybersecurity Legal Task Force. Prior to joining the New York Fed, Ms. Jones served as Chief Legal Counsel for the Ohio Department of Development, and she was a partner in the Cleveland, Ohio firm Hahn, Loeser & Parks LLP.

Joshua H. Lida (Chapter 10: The Development of Nonfungible Tokens) is an attorney with the firm of Attorneys Jo Ann Hoffman & Associates, P.A., where he handles international Defense Base Act Claims. Additionally, as an artist himself, his practices also focuses on the art world and Web3, including NFTs and blockchain, with extensive experience in transactional matters and advising small businesses, artists, and individuals. Josh has presented on NFTs and blockchain for organizations such as the American Bar Association and the Broward County Bar Association. He is an active board member of the Young Lawyer's Section for the Broward County Bar Association and frequently shares insights on emerging legal fields. Josh holds a BA in History from the University of Central Florida and a JD from Nova Southeastern University.

Lisa R. Lifshitz (Chapter 13: A Northern Perspective: Comparative Regulation of Digital Content and Technology in Canada) is a partner in Torkin Manes LLP's Business Law Group, Toronto, and is the leader of the firm's Technology and Privacy & Data Management Groups. Lisa has particular expertise in preparing and negotiating technology agreements, including cloud and managed services, mobile payment, system acquisition, and master services agreements. She also advises on privacy, data security, and cybersecurity legal matters. A prolific speaker and author, Lisa is ranked in Chambers Global, Chambers Canada, LEXPERT, Best Lawyers®, Lexology Index (formerly Who's Who Legal), and the LEXPERT/American Lawyer Guide to the Leading 500 Lawyers in Canada. A prolific writer and speaker, Lisa was named 2025 "Lawyer of the Year" in Information Technology by Best Lawyers®, was recognized by Lexology Index as a 2025 Global Elite Thought Leader in categories of Data Privacy & Protection and Data Security, and was awarded the Lexology Client Choice Award for Data in Ontario. Lisa is currently the Co-Chair of the AI and Robotics Subcommittee, Cyberspace Law Committee of the ABA Business Law Section (BLS), and is the Content Officer of the BLS.

Carla Pompa (Chapter 15: Media Regulation in the European Union) was born in Rome, Italy. She earned her summa cum laude Law Degree from the University of Roma Tre in Italy, where her thesis explored the intersection of digital consumer rights and health data protection in the European Union and the United States, focusing on international contracts and data protection. Following graduation, she became a dual-degree law student at Nova Southeastern University's Shepard Broad College of Law, where she graduated summa cum laude in May 2025. At Nova, Carla is a research assistant to Professor Jon Garon, working on artificial intelligence, cybersecurity, and privacy law. She gained practical legal experience through internships at Florida Legal Services and assisting a solo practitioner in Rome, developing skills in family, tax, and corporate law. A member of the International Trademark Association and a former Model United Nations delegate, Carla speaks also Italian and Spanish, and she is driven by her passion for advancing technology regulation and legal innovation.

Susan H. Stephan (Chapter 11: Digital Money Transfer, Anti-money Laundering, and Related Laws and Regulations; Chapter 12: Securities and Commodities Regulation for Crypto and Other Digital Assets) is the Director of the Master of Legal Studies Program at the University of Cincinnati College of Law. With a JD from Mitchell Hamline School of Law, an MA from New York University, and an LLM in IT from the University of Edinburgh School of Law, her work focuses on antitrust, privacy, cyberlaw, blockchain technologies, and digital currencies. She has published and presented extensively on technology and privacy issues and received the 2019 Florida Distance Learning Association Visionary Award for Leadership. Stephan's career includes legal practice in intellectual property and business law and teaching roles in areas such as privacy, information security, digital assets, and antitrust law. Her expertise in regulation and education makes her a leader in addressing emerging issues in digital finance and law.

Shannon Taub (Chapter 6: Defamation and Tort Law Protections from Harm) completed her Juris Doctor at Nova Southeastern University's Shepard Broad College of Law with a concentration in Intellectual Property Law. At Nova, she served as a research assistant for Professor Jon Garon, focusing on editing and research in intellectual property, cybersecurity, and technology law. She was a Senior Associate for the *Journal of International Law and Comparative Studies*, the 3L Representative for the Intellectual Property Law Society, the Social Media Director for the First Generation Professionals Legal Society, and a member of the Stephen R. Booher American Inn of Court. Shannon gained practical experience at Robinson Mediation, where she honed her skills in estate planning and prepared legal documents, including wills and trusts. She is dedicated to finding creative and effective solutions to the complex legal challenges posed by emerging technologies.